Longman Annotated Anthologies of English Verse
General Editor Alastair Fowler

Volume I

English Verse 1300–1500

Edited by John Burrow

Longman London and New York

Longman Group Limited
Longman House, Burnt Mill, Harlow, Essex CM20 2JE, England
Associated companies throughout the world

Published in the United States of America
by Longman Inc., New York

First published 1977
Second impression 1986

Library of Congress Cataloging in Publication Data

Main entry under title:

English verse, 1300–1500.

(Longman annotated anthologies of English verse; v. 1)
Bibliography; p. 391.
Includes index.
1. English poetry—Middle English, 1100–1500.

I. Burrow, John Anthony.

PR1203.E5 821'.1'08 76-7591

ISBN 0-582-48368-9

Set in Times New Roman

Produced by Longman Singapore Publishers (Pte) Ltd.
Printed in Singapore.

Contents

	Note by the General Editor	vii
	Acknowledgements	ix
	Abbreviations	x
	Chronological Table	xii
	Introduction	xv
1	Four Rawlinson Lyrics	1
	1 'Of everykune tree'	2
	2 'Ich am of Irlaunde'	2
	3 'Maiden in the mor lay'	2
	4 'Alnight by the rose . . .'	3
2	*Sir Orfeo*	4
3	*Thole a Little*	28
4	'Lollay, lollay, littel child'	28
5	*I would be Clad in Christ's Skin*	31
6	*Penny*	31
7	*Winner and Waster*: extract	32
	The 'Gawain' - poet	46
8	*Patience*: extract	47
9	*Pearl*: extract	61
10	*Sir Gawain and the Green Knight*: extract	76
	William Langland	105
11	*Piers Plowman* B Text: extracts	105
	1 Passus 6	107
	2 Passus 18	123
	Geoffrey Chaucer	146
12	*Troilus*: extract	147
13	*To Rosemounde*	188
14	'Hide, Absolon, thy gilte tresses clere'	190
15	Two Roundels	192
	1 'Your eyen two . . .'	192
	2 'Syn I fro Love . . .'	193
16	*Envoy to Scogan*	194
17	*Balade de Bone Conseyl*	197
18	*The Canterbury Tales*: extract	200
	including *The Shipman's Tale*	201
	and *The Prioress's Tale*	221

	John Gower	234
19	*Confessio Amantis*: extract	235
20	*This World Fares as a Fantasy*	250
21	*Mum and the Sothsegger*: extract	257
	Thomas Hoccleve	265
22	*Hoccleve's Complaint*: extract	265
	John Lydgate	280
23	*As a Midsummer Rose*	281
	Charles d'Orléans	289
24	Four Lyrics from the 'Livre de prison'	290
	1 'Not long ago . . .' 290	
	2 'Your mouth hit saith me . . .' 292	
	3 'My gostly fader . . .' 293	
	4 'O sely anker . . .' 294	
25	Five Sloane Lyrics	295
	1 'Kyrie, so kyrie' 296	
	2 'I have a yong suster . . .' 298	
	3 'Saint Steven was a clerk . . .' 299	
	4 'Adam lay ybounden . . .' 300	
	5 'I singe of a maiden . . .' 301	
26	*God Speed the Plough*	301
27	*Corpus Christi Carol*	303
28	'Farewell this world . . .'	306
29	*Christ Triumphant*	309
	Robert Henryson	310
30	*The Testament of Cresseid*: extract	310
31	*Moral Fables*: extracts	323
	1 The Preiching of the Swallow 324	
	2 The Tale of the Uplandis Mous and the Borowstown Mous 338	
32	*The Hunting of the Cheviot*	349
	William Dunbar	362
33	*Lament: When He Wes Sek*	363
34	*Meditatioun in Wyntir*	369
35	'All erdly joy returns in pane'	372
36	*Of the Nativitie of Christ*	374
37	*Of the Resurrection of Christ*	377
38	*The Tretis of the Twa Mariit Wemen and the Wedo*: extract	380
	Select Bibliography	391
	Index of Titles and First Lines	395

Note by the General Editor

This series is meant to provide period anthologies of representative English and Scottish poems, with full annotation of the kind that any serious reading will require. Most period anthologies offer little or no annotation, apparently on the assumption that only the learned will wish to read a variety of authors. Yet it is very often the beginner who samples a period through an anthology. Course readers designed for beginners, on the other hand, mostly treat their users as a species of idiot, to be written down to. The present series addresses itself to intelligent readers, who may nevertheless not know what needs to be known in order to make sense of the poems. It attempts to provide a reading instrument that will ease immediate difficulties and, by reference to fuller treatments elsewhere, open ways to deeper understanding for those who care to take them. Where the anthologies are used in teaching they should make for a quicker advance, beyond exchange of information, to critical discussion. More generally, they may serve to introduce the non-specialist to some of the best critical thought about an unfamiliar period of literature.

Incidentally, several anonymous or minor classics here receive for the first time explanatory and critical commentary – an attention previously confined to a comparatively small number of poets. In this way the series forms a natural extension of the Longman Annotated English Poets. Indeed, the two series overlap (though without coinciding), in that a few poems already edited have been allowed to reappear in their period context, with different annotation. A similar redundancy is tolerated in divisions of material between periods. Here, overlaps help to avoid specious discontinuities of periodization; and they may have positive interest in offering different editors' views of the same poet or poem.

In textual presentation the series tries to acknowledge the distinct needs of different periods and different kinds of writing. In general, unless there is indication to the contrary spelling is modernized or normalized but old punctuation kept. Old spelling hardly repays keeping, except in a textual edition, since orthographic structures mainly signal a vocabulary selection – take this word, not that. Such signals, where they are unambiguous, can be replaced with modern signals without loss: and where they are ambiguous they need a note anyway. With punctuation, no such direct translation can be performed satisfactorily, because there are no entities so publicly and clearly recognized as words. Elizabethan comma does not equal modern full stop. Or not always. Nevertheless, punctuation has far too important a role in grammatical structure, and hence in the communication of meaning, for us to set light to it by modernizing casually, at our convenience. This (the usual practice) would be to impose an editor's reconstruction of meaning so secretly that the reader would be in no position to disagree. Thus, the series aims at combining maximum ease in reading with as much as possible of the textual evidence on which sound interpretation must ultimately be based.

This general policy cannot be imposed uniformly. In medieval texts much old spelling has to be retained, for a variety of reasons. Intervening sound changes, for example, are so great that the metrical and assonantal patterns would otherwise be lost. Again, MS. texts in all periods may have little or no punctuation; and then an editor is reasonably expected to supply it – and to say that he has done so. Further problems are presented by Scots and by dialectal spellings. When the poet aimed to write in 'standard Scots', the editors aim at a regionally neutral regularization that designates words without specifying any particular variants of them. But where regional flavour matters (as with Barnes and sometimes with Burns), this policy would obviously lose more than it gained. Each editor explains his own practice in textual matters, and draws attention to local exceptions. In this way we hope always to keep the evidential status of the text as clear as possible.

Acknowledgements

The editor of an anthology such as this incurs many obligations. I am most in debt to the general editor of the series, Professor Fowler. He dealt promptly and patiently with all my questions; and my notes owe much more than I have been able to acknowledge to his thorough criticism and valuable suggestions. Mr. A. J. Aitken, Professor E. J. Dobson and Mr. T. N. Turville-Petre have given me generous help. I should like also to thank Miss E. Kennedy, Miss M. A. Levy, Professor J. MacQueen, Professor A. McIntosh, Mr. J. D. North, Mr. M. B. Parkes, Miss Ruth Pryor and Mr. P. Sims-Williams. Dr. A. B. Cottle kindly read the proofs and suggested several improvements.

I am grateful to the following libraries for allowing me to consult their manuscripts, or for supplying me with photographs: National Library of Scotland, National Library of Wales, British Library, Coventry City Reference Library, Bodleian Library, Cambridge University Library, Durham University Library; the libraries of St. John's College, Gonville and Caius College, and Magdalene College, Cambridge; the libraries of Balliol College and New College, Oxford.

J.A.B.

Jesus College, Oxford
September 1975

Abbreviations

Periodicals

Ang.	*Anglia*
Archiv	*Archiv für das Studium der neueren Sprachen*
Ch. R.	*Chaucer Review*
E & S	*Essays and Studies*
EC	*Essays in Criticism*
EGS	*English and Germanic Studies*
ELH	*Journal of English Literary History*
ELN	*English Language Notes*
ES	*English Studies*
JEGP	*Journal of English and Germanic Philology*
Med. Aev.	*Medium Aevum*
Med. Stud.	*Mediaeval Studies*
MLN	*Modern Language Notes*
MLQ	*Modern Language Quarterly*
MLR	*Modern Language Review*
MP	*Modern Philology*
N & Q	*Notes and Queries* (volume numbers refer to New Series)
Neophil.	*Neophilologus*
Neuphil. Mitteil.	*Neuphilologische Mitteilungen*
PBA	*Proceedings of the British Academy*
PMLA	*Publications of the Modern Language Association of America*
PQ	*Philological Quarterly*
RES	*Review of English Studies* (n.s. = new series)
SHR	*Scottish Historical Review*
SP	*Studies in Philology*
Spec.	*Speculum*
SSL	*Studies in Scottish Literature*
Stud. Neophil.	*Studia Neophilologica*
TLS	*Times Literary Supplement*
Trad.	*Traditio*
UTQ	*University of Toronto Quarterly*

Other Abbreviations

ALMA	*Arthurian Literature in the Middle Ages*†
A.V.	Authorized Version of the Bible (King James, 1611)
B.L.	British Library (formerly British Museum)
Child	Child, F. J., ed. *The English and Scottish Popular Ballads*†
C.T.	Chaucer's *Canterbury Tales*
D.	Duke
DOST	*A Dictionary of the Older Scottish Tongue*†
E.	Earl

EDD	*The English Dialect Dictionary*†
EETS	Early English Text Society (o.s. = original series, e.s. = extra series)
Fr., It. etc.	French, Italian etc.
L.G.W.	Chaucer's *Legend of Good Women*
ME	Middle English
MED	*Middle English Dictionary*†
Migne. *P.L.*	Migne, J.-P. ed. *Patrologia Latina*†
MS.	manuscript
Mustanoja	Mustanoja, T. F., *A Middle English Syntax*†
N.L.S.	National Library of Scotland
N.T.	New Testament
OE	Old English
OED	*Oxford English Dictionary*
O.T.	Old Testament
Piers	Langland's *Piers Plowman*
R. de la Rose	*Le Roman de la Rose*, ed. Lecoy†
SATF	Société des Anciens Textes Français
STS	Scottish Text Society
U.P.	University Press
Whiting	Whiting, B. J., ed. *Proverbs, Sentences, and Proverbial Phrases From English Writings Mainly before 1500*†

*indicates a word or form not actually found, but of which the existence is inferred.

†See Bibliography p. 391.

Chronological Table

	Literary events		*Other events*
		1307	Death of Edward I; accession of Edward II.
		1314	Robert Bruce defeats English at Bannockburn.
		1327	Accession of Edward III; murder of Edward II.
c. 1330	Compilation of Auchinleck Manuscript. Gower born.		
		1337	Hundred Years War between France and England begins.
c. 1343	Chaucer born.		
		1346	Edward defeats French at Crécy.
		1348–49	Black Death (also 1361–62, 1369).
1349	Richard Rolle dies.	1349	William of Occam dies. Edward establishes Order of Garter.
		1351	Statute of Labourers regulates wages.
1352–3	*Winner and Waster.*		
		1356	English defeat French at Poitiers.
		1360	Treaty of Calais between English and French.
		1362	Statute decrees use of English in law courts.
		1363	Chancellor first opens Parliament in English.
1368/9	Hoccleve born.		
1369	Chaucer's *Book of the Duchess.*		
c. 1370	Langland's *Piers Plowman:* A Text. Lydgate born.		
		1376	Black Prince dies.
1377–9	Langland's *Piers Plowman:* B Text.	1377	Death of Edward III; accession of Richard II.
		1378	Great Schism begins (two Popes).

	Literary events		*Other events*
		1379	William of Wykeham founds New College, Oxford.
		1381	Peasants' Revolt under Wat Tyler.
		1384	John Wyclif dies.
1386	Chaucer completes *Troilus*.		
1387	Chaucer begins *Canterbury Tales*.	1387	Lords Appellant restrict authority of Richard II.
1388	Thomas Usk executed.	1388	Scots under Douglas defeat English at Otterburn.
c. 1390	Gower completes *Confessio Amantis* (first version).		
1391	Sir John Clanvowe dies.		
1394	Charles d'Orléans born.		
1395	John Barbour dies.		
1396	Walter Hilton dies.		
		1399	Deposition of Richard II; accession of Henry IV.
1400	Chaucer dies.	1400	Murder of Richard II.
		1401	Statute *De heretico comburendo* against Lollards.
1402	John Trevisa dies.	1402	Percies defeat Scots at Homildon Hill.
		1406	James I of Scotland captured.
1408	Gower dies.		
		1413	Death of Henry IV; accession of Henry V.
1415	Charles d'Orléans captured by English.	1415	Henry defeats French at Agincourt.
		1417	Great Schism ends.
1420	Lydgate completes *Troy Book*.		
		1422	Death of Henry V; accession of Henry VI.
1426	Hoccleve dies.		
		1431	Joan of Arc burnt at Rouen.
		1437	Accession of James II of Scotland.
1438/9	Lydgate completes *Fall of Princes*.		

	Literary events		Other events
1440	Charles d'Orléans released.		
		1441	Henry VI founds Eton and King's College, Cambridge.
1449/50	Lydgate dies.		
		1451	Glasgow University founded.
		1453	End of Hundred Years War.
		1455	York defeats royal forces at St. Albans: beginning of Wars of Roses.
1456?	Dunbar born.		
		1460	Accession of James III of Scotland.
		1461	Deposition of Henry VI; accession of Edward IV.
1465	Charles d'Orléans dies.		
1469	Malory completes *Morte D'arthur*.		
		1470	Henry VI reinstated by Warwick.
		1471	Deposition and death of Henry VI; accession of Edward IV.
1473/4	First book printed in English: Caxton's *History of Troy*.		
1475?	Gavin Douglas born.		
1476	Caxton establishes a press in Westminster.		
1478	Caxton prints *Canterbury Tales*.		
1483	Caxton prints *Confessio Amantis*.	1483	Death of Edward IV; accession of Edward V; usurpation by Richard III.
1484	Caxton prints *Troilus*.		
1485	Caxton prints *Morte D'arthur*.	1485	Richard III killed at Bosworth; accession of Henry VII, first of the Tudors.
		1488	Accession of James IV of Scotland.
1491	Caxton dies.		
		1496	Colet begins to lecture at Oxford.
1513?	Dunbar dies.	1513	James IV of Scotland killed at Flodden.

Introduction

The poetry of the two centuries represented in this anthology exhibits great diversity, both in form and in content. This diversity is in no way surprising. Even in the Middle Ages two hundred years was a long time – long enough for many important changes to occur between 1300 and 1500. Furthermore, the life of an Englishman or Scotsman before 1500 was still governed by traditions which, though very powerful, were often peculiar to a specific locality or institution. The development and establishment of a standard written language in the course of the fifteenth century, together with the centralizing policies of the Tudor monarchy and other like factors, were to create in the sixteenth century, for the first time in England, a unified national literature, a single literary scene; but in the fifteenth century, and still more in the fourteenth, English poetry had many traditions and many centres, of which London and Edinburgh were only the most important. One may think of the poets of these centuries as working in many cells, divided from each other, often, by regional, social and educational differences more drastic than we are accustomed to observe in the English literature of modern times. In modern literature, for example, 'dialect poetry' such as that of William Barnes is an occasional phenomenon; but practically all the poetry in this book, including Chaucer's, is dialect poetry. Its language, that is, reflects, to a greater or less extent, the regional varieties of spoken and written English. This 'diversité in English and in writing of oure tonge', observed by Chaucer (*Troilus* 5.1793–4), is both a minor cause and (for the literary student) a major symptom of the diverse and uncentralized vernacular culture before 1500. The lack of a commanding centre makes it difficult, perhaps impossible, to give a single, unified account of the English poetry of these two centuries. I can do no more here than distinguish and briefly describe three different kinds of poetry which the reader will find in this anthology.

I

Many people believe that English poetry started with Geoffrey Chaucer (1343?–1400). This belief is so widespread and of such long standing that even if it were entirely groundless (which it is not) it would still count as an important fact in the history of English poetry. For centuries poets have shared with their readers this myth about the origins of the craft – in its perfected, modern form – in England. The chief founding father is Chaucer, flanked by his friend and contemporary John Gower (1330?–1408) and followed by John Lydgate (1370?–1449?). From this group there derives a succession of English and Scottish 'Chaucerians', who in turn are succeeded by the Tudor poets. Thus the great poetry of the age of Richard II is connected by a direct line of descent to the great poetry of the age of Elizabeth I. One version of this 'genealogy' of English poetry is given by the Elizabethan writer George Puttenham, in his *Art of English Poesy* (1589), who says that there is little or no English poetry 'worth commendation' before the reigns of Edward III and Richard II:

> Those of the first age were Chaucer and Gower, both of them, as I suppose, knights. After whom followed John Lydgate, the monk of Bury, and that nameless, who wrote the Satire called *Piers Plowman*: next him followed Hardyng, the Chronicler; then, in king Henry the eight's time, Skelton, (I wot not for what great worthiness) surnamed the Poet Laureate. In the latter end of the same king's reign sprong up a new company of courtly makers, of whom Sir Thomas Wyatt the elder and Henry Earl of Surrey were the two chieftains.[1]

Another version of the genealogy was given, about 1506, by the Scottish poet William Dunbar, in his *Lament* (No. 33 here, lines 49–92). Dunbar's list of 'makers' destroyed by death begins, like Puttenham's, with Chaucer, Gower and the Monk of Bury. The rest of the list is entirely different from Puttenham's, being devoted to Scottish poets past and present. But the purpose is the same in each case: Dunbar and Puttenham are both claiming for themselves and their contemporaries a place in the great tradition of English poetry. This is the tradition to which Poets Laureate such as Skelton belong. It is also a tradition of '*courtly* makers': Dunbar numbers four knights among his Scottish predecessors, and Puttenham even bestows knighthoods on Chaucer and Gower.

Belief in this courtly or 'laureate' tradition stemming from Chaucer played an important part in establishing the idea of English poetry as an independent and flourishing growth, especially in the years between Chaucer and Shakespeare. It acted as a kind of 'foundation myth'. Unlike many such myths, however, this one contains a good deal of truth. There does exist a tradition of learned, courtly poetry, such as Puttenham describes. It is represented in this anthology by the works of Chaucer (Nos. 12–18), Gower (No. 19), Hoccleve (No. 22), Lydgate (No. 23), Charles d'Orléans (No. 24), Henryson (Nos. 30–1) and Dunbar (Nos. 33–8).

It is partly a matter of chance that all these poems can be ascribed to specific, identifiable 'makers'. I might have included *The Flower and the Leaf*; and that undoubtedly courtly poem is anonymous (though it used to be ascribed to Chaucer). Conversely, *Piers Plowman* belongs outside the courtly tradition, but is not anonymous (though it hovers on the brink of anonymity, for little is known about 'that nameless, who wrote the Satire called *Piers Plowman*' except that he was called William Langland). However, it is a fact that poems in the courtly tradition are much more likely than other poems of the period to be the work of an identifiable poet. Explanations for this fact are not hard to find. If a poet writes with one eye on the purse, or at least the favour, of a king or great lord, as Chaucer, Gower, Hoccleve, Lydgate and Dunbar sometimes do, he will want to 'sign' his work. Again, if the poet is himself a great lord, like Charles d'Orléans, or a landed gentleman, like Gower, or a servant of the King in some capacity, like Chaucer and Hoccleve (both 'civil servants'), Lydgate (a monk patronized by royalty), or Dunbar (a royal secretary and chaplain), his name will tend to be traceable in the historical records, as Langland's, for instance, is not.

Such considerations point towards a general observation of some literary significance. The conditions of court life and of royal service – even such relatively humble service as Hoccleve's in the Privy Seal Office – encouraged a much stronger sense of individual interest and particular identity than was common in medieval society as a whole. As Chaucer's Arcite says:

> And therfore, at the kinges court, my brother,
> Ech man for himself, there is non other (*C.T.* I 1181–2).

Accordingly, the poet's sense of 'himself' comes out much more strongly in the poems of the courtly makers than in other poetry of the period. Each of the makers represented here, certainly, has his own distinctive personal tone; and each writes his own kind of poetry. Hoccleve exploits the autobiographic vein already present in his master Chaucer and in Gower. Lydgate, just as characteristically, does not. Charles d'Orléans, son of the King of France, strikes the traditional attitudes of courtly love with splendid dash and hauteur. Henryson is perhaps nearest to Chaucer in his cultivation of a narrative poetry shot through with an elusive, dry irony. Dunbar, on the other hand, shows little interest in traditional narrative subjects, and displays his powers best in short pieces of great brilliance.

Unlike many medieval writers, then, these poets can offer a modern reader something of the variety and individuality to which he is accustomed in more recent work. At the same time, they are all practitioners of the same art or craft of 'making', sharing many of the professional secrets of what Dunbar calls their 'faculty' (No. 33 line 47). Thus they all exhibit a similar control of varieties of diction and syntax. The principle governing this particular skill is stated by Chaucer: 'The wordes mote be cosin to the dede' (*C.T.* I 742). Style, that is, must suit subject and context. Chaucer himself provides a striking instance of this principle in his *Canterbury Tales*, in the adjacent tales of the Shipman and the Prioress (No. 18 here). At the beginning of the latter tale, diction (e.g. the word 'laude'), rhetorical figures (e.g. the invocation), word order and syntax combine to establish a stylistic register appropriate to a Miracle of the Virgin and unmistakably different from that prevailing in the preceding fabliau. The repertoire of contrasting styles in the works of Hoccleve and Lydgate owes much to Chaucer. Thus Hoccleve, at the beginning of his *Complaint* (No. 22), imitates the sustained syntax which contributes to the grandeur of the opening of the *Canterbury Tales.* Lydgate's high style, however, is distinguished from Chaucer's by a more deliberate exploitation of unusual Latinate words ('aureate diction'). The influence of this may be seen in Dunbar's sonorous liturgical lyrics (Nos. 36 and 37). Dunbar's *Twa Mariit Wemen and the Wedo* (No. 38), like Henryson's *Fables* (No. 31), shows how a skilled maker can play high style off against low to create comic or satiric effects.

There is one aspect of this craft of making that a modern reader may neglect. No treatises on the 'art of English poesy' survive from the period covered by this anthology; but the French treatises from this period (known as 'arts of second rhetoric'), as well as English treatises of the sixteenth century, strongly suggest that the makers paid close attention to the selection and manipulation of stanza forms. The couplet was not highly thought of. Gower followed French narrative poets of the high Middle Ages (and their English derivatives) in using octosyllabic couplets in *Confessio Amantis* (No. 19); but Chaucer apparently abandoned the form after the *House of Fame*; and fifteenth-century poets used it rather little, regarding it perhaps as a 'light', old-fashioned form, and associating it with minstrel narrative such as *Sir Orfeo* (No. 2). Even the long, decasyllabic couplet, introduced by Chaucer to such good effect in his *Legend of Good Women* and several Canterbury Tales, was regarded by sixteenth-century theorists (who called it 'riding rhyme') as suitable mostly for 'light enterprises'. With a few notable exceptions (Chaucer's *Knight's Tale* and its pendant, Lydgate's *Siege of Thebes*), earlier usage conforms to this principle. Chaucer's practice in No. 18, where the transition from fabliau to pious tale is marked by a shift from long couplet to rhyme royal, agrees exactly with the rule stated by George Gascoigne in 1575: 'As this riding rhyme serveth most aptly to write a merry tale, so Rhyme royal is fittest for a grave discourse.'[2]

Rhyme royal itself was perhaps Chaucer's greatest single contribution to the art of the makers. Chaucer uses it in his *Troilus* (No. 12), in four of the more serious Canterbury Tales (including the *Prioress's Tale*), and in grave ballades such as Nos. 14 and 17, as well as in the lighter No. 16. It became in the fifteenth century the most highly esteemed form, especially for narrative poetry (examples here are Nos. 22, 30 and 31). Its peculiar flexibility and liveliness derive largely from the fact that it consists of a quatrain (*abab*) overlapping, as it were, with a pair of couplets (*bbcc*) thus: *ababbcc*. The fourth line, where the overlap occurs, belongs to both systems; and this keeps the stanza going at the point where it might sag. By comparison, the other stanza form specially favoured by makers in this anthology, the eight-line '*Monk's*

Tale stanza', creates a more massive and static effect, because it consists of two equally balanced quatrains: *ababbcbc*. Chaucer uses this stanza in his skittish ballade *To Rosemounde* (No. 13, cf. No. 24.4); but it is best suited for the measured utterance of moral poems such as Lydgate's *As a Midsummer Rose* (No. 23) or religious poems such as Dunbar's *Of the Resurrection of Christ* (No. 37). Henryson exploits the contrast between the two forms when he shifts from narrative in rhyme royal to a *Moralitas* in the eight-line stanza in his Fable of the two mice (No. 31.2).

In general, the stanza forms used by the English makers derive from those current among the courtly poets of France in their day. From the same source they borrowed certain 'poem forms', notably the ballade (see headnote to No. 13) and the roundel (headnote to No. 15). Their rhyming techniques are also much influenced by French practice. But the rhythms of their lines inevitably differed from the French, because of the strong stress in English. With three exceptions (Nos. 19, 24.3 and 36 are octosyllabic) all the maker's pieces in this anthology employ the longer line conventionally described as an iambic pentameter. This kind of line is, of course, entirely familiar to readers of later English poetry, but the version used by Chaucer and his successors presents several knotty problems. Most people believe that Chaucer himself wrote a regular five-stress iambic line (with normal licences, which present no problem to our ear), and that it is important, in order to appreciate this, to sound the final *-e* (as in 'chin*a*') so as to give an extra syllable in words such as 'lovė', except where a following word beginning with a vowel or weak *h* causes elision. There is, however, a joker in the pack, for Chaucer seems to have availed himself wherever it suited him (except, probably, in rhyme) of variant forms without final *-e* which were already widely current in the spoken language of his time.[3]

Lydgate and Hoccleve also took advantage of such variants; but it is more difficult with them, especially with Lydgate, to determine which variant is intended in any particular case. Lydgate certainly allowed himself considerable liberties, both in stress-placing and in syllable count. Hoccleve is nearer to Chaucerian norms, but not consistently so. In the poetry of the Scotsmen Henryson and Dunbar there is no question of sounding final *-e*, partly because of their later date, and partly because final *-e* had in any case ceased to be pronounced much earlier in the North than in the South. Their work is distinguished by a mastery of metre almost equal to Chaucer's, and presents few problems to the ear.

II

The tradition of the courtly makers, beginning with Chaucer, represents the first phase of English poetry as most readers have known it since Tudor times. Any reader of this anthology who confined himself to the poems so far mentioned here should therefore feel himself at home, despite many minor difficulties of a historical and linguistic kind. For Chaucer and Gower, Hoccleve and Lydgate, Henryson and Dunbar, all set before themselves ideals of poetic achievement which are in many ways not unlike those prevailing in modern times. Once we step outside this tradition we find ourselves in a less familiar world: an anonymous world of clerks and minstrels, monks and friars, whose identities and purposes we can often only guess at.

The work of these anonymous poets is not necessarily very different from that of the courtly makers. The Latin and French writers who so influenced Chaucer and his successors exerted some influence also, directly or indirectly, on practically all other English verse in this period. Nor were the makers themselves uninfluenced by, or without influence on, their fellow English poets. Thus the anonymous minstrel romance *Sir Orfeo*, one of the earliest pieces in this collection (No. 2), is not so very unlike the narrative poetry of Gower, or even of Chaucer. This is partly because the earlier English poet was open to some of the same French influences (in this case, from the Breton lays) which so affected Chaucer and Gower; and partly because Chaucer, in particular, was demonstrably aware of, and indebted to, the kind of English poetry which *Orfeo* represents. He may even at one time have owned or consulted the Auchinleck MS., a large collection of English writings (compiled about 1330) which includes the best surviving text of *Orfeo*. Again, the present anthology contains four poems on the instability of human life, one of them (No. 23) by Chaucer's disciple, Lydgate, and three by anonymous moralists. One of the three (No. 4) is possibly by an early fourteenth-century friar, another (No. 20) by an anonymous contemporary of Chaucer (again possibly a friar), and a third (No. 28) by a poet of the mid fifteenth century. These four poems have much in common. Lydgate's piece is perhaps the most polished, and certainly the most 'literary'; but it draws much from the traditions of common Middle English religious-didactic verse, represented in the other three poems. Conversely, No. 28 exhibits unmistakably, by its use of the rhyme royal stanza, the influence of Chaucerian verse.

But not all anonymous poetry can usefully be related in this way – as antecedent, derivative, or congener – to the work of Chaucer and his successors. In the multicellular world of late medieval English poetry, other traditions could also flourish. Much the most important example of such an independent tradition is that of alliterative verse, represented here by seven pieces: No. 7 (from *Winner and Waster*), No. 8 (from *Patience*), No. 9 (from *Pearl*), No. 10 (from *Sir Gawain and the Green Knight*), No. 11 (from *Piers Plowman*), No. 21 (from *Mum and the Sothsegger*), and No. 38 (from Dunbar's *Twa Mariit Wemen and the Wedo*). These pieces sufficiently illustrate the vitality of alliterative verse in this period, and the variety of its uses – for comedy, satire, romance and religious vision. Yet relations between this large body of verse and what for us is the central tradition of the courtly makers are, in general, very difficult to trace. This rather extraordinary situation may be summed up by observing that two great English poets, Chaucer and Langland, probably very near neighbours in the London of the 1370s and 1380s, show no clear sign of having read each other's work.

In some ways Langland's *Piers Plowman* is a poem untypical of the so-called Alliterative Revival. It is in fact the only alliterative poem (Old or Middle English) which has always formed part of the canon of English poetry. It was widely read in the fifteenth century and printed in the sixteenth. Puttenham, as we have seen, mentioned it in his survey of poetic predecessors, and both Spenser and Milton knew something of it. There is, accordingly, a certain aptness in the fact that Langland lived, by his own account, in London.

More typical are such alliterative poets as the 'Western man' who wrote *Winner and Waster*, or the Cheshire or Staffordshire man who wrote *Sir Gawain* and *Pearl*. For the 'revival' of alliterative verse seems, on surviving evidence, to have started in the middle of the fourteenth century in the western and north-western counties of England. Later it spread northwards to Scotland. Chaucer certainly associated such verse with the north, for he has his Parson say:

> But trusteth well, I am a southren man,
> I can nat geeste [tell tales] 'rum, ram, ruf', by lettre (*C.T.* X 42–3).

His Scottish followers, not surprisingly, included alliterative verse as one item in their repertoire (e.g. Dunbar's No. 38 here); but neither Chaucer himself nor his English followers attempted it. Nor did the alliterative poets take much notice of Chaucer. I have argued elsewhere (*Ricardian Poetry* 1971) that the two great alliterative poets of the age of Richard II, Langland and the *Gawain*-poet, do indeed share certain period characteristics with their contemporaries, Chaucer and Gower. All four are essentially narrative poets, employing traditional story-telling styles, but with a certain idiosyncratic irony and detachment. But the two traditions which they represent retain their strong and separate identities.

It would be easier to understand this state of affairs, perhaps, if we knew as much about the alliterative poets as we do about the courtly makers. Who and what were they, and for whom did they write? One hypothesis attempts to associate the Alliterative Revival, at least in its early phase, with the great baronial households of the Welsh Marches and the north-west; but the evidence (which is very slight) may point rather towards the more modest, but still often substantial, country gentry as the class most often concerned with this kind of poetry.[4] The latter hypothesis would agree well enough with the view of social and political matters expressed in *Winner and Waster* and *Mum and the Sothsegger*; and it would agree better than might at first appear with the loving portrayal of courtly life in *Sir Gawain* and other alliterative romances. Country gentlemen such as the Franklin in Chaucer's *Canterbury Tales* (and cf. No. 21 here, lines 945 f.) might identify themselves strongly with the world of the court, in which, ideally, their own 'gentillesse' achieved its perfection.

The long alliterative line, employed without rhyme in Nos. 7, 8, 11, 21 and 38 here, is unfamiliar to readers of modern English poetry, despite recent revivals by poets such as W. H. Auden. The Middle English variety descends from the poetry of the Anglo-Saxons, which is one branch of Germanic alliterative verse. The gap of time separating the earliest poetry of the Revival (about 1350) from the *Brut* of Layamon (about 1200), not to speak of the questionable character of the latter's technique, makes the history of Middle English alliterative verse a controversial subject; but its descent from Anglo-Saxon verse is not seriously in doubt. As might be expected, given its Germanic ancestry, the principles governing this verse differ radically from those governing 'metrical' rhyming verse, the origins of which lie in the Latin culture of *Romania* rather than in *Germania*. The units of verse (half-lines rather than lines) are linked not by end-rhyme but by head-rhyme, i.e. alliteration. It is a general rule that each pair of half-lines should be linked by alliteration between at least one syllable in each. Usually two, and sometimes three, syllables in the first half-line participate in this alliteration; and occasionally a second syllable in the second half-line also participates. The most common pattern is *aa* / *ax*, thus:

And ye *l*ovely *l*adies / with your *l*onge fingres.

The required alliteration (which is not to be confused with the optional, expressive alliteration of modern verse) is assisted by traditional alliterating collocations ('lovely ladies', in the example from Langland), which function like the traditional rhyme pairs in rhyming verse. The poets also drew upon the remains of a special poetic diction, which provided alternative ways of expressing common notions such as 'man' or 'horse' in accordance with differing alliterative requirements.

Some Middle English alliterative poets evidently felt dissatisfied with a form which, like the short couplet of metrical verse, linked no more than two short neighbouring units together. One way to be more ambitious was to sustain the same alliterating sound over more than one line, as Dunbar often does in his *Twa Mariit Wemen and the Wedo* (see headnote to No. 38). Another way was to superimpose stanzaic end-rhyming upon the alliterative verse. *Sir Gawain* does this in a unique way. The poet breaks up the main body of unrhymed alliterative lines into paragraphs, by introducing at irregular intervals a group of five shorter rhymed lines (the 'bob and wheel': see headnote to No. 10). The same poet's *Pearl* lies on the border between alliterative and metrical verse. It is fully stanzaic, and its lines might appear to be very loose iambic octosyllables; but the coupling of heavy alliteration with a four-stress movement brings the poem close to alliterative verse (much closer than No. 20, which it otherwise resembles in metrical form).

The rhythm of alliterative verse is governed by rules different from those observed by Chaucer and his successors. Normally each unit of verse, or half-line, has two main stresses, though first half-lines sometimes have an extra, lesser, stress. It is customary for the alliteration to be carried by these stressed syllables, though unstressed syllables sometimes carry it (a liberty not taken by Old English alliterative poets). The number of unstressed syllables in a half-line is (within reason) a matter of indifference; so the problem of final *-e* has little metrical significance here. The rhythmical pattern of each half-line (i.e. the ordering of stressed and unstressed elements) is in principle independent of its neighbours. But certain patterns were strongly favoured, notably the so-called 'rising-falling' pattern: x (x) / x x / x. These patterns are, in fact, simply a selection from the patterns which actually occur in English speech; and alliterative verse can therefore approach very close to the general rhythms of ordinary speech (e.g. in *Piers Plowman*). But Middle English alliterative verse is generally not colloquial or familiar in manner – less so than much verse in the Chaucerian tradition. The alliterative poets seem to have inherited from their Old English predecessors a certain formality and impersonality of manner, not unconnected, perhaps, with a sense of the dignity and antiquity of their craft. They do not cultivate the courtly graces of self-depreciation. They offer themselves, most often, as custodians of tradition, moral 'truth-tellers', or even visionaries.[5]

III

There remain certain poems which, unlike any so far mentioned, may seem to invite the label 'folk poetry'. The literary antiquarians of the Romantic and Victorian periods are nowadays generally held to have affixed the 'folk' label too freely to medieval poems (as to other products of medieval civilization). In this matter, certainly, first impressions are not to be trusted. *God Speed the Plough* (No. 26), for example, might seem to be a genuine ploughman's shanty; but the character of the manuscript in which it survives strongly suggests that it is a sophisticated piece, designed perhaps for performance by choristers on Plough Monday (see headnote to No. 26). Yet I think that modern scholars have here reacted too far against the undoubted excesses of earlier romantic historicism. Presumably the common people of medieval towns and villages did have a stock of traditional songs and poems, and presumably these were not all the work of monks and friars writing in the popular manner for purposes of edification. Such folk poems would obviously have a poorer chance of survival than other kinds of poetry, but it is not likely that every single one has been lost. As a matter of fact there are some poems surviving, including some in this anthology, of which one can at least say that, if they are not folk poems, they are *something* special. Those who deny these poems folk status must produce some alternative specification to account for their unique and haunting qualities.

Such poems in the present collection are: the four lyrics from the early fourteenth-century Rawlinson MS. (No. 1), the five lyrics from the early fifteenth-century Sloane MS. (No. 25), the *Corpus Christi Carol* (No. 27) and *The Hunting of the Cheviot* (No. 32). These poems are of varying types (love song, border ballad, religious lyric, etc.), and three of them present intractable problems of interpretation – evidence in itself, perhaps, of an origin outside the usual literary circles. Certain general observations are possible, however. First, three of the poems have some connection with pieces recorded in post-medieval times in popular tradition: nursery rhyme, ballad and riddle in the case of 'I have a yong suster'; folk song in the case of the *Corpus Christi Carol*; ballad in the case of *The Hunting of the Cheviot.*[6] Such connections cannot prove the popular character of a medieval text, of course; but they establish a likelihood. The verse forms are also suggestive: the 'carol' (see headnote to No. 1.2, and Nos. 25.1 and 27) and the ballad stanza (No. 32) are both popular forms; and the 'long couplet' of the Sloane poems is closer to the ballad stanza than to Chaucer's decasyllabic couplet (headnote to No. 25). Most readers would agree, also, that the movement and manner of some of these poems strongly suggests popular dance and song: especially the Rawlinson poems, but also No. 25.2. Finally, the circumstances in which these pieces have survived are at least consistent with popular origin. The Rawlinson MS. is a single separate scrap of parchment; the *Corpus Christi Carol* survives in a Tudor grocer's commonplace book; *The Hunting of the Cheviot* is scribbled down in the repertoire book of an Elizabethan minstrel. The problem case is the Sloane MS., which recent opinion would connect with the monastery of Bury St. Edmunds (see headnote to No. 25). This hypothesis, if it were established, would place the Sloane poems under clerical auspices, like *God Speed the Plough* – a conclusion which would challenge our image of Lydgate's monastery just as much as our reading of the poems. However we take it, in fact, a volume such as the Sloane MS. stands as a salutary reminder of how imperfectly we understand the diverse and complex culture of late-medieval England.

Presentation

This anthology contains about 7,500 lines of poetry, selected to represent the non-dramatic verse of two centuries. The inevitable difficulties of any such selection are compounded in this case by the fact that so much of the best poetry of this period is long. Lengthy chronicle poems such as Barbour's *Bruce* have had to be excluded; and several other important poems are represented by extracts. I have confined myself to a single continuous extract, except in Nos. 11 and 31 (where there are two). Thus *Canterbury Tales* is represented by the linked tales of Shipman and Prioress (*C.T.* VII 1–690). The extracts are all, I hope, sufficiently substantial and shapely; but interested readers will want to go on to the complete works.

Each piece has been newly edited from the MS. or print specified in its headnote. All significant departures from this base text are indicated in textual notes (distinguished by square brackets after the lemmas). I have recorded the readings of other MSS. (specified in headnotes) much more selectively, either to justify or to suggest emendation of the base text.

In accordance with the policy of the series, the spelling of the base texts has been normalized and modernized, but only in part. My intention has been to assist identification of words without prompting mispronunciations or obscuring rhymes. Certain letter pairs have in most cases been modernized: *c/k*, *f/v*, *i/j*, *i/y*, *u/v*, *u/w*, *ei/ai*. So have certain letter clusters: *ht* becomes *ght*, *sch* becomes *sh*, *quh* (in Scots poems) becomes *wh*. The prefix *bi-* becomes *be-*. Where appropriate, *e* and *o* have been doubled to indicate long vowels. Inflexional *-is* and *-id* become *-es* and *-ed*, except in Scots texts, where *-id* and syllabic *-is* have been preserved. The forms of certain common words have been systematically distinguished: *be/by*, *of/off*, *the/thee*, *then/than* (except in Scots), *to/too*, *ye/yea*. *Hir* 'her' is distinguished from *her* 'their'. In poems where final *-e* is pronounced, my intention has been to remove such *-e*'s as are merely scribal. The spelling of Latin quotations has been modernized.

The policy of the series is to preserve original punctuation, but the punctuation of the MSS. is at best very sketchy, and I have therefore been obliged to punctuate the texts myself. The punctuation, accordingly, has no more than editorial authority, and follows modern conventions, which are not always suited to the fluid syntax of ME poetry. Readers should feel free to ignore it. Capitalization is also editorial, and may also be questionable where personal names and personifications are concerned.

In the notes I have tried to provide the information a non-specialist reader will need, together with a necessarily limited amount of critical comment. Since there is no general glossary, all difficult words are explained in the notes. Words occurring more than once within an individual piece are normally glossed only at their first appearance there.

Works cited in brief form, by author and/or cue-title, are listed in the Bibliography. Thus 'Wimberly 63' refers to p. 63 of the work listed in the Bibliography under 'Wimberly'. Classical titles may be abbreviated according to the usage of the *Oxford Classical Dictionary*. Place of publication, where not given, is London, except in the case of University Presses. Biblical quotations are from the Douai-Reims version, which best represents the Latin Vulgate most used by the poets. Chaucer quotations are from *Works* ed. F. N. Robinson (2nd edn, Oxford University Press 1957), Shakespeare quotations from *Works* ed. P. Alexander (Collins 1951).

Pronunciation

The following general observations on pronunciation may be helpful. Short vowels are much as in modern English, except *a* (as in French 'Paris') and *u* (always as in 'full', never as in 'dull'). Final unstressed *-e* is to be pronounced (as in 'Chin*a*') in most fourteenth-century poems, though not all writers are as consistent in this matter as Chaucer or Gower. In the northern dialect of the *Gawain*-poet, *-e* is usually not pronounced; fifteenth-century poets treat syllabic *-e* as an optional, and increasingly occasional, poeticism; the Scottish poets do not use it. Long vowels (often indicated in Scottish spelling by a following *i*: *woik* = 'woke') generally have their continental values. Long *a* is short *a* lengthened, approximately as in modern 'father'. Long *e* is either 'open' (pronounced like French *è*, or roughly as in English 'there'), chiefly in words now spelt with *ea*, or *e* + consonant + *e*; or 'close' (as in German 'mehr', or roughly as in English 'mate'), chiefly in words now spelt with *ee* or *ie*. Long *o* is also either 'open' (pronounced as in 'broad'), chiefly in words now pronounced with 'long *o*', like 'boat' and 'dole'; or 'close' (as in German 'Sohn', or roughly as in English 'note'), chiefly in words now spelt with *oo* like 'boot' and 'book'. Long *i* is pronounced as in 'machine'. In words like *hous*, *out*, *how*, the spelling *ou* / *ow* stands for a long *u* vowel as in modern 'loose'. The diphthong variously spelt *ai* or *ei* is like that in modern 'mile', not 'mail'; *au* is pronounced as in modern 'house'. Initial consonant groups *gn-*, *kn-*, and *wr-* are to be pronounced as written, and *wh-* is pronounced *hw-*. The *l* is sounded in words like 'half'; *r* is always pronounced wherever written; and *-gh* represents the spirants of German 'ich' or 'ach'. The placing of stress in polysyllabic words often differs from modern usage, especially in French and Latin loan words, which are often stressed on the last or second-last syllable, especially at the end of verse lines. Secondary stress is more common than in modern English, as when Hoccleve rhymes *impáciènce* with *offénce* (No. 22 lines 177–9). Ideally the verse should be read aloud, not too quickly, giving due emphasis to the rhymes, and to the alliteration in alliterative verse.

Notes

1. G. G. Smith, ed. *Elizabethan Critical Essays* 2 vols. (Oxford U.P. 1904) 2.62.
2. Smith 1.56.
3. See the brief account by Prof. N. Davis in D. S. Brewer, ed. *Geoffrey Chaucer* (1974) 68–71. Davis observes that 'the use of alternative forms of various kinds can be seen to be a common feature of Chaucer's language'.
4. The baronial hypothesis was stated by J. R. Hulbert *MP* 28 (1930–1) 405–22 and modified by E. Salter *MP* 64 (1966–7) 146–50, 233–7. T. Turville-Petre argues the case for the gentry in a forthcoming study of the Alliterative Revival.
5. See G. Shepherd 'The nature of alliterative poetry in late medieval England' *PBA* 56 (1970) 57–76.
6. Details are given in the headnotes to Nos. 25.2, 27 and 32.

1 Four Rawlinson lyrics

Manuscript A single parchment strip, bound as part of Bodleian MS. Rawlinson D. 913, contains 12 short pieces (items a–l) of English and French verse. First printed by Heuser *Ang.* 30 (1907) 173–9; new MS. readings by Dronke *N & Q* 8 (1961) 245–6; and see Wilson *Lost Literature* 169–70. The strip 'looks like a loose sheet that a minstrel might carry' (Davis *RES* n.s. 22 (1971) 323); but R. L. Greene thinks the scribe was a monk at the monastery of Coggeshall, Essex (mentioned in item d): see *The Lyrics of the Red Book of Ossory* (Oxford, Blackwell 1974) x. The strip dates from second quarter of C14. Its contents seem mostly popular songs. Some are probably dance songs: see the references to dancing (e.g. No. 1.2 line 6), frequent repetitions of single words (*Irlaunde* in No. 1.2, *rose* in No. 1.4), and repetitions of whole lines (in Nos. 1.1, 1.3, 1.4).

No. 1.1 (item a in MS.) expresses in hypnotic rhyme (*aaba aaca*) a young man's image of what his mistress will be. Unrhyming lines 3 and 7 are linked by superlatives, *swotes* ('sweetest') and *fairest*.

No. 1.2 (item g) was made famous by Yeats's 'I am of Ireland' (*Winding Stair* 1933), on the genesis of which see R. Ellmann *The Identity of Yeats* (Macmillan 1954) 280. Formally it is a medieval 'carol', or dance song with burden: first (1–3) a burden, or refrain, to be sung by all the dancers together; then a stanza (4–7) sung by soloist/leader. Normally there is more than one stanza, each followed by repetition of burden. This piece may be fragmentary. The stanza form is common in 'carol': three lines rhyming, with the fourth leading on to the burden (Greene *Carols* xxxvi–xxxvii).

No. 1.3 (item h) was a popular C14 song, as two allusions prove. A Latin sermon (copied *c.* 1360), talking of men's life in the Age of Gold, asks 'What was their drink?' (cf. line 16): 'The answer appears in a certain song, namely a *karole* that is called "the mayde be wode lay"'; see S. Wenzel *Spec.* 49 (1974) 69–74. The other allusion is discussed by Greene *Red Book* ix–xiii and in *Spec.* 27 (1952) 504–6. Richard de Ledrede (Bishop of Ossory 1317–60) disapproved of his clergy's profane songs, and composed Latin verses in similar metres to be sung to the secular tunes. Scraps of profane original text indicate appropriate tunes, one being 'mayde yn the moore lay'. This is attached to a Latin Nativity poem, which helps us reconstruct the stanza form of the English (written as prose, with frequent non-indication of repeated lines, in Rawlinson MS: see notes). The first stanza (Greene's text) runs: 'Peperit virgo, | Virgo regia, | Mater orphanorum, | Mater orphanorum; | Peperit virgo, | Virgo regia, | Mater orphanorum, | Mater orphanorum, | Plena gratia'. Greene proposes expansion of English stanza to nine lines, matching second repetition of 'mater orphanorum' in Latin. **Interpretation** D. W. Robertson *English Institute Essays 1950* (Columbia U.P. 1951) 26–7 sees the maiden as the Virgin Mary; to which J. Harris *Journal of Medieval and Renaissance Studies* 1 (1971) 59–87 adds a possible influence from ballads of Mary Magdalene's penance in the wilderness. Such religious-symbolic interpretations are convincingly criticized by Greene *Red Book* xi–xiii, asserting the 'secular and popular character of the song'. But who then was the maiden? Speirs 59–64 sees her as the spirit of the well, P. Dronke *The Medieval Lyric* (Hutchinson 1968) 195–6 as 'a kind of water-sprite living in the moors'.

No. 1.4 (item j) seems, like No. 1.1, to be a scrap of popular love poetry.

[1]

1.1 'Of everykune tree'

Of everykune tree,
Of everykune tree,
The hawethorn blowet swotes
Of everykune tree.
My lemmon she shall be,
My lemmon she shall be,
The fairest of every kune
My lemmon she shall be.

1 etc. everykune every kind of.
3 blowet swotes blooms most sweetly.
5 lemmon mistress (in common, as against courtly, usage).
7 every] So Dronke. Earlier editors read *erthkinne* 'earth-kind'. MS. almost obliterated here. **kune** kind.

1.2 'Ich am of Irlaunde'

Ich am of Irlaunde
Ant of the holy londe
Of Irlaunde.

Gode sire, pray ich thee
For of sainte charité
Come ant daunce wit me
In Irlaunde.

1 Ich I.
2 Ireland, 'land of the saints'.
4 thee] ye MS. But *ye* for accusative *you* does not occur this early.
5 The Fr. phrase 'par seinte charite' gives 'for sainte charite' in ME. The *of* is redundant.

1.3 'Maiden in the mor lay'

Maiden in the mor lay,
In the mor lay,
Sevenight fulle ant a –
Sevenight fulle ant a –
Maiden in the mor lay,

1 Cf. the variant versions (see headnote): 'the mayde be [by] wode lay' and 'mayde yn the moore lay'. 'Wode' for 'mor' is suspect; but 'maide' for 'maiden' brings the rhythm closer to that of *Peperit Virgo*.
3–4 The first two sts, unlike the last two (see *n.* to 15–28), seem to be written out in full in MS. These two lines have therefore been left by editors as they stand: 'sevenyst fulle | sevenist fulle'. But comparison with the second stanza suggests addition of 'ant a –', as does comparison with Ledrede's Latin (see headnote), where the corresponding lines have six syllables ('mater orphanorum').
3 etc. Sevenight fulle a whole week.

In the mor lay,
Sevenightes fulle ant a day.

Well was hir mete,
What was hir mete?
The primerole ant the –
The primerole ant the –
Well was hir mete,
What was hir mete?
The primerole ant the violet.

Well was hir dring,
What was hir dring?
The chelde water of the –
The chelde water of the –
Well was hir dring,
What was hir dring?
The chelde water of the welle spring.

Well was hir bour,
What was hir bour?
The rede rose ant the –
The rede rose ant the –
Well was hir bour,
What was hir bour?
The rede rose ant the lilie flour.

8 'Good was her food.'
10 primerole primrose.
15–28 Drastically abbreviated in MS: 'Welle [was hir dryng *omitted in error*?] wat was hir dryng, the chelde water of the welle spring; Welle was hire bour, wat was hire bour, the rede rose ante lilie flour.'
15 'Good was her drink.'
17 etc. chelde a southern form of 'cold' (not 'chilled').
21 welle spring not a 'well' in the modern sense (which would suggest human habitation) but the source of a stream.
22 etc. bour lady's chamber. The later sense of *bower* ('arbour, leafy covert') is to be excluded. One could not speak of a 'bower of roses' in ME. Hence the rose of line 24 is a pure surprise.

1.4 'Alnight by the rose . . .'

Alnight by the rose, rose,
Alnight by the rose I lay.
Darst ich nought the rose stele
And yet I bar the flour away.

1 rose The image of the rose as mistress was commonplace in the Middle Ages as now. *R. de la Rose* provides an example.
3 darst dared (read *darf* by editors before Dronke).
4 bar bore. **flour** the flower of virginity. Cf. Gower *Confessio Amantis* 5.5381–2: 'All prively betwen hem tweye | The ferste flour he tok aweye.'

2 Sir Orfeo

Sir Orfeo is the best-known ME example (two others are *Sir Launfal* and *Le Freine*) of the medieval 'Breton lay': a kind of short romance, usually involving love and the 'fairy', and often claiming descent from 'lays' sung by Bretons (so *Orfeo* 13–20). The genre was established in French by Marie de France, whose twelve lays (ed. A. Ewert, Oxford, Blackwell 1944) were dedicated to Henry II of England (reigned 1155–89). Marie claims to be following minstrels of Brittany, who apparently introduced performances of native Breton songs (the Celtic 'lay' proper) with explanations of the 'story' of the song for their French-speaking audience. Marie narrates such stories in elegant octosyllabic couplets. See Bliss's edn of *Orfeo* (below) xxvii–xxxi; E. Hoepffner 'The Breton Lais', Ch. 11 in *ALMA*; C. Bullock-Davies *Med. Aev*. 42 (1973) 18–31. The immediate source of *Orfeo* itself was probably a French lay now lost (see also below); but it is doubtful whether a genuine Breton lay of Orpheus (see Bliss xxxi–xxxii) lay behind the French. 'Celtic elements' in *Orfeo* may be due to a French poet reworking the Orpheus story in the Breton manner.

Orpheus and Orfeo The classical story of Orpheus was known in the Middle Ages chiefly through Ovid *Met*. 10–11, Virgil *Georg*. 4, and Boethius *De consolatione* 3 metre 12. The peculiarities of the *Orfeo* version have three main causes. First, influence of folk beliefs, especially Celtic: e.g. the 'imp-tree' (70 and *n*.), the otherworld (351 f. and *n*.), and (most important) the idea of being 'taken' by the fairy, on which see D. Allen 'Orpheus and Orfeo: the Dead and the *Taken*' *Med. Aev*. 33 (1964) 102–11 (see *n*. to 387–408). The Irish legend *The Wooing of Etain*, proposed as a specific source e.g. by G. V. Smithers *Med. Aev*. 22 (1953) 85–8, 'can be considered only as a story in which a number of the Celtic motifs found in *Sir Orfeo* happen to reappear in combination' (Bliss liv). Second, the preference in Breton lays, as in romances generally, for happy endings. For general consideration of *Orfeo* as romance, see J. B. Friedman *Orpheus in the Middle Ages* (Harvard U.P. 1970). But a happy-ending version of the Orpheus story existed in antiquity (first recorded in Euripides). Third, development by the medieval poet (French and/or English) of the theme of fidelity or 'truth'. Orfeo is the type of faithful lover-husband ('In luve none leler than Schir Orpheus', Henryson *Orpheus and Eurydice* 207). His fidelity to Heurodis is matched by the Steward's fidelity to him: see D. M. Hill 'The structure of *Sir Orfeo*' *Med. Stud*. 23 (1961) 136–53. Orfeo also tests (see *n*. to 452) the Fairy King's fidelity to his pledged word. Thus two intrusive folk motifs, Disguised Return and Rash Promise, serve simple thematic purposes. The exemplary fidelity of all concerned is a condition of the happy ending, as in other lays (cf. *Franklin's Tale*, Chaucer's imitation of the Breton lay). But Doob 164–207 interprets the poem as a Christian allegory, with Orfeo representing Christ.

Manuscripts and versions Three MSS., all edited by A. J. Bliss *Sir Orfeo* (2nd edn, Oxford U.P. 1966): Auchinleck MS., N.L.S. MS. Advocates' 19.2.1 (= *Auch*); B.L. MS. Harley 3810 (= *H*, early C15); Bodleian MS. Ashmole 61 (= *Ashm*, late C15). Wide textual variations suggest transmission by minstrels (adapting, abbreviating, half-remembering): see Baugh *Spec*. 42 (1967) 1–31. The present text (except lines 1–38: see *n*.) is based on *Auch*. This MS., compiled *c.*1330, not long after *Orfeo*'s composition, was perhaps known to Chaucer, whose *Franklin's Tale* may owe something to *Orfeo*; L. H. Loomis 'Chaucer and the Breton Lays of the Auchinleck MS.' *SP* 38 (1941) 14–33. Two fragments (copied *c.*1585) of a Scottish text closely related to *Orfeo*, ed. M. Stewart *Scottish Studies* 17 (1973) 1–16, may represent another, independent version of the lost French source. The story survives in northern folk tradition, and ballad versions have been collected in Shetland in C19 (Bliss l–li, Child 1.217) and in mid C20: B. H. Bronson *Traditional Tunes of the Child Ballads* 4 vols. (Princeton U.P. 1959–72) 4.455–6, with tune.

We reden ofte and finde ywrite,
As clerkes don us to wite,
The layes that ben of harping
Ben yfounde of ferly thing.
Som ben of wer and som of wo
And som of joy and mirthe also,
Som of trechery and som of gile
And som of happes that fallen by while,
Som of bourdes and ribaudy,
And many there ben of the fairy.
Of alle thing that men may see
Most o love forsothe they be.
In Bretain thise layes arn ywrought,
First yfounde and forth ybrought,
Of aventures that fallen by dayes,
Wherof Bretouns made her layes.

1–38 These lines, missing from *Auch* through loss of a leaf, are supplied from *H*. The *H* prologue closely resembles the prologue to *Lay le Freine*, another Breton lay, in *Auch*. Bliss bases his reconstructed *Auch Orfeo* prologue on the latter: *EGS* 5 (1953) 7–14. (It is not clear which lay borrowed from which: Bliss Introd. xlvi–xlvii.) The *Ashm* prologue, though much distorted in transmission, shares some readings against *H* with the *Auch Freine* prologue. These have been adopted where indicated.
2 don us to wite inform us.
3 layes On Breton lays, see headnote above.
4 yfounde devised. **ferly** wonderful (so *Auch Freine*; *H* has 'frely').
5 wer war (so *Auch Freine*, *Ashm*; wele *H*).
7–8 follow 10 in *H*.
8 by while from time to time.
9 bourdes jests. **and**] *Auch Freine*; and sum of *H*.
10 many] *Auch Freine*, *Ashm*; sum *H*.
12 o love of love (so *Auch Freine*, *Ashm*; *H* has *to lowe* 'to praise').
13 Bretain Brittany, 'Little Britain'. **ywrought**] *Ashm*; wrought *Auch Freine*; ywritt *H*.
14 ybrought] brought *Ashm*; ygete *H*.
15–16 Cf. Chaucer *Franklin's T.*, *C.T.* V 709–10: 'Thise olde gentil Britouns in her dayes | Of diverse aventures maden layes.' Such opening remarks about the Bretons were customary in lays, following Marie de France. **her** their.

[2]

When they might owher heren
Of aventures that there weren,
They toke her harpes with game,
Maden layes and yaf it name.
Of aventures that han befalle
I can som telle but nought alle.
Herken, lordinges that ben trewe,
And I woll you telle of Sir Orphewe.

Orfeo most of any thing
Loved the glee of harping;
Siker was every good harpour
Of him to have moche honour.
Himself he lerned forto harpe
And laid theron his wittes sharpe;
He lerned so, there nothing was
A better harper in no plas.
In the world was never man born
That ones Orfeo sat beforn,
And he might of his harping here,
He sholde thinke that he were
In oon of the joys of Paradis,
Such melody in his harping is.

Orfeo was a king,
In Inglond an hye lording,
A stalworth man and hardy bo,
Large and curteis he was also.

17 owher anywhere.
20 yaf gave. Peculiar significance attached to the titles of Breton lays. They often, like *Orfeo* 600, describe how they got their names.
23 The address to the audience is in the minstrel manner, parodied by Chaucer at the beginning of *Sir Thopas*: 'Listeth, lordes, in good entent' (*C.T.* VII 712).
25–38 These lines on Orfeo's love of the harp follow 46 in *H*; but Bliss argues convincingly that they were among the lost lines in *Auch*, and therefore preceded the lines on Orfeo's royal descent (39–46). This order points up Orfeo's kinship with the Breton minstrels.
26 glee of harping music of the harp.
27 Siker certain. The 'honour' paid by Orfeo to harpers anticipates that paid by the Fairy King at the climax of the story.
29 he lerned] *Ashm*; loved *H*.
34 'Who once sat before Orfeo.'
35 And if.
36 He sholde . . . Confused construction. Bliss emends to 'Bot he schuld . . .', following *Ashm*.
38 melody] joy and melody *H*.
39 Here *Auch* begins.
41 hardy bo courageous too.
42 Large generous.

His fader was comen of King Pluto
And his moder of King Juno,
That s[illegible]time were as goddes yhold
For [illegible]hat they dede and told.
Thi[illegible] Traciens,
Th[illegible]fens:
F[illegible]
T[illegible]

43–6 [illegible]ryson *Orpheus and Eurydice* 29–63) to [illegible]d the muse Calliope, neither descended from [illegible] ignorance also appears in his failure to identify Plut[illegible]and of Fairyland (Chaucer *C.T.* IV 2227) and hence the very [illegible]rfeo's wife. However, his identification of Pluto and Juno as kings [illegible] time, become 'gods' in pagan eyes because of their feats, belongs to a [illegible]pectable euhemeristic tradition in medieval thought: J. Seznec *The Survival of the Pagan Gods* tr. B. F. Sessions (New York, Pantheon 1953) Pt 1 Ch. 1.
44 King Juno The poet may have gathered this error from a MS. in which 'Joue' was corrupted to 'Juno', as in No. 23 below, line 60; or 'King' may be a scribal error carried down from 43.
47 Traciens Orpheus was a Thracian. Probably the poet had a (lost) French original which referred to him as 'reis Traciens', 'Thracian king'.
48 of noble defens strongly fortified.
49–50 Not in *Ashm* or *H*, and perhaps interpolated by a minstrel seeking local colour. However, 'Winchester was the old capital of England, and therefore the conventional seat of an English king' (Sisam); and the name may reflect a place-name in the French original (Caruent?).
49 tho then.
50 withouten no undeniably.
51 of pris excellent.
53 levedy lady. **for the nones** 'for the nonce', a tag.
56 Ac but.
57 comessing 'commencing'.
61 breme bright.
63 ich same.

Took two maidens of pris
And went in an undrentide
To play by an orchard side,
To see the floures sprede and spring
And to here the fowles sing.
They set hem down all three
Under a fair impe-tree,
And well sone this fair quene
Fell on slepe opon the grene.
The maidens durst hir nought awake
Bot lete hir ligge and rest take.
So she slepe till after none,
That undrentide was all ydone.
Ac as sone as she gan awake
She cried and lothly bere gan make;
She froted hir honden and hir feet
And cracched hir visage, it bled weet;
Hir riche robe hie all to-rett
And was reveyd out of hir wit.
The two maidens hir beside
No durst with hir no leng abide,
Bot urn to the palais full right
And tolde bothe squier and knight
That her quene awede wold,
And bad hem go and hir athold.
Knightes urn and levedis also,
Damisels sexty and mo.

65 undrentide 'the time of undern', here midday (cf. 75–6). The heat of the day, when people take siestas (cf. 402), is the time when fairies are about (cf. 282). J. B. Friedman *Spec.* 41 (1966) 22–9 compares the 'noon-day demon' of *Ps.* 90.6 (A.V. 91.6).
66 play amuse herself, relax.
70 impe-tree apparently a grafted tree, such as might grow in an orchard. The idea that lying under a tree places one in fairy power is found in other English and French lays (Bliss Introd. xxxv–xxxvi) and English ballads (Child 1.340).
74 ligge lie.
78 bere outcry. The cause of Heurodis's distress is not revealed until 133 f. Such use of suspense is characteristic of the poem (Bliss xlii), and contributes to its narrative power.
79 froted rubbed together.
80 cracched scratched. **it bled weet** until it was wet with blood.
81 hie she. **to-rett** tore to pieces.
82 reveyd hunted, driven (*OED* s.v. *Revay* v.).
84 leng longer.
85 urn ran.
87 awede go mad.
88 athold restrain.

In the orchard to the quene hie come
And hir up in her armes nome
And brought hir to bed atte last
And held hir there fine fast.
Ac ever she held in o cry
And wold up and owy.
  When Orfeo herd that tiding,
Never him nas wers for no thing.
He com with knightes tene
To chaumber right before the quene
And beheld and said with grete pité:
'O leef lif, what is te,
That ever yet hast ben so stille
And now gredest wonder shille?
Thy body, that was so white ycore,
With thine nailes is all totore.
Allas, thy rode, that was so red,
Is all wan as thou were ded,
And also thine fingres smale
Beth all blody and all pale.
Allas, thy lovesom eyen two
Looketh so man doth on his fo!
A, dame, ich beseche mercy.
Let ben all this rewful cry
And tell me what thee is and how,
And what thing may thee helpe now.'
  Tho lay she stille atte last
And gan to wepe swithe fast

92 nome took.
94 fine fast very firmly.
95 'But she kept crying out the same thing', i.e. that she wanted to be 'up and away' (96). Heurodis does not hope to escape from the fairy (126). Rather, in her hysteria, she wants to go to them before they come for her.
98 nas was not. The triple negative (idiomatic in ME) emphasizes the shock to Orfeo.
102 'O beloved one, what is the matter with you?' *te* is a form of 'thee'.
103 yet up to now.
104 gredest cry out. **shille** loudly.
105–12 The pathos of Orfeo's plight is later described in a similar passage of antitheses, 241–56.
105 ycore excellently.
107 rode countenance, complexion.
109 smale slender (a sign of good breeding).
112 so as.
114 rewful piteous.
115 'And tell me what is wrong with you, and how it happened.'
118 swithe fast very hard.

[2]

And saide thus the king to:
'Allas, my lord Sir Orfeo,
Sethen we first togider were
Ones wroth never we nere,
Bot ever ich have yloved thee
As my lif, and so thou me.
Ac now we mot delen atwo;
Do thy best, for I mot go.'
'Allas,' quath he, 'forlorn icham.
Whider wiltow go and to wham?
Whider thou gost ichill with thee,
And whider I go thou shalt with me.'
'Nay, nay, sir, that nought nis.
Ichill thee telle all how it is.
As ich lay this undrentide
And slepe under our orchard side,
There come to me two faire knightes
Wele y-armed all to rightes,
And bad me comen an heighing
And speke with her lord the king;
And ich answerd at wordes bold,
I no durst nought, no I nold.
They pricked ayain as they might drive.
Tho com her king also blive
With an hundred knightes and mo
And damisels an hundred also,
All on snowe-white stedes;
As white as milke were her wedes.
I no seigh never yet before

121 Sethen since.
122 nere were not. Emphatic double negative.
125 'But now we must part from each other.'
126 Do thy best get on as best you can.
127 icham I am.
129 ichill I will.
131 nought nis is quite impossible.
133 f. Heurodis does not describe a dream. 'The "soul" or "self" is able [according to folk belief] to wander from the body on adventures of its own', D. Allen *Med. Aev.* 33 (1964) 102–3.
136 to rightes as was proper.
137 an heighing in haste.
140 no I nold neither did I wish to.
141 'They rode away as fast as they could spur.'
142 also blive immediately.
145 White steeds are characteristic of fairy riders: cf. No. 19 below, lines 1310–14 and *n.*
146 See No. 19 below, *n.* to lines 1305 f.

So faire creatours ycore.
The king had a crown on hed;
It nas of silver no of gold red,
Ac it was of a precious ston,
As bright as the sunne it shon.
And as sone as he to me cam,
Wold ich, nold ich, he me nam
And made me with him ride
Opon a palfray by his side,
And brought me to his palais,
Wele atird in ich ways,
And shewed me castels and tours,
Rivers, forestes, frith with flours,
And his riche stedes ichon,
And sethen me brought ayain hom
Into our owen orchard,
And said to me thus afterward:
"Loke, dame, tomorwe thatow be
Right here under this impe-tree,
And then thou shalt with us go
And live with us evermo;
And yif thou makest us ylet,
Whar thou be, thou worst yfet,
And totore thine limes all,
That nothing help thee no shall.
And thei thou beest so totorn,
Yet thou worst with us yborn."'
   When King Orfeo herd this cas,
'O we!' quath he, 'allas, allas.

148 ycore and excellent.
151 The crown made of a single precious stone may be compared with that worn by Alceste in Chaucer's *L.G.W.* F Prol. 221. The wealth here and at 357–76 is characteristic of the fairy world (Wimberly 180–6) and of 'other worlds' in general (Patch *Other World*).
154 'Whether I was willing or not, he took me.'
158 'Well equipped in every way.' Description of the fairy palace is postponed until 355.
160 frith woodland.
161 stedes estates. **ichon** each one.
165 thatow that thou.
169 'And if you cause us to be hindered.'
170 'Wherever you are, you will be fetched.'
171 totore torn to pieces.
173 thei even though.
174 worst will be.
176 we woe.

[2]

Lever me were to lete my lif
Than thus to lese the quene my wif.'
He asked conseil at ich man,
Ac no man him help no can.
Amorwe the undrentide is come,
And Orfeo hath his armes ynome
And wele ten hundred knightes with him,
Ich y-armed stout and grim;
And with the quene wenten he
Right unto that impe-tree.
They made sheltrom in ich a side
And said they wolde there abide
And die there everichon
Ere the quene sholde fram hem gon.
Ac yet amiddes hem full right
The quene was oway ytwight,
With fairy forth ynome.
Men wist never where she was become.
  Tho was there crying, wepe and wo.
The king into his chaumber is go,
And oft swoned opon the ston
And made swich diol and swich mon
That neigh his lif was yspent.
There was non amendement.
He cleped togider his barouns,
Erles, lordes of renouns;
And when they all ycomen were,
'Lordinges,' he said, 'before you here
Ich ordainy myn hye steward
To wite my kingdom afterward.
In my stede ben he shall
To kepe my londes overall.
For now ichave my quene ylore,

177 lete give up.
181 Amorwe on the next day.
182 ynome taken.
185 he they.
187 made sheltrom formed themselves into a compact troop (OE *scieldtruma* 'shield-troop').
192 oway ytwight snatched away.
193 fairy enchantment, magic.
194 was become had got to.
198 diol lamentation.
205 ordainy appoint.
206 wite keep.
209 ylore lost.

The fairest levedy that ever was bore,
Never eft I nill no woman see.
Into wilderness ichill tee
And live there evermore
With wilde bestes in holtes hore.
And when ye understond that I be spent,
Make you then a parlement
And chese you a newe king.
Now doth your best with all my thing.'
Tho was there weping in the halle
And grete cry among hem alle;
Unethe might old or yong
For weping speke a word with tong.
They kneled adown all yfere
And prayed him, yif his wille were,
That he no shold nought fram hem go.
'Do way,' quath he, 'it shall be so.'
All his kingdom he forsook;
Bot a sclavin on him he took.
He no had kirtel no hood,
Shert, no non other good,
Bot his harp he took algate
And dede him barfoot out atte yate;
No man most with him go.

211 nill will not. Emphatic triple negative. Ovid says that Orpheus, after his final loss of Eurydice, gave up the company of women because of a vow: *Met*. 10.79–81.
212 When he goes into the 'wilderness', Orfeo has no intention of searching for Heurodis: see K.R.R. Gros Louis *RES* n.s. 18 (1967) 245–52. Louis suggests that his time in the wilderness (like Lear's on the heath) is one of 'humility and sacrifice', a purgatorial experience after which he is rewarded with Heurodis; and Doob (164–207) considers Orfeo as a 'Holy Wild Man', comparing him with Christ in the wilderness. But Orfeo's 'self-exile' is no more (and no less) than a manifestation of his grief and his devotion to Heurodis.
212 tee go.
214 hore grey, i.e. ancient. A traditional epithet for woods.
215 spent finished.
221 Unethe hardly.
223 yfere together.
226 Do way enough.
228 Bot a sclavin only a pilgrim's mantle.
229 kirtel short coat.
230 no non other good nor any other possession. So (with *ne* for *no*) *Ashm*; no nother gode *Auch*.
231 algate at any rate.

[2]

O way! what there was wepe and wo
When he that had ben king with crown
Went so poverlich out of town.
Thurgh wode and over heth
Into the wilderness he geth.
Nothing he fint that him is ais,
Bot ever he liveth in gret malais.
He that had ywerd the fowe and gris
And on bed the purper bis,
Now on hard heth he lith,
With leves and gresse he him writh.
He that had had castels and tours,
River, forest, frith with flours,
Now, thei it comency to snewe and frese,
This king mot make his bed in mese.
He that had yhad knightes of pris
Before him kneland, and levedis,
Now seeth he nothing that him liketh
Bot wilde wormes by him striketh.
He that had yhad plenté
Of mete and drink, of ich dainté,
Now may he all day digge and wrote
Ere he finde his fill of rote.
In somer he liveth by wild frut
And berien bot gode lite;
In winter may he nothing finde

234 way woe.
239 'He finds nothing to give him comfort.'
241–56 The sustained antithesis (cf. 105–12 and 235–6) carries here a faint moral implication, suggesting the traditional *ubi sunt* ('Where are now his robes, his castles . . . ?'). See No. 23 below, lines 65–96. Bliss Introd. xxxvii and lvi traces the account of Orfeo's life in the wilderness to 'the Celtic tradition of the wild man of the woods', as well as to the classical story. Cf. especially the story of Merlin taking to the woods as a wild man, in early Welsh poetry, whence Geoffrey of Monmouth's *Vita Merlini* and French treatments.
241 ywerd worn. **fowe and gris** rich furs, striped (*fowe*) and grey.
242 purper bis dark purple cloth.
244 writh covers.
245–6 This couplet virtually repeats 159–60. Such repetitions are common in minstrel verse.
248 mese moss.
251 liketh pleases.
252 'Save fearsome snakes which slip past him.'
255 wrote grub.
258 'And berries of very little worth.'

Bot rote, grases and the rinde.
All his body was oway dwine
For missais and all tochine.
Lord! who may telle the sore
This king sufferd ten yere and more?
His here of his berd, black and rowe,
To his girdelstede was growe.
His harp, wheron was all his glee,
He hidde in an holwe tree;
And when the weder was clere and bright
He took his harp to him well right
And harped at his owen wille.
Into alle the wode the soun gan shille,
That alle the wilde bestes that there beth
For joye abouten him they teth,
And alle the fowles that there were
Com and sete on ich a brere
To here his harping afine,
So miche melody was therin;
And when he his harping lete wold,
No beste by him abide nold.
  He might see him besides
Oft in hot undrentides
The king o fairy with his rout
Come to hunt him all about
With dim cry and blowing,

260 rinde bark.
261 oway dwine wasted away.
262 missais hardship. **tochine** scarred.
265 rowe rough (cf. 459).
266 girdelstede waist.
272 gan shille rang out.
273–80 The classical account of how Orpheus with his lyre moved not only beasts but also trees and stones (Ovid *Met*. 11.1 f.) is here somewhat rationalized. Only animals and birds respond.
274 teth come.
276 sete sat.
277 afine to the end.
279 lete leave, cease.
281–96 The fairy hunt and army are both traditional, particularly in Celtic sources. Walter Map (twelfth century) gives a notable account of Herla and the fairy hunt (*De nugis curialium* Dist.i Cap. xi, summarized Bliss xxxviii).
282 See 65 *n*.
283 rout company.
285 dim cry] *Auch*; dynne cry *Ashm*; dunnyng *H*. Hill *Med. Stud*. 23 (1961) 136–8 argues that 'dim' in *Auch* is a scribal error for 'din' adopted by editors on account of its Tennysonian flavour; but 'dim' was quite commonly applied to sounds in ME: see *MED* s.v. sense 4.

[2]

And houndes also with him berking;
Ac no beste they no nome,
No never he nist whider they become.
And other while he might him see
As a gret ost by him tee,
Wele atourned, ten hundred knightes,
Ich y-armed to his rightes,
Of cuntenaunce stout and fers,
With many desplayd baners,
And ich his swerd ydrawe hold;
Ac never he nist whider they wold.
And other while he seigh other thing:
Knightes and levedis com dauncing
In queint atire, gisely,
Queint pas and softly;
Tabours and trumpes yede hem by
And all maner minstracy.
And on a day he seigh him beside
Sexty levedis on hors ride,
Gentil and jolif as brid on ris.
Nought o man amonges hem there nis,
And ich a faucoun on hond bere,
And riden on hawkin by o rivere.
Of game they founde well good haunt,
Maulardes, hairoun and cormeraunt.

288 'Nor did he ever know where they went' (cf. 194 and 296).
290 As a gret ost what seemed a great army.
291 atourned equipped.
292 to his rightes as was proper for him.
293 fers proud, fierce.
296 'But he never knew where they were going.'
298–302 The fairy dance was traditional, e.g. in ballads (Wimberly 191–4). Here the dance with its 'knights and ladies' forms a transition from the all-male hunt and army to the all-female hawking party which follows.
299 'In elegant dress, skilfully.'
300 Queint pas with elegant steps.
301 Tabours drums. **yede** went.
303–13 Ladies did accompany men on hawking-parties (see e.g. the August illustration in *Très Riches Heures du Duc de Berry*); but a party entirely composed of ladies is strange.
305 'Graceful and joyous as bird on branch.'
308 'And they rode a-hawking by a river-bank.'
309 haunt profusion.
310 Maulardes wild ducks. **hairoun** heron. Frederick II devoted Book 5 of his treatise on hawking to heron-hawking.

The fowles of the water ariseth,
The faucouns hem wele deviseth;
Ich faucoun his prey slough.
That seigh Orfeo and lough:
'Parfay,' quath he, 'there is fair game;
Thider ichill, by Goddes name.
Ich was ywon swich werk to see.'
He aros and thider gan tee.
To a levedy he was ycome,
Beheld and hath wele undernome
And seeth by all thing that it is
His owen quene, Dame Heurodis.
Yern he beheld hir, and she him eke,
Ac noither to other a word no speke.
For missais that she on him seigh
That had ben so riche and so heigh
The teres fell out of hir eighe.
The other levedis this yseighe
And maked hir oway to ride;
She most with him no lenger abide.
'Allas,' quath he, 'now me is wo.
Why nill deth now me slo?
Allas, wrocche, that I no might
Die now after this sight.
Allas, too long last my lif,
When I no dar nought with my wif,

312 deviseth mark.
313 The contrast with 287 is notable: 'Orfeo is now to meet his wife, and must be in no doubt that she is really alive and not merely an illusion' (Bliss Introd. xlii).
315 Parfay by my faith.
316 Thider ichill I shall go there.
317 ywon accustomed. Hawking was a favourite activity of medieval lords.
320 undernome observed.
323–30 The discovery of a known person among a band of fairy riders (leading to a rescue attempt) suggests the ballad of Tam Lin. And cf. Gower's story of Rosiphelee, No. 19 below.
323 Yern eagerly.
324 noither neither. Orfeo and Heurodis are still constrained by the power of the fairy: cf. 336–7. See Owen *Med. Aev.* 40 (1971) 249–53. The scene may be compared with the meeting of Troilus and Cresseid in Henryson's *Testament*, No. 30 below, lines 484–525.
330 most might.
333 wrocche wretch.
335 last lasts.

[2]

Ne hie to me, o word speke.
Allas, why nill myn hert breke?
Parfay,' quath he, 'tide what betide,
Whider so thise levedis ride,
The selve way ichill strecche.
Of lif no deth me no recche.'
His sclavin he dede on also spack
And heng his harp opon his back,
And had well gode will to gon;
He no spard noither stub no ston.
In at a roche the levedis rideth
And he after and nought abideth.
When he was in the roche ygo
Wele three mile other mo,
He com into a fair cuntray
As bright so sunne on somers day,
Smothe and plain and all grene,
Hill no dale nas there non ysene.
Amidde the lond a castel he seigh,
Riche and real and wonder heigh.
All the utemaste wall
Was clere and shine as cristal;
An hundred tours there were about,

337 hie she.
339 tide what betide come what may.
341 'I shall travel the same way.'
342 me no recche I do not care.
343 also spack straight away.
346 spard stopped for. **stub** stump.
347–8 In Walter Map's story (*n.* to 281–96 above) Herla comes to the pygmy's palace through a cave in a cliff. On fairies living in hills, see Wimberly 130–2.
347 roche rock.
350 other mo or more.
351 f. Bliss Introd. xxxix cites Celtic parallels for the flat greenness of fairy-land, and also for the crystal wall, gold pillars, and jewel houses; but parallels will also be found in English ballads: Wimberly Ch. 5 (e.g. p. 146: 'The roof was o the beaten gowd, | The flure was o the crystal a'). See generally Patch *Other World.*
353 plain flat. The flatness of Paradise (attractive to an agricultural society) is emphasized in OE *Phoenix*.
356 real royal.
357 utemaste outermost.
358 shine bright.

Degiselich and bataild stout;
The butras com out of the diche
Of rede gold y-arched riche;
The vousour was avowed all
Of ich maner divers aumal.
Within there were wide wones
All of precious stones;
The werst piler on to behold
Was all of burnist gold.
All that lond was ever light,
For when it shold be therk and night
The riche stones light gunne
As bright as doth at none the sunne.
No man may telle no thenche in thought
The riche werk that there was wrought.
By all thing him think that it is
The proude court of Paradis.
In this castel the levedis alight;
He wolde in after, yif he might.
  Orfeo knocketh atte gate;
The porter was redy therate
And asked what he wold have ydo.
'Parfay,' quath he, 'icham a minstrel, lo!
To solas thy lord with my glee,
Yif his swete wille be.'
The porter undede the yate anon
And lete him in to the castel gon.

360 'Wonderful and strongly battlemented.'

361 diche i.e. moat.

363–4 'The vaulting [i.e. in the arches of the flying buttresses] was all decorated with every kind of different enamel.' *avowed* ('decorated', OE **afagod*) is doubtful, and might be emended to *anowrned* 'adorned'.

365 wones halls.

370 therk dark.

371 light gunne shone. Jewels were commonly thought to give off light in Middle Ages.

373 thenche think.

375 him think it seems to him.

376 The Heavenly Jerusalem in *Rev.* Ch. 21 (followed in *Pearl* 977 ff.) is of pure gold, with walls of jasper and foundations of precious stones: 'And the light thereof was like to a precious stone, as to the jasper stone, even as crystal' (21.11).

378 wolde wanted to go.

381 wold have ydo wanted to be done.

383 glee music.

Then he gan behold about all
And seigh liggeand within the wall
Of folk that were thider ybrought,
And thought dede and nere nought.
Som stode withouten hade,
And som non armes nade,
And som thurgh the body hadde wounde,
And som lay wode ybounde,
And som armed on hors sete,
And som astrangled as they ete,
And som were in water adreint,
And som with fire all forshreint.
Wives there lay on childbedde,
Som dede and som awedde,
And wonder fele there lay besides
Right as they slepe her undrentides.
Ech was thus in this warld ynome,
With fairy thider ycome.
There he seigh his owen wif,
Dame Heurodis, his leef lif,

387–408 R. B. Mitchell *Neophil.* 48 (1964) 155–9 suggests that lines 391–400, which have no equivalent in MS. *H*, were interpolated by a scribe, giving rise to inept contradiction between 400 and 390. Others trace this contradiction back to the difficulty of blending the classical Hades (land of the dead – Eurydice dies of snakebite in classical versions) and the Celtic Fairyland ('land of the living'). The difficulty is resolved by D. Allen *Med. Aev.* 33 (1964) 102–11 by reference to folk beliefs (especially Celtic). Fairies will 'take' people, not only when peacefully asleep under trees, but also in the throes of death. Thus in Henryson's *Orpheus and Eurydice*, the Queen, having suffered a mortal snakebite in the classical manner, is nevertheless 'with the phary tane' in her death-swoon (lines 110–19). What Orfeo sees within the wall of the fairy city is the 'taken', each in the state in which he was taken. The catalogue is organized around pairs of opposites: head/arms (391–2), body/mind (393–4), war/peace (395–6), water/fire (397–8), and finally (for women) childbed/daybed (399–402).
388 liggeand lying. *Auch* has 'ful liggeand', where 'ful' might be emended to 'fele' ('many') as at 401.
390 nere were (not).
391 hade head.
394 wode mad. It was customary to confine madmen.
396 astrangled choked.
397 adreint drowned.
398 forshreint scorched to death.
400 awedde mad.
401 fele many.
402 See 65 *n*.

Slepe under an impe-tree:
By hir clothes he knew that it was he.
And when he had behold thise mervails alle,
He went into the kinges halle.
Then seigh he there a semly sight,
A tabernacle blissful and bright.
Therin her maister king sete,
And her quene fair and swete.
Her crownes, her clothes shine so bright
That unethe behold he hem might.
When he had beholden all that thing,
He kneled adown before the king:
'O lord,' he said, 'yif it thy wille were,
My minstracy thou shust yhere.'
The king answerd, 'What man artow
That art hider ycomen now?
Ich no non that is with me
No sent never after thee.
Sethen that ich here regny gan
I no fond never so folehardy man
That hider to us durst wende
Bot that ichim wald ofsende.'
'Lord,' quath he, 'trowe full well,
I nam bot a pover minstrel,
And, sir, it is the maner of ous
To seche many a lordes hous.
Thei we nought welcom no be,
Yet we mote profery forth our glee.'
Before the king he sat adown
And took his harp so mirry of soun
And tempreth his harp as he wele can,
And blissful notes he there gan,
That all that in the palais were
Com to him forto here

407 See 70 *n*.
408 he she.
412 tabernacle canopy over a throne.
413 maister lord.
420 shust shouldst.
423 'Neither I nor any of my men.'
425 'Since I began to reign here.'
428 'Unless I was pleased to send for him.'
431–4 These reflections on a minstrel's life support the theory that *Orfeo* itself is of minstrel origin.
434 profery offer.
437 tempreth tunes.

[2]

And liggeth adown to his fete,
Hem thenketh his melody so swete.
The king herkneth and sit full stille;
To here his glee he hath good wille.
Good bourde he had of his glee,
The riche quene also had he.
When he had stint his harping,
Then said to him the king:
'Minstrel, me liketh well thy glee.
Now aske of me what it be,
Largelich ichill thee pay.
Now speke, and tow might asay.'
'Sir,' he said, 'ich beseche thee
Thatow woldest yive me
That ich levedy bright on blee
That slepeth under the impe-tree.'
'Nay,' quath the king, 'that nought nere,
A sorry couple of you it were!
For thou art lene, rowe and black,
And she is lovesom, withouten lack.
A lothlich thing it were forthy
To seen hir in thy compainy.'
'O sir,' he said, 'gentil king,
Yet were it a wele fouler thing
To here a lesing of thy mouthe.
So, sir, as ye said nowthe,

441 liggeth lie. The fairy inhabitants behave like tamed animals.
442 Hem thenketh seems to them.
445 bourde entertainment.
446 'And so also had the noble queen.'
450 what whatever.
451 'I will reward you generously.'
452 and tow might asay if you can bring yourself to. Or perhaps, 'if you are able to put me to the test'? Orfeo is to test the Fairy King, as he later 'assays' the Steward (568); but the King perhaps doubts whether this humble minstrel can frame a request great enough truly to test him.
455 ich same. **blee** face.
457 that nought nere that would be no good at all.
458 'You two would make an ill-matched pair.' The episode of the Fairy King's Rash Promise (a common folk-tale motif) is weakened by his lack of any powerful reason for wishing to refuse the resulting request.
459 rowe and black shaggy and swarthy, i.e. like a churl.
460 lack fault.
461 forthy therefore.
465 lesing lie (dishonoured promise). Orfeo's reply points the theme of 'truth': see headnote.
466 nowthe just now.

What ich wold asky have I shold,
And nedes thou most thy word hold.'
The king said, 'Sethen it is so,
Take hir by the hond and go;
Of hir ichill thatow be blithe.'
He kneled adown and thonked him swithe.
His wif he took by the hond
And dede him swithe out of that lond
And went him out of that thede;
Right as he com the way he yede.
So long he hath the way ynome
To Winchester he is ycome,
That was his owen cité;
Ac no man knew that it was he.
No forther than the townes ende
For knowleche no durst wende;
Bot with a begger, ybilt full narwe,
There he took his herbarwe
To him and to his owen wif,
As a minstrel of pover lif,
And asked tidinges of that lond
And who the kingdom held in hond.
The pover begger in his cote
Told him everich a grot:
How her quene was stole owy
Ten yere gon with fairy,
And how her king en exile yede,
Bot no man nist in whiche thede,
And how the steward the lond gan hold,
And other many thinges him told.

471 'I wish you joy of her.'
472 swithe very much.
474 dede him swithe made his way quickly.
475 thede country.
476 yede followed.
477 'He has travelled the way so far.'
478 Winchester] Trasyens *Ashm*; Crassens *H*. See 49–50 *n*.
482 'He dared not go for fear of being recognized.'
483 ybilt full narwe very meanly lodged.
484 herbarwe lodging.
489 cote hovel.
490 everich a grot every single detail.
492 gon ago.
493 en exile yede went into exile. A French phrase ('en exile') perhaps carried over from the lost Fr. original.

[2]

Amorwe, ayain none tide,
He maked his wif there abide;
The beggers clothes he borwed anon
And heng his harp his rigge opon,
And went him in to that cité
That men might him behold and see.
Erles and barounes bold,
Burjais and levedis him gun behold:
'Lo,' they said, 'swich a man!
How long the here hongeth him opan!
Lo how his berd hongeth to his knee!
He is yclungen also a tree.'
And as he yede in the strete,
With his steward he gan mete,
And loude he set on him a cry:
'Sir steward,' he said, 'mercy!
Icham an harpour of hethenesse;
Help me now in this distresse.'
The steward said, 'Come with me, come;
Of that ichave thou shalt have some.
Everich good harpour is welcom me to
For my lordes love Sir Orfeo.'
In the castel the steward sat atte mete,
And many lording was by him sete.
There were trompours and tabourers,
Harpours fele and crowders.
Miche melody they maked alle,
And Orfeo sat stille in the halle

497 'The next day, towards noon.'
499 Orfeo took only a *sclavin* into the wilderness (228–30), and even a beggar's clothes are better than what he now has.
500 rigge back.
504 Burjais citizens. **gun behold** looked at.
505 swich what.
507 Orfeo's beard reached no further than his waist at 266.
508 yclungen shrunk. **also** like.
512 mercy take pity.
513 hethenesse heathen lands. The folk motif of the hero's disguised return is best known from the *Odyssey*.
516 that what.
518 'For the love of my lord, Sir Orfeo' (regular ME word order).
519 The abrupt transition recalls the close kinship between metrical romance and ballad.
521 tabourers drummers.
522 'Many harpers and fiddlers.'

And herkneth when they ben all stille.
He took his harp and tempred shille;
The blifulest notes he harped there
That ever any man yherd with ere;
Ich man liked wele his glee.
The steward beheld and gan ysee
And knew the harp also blive.
'Minstrel', he said, 'so mot thou thrive,
Where haddestow this harp and how?
I pray that thou me telle now.'
'Lord,' quath he, 'in uncouth thede.
Thurgh a wilderness as I yede,
There I found in a dale
With liouns a man totorn smale,
And wolves him frete with teeth so sharp.
By him I fond this ich harp.
Wele ten yere it is ygo.'
'O,' quath the steward, 'now me is wo!
That was my lord Sir Orfeo.
Allas, wrecche, what shall I do
That have swich a lord ylore?
A, way, that ich was ybore!
That him was so hard grace iyarked
And so vile deth ymarked!'
Adown he fell aswon to grounde.
His barouns him took up in that stounde,
And telleth him how it geth:
It nis no bot of mannes deth.

525 'And listens for when they are all silent.' Editors put a semicolon or stop after *herkneth*; but the translation suggested here avoids an awkward and uncharacteristic stop in the verse, and is supported by *Ashm*: 'And lystynd to [until] thei wer styll.' The change of tense is quite normal.
526 tempred shille tuned it loudly.
527 blifulest most joyful (form of 'blitheful').
531 also blive immediately.
532 mot mayst.
535 uncouth thede a strange land.
539 frete devoured.
546 A, way alas.
547 'That so hard a fate was ordained for him.'
548 ymarked marked out.
549 aswon in a swoon.
550 in that stounde thereupon.
551 how it geth how life goes.
552 'There is no remedy for a man's death.' Proverbial: Whiting D78.

[2]

King Orfeo knew wele by than
His steward was a trewe man
And loved him as he aught to do,
And stont up and seith thus, lo:
'Steward, herkne now this thing
Yif ich were Orfeo the king,
And had ysuffred full yore
In wildernesse miche sore,
And had ywon my quene owy
Out of the lond of fairy,
And had ybrought the levedy hende
Right here to the townes ende,
And with a begger hir in ynome,
And were myself hider ycome
Poverlich to thee thus stille
Forto asay thy gode wille,
And ich founde thee thus trewe,
Thou no shust it never rewe:
Sikerlich, for love or ay,
Thou shust be king after my day.
And yif thou of my deth hadest ben blithe.
Thou shust have voided also swithe.'
Tho all tho that therin sete
That it was King Orfeo underyete,
And the steward him wele knew:
Over and over the bord he threw

553 King Orfeo The title has been used only once before, at 175. It here marks Orfeo's resumption of his normal role: cf. 576, 593. **by than** by that.

554 The disguised lord has tested his substitute, as in Shakespeare's *Measure for Measure*.

556 stont stands. **lo** more likely a minstrelish introduction to the speech than the first word of it (as taken by editors).

558 The series of conditional clauses lasts until line 569, to dramatic effect.

559 fule yore for a long time.

561 ywon . . . owy won away.

563 hende gracious.

565 'And taken lodgings for her with a beggar.' On the translation, see D. Gray *Archiv* 198. (1962) 167–9.

567 stille quietly.

570 'You would never regret it.'

571 Sikerlich certainly. **for love or ay** despite any feelings to the contrary (*ay* 'fear').

574 'You would have cleared out at once.'

575 Tho all tho then all those.

576 underyete understood.

578 Trestle tables were used in halls. The steward knocks one over in his eagerness to get to his king.

And fell adown to his fete;
So dede everich lord that there sete;
And all they said at o crying:
'Ye beth our lord, sir, and our king.'
Glad they were of his live.
To chaumber they ladde him als bilive
And bathed him and shaved his berd
And tired him as a king apert;
And sethen with grete processioun
They brought the quene into the town
With all maner minstracy.
Lord, there was grete melody!
For joye they wepe with her eighe
That hem so sounde ycomen seighe.
  Now King Orfeo newe coround is,
And his quene Dame Heurodis,
And lived long afterward,
And sethen was king the steward.
Harpours in Bretain after than
Herd how this mervail began
And made herof a lay of good liking
And nempned it after the king:
That lay 'Orfeo' is yhote;
Good is the lay, swete is the note.
Thus com Sir Orfeo out of his care.
God graunt us alle wele to fare. Amen.

581 at o crying with one cry. The acclamation marks the lords' acceptance of Orfeo as king once more.
584 als bilive immediately.
586 tired robed. **apert** for all to see.
589 Music and pageants were often arranged by cities to welcome a royal arrival (see Wickham).
592 'Seeing them returned so safe.'
597 after than after that.
599 of good liking well-pleasing.
600 nempned named. The name of a Breton lay is often recorded in the text, as a matter of special significance: see *ALMA* 113.
601 yhote called.
602 note tune. See headnote.
604 The first-person plural prayer is common at the end of minstrel pieces.

3 Thole a Little

This poem occurs in a Latin sermon in New Coll. Oxford MS. 88, immediately following the passage from St Augustine's *Confessions* (Bk 8 Ch. 5) of which it is a version: 'When You said to me "Awake, thou that sleepest and rise up from the dead, and Christ shall give thee light" [*Eph.* 5.14], I had no answer for you . . . except slow and sleepy words [*verba lenta et sompnolenta*]: "Shortly, now, shortly. Have patience a little". But "shortly" and "shortly" had no limit [*Sed modo et modo non habebant modum*], and "have patience a little" went on a great while.' Augustine refers to his own slow conversion. Delay in confession is the preacher's topic. Formal analysis in R. D. Stevick 'The criticism of ME lyrics' *MP* 64 (1966–7) 105–8, with references to other discussions. The poem is No. 5 in Brown *XIVth-Century Religious Lyrics.*

Loverd, thou clepedest me
An ich naght ne answarede thee
Bute wordes slowe and slepye:
'Thole yet! Thole a littel!'
Bute 'yet' and 'yet' was endelis
And 'thole a littel' a long way is.

1 'Lord, you called to me.'
4 Thole wait. This colloquial sense ('hang on a bit') does not exclude the original sense 'suffer': both the long-suffering Lord and the suffering Christ are addressed.
5 In the Latin the repetition here of *modo* ('shortly') arises from a repetition in the speaker's reply to Christ: 'Modo, ecce, modo.' In the English the effect is more mysterious and incantatory.

4 'Lollay, lollay, littel child . . .'

No true (i.e. non-literary) lullabies survive from the Middle Ages, but evidence cited by Woolf *Lyric* 151 shows that mothers sang to babies about their future. This poem (the earliest surviving lullaby text) takes the mother's presumably romantic and optimistic prophecy and substitutes a grimly didactic and pessimistic one. Cf. Robert Greene *Sephestia's Lullaby* (1589): 'Weep not my wanton, smile upon my knee, | When thou art old there's grief enough for thee.' All other ME lullabies concern the Christ-child: one example, No. 65 in Brown *XIVth-Century Religious Lyrics*, is probably an imitation of the present poem: Woolf *Lyric* 155–6. See generally F. E. Budd *A Book of Lullabies 1300–1900* (London, Partridge 1930).

Manuscript B.L. MS. Harley 913, an Anglo-Irish MS. of the first third of C14. Some of its contents – and possibly the present poem – are the work of Friar Michael of Kildare. See W. Heuser, ed. *Die Kildare-Gedichte* (Bonn 1904). This poem is No. 28 in Brown *XIVth-Century Religious Lyrics*, and No. 82 in Gray *Selection.*

Lollay, lollay, littel child, why wepestow so sore?
Nedes mostow wepe, hit was iyarked thee yore
Ever to lib in sorow, and sich and mourn therfore,
As thyn eldren did ere this, whil hi alives wore.
  Lollay, lollay, littel child, child, lollay, lullow,
  Into uncuth world ycomen so ertow.

Bestes and thos fowles, the fisses in the flood,
And euch shef alives, ymaked of bone and blood,
Whan hi cometh to the world hi doth hamsilf som good,
All bot the wrecche broll that is of Adames blood.
  Lollay, lollay, littel child, to care ertow bemet,
  Thou nost noght this world is wild before thee is yset.

Child, if betideth that thou shalt thrive and thee,
Thench thou were yfostred up thy moder knee;
Ever hab mund in thy hert of thos thinges three,
Whan thou comest, whan thou art, and what shall come of thee.

2 'You must indeed weep – it was ordained for you of old.'
3 lib live. **sich** sigh. **therfore**] suggested by Brown *XIVth-Century Religious Lyrics* instead of MS. *euer* to restore rhyme. Heusler proposed *evermore*. On traditional interpretations of the child's first cries, see Gray 211. Sometimes the baby is represented as weeping because it realizes what its new world is like ('When we are born, we cry that we are come | To this great stage of fools' *Lear* 4.6.183–4). But in this version the baby is ignorant (line 12).
4 whil hi alives wore while they were alive. **wore**] were MS. See *n.* to 3.
5 Lollay, lollay] Lollai MS.
6 'Thus you have come into an alien world.'
8 euch shef alives every living creature.
9 'When they are first born they are able to do some things for themselves', i.e. newborn animals etc. are not as helpless as human babies. An unfinished Latin version of the poem (first 2 sts only) on f. 63b of the MS. renders: 'Sibi prosunt aliquid vivamen prestantes' ('benefit themselves by providing some livelihood'). Cf. *Castle of Perseverance* 329–30: 'For iche creature helpeth himself bedene | Save only man at his cominge.'
10 wrecche broll wretched brat.
11 to care ertow bemet you are destined for sorrow.
12 'You do not know that this world which is set before you is a wilderness.'
13 thee prosper.
14 Thench think. **up** upon.
15 hab mund have mind, take thought.
16 Whan . . . whan whence . . . whence. Davies emends the second *whan* to *what*, citing Alanus de Insulis: 'Consider carefully what you were when you came to be born, what you are now, and what you will be' ('. . . Quid sis praesens, quid futurus', Migne *P.L.* 210.580); but the present context might encourage double stress on maternal origins. Man's origin in the womb, as represented by medieval moralists, is just as chastening as his destination in the tomb.

Lollay, lollay, littel child, child, lollay, lollay,
With sorow thou com into this world, with sorow shalt wend away.

Ne tristow to this world, hit is thy fulle vo;
The rich he maketh pover, the pore rich also;
Hit turneth wo to wele and eke wele to wo.
Ne trist no man to this world whil hit turneth so.
Lollay, lollay, littel child, the foot is in the whele;
Thou nost whoder turne to wo other wele.

Child, thou ert a pilgrim in wickedness yborn;
Thou wandrest in this fals world – thou loke thee beforn!
Deth shall come with a blast ute of a well dim horn
Adames kin down to cast, himsilf hath ydo beforn.
Lollay, lollay, littel child, so wo thee worth Adam
In the lond of Paradis throgh wickedness of Satan.

Child, thou nert a pilgrim bot an uncuthe gest,
Thy dawes beth ytold, thy jurneys beth ycest.
Whoder thou shalt wend north other est,
Deth thee shall betide with bitter bale in brest.
Lollay, lollay, littel child, this wo Adam thee wroght
When he of the appil ete and Eve hit him betoght.

19 tristow trust thou. **fulle vo** declared enemy: *MED* s.v. *Ful* adj. 5(f).
21 wele prosperity, joy.
22 turneth The earth did not rotate in medieval cosmology. The underlying image in this passage is that of Fortune and her turning wheel (cf. 23–4), on which see H. R. Patch *The Goddess Fortuna in Medieval Literature* (Harvard U.P. 1927). Lines 19–22 are probably based on a popular quatrain on Fortune (Brown *XIVth-Century Religious Lyrics* No. 42), in one form of which the line corresponding to 22 runs: 'No triste no man to this wele, the *whel* it turnet so.'
24 'You do not know whether it will turn to sorrow or joy.'
26 thou loke thee beforn look ahead.
27 horn] horre MS., which could only represent *MED Herre* n. (1), meaning possibly 'corner', or more likely 'doorway'. But the emendation (Sisam *Med. Eng. Verse*, emending also MS. forms *ibor* 25, *bifor* 26 and *befor* 28) makes better sense. Death summons man with a blast from his horn (cf. No. 28 line 21 and *n.*) *dim* presumably implies uncanny faintness, as in No. 2 line 285.
28 'To knock down Adam's descendants, as he once did Adam himself.'
29 so wo thee worth Adam such ill-luck Adam brought you (literally 'so badly Adam turned out for you'). See *OED* s.v. *Woe* int. and adv. 4. Brown *XIVth-Century Religious Lyrics* emends *worth* to *worp* ('wove, prepared'); but *so* suggests that *wo* is not a noun.
31 'Child, you are not even a pilgrim [see 25], rather an unknown guest.'
32 'Your days are numbered, your travels planned' (Davies).
33 Whoder whether.
34 bale misery.
36 betoght gave.

5 I would be Clad in Christ's Skin

Recorded in N.L.S. MS. Advocates' 18.7.21: a collection of materials for preaching, assembled in 1372 by the Norfolk Franciscan friar John of Grimestone. See E. Wilson *Descriptive Index of the English Lyrics in John of Grimestone's Preaching Book* (Oxford, Blackwell 1973). The poem (No. 71 in Brown *XIVth-Century Religious Lyrics*) would have suited the emotional style of preaching, especially on the Passion, for which friars were famous. It has connections with the cult of Christ's wounds (Gray 133–5), especially with the traditional idea of taking refuge in them (Gray 134, Brown's note). But the exact conceit here has not been paralleled: man can find clothing (3), lodging (5) and food (6) in the body of the crucified Christ.

Gold and all this werdis win
Is nought but Cristes rode.
I wolde ben clad in Cristes skin
That ran so longe on blode,
And gon t'is herte and taken myn in –
There is a fulsum fode.
Then yef I littel of kith or kin,
For there is alle gode.

1 werdis win world's joy.
2 'Is nothing without Christ's cross.'
5 t'is to his. **in** dwelling.
6 fulsum fode plentiful supply of food.
7 'Then I would care little about kith or kin.'

6 Penny

Added in C14 handwriting in Gonville and Caius Coll. Cambridge MS. 261. No. 60 in Robbins *Secular Lyrics*. Versions of lines 1 and 2 were current as proverbs in Tudor times (Tilley G247, S706). They are found together in two C15 proverb collections: 'Spende, and God will sende; | Spare, and evere bare' (Whiting G261). Line 5 suggests popular medieval personifications of 'Sir Penny': see Greene *Carols* 429. The whole is a pithy version of attitudes expressed by Waster in No. 7 below. Cf. also No. 20.

Spende, and God shall sende;
Spare, and ermore care;
Non peny, non ware,
Non catel, non care.
Go, peny, go.

2 Spare save, traditionally coupled with *spend*. Cf. No. 7 line 224 and No. 20 line 125. **ermore care** worry for evermore.
3 Non no.
4 catel goods, property (corresponding to *ware* in the rhetorical climax of 3–4).
5 Like the refrain in *Sir Penny I* (Robbins *Secular Lyrics* No. 57): 'Go bet, peny, go bet, go! | For thou mot maken bothe frind and fo.'

7 Winner and Waster: extract

Winner and Waster, like many medieval poems (e.g. *Owl and Nightingale*), takes the form of a debate. The poet, as in Nos. 9 and 11 below, has a dream. He sees two armies confronting each other on a plain surrounded by wooded hills. Winner leads one army, which includes lawyers, friars, merchants, and the Pope. In Waster's army are 'men of arms, bold squires of blood, bowmen many'. The two leaders are summoned to answer before a King (Edward III) seated in a pavilion above the plain. The debate follows, consisting of eight speeches in which Winner and Waster alternately vie for the King's favour. The one, defective MS. breaks off before the end of the King's speech of judgment: for the time being, Winner is to go abroad to where he is 'most loved', the papal court; while Waster remains in England, conning innocent visitors to London and feasting on the proceeds. But the King promises to summon Winner back in due time, whereupon Waster will go abroad. Like many debate poems, therefore, this one ends without endorsing either party.

Interpretation Gollancz called the poem 'a topical pamphlet in alliterative verse on the social and economic problems of the hour'. Like Stillwell, *ELH* 8 (1941) 241–7, Gollancz identified the two rival parties with the aristocratic or military class (Waster) and the middle or merchant class (Winner). The poem so considered would be an early statement of the conflict between landed and moneyed interests (cf. Roger de Coverley and Andrew Freeport in Addison's *Spectator* papers). But the presence of churchmen in Winner's host, and Waster's last appearance as a London conman, suggest the limitations of a class analysis. Speirs 263–89 rightly stresses the personal, moral issues, upon which the solution of social and economic problems depends. The basic moral groundplan is the Aristotelian *schema* of the two opposed vices of prodigality and niggardliness (*Eth. Nic.* 4.1), a *schema* transmitted e.g. by Aquinas *Summa theologica* II–II qq. 117–9 (cf. Dante *Inferno* Canto 7, Gower *Confessio Amantis* 7.1985–2164). See T. H. Bestul *Satire and Allegory in 'W & W'* (Univ. of Nebraska P. 1974). The poet develops this opposition with finesse, inventiveness and humour, introducing several subordinate moral issues also (see *n.* to 230). The upshot might be clearer if the last lines survived. Everett 49–50 sees the poem as satire: 'A sharp twofold attack upon Edward III for the extravagance of his living, and of his wars, and for the means by which he obtained the money for both.' So too D. J. Williams, in W. F. Bolton, ed. *The Middle Ages* (Barrie and Jenkins 1970) 117–19. But Speirs 289 points the positive significance: 'Winner and Waster could be aspects of the same person. The way of wisdom in the individual life, as in the life of a kingdom, would seem to be to keep a just balance between the two extremes.' The medieval name for the 'just balance' between niggardliness and prodigality was 'liberality' or 'largesse'.

Manuscript and authorship B.L. MS. Additional 31042, imperfect, breaking off after 503 lines. Headed: 'Here Begynnes a Tretys and god Schorte refreyte [? refrain] Bytwixe Wynnere and Wastoure'. First edited by I. Gollancz, 1897. See his edn with trans., 2nd edn (1930 for 1931), reissued Cambridge, Brewer 1974. The anonymous author represents himself as an honest 'Western man' (7). *The Parliament of the Three Ages*, another alliterative debate poem in vision form, is sometimes ascribed to the same poet, without good reason.

Date and influence Gollancz and J. M. Steadman, *MP* 19 (1921–2) 211–19, agree on the winter of 1352–53. William Shareshull (317) was Chief Justice 1350–61. The statement by Winner and Waster that the King 'has us fostered and fed this five and twenty winter' (206) points to 1352, twenty-fifth year of Edward III's reign. The poem is in that case one of the earliest datable monuments of the Alliterative Revival (see Introduction xx–xxiii). It was probably known to Langland, and influenced the *Visio* of *Piers Plowman*: see S. S. Hussey *MLR* 60 (1965) 163–70.

Lines 218–453

Bot then kerpede the king, said, 'Kithe what ye hatten
And why the hates aren so hote your hertes betwene.
If I shall deme you this day, doth me to here.'
'Now certes, lord,' said that one, 'the soth forto telle,
I hat Winner, a wye that all this world helpes,
For I lordes can lere thurgh leding of wit.
Tho that spedfully will spare and spende not too grete,
Live upon littel-whattes, I love him the better.
Wit wendes me with and wisses me faire.
Ay when gader my gudes, then glades myn herte.
Bot this felle false thefe that before you standes
Thinkes to strike or he stint, and stroye me for ever.
All that I winne thurgh wit, he wastes thurgh pride:
I gader, I glene, and he lattes go sone;
I prike and I prine, and he the purse openes.

218 kerpede spoke. **Kithe what ye hatten** make known what you are called.
220 doth me to here let me hear. The King is to judge between (*deme*) the rival claims of Winner and Waster.
222 wye man. A poetic word peculiar to alliterative verse at this time. **world** object of *helpes*.
223 lere instruct. **wit** good sense, intelligence: half-personified, here as at 226.
224 Tho those. **spedfully** in a profitable way. **spare and spende** traditional alliterating opposites, like *win* and *waste*: cf. No. 6 lines 1–2, No. 20 line 125.
225 littel-whattes small portions.
226 Wit see 223 *n*. **wisses** guides.
227 'Always when my goods accumulate . . .' But the word order is unusual. Perhaps a subject *I* is to be understood.
228 felle treacherous. **thefe** see 242 *n*.
229 or he stint before he is done. **stroye** destroy.
230–7 Lines especially notable for variety and expressiveness in the handling of alliterative metre.
230 thurgh wit i.e. by using my head. **pride** In the course of the debate, Winner accuses Waster of the sins of pride, gluttony and lechery; Waster accuses Winner of avarice and sloth (*wanhope* 309, 373).
232 I prike and I prine I make everything trim and tidy (?). Apparently a variant of a phrase *pick and preen* (see *OED* s.v. *Pick* v.^{1} 4, *Preen* v.^{2}, *Prune* v.^{1}) used of birds trimming their feathers, etc.

[7]

Why has this caiteff no care how men corn sellen?
His londes liggen all ley, his lomes aren solde,
Down ben his doufehouses, drye ben his pools.
The devil wonder the wele he weldes at home,
Bot hunger and hye houses and houndes full kene!
Save a sparth and a spere sparred in an hirne,
A brond at his bede hede, biddes he no nother,
Bot a cutted capill to caire with to his frendes.
Then will he boste with his brand and braundeshe him ofte,
This wicked weried thefe that Wastour men calles,
That if he live may longe, this land will he stroye.
Forthy deme us this day, for Drightens love in heven,
To fighte furth with oure folk to outher fey worthe.'
'Yea, Winner,' quod Wastour, 'thy wordes are hye,
Bot I shall telle thee a tale that tene shall thee better.
When thou hast waltered and went and waked all the night,
And ich a wye in this world that wonnes thee aboute,
And has werped thy wide houses full of wolle sackes,
The bemes benden at the rofe, sich bacon there hinges,
Stuffed are sterlinges under stelen boundes –

233 how at what price. Waster comments later on Winner's preoccupation with corn prices (which suffered violent fluctuations in C14): 370–4. Cf. 274.
234–5 D.V. Moran *Neuphil. Mitteil.* 73 (1972) 684 points out a relevant legal sense of 'waste' (*OED* s.v. *Waste* sb. 7): 'Any unauthorized act of a tenant ... which tends to the destruction of the tenement.' Cf. 396 f., 450.
234 ley untilled. **lomes** tools (modern 'loom').
235 pools fishponds. Fish, like doves, supply food to the prudent householder.
236 wonder] wounder one MS. Emended by Gollancz: 'There is nothing at all marvellous about the wealth he has at home.' Colloquial scorn.
237 hye houses high houses, suggesting extravagant impracticality (cf. *Mum and Sothsegger* 3.217). **kene** fierce (through hunger?).
238–40 'He asks nothing but a halberd and a spear tucked away in a corner, a sword at his bed's head, and a gelding to go to his friends on.'
241 boste threaten. **brand** sword. **braundeshe him** strut about (reflexive).
242 weried accursed. **thefe** The term 'wastour' is used in a statute of Edward III to designate a class of thief: see *OED* s.v. *Roberdsmen.*
244 Forthy so. **Drightens** the Lord's. Cf. 255 and *n.*
245 to outher fey worthe until one of us die (literally 'become doomed').
247 tene vex.
248 waltered and went tossed and turned.
249 ich a wye every man (222 *n*). **wonnes thee aboute** lives in your household. Both contestants usually address each other with the familiar and here aggressive singular pronoun, instead of the polite *you.*
250 werped crammed.
251 hinges hangs.
252 sterlinges silver coins. **stelen boundes** bands of steel (on a treasure chest).

What sholde worthe of that wele if no waste come?
Some rote, some ruste, some ratouns fede.
Let be thy craming of thy kistes, for Cristes love of heven!
Let the peple and the pore have part of thy silver;
For if thou wide-whare sholde walke and waiten the sothe,
Thou sholdest reme for reuthe, in sich rife ben the pore.
For, and thou lenger thus live, leve thou no nother,
Thou shall be hanged in helle for that thou here sparest.
For sich a sin hast thou sold thy soule into helle,
And there is ever wellande wo, world withouten ende.'
'Let be thy word, Wastour,' quod Winner the riche,
'Thou mellest of a mater, thou madest it thyselven.
With thy sturt and thy strife thou stroyest up my gudes,
In playing and in waking in wintres nightes,
In outrage, in unthrift, in angarte pride.
There is no wele in this world to washen thyn handes
That ne is given and grounden ere thou it geten have.
Thou ledes renkes in thy route well richly attired;

253 worthe of become of. **wele** wealth. Waster's argument, here and at 384 f., anticipates that of Milton's Comus: *Masque* 727 ff.
254 ratouns rats.
255 kistes chests. **for Cristes love of heven** for the love of Christ in heaven (normal ME word order).
256 A similar argument is used against niggardliness in *Jacob's Well* ed. A. Brandeis EETS o.s. 115 (1900) p. 121: 'right hard and spending littel in good use, ne having no reuthe ne pité on the pore'. But the piety of Waster's tone is suspect.
257 wide-whare far and wide. **waiten** observe.
258 reme cry out. **in sich rife** so numerous.
259 and if. **leve thou no nother** don't doubt it.
261 sin Avarice, or covetousness, was one of the Seven Deadly Sins.
262 wellande wo boiling sorrow (a phrase traditionally applied to Hell pains).
264 'You are talking about something [poverty] which you yourself are responsible for.'
265 sturt quarrelling.
267 'In excess, prodigality, and overweening pride.'
268–9 'There is no wealth in this world in which your hands may dip [? so Gollancz] that is not given and granted even before you have got it.' The collocation with *given* establishes *grounden* as a rare form of *graunten*. The phrase 'given and granted' is a legalism, rendering Latin 'datum et concessum': cf. *MED* s.v. *Graunten* v. 4(a) and *Piers* No. 11.2 below, line 183. Line 268b is obscure: Prof. Fowler refers me to the proverb 'For washing his hands none sells his lands' (Tilley W75).
270 renkes men. **route** company.

[7]

Some have girdills of gold that more gude coste
Than all the faire free lond that ye before haden.
Ye folowe noght your faders, that fosterde you alle,
A kinde hervest to cacche and cornes to winne
For the colde winter and the kene with gleterande frostes,
Sithen dropeless drye in the dede moneth.
And thou woll to the taverne before the town-hede,
Ich berin redy with a bolle to bleren thyn eyen,
Hete thee what thou have shalt and what thyn hert likes,
Wife, wedowe or wenche that wonnes theraboute.
Then is there bot "fille in" and "fecche forth", florenes to shewe,
"Wee hee" and "worthe up", wordes ynewe.
Bot when this wele is away, the wine most be payed for;
Then limpes you weddes to laye, or your lond selle.
For sich wicked werkes, wery thee oure Lord!
And forthy God laughte that he lovede and levede that other,

271–2 Waster has sold off his paternal acres to buy rich gifts for his followers. Such 'outrageous array' is treated as a kind of pride (cf. 267) by Chaucer's Parson (*C.T.* X 409 f.) and other moralists.
272 free freehold.
273 fosterde trained, brought up.
274 'To get a good harvest and bring in the corn.'
275 gleterande glittering. Gollancz emends to *clengande*; but alliteration of *c* and *g* is sometimes permitted in ME.
276 'And then the rainless drought in the dead month.' Probably a reference to the 'drought of March' coming after the cold winter. Cf. No. 11.1, line 289.
277 woll to will go to. **town-hede** upper end of the town, 'beyond the jurisdiction of the authorities' (Gollancz).
278 berin man. **bolle** drinking-bowl. **bleren thyn eyen** befuddle you.
279 Hete thee promise you.
280 wonnes lives.
281 'Then there is nothing but "pour out" and "fetch out", to make florins appear.' Gollancz takes MS. *florence* as the girl's name, meaning a 'wanton woman'; but this meaning is not recorded until much later. *florence* is a ME spelling of 'florins'.
282 Wee hee a neighing noise. **worthe up** get up (used of getting up on horseback). Cf. *Piers* B 7.91–2, describing the sexual animality of beggars: 'But as wilde bestes with wehe worthen uppe and worchen, | And bringeth forth barnes that bastardes men calleth.' **wordes ynewe** words sufficient, i.e. no further 'love-talking' is necessary.
283 'But when this money is gone . . .'
284 'Then you must give pledges . . .'
285 wery curse.
286 forthy because. **laughte** took.

Ich freke on felde ogh the ferder be to wirche.
Teche thy men for to tille and timen thyn feldes,
Raise up thy rent-houses, rime up thy yerdes,
Outher have as thou hast done and hope after werse –
That is first the failing of fode, and then the fire after
To brenne thee all at a birre for thy bale dedes.
The more cold is to come, als me a clerk tolde.'
'Yea, Winner,' quod Wastour, 'thy wordes are vaine.
With oure festes and oure fare we feden the pore.
It is plesing to the prince that paradise wroghte;
When Cristes peple hath parte him payes all the better
Than here ben hodird and hid and happed in cofers,
That it no sunne may see thurgh seven winter ones,
Outher freres it fecche when thou fey worthes,
To painten with their pelers or pergette with their walles.

287 Ich freke every man. **ogh** must. **ferder** more eager. In the last part of his speech, Winner uses apocalyptic language, referring here to Christ's prophecy of the Last Days: 'Then two shall be in the field. One shall be taken and one shall be left' (*Matt*. 24.40).
288 timen Gollancz emends to *tinen*, glossing 'fence, hedge in'. The existence of a verb *tine* 'to harrow' is to be noted (*OED Tine* v.[3], and cf. ME *tine* sb. 'prong of a harrow'), particularly as *Scottish National Dictionary* records a variant *time* in Modern Scots. 'Harrow' would make good sense here.
289 Raise up restore. **rime up** clear out.
290 'Or else get what your actions deserve, and live in expectations of worse.' The first half-line is proverbial: Whiting H185.
291–3 Winner's prophecy of famine, fire and a great cold, is in the manner of much C14 apocalyptic prophecy: see Bloomfield *Piers* 91–4. Bennett 215 suggests that the present passage may have influenced Langland, No. 11.1 below, lines 319–31, where the prophecy arises, as here, out of exhortations to work.
292 at a birre at one rush, instantly. **bale** wicked. The world is to be destroyed by fire at the end of time.
293 Referring perhaps to the extreme cold which traditionally alternates with the extreme heat of the medieval Hell.
295 This reply to Winner's accusation that Waster creates poverty (264) employs an argument used elsewhere to prove that prodigality is less harmful than niggardliness: Hoccleve *Regement of Princes* 4641. **fare** feasting.
297 him payes it pleases him (Christ). Cf. *Matt*. 19.21.
298 hodird covered up. **happed** wrapped.
299 Gold was thought to mature in the sun.
300–1 People often left their money, in return for prayers, to the Friars, who were held to spend too much of it on elaborate church buildings: cf. Chaucer *Summoner's T.* and *Piers* B 3.48 f. Friars form part of Winner's army, as described in the First Fitt.
300 Outher or else. **fey worthes** die.
301 pelers pillars. **pergette** plaster.

[7]

Thy sone and thy sectours ichone slees other,
Maken dale after thy day, for thou durste never
Maungery ne mindale, ne never mirthe lovedest.
A dale after thy day dos thee no mare
Than a light lanterne late upon nighte
When it is borne at thy backe, berin, by my trouthe.
Now wolde God that it were als I wisse couthe,
That thou, Winner, thou wricche, and Wanhope thy brother
And eke imbrene dayes and evenes of saintes,
The Friday and his fere on the ferrer side,
Were drowned in the depe see there never droght com,
And dedly sin for their dede were endited with twelve;
And thise berins on the binches with howes on lofte
That ben knowen and kidde for clerkes of the beste,
Als gude als Arestotle or Austin the wise,
That alle shent were those shalkes and Sharshull itwiste,
That said I prickede with powere his pese to distourbe!

302 sectours executors. **slees** destroys. The rascality of executors formed one of the commonplaces of medieval satire and preaching against avarice.
303–4 'They distribute alms after your lifetime, just because you never dared to have a banquet or a mind-ale.' **dale** distribution of alms. **mindale** 'an ale-drinking or feast in memory of a person' (Gollancz).
305 dos thee no mare is no more use to you.
308 als I wisse couthe as I could devise it.
309 Wanhope a form of sloth or *acedia*: specifically, despair of God's mercy, often leading to suicide (373–4). See S. Wenzel *The Sin of Sloth* (Univ. of N. Carolina Press 1967).
310 imbrene dayes ember days, periods of fasting and prayer. The eves of saints' days were also fasts.
311 Friday was a regular fast day. Its 'companion on the further side', i.e. Saturday, was also kept as a fast by devotees of the Virgin, whose votive mass was then.
313 their dede their death, i.e. the drowning of Winner, Wanhope etc. **endited with twelve** indicted with a jury (the procedure in homicide cases). Waster's fantasy leads on to the attack on lawyers which follows.
314 berins on the binches men on the benches, i.e. judges. **howes** lawyers' caps. Alliteration fails: Gollancz emended to *biggins*.
315 kidde renowned. **clerkes** learned men.
316 Austin St Augustine.
317 'That those men were all ruined, and Shareshull with them.' William Shareshull was Chief Justice 1350–61. **itwiste** MS. *it wiste* ('knew it') seems to conceal a form of *MED Itwix* adv.
318 prickede spurred. **powere** body of armed men. In his summons to the 1352 Parliament, Shareshull referred to 'les destourbours de la Pees'. He was involved in quelling such disturbances in 1352 and 1353. See J. M. Anderson *MLN* 43 (1928) 47–9. **his** implies that it was the Chief Justice's peace that suffered, not the King's (whom Waster is addressing).

Forthy, comely king, that oure case heres,
Let us swithe with oure swerdes swingen togeders;
For now I see it is full soth that said is full yore:
The richer of rank wele, the rather will drede;
The more havand that he hath, the more of herte feble.'
    Bot then this wrecched Winner full wrothly he lukes,
Says, 'This is spedless speche to speken thise wordes.
Lo this wrecched Wastour, that wide-whare is knawen!
Ne is nother kaiser ne king ne knight that thee folowes,
Baron ne bachelere ne berin that thou lovest,
Bot foure felawes or five that thee faith oweth.
And he shall dighte them to dine with dainteths so many
That ich a wye in this world may wepen for sorowe.
The bores hede shall be broght with plontes upon lofte,
Buck-tailes full brode in brothes there beside,
Venison with the frumenté, and fesantes full riche,
Baken mete therby on the borde set,
Chewettes of chopped flesh, charbiand fowles;
And ich a segge that I see has sex mens doke.
If this were nedeless note, another comes after:
Roste with the riche sewes and the ryal spices,
Kiddes cloven by the rigge, quarterd swannes,

320 swithe quickly. **swingen togeders** come to blows.
321 yore long since.
322 'The richer of abundant wealth [a man is], the readier he will be to feel fear.'
323 havand possessions.
325 spedless profitless.
326 Lo look at. The line is ironical. Waster is such an obscure, small-time leader (329) that Winner does not want to waste time on him.
327 'There is neither emperor . . .'
328 bachelere young knight.
329 that thee faith oweth who owe you loyalty.
330–63 The three-course banquet served by Waster to his few followers, as described by the indignant Winner, is highly extravagant even by medieval standards.
330 dighte them to dine prepare dinner for them.
332 plontes upon lofte plants on top. The boar's head would be decked with bays, rosemary, etc.
333 Buck-tailes hindquarters of a deer.
334 frumenté 'a dish made of hulled wheat boiled in milk, and seasoned with cinnamon, sugar, etc' (*OED* s.v. *Frumenty*).
335 Baken mete pastry dishes, such as meat pies and tarts.
336 Chewettes meat pies. **charbiand** roasted (obscure and uncertain).
337 segge man. **sex mens doke** duck enough for six.
338 nedeless note an unnecessary business. **another** i.e. the second course.
339 sewes broths. **ryal** royal.
340 cloven by the rigge split down the back.

[7]

Tartes of ten inch, that tenes myn herte
To see the borde overbrade with blasande dishes,
Als it were a railed rood with ringes and stones.
The thirde mese to me were mervelle to recken,
For all is Martinmesse mete that I with moste dele,
Noght bot wortes with the flesh, without wild fowl,
Save an hen to him that the house oweth;
And he will have birdes boun on a broche riche,
Barnakes and buturs and many billed snipes,
Larks and lingwhittes lapped in sogoure,
Woodcockes and woodwales full wellande hote,
Teeles and titmoises, to take what him likes;
Caudels of coninges and custades swete,
Dariols and dish-metes that full dere coste,
Mawmene that men clepen, your mawes to fille:
Ich a mese at a merke betwene twa men,
Whiche bot brinneth for bale your bowels within!
Me teneth at your trompers, they tounen so hye
That ich a gome in the gate goulling may here.

341 tenes hurts.
342 overbrade overspread. **blasande** shining.
343 railed rood bejewelled cross.
344 mese course.
345–6 'For *I* have to make do with salted meat, and nothing but vegetables with it . . .' Cattle were commonly slaughtered at Martinmas (11 Nov.) for winter provisions.
347 oweth owns. The owner is presumably Winner himself, who allows himself a little chicken as a treat.
348 boun on a broche ready on a spit.
349–52 The *wild fowl* specified are: goose, bittern, snipe, lark, linnet, woodcock, oriole (?), teal and tit.
350 sogoure sugar.
351 wellande boiling.
353–60 A tear in the MS. cuts off the first letters of each line. Restorations as follows: [Caude]ls (Gollancz), [Dario]ls (Goll.), [Mawm]ene (Goll.), [Ich a] mese, [Whic]he, [Me ten]eth (Goll.), [That ich] a (Goll.), [Then] will (Goll.).
353 Caudels of coninges rabbit broths.
354 Dariols pastries. **dish-metes** food cooked in dishes.
355 Mawmene that men clepen 'what men call "mawmene"', a delicacy with wine in it.
356 'Each portion for two men is worth a mark.' Diners ate in pairs, sharing a set of dishes: each course for one such pair was worth 66·6p.
357 'Which does nothing but make your bowels burn with pain!'
358 'I grieve at your trumpeters, they blow so loud.' Blowing of trumpets accompanied the entry of each course at a banquet.
359 gome in the gate person in the road outside. **goulling** yowling.

[7]

Then will they say to themselve as they samen ride
Ye have no mister of the help of the heven king.
Thus are ye scorned by skill and scathed therafter
That rechen for a repaste a raunsom of silver.
Bot ones I herd in a halle of a herdmans tong:
Better were meles many than a mirry night.'
  And he that wilnes of this werke forto wete forther,
Full freshly and faste, for here a fit endes.

Fitt III

'Yea, Winner,' quod Wastour, 'I wot well myselven
What shall limpe of thee, lede, within fewe yeres.
Thurgh the pure plenté of corn that the peple sowes,
That God will graunte of his grace to growe on the erthe,
Ay to appaire the pris and it passe not too hye,
Shall make thee to waxe wood for wanhope in erthe,
To hope after an hard yere, to honge thyselven.
Woldest thou have lordes to live as laddes on fote?
Prelates als prestes that the parishen yemes?

360 samen together.
361 mister need.
362 by skill with reason. **scathed therafter** harmed as a result.
363 rechen give out.
364 ones] one MS. Emended by Gollancz. **herdmans** probably not 'herdsman's' (so Gollancz): proverbs were not especially associated with rustics at this time. Rather 'a member of a noble household' (OE *hiredman*). Hence *in a halle* (cf. *Gawain* 302).
365 Proverbial: Whiting M434. **a** a single.
366 wilnes wishes. **wete** know.
367 Full freshly fill up quickly. The appeal for drinks all round is in the minstrel manner. J. D. James finds an 'ironic contradiction' with Winner's attack on 'merry nights': *MLQ* 25 (1964) 243–58. **fit** fitt, a term for a section in a poem (=*passus*), going back to the Dark Ages. Cf. No. 32.
368 wot know.
369 limpe become. **lede** man.
370 pure] poure MS.
372 appaire spoil (i.e. reduce). **and** so that **it**] MS. omits.
373 A shift of syntax: '(the abundant harvest) will make you go mad for despair.' **in erthe** probably a mere tag, but possibly with word play on *MED Erthe* n.(2) 'ploughing'.
374 The unnaturalness of avarice appears in both the hoping for scarcities and the self-murder. Gollancz compares Shakespeare *Mac*. 2.3.5–6: 'Here's a farmer that hang'd himself on th'expectation of plenty.' Cf. also Lydgate *Pilgrimage of the Life of Man*: the usurer 'In gerneres shette up his grain, | Abidinge with an hevy chere | Till there come a dere yere', ed. Furnivall EETS e.s. 83 (1901), 17667–73. See Bestul 22.
375 laddes on fote common people without horses.
376 'Lords of the Church like parish priests?' **yemes** look after.

Proude marchandes of pris as pedders in town?
Let lordes live as them liste, laddes as them falles;
They the bacon and beef, they buturs and swannes,
They the rough of the rye, they the rede whete,
They the grewel gray, and they the gude sewes;
And then may the peple have part, in povert that standes,
Som gude morsel of mete to mend with their chere.
If fewles flye shold forth and fongen be never,
And wild bestes in the wode wone all their live,
And fishes flete in the flode and ichone ete other,
An henne at an halpeny by half yeres ende –
Shold not a ladde be in londe a lord forto serve.
This wot thou full wele witterly thyselven:
Whoso wele shall winne, a wastour moste he finde,
For if it greves one gome, it gladdes another.'
'Now,' quod Winner to Wastour, 'me wonders in herte
Of thise poure peniless men that pelour will bye,
Sadills of sendal, with sercles full riche.
Less that ye wrothe your wives, their willes to folowe,
Ye sellen wode after wode in a wale time,
Both the oke and the ash and all that there growes.
The spires and the yonge spring ye spare to your children

377 of pris of consequence. **pedders in town** village pedlars.
378 them liste they please. **them falles** they must. The division of the alliterative line here yields an epigrammatic antithesis.
379 beef in conjunction with bacon, suggests salt beef. Neither were highly thought of: cf. 345, and No. 11.1 below, line 310; also *C.T.* III 1753. **buturs** bitterns: cf. 349.
380 Fine wheat loaf is contrasted with rye bread.
382–3 Waster reverts to a favourite argument: that the high living of some alleviates the poverty of others. Cf. 295 *n.*
383 to mend with their chere to raise their spirits.
384 f. See 253 *n.* **fongen** taken, snared.
385 wone dwell.
386 flete swim.
387 'Then after six months you would be able to buy a hen for a halfpenny.' An argument calculated to weigh with Winner, who has an interest in high prices.
388 If the gentry did not deplete the countryside by huntin, shootin and fishin, they would not be able to attract servants.
389 witterly certainly.
391 gome man.
393 pelour fur.
394 sendal rich silken material. **sercles** rings.
395 Less that (less and MS.) lest. **wrothe** anger.
396 wale short (so Gollancz, comparing *Wars of Alexander* 4597 etc.).
398 spires seedlings. **spring** sapling.

And sayen God will grant it his grace to grow at the laste
Forto shadewe your sones – bot the shame is your owen.
Nedeless save ye the soile, for sell it ye thinken.
Your forfaders were faine, when any frend com,
Forto shake to the shawe and shewe him the estres,
In ich holt that they had an hare forto finde,
Bring to the brode launde buckes ynewe,
To lacche and to late go, to lighten their hertes.
Now is it set and sold, my sorow is the more,
Wastes all wilfully your wives to paye.
That are had lordes in londe and ladies riche,
Now are they nisottes of the new get, so nisely attired,
With side slabbande sleves sleght to the grounde,
Ourled all umbtourne with ermin aboute,
That is as hard, as I hope, to handele in the derne
Als a sely simple wenche that never silk wroghte.

400 shadewe Gollancz's attractive emendation for MS. *save to*; *save* in the next line possibly caused the error.
401 i.e. 'Nor do you need to keep the soil in good heart, for you intend to sell that too, as well as the timber.'
402–6 Winner evokes, eloquently but not quite convincingly, the hospitality of landowners in the good old days.
403 shake to the shawe go out to the wood. **estres** coverts.
404 holt wood.
405 brode launde wide glade. **ynewe** enough.
406 lacche catch. **late go** release. The reference is perhaps to bucks brought (cf. 405) to be hunted and then released; or possibly to the unleashing of hunting dogs (cf. Chaucer *L.G.W.* 1213).
407 set leased.
408 'Is consumed quite deliberately to please your wives.'
409–10 'Those who are considered masters in the land and noble mistresses nowadays are wantons of the latest fashion, attired with foolish refinement.' But *that are* may mean 'Those who previously [*are*] had'. The text is suspect here and in several places following.
410 of the new get Cf. Chaucer's Pardoner: 'Him thoughte he rood all of the newe jet', *C.T.* I 682.
411 'With ample sleeves trailing in the mud, let down to the ground.' Broad trailing sleeves were fashionable. **side**] elde MS.
412 Ourled all umbtourne bordered all round.
413 hope think. **derne** darkness.
414 sely poor. Silk was an aristocratic material. The point of this line is not clear. Gollancz takes line 413 as referring to the fashionable 'wantons'; but why should they be called 'as hard to handle in the dark' as a simple girl? Should they not be harder? Line 413 seems more naturally to refer to the difficulty of handling the sleeves; but the comparison in 414 makes equally little sense in that case. Perhaps there was originally a different comparison, lost by scribal eyeskip to the present line 414?

[7]

Bot whoso lukes on hir lire, oure lady of heven,
How she fled for ferd ferre out of hir kithe
Upon an amblande asse withouten more pride
Save a barn in hir barme and a broken heltre
That Joseph held in his hande that hend forto yeme,
Althof she walt all this werld, hir wedes were pore,
Forto give ensample of sich, forto shewe other
Forto leve pompe and pride – that poverté ofte shewes.'
  Then the wastour wrothly castes up his eyen
And said, 'Thou Winner, thou wricche, me wonders in herte.
What have oure clothes cost thee, caitif, to bye,
That thou shall birdes upbraid of their bright wedes,
Sithen that we vouche safe that the silver payen?
It lies well for a lede his lemman to finde
After hir faire chere, to forther hir herte.
Then will she love him lelely as hir life one,
Make him bold and boun with brandes to smite,
To shonne shenship and shame there shalkes are gadred.
And if my peple ben proude, me payes all the better,

415–22 Winner ends his speech piously with an extended *exemplum* (*ensample* 421). The Virgin Mary on the flight into Egypt is presented as an example of humble poverty, in the manner of devotional treatises such as N. Love *The Mirrour of the Blessed Lyf of Jesu Christ* ed. L. F. Powell (Oxford U.P. 1908), Ch. X, which emphasizes the poverty, humility and patience of the Holy Family during the flight.

415 'But if one looks at her hardship, our Lady of Heaven's' (taking *lire* as *MED Lire* n.(1)).

416 ferd fear. **ferre** far. **kithe** homeland.

418 barme bosom. **heltre** halter.

419 that hende forto yeme to look after that gracious lady. In the conventional iconography of the flight into Egypt, Joseph is seen on foot, leading by the bridle an ass on which Mary sits holding Jesus: Réau 2.2.275–6.

420 walt ruled. **wedes** garments (wordes MS.).

421–2 'In order to give an example of this (i.e. poverty) so as to show others that they must abandon pomp and display – something that poverty often demonstrates.' A halting couplet, reflecting either textual corruption or the insincerity of Winner's praise of poverty.

424 Echoing the beginning of Winner's last speech (392): 'Now *I* am astonished.'

426 birdes damsels. A high-flown word.

427 'Since we who pay the money permit it?'

428–9 'It is fitting for a man to provide for his mistress in a way appropriate to her good reception of him, so as to increase her love.'

430 lelely faithfully.

431 boun eager. The old idea of chivalry inspired by beauty receives more romantic expression in *Troilus* 3.1772 f.

432 shenship dishonour. **shalkes** men (of war). The style of this reference to the battlefield is very archaic.

433 me payes it pleases me.

To see them faire and free toforewith myn eyen.
And ye negardes upon nighte ye nappen so harde,
Routen at your raxilling, raisen your hurdes.
Ye beden waite on the weder, then wery ye the while
That ye nad hightild up your houses and your hine raised.
Forthy, Winner, with wronge thou wastes thy time,
For good day ne glad getes thou never.
The devil at thy dede day shall delen thy gudes.
Tho thou woldest that it were, winne they it never;
Thy skathill sectours shall sever them aboute,
And thou have helle full hot for that thou here saved.
Thou tast no tent on a tale that told was full yore.
I hold him mad that mournes his make forto winne;
Hent hir that hir have shall, and hold hir his while.
Take the coppe as it comes, the case as it falles.
For whoso live may lengest limpes to fecche
Wode that he waste shall to warmen his heles
Ferrer than his fader did by fivetene mile.
Now can I carpe no more; bot, sir king, by thy trouthe,
Deme us where we dwell shall: me think the day hies.'

434 see] fee MS. The MS. reading ('enfeoff') may be right. **free** noble. **toforewith** before.
436 'You snore as you stretch and lift your buttocks.' This image of Winner fast asleep conflicts with Waster's earlier attack on his anxious sleeplessness (248). The point here is that Winner, paradoxically, wastes his night time (439) by sleeping, while Waster uses it in feasts and revelry.
437–8 'You give orders to wait and see how the weather turns out, and then curse the day that you did not improve your buildings and muster your workmen.' Obscure. Apparently Winner is accused of further 'wasting time' by keeping a small establishment and putting off necessary improvements to barns etc. (cf. use of *houses* at 250) in case bad weather causes a small harvest. If the harvest then turns out good, he curses himself because he cannot reap and store it. Further waste!
441 delen share out.
442 'Those whom you would like to have it . . .'
443 The skathill sectours the rascally executors: cf. 302 *n*. **sever them aboute** divide the goods around.
445 'You pay no attention to a saying . . .' MS. omits *no*.
446 mournes worries. **make** mistress.
447 'Let him who is to have her take her, and keep her for his allotted time.'
448 coppe cup. Proverb recorded only here by Whiting: C631.
449–51–'Waster argues in favour of a short and merry life: the longer you live, the more timber you will use up for fuel, and in your old age you will have to send a long way – fifteen miles further than your father did – for the wood to be wasted merely in getting yourself warm' (Gollancz).
452 carpe speak.

The 'Gawain'-poet

Manuscript B.L. MS. Cotton Nero A. x contains unique texts of four alliterative poems, known by modern titles *Pearl*, *Purity* (or *Cleanness*), *Patience*, and *Sir Gawain and the Green Knight*, together with twelve illustrations apparently copied from more accomplished originals. Facsimile edn I. Gollancz EETS 162 (1923). All four texts exhibit the same N.W. Midland dialect, variously identified as that of Cheshire, S. Lancashire, N.W. Derbyshire, or (most recently) 'either in S.E. Cheshire or just over the border in N.E. Staffordshire': A. McIntosh *ES* 44 (1963) 1–11. The MS. 'can hardly be later than 1400' (*Gawain* ed. Davis xxv).

Authorship Most critics now suppose that all four Cotton Nero poems are by one man ('*Gawain*-poet' or '*Pearl*-poet'). Evidence, though all internal, is strong. There are similarities of dialect, diction, metre, imagery (e.g. pearl imagery, as in No. 9 and No. 10 line 2364), and structure (e.g. repetition of first line at end of *Patience*, *Gawain* and *Pearl*, see *n.* to No. 10 line 2525). Recurrence of certain moral and religious preoccupations, e.g. courtesy and 'cleanness', the Beatitudes and heavenly rewards, points in the same direction. Some would regard *St Erkenwald* as the same poet's work: it is included with the Cotton Nero poems in *A Concordance to Five ME Poems* ed. B. Kottler and A. M. Markman (Univ. of Pittsburgh P. 1966). But see contrary arguments of L. D. Benson *JEGP* 64 (1965) 393–405.

The poet's own dialect differed little from that of the MS. He is therefore presumed to have lived and worked in N.W. Midlands. Perhaps some aristocratic household there (John of Gaunt's?) provided the kind of audience – interested in hunting, armour, architecture, fine points of courtesy – implied by the poems. For connections between Alliterative Revival and baronial households of W. and N.W., see J. R. Hulbert *MP* 28 (1930–1) 405–22 and E. Salter *MP* 64 (1966–7) 146–50, 233–7. However, the poems may have been composed for country gentlemen of refined tastes. The poet's identity is not known. Earlier suggestions (Strode, Huchown etc) are now discounted; and research has concentrated on families within the N.W. Midland dialect area, especially the Cheshire families of Newton, Booth and Massey. Several critics believe that the author of *Pearl* was a Massey ('Mascy' in C14; cf. 'mascelless' in *Pearl* 732 etc). O. Greenwood favours Hugh Massey, in Introd. to his trans. of *Sir Gawain* (London, Lion & Unicorn Press 1956). B. Noland and D. Farley-Hills, *RES* n.s. 22 (1971) 295–302, propose John Massey; on whom see also *RES* n.s. 25 (1974) 49–53, 257–66. The identification is questioned in n.s. 26 (1975) 129–43.

Dates Order and date of composition of the four poems are matters of speculation. None can be later than about 1400, the date of the MS. Language and styles of architecture and costume suggest middle or later C14, and most scholars regard *c.*1360 as an earliest likely date. *Purity* and *Patience* are commonly considered less artistically mature and therefore earlier than *Pearl* or *Gawain*: see R. J. Menner, ed. *Purity* (Yale U.P. 1920) xxvii–xxxviii. But even if this is accepted, the relative order of *Pearl* and *Gawain* remains entirely speculative.

Reputation No contemporary allusions to the *Gawain*-poet survive. *The Squire's Tale* suggests to some that his work was known to Chaucer: C. O. Chapman *MLN* 68 (1953) 521–4. He exerted some influence on C15 alliterative verse such as *Death and Life*; and a tail-rhyme reworking of *Gawain* survives from the same period: *The Green Knight*, ed. Hales and Furnivall in *Bishop Percy's Folio MS* 2 (1868) 56–77. By *c.*1500 knowledge of his work is evidenced only in Cheshire: see R. H. Robbins on the commonplace book of Humfrey Newton (1466–1536), *MLN* 58 (1943) 361–6 and *PMLA* 65 (1950) 249–81. The surviving MS. came into the library of the Yorkshireman Henry Savile (1568–1617), whence it passed via Sir Robert Cotton to the British Library; but nothing was printed until Thomas Warton quoted short passages from *Pearl* and *Purity* in his *History of English Poetry* (1774–81). *Gawain* was the first to be printed entire, with encouragement from Sir Walter Scott, by F. Madden in 1839. The other three were edited by R. Morris for EETS in 1864. The Pre-Raphaelite Holman Hunt designed a frontispiece for Gollancz's 1891 edition of *Pearl*, which enjoyed some vogue about then. For C20 studies, see individual headnotes. A rather speculative general biographical study is H. L. Savage *The Gawain-Poet*: *studies in his personality and background* (Univ. of N. Carolina Press 1956). The best general literary study is A.C. Spearing *The Gawain-Poet: a critical study* (Cambridge U.P. 1970).

8 Patience: extract

After an introductory passage on the virtue of patience (1–60), *Patience* narrates the story of Jonah as an example of man's impatience and God's patience. This structure, with statement of theme followed by illustrative *exemplum*, recalls the techniques of medieval preaching: see C. F. Moorman *MP* 61 (1963–4) 90–5 and O. G. Hill *MP* 66 (1968–9) 103–9. The *exemplum* is exceptionally rich and complex, and the theme, 'patience', is less simple than the modern word suggests. The poem concerns control of impulse and consequent submission to reality, which, for the poet, means God. See D. J. Williams 'The point of *Patience*' *MP* 68 (1970–1) 127–36. The poet's main source was the *Book of Jonah* (Vulgate Latin version), which he fills out with much narrative and descriptive detail: see A. C. Spearing *Gawain-Poet* Ch. 3, stressing comic elements in Jonah's encounter with the Almighty; also Everett 69–74. Emerson *PMLA* 10 (1895) 242–8 and Hill *JEGP* 66 (1967) 21–5 propose a late Latin poem, *De Jona* (ascribed to Tertullian), as source for the much amplified account of the storm at sea; but see Liljegren, *Englische Studien* 48 (1914–15) 337–41, and Jacobs (*n.* to 133–64) on the common *topos* of the storm. E. M. Kelly *ELN* 4 (1966–7) 244–7 cites another reworking of *Jon.* by Prudentius, *Hymnus jejunantium* (Loeb edn, Vol. 1, pp. 56–71), which the poet probably knew (cf. *Hymnus* 163–9 with *Patience* 391–4). But the English poet was probably not much dependent on non-biblical authorities. R. H. Bowers *The Legend of Jonah* (The Hague, Nijhoff 1971) concludes: '[*Patience*] is the only homily I have encountered that extracts the theme of divine patience from the Book of Jonah; and . . . the author evidences no interest in traditional allegorical expositions' (62).

[8] The 'Gawain'-poet

Metrical form The 531 unrhymed alliterative long lines are marked off into groups of 4 by marginal slanting double lines (used in *Pearl* and *Gawain* to mark off stanzas). These four-line groups, though not always coinciding with units of syntax or sense (e.g. 104–5, 184–5), cannot be dismissed as scribal, as by W. W. Greg *MLR* 19 (1924) 223–4. The four special capital letters dividing *Patience* into sections (at 61, 245, 305, 409) all occur at the beginning of a four-line group, and only the last section (409–531) fails to divide by four, for reasons which can be explained (see Anderson's note to 509–15). Similar four-line groupings have been detected in other unrhymed ME alliterative poems: see J. R. Hulbert *MP* 48 (1950–1) 73–81. The significance of these groupings is uncertain, since they have no formal exponent in the text (e.g. a rhyme scheme) and depend upon scribal indications for their recognition.

Editions H. Bateson (2nd edn, Manchester U.P. 1918) and I. Gollancz (2nd edn 1924) are superseded for most purposes by J. J. Anderson (Manchester U.P. 1969).

Manuscript, date, authorship See above, 'The *Gawain*-poet'.

Lines 61–296

Hit betidde somtime in the termes of Judé
Jonas joined was therinne gentile prophete;
Goddes glam to him glod that him unglad made,
With a roghlich rurd rouned in his ere:

'Rise radly,' he says, 'and raike forth even,
Nim the way to Ninivé withouten other speche,
And in that ceté my sawes sowe alle aboute
That in that place at the point I put in thy hert.

61 somtime once. **termes of Judé** borders of Judea. Cf. *2 Kings* 14.25: 'He [Jeroboam] restored the borders of Israel . . . according to the word of the Lord the God of Israel, which he spoke by his servant Jonas the son of Amathi, the prophet, who was of Geth, which is in Opher.' *Jonah* itself opens abruptly: 'Now the word of the Lord came to Jonas the son of Amathi . . .'

62 joined appointed. **gentile prophete** prophet to the Gentiles (? or 'a noble prophet').

63 glam voice. **glod** came stealing ('glided').

64 roghlich rurd harsh sound. **rouned** murmured.

65–72 Expanded from *Jon.* 1.2: 'Arise, and go to Ninive the great city and preach in it: for the wickedness thereof is come up before me.'

65 radly quickly. **raike** go. **even** directly.

66 Nim take.

67 sawes sayings. **sowe** spread.

'For ywis hit arn so wicke that in that won dwelles
And her malis is so much, I may not abide,
Bot venge me on her vilanye and venim bilive.
Now sweye me thider swiftly and say me this arende.'

When that steven was stint that stouned his minde
All he wrathed in his wit and witherly he thoght:
'If I bowe to his bode and bring hem this tale
And I be nummen in Ninivé, my nyes beginnes.

'He telles me those traitoures arn tipped shrewes:
I come with those tithinges, they ta me bilive,
Pines me in a prisoun, put me in stockes,
Writhe me in a warlock, wrast out myn eyen.

'This is a mervail message a man forto preche
Among enmies so mony and mansed fendes –
Bot if my gainlich God such gref to me wolde,
For desert of som sake, that I slain were.

'At alle periles,' quoth the prophete, 'I aproche hit no nerre.
I will me som other way that he ne waite after;
I shall tee into Tarcé and tary there a while,
And lightly when I am lest he letes me alone.'

69 hit arn they are. **won** city.
71 bilive at once.
72 sweye hasten. **arende** message. The two *me*'s are 'ethic datives', declaring the interest of the speaker: here roughly 'on my behalf'. See No. 10 line 2014 and *n*.
73 steven voice. **stint** finished. **stouned** astonished.
74 witherly rebelliously, in a 'contrary' fashion.
75–88 Jonah's reflections have no basis in *Jon*. Spearing 86–7 points out that Jonah later (417–24) gives a different, and more creditable, account of his reasons for not obeying God.
75 bode command.
76 'And I am taken captive in Nineveh, my troubles will begin.' *-s* is a regular northern plural indicative ending, common in this MS.
77 tipped consummate.
78 I come if I come. **ta** will take.
79 Pines confine.
80 'Fasten me in foot-fetters and tear out my eyes.'
82 mansed cursed.
83–4 'Unless this gracious God of mine wishes such harm to me as to want me killed in punishment for some offence.'
85 At alle periles whatever the risk. **nerre** nearer.
86 I will me I will go. **he ne waite after** he is not keeping a watch on.
87 tee travel. **Tarcé** Tarshish.
88 lightly probably. **lest** lost.

Thenne he rises radly and raikes bilive
Jonas toward port Japh, ay janglande for tene
That he nolde thole for no thing non of those pines,
Thagh the fader that him formed were fale of his hele.

'Oure sire sittes,' he says, 'on sege so hye
In his glowande glorye, and gloumbes full littel
Thagh I be nummen in Ninivé and naked dispoiled,
On rood rewly torent with ribaudes mony.'

Thus he passes to that port his passage to seche;
Findes he a fair ship to the fare redy,
Macches him with the marineres, makes her paye,
Forto towe him into Tarcé as tid as they might.

Then he tron on tho trees, and they her tramme ruchen,
Cacchen up the crossail, cables they fasten,
Wight at the windas weyen her ancres,
Spinde spack to the sprete the spare bawe-line,

89 Echoing, with some irony, line 65.

90 Japh Jaffa, Joppa. **ay janglande for tene** grumbling angrily the whole time.

91 thole endure. **pines** torments.

92 fale of his hele unmindful of his wellbeing (? *MED* s.v. *Fale* adj.).

93–6 These reflections, that God does not care and perhaps cannot even see, are not in *Jon*. Here and in 75–88, the poet is emphasizing Jonah's lack of 'patience' or willingness to endure.

93 sege seat.

94 gloumbes will worry ('look glum').

95–6 These lines suggest Christ's stripping and crucifixion. Spearing 87 quotes *Luke* 11.30: 'For as Jonas was a sign to the Ninivites; so shall the Son of man also be to this generation.' The point here is perhaps to contrast Christ's patience with Jonah's impatience. M. Andrew, 'Jonah and Christ in *Patience*' *MP* 70 (1972–3) 230–3, argues that Jonah, though contrasted here, is elsewhere like Christ. Schleusener *PMLA* 86 (1971) 959–65 emphasizes Jonah's ignorance of his figural role as a type of Christ.

96 rewly pitiably. **torent** torn to pieces. **ribaudes** ruffians.

98 fare journey.

99 'Agrees terms with the sailors and pays them' (cf. *Jon*. 1.3).

100 towe take. **tid** quickly.

101 tron stepped. **tho trees** those planks, i.e. the deck.

101–8 This condensed and lively account of the embarkation of a square-rigged ship illustrates the *Gawain*-poet's love of the specialized techniques and terminology of skilled men (sailors, huntsmen, armourers, shipwrights,

Gederen to the gide-ropes, the grete cloth falles.
They laiden in on ladde-borde and the lofe winnes;
The blithe breth at her back the bosum he findes,
He swenges me this swete ship swefte fro the haven.

Was never so joyful a Jewe as Jonas was thenne,
That the daunger of Drighten so derfly ascaped;
He wende well that that wye that all the world planted
Had no maght in that mere no man forto greve.

Lo the witless wrecche! For he wolde noght suffer
Now has he put him in plit of peril well more.
Hit was a wening unwar that welt in his miṇde,
Thagh he were soght fro Samarye, that God sey no firre.

Yise, he blushed full brode, that burde him be sure.
That ofte kid him the carp that king saide,
Dingne David on des, that demed this speche
In a psalme that he set the sauter withinne:

etc.). The sailors first prepare their gear (*her tramme ruchen*), then hoist the square-sail (still reefed to its yard) and make fast the cables which hold it up (102). They then quickly (*wight* 103, *spack* 104) wind in the anchors on the windlass, and attach (*spinde* pa. t.) to the bowsprit (*sprete* 104) a bowline carried in reserve (a rope attached to the weather edge of the sail to keep it steady when sailing close to the wind). Then they tug at (*gederen to*) the guy-ropes (to pull the yard round?), and the sail is released and falls (105). The ship has been anchored into the wind; but by rowing on the port side (*laiden in on ladde-borde*) they bring its head round to starboard until the sail catches the wind. This manoeuvre is called 'winning the luff' (106). As the ship turns to starboard away from land, the wind finds the belly of the sail and swings the ship out of harbour.

108 me see 72 *n*.

110 daunger power. **Drighten** the Lord. **derfly** boldly.

111 wende thought. **wye** man. Such periphrases for God are common in the *Gawain*-poet: cf. 92, 176, 206, 225 etc; also No. 10, lines 2056–7 *n*.

112 mere sea.

114 plit state.

115 wening unwar foolish expectation. **welt** rolled.

116 were soght had gone. **sey no firre** saw no further.

117 'On the contrary, he (God) looked with wide-open eyes, and he (Jonah) should have been sure of that.'

118 kid made known. **carp** words.

119 Dingne noble. **des** dais. **demed** uttered.

120 sauter Psalter.

'O foles in folk, feles otherwhile
And understondes umbestounde, thagh he be stape fole.
Hope ye that he heres not that eres alle made?
Hit may not be that he is blind that bigged uch eye.'

Bot he dredes no dint that dotes for elde,
For he was fer in the flood foundande to Tarcé;
Bot I trow full tid overtan that he were,
So that shomely too short he shot of his ame.

For the welder of wit that wot alle thinges,
That ay wakes and waites, at wille has he slightes.
He calde on that ilk craft he carf with his hondes;
They wakened well the wrothloker for wrothly he cleped:

'Eurus and Aquiloun that on est sittes,
Blowes bothe at my bode upon blo watteres.'
Thenne was no tom there betwene his tale and her dede,
So bain were they bothe two his bone forto wirk.

121–4 *Ps.* 93.8–9 (A.V. 94.8–9): 'Understand, ye senseless among the people: and, you fools, be wise at last. He that planted [*plantavit*, cf. line 111] the ear, shall he not hear? Or he that formed the eye, doth he not consider?'
121 feles otherwhile consider occasionally.
122 umbestounde now and then. **he** Editors emend to *ye*, but *he* makes sense: 'even the man who is a complete fool.'
123 Hope believe.
124 bigged built, made.
125 dint blow. **elde** old age.
126 foundande making his way.
127 full tid very quickly. **overtan** overtaken.
128 shomely shamefully.
129 welder controller. **wit** wisdom. **wot** knows.
130 waites watches. **at wille has he slightes** he has tricks at his command.
131 craft work, creation (*MED* s.v. *Craft* n.(1) 9(a)), i.e. the winds. **carf** made.
132 wrothloker more angrily.
133–64 The description of the storm is much expanded from *Jon.* 1.4–5, under direct or indirect influence from Latin works, especially Guido's *Historia destructionis Troiae*: see N. Jacobs 'Alliterative storms' *Spec.* 47 (1972) 695–719.
133 Eurus the east wind. **Aquiloun** Aquilo, a violent wind that 'sits' a little east of due north. The two combine to produce a N.E. wind (137). Cf. the 'tempestuous wind called Euroaquilo' which wrecked St Paul (*Acts* 27.14). See also Jacobs 705, 707.
134 bode command. **blo** dark.
135 tom delay. **tale** utterance.
136 bain willing. **bone** bidding.

Anon out of the north-est the nois beginnes
When bothe brethes con blowe upon blo watteres.
Rogh rackes there ros with rudning anunder;
The see soughed full sore, gret selly to here.

The windes on the wonne water so wrastel togeder
That the wawes full wood waltered so hye
And eft bushed to the abyme, that breed fishes
Durst nowhere for rogh arest at the bothem.

When the breth and the brok and the bote metten
Hit was a joyless gin that Jonas was inne,
For hit reled on roun upon the roghe ithes;
The bur ber to hit baft, that braste alle her gere.

Then hurled on a hepe the helme and the sterne;
First tomurte mony rop and the mast after;
The sail sweyed on the see; thenne suppe behoved
The coge of the colde water, and then the cry rises.

Yet corven they the cordes and kest all theroute;
Mony ladde there forth lep to lave and to kest,
Scopen out the scathel water, that fain scape wolde;
For be monnes lode never so luther, the lif is ay swete.

138 con began to.
139 rackes storm-clouds. **rudning** red glare.
140 selly wonder.
141–2 Jacobs 710 traces the motif of the conflict of the winds back to antiquity, especially Ovid *Met*. 11.490–1: 'omnique e parte feroces | bella gerunt venti fretaque indignantia miscent' ('from every quarter the raging winds make their attacks and stir up the angry waves').
141 wonne dark.
142 wawes waves. **wood** furious. **waltered** rolled up.
143 bushed plunged. **abyme** depths of the sea. **breed** terrified (*MED* s.v. *Breen* v.).
144 rogh roughness, turbulence. **arest** lie still. Cf. line 248.
145 brok sea.
146 gin craft.
147 on roun around. **ithes** waves.
148 'The gale came upon it abaft so that all their gear was smashed.'
150 tomurte broke.
151–2 'The sail fell onto the sea; then the boat had to drink . . .' A *cog* was a medium-sized, single-masted ship, with high prow and stern.
153 corven cut. **kest** threw.
154 lep leapt. **lave** bale.
155 Scopen scooped. **scathel** harmful. **that** referring to the *laddes*.
156 'For however difficult a man's journey may be . . .'

There was busy overborde bale to kest,
Her bagges and her fether beddes and her bright wedes,
Her kistes and her coferes, her caraldes alle,
And all to lighten that lome, if lethe wolde shape.

Bot ever was yliche loud the lote of the windes
And ever wrother the water and wodder the stremes.
Then tho wery forwroght wist no bote
Bot uchon glewed on his god that gained him beste.

Some to Vernagu there vouched avowes solemne,
Some to Diana devout and derf Nepturne,
To Mahoun and to Mergot, the mone and the sunne,
And uch lede as he loved and laid had his hert.

Thenne bespeke the spackest, despaired well nere:
'I leve here be som losinger, som lawless wrecche,
That has greved his god and gos here among us.
Lo, all sinkes in his sinne and for his sake marres.

'I louve that we lay lots on ledes uchone,
And whoso limpes the loss, lay him theroute;
And when the gulty is gon, what may gome trawe
Bot he that rules the rack may rewe on those other?'

157 busy bustle (*MED* s.v. *Bisi* adj. as n.). **bale** packages: 'They cast forth the wares that were in the ship', *Jon.* 1.5.
159 kistes chests. **caraldes** casks.
160 lome craft. **if lethe wolde shape** 'to see if an easing would follow' (Sisam *Med. Eng. Verse*).
161 yliche equally, no less. **lote** roaring.
162 wodder madder. **stremes** currents.
163 tho wery forwroght those men tired out with work. **bote** remedy.
164–8 Cf. *Jon.* 1.5: 'And the mariners were afraid and the men cried to their god.'
164 glewed called. **gained** pleased.
165 Vernagu a giant Saracen (not a god) in Charlemagne romances. There is a ME poem *Roland and Vernagu*. **vouched** offered.
166 devout sacred. **derf** dread.
167 Mahoun Mahomet, considered as a pagan god. **Mergot** Margot, a heathen god in Charlemagne romances, probably from biblical Magog (*Gen.* 10.2).
168 lede man.
169 spackest wisest. **well nere** well-nigh.
170 leve believe. **losinger** miscreant.
173 louve] lovue *or* lovne MS. The word obviously means 'propose'; but its form and identity are in doubt: see *DOST* s.v. *Love* v.
174 'And throw overboard whoever is the loser.'
175 gome man. **trawe** believe.
176 See 111 *n*.

This was set in asent, and sembled they were,
Heryed out of uch hirne to hent that falles.
A lodesman lightly lep under hacches
Forto laite mo ledes and hem to lot bringe.

Bot him failed no freke that he finde might
Saf Jonas the Jewe that jowked in derne:
He was flowen for ferde of the flood lotes
Into the bothem of the bote, and on a brede ligged,

Onhelde by the hurrock for the heven wrache,
Slipped upon a sloumbe-slepe, and sloberande he routes.
The freke him frunt with his foot and bede him ferk up,
There Ragnel in his rakentes him rere of his dremes!

By the hater hasped he hentes him thenne
And broght him up by the brest and upon bord sette,
Arained him full runishly what raisoun he had
In such slaghtes of sorwe to slepe so faste.

178 Heryed dragged. **hirne** corner. **hent** take.
179 lodesman steersman. In *Jon.* 1.6 the *gubernator* comes upon Jonah and bids him call upon his god before the casting of lots is proposed. The poet's order explains why Jonah should have been routed out.
180 laite search for. **lot** lot-casting.
181 freke man.
182 Saf except. **jowked in derne** lay asleep in a hiding place. *jowk* is originally a term of falconry: 'roost'.
183 ferde fear.
184 brede plank.
185 'Huddled up in the stern part because of heaven's vengeance'. The meaning of *hurrock* is uncertain: see Anderson's note.
186 sloumbe-slepe deep sleep. **sloberande** slobbering (a word not recorded in this sense before C18, but cf. *MED* s.v. *Bislobben*; emendation to *slomberande* has been proposed). **routes** snores: *Jon.* 1.5, 'and fell into a deep sleep'. The fact that he snores in *De Jona* has been held to point to the poet's use of that work; but he also snores in the Septuagint (cited by St Jerome): 'et dormiebat, et stertebat' (see *N & Q* 18 (1971) 125–6).
187 frunt kicked. **ferk up** jump up, look lively.
188 'And may Ragnel in his fetters wake him from his dreams.' *Ragnel* occurs as a devil's name in Miracle plays.
189 hater garment. MS. omits. Anderson defends MS. *haspede* as in itself a noun = 'hasp-hede' i.e. 'clasp-head' or brooch buckling the cloak. But the compound is doubtful and the line too short. Ekwall supplied *hater*; Gollancz suggested *here* 'hair'. Translation: 'He seizes him by his clothing and drags him away.'
190 bord deck.
191 Arained questioned. **runishly** roughly.
192 slaghtes strokes, onsets.

Sone haf they her sortes set and serelich deled,
And ay the lot upon laste limped on Jonas.
Thenne ascried they him skete and asked full loude:
'What the devel has thou don, doted wrecche?

'What seches thou on see, sinful shrewe,
With thy lastes so luther to lose us uchone?
Has thou, gome, no governour ne god on to calle,
That thou thus slides on slepe when thou slain worthes?

'Of what londe art thou lent, what laites thou here,
Whider in worlde that thou wilt, and what is thyn arende?
Lo, thy doom is thee dight for thy dedes ille.
Do, gif glory to thy god ere thou glide hens.'

'I am an ebru,' quoth he, 'of Israyl born.
That wye I worship, ywis, that wroght all thinges,
All the world with the welkin, the wind and the sternes,
And all that wones there withinne, at a word one.

'All this meschef for me is made at this time
For I haf greved my God and gulty am founden;
Forthy beres me to the borde and bathes me theroute;
Ere gete ye no happe, I hope for sothe.'

193 sortes lots. **serelich** severally.
194 limped fell.
195 ascried shouted at. **skete** at once.
196–204 Cf. *Jon.* 1.8: 'And they said to him: Tell us for what cause this evil is upon us. What is thy business? Of what country art thou and whither goest thou? Or of what people art thou?'
198 'To ruin all of us with your wicked crimes.'
200 when thou slain worthes when you are meeting your death.
201 lent come.
202 'Where in the world do you want to go . . . ?'
203 thee dight settled for you.
204 Do go on. Prefixed to imperatives to make them more urgent: cf. *Gawain* 1533.
207 sternes stars.
208 wones dwells. **at a word one** with a single word. Cf. *Piers* B 9.32, citing *Ps.* 148.5: 'For he spoke, and they were made.'
211 Forthy therefore. **borde** ship's side.
212 'You will not get any good fortune until then, I truly believe.'

He ossed hem by unninges that they undernomen
That he was flawen fro the face of frelich Drighten.
Thenne such a ferde on hem fell and flayed hem withinne
That they ruit hem to rowe and letten the rink one.

Hatheles hied in haste with ores full longe,
Syn her sail was hem aslipped, on sides to rowe,
Hef and haled upon hight to helpen hemselven;
Bot all was nedless note, that nolde not betide;

In bluber of the blo flood bursten her ores.
Thenne had they noght in her honde that hem help might;
Thenne nas no coumfort to kever, ne counsel non other,
Bot Jonas into his juis jugge bilive.

First they prayen to the prince that prophetes serven
That he gef hem the grace to greven him never
That they in baleless blood there blenden her handes,
Thagh that hathel were his that they here quelled.

Tid by top and by to they token him synne,
Into that lodlich loghe they luche him sone.
He was no titter out-tuld that tempest ne sesed;
The see saghtled therwith as sone as ho moght.

213 'He showed them by signs which they understood.'
214 flawen fled. **frelich** glorious.
215–6 A typical amplification. *Jon.* 1.13, after reporting Jonah's speech, continues: 'And the men rowed hard to return to land.' Why did they not throw him straight overboard? The poet explains.
215 flayed terrified.
216 ruit hurried. **letten the rink one** left the man alone.
217 Hatheles hied men hurried.
218 Syn since.
219 Hef heaved. **haled** (hale MS.) pulled. **upon hight** strongly.
220 nedless note useless effort. Cf. *Jon.* 1.13.
221 bluber seething.
223 to kever to be had.
224 'Save to condemn Jonah to his punishment forthwith.'
227 baleless innocent: cf. *Jon.* 1.14. **blenden** steep.
228 'Even though the man they here killed belonged to him', i.e. to the God of the Prophets.
229 Tid quickly. **to** toe. **synne** afterwards.
230 lodlich loghe terrible sea. **luche** threw.
231 'No sooner was he thrown out than the storm stopped.'
232 saghtled quietened.

Thenne thagh her tackel were torn that totered on ithes.
Stiffe stremes and streght hem strained a while
That drof hem drylich adown the depe to serve,
Till a swetter full swithe hem sweyed to bonk.

There was loving on lofte, when they the lond wonnen,
To oure merciable God on Moyses wise,
With sacrafise up set and solempne vowes,
And graunted him oon to be God and graithly non other.

Thagh they be jolef for joye, Jonas yet dredes;
Thagh he nolde suffer no sore, his seele is on anter;
For what so worthed of that wye fro he in water dipped,
Hit were a wonder to wene, yif holy writ nere.

Now is Jonas the Jewe jugged to drowne;
Of that shended ship men shouved him sone.
A wild walterande whal, as wird then shaped,
That was beten fro the abyme, by that bote flotte,

233–6 Much ship's tackle has gone overboard with the mast and is tossing (*OED* s.v. *Totter* v. 2) on the waves. But the ship is driven on by currents (*stremes*).

234 streght strong. **strained** constrained.

235 drylich relentlessly. **the depe to serve** to keep to the deep sea.

236 swetter sweeter, more welcome. **swithe** swiftly. **bonk** land.

237 loving on lofte praise raised up.

238 on Moyses wise in the manner of Moses (as laid down in Pentateuch): 'And the men feared the Lord exceedingly and sacrificed victims to the Lord and made vows', *Jon.* 1.16.

240 oon alone (un MS.). **graithly** truly.

241 jolef happy.

242 'Though he did not want to endure any hardship, his happiness is in jeopardy.' Cf. Jonah's statement at line 91 and the poet's reflections at 113–4. Also 276.

243 worthed of became of. **fro** from the time that.

244 'It would be a strange thing to believe if it were not Holy Writ.'

245–6 The poet, having disposed of the sailors (231–40), returns to Jonah and repeats 229–30. Such overlaps are common in medieval narrative. An extra-large capital at 245 marks the beginning of a new section.

246 shended damaged.

247 Vulgate *Jon.* speaks only of a 'big fish' (*piscem grandem* 2.1); but this is identified as a whale in the Septuagint *Jon.* and in *Matt.* 12.40. **walterande** rolling. **wird** fate. **shaped** decreed.

248 Cf. 143–4, an amplification designed to prepare for the appearance of the whale here. **flotte** floated.

And was war of that wye that the water soghte,
And swiftly swenged him to swepe and his swolwe opened.
The folk yet haldande his feet, the fish him tid hentes;
Withouten touche of any tooth he tult in his throte.

Thenne he swenges and swaives to the see bothem
By mony rockes full roghe and ridelande strondes,
With the mon in his mawe malskred in drede –
As littel wonder hit was yif he wo dreyed,

For nad the hye heven king thurgh his hond-might
Warded this wrecche man in warlowes guttes,
What lede moght leve by lawe of any kind
That any lif might be lent so longe him withinne?

Bot he was socored by that sire that sittes so hye,
Thagh were wanless of wele in wombe of that fishe
And also driven thurgh the depe and in derk walteres.
Lord, cold was his cumfort and his care huge,

249 war aware. **soghte** was going into.

250 'And quickly swung round to swoop, and opened his gaping mouth.'

251 In medieval illustrations, such as that in the Cotton Nero MS. itself (f.82), Jonah is commonly portrayed as still held by the heels when the whale gets him: Williams *MP* 68 (1970–1) 133.

252 tult tumbled.

253 swaives glides.

254 ridelande strondes Obscure. *strondes* is apparently *OED Strand* sb.[1] meaning something like 'sandbank'; *ridelande* is doubtfully referred by *OED* (s.v. *Rideling*) to *ridel* 'to fall', but may rather be connected with *riddle* 'a sieve', in which case it alludes to the shifting movement of small particles: cf. *Purity* 953.

255 malskred bewildered.

256 dreyed suffered.

257 nad had not.

258 Warded guarded. **warlowes** the devil's. References to the Devil in connection with the whale have been held to suggest the Gospel interpretation (*Matt*. 12.40) of Jonah's three days in the whale's belly as a type of Christ's three days in hell (Spearing 85); but the poet's interests seem concentrated on the literal story, here and at 274–5. See headnote.

259 leve believe (live MS.). **lawe of any kind** any law of nature. Cf. Dunbar, No. 38 line 58 below.

260 'That any living creature could have survived so long inside him' (or 'That any life could have remained so long within him').

262 'Though he was without hope of happiness . . .'

For he knew uch a case and cark that him limped:
How fro the bote into the bluber was with a beste lacched,
And threw in at hit throte withouten thret more,
As mote in at a munster dor, so muckel wern his chawles.

He glides in by the giles thurgh glaimande glette,
Relande in by a rop, a rode that him thoght,
Ay hele over hed hourlande aboute,
Till he blunt in a block as brod as a hall;

And there he festnes the feet and fathmes aboute
And stood up in his stomak, that stank as the devel.
There in saim and in sorwe that savoured as helle
There was bilded his bour that will no bale suffer.

And thenne he lurkes and laites where was lee best
In uch a nook of his navel, bot nowhere he findes
No rest ne recoverer bot ramel and mire
In which gut so-ever he gos; bot ever is God swete.

And there he lenged at the last and to the lede called:
'Now, prince, of thy prophete pité thou have.
Thagh I be fool and fickel and false of my hert,
Devoid now thy vengaunce thurgh vertu of rauthe.

265 case chance. **cark** trouble.
266 'How he was snatched from the boat into the seething water by some creature.'
267 threw rushed. **hit** its. **thret** resistance.
268 The simile of the mote and the minster door illustrates the poet's mastery of bold or 'drastic' comparisons: Burrow *Ricardian Poetry* 134–5. **chawles** jaws.
269 giles gills. **glaimande glette** sticky slime: *MED* s.v. *Gleimen* 1(c).
270 rop gut. **rode** road.
271 hourlande tumbling.
272 blunt came to a stop. **block** 'enclosed space, cavern' (Anderson). A unique word, of doubtful identity. In *Gawain* 440 *bluk* refers to the Green Knight's beheaded torso. Could *block* be the same word (presumably related to *bulk* 292), referring to the main part of the whale?
273 fathmes gropes.
275 saim grease. **sorwe** filth.
276 See 242 *n*.
277 lurkes lies low. **laites** looks **lee** shelter.
279 recoverer remedy. **ramel** muck.
281 lenged stood still.
282–8 This speech is added by the poet. His version of Jonah's speech in *Jon*. 2.3–10 comes later (305 ff.).
284 Devoid withdraw. **rauthe** mercy.

'Thagh I be gulty of gile, as gaule of prophetes,
Thou art God and all goodes are graithly thyn owen;
Haf now mercy of thy man and his misdedes
And preve thee lightly a lord in londe and in water.'

With that he hitte to a hirne and held him therinne,
There no defoule of no filth was fest him aboute.
There he sete also sound, saf for merk one,
As in the bulk of the bote there he before sleped.

So in a bowel of that beste he bides on live
Three dayes and three night, ay thenkande on Drighten,
His might and his mercy, his mesure thenne.
Now he knawes him in care that couthe not in sele.

285 gaule of prophetes 'the scum of the prophets': *MED* s.v. *Galle* n.(2) 2(b).
288 preve thee lightly prove yourself easily.
289 hitte to got to. **hirne** corner.
290 fest close.
291 saf for merk one except only for the darkness.
292 bulk main body. See 272 *n.*
293 on live alive.
294 three night] the nyght MS.
295 mesure moderation, restraint in punishing.
296 sele happiness.

9 Pearl: extract

Pearl is a dream-vision poem, like Nos. 7 and 11. It is divided into 20 sections (see below) symmetrically organized as follows:

Prologue	Section I	Loss of the pearl in the garden
Dream	Sections II–IV	Vision of Earthly Paradise and of Pearl
	Sections V–XVI	Dialogue with Pearl
	Sections XVII–XIX	Vision of Heavenly Jerusalem
Epilogue	Section XX	Back in the garden. Reconcilement to loss.

The loss of the pearl in Section I is enigmatic; but later indications, at 233 (see *n.*), 412, 483 and 1208, suggest it should be understood allegorically as referring to the death of an infant daughter. Rival allegorical interpretations see the pearl as representing maidenhood (W. H. Schofield *PMLA* 19 (1904) 154–215) or the soul (M. P. Hamilton, in Blanch below). The question whether poet (or patron?) really lost such a daughter is separate, and open. Comparison with Dante's Beatrice, or the dead daughter of Boccaccio's elegy (a

Latin eclogue, printed with trans. in Gollancz's *Pearl*), suggests that 'Pearl' did exist (called Margery? see *n.* to 199). *Pearl* might then be considered alongside the ornate funerary art of late Middle Ages (e.g. canopied tombs). The loss, whether real or fictional, receives consolation in the central vision. This proves from Scripture (Parable of the Vineyard, St John's vision of Heaven) that the girl is one of the followers of the Lamb. On *Pearl* as an example of the genre *consolatio mortis*, see I. B. Bishop *'Pearl' in its setting* (Oxford, Blackwell 1968) and V. E. Watts *Med. Aev.* 32 (1963) 34–6. The immediate theological issue is the 'salvation of the innocent', on which see R. Wellek, in Blanch (below); but the case raises for the dreamer the question of his and all men's salvation, since all must become 'as little children' to enter Heaven. On the importance of the dreamer, see C. Moorman *MP* 53 (1955–6) 73–81 (in Conley below), and Spearing Ch. 4.

Traditional symbolism of pearls is fully exploited. See, besides Bishop and Spearing, the very detailed study by P. M. Kean *'The Pearl': an interpretation* (Routledge 1967). The symbolic logic runs as follows: Pearl (? Margery), through the pearly whiteness and perfection of her maiden innocence, wins the 'pearl of great price' of *Matt.* 13.46, i.e. the Kingdom of Heaven (see *n.* to 221–8). She has her right 'setting' in Heaven; and the dreamer (spoken of in Section V as a 'jeweller') must no longer regard her as his.

Metrical form etc. Four-stress lines with heavy alliteration rhyme in twelve-line stanza: *ababababbcbc*; cf. No. 20 below. Stanzas are grouped in sections of five (Section XV has six) by a common 'link word' (e.g. 'more' in Section III here), occurring in rhyme at the end of one stanza and within the first line of the next. The link word may be supported by other repeated words (e.g. in IV 'precios' and 'perle', as well as 'pight'). The 20 five-stanza sections are all (except XII–XIII) joined by link words (e.g. 'more' 181). The link word of the last section occurs in the first line of the poem, creating a circular effect (cf. Donne's *La Corona*). This formal circularity corresponds to the 'endless round' (738) of the pearl, just as the formal circularity of *Sir Gawain* corresponds to the 'endless knot' (630) of the pentangle. The idea of moral perfection is symbolically suggested in both cases. Like *Gawain*, too, *Pearl* has 101 stanzas, suggesting perhaps 'the completion of one cycle and the beginning of another': M.-S. Røstvig *ES* 48 (1967) 326–32. See also Kean *N & Q* 12 (1965) 49–51 and Bishop 27–31.

Editions and critical anthologies The best edn is by E. V. Gordon (Oxford U.P. 1953), which largely supersedes those of I. Gollancz (1891, rev. 1921) and C. G. Osgood (Boston 1906). Gordon's Introd. contains excellent critical discussion. A useful working text is A. C. Cawley *'Pearl' and 'Sir Gawain and the Green Knight'* (Dent, Everyman Lib. 1962). Critical articles are collected in R. J. Blanch, ed. *'Sir Gawain' and 'Pearl': critical essays* (Indiana U.P. 1966) and J. Conley, ed. *The ME 'Pearl': critical essays* (Univ. of Notre Dame P. 1970).

Manuscript, date, authorship See above, 'The *Gawain*-poet'.

Lines 121–360

III

The dubbement dere of down and dales,
Of wode and water and wlonk plaines,
Bilde in me bliss, abated my bales,
Fordidden my stresse, destryed my paines.
Down after a strem that drighly hales
I bowed in bliss, bredful my braines;
The firre I folwed those floty vales
The more strength of joye myn herte straines.
As fortune fares theras ho fraines,
Whether solace ho sende other elles sore,
The wye to wham hir wille ho waines
Hittes to have ay more and more.

More of wele was in that wise
Than I couthe telle thagh I tom hade,
For erthly herte might not suffise
To the tenthe dole of tho gladnes glade;

121–4 The previous five stanzas describe the strange landscape seen by the dreamer's spirit at the beginning of its vision: shining cliffs and rocks, trees with silver leaves, pearls under foot, gaudy birds, and a river with banks of beryl and pebbles of precious stone: see 137 *n*.
121 dubbement dere rich splendour. *(a)dubbement*, coupled with *dere*, is the link word of the previous section.
122 wlonk rich, fertile.
123–4 The sorrow (*bales*), grief (*stresse*) and pains are those attending the dreamer's loss of his pearl, described in the first section.
123 Bilde raised.
124 Fordidden dispelled.
125 Later (974), Pearl invites him to walk *up* towards the stream's source – presumably the better direction, since the stream flows out of Paradise. **after** along beside. **drighly hales** flows strongly.
126 bowed went. **bredful** brimful.
127 firre further. **floty** watery.
129–32 'As is the way with Fortune whenever she is making trial, whether sending joy or else sorrow – the man to whom she sends what she chooses is likely to have ever more and more of it.' Fortune tests men with runs of good or bad luck. The Dreamer, whose reflections are not profound, thinks he is enjoying a good run.
133 wele delight.
134 tom leisure.
136 dole part. **tho gladnes glade** those joyful joys (?); but the whole line might be interpreted: '(even if one were only) glad to the extent of one tenth of those joys'.

[9] The 'Gawain'-poet

Forthy I thoght that Paradise
Was there other gain tho bonkes brade.
I hoped the water were a devise
Betwene mirthes by meres made.
Beyonde the brook, by slent other slade,
I hoped that mote merked wore.
Bot the water was depe, I dorst not wade,
And ever me longed ay more and more.

More and more and yet well mare
Me liste to see the brook beyonde;
For if hit was fair there I con fare,
Well loveloker was the firre londe.
Aboute me con I stote and stare,
To finde a forth faste con I fonde.
Bot wothes mo ywis there ware

137 Forthy therefore. **Paradise** Kean (Pt 2 Ch. 1) shows that the landscape here resembles medieval descriptions of the country surrounding the Earthly Paradise; and identifies the river with Phison, one of the four rivers arising in Paradise or Eden, which had a bed of precious stones (cf. *Gen.* 2.11–12). Earthly Paradise is 'a natural and proper meeting-place for the blessed spirits of the dead and the living. In the *Divina Commedia* it is in the Earthly Paradise . . . that Dante first encounters Beatrice' (Kean 91). See also Patch *Other World.*
138 other gain or opposite, i.e. on the other side of the river. Emendation to *over gain* 'over beyond' is tempting, in view of 141. **brade** broad.
139–40 Obscure. Perhaps: 'I supposed the stream was a dividing-line between delightful places made by waters.' **hoped** supposed. **devise** recorded in C15 and C16 Scots, meaning 'division'. Or 'device (i.e. an artificial conduit)' (Cawley)? **mirthes** probably just the delights on both sides of the stream; but can mean 'pleasure garden'. **by meres** probably referring to the stream itself (cf. 1166 and 158), though *mere* usually means 'pool'. For other interpretations of the passage, see Fowler *MLQ* 21 (1960) 27–9 (*devise* = deception); Gollancz, *n.* in edn (emends: 'Betwene meres by Mirthe made'); Hillmann, *n.* to transl. (*meres* = boundaries).
141 slent slope. **slade** valley.
142 'I supposed that city [Heavenly Jerusalem] was situated.' **hoped]** hope MS.
146 Me liste I longed.
147 there where. **con fare** walked. *con* is past tense auxiliary, as at 149, 150, 157 etc.
148 loveloker lovelier.
149 stote stop.
150 forth ford. **fonde** try.
151 wothes mo more perils. The river gets wider as the dreamer follows it downstream. **ywis** indeed.

The firre I stalked by the stronde.
And ever me thoght I sholde not wonde
For wo there weles so winne wore.
Thenne newe note me com on honde
That meved my mind ay more and more.

More mervaile con my doom adaunt.
I sey beyonde that mirry mere
A crystal cliff full relusaunt;
Mony ryal ray con fro hit rere.
At the foot therof there sete a faunt,
A maiden of mensk full debonere;
Blisnande whit was hir bleaunt.
I knew hir well, I had seen hir ere.
As glisnande gold that man con shere,
So shon that shene anunder shore.
On lenghe I loked to hir there;
The lenger, I knew hir more and more.

The more I fraiste hir faire face,
Hir figure fin when I had font,

152 'The farther I walked along the bank.'
153 wonde hesitate, draw back.
154 'Because of any difficulty, where joys were so delightful.' Gollancz emended *wo* 'woe' to *wothe* 'peril', comparing *Gawain* 488; cf. 151 above.
155 'Then a new thing came to my notice' (Cawley).
157 'A greater marvel overcame my powers of judgment.'
158 mirry mere beautiful water.
159 relusaunt casting back light. A rare Fr. loan word, here first recorded in English.
160 'Many a ray of royal spendour sprang from it' (Cawley). On the poet's imagery of light, see L. Blenkner *SP* 68 (1971) 28–36.
161 faunt child.
162 of mensk courteous. **debonere** gracious of demeanour.
163 Blisnande shining. **bleaunt** mantle. The poet emphasizes the whiteness of the maiden's clothes, of the pearls on her dress and crown, and of her face. The basic meaning is innocence. Bishop 118 compares the white vestments worn by the newly baptized, which 'signify the innocence which was lost through Adam and restored through the sacrament of baptism'. See also 197 *n*.
165 con shere cut, i.e. into fine gold thread. No doubt referring to the damsel's hair: cf. 213.
166 shene bright one. **anunder shore** at the foot of the cliff.
167 On lenghe for a long time.
169 fraiste examined.
170 'Once I had caught sight of [found] her delicate form.' *fin* implies slenderness which, together with the dazzling light, would make Pearl hard to see against the crystal cliff.

Such gladande glory con to me glace
As littel before therto was wont.
To calle hir liste con me enchace,
Bot baisment gef myn herte a brunt:
I sey hir in so strange a place.
Such a bur might make myn herte blunt.
Thenne veres ho up hir faire frount,
Hir visage whit as plain ivore,
That stong myn herte full stray atount,
And ever the lenger, the more and more.

IV

More than me liste my drede aros.
I stood full stille and dorste not calle;
With eyen open and mouth full clos
I stood as hende as hawk in halle.
I hoped that gostly was that porpos.
I dred onende what sholde befalle
Lest ho me eschaped that I there chos
Ere I at steven hir moght stalle.
That gracios gay withouten galle,
So smooth, so small, so seme slight,

171 gladande gladdening. **con to me glace** stole over me.
172 'As had rarely enough come to me before' (Sisam *Med. Eng. Verse*).
173 liste desire (noun). **enchace** urge.
174 baisment confusion. **brunt** blow. The Dreamer is abashed. Kean 123 compares Dante's reactions on seeing Beatrice across the stream in Earthly Paradise (*Purg*. 30.34 ff.).
176 bur blow. **blunt** stupid.
177 veres turns. **ho** she. **frount** brow.
178 plain ivore smooth ivory. Pearl's complexion is pure white (cf. 212), as her name requires, instead of the conventional blend of red and white: Bishop 112.
179 stong stung, pierced. **stray** in bewilderment. **atount** astounded.
184 hende meek, quiet. The poet blends the alliterative phrase 'hend in hall' (see *MED* s.v. *Hend(e* adj. 1(a)) with the proverbial 'hend as hawk' (Whiting H195), giving an image of a hooded falcon sitting on a perch in a hall: cf. Chaucer *C.T.* I 2204.
185 'I hoped that the affair had a spiritual meaning' (?). MS. reads *hope* as at 142. Occurrence of *dred* at 186 suggests the modern meaning for *hope* here.
186 I dred onende I was afraid concerning.
187 chos perceived.
188 'Before I could stop her for a meeting.'
189 gay fair damsel. **galle** impurity.
190 small slender. **seme** becomingly.

Rises up in hir aray ryalle,
A precios piece in perles pight.

Perles pight of ryal pris
There moght mon by grace haf sene,
When that fresh as flor-de-lis
Down the bonk con bowe bidene.
All blisnande whit was hir beau bis,
Open at sides and bounden bene
With the mirriest margarys at my devis
That ever I sey yet with myn ene,
With lappes large, I wot and I wene,
Dubbed with double perle and dight;
Hir cortel of self sute shene,
With precios perles all umbepight.

A pight coroune yet wer that girle
Of margarys and non other ston,

192 piece person: *OED* s.v. 9. **pight** adorned.
193–228 As the maiden approaches the river and the Dreamer, he gives a more detailed description. A similar technique of long-shot followed by close-up is used in the description of the castle in *Gawain* 764–802.
193 pris excellence.
194 moght could.
195 The comparison with the fleur-de-lis (lily) is proverbial (Whiting F276–8). Cf. Chaucer *C.T.* I 238.
196 bidene straightaway.
197 Cf. 163. **beau bis**] beaumys *or* beauuiys MS. Gollancz reads MS. *mys*, aphetic for *amice*, meaning 'surcoat'; but the MS. is better read *uiys*, emended to *biys* (so Gordon, *b* and *v* being alike in hands of this period), and translated 'fine linen'. Cf. *Rev.* 19.8: 'And it is granted to [the Bride of the Lamb] that she should clothe herself with fine linen (*byssinum*), glittering and white.' Pearl is one of the Brides, as the Dreamer later sees. See Bishop 118–19.
198–202 The mantle (*bleaunt* 163) of white linen is slit down the sides and has hanging sleeves (*lappes* 201), all trimmed with single or double pearl. The fashion is contemporary.
198 bounden bene beautifully trimmed.
199 margarys pearls. The dead child was probably called Margaret or Margery. Cf. Chaucer's play on the name Blanche/White in *Book of the Duchess* and Langland's play on his own name, Will, in *Piers*. Such play with names was common. **at my devis** in my judgment.
201 lappes large broad hanging sleeves.
202 Dubbed adorned. **dight** set.
203 cortel kirtle, dress worn under the mantle. **of self sute** exactly matching. **shene** bright.
204 umbepight adorned round about.
205–6 'Furthermore that girl wore a crown adorned with pearls . . .' Pearl is a Queen of Heaven, as she explains at 415 etc.

Hye pinacled of cler whit perle
With flurted floures perfet upon;
To hed had ho non other werle.
Hir here leke all hir umbegon,
Hir semblaunt sad for doc other erle,
Hir blee more blaght than whales bon
As shorn gold shir hir fax thenne shon
On shilderes that legh unlapped light.
Hir depe colour yet wanted non
Of precios perle in porfil pight.

Pight was poined and uch a hemme
At honde, at sides, at overture,
With white perle and non other gemme,
And bornist white was hir vesture.
Bot a wonder perle withouten wemme
Inmiddes hir brest was set so sure;

208 'With exquisite flowers figured upon it'; perhaps the 'pinnacles' are in the shape of fleurs-de-lys.

209 'She had no other headcovering.' **werle** obscure, possibly 'circlet'.

210 here] lere MS. *lere* ('face', cf. 398) seems appropriate in itself, but makes hard sense with the rest of the line: e.g. 'Her face was enclosed all round (i.e. with a wimple)' (Cawley). *leke* appears to be the past tense of *louke* 'lock', used intransitively as in *Gawain* 1830, where it refers to the girdle fitting closely round the lady. So perhaps: 'Her hair fitted closely all round her', i.e. lay close round her head and face, before spreading out on her shoulders (213–14). Gordon takes the verb as transitive, with the next line: 'Her hair, lying all about her, enclosed her countenance.'

211 'Her expression was grave enough for duke or earl.'

212 blee complexion. **blaght** white. The comparison with ivory was conventional: Whiting W203.

213 'As bright, cut gold . . .' Cf. 165. **fax** hair.

214 unlapped unbound.

215–16 'The deep white of her complexion lacked nothing of the colour of the precious pearls set in the embroidery.' So Gordon. But *yet* may suggest that a new item is being introduced (cf. 205), and *colour* could mean 'collar': 'Furthermore, her high collar was not lacking in precious pearls set in the embroidery.' So Cook *MP* 6 (1908–9) 197–200.

217 poined wristband (Fr. *poignet*).

218 overture opening (at neck).

220 bornist burnished.

221–8 The great pearl is later identified with the 'pearl of great price' of *Matt.* 13.46, which itself is 'like the Kingdom of Heaven' (729–42).

221 wemme blemish.

A mannes doom moght drighly demme
Ere mind moght malte in hit mesure.
I hope no tong moght endure
Ne saverly saghe say of that sight,
So was hit clene and cler and pure
That precios perle there hit was pight.

Pight in perle that precios piece
On wither-half water com down the shore;
No gladder gome hethen into Grece
Than I when ho on brimme wore.
Ho was me nerre than aunte or nece;
My joye forthy was much the more.
Ho profered me speche, that special spece,
Enclinande lowe in woman lore,
Caghte off hir coroune of grete tresore
And hailsed me with a lote light.
Well was me that ever I was bore
To sware that swete in perles pight.

223–6 ‘A man’s judgment could be utterly baffled [lit. ‘dam up’] before his mind could enter into [lit. ‘melt into’] its degree of excellence. I think no tongue would be able to find words adequate to that vision.’
228 there where.
230 On wither-half water on the opposite side of the water.
231 ‘There was no happier man from here to Greece.’ Conventional form of hyperbole in ME and Fr. Cf. No. 10 below, line 2023.
232 brimme brink.
233 nerre nearer. The audience is to identify Pearl as a close relative. Line 483 (‘Thou lifed not two yer in oure thede’) and the parental formula at 1208 together point to an infant daughter: cf. 236 *n.* Spearing comments on the Dreamer ‘continuing to think . . . in naively familial terms, comically and pathetically unaware of their inadequacy’ (Blanch 108).
235 spece] spice MS. (spoiling the rhyme). *spece* and *spice* both derive from Lat. *species* and function in ME as alternative forms of the same word, meaning ‘species’, ‘appearance’, or ‘spice’. The poet’s use of *special* (here ‘precious’) suggests that he knew the etymology; but the sense of *spece* is uncertain. Spices are mentioned as growing out of the grave in Sect. I; so perhaps Pearl is a ‘precious spice’.
236 Enclinande bowing the head. **in woman lore** in a womanly way. Women do not bow to men as a matter of course. The Pearl appears to be acting towards the Dreamer as daughter to father. Cf. 233 *n.* and 257 *n.*
237 Caghte took.
238 hailsed greeted. **lote light** pleasant word.
239 i.e. I was glad to be alive.
240 sware answer.

V

‘O perle,’ quod I, ‘in perles pight,
Art thou my perle that I haf plained,
Regretted by myn one on night?
Much longing haf I for thee lained
Sithen into gress thou me aglight.
Pensif, paired, I am forpained,
And thou in a lif of liking light
In Paradis erde, of strif unstrained.
What wird has hider my juel wained
And don me in this doel and gret daunger?
Fro we in twinne wern towen and twained
I haf ben a joyless jueler.’

That juel thenne in gemmes gent
Vered up hir vise with eyen gray,
Set on hir coroune of perle orient,
And soberly after thenne con ho say:
‘Sir, ye haf your tale mistent

242 plained lamented.
243 by myn one on my own.
244 lained concealed. In this stanza, as in Sect. I, the Dreamer speaks of his relation with Pearl as a kind of romantic love. The idea of concealing grief and the term *longing* both belong to courtly love traditions. Cf. 250 *n*.
245 ‘Ever since you slipped away from me into the grass.’ In Sect. I the loss of the child is described allegorically as a jeweller’s losing a pearl in the grass in a garden.
246 paired worn out. **forpained** tormented.
247 liking pleasure. **light** settled.
248 erde land. **unstrained** untroubled.
249 wird fate. The Dreamer’s references to fate, and fortune (129), are characteristic of his limited perception of God. **wained** carried off.
250 don put. **doel** grief. **daunger** frustration. Another term of romantic love: cf. 244 *n*.
251 ‘From the time that we were dragged apart and separated.’
253 gent noble.
254 Vered lifted. **vise** face. Pearl has been standing before the Dreamer with head bowed. **eyen gray** The eyes of beautiful women are conventionally gray.
255 orient from the East. Oriental pearls were specially prized.
257 ye The Dreamer addressed Pearl with the familiar (fatherly?) singular *thou* (242, 244, 245, 247). Pearl begins her reply with the respectful (filial?) *you*, but soon drops into the singular (263, 264 etc.). **your tale mistent** not attended to what you are saying.

To say your perle is all away,
That is in cofer so comly clent
As in this gardin gracios gay,
Hereinne to lenge for ever and play
There miss ne morning com never here.
Here were a forser for thee, in fay,
If thou were a gentil jueler.

'Bot, jueler gent, if thou shall lose
Thy joye for a gemme that thee was lef,
Me think thee put in a mad porpose
And busies thee aboute a raisoun bref.
For that thou lestes was bot a rose
That floured and failed as kind hit gef;
Now thurgh kind of the kiste that hit con close
To a perle of pris hit is put in pref.
And thou has called thy wird a thef,
That oght of noght has made thee cler;
Thou blames the boot of thy meschef,
Thou art no kinde jueler.'

259 cofer coffer. The image of the jewel casket (also called *forser* 263 and *kiste* 271) adapts Pearl's first explanations to the 'jeweller's' understanding. **clent** made fast ('clenched').

261 lenge dwell. **play** enjoy herself.

262 'Here where loss or grief never come.' Redundant *here* inside the subordinate clause is idiomatic ME, though editors emend to *nere*.

263 forser casket. **in fay** truly. Double meaning: 'This would seem a (fitting) casket to you' (Cawley), and 'This would be a fitting casket *for* you', i.e. for your soul after death.

264 gentil noble.

266 thee was lef was dear to you.

267–8 'It seems to me you are engaged in a mad enterprise, and are troubling yourself for a shortlived cause.'

269 lestes lost.

270 as kind hit gef as nature granted to it.

271 kind nature. **kiste** chest (jewel-casket, but also suggesting coffin).

272 'It has proved to be a pearl of great price.'

274 'Who out of absolutely nothing has made you something.' Man is created from nothing by God: cf. No. 17 below, line 25, and *Piers* B 5.489. 'The dreamer, instead of complaining against God for a supposed injustice, should be praising God for his very existence', Kellogg *Trad.* 12 (1956) 406–7 (reptd Conley). **cler** completely: *MED* adv. 3(a).

275 'You are blaming your trouble on its remedy.'

276 kinde courteous. The Dreamer is showing unnatural ingratitude (cf. *kind* 270, 271) towards God.

A juel to me then was this geste
And jueles wern hir gentil sawes.
‘Ywis,’ quod I, ‘my blissful beste,
My grete distresse thou all todrawes.
To be excused I make requeste.
I trawed my perle don out of dawes;
Now haf I fonde hit, I shall ma feste
And wony with hit in shir wode-shawes
And love my lorde and all his lawes
That has me broght this bliss ner.
Now were I at you beyonde thise wawes
I were a joyful jueler.’

‘Jueler,’ said that gemme clene,
‘Why borde ye men? So madde ye be!
Three wordes has thou spoken at ene;
Unavised forsothe wern all three.
Thou ne wost in worlde what oon dos mene;
Thy word before thy wit con flee.
Thou says thou trawes me in this dene
Because thou may with eyen me see;
Another thou says, in this countré

277 geste newcomer.

278 sawes utterances. Cf. *Matt*. 7.6 (‘Neither cast ye your pearls before swine’); for in what follows the Dreamer is pig-headed: Rupp *MLN* 70 (1955) 558–9.

280 todrawes dispel.

282 ‘I thought my pearl was dead’ (literally ‘put out of days’).

283 ma feste celebrate.

284 wony dwell. **shir wode-shawes** bright groves.

285 love praise (OE *lofian*, not *lufian* ‘love’).

287 at you in your company. **wawes** waves.

290 borde jest. All men seem, from the Pearl’s vantage-point, to speak without proper seriousness.

291 at ene at one time. In the style of a formal disputation, Pearl goes on to itemize the three erroneous propositions (*wordes*) in the Dreamer’s last speech, discussing them in turn in the next two stanzas: (*a*) he believes only what he sees (295–6, 301–12); (*b*) he thinks he can stay with her in the heavenly country (297–8, 313–17); (*c*) he thinks he can cross the stream (299, 318–24).

292 Unavised ill-considered.

293 wost know.

294 i.e. he speaks before he thinks.

295 dene valley. ‘She is not saying that he is mistaken in trusting the evidence of his eyes that she is “in this dene” of paradise, but that he is mistaken in believing her to be there *only* because he can see her with his eyes’, Spearing 151.

Thyself shall won with me right here;
The thridde, to passe this water free –
That may no joyful jueler.

VI

'I halde that jueler littel to praise
That leves well that he sey with yë,
And much to blame and uncortaise
That leves oure lorde wolde make a lie,
That lelly highte your lif to raise
Thagh fortune did your flesh to die.
Ye setten his wordes full westernais
That leves no think bot ye hit sye.
And that is a point o sorquidrye
That uch good mon may evel beseme,
To leve no tale be true to trye
Bot that his one skill may deme.

'Deme now thyself if thou con daily
As man to God wordes sholde heve:
Thou says thou shall won in this baily.
Me think thee burde first aske leve,
And yet of graunt thou mightes faile.

299 free without hindrance (or 'noble'?).
302 leves believes (MS. reads 'loves' here and at 308). **that he sey with yë** (only) what he saw with his own eyes.
305 lelly highte faithfully promised.
306 did caused.
307–8 'You twist his words quite awry if you believe nothing without having seen it.' Alluding to Christ's words to Doubting Thomas: 'Because thou hast seen me, Thomas, thou hast believed: blessed are they that have not seen and have believed' *John* 20.29. **westernais** apparently an altered form of Fr. *bestorneis* 'awry'.
309 o sorquidrye of pride.
310 'Which ill becomes any good man.'
311 trye test out.
312 his one skill his reason alone.
313–14 'Judge now for yourself whether you spoke in the courteous manner in which one should address God.' Pearl turns from a 'point of pride' to one of discourtesy: the Dreamer has said he will stay with her in God's domain without asking His permission. **daily** speak courteously: cf. C. A. Luttrell *N & Q* 9 (1962) 447–8.
315 baily domain.
316 thee burde you ought.
317 yet even so. **graunt** permission.

Thou wilnes over this water to weve.
Ere moste thou kever to other counsaile:
Thy corse in clot mot calder keve.
For hit was forgart at Paradis greve;
Oure yorefader hit con misyeme.
Thurgh drury deth bos uch man dreve
Ere over this dam him Drighten deme.'

'Demes thou me,' quod I, 'my swete,
To doel again, thenne I dowine.
Now haf I fonte that I forlete,
Shall I eft forgo hit ere ever I fine?
Why shall I hit both misse and mete?
My precios perle dos me gret pine.
What serves tresor bot gares men grete
When he hit shall eft with tenes tine?
Now recche I never forto decline
Ne how fer of folde that man me fleme.
When I am partless of perles mine,
Bot durande doel what may men deme?'

'Thou demes noght bot doel distresse,'
Thenne said that wight, 'Why dos thou so?

318 wilnes wish. **weve** pass.

319–20 'First you must adopt a different course: your body must sink down more cold into the earth.'

321 forgart forfeited. **greve** grove.

322 'Our father of old [Adam] abused it.' The stream forms a barrier between man and the lost paradise which, since the Fall, he can recover only after death. Cf. Patch *Other World* on 'water barriers' (Index s.v. 'river, stream').

323–4 'Every man must pass through cruel death before the Lord will allow him across this body of water.'

326 dowine will pine away. The previous clause is conditional.

327 fonte found. **forlete** lost.

328 fine end (my life).

329 'Why must I both lose and find it?' (i.e. lose it as soon as I have found it).

330 pine grief.

331–3 'What good is treasure except to make a man weep when later he has to lose it with pain? Now I do not care how low I fall.'

334 folde land. **fleme** drive away.

335 partless deprived. **perles** Editors emend this to *perle*; but the Dreamer may be speaking generally as a 'jeweller'.

336 'What can men call it but lasting grief?'

337 doel distresse the distress of grief.

For dine of doel of lures lesse
Ofte mony mon forgos the mo.
Thee oghte better thyselven blesse
And love ay God in wele and wo,
For anger gaines thee not a cresse.
Who nedes shall thole, be not so thro.
For thogh thou daunce as any do,
Braundish and bray thy brathes breme,
When thou no firre may, to ne fro,
Thou moste abide that he shall deme.

'Deme Drighten, ever him adite,
Of the way a foot ne will he writhe.
Thy mendes mountes not a mite
Thagh thou for sorwe be never blithe.
Stint of thy strot and fine to flite
And sech his blithe full swefte and swithe.
Thy prayer may his pité bite
That mercy shall hir craftes kithe.
His comforte may thy langour lithe
And thy lures off lightly leme;

339–40 'In the clamour of grief over lesser losses, many men often lose the greater good.' The Dreamer's salvation is the greater good.
341 thyselven blesse cross yourself.
342 love praise.
343 'For anger will not help you a bit.'
344 thole suffer. **thro** impatient.
345 do doe.
346 'Rush around and cry out your intense indignation.' The image of the stricken doe, like that of the docile hawk (184), contributes to an unheroic, even comic, view of the Dreamer: Spearing 153–4.
349–52 'Though you judge the Lord and arraign him for ever, he will not turn aside (*writhe*) one foot from his path. You will not get the slightest extra relief [from the troubles God has in store] even if you go on feeling miserable for ever.'
353 Stint] stynst MS. **strot** wrangling. **fine to flite** stop disputing.
354 blithe mercy. **swithe** at once.
355 bite i.e. gain.
356 hir craftes kithe show her power. Mercy is personified as a damsel in No. 17.2 below.
357 langour sorrow. **lithe** assuage.
358 lures losses, sorrows. **off lightly leme** easily drive away: *MED Lemen* v.(1)? But *leme*, a word of doubtful form and meaning, may be emended to *fleme* 'drive away' (cf. 334), which, however, does not elsewhere go with *off*.

For marre other madde, morne and mithe,
All lis in him to dight and deme.'

359–60 'For whether you lament or rave, or grieve and conceal your feelings, everything lies in God's power to dispose and judge.' Patient acceptance of God's will is a favourite theme of the *Gawain*-poet: cf. *Patience* (No. 8 above) and *Gawain* (No. 10 below, lines 2208–9).

10 Sir Gawain and the Green Knight: extract

Sir Gawain and the Green Knight belongs to the type of Arthurian romance which takes a single adventure as its subject: in this case, the Adventure of the Green Chapel, in which Sir Gawain confronts a magic adversary. Four large capitals in MS. divide the action into four 'fitts' or sections: Fitt I feasting at Camelot; the Green Knight's challenge; Fitt II Gawain's journey; entertainment at Hautdesert; Fitt III three days of hunting and festivity; the lady's three visits to Gawain; Fitt IV (here printed) Gawain's encounter with the Green Knight at the Green Chapel; his return to Camelot.

Like French courtly romances, upon which it draws heavily, *Gawain* gives pride of place to ideals of knightly conduct (on which see Mathew, Chs. 13–15), symbolized by the pentangle on Gawain's shield (625–65). The hero is an outstanding representative of an outstanding fellowship of knights. Perhaps, as A. M. Markham says, the poem simply 'exists to show us what a splendid man he is', *PMLA* 72 (1957) 574–86 (in Blanch below). But Gawain does not survive the Adventure without a fault, for he deceives his host at the Exchange of Winnings in Fitt III, so failing in the chief point of the pentangle ideal, 'trawthe': see Burrow *Reading of SGGK* (1965) and G. M. Shedd *MLR* 62 (1967) 3–13. The nature and gravity of this failing have been much debated: see e.g. G. J. Engelhardt *MLQ* 16 (1955) 218–25 and P. J. C. Field *SP* 68 (1971) 255–69. See also *n.* to line 2374. Those who stress the comic, Christmassy character of the poem tend to exculpate its hero: e.g. M. Stevens 'Laughter and game in *SGGK*' *Spec.* 47 (1972) 65–78. See also Spearing Ch. 5. But the poem leaves its hero in deep self-reproach (2505–12). Is he merely being hypersensitive?

Does the poet question the knightly ideal itself? Speirs 215–51 sees him as working towards 'a kind of adjustment . . . between man and nature, between the human and the other than human', with Gawain (civilization) coming to terms with Nature (the Green Knight). True, Gawain comes to realize the insidious natural force of fear; but the consequent 'adjustment' seems more penitential than Lawrentian. L. D. Benson, in the most complete critical study, also sees the Green Knight as a 'churlish' figure, representing Nature, before whom the courtly values of Camelot appear limited and slightly absurd: *Art and Tradition in SGGK* (Rutgers U.P. 1965). But the poem seems more interested in the limitations of people than in the limitations of their ideals. Fully allegorical interpretations, e.g. H. Schnyder *SGGK: an essay in interpretation* (Bern, Francke 1961), are convincingly criticized by M. Mills

'Christian significance and romance tradition in *SGGK*' *MLR* 60 (1965) 483–93 (in Howard and Zacher, below).

Metre 2530 lines divided into 101 verse paragraphs (cf. 101 stanzas in *Pearl*). Each paragraph consists of an irregular number of unrhymed alliterative long lines (varying from 12 to 37) terminated by five short lines rhyming *ababa*. The first short line ('bob') has a single stress; the other four ('wheel') form a quatrain of three-stress lines. This unusual combination of rhymed and blank verse allows the poet to punctuate his narrative at convenient moments with a bob-and-wheel, often summarizing or clinching a point. See M. Borroff *SGGK: a stylistic and metrical study* (Yale U.P. 1962) Pt 2.

Style etc. The vocabulary is exceptionally rich, drawing on the special terminology of armoury, hunting, castle architecture etc, and also on the formulaic diction of alliterative verse: see Pt 1 of Borroff's *Study*. Speech is rendered more formally than e.g. in Langland, but with considerable vigour and variety. Different kinds of syntax characterize the speeches of Gawain (complex and subtle) and the Green Knight (brusque and paratactic): Spearing *Criticism* 43–50 and C. Clark, *EC* 16 (1966) 361–74. In narrative and description, the poet tends to adopt the point-of-view of his hero, especially at moments of suspense, e.g. the arrival at the Green Chapel (2163 f.).

Structure The four fitts are elaborately patterned, and linked by parallelisms (e.g. between the three hunts and the three 'temptations' in Fitt III, between the two arming scenes of Fitts II and IV, between the two confession scenes of Fitts III and IV) and by contrasts (notably between indoor Christmas festivity and outdoor winter hardship). See D. Howard 'Structure and symmetry in *SG*' *Spec.* 39 (1964) 425–33 (in all three critical anthologies, below). The last long line of the poem (2525, see *n.*) repeats the first, creating a circularity which matches the 'endlessness' of the pentangle (630) which is the heraldic and mystical symbol of Gawain's virtue. Cf. headnote to No. 9 above. Numerological analysis by A. K. Hieatt in A. Fowler, ed. *Silent Poetry* (Routledge 1970) 116–40.

Sources The poem displays intimate knowledge, unusual in ME, of the conventions and procedures of French courtly romances: e.g. the Vulgate *Lancelot* (prose) and the Continuations of Chrétien's *Perceval* (verse). The sources of the story of the Adventure of the Green Chapel were probably Fr., but have not been certainly identified. The 'Beheading Game' story, which lies behind the 'outer test' in *Gawain* (Fitts I and IV), occurs in the Irish saga *Fled Bricrend* (in a MS. of *c.* 1100). From Celtic sources it passed into French romance, where several versions occur, notably in *Le Livre de Caradoc* (part of the First Continuation of Chrétien's *Perceval*) and *La Mule sans frein*. The former is adduced as the poet's source by Benson *Art and Tradition* Ch. 1 and *MP* 59 (1961) 1–12; the latter in R. C. Johnston and D. D. R. Owen, eds. *Two Old French Gauvain Romances* (Edinburgh, Scottish Academic P. 1972). But neither accounts for everything the poet knows of the traditional story. Furthermore, no known text combines the Beheading Game with a Temptation (as in the 'inner test' in Fitt III), though scenes of temptation are in themselves not uncommon. Nor is the Exchange of Winnings motif, which links Temptation to Beheading, paralleled at all in romance. Discussons by G. L. Kittredge *A Study of GGK* (Harvard U.P. 1916), brought up to date by L. H. Loomis in *ALMA* Ch. 39. Celtic and French analogues transl. in E. Brewer *From Cuchulainn to Gawain* (Cambridge, Brewer 1973).

[10] The 'Gawain'-poet

Editions and critical anthologies The best edn is that of J. R. R. Tolkien and E. V. Gordon, 2nd edn revised by N. Davis (Oxford U.P. 1967, cited as 'Davis'), though I. Gollancz's EETS edn (1940) retains value. Student's edns by A. C. Cawley (Dent, Everyman Lib. 1962), R. A. Waldron (E. Arnold 1970), and J. A. Burrow (Penguin 1972). The best translation (in verse) is by M. Borroff (New York, Norton 1967). Critical articles are collected in R. J. Blanch '*Sir Gawain' and 'Pearl': critical essays* (Indiana U.P. 1966); D. R. Howard and C. Zacher *Critical Studies of SGGK* (Univ. of Notre Dame P. 1968); D. Fox *Twentieth Century Interpretations of SGGK* (Englewood Cliffs, N.J., Prentice-Hall 1968), the last with excellent Introd. Studies of *Gawain* up to 1960 are critically surveyed by M. W. Bloomfield *PMLA* 76 (1961) 7–19 (in Howard and Zacher).
Manuscript, date, authorship See above, 'The *Gawain*-poet'.

Lines 1998–2530

Now neghes the New Yere and the night passes,
The day drives to the derk, as Drighten biddes.
Bot wilde wederes of the worlde wakned theroute,
Cloudes kesten kenly the colde to the erthe,
With nye innogh of the northe the naked to tene;
The snaw snitered full snart, that snaiped the wilde;
The werbelande wind wapped fro the highe
And drof uch dale full of driftes full grete.
The leude listened full well that lay in his bedde,
Thagh he loukes his liddes full littel he slepes;
By uch cock that crue he knew well the steven.
Deliverly he dressed up ere the day sprenged,
For there was light of a laumpe that lemed in his chambre.
He called to his chamberlain, that cofly him swared,

1998 neghes approaches.
1999 'Daylight comes up on the darkness . . .' (Davis). **Drighten** the Lord.
2000 theroute out of doors.
2001 kenly bitterly.
2002–3 'With trouble enough from the north to torment the unprotected flesh; the snow drove down very bitterly, stinging the wild creatures.'
2004 werbelande whistling. **wapped** rushed. **highe** high ground.
2006 leude man.
2007 loukes locks tight.
2008 steven appointed day, i.e. the New Year's Day appointed for Gawain to receive the return blow from the Green Knight. Gawain follows the approach of daybreak by the cocks, thought to crow three times (at midnight, 3 a.m., and an hour before dawn). He gets up after third cockcrow, before dawn (cf. 2009, 2085), being determined not to miss his appointment.
2009 'He got up quickly . . .'
2010 lemed gleamed.
2011 chamberlain servant appointed to wait in the chamber. **cofly** promptly. **swared** answered.

And bede him bring him his bruny and his blonk sadel.
That other ferkes him up and fecches him his wedes
And graithes me Sir Gawain upon a gret wise.
First he clad him in his clothes the colde forto were,
And sithen his other harnais, that holdely was keped,
Both his paunce and his plates piked full clene,
The ringes rocked of the roust of his riche bruny;
And all was fresh as upon first, and he was fain thenne
To thonk.
He had upon uch pece
Wipped full well and wlonk,
The gayest into Grece;
The burn bede bring his blonk.

While the wlonkest wede he warp on himselven,
His cote with the conisaunce of the clere werkes
Ennurned upon velvet, vertuus stones
Aboute beten and bounden, enbrauded semes,
And faire furred withinne with faire pelures,

2012 bruny shirt of mail. **his blonk sadel** saddle his horse.
2013 ferkes him up jumps up (having answered from bed).
2014 graithes me dresses. *me* is an 'ethic dative', expressing the speaker's involvement (here untranslatably slight) in what he says. Cf. 2144, 2459.
2015 were ward off.
2016 sithen afterwards. **harnais** equipment. **holdely** carefully.
2017–8 The plate armour (*paunce* armour for the stomach) has been carefully polished (*piked*) and the chainmail rolled (*rocked*) in sand to get the rust off.
2019 upon first at first.
2020 thonk express his thanks.
2021–3 'He had on all his pieces of armour, polished (*wipped*) well and nobly, the finest knight this side of Greece.' Cf. the similarly intensifying reference to Greece, No. 9 line 231.
2024 'The man commanded his horse to be brought out.'
2025 wlonkest wede the noblest of all his pieces of equipment, i.e. the cloth coat-armour, worn over the shirt of mail. MS. has *wedes* for *wede* (cf. 987); but this has forced editors to treat 2026–9 as a long and awkward parenthesis, specifying just one of the *wedes*. **warp** put.
2026 'His coat-armour with the device of pure deeds', referring to Gawain's heraldic device, the pentangle, carried on shield and *cote* (cf. 637). *clere werkes* may refer either to the fine embroidery or to the virtuous conduct which the emblem represents.
2027 Ennurned ornamentally worked. **vertuus stones** gems of special power. Precious stones were held to possess protective *vertu* or power.
2028 '[Gems] set and attached all round, seams embroidered.'
2029 pelures furs.

Yet laft he not the lace, the ladies gift –
That forgat not Gawain for gode of himselven.
By he had belted the bronde upon his balwe haunches,
Then dressed he his drurye double him aboute,
Swithe swethled umbe his swange swetely that knight.
The girdel of the grene silk that gay well besemed,
Upon that ryal red clothe that riche was to shewe.
Bot wered not this ilk wye for wele this girdel,
For pride of the pendauntes, thagh polist they were,
And thagh the gliterande gold glent upon endes,
Bot forto saven himself when suffer him behoved,
To bide bale withoute debate, of bronde him to were
Other knive.
By that the bolde mon boun
Winnes theroute bilive,
All the meiny of renown
He thonkes ofte full rive.

Then was Gringolet graith, that gret was and huge,
And had ben sojourned saverly and in a siker wise;

2030 f. The 'love-lace' given by the lady to Gawain assumes the place of honour occupied by the pentangle in the earlier account of his arming at Camelot (566–665): Burrow *Reading* 114–17; Howard 'Structure and symmetry'.
2031 The lady promised Gawain that the lace would magically protect him against harm (1851–4).
2032 By when. **bronde** sword. **balwe** swelling.
2033 drurye love-token.
2034 'Quickly and gracefully that knight wound it round his waist.'
2035 that gay well besemed suited that gallant well: an echo of 622, where the pentangle was in question.
2036 ryal royal. **shewe** look at. The gold pentangle is on a red ground ('gules' 619); so the red cloth of the coat-armour forms a background also for the green lace wound over it.
2037–9 Poet, Bertilak (2367) and Gawain himself (2430–2) all insist that the hero was not attracted by the splendour of the lace.
2037 wye man. **for wele** because of its costliness.
2039 glent glinted.
2041–2 'To suffer destruction without resistance to protect himself against sword or knife.' Gawain does not yet know which weapon he has to face.
2043 boun ready.
2044 Winnes goes. **bilive** quickly.
2045 meiny household. In the castle courtyard Gawain politely thanks grooms, valets etc. As often, the wheel (quatrain) anticipates an event described more fully in the next stanza.
2046 rive abundantly.
2047 Gringolet traditional name of Gawain's horse (? from Welsh **Gwyngalet* 'white-hard'). **graith** ready.
2048 sojourned lodged, stabled. **saverly** to his taste. **siker** secure.

Him list prick for point, that proude hors thenne.
The wye winnes him to and wites on his lire,
And said soberly himself and by his soth sweres:
'Here is a meiny in this mote that on mensk thenkes.
The mon hem maintaines, joy mot he have!
The leve lady on live, luf hir betide!
Yif they for charité cherisen a gest
And halden honour in her honde, the hathel hem yelde
That haldes the heven upon highe, and also you all!
And yif I might lif upon londe lede any while,
I sholde reche you som reward redily if I might.'
Then steppes he into stirop and strides aloft;
His shalk shewed him his shelde, on shulder he hit laght,
Gordes to Gringolet with his gilt heles,
And he startes on the stone, stood he no lenger
To praunce.
His hathel on hors was thenne,
That bere his spere and launce.
'This castel to Crist I kenne;
He gef hit ay good chaunce.'

The brigge was brayd down and the brode yates
Unbarred and borne open upon bothe halve.

2049 'The high-spirited horse was ready for a gallop then because of his good condition.' Cf. 2064.

2050 wites on his lire inspects his coat.

2052 mote castle. **mensk** honour.

2053 'The man who supports them, may he have joy!' MS. has *thay* for *he*; but Gollancz's emendation gives better sense, acceptable syntax (the subject relative pronoun can be omitted in ME), and a rhetorical parallel with 2054.

2054 leve dear. **on live** alive (tag: cf. 2095).

2056–7 '... may He who holds up the heavens reward them ...' Such periphrastic references to God are common in ME poetry and in the *Gawain* MS: cf. No. 8 above, 111 *n.* Borroff 22–3 detects a correlation between 'the degree of expansion of references to God made in speech by the characters, and the solemnity or importance of the occasion'. Cf. the further 'expansion' at 2441–2.

2059 reche give. A departing guest would normally tip a servant; but Gawain (see 1808 f.) has brought nothing with him on his quest.

2061 shalk man (allotted to him as guide and temporary squire by the lord of the castle). **laght** took.

2062 Gordes to strikes spurs into.

2067 kenne commit.

2068 'May he always grant it good fortune.'

2069 'The drawbridge was pulled down ...'

The burn blessed him bilive and the bredes passed,
Praises the porter – before the prince kneled,
Gef him God and good day, that Gawain he save –
And went on his way with his wye one,
That sholde teche him to tourne to that tene place
There the ruful race he sholde resaive.
They bowen by bonkes there boghes are bare,
They clomben by cliffes there clenges the colde.
The heven was uphalt, bot ugly therunder.
Mist muged on the mor, malt on the mountes,
Uch hill had a hatte, a mist-hakel huge.
Brokes biled and breke by bonkes aboute,
Shire shaterande on shores there they down shouved.
Wela wille was the way there they by wode sholden,
Till hit was sone sesoun that the sunne rises
That tide.
They were on a hill full hye,
The white snaw lay beside.
The burn that rode him by
Bede his maister abide,

2071 'The knight crossed himself swiftly and passed across the planks.'

2072–3 'Compliments the porter – [the porter] knelt before the prince, commended him to God and wished him good day, praying that He would save Gawain.' Three forms of greeting are abruptly compressed into the indirect speech of 2073: 'I commend you to God', 'I wish you good day', and 'God save you'. See Davis *N & Q* 17 (1970) 163–4.

2075 tene perilous.

2076 'Where he was to receive the grievous blow.'

2077 bowen passed. **bonkes** slopes.

2078 clenges clings.

2079 'The cloud cover was high, but it looked threatening underneath.'

2080 muged drizzled (cf. *mug* in modern dialects). **malt** melted, i.e. condensed?

2081 mist-hakel cloak of mist. A compound apparently formed on analogy of *mass-hackle* 'chasuble'. Hills wearing hats etc. appear as signs of bad weather in local weather-lore.

2082 biled and breke boiled (cf. 2174) and broke.

2083 'Dashing white against their banks as they forced their way down.' Waldron takes the second half-line to refer to the riders; but they are still climbing.

2084 'Very devious was the path they had to take through the wood.'

2086 'At that time of the year' (Waldron).

2089 burn man.

'For I have wonnen you hider, wye, at this time,
And now nare ye not fer fro that note place
That ye han spied and spuried so specially after.
Bot I shall say you for sothe, sithen I you knowe
And ye are a leude upon live that I well lovie;
Wolde ye worch by my wit, ye worthed the better.
The place that ye prese to full perelous is halden.
There wones a wye in that waste the worst upon erthe,
For he is stiff and sturn and to strike lovies,
And more he is than any mon upon middelerde,
And his body bigger than the best foure
That are in Arthures house, Hestor other other.
He cheves that chaunce at the Chapel Grene,
There passes non by that place so proud in his armes
That he ne dinges him to dethe with dint of his honde,
For he is a mon methless and mercy non uses.
For be hit chorle other chaplain that by the chapel rides,
Monk other masseprest other any mon elles,
Him think as queme him to quelle as quick go himselven.

2091–155 The Guide makes his contribution to Gawain's moral ordeal, whether as a clumsy well-wisher (2095, cf. 2468), an agent of Morgan and Bertilak, or Bertilak himself in another guise (Gollancz Introd. xxxvi). See P. Delany 'The role of the guide in *SGGK*' *Neophil.* 49 (1965) 250–5 (in Howard and Zacher), and Benson 226–31.
2091 wonnen brought.
2092 nare are not. **note** well-known.
2093 spuried asked.
2096 'If you would act according to my judgment, you would be the better for it.'
2097 prese to press forward towards.
2098 wones dwells.
2099 stiff strong.
2100 more bigger. **middelerde** earth.
2102 Hestor other other Hector or any other. Would such a speaker refer to Hector of Troy? Since everyone in the poem is represented as knowing about the Round Table, the Guide's words are best taken as referring to Sir Hector de Maris, one of the greatest of Arthur's knights in the Vulgate *Lancelot* (ed. H. O. Sommer Vol. 3) and closely connected there with Gawain.
2103 'He brings it about . . .'
2105 dinges] dinnes MS.
2106 methless without moderation, pitiless.
2107–8 Unlike the usual 'felon knight', the Green Knight, according to the Guide, attacks not only all knights (2104) but also churls and churchmen – i.e. all three orders of medieval society. Thus he appears for a moment like Death
2109 'It seems to him as pleasant a thing to kill him as to be alive himself.'

Forthy I say thee as soth as ye in sadel sitte,
Come ye there, ye be killed, may the knight rede,
Trowe ye me that truely, thagh ye had twenty lives
To spende.
He has woned here full yore,
On bent much baret bende;
Ayain his dintes sore
Ye may not you defende.

'Forthy, good Sir Gawain, let the gome one
And gos away som other gate, upon Goddes halve.
Caires by som other kith, there Crist mot you spede,
And I shall hie me home ayain, and hete you firre
That I shall swere by God and all his gode halwes,
As help me God and the halydam, and othes innowe,
That I shall lelly you laine and lause never tale
That ever ye founded to flee for freke that I wist.'
'Grant merci,' quoth Gawain, and grucching he saide,
'Well worth thee, wye, that woldes my gode,
And that lelly me laine I leve well thou woldes.
Bot helde thou hit never so holde, and I here passed,
Founded for ferde forto flee in forme that thou telles,
I were a knight cowarde, I might not be excused.

2110 Forthy therefore.
2111 'If you come there you will be killed, if the knight has his way.' Sisam suggests an emendation, 'I may thee, knight, rede' ('I can tell you that, knight'), which better preserves the Guide's emphatic tone.
2114 full yore for a very long time (difficult to reconcile with 2445 f.).
2115 'Brought about much strife in that field.'
2118 let the gome one leave the man alone.
2119 gate way.
2120 Caires ride. **kith** country.
2121 hete you firre promise you in addition.
2122 halwes saints.
2123 'So help me God and the holy relic, and many other oaths.'
2124 lelly you laine faithfully hide your secret. Gawain earlier promised the lady to 'lelly laine' the lace from her husband (1863); so the phrase here (and cf. 2128) has associations with an earlier 'temptation': see Delany. **lause never tale** never utter a word.
2125 founded set out. **freke** man.
2126 Grant merci many thanks. **grucching** with displeasure.
2127 'May good fortune befall you . . .'
2128 leve believe.
2129 'But no matter how faithfully you concealed the matter, if I left this place.'
2130 ferde fear. Cf. 2125: Gawain spells out the implications.

Bot I will to the chapel, for chaunce that may falle,
And talk with that ilk tulk the tale that me list,
Worth hit wele other wo, as the wird likes
Hit have.
Thagh he be a sturn knape
To stightel, and stad with stave,
Full well con Drighten shape
His servauntes forto save.'

'Mary!' quoth that other mon, 'now thou so much spelles
That thou wilt thyn awen nye nime to thyselven,
And thee list lese thy lif, thee lette I ne kepe.
Have here thy helme on thy hed, thy spere in thy honde,
And ride me down this ilk rake by yon rock side
Till thou be broght to the bothem of the breme valay.
Thenne loke a littel on the launde on thy lifte honde,
And thou shall see in that slade the self chapel
And the borelich burn on bent that hit kepes.
Now fares well on Goddes half, Gawain the noble;
For all the gold upon grounde I nolde go with thee,
Ne bere thee felawship thurgh this frith oon foot firre.'
By that the wye in the wode wendes his bridel,
Hit the hors with the heles as hard as he might,
Lepes him over the launde and leves the knight there
All one.

2132 'But I am resolved to go to the Chapel, despite anything that may happen.'
2133 tulk man. **tale** conversation.
2134 'Whether good or ill come of it . . .' **wird** fate.
2136 knape fellow.
2137 'To deal with, and standing there with a club.' The club is a churlish weapon. See Benson 72 f. on the Green Knight as 'wild man'.
2138 shape contrive.
2140 Previously (except 2110) the Guide addressed Gawain with polite plural *you*. The shift to singular *thou* in this speech marks a new tone of dismissive familiarity: see Metcalf *Ch. R.* 5 (1971) 165–78. **now** now that. **spelles** speak.
2141 nye harm. **nime** take.
2142 'And it pleases you to lose your life, I have no wish to stop you.'
2144 me See 2014 *n*. **rake** path.
2145 breme wild.
2146 launde glade. **lifte** left (side of ill omen).
2147 slade valley.
2148 borelich massive. **bent** field.
2151 frith wood. **firre** further.
2152 wendes turns.

[10] The 'Gawain'-poet

'By Goddes self,' quoth Gawain,
'I will nauther grete ne grone.
To Goddes wille I am full bain,
And to him I have me tone.'

Thenne girdes he to Gringolet and gederes the rake,
Shouves in by a shore at a shawe side,
Rides thurgh the roghe bonk right to the dale.
And thenne he waited him aboute, and wilde hit him thoght,
And sey no singne of resette besides nowhere,
Bot hye bonkes and brent upon bothe halve
And rogh knokled knarres with knorned stones;
The skues of the scoutes skained him thoght.
Thenne he hoved and withheld his hors at that tide,
And ofte chaunged his chere the chapel to seche.
He sey non such in no side, and selly him thoght,
Save a littel on a launde, a lawe as it were,
A balwe berwe by a bonk the brimme beside,
By a forw of a flood that ferked thare;
The borne blubred therinne as hit boiled had.

2157 grete weep.
2158 bain obedient.
2159 me tone committed myself.
2160 gederes picks up.
2161 'Pushes his way down by a bank at the side of a wood.'
2163 waited looked.
2164 resette habitation. **besides** nearby.
2165 brent steep.
2166 'And rough, knobby crags with gnarled rocks' (pronounce *kn-*).
2167 'The clouds seemed to him to be grazed by the crags' (Davis).
2168 hoved drew up.
2169 chaunged his chere looked this way and that.
2170–84 The description of the Green Chapel in its setting is so specific and so unconventional that it seems likely that the poet had a particular place in mind (cf. earlier references to Anglesey, Wirral etc., 697 f.). Most likely is the cave at Wetton Mill, N. Staffs, first proposed by Day (Introd. to Gollancz's edition, xx): study with photographs by Kaske in *Utley Studies* 111–21. A possible alternative is 'Lud's Church', also N. Staffs: see R. W. V. Elliott in Fox *Twentieth Century Interpretations* 106–9. Both fall within the area of the dialect of the MS. The poet may have been introducing 'a local landmark of sinister repute' (Kaske).
2170 selly strange.
2171 'Except a kind of mound (*lawe*) a little way off in a clearing.' Cf. 2146.
2172 balwe berwe smooth-surfaced barrow. **brimme** water's edge.
2173 forw channel. See note in Davis. **ferked** ran.
2174 blubred bubbled.

The knight cacches his caple and com to the lawe,
Lightes down luflily and at a linde tacches
The reine, and hit riches with a rogh braunch.
There he bowes to the berwe, aboute hit he walkes,
Debatande with himself what hit be might.
Hit had a hole on the ende and on aither side,
And overgrowen with gresse in glodes aywhere,
And all was holw inwith, nobot an olde cave
Or a crevisse of an olde cragge, he couth hit noght deme
With spelle.
‘We! lorde,’ quoth the gentil knight,
‘Whether this be the Grene Chapelle?
Here might aboute midnight
The dele his matines telle.

‘Now ywis,’ quoth Gawain, ‘wisty is here.
This oritore is ugly, with erbes overgrowen;
Well besemes the wye wruxled in grene
Dele here his devocioun on the develes wise.
Now I fele hit is the fende, in my five wittes,
That has stoken me this steven to strye me here.
This is a chapel of meschaunce, that check hit betide!
Hit is the corsedest kirk that ever I com inne.’
With hye helme on his hed, his launce in his honde,

2175 cacches his caple urges on his horse.
2176 luflily graciously. **linde** tree. **tacches** attaches.
2177 hit riches] his riche MS. (‘his noble steed’?). Reading and meaning uncertain. *riche* occurs as a verb with *rein* in the alliterative *Destruction of Troy* (e.g. 2370), apparently meaning ‘draw out tight’. So perhaps here: ‘and draws it tight by means of a rough branch’.
2180 The barrow evidently protrudes out from the bank of 2172, and hence has only one *ende*.
2181 glodes patches (?).
2182 holw inwith hollow inside. **nobot** nothing but.
2183–4 ‘Or a fissure in an old crag – he could not say what it was.’
2186 Whether commonly introduces direct question in ME.
2188 dele Devil. **matines** Matins, properly performed at midnight or just after.
2189 ywis indeed. **wisty** desolate.
2190 oritore chapel. **erbes** plants.
2191 wruxled wrapped.
2192 Dele perform.
2193 D. Randall *SP* 57 (1960) 479–91 itemizes the ‘fiendish’ features of the Green Knight: notably, tempting function, green colour, and northerly abode. See also McAlindon *RES* n.s. 16 (1965) 121–39. **wittes** senses.
2194 stoken appointed. **strye** destroy.
2195 that check hit betide and may ill fortune befall it.

He romes up to the roffe of tho rogh wones.
Then herd he of that hye hill, in a hard roche,
Beyonde the broke in a bonk, a wonder breme noise.
What, hit clatered in the cliff as hit cleve sholde,
As one upon a grindelston had grounden a sythe;
What, hit wharred and whette as water at a mulne;
What, hit rushed and rong, rauthe to here.
Then 'By God,' quoth Gawain, 'that gere, as I trowe,
Is riched at the reverence me, renk, to mete
By rote.
Let God worch! We loo!
Hit helpes me not a mote.
My lif thagh I forgoo,
Drede dos me no lote.'

Thenne the knight con calle full hye:
'Who stightles in this sted me steven to holde?
For now is good Gawain goande right here.

2198 roffe roof. **wones** dwellings.
2199 roche rock.
2200 breme fiercely loud.
2201 as hit cleve sholde as if the cliff would split.
2202 sythe scythe.
2203 wharred and whette whirred and made a grinding noise. **mulne** (water) mill. Gawain, looking across the stream, hears both water rushing (2173–4) and a grinding, sounds commonly heard together at a water-mill.
2204 rong rang out. **rauthe** a grievous thing.
2205–7 Obscure. Perhaps: 'That equipment, I believe, is being prepared in honour of meeting me, a knight, in customary fashion.' Gawain identifies the sound as that of knightly equipment (cf. *gere* 569) being prepared (cf. *riched* 599) for action. 2206b appears to be a version (clumsy, because Gawain is referring to himself) of a normal half-line 'the renk forto mete' (*Destruction of Troy* 6693). But Waldron translates: 'in honour of marking out (*to mete*, literally 'measure') the field of combat (*renk*) for me', i.e. challenging me to a duel. **By rote**, if it means 'in customary fashion' ('by the way' is possible), suggests that Gawain was expecting something more outlandish.
2208–11 'Let God do his will. Ah well, it does not help me a bit. Even though I lose my life, no noise (*lote*) will make me afraid.' 2208–9 are obscure. *We loo* might be understood in quotation marks: 'to say "alas" does not help . . .' Otherwise Gawain may mean that thinking about providence will not help (since God's intentions cannot be foreseen). 'Let God work' was a traditional expression of submission to providence.
2212 con calle called.
2213 stightles is master. **sted** place.
2214 goande walking (dismounted).

If any wye oght will, winne hider fast,
Other now other never, his nedes to spede.'
'Abide,' quoth oon on the bonk aboven over his hed,
'And thou shall have all in hast that I thee hight ones.'
Yet he rushed on that rurde rapely a throwe
And with whetting awharf ere he wolde light;
And sithen he keveres by a cragge and comes of a hole,
Whirlande out of a wro with a felle weppen,
A denes ax newe dight the dint with to yelde,
With a borelich bitte bende by the halme,
Filed in a filor, foure foot large –
Hit was no lasse, by that lace that lemed full bright!
And the gome in the grene gered as first,
Both the lire and the legges, lockes and berd,
Save that faire on his fote he foundes on the erthe,
Sette the stele to the stone and stalked beside.

2215–6 'If any person wants anything, let him come here quickly, either now or never, to get his business done.'
2218 hight promised. Referring to the return blow promised by the Green Knight in Fitt I.
2219–20 'Still he swished on hastily with that noise for a while and turned back to his sharpening before he would come down' (Waldron).
2221 keveres makes his way.
2222 wro nook. Here and at 2199–201 the Green Knight seems to display the fairy power of existing inside hills (cf. No. 2 above, 347–8 *n.*). Yet crags such as those opposite Wetton Mill (Kaske *art. cit.* 118–19) might provide a naturalistic explanation. Such overlap of supernatural and natural is characteristic of the whole poem. **felle** terrible.
2223 'A Danish axe newly prepared to return the blow with.' A 'Danish axe' was a kind of battle-axe.
2224–5 'With a massive cutting-edge curving back along by the handle, sharpened in a sharpener and four foot long.'
2226 lemed gleamed. An obscure line. Davis takes *by* as 'measured by', and refers to the lace wrapped round the handle of the other axe used by Gawain in Fitt I (217–20). But why should one measure the blade of one axe by a cord wrapped round the handle of another? Malarkey and Toelken *JEGP* 63 (1964) 14–20 (in Howard and Zacher) suggest a reference to the lady's *lace*; and Waldron sees the line as an oath by that lace 'spoken *in petto* by Gawain', whose thoughts turn to his magic protection when he first sees the axe blade. This seems best.
2227–9 The Green Knight reappears exactly as he was in Fitt I, except that there he rode into Arthur's hall on a green horse.
2228 lire face.
2229 foundes hastens.
2230 stele handle. **stalked** walked with long strides. The Green Knight uses his axe as walking-stick and vaulting-pole.

When he wan to the water, there he wade nolde,
He hipped over on his ax and orpedly strides,
Bremely brothe on a bent that brode was aboute
        On snowe.
    Sir Gawain the knight con mete,
    He ne lutte him nothing lowe.
    That other said, 'Now, sir swete,
    Of steven mon may thee trowe.

'Gawain,' quoth that grene gome, 'God thee mot loke!
Ywis thou art welcom, wye, to my place,
And thou has timed thy travail as true mon sholde,
And thou knowes the covenauntes kest us betwene:
At this time twelmonith thou toke that thee falled,
And I sholde at this New Yere yeply thee quite.
And we are in this valay veraily oure one;
Here are no renkes us to rid, rele as us likes.
Haf thy helme of thy hed and haf here thy pay.
Busk no more debate than I thee bede thenne
When thou wipped off my hed at a wap one.'
'Nay, by God,' quoth Gawain, 'that me gost lante,
I shall grucche thee no grue for greme that falles.

2231 wan to arrived at. **nolde** did not wish to. The Green Knight has a special reason for avoiding contact with water, which dissolves spells (cf. *Tam o Shanter*): C. Dean *Explicator* 22 (April 1964) No. 67.
2232 hipped hopped. **orpedly** boldly.
2233 Bremely brothe fierce and vigorous.
2234 'Covered in snow'.
2236 lutte bowed. A striking omission in the knight of courtesy.
2238 'One can trust you to keep an appointment.'
2239 God thee mot loke may God protect you.
2240 Echoing the words with which Arthur welcomed the Green Knight to Camelot: 'Wye, welcom ywis to this place' (252).
2241 travail journey.
2242 kest agreed.
2243 'A year ago today you accepted what fell to your lot', i.e. the chance to deliver the first blow.
2244 yeply promptly. **quite** requite.
2245 oure one on our own.
2246 rid separate. **rele as us likes** however much we like to struggle.
2248 'Offer no more resistance than I offered you then.'
2249 wap one single stroke.
2250 that me gost lante who gave me a soul.
2251 'I shall bear you not the slightest grudge, whatever injury happens to me.' **grue** grain i.e. whit. Gawain speaks with grim irony.

Bot stightel thee upon oon stroke, and I shall stonde stille
And warp thee no werning to worch as thee likes
Nowhare.'
He lened with the neck and lutte
And shewed that shire all bare
And let as he noght dutte;
For drede he wolde not dare.

Then the gome in the grene graithed him swithe,
Gederes up his grimme tole Gawain to smite;
With all the bur in his body he ber hit on lofte,
Munt as maghtily as marre him he wolde.
Had hit driven adown as dregh as he atled,
There had ben ded of his dint that doghty was ever;
Bot Gawain on that giserne glifte him beside,
As hit com glidande adown on glode him to shende,
And shrank a littel with the shulderes for the sharp irn.
The other shalk with a shunt the shene withhaldes,
And thenne repreved he the prince with mony proude wordes:
'Thou art not Gawain,' quoth the gome, 'that is so good halden,
That never arwed for no here by hille ne by vale,
And now thou flees for ferde ere thou fele harmes!
Such cowardise of that knight couth I never here.
Nauther fiked I ne flagh, freke, when thou mintest,
Ne kest no cavelacioun in kinges hous Arthur.

2252 'Just confine yourself to a single blow . . .'
2253 'And offer you no resistance . . .'
2255 lutte cf. 2236.
2256 shire white (flesh).
2257 'And acted as if he feared nothing.'
2258 dare cower.
2259 graithed him swithe got ready quickly.
2261 bur force.
2262 'Prepared to strike as forcibly as if he wanted to destroy him.'
2263–4 'If it had come down as hard as he threatened, the man who had always been valiant would have died there from his blow.'
2265 giserne axe. **glifte him beside** glanced sideways.
2266 'The content of the adverbial clause, which occupies an entire line, is superfluous, but the drawing out of the instant of suspense is psychologically valid', Borroff 127. **on glode** on the ground (tag). **shende** destroy.
2268 shunt abrupt stop. **shene** bright (blade)
2271 arwed was afraid. **here** army.
2272 flees flinch.
2274–5 'I neither jumped nor flinched, sir, when you prepared to strike, nor raised any objection in King Arthur's hall.'

My hed flagh to my fote and yet flagh I never,
And thou, ere any harme hent, arwes in hert;
Wherfore the better burn me burde be called
Therfore.'
Quoth Gawain, 'I shunt ones,
And so will I no more.
Bot thagh my hed falle on the stones
I con not hit restore.

'Bot busk, burn, by thy faith, and bring me to the point,
Dele to me my destiné and do hit out of honde;
For I shall stonde thee a strok and start no more
Till thyn ax have me hitte, haf here my trauthe.'
'Haf at thee thenne!' quoth that other, and heves hit alofte
And waites as wrothly as he wood were.
He mintes at him maghtily bot not the mon rines,
Withheld heterly his honde ere hit hurt might.
Gawain graithly hit bides and glent with no membre,
Bot stood stille as the ston, other a stubbe other
That ratheled is in roché grounde with rotes a hundreth.
Then murily eft con he mele, the mon in the grene:
'So, now thou has thy hert hole, hitte me behoves.
Holde thee now the hye hode that Arthur thee raght,
And kepe thy kanel at this kest, yif hit kever may.'

2276 flagh . . . flagh flew (from *fly*) . . . flinched (from *flee*). Wordplay.
2277 'And you, before receiving any injury, are afraid in your heart.'
2278 me burde I must.
2280 shunt jerked.
2282–3 The Green Knight had nothing to fear from losing *his* head, as he did at Camelot.
2284 busk hurry up. **point** Waldron suggests wordplay: cf. 2392.
2286 'For I shall stand and take a blow from you and jump no more.'
2289 waites looks. **wrothly** angrily. **wood** mad.
2290 'He aims a mighty blow at the man, but does not touch him.'
2291 heterly suddenly.
2292 graithly duly. **glent** flinched.
2293–4 The double simile of rock and tree stump is based on the proverbial coupling of stock and stone: Whiting S745–6. Cf. No. 2 line 346.
2293 other . . . other or else.
2294 ratheled entwined. **roché** rocky.
2295 eft again. **mele** speak.
2296 hole whole (i.e. 'now you have regained your self-possession'). **hitte me behoves** it is time for me to strike.
2297–8 'May the noble order which Arthur bestowed upon you [knighthood] preserve you now and protect your neck at this stroke, if it can succeed in doing so.'

Gawain full grindelly with greme thenne saide:
'Wy! thresh on, thou thro mon, thou thretes too longe.
I hope that thy hert arwe with thyn awen selven.'
'For sothe,' quoth that other freke, 'so felly thou spekes,
I will no lenger on lite lette thyn ernde
Right now.'
Thenne tas he him strithe to strike
And frounses both lippe and browe.
No mervail thagh him mislike
That hoped of no rescowe.

He liftes lightly his lome and let hit down faire
With the barbe of the bit by the bare neck;
Thagh he homered heterly, hurt him no more
Bot snirt him on that oon side, that severed the hide.
The sharp shrank to the flesh thurgh the shire grece,
That the shene blood over his shulderes shot to the erthe.
And when the burn sey the blood blenk on the snawe,
He sprit forth spenne-foot more than a spere lenthe,
Hent heterly his helme and on his hed cast,
Shot with his shulderes his fair shelde under,
Braides out a bright bronde, and bremely he spekes –
Never syn that he was burn born of his moder

2299 grindelly fiercely. **greme** anger.
2300 Wy interjection ('Oh, for God's sake'). **thresh** strike. **thro** fierce.
2301 'I believe that your own heart is afraid within you': see Davis Glossary s.v. *with*.
2302 felly fiercely.
2303 on lite lette hinder with delays. **ernde** mission.
2305 tas . . . strithe takes stance.
2306 frounses puckers.
2307–8 'No wonder if he found it unpleasant, having no hope of rescue.'
2309 lome tool.
2310 the barbe of the bit 'the hooked part of the blade': Luttrell *Neophil.* 40 (1956) 292. This time the Green Knight does not withhold the stroke, but lets it fall to one side of Gawain's neck, cutting him with the *barbe*.
2311 homered heterly struck fiercely.
2312 'But nicked him on the one side, so that the skin parted.'
2313 shire grece white fat (cf. 425).
2315 blenk gleam. The blood on the snow provides evidence that the return blow has been duly delivered. Gawain is now free to defend himself.
2316 sprit sprang. **spenne-foot** with feet together, in a standing jump.
2318 'Jerked with his shoulders his fair shield round under his arm.' The shield has been slung on his back.
2319 Braides draws. **bronde**] sworde MS. Emendation suggested by Borroff 239. Cf. No. 32 below, line 126. **bremely** fiercely.

Was he never in this worlde wye half so blithe –
'Blinne, burn, of thy bur, bede me no mo!
I haf a stroke in this sted withoute strif hent,
And if thou reches me any mo, I redily shall quite
And yelde yederly ayain, and therto ye trist –
And foo.
Bot oon stroke here me falles;
The covenaunt shop right so
Festned in Arthures halles;
And therfore, hende, now hoo!'

The hathel helded him fro and on his ax rested,
Sette the shaft upon shore and to the sharp lened
And loked to the leude that on the launde yede,
How that doghty dredless dervely there stondes
Armed, full awless; in hert hit him likes.
Then he meles murily with a much steven
And with a rickande rurd he to the renk saide:
'Bold burn on this bent be not so grindel.
No mon here unmanerly thee misboden habbes,
Ne kid bot as covenaunt at kinges court shaped.
I hight thee a stroke and thou hit has; halde thee well payed.

2322 Blinne cease. **bur** violence.
2323 hent taken.
2324 reches offer.
2325–6 'And repay promptly, you may be sure of that – and fiercely too.'
2327 'Only one blow is due to me here.'
2328 shop ordained.
2329 Festned in] MS. illegible, though *Fe* can be seen in offset. With *festned* 'made fast' cf. 1783. Other conjectures are *fermed* and *fettled*.
2330 hende good sir. **hoo** whoa, enough. A word used for stopping combat in jousts etc. (e.g. Chaucer *C.T.* I 2656).
2331 helded stepped away.
2332 upon shore 'at a slant': A. McIntosh, in *Schlauch Studies* 255–60, referring to *OED A-shore* adv. phr. and *MED Ashore* adv. The Green Knight puts the handle (*shaft*) of the axe at a slant to the ground and leans on the head (*sharp*): a typically relaxed, insouciant attitude.
2333 yede went.
2334 dervely boldly.
2335 awless fearless. **likes** pleases. A rare glimpse into the Green Knight's mind.
2336 meles speaks. **much steven** big voice.
2337 rickande loud (rattling?): *EDD Rick* v³. **rurd** voice.
2338 grindel fierce.
2339–40 'No one here has mistreated you in unmannerly fashion, or acted towards you otherwise than as the agreement at the King's court laid down.'

I relece thee of the remnaunt of rightes all other.
If I deliver had ben, a boffet paraunter
I couth wrothloker haf wared, to thee haf wroght anger.
First I mansed thee murily with a mint one
And rove thee with no rof-sore, with right I thee profered
For the forward that we fest in the first night,
And thou tristily the trauthe and truly me haldes;
All the gaine thou me gef as good mon sholde.
That other mint for the morn, mon, I thee profered;
Thou kissedes my clere wif, the cosses me raghtes.
For both two here I thee bede bot two bare mintes
Boute scathe.
True mon true restore,
Thenne thar mon drede no wathe.
At the thrid thou failed thore,
And therfore that tappe ta the.

'For hit is my wede that thou weres, that ilk woven girdel,
Myn owen wif hit thee weved, I wot well for sothe.
Now know I well thy cosses and thy costes als,
And the wowing of my wif, I wroght hit myselven.

2342 The Green Knight's reference to other *rightes*, which he is ready to waive, can be understood only in the light of his later explanations.
2343 deliver quick.
2344 'I could have struck more in anger and done you some damage.'
2345–7 'First I threatened you in sport with a single aimed blow and cut you with no gash: with justice I made you the offer [of that undelivered blow] in view of the agreement we made on the first night.' Spearing 190 points out that the identity of the Green Knight with Gawain's host at the castle, with whom he three times engaged in the Exchange of Winnings pact, 'is never formally disclosed at all, but simply implied by the *we*' of line 2347.
2348 tristily in a trusty fashion. **trauthe** compact.
2349 gaine winnings. Gawain received one kiss from the lady on the first day and 'paid' it to the host on his return from the hunt.
2350 the morn i.e. the next day after Gawain first honoured his agreement.
2351 the cosses me raghtes (you) handed over the kisses to me.
2352 bede offered. **bare mintes** simple aimed (undelivered) blows.
2353 Boute scathe without harming you.
2354–5 'A true person must (*mon*) make true restitution; then a man need fear no danger.'
2356 thrid third occasion: when Gawain failed to pay over the lace. **thore** there.
2357 ta the take to yourself. *the* is an unstressed form of *thee*.
2358 '*My* wede' because it should justly be his under the Exchange agreement.
2359 weved gave (with play on *woven*).
2360 costes qualities.
2361 'And my wife's wooing (of you) . . .'

I sende hir to assay thee, and sothly me thinkes
Oon the fautlest freke that ever on fote yede.
As perle by the white pese is of pris more,
So is Gawain in good faith by other gay knightes.
Bot here you lacked a littel, sir, and lewté you wonted;
Bot that was for no wiled werk, ne wowing nauther,
Bot for ye lufed your lif – the lasse I you blame.’
That other stiff mon in study stood a gret while,
So agreved for greme he gryed withinne:
All the blood of his brest blende in his face,
That all he shrank for shome that the shalk talked.
The forme word upon folde that the freke meled:
‘Corsed worth cowardise and covetise both!
In you is vilany and vise that vertue distryes.’
Thenne he caght to the knot and the kest lauses,
Braide brothly the belt to the burn selven:
‘Lo there the falsing, foule mot hit falle!

2362–3 ‘I sent her to try you – truly, it seems to me, quite the most faultless man that ever trod ground.’ *one* strengthens the superlative in ME (contrast Modern Eng. ‘one of’).
2364 ‘As a pearl by comparison with the white pea is of greater value.’ A dried pea might be mistaken for a pearl.
2366 you lacked a littel a little was lacking in you. Previously in this scene the Green Knight has consistently used the singular *thou*, suggesting masterful familiarity. Here he shifts to a more formal plural (N.B. *sir*) appropriate for his measured judgment. See 2140 *n*. **lewté** loyalty, fidelity. Gawain’s chief failure is one of *lewté* or *trauthe*, in failing to honour the Exchange of Winnings agreement: cf. 2381–3, 2499, 2509.
2367 wiled werk skilled workmanship (of the lace: 2037–9 *n*.). ‘Wild work’ could mean ‘sexual intercourse’ in ME (*N & Q* 13 (1966) 451–2); but *wiled* (MS. *wylyde*) ‘seems rather to be an adj. formed on *wile* “skill”’ (Davis). **wowing** wooing.
2370 greme mortification. **gryed** shuddered.
2371 blende mingled, streamed together. Davis compares 2503.
2373 forme first. **folde** earth.
2374 worth be. **covetise** covetousness. Gawain three times accuses himself of *covetise* as well as cowardice (cf. 2380, 2508); but he did *not* desire the girdle for its richness or workmanship (cf. 2037–9 *n*.). The act of withholding something justly due to another was classed among the acts of covetousness in medieval manuals; and that is what Gawain did when he hid the girdle from his host. D. F. Hills *RES* n.s. 14 (1963) 124–31 (in Howard and Zacher) takes *covetise* to denote ‘any turning away from God’s love’; but this broad sense seems excluded by 2379–81, where *covetise* is secondary to cowardice and opposed to *largesse*: *RES* n.s. 15 (1964) 56.
2376 the kest lauses releases the fastening.
2377 Braide brothly angrily threw.
2378 falsing (occasion of) breaking faith.

For care of thy knocke cowardise me taght
To acorde me with covetise, my kinde to forsake,
That is largesse and lewté that longes to knightes.
Now am I fauty and falce, and ferde haf ben ever
Of trecherye and untrauthe – both betide sorwe
And care!
I beknowe you, knight, here stille,
All fauty is my fare.
Letes me overtake your wille
And eft I shall be ware.'

Then logh that other leude and luflily saide:
'I halde hit hardily hole the harme that I had;
Thou art confessed so clene, beknowen of thy misses,
And has the penaunce apert of the point of myn egge.
I halde thee polised of that plight and pured as clene
As thou hades never forfeted sithen thou was first born.
And I gif thee, sir, the girdel that is gold-hemmed;
For hit is grene as my gowne, Sir Gawain, ye may
Thenk upon this ilk threpe there thou forth thringes
Among princes of pris, and this a pure token
Of the chaunce of the Grene Chapel at chevalrous knightes.

2380 acorde me come to terms. Gawain speaks in quasi-allegorical terms. **kinde** nature.
2381 *Largesse* and *lewté* are the exact and formal opposites of *covetise* and *trecherye* (otherwise *untrauthe*) respectively.
2382 fauty faulty. **ferde** afraid.
2385 beknowe confess to. **stille** 'between ourselves'? or 'without protest, humbly' (Davis).
2386 fare behaviour.
2387 '"Let me understand your will", i.e. what do you want me to do now? Gawain, having confessed, asks for penance' (Gollancz).
2389 logh laughed. **luflily** amiably.
2390 hardily hole quite mended.
2391–4 The scene follows the order of the confessional: the Green Knight, having observed Gawain's contrition and heard his confession, and having already administered the right measure of penance with his axe, is now able to absolve the hero: see Burrow *MP* 57 (1959–60) 73–9 and *Reading* 127–33.
2391 misses faults.
2392 penaunce apert open penance; alluding to the practice of public penance. Gawain's cut will be visible to all. **point** 2310 *n.*
2393 plight offence.
2394 Cf. Chaucer *C.T.* VI 913–5: 'I you assoille . . . as clene and eek as cleer | As ye were born.'
2396–9 'Because it is as green as my gown, you can be reminded of this same contest, Sir Gawain, when you make your way among noble princes; and this will be an excellent token of the Adventure of the Green Chapel among chivalrous knights.'

And ye shall in this New Yere ayain to my wones,
And we shyn revel the remnaunt of this riche fest
Full bene.'
There lathed him fast the lorde
And saide, 'With my wif, I wene,
We shall you well acorde,
That was your enmy kene.'

'Nay, for sothe,' quoth the segge, and sesed his helme
And has hit off hendly and the hathel thonkes:
'I have sojorned sadly; sele you betide
And he yelde hit you yare that yarkes all menskes!
And comaundes me to that cortais, your comlich fere,
Both that oon and that other, myn honoured ladies,
That thus her knight with her kest han kointly begiled.
Bot hit is no ferly thagh a fole madde,
And thurgh wiles of wimmen be wonen to sorwe;
For so was Adam in erde with one begiled,
And Salamon with fele sere; and Samson eftsones,

2400 ayain (come) back.
2401 shyn shall. **remnaunt** remainder. Gawain spent 7 days of Christmas feast at Hautdesert; but at Camelot the feast lasted 15 days (44).
2402 bene pleasantly.
2403 lathed him fast invited him insistently.
2405 We a colloquially reassuring usage, as in Mod. Eng.
2407 segge man.
2408 hendly courteously.
2409–10 'I have stayed with you long enough. May good fortune befall you, and may He who bestows all honours [2056–7 *n.*] soon repay you.'
2411 comaundes commend. **fere** companion, wife.
2412 other referring to the mysterious old lady at Hautdesert.
2413 her knight Gawain declared himself the 'servant' of both ladies (976). **kest** tricks. **kointly** skilfully. It is not clear why Gawain here includes the old lady in his suspicions.
2414–26 Lists of great men ruined by women were common. The same four O.T. examples are listed in *Kyng Alisaunder* (B text) 7703–9. M. Dove *Med. Aev.* 41 (1972) 20–6 produces evidence that Gawain was traditionally a distruster of women, e.g. *Chevalier à l'épée* 1168–88 (see Johnston and Owen 201–2). Burrow *Reading* 147–8 suggests that either hero or poet is here somewhat carried away by antifeminist feeling; but P. J. Lucas *N & Q* 15 (1968) 324–5 finds Gawain's parallels justified almost completely. D. Mills *Neuphil. Mitteil.* 71 (1970) 635–40 reads the tone as courteous and bantering, reflecting newly regained self-control.
2414 ferly marvel. **madde** act madly.
2416 erde earth.
2417 fele sere many and various (women).

Dalida dalt him his wird; and Davith therafter
Was blended with Barsabe, that much bale tholed.
Now these were wrathed with her wiles, hit were a winne huge
To luf hem well and leve hem not, a leude that couth.
For these were forne the freest, that folwed all the sele
Exellently of all these other under hevenriche
That mused;
And all they were bewiled,
With wimmen that they used.
Thagh I be now begiled,
Me think me burde be excused.

'Bot your girdel,' quoth Gawain, 'God you foryelde!
That will I welde with good wille, not for the winne gold,
Ne the seint, ne the silk, ne the side pendauntes,
For wele ne for worship, ne for the wlonk werkes,
Bot in singne of my surfet I shall see hit ofte,
When I ride in renown remorde to myselven
The faut and the faintise of the flesh crabbed,
How tender hit is to entise teches of filthe;
And thus, when pride shall me prick for prowess of armes,
The loke to this luf-lace shall lethe my hert.
Bot oon I wolde you pray, displeses you never:

2418 'Delilah dealt him his doom . . .'
2419 blended blinded. **that much bale tholed** and suffered much misery. David did penance after the death of Bathsheba's husband (2 *Sam.* 12).
2420–4 'Since these were afflicted through their wiles, it would be a great advantage to love them well and not trust them at all, if a man could. For these were the noblest of former times, and every prosperity attended them preeminently above all others who lived ['thought'] under the heavens.' *winne* (2420) may be 'joy' rather than 'gain, advantage'.
2426 used had sexual intercourse with (*OED* s.v. *Use* v. 10b). Editorial gloss 'had dealings with' gains only doubtful support from *OED* sense 17a, and seems too bland for a line which expresses a degree of revulsion.
2428 'It seems to me that I should be excused.'
2429 you foryelde repay you for it.
2430–2 See 2037–9 *n.*
2430 welde take possession of. **winne** splendid.
2431 seint woven part of the girdle (Fr. *ceint*). **side** long.
2432 wlonk werkes rich workmanship.
2433 surfet transgression.
2434 remorde to myselven recall with remorse.
2435 faut faultiness. **faintise** probably 'treacherousness' (*MED* s.v. *Feintise* n. 1(a)); but possibly 'frailty'. **crabbed** perverse.
2436 'How liable it is to attract blemishes of sin.'
2438 The loke to looking at. **lethe** make humble.
2439 'But there is one thing I should like to ask you – do not be displeased.'

Syn ye be lorde of the yonder londe that I haf lent inne
With you with worship – the wye hit you yelde
That uphaldes the heven and on high sittes –
How norne ye your right name, and thenne no more?'
'That shall I telle thee truly,' quoth that other thenne:
'Bertilak de Hautdesert I hat in this londe.
Thurgh might of Morgne la Faye, that in my hous lenges,
And kointise of clergye by craftes well lerned,
The maistrés of Merlin mony has taken;
For ho has dalt drury full dere somtime
With that conable clerk, that knowes all your knightes
At hame.

2440 lent stayed.
2441–2 See 2056–7 *n*.
2443 How norne ye what do you call. **right name** The adversary announced himself in Fitt I as 'the Knight of the Green Chapel' (454). Gawain now wants to know his true, everyday name. Cf. Malory: 'He was called in the courte of king Arthur Bewmaynes, but his right name is sir Gareth of Orkeney' (Burrow *Reading* 124).
2444 that other Alliteration requires *the tother* (Davis).
2445 Bertilak an Eng. form of Fr. *Bertolais*. Knights who bear this name in Fr. romance display no special resemblance to Bertilak. The English poet perhaps chose the name as being established but unremarkable. **Hautdesert** the name of Bertilak's regular home, i.e. the castle where Gawain spent Christmas. The name means 'high and lonely place'. **hat** am called.
2445 ff. Syntax and punctuation very uncertain. If 2446 begins a new sentence (Bertilak can hardly say that he owes his right name to Morgan), one would look for the main clause in 2448, which is however corrupt: at 2448b MS. reads 'mony ho taken'. If MS. *ho* ('she', Morgan) is preserved (reading perhaps 'mony ho has taken'), this clause cannot belong with 2446–7; and 2448–55 may be put in parenthesis, leaving the main sentence to be resumed at 2456 (so Waldron), or else a line providing the main clause for 2446–7 may be supposed lost (so Gollancz). But if *ho* is emended to *has* (so Davis and here), 2446–51 may be translated: 'Through the agency of Morgan le Fay, who is staying in my house, and through learned skills well and artfully mastered, many people have experienced the magic powers of Merlin; for she formerly had a very intimate love-affair with that excellent scholar, as all your knights at home know.' Morgan, that is, mastered the learned skills (cf. No. 20 line 118) of her lover; and so, through her agency, Merlin's magic came to be exercised on people like Bertilak. The difficulty here lies in the sense required for *taken*.
2446 Morgne la Faye Morgan's love-affair with Merlin and her consequent possession of magic arts are well-known facts of Arthurian romance. In the Fr. Vulgate *Lancelot*, 'supernatural' events are regularly explained by reference to Morgan's magic. On the role of Morgan in *Gawain*, see A. B. Friedman *Spec*. 35 (1960) 260–74.

Morgne the goddess
Therfore hit is hir name;
Weldes non so high hautesse
That ho ne con make full tame.

'Ho wained me upon this wise to your winne halle
Forto assay the surquidré, yif hit soth were
That rennes of the grete renown of the Rounde Table.
Ho wained me this wonder your wittes to reve,
Forto have greved Gainour and gart hir to die
With glopning of that ilk gome that gostlich speked
With his hed in his honde before the high table.
That is ho that is at home, the auncian lady;
Ho is even thyn aunt, Arthures half-suster,
The Duchess doghter of Tintagelle, that dere Uter after
Had Arthur upon, that athel is nowthe.
Therfore I ethe thee, hathel, to come to thyn aunt.
Make mirry in my house; my meiny thee lovies,
And I woll thee as well, wye, by my faith,
As any gome under God, for thy grete trauthe.'
And he nicked him nay, he nolde by no wayes.
They acolen and kissen, bekennen aither other

2452–3 Morgan is called 'la déesse' in the Vulgate *Lancelot*: see Davis *n.*
2454 Weldes possesses. **hautesse** pride.
2456 Ho wained she sent.
2457 surquidré pride.
2458 That rennes of what is currently said about. On the theme of 'renown' in *Gawain*, see Benson Ch. 5.
2459 'She sent this marvel . . .' *me* is not obj. as at 2456, but an ethic dative (2014 *n.*). **reve** take away.
2460 gart caused. Morgan's hatred of Guinevere is explained in Fr. Vulgate romances by a story of how the Queen frustrated her in a secret love-affair: see Davis *n.*
2461 glopning of dismay at. **gome** man. MS. reading *gomen*, defended by Gollancz ('trick or machination'). **gostlich** in a ghostly or uncanny way.
2464–6 The Duchess of Tintagel, before becoming the mother of Arthur by Uther Pendragon, had daughters by her husband, one of whom was Morgan, another (Morgawse in Malory) the mother of Gawain.
2465 dere noble.
2466 athel noble. **nowthe** now.
2467 ethe entreat.
2469–70 'And I wish you as well, sir, by my faith, as any man on earth, because of your great integrity.' Bertilak places his last emphasis on *trauthe*, the quality symbolized by Gawain's pentangle (625–6).
2471 'And he said to him no, he would by no means.'
2472 acolen embrace. **bekennen** commit (MS. omits).

To the prince of paradise, and parten right there
On colde.
Gawain on blonk full bene
To the kinges burgh buskes bolde,
And the knight in the enker grene
Whiderward-so-ever he wolde.

Wilde wayes in the worlde Wawain now rides
On Gringolet, that the grace had geten of his live.
Ofte he herbered in house and ofte all theroute,
And mony aventure in vale he venquist ofte
That I ne tight at this time in tale to remene.
The hurt was hole that he had hent in his neck,
And the blickande belt he bere theraboute
Abelef as a bauderik bounden by his side,
Loken under his lift arme, the lace, with a knot,
In tokening he was tan in tech of a faut;
And thus he comes to the court, knight all in sounde.
There wakned wele in that wone when wist the grete
That good Gawain was comen; gain hit hem thoght.
The king kisses the knight, and the quene als,

2475 blonk full bene his very excellent steed.
2476 buskes hastens.
2477 enker bright.
2478 This vague form of dismissal (not 'Bertilak hastened back to Hautdesert') allows the Green Knight to leave a whiff of mystery behind, despite his explanations. Contrast No. 18, lines 323–4.
2480 grace Bertilak had an absolute, unqualified right to chop Gawain's head off, under the Beheading Agreement.
2482 he venquist he was victorious in. Emendation by Gollancz of MS. '& venquyst', which leaves the syntax of 2483 obscure.
2483 tight intend. **remene** recall. The rhetorical device *occupatio*, used to pass over marginal matter, is characteristic of the author's concentration on his one topic, the Adventure of the Green Chapel. Cf. 715–25.
2485 blickande gleaming.
2486 Abelef slantwise. **bauderik** baldric, strap (for shield etc.) worn diagonally across the body.
2487 Loken fastened.
2488 tan taken. **tech** spot, stain. In itself the girdle is a *token* of Gawain's weakness (cf. 2433) simply because of the manner in which he obtained it (Burrow *Reading* 158). But it acquires a certain symbolic appropriateness from the way he wears it: round his neck like the halters sometimes worn by penitents, and knotted in a fashion which recalls the *endless knot* of the pentangle (Hieatt in *Silent Poetry* 120). There is also mention of the left, or evil, side at 2487.
2490 wele joy. **when wist the grete** when the great ones (nobles) learned.
2491 gain good.

And sithen mony siker knight that soght him to hailse,
Of his fare that him frained; and ferlily he telles,
Beknowes all the costes of care that he had,
The chaunce of the chapel, the chere of the knight,
The luf of the lady, the lace at the last.
The nirt in the neck he naked hem shewed
That he laght for his unlewté at the leudes hondes
For blame.
He tened when he sholde telle,
He groned for gref and grame;
The blood in his face con melle
When he hit sholde shewe, for shame.

'Lo, lorde,' quoth the leude, and the lace hondeled,
'This is the bende of this blame I bere in my neck,
This is the lathe and the losse that I laght have
Of cowardise and covetise that I haf caght thare;
This is the token of untrauthe that I am tan inne,
And I mot nedes hit were while I may last.
For non may hiden his harme bot unhap ne may hit,
For there hit ones is tacched twinne will hit never.'

2493 siker trusty. **hailse** greet.
2494 'Who asked him how he got on; and he tells of wonders.'
2495 Beknowes confesses. The parallel with 2385 is one of several between this scene and the earlier confession to the Green Knight. Cf. 2502–4. **costes of care** difficulties.
2496 chaunce adventure. **chere** behaviour.
2498 nirt slight cut.
2499 laght received.
2501 tened felt pain.
2502–4 The sequence of mortification, blushing and shame recalls 2370–2.
2502 grame mortification.
2503 melle mingle (cf. 2371).
2506 A *bende* was a ceremonial sash, and also a heraldic device: a band running diagonally from heraldic top r. to bottom l. (cf. 2487) of a shield. The *blame* is the scar. **in]** MS. omits.
2507 lathe injury.
2508 covetise See 2374 *n*.
2510 were wear.
2511–2 Meaning uncertain. Perhaps: 'For no one can conceal his guilt without misfortune befalling (*hit*), for where it once becomes fixed it will never be separated.' This involves doubtful translation of 2511b (superfluous *ne* is difficult), but otherwise makes sense of MS: Gawain had concealed his guilt even from himself, and now suffers the misfortune of wearing a 'token of untruth' for the rest of his life. But Davis, emending *non* to *mon*, and taking *unhap* as verb and *hit* as pronoun, translates: 'For a man may hide his (spiritual) harm, but cannot unfasten (get rid of) it.'

The king comfortes the knight, and all the court als,
Laughen loude therat and luflily acorden
That lordes and ledes that longed to the Table,
Uch burn of the brotherhede, a bauderik sholde have,
A bende abelef him aboute of a bright grene,
And that for sake of that segge in sute to were.
For that was acorded the renown of the Rounde Table
And he honoured that hit had evermore after,
As hit is breved in the best boke of romaunce.
Thus in Arthures day this aunter betidde,
The Brutus bokes therof beres witnesse.
Sithen Brutus the bold burn bowed hider first,
After the sege and the asaute was sesed at Troye,
Ywis,
Mony aunteres here beforn
Haf fallen such ere this.
Now that bere the crown of thorn,
He bring us to his bliss. Amen.

2515 ledes] ladis MS. The scribe apparently wrote *ladis* (ladies) for *ledis* (knights) under the influence of a well-known phrase. It is irregular for ladies to belong to the Round Table, and the language of the following lines is entirely masculine (2516–20). *ledes* is coupled with *lorde* in a similar context at 38–9: *N & Q* 19 (1972) 44–5.
2518–9 'And wear that to match (Gawain's) for that man's sake. For this was agreed to be to the honour of the Round Table.'
2521 breved declared.
2522 aunter adventure.
2523 Brutus bokes chronicles of Britain. Brutus, mentioned in the first stanza (13), was the legendary founder of Britain. He was a great-grandson of Aeneas, and came to Britain from Rome, as Aeneas came from Troy to Rome.
2524 Sithen ever since.
2525 Repeating the poem's first line. See headnote, under Structure.
2527–8 'Many adventures such as this have occurred here in times past.'
2529 'Now may He who bore the crown of thorns.'
2530 The motto of the Order of the Garter, 'Hony soyt qui mal pence', is appended to the text in the MS. This suggests that the closing episode represents the founding of a new chivalric order. However, the Arthurian Order of the Green Lace, if such it be, cannot be identified with the Garter or any other known C14 order. See Savage, *Gawain-Poet* App. J.

William Langland

Piers Plowman survives in three versions (A, B, C). Whether one man produced all three has been much debated, and the case for multiple authorship is still stated by D. C. Fowler *PP: literary relations of the A and B Texts* (Univ. of Washington P. 1961); but opinion now generally favours a single author. See especially G. Kane *PP: the evidence for authorship* (Athlone Press 1965). Kane accepts 'William Langland' as the author's name, on the strength of wordplay at B 15.148 ('I haue lyued in *londe* . . . my name is *longe wille*') and a note (*c.* 1400) in Trinity Coll. Dublin MS. D.4.1. The biographical information in the latter may well be correct: 'Note that Stacy de Rokayle was father of William de Langlond, the which Stacy was a gentleman dwelling and holding land from Lord le Spenser at Shipton-under-Wychwood in the county of Oxfordshire, the which aforesaid William made the book which is called *Perys ploughman.*' See Kane 26 f. This evidence is not inconsistent with an association between Langland and the Malvern Hills (suggested by references in the *Visio*, Prol. 5 and 7.141, and by evidence on the circulation of C-Text MSS.), or with 'autobiographical' passages in the poem which represent 'Will' the dreamer as living with his family in humble circumstances in Cornhill, London (C 6.1–104, and cf. No. 11.2 here, line 425). The mobility of medieval populations has been generally underestimated. Kane's Chambers Memorial Lecture, 'The Autobiographical Fallacy in Chaucer and Langland Studies' (London, H. K. Lewis 1965), stresses the need for caution in interpreting 'autobiographical' passages; but the passage in C 6 is very circumstantial. See E. T. Donaldson *PP: the C-Text and its poet* (Yale U.P. 1949; 2nd edn London, Cass 1966) Ch. 7, summarizing Will's description of his occupation as follows: 'a married clerk, of an order certainly no higher than acolyte, who made his living in an irregular fashion by saying prayers for the dead or for the living who supported him' (219). So at the time of writing C Text (in circulation by 1388, see below) Langland was probably living the life of the 'clerical proletariat' in London. The date of his death is unknown.

11 Piers Plowman B Text: extracts

Piers Plowman is a long allegorical poem in alliterative verse concerned with the reformation of Society and the Church, and with individual salvation. For basic introductions, see R. W. Chambers *Man's Unconquerable Mind* (Cape 1939) 88–171, and N. Coghill *Langland: PP* (Writers and their Work, British Council: Longmans 1964). For fuller general studies, see E. Salter *PP: an introduction* (Oxford, Blackwell 1962; 2nd edn 1969), and J. Lawlor *PP: an essay in criticism* (E. Arnold 1962).

Like Nos. 7 and 9 above, *Piers* is a dream-poem; but it is unusual in describing several dreams – ten in B Text, to which the following summary refers. (The most helpful study of B Text is R. W. Frank *PP and the Scheme of Salvation* (Yale U.P. 1957).) The first two dreams constitute the *Visio* section (Prol. and Passus 1–7). The First contrasts Lady Holy Church, who instructs Will the dreamer, with Mede, who represents corruption; and culminates in the purging of corruption at the King's court. The Second Dream (from which No. 11.1 comes) represents an attempted conversion of the whole community to the life of truth, culminating in the Pardon sent to Piers promising salvation to those who 'do well'. This concludes the *Visio*. The rest of the poem (Passus 8–20) is divided by MS. headings into three sections: *Do-Well*, *Do-Bet*, *Do-Best*. The Third Dream (Passus 8–12, with inner dream in 11) attempts definitions of Do-Well (with Do-Bet and Do-Best), and tackles theological difficulties raised by the Pardon. The Fifth Dream (Passus 13–14) centres on the virtue of patience (cf. No. 8 above), which leads on to *Do-Bet*, whose chief subject is charity. The Sixth Dream (Passus 15–17, with inner dream in 16) includes the Tree of Charity, and leads up to Christ's redemption of man, represented as a joust against the Devil. This supreme act of charity is the subject of the Eighth Dream (Passus 18; No. 11.2 here). The two dreams of *Do-Best* (Passus 19–20) concern the Church, as founded by Christ, and as corrupted in modern times. On them, see especially M. W. Bloomfield *PP as a C14 Apocalypse* (Rutgers U.P. 1961).

Piers is the only English alliterative poem to be known and read continuously from the time of its composition to the present. It circulated widely in MS., especially among fellow clerks and pious layfolk: see Burrow *Ang.* 75 (1957) 373–84; and it attracted C15 imitators, such as the author of *Mum and the Sothsegger* (No. 21 below). It was first printed in 1550 by the Puritan Crowley as an anti-Catholic piece 'crying out against the works of darkness' (though Langland was in fact orthodox both in social and ecclesiastical ideals). C16 and C17 authors knew *Piers* chiefly as a 'satire' (see above p. xvi). In C18 Thomas Warton praised Langland's humour and sublimity, as well as his satiric verve (*History of English Poetry*). Modern criticism has tended to stress the religious and devotional side of the poem. Many of the best modern articles are collected by E. Vasta, ed. *Interpretations of PP* (Univ. of Notre Dame P. 1968), and R. J. Blanch, ed. *Style and Symbolism in PP* (Univ. of Tennessee Press 1969). See also collection of new essays in S. S. Hussey, ed. *PP: critical approaches* (Methuen 1969).

Allegory Langland's allegorical techniques are bold and varied. He employs much relatively straightforward 'personification allegory' (e.g. Hunger in No. 11.1, the Four Daughters in No. 11.2), following French religious allegorical poets such as Deguileville: see D. L. Owen *PP: a comparison with some earlier and contemporary French allegories* (London, Folerofe 1912). Vernacular preachers are also important here: see Owst *Literature and Pulpit* Ch. 9. In the case of more complex, multilayered allegories, some critics detect the influence of four-level scriptural allegorizing: D. W. Robertson and B. F. Huppé *PP and Scriptural Tradition* (Princeton U.P. 1951), and B. H. Smith *Traditional Imagery of Charity in PP* (The Hague, Mouton 1966). But Langland's layers coincide only intermittently with the scriptural 'levels'; and his profoundest allegories appear to depart from all medieval norms: see R Woolf 'Some non-medieval qualities of *PP*' *EC* 12 (1962) 111–25, and D. Aers *PP and Christian Allegory* (E. Arnold 1975). Piers Plowman himself, in particular, is neither a simple personification nor a four-level allegory. In the *Visio* he embodies the life of truth or Do-Well: see N. Coghill *Med.*

Aev. 2 (1933) 108–35 (in Vasta, above). In *Do-Bet* he is associated with charity and the human nature of Christ. In *Do-Best* he represents the apostolic ideal first realized by St Peter. In each case he represents the spiritual reality (as against external forms and intellectual formulations) sought at that stage by the dreamer.

Texts and editions The poem survives in more than 50 complete or nearly complete MSS. (listed in Donaldson *C-Text* 227–31). Only three ME poems have more MSS: *Prick of Conscience*, Chaucer's *Canterbury Tales*, Lydgate's *Dietary*. The MSS. exhibit the poem in three versions: the A Text, which breaks off unfinished in the middle of the Third Dream (= end of Passus 10 in B); the B Text, which incorporates the A Text revised, and continues to 20 passus; the C Text, which represents an unfinished revision of B up to, but not including, *Do-Best*. Edn of all three texts by W. W. Skeat, EETS o.s. 28, 38, 54, 67, 81 (1867–84), to which line references here refer. Parallel text edn also by Skeat, 2 vols (Oxford U. P. 1886). Two volumes of the London edn, superseding Skeat, have appeared: A Text ed. G. Kane (Athlone Press 1960), B Text ed. G. Kane and E. T. Donaldson (Athlone Press 1975). B-Text *Visio* ed. with excellent notes by J. A. W. Bennett (Oxford U.P. 1972). C-Text selections ed. E. Salter and D. Pearsall (E. Arnold 1967). The present text is based on Bodleian MS. Laud Misc. 581 (= *L*), one of 17 authorities for the B Text listed by Kane and Donaldson (whose sigils I use). Only a few textual variants are reported here. A full record is given by Kane and Donaldson, who show that all B MSS. descend from a source itself seriously corrupt. Their edn appeared too late for me to take full account of their emendations.

Dates The three versions can be dated only roughly on internal evidence. Skeat dated the A Text 1362–3; but J. A. W. Bennett *PMLA* 58 (1943) 566–72 gives grounds for a date around 1370. Skeat dated the B Text 1377; Bennett *Med. Aev.* 12 (1943) 55–64 suggests 1377–79. Skeat dated the C Text 1393; but Thomas Usk, executed in 1388, appears to echo this version (as well as Chaucer's *Troilus*) in his *Testament of Love*. If this is so, the C Text must have been in circulation before 1388.

11.1 Passus 6

'This were a wicked way, but whoso hadde a gide
That wolde folwen us eche a foot,' thus this folk hem mened.
Quath Perkin the Plowman, 'By saint Peter of Rome,
I have an half acre to erie by the hye way;
Hadde I eried this half acre and sowen it after,
I wolde wende with you and the way teche.'

1 but whoso hadde unless one had. Piers had just described the pilgrimage road to Truth's castle, leading through the Ten Commandments.
2 hem mened complained.
3 Perkin diminutive of Peter/Piers.
4 Half-acre strips of land frequently appear in the records. Perhaps 'the amount of land which was expected in custom to be plowed in . . . a long morning's work' (Homans 49). **erie** plough.
6 wolde] wil *L* etc.

'This were a long letting,' quod a lady in a sklaire,
'What sholde we wommen worche therewhiles?'
'Some shall sowe the sack,' quod Piers, 'for sheding of the whete;
And ye lovely ladies with your longe fingres,
That ye han silk and sendal to sowe, whan time is,
Chesibles for chapelaines, cherches to honoure.
Wives and widwes, wolle and flex spinneth,
Maketh cloth, I conseille you, and kenneth so your doughtres.
The needy and the naked, nimmeth hede how hi liggeth,
And casteth hem clothes, for so comaundeth Treuthe;
For I shall lene hem liflode but yif the lond faille,
Flesh and bred bothe to riche and to pore,
As longe as I live, for the lordes love of hevene.
And alle manere of men that thurgh mete and drink libbeth,
Helpeth him to worche wightliche that winneth your fode.'
  'By Crist,' quod a knight tho, 'he kenneth us the beste;
Ac on the teme trewely taught was I nevere.
Ac kenne me,' quod the knight, 'and by Christ I will assaye.'
'By saint Poule,' quod Perkin, 'ye profre you so faire
That I shall swinke and swete and sowe for us bothe
And other laboures do for thy love all my lif time,
In covenaunt that thou kepe holikirke and myselve
Fro wastoures and fro wicked men that this world struyeth,

7 letting delay. **sklaire** veil (worn by ladies of rank).
8 therewhiles in the meantime.
9 the sack] sakke *L.* **for sheding** to prevent spilling.
11 sendal a fine silk.
12 Chesibles chasubles. England was famous for richly embroidered vestments. Cf. No. 19 lines 1174–5.
14 kenneth teach.
15 nimmeth take. **how hi liggeth** how they lie i.e. of their conditions.
16 casteth hem contrive for them. **Treuthe** represents in the *Visio* primarily the just God.
17 lene hem liflode furnish them with food. **but yif** unless.
18 Kane and Donaldson reject this line (non-alliterating, and absent in A and C) as scribal.
19 lordes love of hevene regular ME word order.
21 'Vigorously help those who obtain your food to carry on their work.'
22 tho then.
23 the teme that subject (i.e. of assisting with manual work), with wordplay on *team* ('I was never taught to plough').
25 Poule Paul. **profre you** offer yourself.
28 In covenaunt that on condition that.
29 wastoures layabouts. The word has a less general, more colloquial sense here than in No. 7 above. **struyeth** destroy.

And go hunte hardiliche to hares and to foxes,
To bores and to brockes that breketh adown mine hegges,
And go affaite thee faucones, wilde fowles to kille,
For suche cometh to my croft and croppeth my whete.'
Curteislich the knight thenne comsed thise wordes:
'By my power, Piers, I plighte thee my treuthe
To fulfille this forward though I fighte sholde;
Als longe as I live I shall thee maintene.'
'Yea, and yit a point,' quod Piers, 'I praye you of more.
Loke ye tene no tenaunt but Treuthe will assente;
And though ye mowe amercy hem, late mercy be taxoure
And mekenesse thy maister, maugré Medes chekes.
And though pore men profre you presentes and yiftes,
Nim it naught, an aventure ye mowe it naught deserve;
For thou shalt yelde it ayain at one yeres ende
In a full perillous place, purgatorye it hatte.
And misbede nought thy bondemen, the better may thou spede;
Though he be thyn underling here, well may happe in hevene
That he worth worthier set and with more blisse:
Amice, ascende superius.
For in charnel atte chirche cherles ben ivel to knowe,
Or a knight fram a knave there, knowe this in thyn herte.

30 hardiliche boldly.
31 bores boars. **brockes** badgers.
32 affaite thee tame for yourself.
33 croft enclosed field.
34 comsed began.
35 Piers] Pieres quod he B MSS. *quod he* is absent in A and C MSS. and probably scribal.
36 forward agreement.
38 yit a point one further point.
39 tene injure.
40 'And if you do have reason to fine them, let Mercy be the assessor.'
41 maugré Medes chekes in spite of Mede. Here, as in the first dream of the *Visio*, Mede represents the desire for inordinate unfair gain.
43–4 'Take it not, for fear you may not deserve it, for you will have to pay it back sooner or later.'
45 hatte is called.
46 misbede maltreat. **spede** prosper.
48 worth worthier set will be seated in a more honourable place. Cf. parable of the wedding guests, *Luke* 14.8–11, from which the Lat. quotation comes: 'Friend, go up higher.'
49 charnel 'the charnel-house being the place (usually beneath the church) where bones disturbed when dug up to make room for new burials were deposited indiscriminately' (Bennett). **ivel to knowe** hard to recognize.

And that thou be trewe of thy tong and tales that thou hatie,
But if they ben of wisdom or of wit thy werkmen to chaste.
Holde with none harlotes ne here nought her tales,
And namelich atte mete suche men eschue,
For it ben the develes disoures, I do thee to understande.'
'I assente, by saint Jame,' saide the knight thenne,
'Forto worche by thy wordes the while my lif dureth.'
 'And I shall apparaille me,' quod Perkin, 'in pilgrimes wise,
And wende with you I will till we finde Treuthe,
And caste on my clothes, yclouted and hole,
My cockeres and my coffes for colde of my nailles,
And hange myn hoper at myn hals in stede of a scrippe.
A bushel of bredcorn bringe me therinne,
For I will sowe it myself and sithenes will I wende
To pilgrimage as palmers don, pardoun forto have.
Ac whoso helpeth me to erie or sowen here ar I wende
Shall have leve, by oure lorde, to lese here in hervest
And make hem merry theremid, maugré whoso begruccheth it.
And alkin crafty men that konne liven in treuthe,

51 tales that thou hatie that you hate idle chatter.
52 wit good sense. **chaste** chastise.
53 harlotes rogues.
54 nameliche atte mete especially at mealtimes.
55 'For they are minstrels of the devil, I tell you.'
56 Jame St James of Compostella (Spain) was a favourite object of English pilgrimage. The Knight has just set out on his own pilgrimage.
58–65 This passage contains the first hint that the Pilgrimage to Truth, proclaimed as a penance for the people (Passus 5 line 58), may get no further than the half-acre. By the beginning of Passus 7, when Truth's pardon (the goal of a pilgrimage, cf. 65 here) is achieved, it becomes evident that the life of the half-acre, properly lived, *is* the pilgrimage: see Burrow *EC* 15 (1965) 247–68.
60 on] on me *LR*. **yclouted** patched. **hole** obscure: 'whole, entire', i.e. 'neatly mended' (Skeat), or 'full of holes' (Bennett). But the variant *ihole* in *R* (also in one A MS.) must represent the strong past participle of the vb *hele* 'cover'; so *yclouted and hole* may mean, by hendiadys, 'covered with patches'.
61 cockeres leggings. **coffes** gloves.
62 hoper seed-basket. **hals** neck. **scrippe** pilgrim's bag (for food).
63 'A bushel was the regular allowance of seed for half an acre' (Bennett).
64 sithenes afterwards.
65 palmers pilgrims. Properly, those returned from the Holy Land; whence 'full-time pilgrims'. **pardoun** The object of pilgrimage was partly to receive at the shrine of the saint the pardon attached to it.
66 Ac but. **ar** ere, before.
67 lese glean. See 115 *n.*
68 theremid therewith, with the gleanings. **begruccheth** begrudges.
69 alkin crafty men all kinds of skilled men. **in treuthe** honestly.

I shall finden hem fode that faithfulliche libbeth;
Save Jack the jogeloure and Jonet of the stues
And Daniel the dis-playere and Denote the bawde
And frere the faitoure and folk of his ordre
And Robin the ribaudoure for his rusty wordes.
Treuthe tolde me ones and bad me tellen it after,
Deleantur de libro viventium, I sholde nought dele with hem,
For holicherche is hote of hem no tithe to take,
Quia cum iustis non scribantur.
They ben ascaped good aventure; now God hem amende!'
Dame 'Worche whan time is' Piers wif highte;
His doughter highte 'Do right so or thy dame shall thee bete';
His sone highte 'Suffre thy sovereines to haven her wille,
Deme hem nought, for if thou dost thou shalt it dere abugge;
Late God yworth with all, for so his word techeth.
For now I am old and hore and have of myn owen,
To penaunce and to pilgrimage I will passe with thise other;
Forthy I will, or I wende, do write my bequeste.
In Dei nomine, *amen*, I make it myselven.

70 finden provide.
71 jogeloure buffoon. **stues** brothel.
72 dis dice. **Denote** Dennet, a pet form of Denise.
73 faitoure deceiver. Langland is consistently hostile to the Friars.
74 ribaudoure teller of dirty stories. **rusty** foul.
76–7 *Ps.* 68.29 (A.V. 69.28): 'Let them be blotted out of the book of the living: and with the just let them not be written.'
77 hote commanded. ***Quia*** because (replacing *et* of Vulgate).
78 'They have been lucky to escape so long', i.e. to have been spared God's punishment. Cf. 145.
79 'Piers's wife was called Mrs "Work-while-there-is-time".'
80 thy dame your mother. The names take the form of instructions given by Piers to wife, daughter and son. This is why the son's name, the last, can shade off into a speech by Piers.
82 Deme judge. **abugge** pay for.
83 This line carries us straight on from the son's name to Piers's speech (80 *n.*). Scribes did not have to decide where to put inverted commas, which they did not use; and the passage reads quite smoothly in MSS. **Late God yworth with all** let God do his will in all things: cf. 227 below, and No. 10 line 2208. **his word** presumably 'Thy will be done'.
84 have of myn owen have property of my own.
85 penaunce . . . pilgrimage Hendiadys: the pilgrimage is the penance, as commonly imposed by confessors.
86 Forthy and so. **or** ere, before. **do write** cause to be written (a ploughman would be illiterate). **bequeste** will. 'To make a will was a normal preliminary to a pilgrimage' (Bennett). Piers's will observes the forms of C14 testaments, opening 'In God's name', first bequeathing the soul to God, etc.

He shall have my soule that best hath yserved it,
And fro the fende it defende, for so I beleve,
Till I come to his acountes as my *Credo* me telleth;
To have a relees and a remissioun on that rental I leve.
The kirk shall have my caroigne and kepe my bones,
For of my corn and catel he craved the tithe;
I payed it him prestly for peril of my soule,
Forthy is he holden, I hope, to have me in his masse
And mengen in his memorye among alle cristene.
My wif shall have of that I wan with treuthe and nomore,
And dele among my doughtres and my dere children;
For though I deye today my dettes are quit,
I bare home that I borwed ar I to bedde yede.
And with the residue and the remenaunt, by the rood of Lukes,
I will worship therewith Treuthe by my live,
And ben his pilgrim atte plow for pore mennes sake.
My plow-pote shall be my pikstaff and picche atwo the rotes
And helpe my culter to cerve and clense the forwes.'
  Now is Perkin and his pilgrimes to the plow faren;
To erie this halve acre holpen him manye.
Dikeres and delveres digged up the balkes;

88 yserved deserved.
90 Referring to the Last Judgment, mentioned in the Creed.
91 relees . . . remissioun a legalistic word-pair. Piers hopes to be released from his 'debts' at the great Day of Accounts. **rental** rent-roll. **leve** trust.
92 caroigne body.
93 catel property. **he** the Church, in the person of the parson.
94 prestly promptly.
95–6 Referring to the Commemoration for the Dead at Mass, where individual names were often remembered.
95 holden bound.
96 mengen remember.
97 wan got.
98 dele divide. After all debts paid, remaining personal property was divided in three: one part each for widow and children, and one 'dead's part' (101) as the testator chose. See Bennett.
100 bare home took back (to its home). **yede** went. Cf. *Deut*. 24.12–13.
101 Lukes Lucca, where there was a famous icon of Christ.
103–5 See 58–65 *n.*
104 plow-pote] *RF* and A MSS.; plowfote *L* etc. A *plowpote* was a long-handled spade used by ploughmen to clear away obstacles, clinging earth etc. **pikstaff** pilgrim's staff. **picche atwo** cut in two.
105 culter front cutting-blade of plough.
108 Dikeres ditchers. **balkes** unploughed places. Perhaps any scraps of land missed by the plough were dug by hand.

Therewith was Perkin apayed and praised hem faste.
Other werkmen there were that wroughten full yerne,
Eche man in his manere made himself to done,
And some to plese Perkin piked up the wedes.
At hye prime Piers lete the plow stonde
To overseen hem himself, and whoso best wroughte
He shulde be huired therafter whan hervest time come.
And then seten some and songen atte nale
And hulpen erie his half acre with 'how, trolly lolly'.
'Now by the peril of my soule,' quod Piers all in pure tene,
'But ye arise the rather and rape you to worche,
Shall no graine that groweth glade you at nede,
And though ye deye for dole, the devel have that reccheth!'
Tho were faitoures aferde and feined hem blinde;
Some laide her legges aliry as suche loseles conneth
And made her mone to Piers and prayde him of grace:
'For we have no limes to laboure with, lorde, ygraced be ye!
Ac we praye for you, Piers, and for your plow both,
That God of his grace your grain multiplye
And yelde you of your almesse that ye yive us here,
For we may nought swinke ne swete, such sikenesse us aileth.'

109 apayed gratified.
110 yerne eagerly.
112 piked hoed.
113 hye prime about 9 a.m., at the end of the first part of the day (*prime*). People began work at sunrise.
115 'He would be paid accordingly (in kind) when harvest time should come' (Bennett). Or does Piers intend to employ the best men again for the harvest? Either way, there seems to be a passing hint, here as at 67, of God's harvest of souls at the Judgment: 'the harvest is the end of the world' (*Matt*. 13.39).
116 atte nale over their beer.
117 how, trolly lolly a snatch of a popular song.
118 tene anger.
119 But unless. **rape you** hurry.
121 'And the Devil take anyone who bothers about you, even though you are dying in misery.'
122 faitoures malingerers.
123 laide her legges aliry 'they put their legs into such a posture as to make them appear to be maimed (or paralysed)', Dobson *EGS* 1 (1947–8) 61. The leg may have been strapped back on itself to simulate amputation: Colledge *Med. Aev.* 27 (1958) 111–13. *aliry* is a cant word of disputed etymology. **loseles** good-for-nothings.
125 ygraced be ye our thanks to you. The *lorde* is presumably Piers, addressed with wheedling flattery.
128 yelde reward. **almesse** alms.

'If it be soth,' quod Piers, 'that ye seyn, I shall it sone aspie.
Ye ben wastoures, I wot well, and Treuthe wot the sothe;
And I am his olde hine and highte him to warne
Which they were in this worlde his werkmen appeired.
Ye wasten that men winnen with travaille and with tene;
Ac Treuthe shall teche you his teme to drive,
Or ye shall ete barly bred and of the brook drinke.
But if he be blinde or broke-legged or bolted with irnes,
He shall ete whete bred and drinke with myselve
Till God of his goodnesse amendement him sende.
Ac ye might travaille as Treuthe wolde and take mete and huire
To kepe kine in the felde, the corn fro the bestes,
Diken or delven or dingen upon sheves,
Or helpe make morter, or bere mucke afelde.
In lecherye and in losengerye ye liven, and in sleuthe,
And all is thurgh suffrance that venjaunce you ne taketh.
Ac ancres and heremites that eten but at nones
And namore ere morwe, mine almesse shull they have,
And of my catel to cope hem with that han cloistres and cherches.
Ac Robert Renne-aboute shall nought have of mine,
Ne posteles, but they preche conne and have powere of the bishop;
They shall have pain and potage and make hemself at ese,

130 aspie find out.
132 olde Kane and Donaldson conjecture that the original had *holde* 'faithful', as in Kane's A Text. **hine** servant. **highte him to warne** promised to inform him. Piers, being a 'lord's ploughman' (Homans 241), has a special relationship with the lord of the manor, Truth.
134 Cf. *Winner and Waster*, No. 7 above. **tene** trouble.
135 teme the plough-team of oxen.
136 barly bred inferior to the wheat bread of 138. Cf. Chaucer *C.T.* III 143–4.
137 blinde or] blynde and *L.* **bolted** 'supported by iron bands' as a cripple (Bennett). Or 'shackled'?
140 huire pay
142 Diken ditch. **dingen upon** strike (with threshing-flails, cf. 186).
144 losengerye lying flattery (e.g. 125 f. above).
145 Cf. 78 and *n.* 'It is entirely through (God's) forbearance that vengeance does not fall on you.'
146 ancres anchorites. **but at nones** only at noon (making every day a fast day).
148 'And those who have cloisters and churches shall get part of my goods to provide them with cloaks' – referring primarily to monks.
149 Robert Renne-aboute a wandering hermit or priest.
150 posteles itinerant preachers. **powere** i.e. licence.
151 The competent, licensed preachers will be given bread and soup.

For it is an unresonable religioun that hath right nought of certeine.'
And then gan a wastoure to wrathe him and wolde have yfought,
And to Piers the Plowman he profered his glove.
A Britonere, a braggere, abosted Piers als
And bad him go pissen with his plow, forpined shrewe.
'Wiltow or niltow, we will have oure wille
Of thy flour and of thy flesh, fecche whan us liketh,
And make us mirry thermid, maugré thy chekes.'
Then Piers the Plowman plained him to the knighte
To kepe him, as covenaunt was, fram cursed shrewes
And fro thise wastoures wolveskinnes that maketh the world dere,
'For tho waste and winnen nought, and that ilke while
Worth never plenté among the poeple the while my plow liggeth.'
Curteisly the knight then, as his kinde wolde,
Warned Wastoure and wissed him bettere,
'Or thou shalt abugge by the lawe, by the ordre that I bere.'
'I was nought wont to worche,' quod Wastoure, 'and now will I nought beginne!'
And lete light of the lawe and lasse of the knight
And sette Piers at a pees and his plow bothe
And manaced Piers and his men yif they mette eftsone.
'Now, by the peril of my soule,' quod Piers, 'I shall apeire you alle,'
And houped after Hunger, that herde him atte firste:

152 Men of religion should not be expected to live without some fixed and regular provision.
153 wrathe him grow angry.
155 Britonere boaster. Bretons were notorious boasters. **abosted** threatened boastfully.
156 forpined wretched.
157 'Whether you wish it or not . . .'
159 thermid with it. **maugré thy chekes** despite you.
162 wolveskinnes of wolfish kind. **dere** expensive. Cf. No. 7 above, line 387.
163 ilke same.
164 Worth never there will never be. **the while]** ther while *L* etc. **liggeth** lies idle.
165 kinde nature.
166 wissed advised.
167 abugge pay for it. **ordre** i.e. of knighthood.
169 lete made.
170 pees pea (singular), a measure of contempt.
171 eftsone again.
172 apeire injure.
173 houped after shouted for.

'Awreke me of thise wastoures,' quod he, 'that this world shendeth.'
Hunger in haste tho hente Wastoure by the mawe
And wrong him so by the wombe that all watered his eyen.
He buffeted the Britoner aboute the chekes
That he loked like a lanterne all his lif after.
He bette hem so bothe he barste nere her guttes.
Ne hadde Piers with a pese-lof prayed Hunger to cesse
They hadde ben dolven bothe, ne deme thou non other:
'Suffre hem live,' he saide, 'and lete hem ete with hogges,
Or elles benes and bren ybaken togideres,
Or elles melk and mene ale,' thus prayed Piers for hem.
Faitoures for fere herof flowen into bernes
And flapten on with flailes fram morwe till even,
That Hunger was nought so hardy on hem forto loke.
For a potful of peses that Piers hadde ymaked
An heep of heremites henten hem spades
And ketten her copes and courtpies hem made
And wenten as werkmen with spades and with shoveles
And dolven and dikeden to drive away Hunger.
Blinde and bedreden were botened a thousand;
That seten to begge silver, sone were they heled.

174 Awreke avenge. **shendeth** ruin.
175 mawe belly.
176 wrong wrung. **all watered his eyen]** *R* and A and C MSS.; bothe his eyen wattered *L* etc.
178 'One could see through him' (Skeat). The translucent cheeks of an emaciated man are compared to the sides of a horn lantern.
179 barste burst.
180 Ne hadde had not. **pese-lof** bread made of peas, eaten by the poor.
181 dolven dug under, buried.
183 Bread made of beans and bran was eaten by poor men, dogs and horses; cf. 195, 216, 284, 304.
184 mene poor. Some MSS. read *meyne*, *meynye* 'household' (servant's ale?). Kane and Donaldson regard the whole line as spurious.
185 flowen flew. **bernes** barns.
186 Threshing. The time-scheme of the 'long morning's work' here disintegrates, giving place to the time-scheme of the husbandman's year from Michaelmas to Michaelmas. Threshing in the barn follows the sowing of the winter corn: Homans 356.
187 hardy bold.
189 henten hem took for themselves.
190 'And cut down their cloaks to make short coats.' Long, trailing clothes distinguished clergy and aristocracy.
193 bedreden bedridden. **botened** cured. An ironic sort of miracle.
194 That seten those who sat.

For that was bake for Bayarde was boot for many hungry,
And many a beggere for benes buxom was to swinke,
And eche a pore man well apayed to have pesen for his huire,
And what Piers prayed hem to do as prest as a sperhawk.
And therof was Piers proude, and putte hem to werke,
And yaf hem mete as he mighte aforthe and mesurable huire.
  Then hadde Piers pité and prayed Hunger to wende
Home into his owne erde and holden him there,
'For I am well awroke now of wastoures thurgh thy might.
Ac I praye thee, ar thou passe,' quod Piers to Hunger,
'Of beggeres and of bidderes what best be to done?
For I wot well, be thou went, they will worche full ille;
For mischief it maketh they beth so meke nowthe,
And for defaute of her fode this folk is at my wille.
They are my blody bretheren,' quod Piers, 'for God boughte us alle;
Treuthe taughte me ones to lovie hem uchone,
And to helpen hem of alle thing ay as hem nedeth.
And now wolde I witen of thee what were the best,
And how I mighte amaistrien hem and make hem to worche.'
'Here now,' quod Hunger, 'and holde it for a wisdom:
Bolde beggeres and bigge that mowe her bred beswinke,
With houndes bred and hors bred holde up her hertes,
Abave hem with benes for bolling of her wombe;
And yif the gomes grucche, bidde hem go swinke,

195 'For what was baked for Bayard [a horse-name: the reference is to bean-bread, 183 *n.*] served as relief to many hungry folk.'
196 buxom obediently ready.
198 prest prompt. **sperhawk** sparrowhawk.
200 aforthe afford. **mesurable huire** fair reward: a phrase used in the first dream of the *Visio* (3.254) in contrast to 'meed' or 'measureless' reward.
202 erde land.
203 awroke avenged Cf. 174.
205 to] *L* omits.
206 be thou went once you are gone.
207 'For it is hardship which causes them to be so obedient at present.'
208 defaute lack.
209 blody by blood. Cf. No. 11.2 below, line 375.
213 amaistrien master, control.
215 bigge robust. **beswinke** earn by work.
216 See 183 *n.*
217 Abave] Abate B MSS. The B reading ('appease'?) is probably a scribal error for *abave* 'confound' in A and C (Kane and Donaldson). **for bolling of her wombe** for fear of their belly swelling. Ironical.
218 gomes grucche men grumble.

And he shall soupe swettere whan he it hath deserved.
Ac if thou finde any freke that fortune hath appeired
Or any maner fals men, fonde thou such to knowe,
Comforte hem with thy catel for Cristes love of hevene,
Love hem and lene hem, so lawe of God techeth:
Alter alterius onera portate.
And alle maner of men that thou mighte aspye
That needy ben and naughty, helpe hem with thy godes,
Love hem and lacke hem nought – late God take the venjaunce.
Theigh they don ivel, late thou God yworthe:
Mihi vindictam et ego retribuam.
And if thou wilt be gracious to God, do as the gospel techeth
And belove thee amonges lowe men, so shaltow lacche grace:
Facite vobis amicos de mammona iniquitatis.'
'I wolde nought greve God,' quod Piers, 'for all the good on grounde.
Might I sinnelees do as thou saist?' saide Piers thenne.
'Yea, I behote thee,' quod Hunger, 'or elles the Bible lieth.
Go to Genesis the giaunt, the engendrour of us alle:
In sudore and swinke thou shalt thy mete tilie,
And laboure for thy liflode, and so our lorde highte.

219 swettere the more sweetly.
220–1 'But if you find any man whom Fortune or any kind of trickster has ruined, endeavour to become acquainted with him.'
220 Ac but (so *R* and A MSS; And *L* etc.).
222 hem] him *L* etc.
223 lene hem give to them. ***Alter . . . portate*** 'Bear ye one another's burdens' (*Gal.* 6.2).
225 naughty penniless. On Langland's attitude to beggars, see Coghill *RES* 8 (1932) 303–9 and Donaldson *Piers* 130–6.
226 lacke criticize.
227 late thou God yworthe See 83 *n.* ***Mihi . . . retribuam*** 'Revenge is mine, I will repay' (*Rom.* 12.19). *vindictam* is an error for *vindicta.*
228 gracious pleasing.
229 belove thee make yourself loved (*L* etc. have *bilowe* 'humble').
lacche get. ***Facite . . . iniquitatis*** 'Make unto you friends of the mammon of iniquity' i.e. make friends with your riches (*Luke* 16.9).
231 'Piers is evidently still in doubt about Hunger's primary advice that able-bodied vagrants are to be given only the barest necessities' (Bennett).
232 behote promise.
233–53 Langland may have found a gathering of scriptural passages on work in some exegetical treatise or *catena.*
233 Genesis a *giaunt* because it is the second longest book in the Bible, and refers to giants (6.4), *engendrour* because it describes Creation.
234 *In sudore* in sweat, *Gen.* 3.19. **mete tilie** earn food by labour.
235 highte commanded.

And Sapience saith the same, I seigh it in the Bible:
Piger pro frigore no feld nolde tilie,
And therfore he shall begge and bidde and no man bete his hunger.
Mathew with mannes face mouthed thise wordes,
That *servus nequam* had a mnam, and for he wolde nought chaffare
He had maugré of his maistre for evermore after,
And benam him his mnam for he ne wolde worche,
And yaf that mnam to him that ten mnammes hadde;
And with that he saide, that holicherche it herde:
"He that hath shall have, and helpe there it nedeth,
And he that nought hath shall nought have, and no man him helpe,
And that he weneth well to have I will it him bereve."
Kind wit wolde that eche a wight wroughte
Or in diking or in delving, or travailling in prayeres,
Contemplatif lif or actif lif, Crist wolde men wroughte.
The Sauter saith in the psalme of *Beati omnes*,
The freke that fedeth himself with his faithful laboure,
He is blessed by the book in body and in soule:
Labores manuum tuarum etc.'

236 Sapience the Book of Wisdom. The ref. is to *Prov*. 20.4: 'Because of the cold (*pro frigore*), the sluggard (*piger*) would not plough: he shall beg therefore in the summer, and it shall not be given him.'
238 bete relieve.
239 Each Evangelist had a symbol: Matthew a man, Mark a lion, Luke a bull, John an eagle. The Parable of the Talents is in *Matt*. 25; but *mnam* points also to Luke's version (19.12 f.).
240 ***servus nequam*** a wicked servant. **mnam** the Vulgate term for the 'talent' of A.V. (*Luke* 19.24). **chaffare** engage in trade.
241 maugré ill will.
242 benam deprived. **him]** *L* omits.
244 he Christ (*Matt*. 25.29).
245 helpe give help: 'and he shall abound' (*Matt*. 25.29).
248 Kind wit natural understanding. Cf. No. 11.2 below, line 220 *n*. **eche a wight** every single person.
250 On medieval conceptions of 'active' and 'contemplative' lives, here simply represented by digging and praying, see T. P. Dunning 'Action and contemplation in *PP*' in Hussey *Critical Approaches* 213–25.
251 Sauter psalter. The reference is to *Ps*. 127 (A.V. 128), beginning 'Blessed are all they that fear the Lord'.
252 freke man.
253 ***Labores*** . . . '[For thou shalt eat] the labours of thy hands: [blessed art thou]' (*Ps*. 127.2).

'Yet I praye you,' quod Piers, '*par charité*, and ye kunne
Eny leef of lechecraft, lere it me, my dere.
For some of my servauntes and myself bothe
Of all a wike worche nought, so oure wombe aketh.'
'I wot well,' quod Hunger, 'what sikenesse you aileth;
Ye han maunged overmoche, and that maketh you grone.
Ac I hote thee,' quod Hunger, 'as thou thine hele wilnest,
That thou drinke no day ar thou dine somwhat.
Ete nought, I hote thee, ar hunger thee take
And sende thee of his sauce to savoure with thy lippes,
And kepe some till soper-time, and sitte nought too longe:
Arise up ar appetit have eten his fulle.
Lat nought Sir Surfait sitten at thy borde;
Leve him nought, for he is lecherous and likerous of tonge,
And after many manere metes his maw is afingred.
And yif thou diete thee thus, I dar legge mine eres
That phisik shall his furred hodes for his fode selle
And his cloke of calabre with alle the knappes of gold,
And be fain, by my faith, his phisik to lete
And lerne to laboure with londe, for liflode is swete;
For morthereres aren mony leches, lorde hem amende!
They do men deye thurgh her drinkes ar destiné it wolde.'
'By saint Poule,' quod Piers, 'thise aren profitable wordes.
Wende now, Hunger, whan thou wilt, that well be thou evere,
For this is a lovely lessoun; lorde it thee foryelde!'

254 Yet i.e. 'one more thing'. **and ye kunne** if you know.
255 leef i.e. page from the 'book' of medicine (*lechecraft*). **lere** teach. **dere** with a pun on *dere* 'famine'.
257 Of all a wike for a whole week.
259 maunged eaten. Not a usual ME loan word; used here in contempt of Frenchified luxury (cf. 312).
260 hote command. **thine hele wilnest** wish for your health. What follows is in the manner of medieval dietary treatises, which handed down lore originating in ancient Greece. Their favourite theme was moderation. Cf. No. 18 below, line 262.
263 savoure with add relish to.
267 Leve trust. **likerous** gluttonous.
268 afingred hungry.
269 legge wager.
270–1 Doctors were often paid with articles of clothing.
271 calabre grey squirrel fur (from Calabria).
272 lete leave.
273 liflode means of life.
275 do men deye cause men to die.
277 that well be thou evere and may you always prosper.
278 foryelde repay.

'Behote God,' quod Hunger, 'hennes ne will I wende
Till I have dined by this day and ydronke bothe.'
'I have no peny,' quod Piers, 'poletes forto bigge,
Ne neither gees ne gris, but two grene cheses,
A fewe cruddes and creem, and an haver cake,
And two loves of benes and bran, ybake for my fauntes;
And yet I say, by my soule, I have no salt bacoun,
Ne no kokenay, by Crist, coloppes forto maken.
Ac I have percil and poret and many kole plantes,
And eke a cow and a calf, and a cart-mare
To draw afelde my dong the while the drought lasteth;
And by this liflode we mote live till Lammasse time,
And by that I hope to have hervest in my croft,
And thenne may I dighte thy diner as me dere liketh.'
Alle the pore peple tho pesecoddes fetten,
Benes and baken apples they broughte in her lappes,
Chibolles and chervelles and ripe chirries manye,
And profred Piers this present to plese with Hunger.
All Hunger eet in hast and axed after more.
Thenne pore folk for fere fedde Hunger yerne
With grene poret and pesen, to peisen him they thoughte.
By that it neighed nere hervest, newe corn cam to cheping.
Thenne was folk fain and fedde Hunger with the best,
With good ale, as Glotoun taughte, and gerte Hunger go slepe.
 And tho wolde Wastoure nought werche but wandren aboute,

279 Behote God I swear to God. **hennes** hence.
281 poletes chickens. **bigge** buy.
282 gris pigs. **grene** unripe ('he cannot afford to keep them until they mature' Bennett).
283 cruddes curds. **haver cake** oatcake.
284 See 183 *n.* **fauntes** children.
286 kokenay small egg. **coloppes** bacon-and-eggs.
287 percil parsley. **poret**] *B R*; porettes *L* etc. A *poret* was a small leek. **kole plantes** cabbages, 'greens'.
289 Dung was spread before the 'drought of March' broke: cf. No. 7 line 276*n.*
290 The beginning of harvest was celebrated at Lammas, 1 Aug.
292 dighte prepare. **as me dere liketh** as well as I would like.
293 pesecoddes fetten fetched peas in the pod.
294 lappes folds of their clothes.
295 Chibolles and chervelles spring onions and chervils (a kind of herb).
299 peisen appease. All B MSS. read *poison*; Skeat's C Text reads *plese*. Both variants occur in A MSS., where Kane plausibly conjectures an original *peysen*, adopted here. **him**] Hunger *L* etc.
300 See 186 *n.* **cheping** market.
302 Glotoun a personification of one of the Seven Deadly Sins, who confess after Reason's sermon in Passus 5. **gerte** caused.

Ne no begger ete bred that benes inne were,
But of coket or clerematin or elles of clene whete,
Ne none halpeny ale in none wise drinke,
But of the best and of the brownest that in borghe is to selle.
Laboreres that have no land to live on but her handes
Deined nought to dine aday night-olde wortes.
May no peny ale hem paye ne no pece of bacoun,
But if it be fresh flesh other fish fried other bake,
And that *chaud* or *plus chaud* for chilling of her mawe.
And but if he be hyelich huired, elles will he chide
And that he was werkman wrought waille the time.
Ayeines Catones conseille comseth he to jangle:
Paupertatis onus patienter ferre memento.
He greveth him ayeines God and gruccheth ayeines resoun,
And thenne curseth he the king and all his conseille after,
Suche lawes to loke laboreres to greve.
Ac whiles Hunger was her maister, there wolde none of hem chide
Ne strive ayaines his statut, so sternliche he loked.
Ac I warne you, werkmen, winneth while ye mowe,
For Hunger hiderward hasteth him faste.
He shall awake with water wastoures to chaste;

305 coket or clerematin kinds of fine white bread. **or elles of clene whete** 'or other kinds of pure wheat' (Bennett).

306 halpeny halfpenny a gallon, cheap.

307 borghe city.

309 'Would not condescend to eat one day vegetables picked the day before.'

310 peny See 306 *n.* **paye** satisfy.

312 *chaud* or *plus chaud* warm or warmer. Phrases from Fr. cookery parlance: see 259 *n.* **for chilling of her mawe** for fear of chilling their stomach.

313 hyelich huired employed for a good wage. The shortage of labour after the Black Death (1349) led to a general rise in wage levels.

314 'And bewail the time he was ever made a workman.'

315 comseth begins. **jangle** quarrel, argue. The quotation is from the 'Distichs of Cato', a collection of maxims (C4?) used in elementary study of Latin: 'Be sure to bear the burden of poverty with patience' (Boas I.21).

316 gruccheth grumbles.

318 loke ordain.

320 'The emphatic *his* points the contrast with the ineffective Statutes of Labourers' (Bennett). The Statutes of Labourers attempted to control workers' demands after the Black Death.

321 winneth make gains, accumulate.

323 awake Cf. the sleep of Hunger, 302. The idea is of floods leading to famine. **chaste** chastise.

Ar five yere be fulfilled such famin shall arise,
Thurgh flodes and foule wederes frutes shull faille,
And so saith Saturne and sent you to warne.
Whan ye see the sunne amiss and two monkes hedes
And a maide have the maistrye, and multiplie by eight,
Thenne shall deth withdrawe and derthe be justice
And Dawe the diker deye for hunger,
But if God of his goodnesse graunte us a trewe.

324 yere] *L* etc. omit, as do some A MSS., perhaps rightly. *Ar five be fulfilled* would be good, mysterious prophetic style: cf. 328.
325 and] and thourgh *L* etc.
326 saith] A and C MSS. B MSS. have *saide*, probably through misunderstanding of *sent* (present tense form, 'sendeth'). **Saturne** the most maleficent of the planets: cf. Chaucer *C.T.* I 2456–69. Floods and famine were among the disasters ascribed to him.
327–31 This passage of darker prophecy, added in B Text, follows the conventions of late medieval prophecy: see Bloomfield *Piers* 91–4, 112, 212.
327 Totally obscure, though eclipses and strange sightings in the sky are common in such prophecies. Kane and Donaldson conjecture *mone* for *sunne*.
328 maide Bloomfield *Piers* 212 refers to the 'general Sibylline idea of the reign of the woman (or virgin) in the last days', Bennett (less convincingly) to the maiden Mede in the first dream (cf. 4.25).
multiplie] multiplied *L* etc. No editor has known what sum to do. H. Bradley suggested that *multiplie* was used in the alchemical sense of multiplying gold: *MLR* 5 (1910) 341.
329 derthe scarcity.
330 Dawe pet form of David.
331 trewe truce, respite.

11.2 Passus 18

Wolleward and wete-shoed went I forth after
As a reccheless renk that of no wo reccheth,
And yede forth like a lorel all my lif time,
Till I wex wery of the world and wilnede eft to slepe
And lened me to a lenten and long time I slepte,

1 Will has just awoken from a dream of Anima and the Good Samaritan. **Wolleward** with wool next to the skin: a form of penance.
2 reccheless renk reckless man.
3 yede went. **lorel** good-for-nothing. In the introduction to the previous dream, Will was described as 'a lorel and loth to reverencen | Lordes or ladies' (15.5–6).
5 lened me to a lenten 'leaned about (idled about) till a Lent-time' (Skeat)? A peculiar phrase, recalling B 8.65: 'And under a linde upon a launde lened I a stounde'. *lenten* takes the place of *linde* 'linden-tree'. C MSS. omit *a*.

Reste me there and rutte faste till *ramis palmarum*.
Of gerles and of *gloria laus* gretly me dremed
And how *osanna* by orgonye olde folk songen,
And of Cristes passioun and penaunce the peple that ofraughte.
One semblable to the Samaritan and somdel to Piers the Plowman
Barfoot on an asse backe bootless cam prickie
Without spores other spere, spackliche he loked,
As is the kind of a knight that cometh to be dubbed,
To geten him gilte spores and galoches ycouped.
Then was Faith in a fenestre and cried 'A, *fili David*!'

6 Reste me rested myself. **rutte faste** snored heavily. ***ramis palmarum*** Palm Sunday, known as *dominica in ramis palmarum* ('the Sunday with the palm branches') in allusion to *John* 12.13. It marks the beginning of Holy Week, the last week of Lent. Will's modern liturgical time synchronizes with that of the events in his dream. Later he wakes from dreaming of the Resurrection on Easter morning (424 f. below)
7–8 The non-biblical distinction between young and old folk appears in pictorial treatments of the Entry into Jerusalem: Schiller 2.20–22.
7 gerles children. Cf. *Ludus Coventriae* p. 241: 'Here Crist passeth forth. There meteth with him a sertain of childerin . . . and they singen Gloria laus'; also *Cursor Mundi* (Cotton) 15033–44. On Palm Sunday boys sang in the processional hymn *Gloria, laus et honor* ('Glory, laud and honour').
8 'And how old folk sang "Hosanna" to the sound of the organ.' Cf. *Matt.* 21.9: 'And the multitudes that went before and that followed cried, saying: Hosanna to the Son of David.' The reference to the organ shows that Langland is also thinking of antiphons to the processional hymn on Palm Sunday.
9 This line follows line 5 in all B MSS. (it is omitted in C). A scribe's eye probably skipped back from *And* (8) to *And* (5). **the peple that ofraughte** that reached the people, 'alluding to the effects of the Passion' (Skeat). A strange expression.
10 semblable to resembling. **somdel** somewhat. The previous dream showed the Samaritan as an example of charity, riding to a joust in Jerusalem (17.47–51). Here he is identified with Christ (cf. Freud's remarks on 'dream-condensation' in *Interpretation of Dreams*). The further resemblance to Piers Plowman is explained below (22–6).
11 prickie riding eagerly. Even without boots or spurs, Christ 'pricks'.
12 other or. **spackliche** eagerly.
13 Referring both to Christ's eagerness and to his lack of spurs, which were buckled on at the dubbing ceremony. See W. Gaffney 'The allegory of the Christ-Knight in *PP*' *PMLA* 46 (1931) 155–68.
14 and] or *L* etc. **galoches ycouped** shoes cut away or slashed in a decorative fashion: 'His shon ycouped as a knight', *Degaré* 790.
15–16 The previous dream showed Faith (Abraham) as a 'herald of arms' (16.177) seeking Jesus. Here he performs a herald's function by identifying Christ from his coat of arms and proclaiming him – but he proclaims only the human title of Christ as 'Son of David' (cf. 22–6).
15 fenestre window. ***fili David*** *Matt.* 21.9. See 8 *n.*

As doth an heraud of armes whan auntrous cometh to joustes.
Olde Jewes of Jerusalem for joye they songen,
'*Benedictus qui venit in nomine Domini.*'
Then I frained at Faith what all that fare bemente
And who sholde jouste in Jerusalem. 'Jesus,' he saide,
'And fecche that the fende claimeth, Piers fruit the Plowman.'
'Is Piers in this place?' quod I, and he preinte on me:
'This Jesus of his gentrice woll jouste in Piers armes,
In his helm and in his haberjoun, *humana natura*,
That Crist be nought beknowe here for *consummatus deus*;
In Piers paltock the Plowman this pricker shall ride
For no dint shall him dere as *in deitate patris.*'
'Who shall jouste with Jesus,' quod I, 'Jewes or scribes?'
'Nay,' quod he, 'the foule fende and fals doom to deye.
Deth saith he shall fordo and adown bringe
All that liveth or loketh in londe or in watere.
Lif saith that he lieth and layth his lif to wedde
That, for all that Deth can do, within three dayes
To walke and fecche fro the fende Piers fruit the Plowman
And legge it there him liketh and Lucifer binde

16 auntrous adventurous (knights).
17 *Benedictus . . . Domini* 'Blessed is he that cometh in the name of the Lord' (*Matt.* 21.9).
18 frained asked (cf. *Matt.* 21.10–11). **fare bemente** affair meant.
20 'And regain what the Devil lays claim to, the fruit of Piers the Plowman.' Referring to Passus 16, where those who lived virtuously before Christ are represented as fruit stolen from Piers's tree by the Devil and hidden in Hell (67–85). This fruit here becomes the prize for which Jesus jousts.
21 preinte on me gave me a meaning look (presumably intended to discourage Will's impertinence: cf. 13.112, 16.64).
22–6 Christ, like Lancelot in romance, borrows the arms of a lesser knight to preserve incognito at the jousts (cf. Malory 1067). Theologically, Christ borrows human nature in order to conceal his divinity.
22 gentrice nobility. **armes** coat of arms (i.e. Piers's heraldic device).
24 beknowe recognized. ***consummatus deus*** perfect God.
25 paltock jacket. **pricker** horseman.
26 dere harm. ***in deitate patris*** in the Godhead of the Father.
28 doom judgment, i.e. that passed by Satan on man (275–83). **to deye]** *R F* and C Text; and deth *L* etc.
29 fordo destroy.
31 Allegorical combat between Death and Life (as between Darkness and Light) is a recurrent motif in this Passus. It derives from the Easter sequence *Victimae paschali*: 'Death and life have fought in a wonderful battle.' Cf. the ME poem *Death and Life* ed. I. Gollancz (1930). **layth his lif to wedde** pledges his life.
34 legge lay (as fruit is laid in a storage place).

And forbete and adown bringe bale Deth for evere.
O mors, ero mors tua.'
Then cam Pilatus with moche peple, *sedens pro tribunali*,
To see how doughtilich Deth sholde do, and deme her botheres right.
The Jewes and the justice ayain Jesu they were
And all her court on him cried '*Crucifige*' sharpe.
Tho put him forth a pelour before Pilat and saide:
'This Jesus of oure Jewes temple japed and despised,
To fordon it on o day and in three dayes after
Edefye it eft newe – here he stant that saide it –
And yit maken it as moche in alle manere pointes,
Both as long and as large by loft and by grounde.'
'*Crucifige*,' quod a cacchepole, 'I warante him a wicche.'
'*Tolle*, *tolle*,' quod an other, and took of kene thornes
And began of grene thorn a gereland to make
And sette it sore on his hed and saide in envye,
'*Ave*, *rabby*,' quod that ribaud, and threw redes at him,
Nailed him with three nailes naked on the rode,

35 forbete thoroughly beat. **bale** destructive. ***O mors . . . tua*** 'O death, I will be thy death' (*Hos.* 13.14), sung in the liturgy of Holy Saturday. On the biblical and patristic idea of Christ as conqueror of death, sin and Satan, see G. Aulén *Christus Victor* (London, S.P.C.K. 1931).
36 *sedens pro tribunali* 'sitting in the place of judgment' (*Matt.* 27.19).
37 deme her botheres right judge the claims of both of them.
38 justice plural. **ayain** against.
40 Tho then. **pelour** appellant, one who brings an accusation. So C MSS. All B MSS. have *pilour* 'pillager', a more common and less apt word. The reference is to the 'false witnesses' of *Matt.* 26.60–1.
41 japed mocked.
42 fordon destroy.
43 Edefye it eft build it again. **stant** stands.
44 moche big.
45 large broad. **by loft and by grounde** above and below.
46 cacchepole an officer of the court who executes its decisions. **wicche** Cf. Passus 16 line 120, citing *John* 10.20 'He hath a devil and is mad.' Accusations of witchcraft are recorded in the apocryphal *Gospel of Nicodemus*, a major source in this Passus: see James *Apocryphal N.T.* 96.
47 *Tolle* 'Away with him' (*John* 19.15). **of** some.
48 grene thorn] C MSS.; kene thorne B MSS. The B reading, probably carried down from 47, spoils the alliteration.
50 Cf. *Matt.* 27.29–30. ***Ave, rabby*** 'Hail, master', form of address used by Judas to Christ at the betrayal (*Matt.* 26.49, cf. *Piers* 16.151). **ribaud** villain.
51 In later medieval iconography, Christ usually has one foot on top of the other, with a single nail through both: e.g. Woolf *Lyric* Pl. 2.

And poisoun on a pole they put up to his lippes
And bede him drinke his deth-evel, his dayes were ydone,
'And yif that thou sotil be, help now thyselven;
If thou be Crist and kinges sone, come down of the rode.
Then shull we leve that Lif thee loveth and will nought lete thee deye.'
'*Consummatum est*,' quod Crist, and comsed forto swowen.
Pitousliche and pale, as a prisoun that deyeth,
The lorde of lif and of light tho layed his eyen togideres.
The day for drede withdrow and derk becam the sunne;
The wall wagged and clef, and all the world quaved;
Ded men for that dine com out of depe graves
And tolde why that tempest so long time dured.
'For a bitter bataille,' the ded body saide;
'Lif and Deth in this derknesse her one fordoth her other.
Shall no wight wite witterly who shall have the maistrye
Ere Sonday aboute sunne risinge,' and sank with that till erthe.
Some saide that he was Goddes sone that so faire deyde,
'*Vere filius Dei erat iste etc.*'
And some saide, 'He was a wicche; good is that we assaye
Wher he be ded or nought ded, down ere he be taken.'
Two theves also tholed deth that time
Upon a cross besides Crist, so was the commune law.

52–3 A sponge filled with vinegar is held up to Christ just before he dies, *Matt*. 27.48, *Mark* 15.36 (and cf. *Luke* 23.36–7, *John* 19.29–30). The C14 commentator Nicholas of Lyra refers to the opinion that the vinegar was meant to speed Christ's death (gloss on *Matt*. 27.34, *John* 19.29): *Biblia Sacra* (Lyon 1590) V cols. 456, 1315.
54 sotil skilful.
56 leve believe.
57 *Consummatum est* 'It is finished' (*John* 19.30). **comsed** began. **swowen** swoon.
58 prisoun prisoner.
59 Unlike the miracle playwrights, L. does not emphasize Christ's suffering. The image here suggests only a temporary loss of life and light.
60–2 *Matt*. 27.45, 51–3.
61 wall C MSS. have 'wall of the temple'. **clef** split.
62 dine din.
64–7 *Gospel of Nicodemus* makes the risen dead men of *Matt*. 27.52–3 testify to the events in Hell: James *Apocryphal N.T.* 119. See 249 *n*. below.
65 her one fordoth her other one of them is destroying the other.
66 witterly truly. **maistrye** mastery, upper hand.
68 *Vere* . . . 'Indeed this was the Son of God' (*Matt*. 27.54).
69 See 46 *n*.
70 Wher whether.
71 tholed suffered.

A cacchepole cam forth and cracked bothe her legges
And her armes after, of either of tho theves.
Ac was no boy so bold Goddes body to touche;
For he was knight and kinges sone, kind foryaf that time
That non harlot were so hardy to layn hand upon him.
Ac there cam forth a knight with a kene spere ygrounde,
Hight Longeus, as the lettre telleth, and longe had lore his sight;
Before Pilat and other peple in that place he hoved.
Maugré his many teeth he was made that time
To take the spere in his honde and jousten with Jesus;
For alle they were unhardy that hoved on hors or stode
To touche him or to taste him or take him down of rode,
But this blinde bacheler, that bar him thurgh the herte.
The blood sprong down by the spere and unspered the knightes eyen;
Then fell the knight upon knees and cried him mercy:
'Ayain my wille it was, lorde, to wounde you so sore.'
He seighed and saide, 'Sore it me athinketh;
For the dede that I have done, I do me in your grace;
Have on me reuth, rightful Jesu!' and right with that he wept.

73–7 See *John* 19.31–3.
75 boy a term of opprobrium in ME: 'fellow'.
76 kind foryaf Nature (i.e. God the Creator) granted.
77 harlot scoundrel. **hardy** bold.
78–91 The soldier who pierced Christ's side (*John* 19.34) is called Longinus in *Nicodemus* (James *Apocryphal N.T.* 113). The story of the blood healing his eyes is from *Legenda aurea* Ch. 47. He became a saint.
79 Hight called. **lettre** biblical text. **lore** lost.
80 hoved waited in readiness: a word used especially of mounted knights (cf. 83 and No. 10 above, line 2168) and hence continuing the tournament allegory.
81 'Despite his teeth' was a proverbial expression (Whiting T406) meaning 'despite his resistance'. *many* simply intensifies.
83 unhardy afraid.
84 taste handle (Fr. *tâter*).
85 bacheler knight. **that]** *R F* and C MSS.; thanne *L* etc.; *W* etc. omit. **bar** pierced.
86 unspered unbarred, opened. On wordplay in *Piers* see B.F. Huppé *ELH* 17 (1950) 163–90.
87–91 Cf. the Longeus episodes in the miracle plays (e.g. *Ludus Coventriae* pp. 309–10, *Towneley Plays* p. 276), where Longeus prays Christ's forgiveness.
89 seighed sighed. **Sore it me athinketh** I bitterly regret it.
90 do me put myself.
91 reuth pity.

Then gan Faith felly the false Jewes despise,
Called hem caitives acursed for evere,
'For this foule vileinye, venjaunce to you falle!
To do the blinde bete him ybounde, it was a boyes conseille.
Cursed caitives! knighthod was it nevere
To misdo a ded body by day or by nighte.
The gree yit hath he geten for all his grete wound;
For your champioun chivaler, chief knight of you alle,
Yelt him recreaunt renning right at Jesus wille.
For be this derknesse ydo, Deth worth yvenkeshed,
And ye, lordeins, han ylost, for Lif shall have the maistrye,
And your fraunchise, that free was, fallen is in thraldom,
And ye cherles and your children chieve shall ye nevere,
Ne have lordship in londe ne no lond tilie,
But all bareine be and usurye usen,
Which is lif that oure lorde in alle lawes acurseth.
Now your good dayes are done, as Daniel prophecied,
Whan Crist cam, her kingdom the crowne sholde lese:
Cum veniat sanctus sanctorum, cessabit unxio vestra.'

92 felly fiercely.
94 falle] *W* etc.; alle *L* etc.
95 'It was a shameful decision to get a blind man to attack a bound one.'
96 caitives] caytyue *L* etc.
98 'He has won the prize, all the same . . .' Faith again performs a herald's function, in declaring the winner of the joust.
100 'Acknowledges himself defeated in the tilt . . .'
101 be this derknesse ydo once this darkness is passed. **Deth worth yvenkeshed**] *R F* and C MSS. ('Death shall be vanquished'); his deth worth avenged *L* etc.
102 lordeins rascals.
103–7 Jews were excluded from many legal rights; but they, unlike Christians, were free to lend money at interest (*usurye* 106). Cf. No. 18 below, 490–1 and *n*.
103 fraunchise freedom.
104 chieve prosper.
105 tilie cultivate.
106 usen practise.
109 lese lose (supplied from *R F*, following Kane and Donaldson; *L* omits). ***Cum . . . vestra*** 'When the Most Holy One comes, your anointing [i.e. the tradition of your kings] shall cease.' This prophecy, remotely based on *Dan*. 9.24, is attributed to Daniel in the pseudo-Augustinian sermon *Contra Iudaeos* (Migne *P.L.* 42.1124), where the preacher attempts to convince the Jews of their error by citing their own prophets. This part of the sermon was familiar as a lesson at Christmas (at Matins on the 4th Sunday of Advent in the Sarum Breviary), and gave rise to the liturgical play *Ordo prophetarum*: see K. Young *Drama of the Medieval Church* (Oxford U.P. 1933) 2.125–71. Cf. *Towneley Plays* p. 63; *Chester Cycle* p. 168.

What for fere of this ferly and of the false Jewes
I drow me in that derknesse to *descendit ad inferna,*
And there I saw sothly *secundum scripturas*
Out of the west coste a wenche, as me thoughte,
Cam walking in the way, to helle-ward she loked.
Mercy highte that maid, a meke thing withalle,
A full benigne buirde and boxom of speche.
Hir suster, as it semed, cam softly walking
Even out of the est, and westward she loked,
A full comely creature, Treuthe she highte;
For the vertue that hir folwed aferd was she never.
Whan thise maidenes mette, Mercy and Treuthe,
Either axed other of this grete wonder,
Of the dine and of the derknesse and how the day rowed,
And which a light and a leme lay before helle.

110 ferly wonder.

111 It is as if, in the course of his dream, Will works through the Apostles' Creed, here reaching 'And descended into Hell'.

112–260 The debate of the Four Daughters of God is a traditional topic, based on *Ps.* 84.10–11 (A.V. 85.9–10): 'Surely his salvation is near to them that fear him: that glory may dwell in our land. Mercy and truth have met each other: justice and peace have kissed.' Cf. line 420 below. 'This famous debate was theological in purpose, being an allegorical method of displaying how, as in Anselm's analysis of the nature of the Redemption, God's justice was reconciled with His mercy' (Woolf *Mystery Plays* 166). Only Langland associates the topic with the approach of Christ bringing 'salvation to them that fear him' in Hell. See H. Traver *The Four Daughters of God* (Philadelphia, 1907); Owst *Literature and Pulpit* 90–2; S.C. Chew *The Virtues Reconciled* (Toronto U.P. 1947).

112 *secundum scripturas* according to the Scriptures. From the Credo of the Mass, where it refers to the Resurrection: 'Et resurrexit tertia die, secundum scripturas'.

113 Mercy and Truth (118) come from W. and E. respectively, Righteousness (163) and Peace (166) from N. and S. Cf. *Isa.* 43.6, where God speaks of 'my daughters from the ends of the earth'. **coste** quarter (not 'coast').

116 buirde damsel. **boxom** mild, submissive.

119 Treuthe Lat. *Veritas*, in the Vulgate *Ps.*

123 rowed was dawning.

124 which what. **leme** glow. **lay before** The phrase suggests a besieging army. Christ's approach is similarly described by the hell-dwellers in *Nicodemus*: 'Now when we were set together with all our fathers in the deep, in obscurity of darkness, on a sudden there came a golden heat of the sun and a purple and royal light shining upon us' (James *Apocryphal N.T.* 123). *Nicodemus* is a prime source for the Harrowing of Hell, directly or indirectly, here as in e.g. *York Plays* 372–95 or *Towneley Plays* 293–305.

'Ich have ferly of this fare, in faith,' saide Treuthe,
'And am wending to wite what this wonder meneth.'
'Have no merveille,' quod Mercy, 'mirthe it betokneth.
A maiden that hatte Marye, and moder without felinge
Of any kinnes creature, conceived thurgh speche
And grace of the holy gost, wex grete with childe,
Withouten wommene wem into this world she brought him;
And that my tale be trewe I take God to witnesse.
Sith this barn was bore ben thritty winter passed,
Which deyde and deth tholed this day aboute midday,
And that is cause of this clips that closeth now the sunne,
In meninge that man shall fro merknesse be drawe,
The while this light and this leme shall Lucifer ablende.
For patriarkes and prophetes han preched herof often,
That man shall man save thurgh a maidenes helpe,
And that was tint thurgh tree, tree shall it winne,
And that deth down broughte, deth shall releve.'
'That thou tellest,' quod Treuthe, 'is but a tale of waltrot;
For Adam and Eve and Abraham with other,
Patriarkes and prophetes that in paine liggen,
Leve thou nevere that yon light hem alofte bringe,
Ne have hem out of helle. Holde thy tong, Mercy.
It is but a trufle that thou tellest – I, Treuthe, wot the sothe –
For that is ones in helle, out cometh it nevere.

125 'I am astonished by this event . . .'
128 **hatte** is named. **felinge** touch.
129 **kinnes** kind of. **speche** i.e. Gabriel's *Ave*.
131 **wommene wem** women's impurity. *wommene* is supplied by Kane and Donaldson from the C Text.
133 See 297 *n*. **Sith** since. **barn** child.
135 **clips** eclipse.
136 **In meninge that** signifying that. **merknesse** darkness.
137 **ablende** blind.
140–1 Such parallelisms (tree for tree, death for death, venom for venom, guile for guile, etc.) are commonplace in meditations on the Redemption. That between the Tree of Transgression and the Tree of the Cross occurs e.g. in *Nicodemus* (James *Apocryphal N.T.* 137, 138) and the hymn *Pange lingua*: 'ipse lignum tunc notavit, damna ligni ut solveret' ('he then marked out a tree to repair the damage done by a tree').
140 **tint** lost.
141 **releve** raise up again.
142 **waltrot** nonsense. A unique, obscure word. See Skeat's note.
145 **Leve** believe.
147 **trufle** nonsense.
148 **that** what.

[11] William Langland

Job the prophete patriarke reproveth thy sawes:
Quia in inferno nulla est redemptio.'
Then Mercy full mildly mouthed thise wordes:
'Thurgh experience,' quod she, 'I hope they shall be saved;
For venim fordoth venim, and that I prove by resoun.
For of alle venimes foulest is the scorpioun;
May no medcine helpe the place there he stingeth,
Till he be ded and do therto; the ivel he destroyeth,
The first venimousté, thurgh vertu of himself.
So shall this deth fordo, I dar my lif legge,
All that deth did firste thurgh the develes entising;
And right as thurgh gile man was begiled,
So shall grace, that began, make a good end,
And begile the gilour, and that is good sleighte:
Ars ut artem falleret.'
'Now suffre we,' saide Treuthe, 'I see, as me thinketh,
Out of the nippe of the north, nought full fer hennes,
Rightwisnesse come renning; reste we the while,
For he wot more than we – he was ere we bothe.'
'That is soth,' saide Mercy, 'and I see here by southe

149 reproveth thy sawes disproves what you say. ***Quia . . . redemptio*** 'There is no release from hell.' From the Office of the Dead, but often ascribed to Job on the strength of *Job* 7.9: 'He that shall go down to hell shall not come up.' See *Castle of Perseverance* 3096–7 and Eccles's note.
151 experience. Mercy previously appealed to the authority of the prophets (138) and was answered with Job. She now appeals to *experience*. For experience/authority, see Wife of Bath, Chaucer *C.T.* III 1.
153–6 Skeat cites Bartholomeus Anglicus and Lily's *Euphues*. A remedy, or 'treacle', against poison was said to be made with scorpion's venom. Henry of Lancaster uses this as an exemplum of sin and confession in *Livre de seyntz medicines* ed. E. J. Arnould (Oxford, Blackwell 1940) 56–7.
155 do therto applied to the place.
156 venimousté venomosity. **vertu**] venym *L* etc.
157 legge wager.
160–1 B MSS. conflate these lines (eyeskip from *good* 160 to *good* 161) to: 'So shall grace that began make a good sleighte.' The missing words are supplied from C.
161 gilour beguiler. **sleighte** trick. 'The guiler beguiled' was proverbial (Whiting G491). ***Ars . . . falleret*** 'Art to deceive art.' From the hymn *Pange lingua* 8.
162 suffre we let us be patient.
163 nippe cold region (or 'darkness'? See *OED* s.v. *Nip* sb.³).
164 Rightwisnesse Latin *Iustitia*, justice.
165 'For she knows more than we – she existed before either of us.' Perhaps alluding to *Ps*. 118.160 (A.V. 119.160): 'The beginning of thy words is truth: all the judgments of thy justice [*iustitia* = righteousness] are for ever.'

Where Pees cometh playing, in pacience yclothed.
Love hath coveited hir longe; leve I none other
But he sent hir some lettre what this light bemeneth
That overhoveth helle thus; she us shall telle.'
Whan Pees, in pacience yclothed, approched nere hem tweine,
Rightwisnesse hir reverenced for hir riche clothing
And prayed Pees to telle hir to what place she wolde,
And in hir gay garnements whom she grete thoughte.
'My wille is to wende,' quoth she, 'and welcome hem alle
That many day mighte I nought see for merknesse of sinne,
Adam and Eve and other mo in helle.
Moises and many mo mercy shall have,
And I shall daunce therto; do thou so, sustre!
For Jesus jousted well, joye beginneth dawe:
Ad vesperum demorabitur fletus, et ad matutinum laetitia.
Love, that is my lemman, such lettres me sente,
That Mercy, my sustre, and I mankinde sholde save,
And that God hath forgiven and graunted me, Pees, and Mercy
To be mannes meinpernoure for evermore after.
Lo here the patent,' quod Pees, '*in pace in idipsum*,
And that this dede shall dure, *dormiam et requiescam*.'
'What, ravestow?' quod Rightwisnesse, 'or thou art right dronke?
Levestow that yond light unlouke mighte helle
And save mannes soule? Suster, wene it nevere.

167 Pees 'the spirit of reconciliation' (Salter and Pearsall). **playing** i.e. walking at her leisure.
168 leve I none other I cannot believe (but that).
170 overhoveth hangs over.
172 reverenced respectfully greeted.
174 'And whom she was intending to welcome, in her fine clothes.'
177 mo more.
178 mercy shall have Kane and Donaldson conjecture *merye shul synge*, which goes better with line 179. C Text has *synge* for *have*.
180 For because. **dawe** dawn. ***Ad . . . laetitia*** 'In the evening weeping shall have place: and in the morning gladness', *Ps.* 29.6 (A.V. 30.5).
181 lemman lover.
183 forgiven and graunted me granted me the right. A legal phrase: see No. 7 above, lines 268–9 and *n*.
184 To be mannes meinpernoure to go bail for mankind.
185 patent letters patent i.e. the Psalm, regarded as a legal document recording the grant to Mercy and Peace.
185–6 *in pace in idipsum . . . dormiam et requiescam* 'In peace in the selfsame I will sleep, and I will rest', *Ps.* 4.9 (A.V. 4.8), set for Holy Saturday.
186 dure endure.
187 ravestow are you mad?
188 unlouke unlock.

[11] William Langland

At the beginning God gaf the doom himselve
That Adam and Eve and alle that hem suwed
Sholde deye downright and dwelle in pine after,
If that they touched a tree and the fruit eten.
Adam afterward ayaines his defence
Frette of that fruit and forsook, as it were,
The love of oure lorde and his lore bothe,
And folwed that the fende taughte and his felawes wille
Ayaines resoun: I, Rightwisnesse, recorde thus with Treuthe
That her paine be perpetual and no prayere hem helpe.
Forthy late hem chewe as they chose, and chide we nought, sustres,
For it is bootless bale, the bite that they eten.'
'And I shall preve,' quod Pees, 'her paine mot have ende,
And wo into well mowe wende atte laste.
For had they wist of no wo, well had they nought knowen;
For no wight wot what well is that nevere wo suffred,
Ne what is hot hunger that had nevere defaute.
If no night ne were, no man, as I leve,
Sholde wite witterly what day is to mene.
Sholde nevere right riche man, that liveth in reste and ese,
Wite what wo is, ne were the deth of kinde.
So God that began alle of his gode wille
Becam man of a maide, mankinde to save,
And suffred to be sold to see the sorwe of deying,
The which unknitteth all care and comsing is of reste.
For till *modicum* mete with us, I may it well avowe,

191 suwed followed.
194 ayaines his defence against his prohibition.
195 Frette ate.
196 lore teaching.
197 felawes companion's (Eve's). Kane and Donaldson emend to *flesshes* (from C Text).
198 I] *L*; and *W* etc. (and C MSS.). The *W* reading requires *recorde* to be taken as an imperative, beginning a new clause.
200 'And so let them chew up what they have chosen to eat . . .'
201 bootless bale an evil without a remedy.
202 mot may.
203 well happiness. **mowe wende** may turn.
204 'For if they had not experienced sorrow, they would not have understood joy.'
206 hot extreme (*MED* s.v. *Hot* adj. 4(b)). **defaute** shortage.
208 witterly for certain.
210 'Know what sorrow is, if it were not for natural death.'
214 comsing beginning.
215 'For until small portions come our way . . .'

Wot no wight, as I wene, what is inough to mene.
Forthy God of his goodnesse the firste gome Adam
Sette him in solace and in sovereign mirthe;
And sith he suffred him sinne, sorwe to fele,
To wite what well was, kindelich to knowe it.
And after, God auntred himself and took Adames kinde,
To wite what he hath suffred in three sondry places,
Both in hevene and in erthe, and now till helle he thinketh,
To wite what all wo is, that wot of all joye.
So it shall fare by this folk: her foly and her sinne
Shall lere hem what langour is and lisse withouten ende.
Wot no wight what werre is there that pees regneth,
Ne what is witterly well till weylowey him teche.'
 Then was there a wight with two brode eyen,
Book highte that beupere, a bold man of speche.
'By Goddes body,' quod this Book, 'I will bere witnesse
That tho this barn was ybore there blased a sterre,
That alle the wise of this world in o wit acordeden
That such a barn was born in Bethleem cité
That mannes soule sholde save and sinne destroye.
And alle the elements,' quod the book, 'herof bereth witnesse.
That he was God that all wroughte, the walken firste shewed:

216 what is inough to mene what it means to have enough.
217 gome man.
219 sith afterwards.
220 kindelich by experience, 'in his bones': see M.C. Davlin '*Kynde Knowyng* as a major theme in *PP*' *RES* n.s. 22 (1971) 1–19.
221 auntred himself put himself at risk.
222 he Adam, who experienced Paradise, Earth and Hell.
223 thinketh intends to go.
226 lere teach. **langour** misery. **lisse** joy.
228 witterly certainly. **weylowey** sorrow, saying 'alas'.
229–58 Book reports the testimonies of Holy Scripture on the divinity of Christ. See Kaske *Ang.* 77 (1959) 117–44.
229 brode broad, wide open.
230 '"Book" was that Father's name': *beupere* was a term of respect for priests.
232 tho when.
233 in o wit acordeden agreed in the one opinion (referring to the Magi).
236–49 All four elements bear witness to Christ's godhead: air (237–40), water (241–3), fire (244–5), earth (246–9). Kaske (*art. cit.* 118–22) traces the theme of the 'witnessing elements' back to its main source in Gregory's sermon on *Matt.* 2.1–12, a passage which was read at Matins at Epiphany (this explains the connection with 232–5).
237 walken welkin, heavens.

Tho that weren in hevene token *stella comata*
And tendeden hir as a torche to reverence his birthe;
The light folwed the lorde into the lowe erthe.
The water witnesseth that he was God, for he wente on it;
Peter the apostel parceived his gate
And, as he wente on the water, well him knew and saide,
"*Iube me venire ad te super aquas*".
And lo how the sunne gan louke hir light in hirself,
Whan she sey him suffre that sunne and see made.
The erthe, for hevinesse that he wolde suffre,
Quaked as quick thing and all bequashte the roche:
Lo, helle mighte nought holde, but opened tho God tholed
And lete out Symondes sones to seen him hange on rode.
And now shall Lucifer leve it, though him loth thinke;
For Gygas the geaunt with a ginne hath engined
To breke and to bete down that ben ayaines Jesus.
And I, Book, will be brent but Jesus rise to live

238 Tho those. ***stella comata*** 'long-haired star', comet.
239 tendeden hir kindled it (*stella* being fem.). Angels hold the streaming comet like a torch to light the nativity: a sublime image.
241 The] That *L* etc. **witnesseth**] witnessed *L* etc.
242 gate manner of going.
243 *Iube . . . aquas* 'Bid me come to thee upon the waters' (*Matt*. 14.28).
244 louke lock (cf. 60, 135).
245 sey saw.
247 quick living. **bequashte** shattered (cf. 61).
248 tho God tholed when God suffered.
249 Symondes sones The two sons of Simeon (cf. *Luke* 2.25–35) are prominent in *Nicodemus* (James *Apocryphal N.T.* 119 f.) among the dead who rise after the Crucifixion. They report the events of the Harrowing, but do not witness the Crucifixion.
250 leve believe (that Jesus is God). **him loth thinke** it is hateful to him.
251 Gygas the geaunt The allusion is to *Ps*. 18.6: 'He hath rejoiced as a giant [*gigas*] to run the way' (differently rendered in A.V. *Ps*. 19.5). This was generally taken as a prophecy of Christ, *gigas* by virtue of his indomitability and double nature: see Kaske *JEGP* 56 (1957) 177–85. C Text has 'Jesus as a giant'. **with a ginne hath engined** has contrived by means of a device. Perhaps *ginne* refers to a siege machine (*MED* s.v. *Ginne* n. 4(a)). *L* etc. omit *hath* (found in *W*), and Kaske takes *with a ginne engined* as adjectival: 'contrived by means of a trick' (the double-natured Christ, devised to trick Satan). But cf. C Text: 'with a gyn cometh yonde.'
252 that those who.
253 'And I, Book, will be burnt unless Jesus rise to life.' The reference to burning is simply the appropriate asseveration for a book – like a man saying 'I will be damned if . . .' On the syntax (correcting Kaske), see E. T. Donaldson, *Schlauch Studies* 103–9 (in Blanch *Style*).

In alle mightes of man and his moder gladie,
And conforte all his kin and out of care bringe,
And all the Jewen joye unjoignen and unlouken;
And but they reverencen his rood and his resurrexioun
And beleve on a newe law, be lost lif and soule.'
'Suffre we,' saide Treuthe, 'I here and see both
How a spirit speketh to Helle and bit unspere the yates.'
Attollite portas etc.
A voice loude in that lighte to Lucifer crieth,
'Princes of this place, unpinneth and unlouketh!
For here cometh with crowne that king is of glorye.'
Then siked Sathan and saide to Helle:
'Such a light ayaines oure leve Lazar it fette.
Care and combraunce is comen to us alle.
If this king come in, mankind will he fecche
And lede it there Lazar is, and lightlich me binde.
Patriarkes and prophetes han parled herof longe,
That such a lorde and a light sholde lede hem alle hennes.'
'Listeneth,' quod Lucifer, 'for I this lorde knowe;
Both this lorde and this light, is longe ago I knew him.
May no deth him dere ne no develes queintise,
And where he will is his waye; ac war him of the periles.

254 The story of Christ's appearance to the Virgin after his Resurrection is non-biblical: Woolf *Lyric* 138.
256 unjoignen and unlouken take apart and undo.
258 The Jews, unless they accept the New Law, will be damned. For a different interpretation, see Hoffman *MLQ* 25 (1964) 57–65.
260 bit unspere the yates commands the gates to be unbàrred. ***Attollite*** . . . 'Lift up your gates, [O ye princes, and be ye lifted up, O eternal gates: and the King of Glory shall enter in]', *Ps.* 23 (A.V. 24) 7 and 9, set for Holy Saturday and generally applied to the Harrowing: cf. *Nicodemus* (James *Apocryphal N.T.* 132).
262 unpinneth unbolt.
264 siked sighed. **Helle**] *R F* and C Text; hem alle *L* etc. Here, and probably at 260, Hell is another name for Lucifer. He is the leading devil, distinguished from Satan. They quarrel, like Hell and Satan in *Nicodemus* (James 136–7).
265 'A light like this carried off Lazarus without our consent.' Cf. *Nicodemus* (James 131).
266 combraunce trouble.
268 Lazar is] *R F* and C Text; hym lyketh *L* etc. **lightlich** easily.
269 parled spoken. Satan confirms that these events fulfil O.T. prophecies.
273 dere harm. **queintise** craftiness.
274 ac war him but let him beware.

If he reve me my right, he robbeth me by maistrye;
For by right and by resoun tho renkes that ben here
Body and soule ben mine, both gode and ille.
For himself saide, that sire is of hevene,
Yif Adam ete the apple alle sholde deye
And dwelle with us develes; this threting he made,
And he that sothnesse is saide thise wordes.
And sithen we han ben yseised seven hundreth winter,
I leve that law nill naught lete him the leest.'
'That is soth,' saide Sathan, 'but I me sore drede,
For thou gete hem with gile and his gardin breke,
And in semblaunce of a serpent sat on the appletree,
And eggedest hem to ete, Eve by hirselve,
And toldest hir a tale, of tresoun were the wordes,
And so thou haddest hem out, and hider atte laste.
It is nought graithly geten there gile is the rote,
For God will nought be begiled,' quod Gobelin, 'ne bejaped.
We have no trewe title to hem, for thurgh tresoun were they dampned.
Certes, I drede me,' quod the devel, 'lest Treuthe will hem fecche.
This thritty winter, as I wene, he wente aboute and preched.
I have assailled him with sinne, and some time y-asked

275 reve take from. **maistrye** superior force.
276 tho renkes those people.
281 that sothnesse is who is Truth itself.
282–3 'And since we have been in possession for 700 years, I am confident that the law will not allow him the least one of them.'
282 we han ben yseised] C MSS.; I seised *L* etc. Kane and Donaldson read *I was seised.* **seven hundreth** a large round number, merely? Estimates of the length of time between Adam and Christ are usually around 4,000 or 5,000 years. See No. 25.4 below, line 2 and *n.* C Text has 'seven thousand', which is too many.
285 breke broke into.
287 'And urged Eve when she was alone that they should eat.'
289 hider (got them) hither.
290 graithly properly. **rote** root, origin.
291 Gobelin a devil, apparently another name for Satan (284); but Kane and Donaldson mark off a separate speech, 290–2. See *OED* s.v. *Goblin.* **bejaped** made a fool of.
293 Treuthe here, as in *Visio*, a name for the just God (not the Daughter of God).
294 thritty winter Christ's ministry began at the age of about 30 (*Luke* 3.23) and lasted only about three years. C Text corrects the blunder. **he wente aboute**] *R F* and C Text; hath he gone *L* etc.
295–6 A reference to the Temptation of Christ (*Matt*. 4.1–11).

Wher he were God or Goddes sone? He gaf me short answere;
And thus hath he trolled forth this two and thritty winter.
And whan I seigh it was so, sleping I wente
To warne Pilates wif what dones man was Jesus,
For Jewes hateden him and han done him to deth.
I wolde have lengthed his lif, for I leved, yif he deyed,
That his soule wolde suffre no sinne in his sighte;
For the body, whil it on bones yede, aboute was evere
To save men from sinne, yif hemself wolde.
And now I see where a soule cometh hiderward sailing
With glorye and with grete light; God it is, I wot well.
I rede we flee,' quod he, 'faste alle hennes,
For us were better nought be than biden his sight.
For thy lesinges, Lucifer, lost is all oure preye.
First thurgh thee we fellen fro hevene so hye,
For we leved thy lesinges, we loupen oute alle;
And now for thy last lesing ylore we have Adam
And all oure lordship, I leve, alonde and awater.
Nunc princeps huius mundi eiicietur foras.'
Eft the light bad unlouke and Lucifer answered,

296 Wher whether.

297 trolled forth rambled about. **two and thritty** Christ's age was calculated by adding two or three years of ministry to the 30 mentioned by Luke (294 *n.*).

298–302 This apocryphal story grew out of *Matt*. 27.19: 'And as he [Pilate] was sitting in the place of judgment, his wife sent to him, saying: Have thou nothing to do with that just man; for I have suffered many things this day in a dream because of him.' The story appears in religious drama: Woolf *Mystery Plays* 243–5.

299 what dones man what kind of man.

300 Suspect in metre and sense. Sense might be improved by adding *wolde* 'intended to' before *han;* but a line may be lost.

303 yede went around. **aboute** busy.

307 rede advise.

308 biden his sight stay and suffer his gaze.

309 lesinges lies.

311–12 All B MSS. except *R* and *F* conflate these lines (by eyeskip from *lesinges* 311 to *lesing* 312) to 'For we leved thy lesinges ylore we have Adam.' The two missing half-lines are supplied from *F*.

311 loupen leapt.

312 ylore lost.

313 *Nunc . . . foras* 'Now shall the prince of this world be cast out', *John* 12.31.

314 Eft once more (referring back to 261–3).

'What lorde artow?' quod Lucifer, '*quis est iste*?'
'*Rex gloriae*,' the light sone saide,
'And lorde of might and of maine and all manere vertues,
Dominus virtutum.
Dukes of this dim place, anon undo thise yates
That Crist may come in, the kinges sone of hevene.'
And with that breth helle brake with Beliales barres,
For any wye or ward, wide opned the yates.
Patriarkes and prophetes, *populus in tenebris*,
Songen seint Johanes song, '*Ecce agnus Dei*'.
Lucifer loke ne mighte, so light him ableinte;
And tho that oure lorde loved, into his light he laughte,
And saide to Sathan, 'Lo here my soule to amendes
For alle sinful soules, to save tho that ben worthy.
Mine they be and of me, I may the bet hem claime.
Although resoun recorde, and right of myself,
That if they ete the apple alle sholde deye,
I behighte hem nought here helle for ever.
For the dede that they dide, thy deceit it made;
With gile thou hem gete again all resoun.
For in my paleis, paradis, in person of an addre,
Falsliche thou fettest there thing that I loved.
Thus ilike a lusarde with a lady visage

315–17 Langland follows his earlier quotation from *Ps.* 23 (A.V. 24) with the answering verse broken into scraps: 'Who is this . . . King of Glory? . . . The Lord of hosts.' See 260 above. Kane and Donaldson solve the metrical problems of 315–16 by combining their English parts into one line: '"What lord artow?" quod Lucifer; the light soone seide.'
320 breth utterance (*MED* s.v. *Breth* n.(1) 3)? But cf. Passus 5.503: Christ 'blewe alle thy blissed into the blisse of paradise.' **barres** Cf. *Ps.* 106 (A.V. 107) 16: 'he hath broken gates of brass and burst iron bars'.
321 'For all that any man or guard could do . . .' **opned]** *W* etc.; opene *L* etc.
322 ***populus in tenebris*** 'the people that walked in darkness [have seen a great light]', *Isa.* 9.2.
323 ***Ecce agnus Dei*** 'Behold the Lamb of God', *John* 1.36.
324 ableinte blinded.
325 lorde] *L* omits. **laughte** took.
326 to amendes as reparation.
328 bet better.
329 right justice.
331 behighte promised.
334 paleis enclosed place (*OED Palis*; not 'palace').
335 fettest fetched.
336 lusarde lizard. **lady** The serpent-tempter is usually represented with a woman's face: 'feet as an edder, a maidens face', *Chester Cycle* Play 2 line 195. The tradition is rabbinic in origin: Woolf *Mystery Plays* 115.

Thevelich thou me robbedest. The olde lawe graunteth
That gilours be begiled, and that is good resoun:
Dentem pro dente et oculum pro oculo.
Ergo, soule shall soule quite and sinne to sinne wende,
And all that man hath misdo, I, man, will amende.
Membre for membre by the olde lawe was amendes,
And lif for lif also, and by that lawe I claime it,
Adam and all his issue at my wille herafter;
And that deth in hem fordid, my deth shall releve,
And bothe quicke and quite that queint was thurgh sinne;
And that grace gile destruye, good faith it asketh.
So leve it nought, Lucifer, ayain the lawe I fecche hem,
But by right and by resoun raunsoun here my liges:
Non veni solvere legem, sed adimplere.
Thou fettest mine in my place ayaines all resoun
Falsliche and felounliche; good faith me it taughte
To recovre hem thurgh raunsoun and by no resoun elles,
So that with gile thou gete, thurgh grace it is ywonne.
Thou, Lucifer, in liknesse of a luther addere
Getest by gile tho that God loved;
And I, in liknesse of a lede, that lorde am of hevene,
Graciousliche thy gile have quit; go gile ayain gile!
And as Adam and alle thurgh a tree deiden,
Adam and alle thurgh a tree shall torne ayain to live;
And gile is begiled and in his gile fallen:
Et cecidit in foveam quam fecit.
Now beginneth thy gile again thee to tourne

338 See 161 *n*. ***Dentem . . . oculo*** 'tooth for tooth, and eye for eye', *Ex*. 21.24.
339 'Therefore one soul shall compensate for another, and one sin [the Crucifixion] go against another.'
345 'And both revive and repay what was quenched by sin.'
346 **asketh** requires.
347 **ayain** contrary to.
348 **liges** liege subjects. ***Non . . . adimplere*** 'I am not come to destroy [the Law], but to fulfil', *Matt*. 5.17.
349 'You got hold of my people in my place [Eden] . . .'
350 **felounliche** treacherously.
352 'So what you got with guile . . .'
353–6 The argument is curious: both Lucifer and Christ 'guilefully' take a step down in the order of creation.
353 **luther** wicked.
355 **lede** man.
356 **go gile** See 161 *n*.
357–8 See 140–1 *n*.
359 ***Et . . . fecit*** 'and he is fallen into the hole he made', *Ps*. 7.16 (A.V. 7.15). See 391 *n*.

And my grace to growe ay gretter and wider.
The bitternesse that thou hast browe, brouke it thyselven;
That art doctour of deth, drinke that thou madest.
For I that am lorde of lif, love is my drink,
And for that drink today I deide upon erthe.
I faughte so, me threstes yet, for mannes soule sake.
May no drink me moiste ne my thruste slake
Till the vendage falle in the vale of Josephath
That I drinke right ripe must, *resurrexio mortuorum*.
And then shall I come as a king crowned with angeles
And han out of helle alle mennes soules.
Fendes and fendekins before me shull stande
And be at my bidding wheresoever me liketh.
Ac to be merciable to man then my kinde it asketh;
For we beth bretheren of blode, but nought in baptesme alle;
Ac alle that beth mine hole bretheren in blode and in baptesme
Shall nought be dampned to the deth that is withouten ende;
    Tibi soli peccavi etc.
It is nought used in erthe to hangen a feloun

362 browe brewed. **brouke** enjoy. A proverbial idea: Whiting B529.
366 'I fought so hard that I am still thirsty . . .' Alluding to Christ's last word on the Cross (quoted in C Text at this point), 'Sitio' ('I thirst'), *John* 19.28, understood as referring to Christ's thirst for the salvation of mankind: cf. *Castle of Perseverance* 3352, and Julian of Norwich: 'the same desire and thirst that he had upon the cross . . . he has still, and shall continue to have until the last soul to be saved has arrived at its blessedness', *Revelations* trans. C. Wolters (Penguin Books 1966) 108–9.
367 thruste thirst.
368–9 'Till the wine-harvest comes in the vale of Jehoshaphat, when I shall drink a well-matured new wine, the resurrection of the dead.' The general resurrection and Last Judgment are to take place in the valley of Jehoshaphat: see *Joel* 3.2, 12–13. *Joel* 3.13 prompts the wine image: 'Put ye in the sickles for the harvest is ripe: come and go down, for the press is full, the vats run over.' The image is taken up in *Rev*. 14.18–20. In both scriptural passages, the wine harvest signifies God's wrathful judgment on his enemies. Langland associates it rather with the mercy of Christ.
371 han have.
372 fendekins small devils (a word found only here).
374 Ac] *R* and C MSS.; and *L* etc. **my kinde it asketh** my nature requires it.
375–6 All men are brothers by blood; but only Christians are brothers also by the water of baptism (which flowed from Christ's side, mingled with blood) and hence full (*hole*) brethren.
377 *Tibi* . . . 'To thee only have I sinned, [and have done evil before thee]', *Ps*. 50.6 (A.V. 51.4), understood as addressed to Christ, who can therefore himself forgive the sin. See 391 *n*.
378 used customary. If a man survived the first attempt to hang him, he was pardoned, e.g. the case at Leicester in 1363 cited by Skeat.

Ofter than ones, though he were a tretour;
And if the king of that kingdom come in that time
There the feloun thole sholde deth or other juwise,
Lawe wolde he yeve him lif if he loked on him.
And I that am king of kinges shall come such a time
There doom to the deth dampneth alle wicked;
And yif lawe will I loke on hem, it lieth in my grace
Whether they deie or deie nought for that they deden ille.
Be it anything abought, the boldnesse of her sinnes,
I may do mercy thurgh rightwisnesse and alle my wordes trewe.
And though holy writ will that I be wroke of hem that deden ille –
Nullum malum inpunitum etc. –
They shull be clensed clereliche and washen of her sinnes
In my prisoun purgatorye till *parce* it hote,
And my mercy shall be shewed to many of my bretheren.
For blood may suffre blood both hungry and akale,
Ac blood may nought see blood bleed, but him rewe.'
Audivi arcana verba, quae non licet homini loqui.
'Ac my rightwisnesse and right shall reulen all helle,
And mercy all mankinde before me in hevene;

381 or other juwise or other punishment. So *W* etc. *L* etc. read *or otherwyse*. Kane and Donaldson adopt *oother Iuwise* 'or punishment' from the C tradition.

382 'The law requires that he grant him his life, if he set eyes on him.'

384 The reference is to Christ's Second Coming at Doomsday.

385 will grants that.

387 'If any payment at all is made for the boldness of their sins.'

389 wroke avenged. ***Nullum* . . .** 'No evil unpunished [and no good unrewarded].' Not from *holy writ*, but from Pope Innocent III, *De contemptu mundi* Bk 3 Ch. 15 (Migne *P.L.* 217.745). Cf. *Piers* 4.143–4.

390 clereliche entirely.

391 *parce* Referring to *Job* 7.16: 'Spare me (*Parce mihi*), for my days are nothing.' See Alford *MP* 69 (1971–2) 323–5, comparing B Text 19.290 and other ME uses. *Parce mihi*, *Domine* opens the first *lectio* of the Office of the Dead, whence its association with purgatory here. Three neighbouring texts from *Psalms* also figure in this Office: cf. 359, 377, 398. **hote** command, i.e. till Christ commands them to be spared.

393 akale acold.

394 but him rewe without taking pity. ***Audivi* . . . *loqui*** 'heard secret words which it is not granted to man to utter', 2 *Cor*. 12.4. Earlier (374–7) Christ promised salvation to his 'full brothers' in blood and baptism; here he seems to promise it to brothers in blood alone, i.e. to all mankind (396). Such doctrine would necessarily be 'arcane': it could not be told to everyone.

For I were an unkinde king but I my kinde holpe,
And namelich at such a nede there nedes help behoveth.
Non intres in iudicium cum servo tuo.
Thus by lawe,' quod oure lorde, 'lede I will fro hennes
Tho that me loved and leved in my coming;
And for thy lesing, Lucifer, that thou lowe till Eve
Thou shalt abye it bittre' – and bond him with chaines.
Astaroth and alle the route hidden hem in hernes;
They dorste nought loke on oure lorde, the boldest of hem alle,
But leten him lede forth what him liked and lete what him liste.
Many hundreth of angeles harpeden and songen,
'*Culpat caro, purgat caro, regnat Deus Dei caro.*'
Than piped Pees of poisye a note,
'*Clarior est solito post maxima nebula phoebus,*
Post inimicitias clarior est et amor.
After sharpe shoures,' quod Pees, 'most shene is the sunne;
Is no weder warmer than after watery cloudes,
Ne no love lever, ne lever frendes,
Than after werre and wo when love and pees be maistres.
Was never werre in this worlde ne wickednesse so kene
That Love, and him liste, to laughing ne broughte,
And Pees thurgh pacience alle perilles stopped.'

397 'I would be an unnatural king if I did not help my own kin.'
398 namelich specially. **there nedes help behoveth** where help is absolutely necessary. ***Non . . . tuo*** 'Enter not into judgment with thy servant', *Ps.* 142.2 (A.V. 143.2). See 391 *n.*
401 lowe lied.
402 abye pay for.
403 Astaroth the Phoenician Venus, one of the strange gods worshipped by Solomon (A.V. 1 *Kings* 11). She is a devil here, as in *York Plays* p. 378 and Milton *Par. Lost* 1.438. **hernes** corners.
405 lete leave behind.
406 *Culpat . . . caro* 'The flesh sins, the flesh atones, the flesh of God reigns as God', from the hymn *Aeterne rex altissime*, sung on Ascension Day.
407 piped sang (suggesting bird-song after rain). **poisye** poetry (usually applied to Lat. in ME). ***Clarior . . . amor*** 'The sun is brighter than usual after the thickest mists, and love also is brighter after strife.' This couplet was current as a learned proverb in the Middle Ages: it is No. 2794 in H. Walter, *Proverbia Sententiaeque Latinitatis Medii Aevi* 6 vols (Göttingen 1963–9), with *nubila* 'clouds' in place of *nebula* 'mists' (?). The latter is ungrammatical, as *nebula* is fem., and also unmetrical.
408 shene bright.
410 lever more dear.
411 Love is spoken of as the lover of Pees at 168.
413 Love] ne love *L* etc. **and him liste** if he pleased.

'Trewes,' quod Treuthe, 'thou tellest us soth, by Jesus.
Clippe we in covenaunt, and uch of us cusse other.'
'And lete no peple,' quod Pees, 'perceive that we chidde,
For inpossible is no thing to him that is almighty.'
'Thou saist soth,' saide Rightwisnesse, and reverentliche hir kiste,
Pees, and Pees hir, *per saecula saeculorum.*
Misericordia et veritas obviaverunt sibi,
iustitia et pax osculatae sunt.
Treuthe tromped tho and song '*Te Deum laudamus*';
And thenne luted Love in a loude note,
'*Ecce quam bonum et quam iocundum etc.*'
Till the day dawed thise damaiseles daunced,
That men rongen to the resurrexioun, and right with that I waked,
And called Kitte my wif and Kalote my doughter:
'Ariseth and reverenceth Goddes resurrexioun
And crepeth to the cross on knees and kisseth it for a juwel.
For Goddes blissed body it bar for oure bote,
And it afereth the fende, for such is the might,
May no grisly gost glide there it shadweth.'

415 Trewes a truce!
416 'Let us embrace as a covenant, and each kiss the other.'
419–20 '. . . and reverently kissed Peace, and Peace kissed her, world without end', i.e. the reconciliation is eternal. ***Misericordia. . . sunt*** See 112–260 *n.*
421 tromped trumpeted. The Matins hymn *Te Deum* ('We praise Thee, O Lord . . .') is associated with the Harrowing of Hell in *Chester Cycle* p. 337 and *Towneley Plays* p. 305.
422 luted played on a lute. ***Ecce . . .*** 'Behold how good and how pleasant [it is for brethren to dwell together in unity]', *Ps.* 132.1 (A.V. 133.1).
424 The sound of Easter bells in the waking world combines with the music in Will's dream to awaken him.
425 *Kitte* (Katherine) is given as the name of Will's wife also at C 6.2. At C 8.304 the word is used generally for 'wife'. *Kalote* is a form of Colette (diminutive from Nichole), according to *Oxf. Dict. of Eng. Christian Names* s.v.; but the form with *a* in first syllable suggests *callot* (*MED* s.v.; *OED* s.v. *Callet*) 'a loose woman'; and three early-modern instances of the phrase 'Kit callot' or 'Kate callot' 'suggest strongly that her name at least is fictitious': see T. F. Mustanoja 'The suggestive use of Christian names in ME poetry' in *Utley Studies* 72–4.
427 'Creeping to the Cross' and kissing it were penitential exercises, practised chiefly on Good Friday.
428 bote benefit.
429 afereth frightens, alluding to the power of the Cross against spirits.

Geoffrey Chaucer

Life Born 1343 or 1344, son of John Chaucer, a wealthy London wine merchant. For immediate social background, see S. L. Thrupp *Merchant Class of Medieval London* (Univ. of Chicago P. 1948). Like other sons of prominent bourgeois, Chaucer was brought up as a gentleman in noble households—as page, 'valet', and esquire. Appears first in service of Countess of Ulster (1357) and of her husband, Lionel, third son of Edward III (1360). Captured by the French in 1360 and ransomed by Edward. In 1366 probably visited Spain, and married Philippa, damsel of the Queen's chamber. In 1367 first appears as a member of King Edward's household. *c.* 1369 *Book of the Duchess*, 'piteously complaining' the death of Blanche, wife of John of Gaunt, d. 1368. In 1372–73 visited Italy, negotiating with the Genoese and visiting Florence. 1374–86 living above gate of Aldgate, acting as Controller of petty custom and wool custom and subsidy in Port of London. In 1378 visited Italy again, negotiating with Barnabo Visconti 'god of delit and scourge of Lumbardye' (*C.T.* VII 2400). *c.* 1380 *House of Fame*; *c.* 1382 *Parlement of Foules*. *c.* 1382 started work on *Troilus*, completed *c.* 1386. 1385–89 Justice of the Peace for Kent, where he probably resided until 1399. 1386 represented Kent in House of Commons and (?) composed *Legend of Good Women*. *c.* 1387 started work on *Canterbury Tales*, unfinished at his death. 1389–91 Clerk of the King's Works. *c.* 1390–1400 forester of the royal forest at N. Petherton, Somerset. 1399 moved to a house adjoining the Lady Chapel of Westminster Abbey. 1400 died and was buried (like other courtiers and royal officials) in the Abbey. The documentary references to Chaucer are collected and interpreted in M. M. Crow and C. C. Olson *Chaucer Life-Records* (Oxford U.P. 1966). For a consecutive account, see D. S. Brewer *Chaucer* (3rd edn, Longman 1973); and for a historian's comments, F. R. H. du Boulay in Brewer, ed. *Geoffrey Chaucer* (Bell 1974) 33–57. For the courtly milieu, see G. Mathew *Court of Richard II* (Murray 1968). Documents illustrating the period generally in E. Rickert, ed. *Chaucer's World* (Columbia U.P. 1948).

Works and editions There is no major disagreement about the canon, thanks largely to Chaucer's own lists of his writings: *L.G.W.* G Prol. 405–20; *Introd. to Man of Law's T.*, *C.T.* II 45–89; *Retraction*, *C.T.* X 1085–8. Beside the four dream-poems, *Troilus* (No. 12 here), and *Canterbury Tales* (No. 18), he also wrote shorter poems (Nos. 13–17), some of which are lost. He translated Boethius *De consolatione philosophiae* and composed a *Treatise on the Astrolabe*. The newly discovered scientific treatise *The Equatorie of the Planetis* ed. D. J. Price (Cambridge U.P. 1955) has been claimed as his. The chronology of his work is doubtful in many particulars: see J. S. P. Tatlock *Development and Chronology of Chaucer's Works* (Chaucer Soc. 1907). The standard large edn is still that of W. W. Skeat, 6 vols (Oxford U.P. 1894), with apocrypha in Vol. 7 (1897). The standard single-volume complete edn is by F. N. Robinson (2nd edn, Oxford U.P. 1957). E. T. Donaldson, ed. *Chaucer's Poetry: an anthology for the modern reader* (New York, Ronald 1958) is notable for its advanced text and sophisticated critical discussions.

There is a Concordance, ed. J. S. P. Tatlock and A. G. Kennedy (Washington, Carnegie Institution 1927).

Reputation Chaucer's successful official career may have owed little to his literary genius; but his poems were read and admired by contemporaries such as Usk and Gower (who saw him as a 'philosophical' poet of love), and imitated by poets of the next generations (Hoccleve, Lydgate, James I of Scotland). The main tradition of C15 and C16 English and Scottish poetry (see Introd. pp. xv–xix) derives largely from him, especially *Troilus* and *Canterbury Tales*, but also *Parlement of Foules*, which influenced Spenser. In C17 Chaucer becomes a historical classic, studied in Speght's edn of 1598. His philosophical and courtly love ideas no longer command assent; and Dryden (*Preface to Fables* 1700) dwells most on the humanity and variety of *Canterbury Tales*. Chaucer emerges as primarily a comic poet in the Augustan period. Romantic critics (e.g. Leigh Hunt) appreciate the pathos which blends with his humour; but Matthew Arnold still finds him defective in 'high seriousness'. Discussions of Chaucer up to 1900 are gathered in C. F. E. Spurgeon, ed. *Five Hundred Years of Chaucer Criticism and Allusion 1357–1900* 3 vols (Cambridge U.P. 1925); and see J. A. Burrow, ed. *Geoffrey Chaucer: a critical anthology* (Penguin Books 1969). Cf. D. S. Brewer's discussion in Brewer, ed. *Chaucer and Chaucerians* (Nelson 1966) 240–70.

Twentieth-century Chaucer criticism, mostly academic in origin and historical in character, is indexed in D. D. Griffith, ed. *Bibliography of Chaucer 1908–1953* (Univ. of Washington P. 1955) and W. R. Crawford, ed. *Bibliography of Chaucer 1954–63* (Univ. of Washington P. 1967). Collections of modern criticism include E. C. Wagenknecht, ed. *Chaucer: modern essays in criticism* (New York, Oxford U.P. 1959), and R. J. Schoeck and J. Taylor, eds. *Chaucer Criticism* Vol. 1 *The Canterbury Tales* (Univ. of Notre Dame P. 1960), Vol. 2 *T & C and the Minor Poems* (Univ. of Notre Dame P. 1961). Useful surveys of modern work in B. Rowland, ed. *Companion to Chaucer Studies* (Toronto and Oxford U.P. 1968). Only four especially influential C20 books may be mentioned here: G. L. Kittredge *Chaucer and his Poetry* (Harvard U.P. 1915); C. S. Lewis *The Allegory of Love* (Oxford U.P. 1936); C. Muscatine *Chaucer and the French Tradition* (Univ. of California P. 1957); D. W. Robertson *A Preface to Chaucer* (Princeton U.P. 1963).

12 Troilus: extract

Chaucer narrates Troilus's 'double sorrow', in winning and losing Criseide, in five books: Bk 1 Troilus in love; Bk 2 approaches to Criseide; Bk 3 consummation; Bk 4 preparations for Criseide's departure; Bk 5 betrayal and death of Troilus. The five-book structure may derive from Boethius *De consolatione philosophiae:* McCall *MLQ* 23 (1962) 297–308; and/or from the five acts of Senecan tragedy: Norton-Smith *Chaucer* 162–9. The resulting structure is strikingly symmetrical: two books for the pains of winning Criseide, one for felicity, and two for the pains of losing her. The narrative method, like that of *Sir Gawain*, is markedly scenic, concentrating on certain chosen episodes and days, and passing summarily over the rest. The present extract from Bk 2, concerning the events of one 4 May, consists of a long scene between Criseide and Pandarus, followed by four short evening scenes:

Criseide's view of Troilus, her soliloquy, Antigone's song in the garden, Criseide's dream. On the evening scenes, see D. R. Howard in *Utley Studies* 173–92, especially his comments on the alternation of inner and outer influences on Criseide's mind.

The narrative method invites comparison with that of modern novels: see J. Speirs *Chaucer the Maker* (Faber 1951) and J. O. Bayley *The Characters of Love* (Constable 1960). Antithetical to this is the reading of *Troilus* as medieval 'tragedye' (Chaucer's own genre-word, 5.1786) in D. W. Robertson's *Preface to Chaucer* (Princeton U.P. 1963). He sees the whole poem as pervaded by ironies which, properly understood, anticipate the explicit condemnation of earthly love pronounced in the so-called Epilogue. Less severe expositions of these ironies may be found in I. L. Gordon *The Double Sorrow of Troilus* (Oxford U.P. 1970); see also T. P. Dunning 'God and Man in *T & C*', in N. Davis and C. L. Wrenn, eds. *English and Medieval Studies Presented to J. R. R. Tolkien* (Allen and Unwin 1962). A different historical approach relates the poem to the dominant French literary culture: see Lewis *Allegory of Love* Ch. 4 and Muscatine *Chaucer and the French Tradition* Ch. 5. Lewis sees the story as an elaborated example of courtly love, in the *Romance of the Rose* tradition. Muscatine stresses also the importance of 'bourgeois' French traditions, represented by Pandarus. But Pandarus, though he naturally does not share Troilus's romantic view of Criseide, is himself a servant of love (see lines 57–63 here). His freedom of speech does not mark him as 'uncourtly.' The sophisticated, courtly delicacy of the whole poem is well caught in Donaldson *Chaucer's Poetry* 965–80.

Troilus was widely admired and imitated by C15 and C16 courtly poets: see Stevens *Music and Poetry*. Caxton printed it in 1484; and Thynne included it, together with Henryson's *Testament* (No. 30 below), in his 1532 edn of Chaucer. Sir Philip Sidney wrote in his *Apology for Poetry*: 'Chaucer, undoubtedly, did excellently in his *Troilus and Criseide*; of whom, truly, I know not whether to marvel more, either that he in that misty time could see so clearly, or that we in this clear age walk so stumblingly after him.' Francis Kynaston translated it into Latin, to preserve it for posterity (first two books published 1635).

Metre 'Rhyme royal', decasyllabic lines rhyming *ababbcc*. Chaucer introduced this stanza into English poetry, probably from the French, where it was used as a stanza in ballades by Machaut and Deschamps. See Introd. pp. xviii–xix.

Sources The main source is Boccaccio's early poem *Il Filostrato* (*c.* 1335): ed. V. Branca in *Tutte le Opere di Giovanni Boccaccio* ed. Branca, Vol. 2 (Milan 1964). Eng. trans. in N. E. Griffin and A. B. Myrick *The Filostrato of Giovanni Boccaccio* (Univ. of Pennsylvania P. 1929), with Italian text parallel; and in R. K. Gordon *The Story of Troilus* (Dent 1934). Chaucer amplifies Boccaccio (5704 lines become 8239 lines), expanding some scenes (e.g. Pandarus's visit to Criseide, below 50–597) and adding others (e.g. Criseide's first sight of Troilus, below 610–93). He also changes the characters of the three main persons, notably that of Pandarus, who in Boccaccio is a young companion of Troilus and cousin of Criseide. Chaucer's Pandarus is Criseide's uncle; and both his humour and his sententiousness are new. The fullest study of Chaucer's treatment of *Filostrato* is S. B. Meech *Design in Chaucer's Troilus* (Syracuse U.P. 1959); and see C. S. Lewis *E & S* 17 (1932) 56–75.

R. A. Pratt *SP* 53 (1956) 509–39 shows that Chaucer probably used a French version of *Filostrato* as well as the Italian. He also collated other versions of the Troy story, notably the C12 *Roman de Troie* (Benoit de Sainte-Maure) and the *Historia destructionis Troiae* (Guido delle Colonne), both already used by Boccaccio. See generally K. Young *The Origin and Development of the Story of Troilus and Criseyde* (Chaucer Soc. 1908).

Chaucer drew on a wide range of other reading in *Troilus*: Boccaccio's *Teseida* (see *n.* to 50–6) and *Filocolo*; Petrarch (a sonnet translated at 1.400–20); Dante; Guillaume de Machaut (see *n.* to 827–75); *R. de la Rose*; Statius; and Ovid (see *n.* to 64–70). For philosophical material he drew especially on Boethius, although this aspect of *Troilus* is scarcely represented here (but see *n.* to 527–8).

Date A decisive *terminus ad quem* is provided by the beheading of Thomas Usk in 1388. In his *Testament of Love*, Bk 3 Ch. 4, Usk makes Love say: 'Mine owne trewe servaunt, the noble philosophical poete in English, which evermore him besieth and travaileth right sore my name to encrese . . . in a tretis that he made of my servant Troilus, hath this matter touched, and at the full this question assoiled', referring to Troilus's Boethian soliloquy on predestination, which Chaucer perhaps added in revision. The (revised?) *Troilus* was therefore available before 1388. Further, Ralph Strode, Oxford logician and London lawyer, and probably the 'philosophical Strode' to whom Chaucer 'directs' his poem (5.1857), died in 1387. *Terminus a quo* is less certain. If 1.171, 'Right as oure firste lettre is now an A', refers to Queen Anne, that line cannot be earlier than 1382, when Richard married her. Chaucer may well have started work on the poem in 1382 or 1383. 3.624–8 describes a rare conjunction of Saturn, Jupiter and Moon in Cancer, which occurred in 1385 for the first time since A.D. 769: see Root and Russell *PMLA* 39 (1924) 48–63 and J. D. North *RES* n.s. 20 (1969) 142–3. Despite O'Connor *JEGP* 55 (1956) 556–62, this suggests that Chaucer was working on Bk 3 around 1385. Conclusions cannot be definite. Chaucer perhaps started serious work on *Troilus* about 1382, and probably completed it about 1386.

Text R. K. Root, in his edn (Princeton U.P. 1926), lists 18 authorities: 16 MSS. and 2 early prints. Short extracts also occur frequently in MSS. The authorities exhibit the poem in a variety of states. Chaucer seems to have subjected his master-copy to much revision: minor verbal changes, re-writings of short passages, and occasional addition of new stanzas (notably Troilus's predestination speech, 4.953–1085, and the flight of his soul, 5.1807–27). See C. Owen, *MP* 55 (1957–8) 1–5 and *Robbins Studies* 303–19. After allowance has been made for scribal error, the MSS. seem to represent a frequently altered original. Three main states or 'versions' have been distinguished: α, the 'first version' (4 authorities in our extract), β (4 or 5 authorities here), and γ (7 or 8 authorities). The relative priority and merits of β and γ are disputed. Root (whose edn contains the fullest, but by no means complete, record of MS. variants) treats unique γ readings as scribal in origin; while F. N. Robinson *Works* p. xl (whose sigils I use) takes the same view of β readings. The present text is based on the excellent β MS., St John's Coll. Cambridge L.1 (= *J*). The extract shows signs of revision particularly from the beginning of Criseide's soliloquy (701ff.); and some examples of 'unrevised' readings are recorded in *nn.* to 110, 115, 478–9, 603, 734–5, 736–8,

761, 792, 908, 922. For an explanation of why *J*, a *β* MS., exhibits unrevised readings in places, see Root pp. lxxx–lxxxi.
Title Chaucer refers to 'the book of Troilus' (*Retraction*, *C.T.* X 1086) and 'Troilus' (*Adam Scriveyn* 2). In *L.G.W.* Cupid accuses Chaucer of being his foe: 'Hast thou nat mad in English ek the bok | How that Criseide Troilus forsok, | In shewing how that wemen han don mis?' (G Prol. 264–6). Lydgate was apparently the first to call the poem 'Troilus and Criseide'.

Book 2, lines 50–931

In May, that moder is of monthes glade,
That freshe floures, blewe and white and rede,
Ben quicke again that winter dede made,
And full of bawme is fleting every mede,
Whan Phebus doth his brighte bemes sprede
Right in the white Bole, it so betidde
As I shall singe, on Mayes day the thridde,

That Pandarus for all his wise speche
Felte eke his part of loves shotes kene,
That, coude he never so wele of loving preche,
It made his hew aday full ofte grene.
So shope it that him fell that day a tene
In love, for which in wo to bedde he wente
And made ere it was day full mony a wente.

50–6 This rhetorical headpiece recalls the description of May by Guillaume de Lorris (see English *Romaunt* 49–89); but the manner is that of Boccaccio's *Teseida* (e.g. 3.5–6), whose 'heightened time descriptions' Chaucer imitates throughout *Troilus*: cf. R. A. Pratt 'Chaucer's use of the *Teseida*' *PMLA* 62 (1947) 598–621, esp. 609–10.
53 'And every meadow is floating full of fragrance.'
54–5 The sun entered Taurus on 12 April, and on 3 May would be past the middle of the sign. The whiteness of the zodiacal Bull (cf. *Complaint of Mars* 86) derives from Virgil's description of spring, *Georg*. 1.217–8: 'Candidus auratis aperit cum cornibus annum | Taurus' ('When the snow-white Bull with gilded horns ushers in the year').
56 Another attack of love-sickness on 3 May is reported by Chaucer's contemporary J. Clanvowe: see line 55 of his *Boke of Cupide* (*Works* ed. Scattergood). McCall *MLN* 76 (1961) 201–5 compares Ovid's account in *Fasti* of the licentious festival of Flora, which culminated on 3 May. But 3 May appears in medieval lists of 'unlucky days', and may be so understood here, as in *Nun's Priest's T.* (*C.T.* VII 3187–97). For a different view, see J. D. North *RES* n.s. 20 (1969) 145–6, 441.
60 hew hue, complexion.
61 So shope it so it happened. **tene** grief.
62 in wo] for wo *J*.
63 wente turn (noun). Such punning rhyme was highly esteemed by French theorists: cf. 191/3, 813/5, 870/3, 898/900, 916/7. See *n.* to No. 19 below, lines 1263–4.

The swallow Proigne with a sorwfull lay,
Whan morwen com, gan make hir waymentinge
Why she forshapen was, and ever lay
Pandare abedde, half in a slomberinge,
Till she so neigh him made hir cheteringe
How Tereus gan forth hir suster take
That with the noise of hir he gan awake,

And gan to calle and dresse him up to rise,
Remembring him his erand was to done
Fro Troilus, and eke his grete emprise,
And caste and knew in good plit was the mone
To don viage, and took his way full sone
Unto his neces paleis there beside.
Now Janus, god of entré, thou him gide.

Whan he was come unto his neces place,
'Where is my lady?' to hir folk quod he;
And they him tolde, and he forth in gan pace,
And fond two other ladies sete and she
Withinne a paved parlour, and they three
Herden a maiden reden hem the geste
Of the sege of Thebes whil hem leste.

64–70 Procne was married to Tereus, who fell in love with her sister Philomela and raped her (69). After taking their revenge, the sisters were transformed into a swallow and a nightingale: Ovid *Met*. 6.412 ff. Chaucer also had Boccaccio (*Teseida* 4.73) and Dante (*Purg*. 9.13–5) in mind. The tragic story contrasts ominously with the spring setting: M. Mudrick, *Hudson Rev*. 10 (1957) 88–95.
65 waymentinge lamentations.
66 forshapen transformed.
71 dresse prepare (*J* reads *dressed*). **him** reflexive.
73 emprise undertaking.
74 caste calculated. **in good plit** in a favourable position. Certain phases of the moon were propitious for journeys: cf. *C.T.* II 306–15. See North 148 and Curry 254–5.
75 viage journey.
76 paleis mansion.
77 Janus The god of entrances (doorways and beginnings) has two faces – a hint at Pandarus's double-dealing with his niece?
82 paved parlour This living room, with its paved or tiled floor, is in keeping with the general grandeur of Criseide's establishment in Chaucer, by comparison with Boccaccio's heroine: Meech 197.
83 geste story.
84 The reference to the *sege of Thebes* recalls the beleaguered state of Troy itself (cf. 123) and also anticipates Cassandra's later account of the death of Tideus, father of Diomede, at the same siege (5.1457 ff.). See 100 *n*. **whil hem leste** for as long as it pleased them.

Quod Pandarus, 'Madame, God you see,
With all your book and all the compaignye.'
'Ey, uncle, now welcome ywis,' quod she,
And up she ros and by the honde in hye
She took him faste and saide, 'This night thrye,
To goode mot it torne, of you I mette.'
And with that word she down on bench him sette.

'Yea, nece, ye shall faren well the bet,
If God woll, all this yere,' quod Pandarus,
'Bot I am sory that I have you let
To herken of your book ye praisen thus.
For Goddes love, what saith it? tell it us,
Is it of love? O, som good ye me lere!'
'Uncle,' quod she, 'your maistresse is nat here.'

With that they gonnen laughe, and tho she seide:
'This romaunce is of Thebes that we rede,
And we han herd how that king Layus deide
Thurgh Edippus his sone, and all that dede,
And here we stinten at thise letteres rede
How the bishop, as the book can telle,
Amphiorax fill thurgh the ground to helle.'

86 So *J* etc. Text uncertain. The reading of γ MSS., 'With al yowre faire bok and al the companye', is hypermetrical; but Chaucer perhaps did introduce *faire* somehow in his master copy to strengthen the effusiveness of Pandarus's entrance.
88 in hye in haste.
89 This night thrye three times last night.
90 mot may. **mette** dreamed. To receive a visit from someone about whom one has dreamed may be lucky.
92 bet better.
93 God woll] good while *J*.
94 let prevented.
95 ye praisen thus which you evidently esteem so much (?).
97 lere teach.
100 romaunce suggests the C12 French *Roman de Thèbes*, as does the reference to *bishop* Amphiorax (105 *n.*); but *bookes twelve* (108 *n.*) points to Statius's *Thebaid*. The reader thus sees Criseide's book as both ancient and modern, like the rest of her world.
101–2 The death of Laius at the hands of Oedipus is narrated in the Fr. romance and alluded to by Statius.
101 that] the *J*.
103 stinten stopped. **letteres rede** rubricated letters, introducing the contents of the next section.
105 Amphiorax Amphiaraus, a soothsayer (or 'archbishop' in *Roman de Thèbes*) who died, as he predicted, at the siege of Thebes: he was swallowed up by the earth.

Quod Pandarus, 'All this knowe I myselve,
And all th'assege of Thebes and the care,
For herof ben there maked bookes twelve.
But lat be this, and tell me how ye fare.
Do way your wimpel and shewe your face bare;
Do way your book; ris up and lat us daunce,
And lat us don to May som observaunce.'

'I, God forbede!' quod she, 'be ye mad?
Is that a widwes lif, so God you save?
By God, ye maken me right sore adrad;
Ye ben so wilde, it semeth as ye rave.
It sate me well bet ay in a cave
To bidde and rede on holy saintes lives;
Lat maidens gon to daunce, and yonge wives.'

'As ever thrive I,' quod this Pandarus,
'Yit coude I telle a thing to do you pleye.'
'Now uncle dere,' quod she, 'tell it us,
For Goddes love; is then th'assege aweye?
I am of Grekes fered so that I deye.'
'Nay, nay,' quod he, 'as ever mot I thrive,
It is a thing well bet than swiche five.'

108 bookes twelve a clear allusion to the twelve books of Statius's Latin epic. Renoir *Stud. Neophil.* 32 (1960) 15 suggests that Pandarus is being superior about Criseide's less authoritative vernacular version; but see 100 *n*.
110 Do way put aside. **wimpel** a modest covering for head, chin and neck, worn by nuns (Prioress in *C.T.*) and widows (the Wife of Bath). *α* and *γ* MSS. read *barbe* 'a chin-band worn by widows'; but Chaucer apparently changed this to *wimpel* as in *J* and other MSS.
112 'The proper observance of May is to go into the fields and gather flowers and greenery, rather than to sit in a "paved parlour" and listen to the tale of *Thebes*' (Root).
113 I possibly a first-person pron. ('Me?'); but MS. variants *ey* and *eighe* suggest *MED Ei* interj: 'an exclamation of surprise'. Cf. *I* (128) and *Ey* (87).
115 By God ye maken me right] Ye make me by Jovis *α* MSS. (a classicizing reading, apparently removed in revision).
117–8 Widowhood was held to be a pious way of life second only to the celibacy of the cloister. Hence Criseide's shocked reaction. Her image of a widow's life recalls the traditional figure of the penitent Mary Magdalen: Kean 1.133. Robertson 483 refers to *1 Tim.* 5.5–6.
117 It sate me well bet it would be much more suitable for me. **a**] *J* omits.
118 bidde pray.
121 do you pleye *make* you enjoy yourself.
123 th'assege the besieging force.
124 fered so so afraid.
126 swiche five five such (events as the raising of the siege).

'Yea, holy God!' quod she, 'what thing is that?
What, bet than swiche five? I, nay ywis!
For all this world ne can I rede what
It sholde ben; som jape I trowe is this!
And but your selven telle us what it is,
My wit is for t'arede it all too lene.
As helpe me God, I not what ye mene.'

'And I your borugh, ne never shall for me
This thing be told to you, so mot I thrive.'
'And why so, uncle myn, why so?' quod she.
'By God,' quod he, 'that woll I telle as blive:
For prouder woman is there non o live,
And ye it wiste, in all the town of Troye.
I jape naught, so ever have I joye!'

Tho gan she wondren more than beforn
A thousand fold, and down hir eyen caste,
For never sith the time that she was born
To knowe thing desired she so faste;
And with a sik, she saide him at the laste:
'Now, uncle myn, I nill you nat displese
Nor axen more that may do you disese.'

So after this with many wordes glade
And frendly tales and with mery chere
Of this and that they playde and gonnen wade
In many an uncouth, glad and deep matere,
As frendes don whan they be met yfere,

128 I See 113 *n.*
129 rede guess, judge (also *arede* 132).
133 not do not know (*ne wot*).
134 And I your borugh I promise you. **for me**] α and γ MSS.; quod he *J* and other β MSS. The αγ reading is far stronger: 'if I have any say in the matter'.
137 as blive at once.
139 And if. **wiste** knew.
143 sith since.
145 sik sigh.
147 do you disese cause you distress.
149 tales conversational exchanges.
150–1 'They amused themselves with this and that, and entered into many an out-of-the-way, entertaining and intimate matter.' **uncouth** Do friends talk more about out-of-the-way matters than strangers? The dictionaries hardly allow Skeat's suggestion that *uncouth* is an adv. 'uncommonly' (cf. Scots *unco*, not recorded until C18).
152 yfere together.

Till she gan axen him how Ector ferde,
That was the townes wall and Grekes yerde.

'Full well, I thonke it God,' quod Pandarus,
'Save in his arme he hath a littel wounde,
And eke his freshe brother Troilus,
The wise, worthy Ector the secounde,
In whom that alle vertu list abounde,
As alle trouthe and alle gentilesse,
Wisdom, honour, fredom and worthynesse.'

'In good faith, em,' quod she, 'that liketh me;
They faren well, God save hem bothe two!
For trewliche I holde it gret deinté
A kinges sone in armes well to do
And be of good condicions therto.
For gret power and moral vertu here
Is selde yseye in o person yfere.'

'In good faith, that is soth,' quoth Pandarus,
'But by my trouthe, the king hath sones tweye,
That is to mene Ector and Troilus,
That certainly, though that I sholde deye,
They ben as voide of vices, dar I seye,
As any men that live under the sunne.
Her might is wide yknowe, and what they cunne.

'Of Ector nedeth no thing forto telle:
In all this world there nis a bettre knight
Than he that is of worthynesse welle;
And he well more vertu hath than might –
This knoweth many a wis and worthy wight.

153 ferde fared.
154 Grekes yerde rod to beat the Greeks.
159 that] *J* omits. **list abounde** pleases to abound.
160 gentilesse nobility.
161 fredom generosity.
162 em uncle. **liketh** pleases.
164 gret deinté a very excellent thing.
166 condicions character.
167–8 The maxim comes, via *R. de la Rose* 5630–2, from Lucan *Pharsalia* 8.494–5: 'virtus et summa potestas | non coeunt' ('virtue and supreme power do not go together'). **yseye** seen.
170 Pandarus corrects Criseide's reference to a single son (165).
175 cunne are capable of.
176 nedeth no thing there is no need.

The same pris of Troilus I seye.
God help me so, I knowe nat swiche tweye.'

'By God,' quod she, 'of Ector that is soth;
Of Troilus the same thing trowe I.
For dredeless men tellen that he doth
In armes day by day so worthily,
And bereth him here at home so gentilly
To every wight, that alle pris hath he
Of hem that me were levest praised be.'

'Ye saye right soth, ywis,' quod Pandarus,
'For yisterday whoso hadde with him ben
Mighte han wondred upon Troilus;
For never yit so thicke a swarm of ben
Ne fleigh, as Grekes fro him gonne flen;
And thurgh the feld in every wightes ere
There nas no crye but "Troilus is there!"

'Now here, now there, he hunted hem so faste
There nas but Grekes blood and Troilus.
Now him he hurte, and him all down he caste.
Ay where he wente it was arayed thus:
He was her deth, and sheld and lif for us,
That, as that day, there durste non withstonde
Whil that he held his blody swerd in honde.

'Therto he is the frendlieste man,
Of gret estat, that ever I say my live,
And where him list, best felawship can
To swich as him thinkth able forto thrive.'
And with that word tho Pandarus as blive
He took his leve and saide 'I woll gon henne.'
'Nay, blame have I, myn uncle,' quod she thenne.

181 pris praise.
182 God help me so] So helpe me god *J*.
184 trowe I I am ready to believe.
188–9 '. . . that he has nothing but praise from those whose praise I most value.'
193 ben bees. A proverbial simile: Whiting B167 and 177. See 63 *n*.
194 fleigh flew. **fro**] for *J*.
198 nas but was nothing but.
200 it was arayed thus this was the state of affairs.
205 my live in my life.
206–7 'And, where it pleases him, he shows the greatest friendliness to those who seem to him worthy to enjoy success.' See *MED* s.v. *Able* adj. 3.
207 swich] which *J*.
209 henne hence.

'What aileth you to be thus weery sone?
And namely of women woll ye so?
Nay, sitteth down. By God, I have to done
With you to speke of wisdom or ye go.'
And every wight that was aboute hem tho
That herde that, gan fer away to stonde
Whil they two hadde all that hem liste on honde.

Whan that her tale all brought was to an ende
Of hir estat and of hir governaunce,
Quod Pandarus, 'Now is time I wende;
But yit I saye, ariseth, lat us daunce,
And cast your widwes habit to meschaunce.
What list you thus your self to disfigure
Sith you is tid so glad an aventure?'

'A, well bethought, for love of God!' quod she,
'Shall I nat witen what ye mene of this?'
'No, this thing axeth leiser,' tho quod he,
'And eke me wolde muche greve ywis
If I it tolde and ye it toke amiss.
Yit were it bet my tonge forto stille
Than saye a soth that were ayain your wille.

'For nece, by the goddesse Minerve
And Jupiter that maketh the thonder ringe,
And by the blissful Venus that I serve,

212 namely especially: 'Will you of all people get quickly tired of a woman's company?' Pandarus is known as a ladies' man.
214 wisdom serious matters. **or** ere.
217 'While those two discussed whatever business they pleased.' **alle that hem liste]** al this matere *J*.
219 'About her position and the management of her affairs.' Since her father's defection to the Greeks, Criseide is dependent on the advice of friendly males in running her affairs.
220 I] to *J*.
221 I saye ariseth] ariseth I seye *J*.
222 habit weeds. Cf. 110.
223 What list you why do you choose.
224 you is tid there has happened to you.
226 witen know.
227 axeth leiser requires leisure.
230 stille hold in silence.
232 Minerve Pallas Athene. The celebration of her feast is the occasion on which Troilus first sees Criseide: 1.155 f.
234 Pandarus *serves* Venus because he is himself a lover: cf. 58.

Ye ben the woman in this world livinge,
Withouten paramours, to my witinge,
That I best love and lothest am to greve,
And that ye witen well your self, I leve.'

'Ywis, myn uncle,' quod she, 'graunt mercy.
Your frendshipe have I founden ever yit.
I am to no man holden, trewely,
So muche as you, and have so littel quit;
And with the grace of God, emforth my wit,
As in my gilt I shall you never offende;
And yif I have or this, I woll amende.

'But for the love of God I you beseche,
As ye ben he that I love most and triste,
Lat be to me your fremde maner speche,
And say to me, your nece, what you liste.'
And with that word hir uncle anon hir kiste
And saide, 'Gladly, leve nece dere;
Tak it for good that I shall say you here.'

With that she gan hir look down forto caste,
And Pandarus to coughe gan a lite
And saide, 'Nece, alway lo to the laste.
How so it be that som men hem delite
With subtil art her tales for t'endite,
Yit for all that in her entencioun
Her tale is all for som conclusioun.

236 Withouten paramours leaving (sexual) love out of account. **witinge** knowledge.
238 leve believe.
239 graunt mercy many thanks (later *gramercy*).
241 holden beholden.
242 quit repaid.
243 emforth my wit so far as I am capable.
248 fremde maner speche way of speaking like a stranger. Criseide recalls their blood-relationship: cf. *nece* 249, *uncle* 250. **fremde**] friende *J*.
254 to coughe gan a lite began to clear his throat a little.
255 alway lo to the laste ('lo alwey to the laste' in some MSS.) always look to the end (?). Perhaps proverbial, equivalent to Lat. proverb *Respice finem*. Cf. Whiting E84: 'Look at the end.' The interjection *lo* (OE *la*) becomes confused in ME with imperative forms of *look* (see *MED* s.v. *Lo* interj. 3). Editors take *lo* here as interjectional ('alway, lo, to the laste, | How so it be . . .'); but the resulting sentence is incoherent, unless one reads (with *J*) *to* for *at*.
257 her tales for t'endite to compose their speeches.
259 for som conclusioun directed towards some end.

'And sithen th'ende is every tales strengthe
And this matere is so behovely,
What sholde I pointe or drawen it on lengthe
To you that ben my frend so faithfully?'
And with that word he gan right inwardly
Beholden hir and loken on hir face,
And saide, 'On swich a mirour goode grace!'

Then thought he thus: 'If I my tale endite
Aught harde, or make a process any while,
She shall no savour han therin but lite
And trowe I wolde hir in my will begile –
For tendre wittes wenen all be wile
Where as they can nat plainly understonde –
Forthy hir wit to serven woll I fonde';

And loked on hir in avisé wise,
And she was war that he behelde hir so
And saide, 'Lorde, so faste ye m'avise!
Sey ye me never or now? What say ye? No?'
'Yis, yis,' quod he, 'and bet woll ere I go.
But, by my trouthe, I thoughte now yif ye
Be fortunate, for now men shall it see.

260 Cf. the proverb 'The last word binds the tale': Whiting W598.

261 behovely fit, seemly.

262 What why. **pointe** go into details (cf. *Troilus* 3.497). This reading of γ MSS. seems better than *peynte* (paint, decorate) found in *J* etc., though either is possible (cf. 424).

264 inwardly intently (*fiso* 'fixedly', *Filostrato* 2.35).

266 'Good luck to such a mirror.' The exact point of this, obviously flattering, remark is not clear.

268 process lengthy exposition.

269 'She will take little pleasure in that.'

270 trowe (she will) believe.

271 wenen all be wile think everything is a trick.

273 'Therefore I will try to adapt myself to her intelligence.'

274 avisé attentive: so MS. Hl^2, an α reading which was apparently corrupted in *J* and the majority of MSS. to the commoner but less apt *a bisy*.

276 m'avise scrutinize me.

277 Sey saw.

278 and bet woll ere I go i.e. I intend to go on looking at you: 'e di vedere intendo', *Filostrato* 2.36.

279–80 'But, by my faith, I was just wondering whether you were lucky – for now we must find that out.'

'For to every wight som goodly aventure
Som time is shape, if he it can receiven,
And if that he woll take of it no cure
Whan that it comth, but wilfully it weiven,
Lo, neither cas ne fortune him deceiven,
But right his owne slouthe and wrecchednesse;
And swich a wight is forto blame, I gesse.

'Good aventure, O bele nece, have ye
Full lightly founden, and ye conne it take;
And for the love of God and eke of me,
Cacche it anon, lest aventure slake.
What sholde I lenger process of it make?
Yif me your hond, for in this world is non,
If that you list, a wight so well begon.

'And sith I speke of good entencioun,
As I to you have told well here beforn,
And love as well your honour and renown
As creature in all this world yborn,
By alle the othes that I have you sworn,
And ye be wroth therfore, or wene I lie,
Ne shall I never see you eft with eye.

'Beth naught agast ne quaketh naught. Wherto?
Ne chaungeth naught for fere so your hewe,
For hardely the werste of this is do.
And though my tale as now be to you newe,
Yit trist alway ye shall me finde trewe –

281–7 Expanded from *Filostrato* 2.44.1–4: the most substantial borrowing from Boccaccio so far in this very freely handled scene.
281 aventure fortune.
282 shape prepared, destined.
283 cure care.
284 that] *J* omits. **weiven** forgo.
285 cas chance.
286 wrecchednesse baseness.
289 and if only.
290 of me] for me *J*.
291 lest aventure slake lest good fortune slacken.
292 process See 268 *n*.
294 well begon fortunate.
295 sith since.
300 And if.
304 hardely assuredly. **do** done, over.
305 my tale what I say.

And were it thing that me thought unsittinge,
To you wolde I non swiche tales bringe.'

'Now, my good em, for Goddes love I praye,'
Quod she, 'come off, and telle me what it is;
For bothe I am agast what ye woll saye
And eke me longeth it to wite, ywis;
For wheither it be well or be amiss,
Say on! lat me nat in this fere dwelle.'
'So will I don. Now herkeneth, I shall telle.

'Now, nece myn, the kinges dere sone,
The goode, wise, worthy, freshe and free,
Which alway forto do well is his wone,
The noble Troilus, so loveth thee
That, but ye helpe, it will his bane be.
Lo, here is all. What sholde I more seye?
Do what you list to make him live or deye.

'But yif ye late him deyen, I woll sterven –
Have here my trouthe, nece, I nill nat lien –
All sholde I with this knife my throte kerven.'
With that the teres bruste out of his eyen,
And saide, 'Yif that ye do us bothe dien
Thus gilteless, then han ye fished faire.
What mende ye if that we bothe apaire?

'Allas, he which that is my lorde so dere,
That trewe man, that noble, gentil knight,
That naught desireth but your frendly chere,
I see him deyen there he goth upright,
And hasteth him with all his fulle might

307 unsittinge unseemly.
310 come off come on (colloquial).
317 free generous.
318 Unusual placing of the relative clause before its noun emphasizes Pandarus's teasing delay in coming to the point. **wone** wont.
323 sterven die.
325 All sholde I even if I have to. Men commonly carried sheath-knives, for cutting food etc. Pandarus points to, or draws, his own, to frighten Criseide.
326 bruste burst.
328 '. . . then you have had a good day's fishing.'
329 What mende ye? What do you gain? *mende* 'improve' and *apaire* 'suffer harm' are antithetical.
332 frendly chere favour as a friend.
333 there he goth upright on his feet.

Forto be slain, if his fortune assente.
Allas, that God you swich a beauté sente!

'If it be so that ye so cruel be
That of his deth you liste nat to recche,
That is so trewe and worthy as we see,
Namore than of a japer or a wrecche,
Yif ye be swich, your beauté may not strecche
To make amendes of so cruel a dede.
Avisement is good before the nede.

'Wo worth the faire gemme vertuless!
Wo worth that herbe also that doth no boote!
Wo worth that beauté that is routheless!
Wo worth that wight that tret ich under foote!
And ye that ben of beauté crop and roote,
Yif therwithal in you there be no routhe,
Then is it harm ye liven, by my trouthe.

'And also thenk well that it is no gaude,
For me were lever thou and I and he
Were hanged than I sholde ben his baude,
Als hye as men might on us alle see.
Ich am thyn em: the shame were to me
As wele as thee, yif that I sholde assente
Thurgh myn abet that he thyn honour shente.

338 you liste nat to recche it pleases you not to care. **you liste**] ye listeth *J.*
340 japer joker (a lover who is not serious).
343 'It is good to take thought before the event requires it' (Donaldson). Proverbial: Whiting A62.
344 Wo worth woe betide (repeated as part of a rhetorical anaphora). **vertuless** i.e. without those natural powers or *virtues* (especially healing) ascribed to gems.
345 boote remedy. Again the reference is to healing wounds, as Criseide's pity might heal Troilus's love-wound.
346 routheless without compassion.
347 tret treads. **ich** everyone.
348 crop top.
349 there be] ne be *J.*
351 gaude joke.
352 thou Previously in this scene Pandarus and Criseide have addressed each other in their usual polite way as *you*, the only exception being 319. The cluster of intimate singular pronouns in this stanza strengthens Pandarus's appeal to family honour.
357 'That he should destroy (*shente*) your honour with my encouragement (*abet*).'

'Now understond, for I you naught requere
To binden you to him thurgh no beheste,
But only that ye make him bettre chere
Than ye have don or this, and more feste,
So that his lif be saved at the leste.
This all and som and plainly oure entente;
God help me so, I never other mente!

'Lo, this requeste is nat but skile, ywis,
Ne doute of resoun pardé is there non.
I sette the worste, that ye drede this:
Men wolde wondren seen him come and gon.
There ayains answere I thus anon:
That every wight, but he be fool of kinde,
Woll deme it love of frendshipe in his minde.

'What, who will demen, though he see a man
To temple gon, that he th'images eteth?
Thenk eke how well and wisly that he can
Governe himself that he no thing foryeteth,
That where he comth he pris and thonk him geteth.
And eke therto, he shall come here so selde,
What fors were it though all the town behelde?

'Swich love of frendes regneth all this town,
And wry you in that mantel ever mo;

359 beheste promise, vow.
361 more feste better welcome.
363 plainly fully.
365 nat but skile only reasonable.
366 doute of resoun reasonable fear. **pardé** by God.
367 sette assume.
368 seen to see.
370 'That every person, unless he is a born fool.'
371 love of frendshipe This phrase (cf. Lat. *amor amicitiae*), used in the English *Romaunt* to render Fr. *amitié*, simply means 'friendship', here as at 2.962. The ideal of friendship, as expounded in Cicero's *De amicitia*, was influential. Versions and perversions of friendship in *Troilus* are discussed by Gaylord, *Ch. R.* 3 (1969) 239–64.
375 foryeteth forgets, omits.
376 pris praise.
377 selde seldom.
378 What fors were it what would it matter.
379 Pandarus reverts to the first of his reassuring arguments, rather awkwardly. Was the previous st. (372–8) an afterthought? **regneth** prevails in (a sense recorded only here).
380 wry wrap.

And God so wis be my savacioun,
As I have said, your beste is to do so.
But, goode nece, alway to stinte his wo
So lat your daunger sucred ben a lite,
That of his deth ye be nat forto wite.'

Criseide, which that herde him in this wise,
Thoughte, 'I shall feelen what he mene, ywis.'
'Now, em,' quod she, 'what wolde ye devise?
What is your rede I sholde don of this?'
'That is well said,' quod he; 'certain, best is
That ye him love ayain for his lovinge,
As love for love is skilful guerdoninge.

'Thenk eke how elde wasteth every houre
In ech of you a partye of beauté;
And therfore, or that age thee devoure,
Go love; for olde, there will no wight of thee.
Lat this proverbe a lore unto you be:
"Too late ywar, quod Beauté whan it paste".
And elde daunteth daunger at the laste.

'The kinges fool is wont to cryen loude,
Whan him thinketh a woman berth hir hye:

381 wis surely.
382 to do so] for to do *J*.
383 stinte stop.
384 daunger standoffishness, reserve. Danger is one of the personifications hostile to the Lover in *R. de la Rose*: see Lewis *Allegory* 123–4. The term formed part of the special language of courtly love literature. **sucred** sugared over.
385 forto wite to blame.
387 feelen explore.
388 devise advise, suggest.
389 rede advice.
392 skilful guerdoninge a reasonable return.
393 elde old age. See discussion of this stanza in Empson 59–61.
394 ech of you i.e. all ladies. **partye** part.
396 'Go and love; for no one will want you when you are old.' Sing. *thee* (see *n.* to 352) here sounds bald and frightening.
397 lore lesson.
398 'Too late aware' was a proverbial phrase: cf. Gower *Confessio*, No. 19 below, line 1421. The full form of Pandarus's proverb is without parallel, but cf. 'Too late to grieve when the chance is past'. Pandarus uses many proverbs.
399 elde daunteth daunger age conquers reserve.
400 The tradition of the wise fool ('fool sage'), who tells lords unpalatable truths, was already established. On the medieval court fool, see E. Welsford *The Fool* (Faber 1935) Ch. 5.
401 berth hir hye conducts herself arrogantly.

"So longe mote ye live, and alle proude,
Till crowes feet be growe under your eye,
And sende you then a mirour in to prye,
In which that ye may see your face amorwe."
I bidde wishe you no more sorwe.'

With this he stinte and caste adown the hede,
And she began to breste awepe anon
And saide, 'Allas, for wo why nere I dede?
For of this world the faith is all agon.
Allas, what sholden straunge to me don,
Whan he that for my beste frende I wende
Ret me to love, and sholde it me defende?

'Allas, I wolde han trusted, douteless,
That yif that I thurgh my disaventure
Hadde loved outher him or Achilles,
Ector, or any mannes creature,
Ye nolde han had no mercy ne mesure
On me, but alway had me in repreve.
This false world, allas, who may it leve?

'What, is this all the joye and all the feste?
Is this your rede? Is this my blissful cas?
Is this the verray mede of your beheste?
Is all this painted process said, allas,

403 Till] To *J.* **crowes feet** First recorded instance of this vivid image. **be]** *J* omits.
404 prye look closely.
405 amorwe of a morning.
406 'I do not choose to wish any greater distress upon you': so Smithers *EGS* 1 (1947–8) 105–6. Pandarus thinks the Fool's threat of crow's feet should be enough for Criseide. Some MSS. add *Nece* at the beginning of the line. This makes clearer the ascription of the line to Pandarus, rather than to the Fool (so Root), but is metrically suspect.
408 breste awepe burst out weeping.
411 straunge strangers.
412 wende 'weened', took.
413 Ret advises. **defende** prohibit.
415 thurgh my disaventure through misfortune.
416 loved outher] outher loved *J.*
418 mesure moderation in judgment (commonly coupled with *mercy*).
419 repreve reproach.
420 See 794–8 *n*.
423 'Is this the true reward you promised me?'
424 painted process specious argument: cf. *process* 268, 292. On the 'Shakespearian' complexity of 421–5, see Empson 58–9, 62–3.

Right for this fin? O lady myn, Pallas,
Thou in this dredful cas for me purveye,
For so astoned am I that I deye.'

With that she gan full sorwfully to sike.
'A, may it be no bet?' quod Pandarus.
'By God, I shall no more come here this wike,
And God toforn! that am mistrusted thus.
I see wele that ye sette lite of us
Or of oure deth. Allas, I woful wrecche!
Might he yit live, of me were naught to recche.

'O cruel god, O despitouse Marte!
O furies three of helle, on you I crye!
So lat me never out of this hous departe
Yif that I mente harm or vileinye!
But sith I see my lorde mot nedes die,
And I with him, here I me shrive and seye
That wickedly ye don us bothe deye.

'But sith it liketh you that I be dede,
By Neptunus, that god is of the see,
Fro this forth shall I never ete brede
Till I myn owen herte blood may see;
For certain I woll deye als sone as he.'
And up he stirte and on his way he raughte
Till she again him by the lappe caughte.

425 fin end. **Pallas** See 232 *n.* Invoked here as a virgin goddess.

426 purveye provide.

428 she] he *J.* **sike** sigh.

431 And God toforn before God.

432 sette lite of us care little for us.

434 recche care.

435 Like other high-style elements in *Troilus* (50–6 *n.*), this invocation is borrowed not from *Filostrato* but from *Teseida*: 'O fiero Marte, o dispettoso iddio' (1.58). **despitouse** pitiless.

436 The three Furies are coupled with Mars again in 4.22–5, as in *Teseida* 3.1.

438 vileinye anything shameful (worthy of a *vilain*).

440–1 Pandarus, on the point of death, has nothing to confess but his niece's wickedness.

443 Neptune, having helped to build Troy and received no reward, works for the destruction of the city (cf. 4.120–6).

447 raughte started.

448 'Till she pulled him back by the sleeve.' Men wore long, flowing sleeves.

Criseida, which that well neigh starf for fere,
So as she was the ferfulleste wight
That mighte be, and herde eke with hir ere
And saugh the sorwful ernest of the knight,
And in his prayer eke saugh non unright,
And for the harm eke that might falle more,
She gan to rewe, and dredde hir wonder sore,

And thoughte thus: 'Unhappes fallen thicke
Alday for love and in such maner cas,
As men ben cruel in hemself and wicke;
And yif this man slee here himself, allas,
In my presence, it nill be no solas.
What men wolde of it deme I can nat saye;
It nedeth me full sleighly forto playe.'

And with a sorwful sik she saide thrye:
'A, lorde! what me is tid a sory chaunce!
For myn estat lith in a jupartye
And eke myn emes lif is in balaunce.
But natheless, with Goddes governaunce,
I shall so don, myn honour shall I kepe
And eke his lif' – and stinte forto wepe.

'Of harmes two the lesse is forto chese.
Yit have I levere maken him good chere
In honour, than myn emes lif to lese.
Ye sain ye no thing elles me requere?'

449 **starf** died.
450 **ferfulleste** most timorous – the most significant of the reasons offered in this breathless stanza for Criseide's taking pity on Troilus: see Lewis *Allegory* 185 f.
453 **eke saugh**] sey ek *J*.
455 **rewe** take pity. **dredde**] drede *J* etc. *J* may intend an infinitive, but writes *drede* for past tense at 482 and 874.
456 **Unhappes** misfortunes.
457 **Alday** all the time. **such maner cas** cases of that sort.
458 **wicke** perverse.
460 **solas** comfort (cf. 325, 437, 445).
462 **sleighly** circumspectly.
463 **thrye** three times ('A, lorde, lorde, lorde').
464 **is tid** has befallen.
465 'For my reputation is in some danger.'
470 **forto chese** the one to choose. Proverbial: Whiting E193. But Criseide believes she can avoid both *harmes*, loss of honour and uncle's death.
471 **have I levere** I would rather.

'No, wis,' quod he, 'myn owne nece dere.'
'Now well,' quod she, 'and I woll do my paine;
I shall myn herte ayain my lust constraine;

'But that I nill naught holden him in honde;
Ne love a man ne can I naught ne may
Ayains my wille; but elles will I fonde,
Myn honour sauf, plese him fro day to day.
Therto nolde I nat ones have said nay
But that I dredde, as in my fantasye.
But cesse cause, ay cesseth maladye.

'But here I make a protestacioun,
That in this process if ye depper go,
That certainly for no savacioun
Of you, though that ye sterven bothe two,
Though all the world on o day be my fo,
Ne shall I never of him han other routhe.'
'I graunte well,' quod Pandare, 'by my trouthe.

'But may I truste well to you,' quod he,
'That of this thing that ye han hight me here
Ye woll it holden trewely unto me?'
'Yea, douteless,' quod she, 'myn uncle dere.'
'Ne that I shall han cause in this matere,'
Quod he, 'to plaine, or ofter you to preche?'
'Why no, pardé.' What nedeth more speche?

474 wis indeed.
475 paine utmost.
476 lust inclination.
477 'Except that I do not wish to keep him in false hopes.' Criseide marks the limits of her concession: she will be nice to Troilus, but not love him.
478–9 In the first (α) version, Criseide states a generalization: 'Ne love a man that can no wight ne may | Ayeins his will.'
479 elles otherwise. **fonde** try.
480 Myn honour sauf saving always my honour. Absolute construction (Lat. *salva fide*): *OED* s.v. *Safe* a.5.
482 dredde was afraid. **fantasye** imagination, mind.
483 cesse cause once the cause ceases, rendering Lat. *cessante causa* in maxims like 'cessante causa, cessat effectus': see Whiting C121.
485 process business. **depper** deeper, further.
489 other routhe i.e. pity beyond that defined in 477–80. Criseide will not give Troilus her heart.
492 hight promised.
496 plaine complain.
497 What nedeth more speche? Some editors include this in Criseide's reply; but it sounds more like a narrator's tag (cf. 2.1541).

Tho fille they in other tales glade
Till at the laste, 'A, good em,' quod she tho,
'For his love which that us bothe made,
Tell me how first ye wisten of his wo.
Wot non of it but ye?' He saide 'No'.
'Can he well speke of love,' quod she, 'I preye?
Tell me, for I the bet me shall purveye.'

Tho Pandarus a littel gan to smile,
And saide, 'By my trouthe, I shall you telle.
This other day, nat gon full longe while,
Within the paleis gardin by a welle,
Gan he and I well half a day to dwelle
Right forto speken of an ordenaunce
How we the Grekes mighten disavaunce.

'Sone after that begonne we to lepe
And casten with oure dartes to and fro,
Till at the laste he saide he wolde slepe,
And on the gres adown he laide him tho;
And I afer gan romen to and fro,

498 'Then they fell into conversation on other cheerful matters.'
500 For his love] For love of god *J* etc.
501 wisten came to know.
502 Wot non does no one know.
503–4 'Love-talking' or 'dalliance' played an important part in the courtly love tradition: see Stevens *Music and Poetry* Ch. 9.
504 purveye prepare.
507–53 This episode, unlike that which Pandarus later recounts (554–74), was not described in Bk 1. Some critics have regarded it as a romantic invention of Pandarus: e.g. Hutson *MLN* 69 (1954) 468–70. See also Donaldson *Chaucer's Poetry* 972: '[The poem] even fails to distinguish clearly between real and illusory pressures exerted on Criseide: for instance, we do not know whether Pandarus' account of his discovering Troilus' love-sicknesses . . . is in the realm of fact or merely a charming invention with which to please Criseide.' But Chaucer, like Boccaccio whom he follows here (*Filostrato* 2.56–61), may simply be narrating his story 'artificially' (out of chronological order).
508 The well-spring (not in Boccaccio) perhaps derives from Guillaume de Lorris (see English *Romaunt* 1456 ff.), whose Garden of Love contains a well.
510 ordenaunce plan.
511 disavaunce set back.
512–3 The allusion is to some game of throwing spears or javelins, or weapon practice.
516 afer afar off. **gan]** gan for to *J*. **to and fro** A bad, identical rhyme, as against the good, punning rhymes of 62/3 etc. See 792 *n*.

Till that I herde, as that I welk allone,
How he began full wofully to grone.

'Tho gan I stalke him softely behinde,
And sikerly the sothe forto saine,
As I can clepe ayain now to my minde,
Right thus to Love he gan him forto plaine:
He saide, "Lorde, have routhe upon my paine;
All have I ben rebel in myn entente,
Now, *mea culpa*, lorde, I me repente.

' "O God, that at thy disposicioun
Ledest the fin, by juste purveiaunce,
Of every wight, my lowe confessioun
Accepte in gree, and sende me swich penaunce
As liketh thee; but from disesperaunce
That may my goste departe away fro thee
Thou be my sheld, for thy benignité.

' "For certes, lorde, so sore hath she me wounded,
That stood in black, with lokinge of hir eyen,
That to myn hertes botme it is ysounded,
Thurgh which I wot that I mot nedes dien.

517 welk walked.
519 stalke steal up. Lovers must be 'secret'; so it is difficult for others to learn of their love, unless they overhear a complaint by chance, as also in *Book of Duchess* 458 f. and *C.T.* I 1540 f. In these circumstances the lover is free of suspicion of 'avaunting' or boasting of his love.
520 sikerly for sure.
521 clepe call.
523 upon] on *J*.
525 *mea culpa* 'Mea culpa, mea culpa, mea maxima culpa' ('By my fault . . .') is part of the *Confiteor*. Troilus's complaint to Cupid takes the form of a deathbed confession. The three parts of the Sacrament of Penance are all present: contrition (525), confession (528) and satisfaction (*penaunce* 529). The 'sin' is that rebellion (524) against Cupid's rule described in Bk 1, where Troilus mocks lovers. The Lover's Confession, familiar from Gower, forms part of what Lewis calls the 'Religion of Love': *Allegory* 18–22, and cf. No. 24.3. here.
526 thy] *J* omits.
527–8 'Appointest the end for every man by just providence . . .' The devout language of Boethius (e.g. *De consolatione* 4 prose 6) is here applied to Cupid.
529 in gree graciously.
530–2 Again the Religion of Love. Despair (*disesperaunce*) may separate (*departe* transitive) a lover's soul (*goste*), like a Christian's, from his God.
534 black Troilus first sees Criseide in her widow's weeds (1.170).
535 ysounded penetrated, sunk. The lady's look wounds the lover, through his eyes, in his heart: cf. Chaucer's roundel, No. 15.1 below, and English *Romaunt* 1727–9.

This is the worste: I dar me naught bewrien;
And well the hotter ben the gledes rede
That men hem wrien with ashen pale and dede."

'With that he smot his hed adown anon
And gan to muttre, I noot what, trewely,
And I with that gan stille away to gon
And let therof as nothing wist hadde I,
And com again anon and stood him by
And saide, "Awake, ye slepen all too longe.
It semeth nat that love doth you longe,

'"That slepen so that no man may you wake.
Who sey ever or this so dull a man?"
"Yea, frend," quod he, "do ye youre hedes ake
For love, and lat me liven as I can."
But though that he for wo was pale and wan,
Yit made he tho as fresh a contenaunce
As though he sholde have led the newe daunce.

'This passed forth till now, this other day,
It fill that I com rominge all alone
Into his chaumbre and fond how that he lay
Upon his bed; but man so sore grone
Ne herde I never; and what that was his mone
Ne wiste I nat, for, as I was cominge,

537 bewrien reveal, make known.
538–9 Cf. Ovid *Met*. 4.64 'quoque magis tegitur, tectus magis aestuat ignis' ('the more the fire was covered up, the more it burned'), referring to the secret love of Pyramus and Thisbe (cf. *L.G.W.* 735–6). The maxim became proverbial.
538 gledes embers.
539 wrien cover (vren *J.*)
540 smot smote, lowered suddenly. The lowered head and muttered words suggest the confessional: 525 *n*. **his**] the *J.*
541 noot do not know.
543 let acted.
546 'It does not appear that love causes you any longing.' Lovers could not sleep: cf. 63.
548 sey saw. **dull** lethargic.
549 do make. Troilus addresses Pandarus and other lovers in his old mocking manner.
551 wo] love *J.*
552 'Yet he assumed then as lively a manner.'
553 'Leading the new dance' suggests the activities of a fashionable young man; but there may be some specific reference now lost.
554–74 This scene has already been described at length: 1.547–1064.
558 mone complaint.

All sodeinly he left his complaininge.

'Of which I took somwhat suspecioun,
And ner I com and fond he weped sore;
And God so wis be my savacioun
As never of thing hadde I no routhe more;
For neither with engin ne with no lore
Unethes might I fro the deth him kepe,
That yit fele I myn herte for him wepe.

'And God wot, never sith that I was born
Was I so besy no man forto preche,
Ne never was to wight so depe ysworn,
Or he me tolde who might ben his leche.
But now to you rehersen all his speche
Or alle his woful wordes forto soune
Ne bid me naught, but ye woll see me swoune.

'But forto save his lif, and elles nought,
And to non harm of you, thus am I driven;
And for the love of God that us hath wrought,
Swich chere him doth that he and I may liven.
Now have I plat to you myn herte yshriven,
And sith ye wot that myn entente is clene,
Tak hede therof, for I no ivel mene.

'And right good thrift I praye to God have ye,
That have swich oon ycaught withoute net;
And, be ye wis as ye be fair to see,
Well in the ring then is the ruby set.

563 so] *J* omits (corrector adds). **wis** surely.
565 engin craft, subtlety. *J* has *eggyng* 'urging', either an authentic reading, or a clever scribal correction. **lore** counsel.
566 Unethes hardly.
568 never sith that] that nevere sith *J*.
571 Or before. **leche** physician. The mistress is traditionally the one 'leech' who can heal her lover.
573 soune utter.
574 but ye woll unless you want to.
578 Swich chere him doth show him such favour.
579 plat flatly. **yshriven** confessed.
582 thrift success.
584–5 From *Filostrato* 2.43, 'Ben è la gemma posta nell' anello, | se tu sei savia come tu sei bella' ('well is the jewel set in the ring, if you are as wise as you are beautiful'); recalling scriptural comparisons between wisdom and jewels (*Job* 28.16–9). A sexual innuendo is to be understood. See Gordon *Double Sorrow* 136–7.
584 be ye] ye be *J*.
585 is the] is thi *J*.

There were never two so well ymet
Whan ye ben his all hool, as he is youre;
There mighty God yit graunte us see that houre.'

'Nay, therof spak I naught, a ha!' quod she,
'As help me God, ye shenden every dele.'
'A, mercy, dere nece,' anon quod he,
'What so I spak, I mente nat but wele,
By Mars, the god that helmed is of stele!
Now be nat wroth, my blood, my nece dere.'
'Now well,' quod she, 'foryeven be it here.'

With this he took his leve and home he wente,
And lorde! so he was glad and well begon.
Criseide aros, no lenger she ne stente,
But streght into hir closet wente anon
And sette hir down as stille as any ston,
And every word gan up and down to winde
That he had said, as it com hir to minde,

And was somdel astoned in hir thought
Right for the newe cas; but whan that she
Was full avised, tho fond she right nought
Of peril, why she ought afered be;
For man may love, of possibilité,
A woman so his herte may tobreste,
And she nat love ayain, but yif hir leste.

But as she sat allone and thoughte thus,

587 hool wholly.
588 There used in ME idiom to introduce wishes etc. **yit]** *J* omits.
589 a ha a ME interjection (other MSS. read 'ha ha') 'used to express indignant reproach or abhorrence in the sense "get out, away with you," etc.' Mustanoja 1.624.
590 ye shenden every dele you are spoiling everything.
598 stente lingered.
599 closet private room, boudoir. The meeting with Pandarus took place in the *parlour* (82 *n.*), with other ladies present.
603 was] wax ('grew') α MSS. **astoned** astonished.
605 Was full avised had fully considered the matter.
608 tobreste break. A MS. stroke after *so* indicates the line's structure.
609 hir leste it please her.
610–51 This episode of Troilus's triumphant re-entry into Troy is not in *Filostrato*. For an analysis of how Chaucer represents the 'drift and settling in [Criseide's] thoughts and feelings' in lines 596–931, see D. R. Howard in *Utley Studies* 173–92.

Ascry áros at scarmuch all withoute,
And men cride in the strete, 'See, Troilus
Hath right now put to flight the Grekes route!'
With that gan all hir meiné forto shoute:
'A, go we see! Caste up the yates wide,
For thurgh this strete he mot to paleis ride,

'For other way is fro the yate non
Of Dardanus, there open is the chaine.'
With that com he and all his folk anon
An esy pas, riding in routes twaine,
Right as his happy day was, soth to saine;
For which men saith, may nat distourbed be
That shall betiden of necessité.

This Troilus sat on his baye stede
All armed, save his hed, full richely,
And wounded was his hors and gan to blede,
On which he rode a pas full softely.
But swich a knightly sighte trewely
As was on him was nat, withoute faille,
To loke on Mars, that god is of bataille.

So lik a man of armes and a knight
He was to seen, fulfild of heigh prowesse;
For bothe he hadde a body and a might

611 The reference is to a battle-cry (*ascry*: 'A Troilus!'?), or a general clamour, at the end of a skirmish (*scarmuch*) in no man's land outside the city wall (*all withoute*). Troy, like Chaucer's London, is small; so Criseide hears the noise.
613 route band.
614 meiné household.
615 Caste up throw open (*OED* s.v. *Up* adv.[1] 16). **yates** probably the main gates leading from the courtyard of Criseide's mansion into the street, thrown open to allow her household to crowd out.
617 is] is ther *J*.
618 Dardanus One of the six gates of ancient Troy, named after an ancestor of Priam. **chaine** used as a barrier. Presumably only one gateway at a time would be unchained.
620 esy gentle.
621 happy fortunate (cf. 680–3). **was**] *J* omits (corr. adds).
622–3 So Boethius complains to Philosophy in Bk 5 of *De consolatione*; but Philosophy refutes his fatalism. A number of circumstances (Troilus's entry, Antigone's song, the nightingale) seem to conspire with Pandarus to make Criseide fall in love; but she is under no absolute necessity.
627 a pas at a walking pace.
629 As was on him as it was to look on him.

To don that thing, as well as hardinesse;
And eke to seen him in his gere him dresse,
So fresh, so yong, so worthy semed he
It was a hevene upon him forto see.

His helm tohewen was in twenty places,
That by a tessew heng his back behinde.
His sheld todashed was with swerdes and maces,
In which men mighten many an arwe finde
That thirled hadde horn and nerf and rinde.
And ay the peple cried, 'Here comth oure joye,
And, next his brother, holder up of Troye!'

For which he wex a littel red for shame,
Whan he the peple upon him herde crien,
That to beholde it was a noble game
How sobrely he caste down his eyen.
Criseida gan all his chere espien,
And let it so softe in hir herte sinke,
That to hirself she saide, 'Who yaf me drinke?'

For of hir owne thought she wex all red
Remembringe hir right thus: 'Lo, this is he
Which that myn uncle swerth he mot be ded
But I on him have mercy and pité.'
And with that thought, for pure ashamed, she

634 that thing i.e. deeds of prowess. **hardinesse** boldness of spirit.

635 him dresse bear himself, i.e. sit upright.

636 worthy] weldy ('vigorous') α and γ MSS. Chaucer apparently revised to the vaguer *worthy*. Why?

639 tessew band of rich material attaching the helmet to the back collar of the shirt of mail.

642 thirled pierced. **nerf** sinew. **rinde** hide, i.e. outer skin of shield.

645 wex grew. **shame** embarrassment.

649 chere appearance.

650 it] *J* omits (corr. adds).

651 'Who has given me a love-potion?' (Skeat). But the reference may simply be to an intoxicating drink.

652 Criseide's blush matches Troilus's. Cf. No. 18 below, line 111: a remarkable example of Chaucer reusing a line in a different context.

654 Which that] Swich as *J*.

656 thought] worde *J*. **for pure ashamed** for very shame. The construction, with preposition preceding a 'semi-substantivized' adjective or participle, is idiomatic: Mustanoja 1.381–2.

Gan in hir hed to pulle and that as faste,
Whil he and all the peple forby paste,

And gan to caste and rollen up and down
Withinne hir thought his excellent prowesse
And his estat, and also his renown,
His wit, his shap, and eke his gentilesse;
But most hir favour was for his destresse
Was all for hir, and thoughte it was a routhe
To slen swich oon, if that he mente trouthe.

Now mighte som envious jangle thus:
'This was a sodein love – how might it be
That she so lightly loved Troilus
Right for the firste sighte? Yea, pardé!'
Now whoso saith so, mot he never ythee!
For every thing a ginning hath it nede
Or all be wrought, withouten any drede.

For I say nat that she so sodeinly
Yaf him hir love, but that she gan encline
To like him first, and I have told you why;
And after that his manhed and his pine
Made love withinne hir forto mine;
For which, by process and by good servise
He gat hir love, and in no sodein wise.

And also blissful Venus well arrayed

657 It is characteristic of Chaucer's sometimes protective handling of Criseide that he did not show her in the undignified act of sticking her head out of the window, but attributed all the curiosity to her household.
658 forby paste passed on by.
659 caste consider.
663 for because.
665 mente trouthe had honourable intentions.
666 jangle raise a carping objection. Throughout *Troilus* Chaucer professes an anxiously defensive attitude towards his audience, who are assumed to be expert in the mysteries of love. For a general discussion of how Chaucer 'engages' his audience, see D. Mehl in *Robbins Studies* 173–89.
670 saith] seyde *J.* **mot he never ythee** may he never prosper.
671 'For everything must necessarily have a beginning.'
672 Or before. **drede** doubt.
673–9 Many of Chaucer's additions to Boccaccio in this part of the poem have the effect of slowing down the yielding of Criseide. On this passage see Donaldson *Chaucer's Poetry* 970.
676 pine suffering.
677 mine The image is from tunnelling at sieges.
680 blissful Venus is a fortunate planet.

Sat in hir seventhe hous of hevene tho,
Disposed wele, and with aspectes payed,
To helpen sely Troilus of his wo;
And soth to sain, she nas nat all a fo
To Troilus in his nativité –
God wot that well the sonner spedde he.

Now lat us stinte of Troilus a throwe
That rideth forth, and lat us torne faste
Unto Criseide, that heng hir hed full lowe,
Theras she sat allone, and gan to caste
Wheron she wolde apointe hir at the laste,
Yif it so were hir em ne wolde cesse
For Troilus upon hir forto presse.

And lorde, so she gan in hir thought argue
In this matere of which I have you told;
And what to don best were and what eschue,
That plited she full ofte in many fold.
Now was hir herte warm, now was it cold;
And what she thoughte somwhat shall I write,
As to myn auctour listeth for t'endite.

681 hous See *MED* s.v. *Hous* n. 6(b): 'One of the twelve divisions of the celestial sphere made by great circles passing through the north and south points of the horizon.' Cf. North *RES* n.s. 20 (1969) 137 and diagram in Curry 173. Planets revolve through all these 'mundane' houses once every 24 hours. The seventh house (*uxor*) is immediately above the W. horizon. Venus located in the W. is the evening star, which gives an appropriate time of day. See North 149 and *n.* to 898 below. Since the seventh house is specially connected with matters of love and marriage, the time when the fortunate planet Venus is in that house would be specially propitious for love-affairs.
682 Disposed wele propitiously situated. **with aspectes payed** with good aspects to Jupiter and Mercury: see North 148–9.
683 sely poor.
684–5 The reference here is to the situation of Venus at the moment of Troilus' birth, as distinct from that of his ride past Criseide's house.
686 sonner sooner. **spedde** prospered.
687 a throwe for a while.
691 'What she would decide upon in the end.'
694 And] A *J.* **thought]** herte *J.*
697 plited folded i.e. turned over in her mind.
700 'As it pleases my author [the authority I am following] to write.' In his account of Criseide's thoughts (701–812), Chaucer follows, but much amplifies and changes, *Filostrato* 2.69–78. From this point on (2.701–1113) Root finds evidence that Chaucer made an unusual number of revisions in individual lines (see his Introd. pp. lxxii–lxxiii and lxxx–lxxxi). I give some of the more interesting examples of 'unrevised' readings.

She thoughte first that Troilus persone
She knew by sight, and eke his gentilesse,
And thus she said: 'All were it nat to done
To graunte him love, yit for his worthinesse
It were honour with playe and with gladnesse
In honesté with swich a lorde to dele
For myn estat, and also for his hele.

'Eke well wot I my kinges sone is he,
And sith he hath to seen me swich delit
Yif I wolde outrely his sighte flee
Peraunter he mighte have me in despit,
Thurgh which I mighte stonde in worse plit.
Now were I wis me hate to purchace
Withoute nede, there I may stonde in grace?

'In every thing, I wot, there lith mesure;
For though a man forbede dronkenesse,
He naught forbet that every creature
Be drinkeless for alway, as I gesse.
Eke sith I wot for me is his destresse,
I ne oughte nat for that thing him despise,
Sith it is so he meneth in good wise.

'And eke I knowe of longe time agon
His thewes goode, and that he is nat nice,
N'avantour, saith men, certain he is non –

701–812 On the 'introspective monologue' as a feature of the courtly tradition (with emphasis on its non-naturalistic character), see Muscatine Ch. 2 and p. 158.
703 *J* has a different version of this line: 'And also thought it nere naught to doone.' **All were it nat to done** although it would not be right.
707 estat position. **hele** wellbeing.
710 outrely entirely.
711 Peraunter perhaps. **have me in despit** feel resentment towards me.
712 plit situation. Criseide is always aware of her situation as a woman whose father is a renegade and whose husband is dead.
713 purchace obtain.
715 'Moderation in all things.' Proverbial: Whiting M464.
716–8 From *R. de la Rose* 5714–6.
717 forbet i.e. commands (lit. 'forbids').
719 sith just because.
720 ne] *J* omits.
721 Sith it is] Yif it be *J*.
723 thewes qualities. **is]** nys *J*. **nice** foolish.
724 avantour braggart, one who boasts of his love conquests: see 519 *n*.

Too wis is he to don so gret a vice,
Ne als I nill him never so cherice
That he may make avaunt, by juste cause;
He shall me never binde in swich a clause.

'Now sette a cas: the hardest is, ywis,
Men mighten demen that he loveth me.
What dishonour were it unto me, this?
May ich him lette of that? Why, nay, pardé!
I knowe also, and alday heere and see,
Men loven women all beside her leve,
And whan hem list namore, lat hem leve.

'I think eke how he able is forto have
Of all this noble town the thriftieste
To ben his love, so she hir honour save;
For out and out he is the worthieste,
Save only Ector, which that is the beste;
And yit his lif all lith now in my cure –
But swich is love, and eke myn aventure.

'Ne me to love a wonder is it naught;
For well wot I myself, so God me spede,
(All wolde I that no man wiste of this thought)
I am oon the faireste, out of drede,

726 cherice show favour, encourage.
729 sette a cas assume a situation.
731 were it unto me] to myn estat is *J*.
732 lette hinder.
734–5 Six MSS. attest an unrevised version: 'Men lovyn wymmen al this toun about. | Be they the wors? Whi, nay, withoutyn dout.' The first line stands closer than the revised version to Boccaccio: 'I do not yet know of a single woman in this land without a lover' (*Filostrato* 2.70).
734 all beside her leve quite without their permission.
735 namore] no lengere *J*. **leve** leave off.
736–8 *J* and two other MSS. attest a more diffuse unrevised version: 'Ek wot I wel he worthy is to have | Of wommen in this world the thriftyeste, | As ferforth as she may hir honour save.'
737 thriftieste worthiest.
738 so provided that.
741 all lith] lith al *J*. **in my cure** under my care: Criseide is Troilus's 'physician'.
742 aventure good fortune.
745 All albeit. **this**] my *J*.
746 oon the faireste quite the most beautiful. *oon* intensifies the superlative in this idiom (unlike modern 'one of'): see Mustanoja 1.297–9. But *J* reads *oon of*. **drede** doubt.

And goodlieste, whoso taketh hede,
And so men sain, in all the town of Troye.
What wonder is though he of me have joye?

'I am myn owne woman, well at ese,
I thank it God, as after myn estat,
Right yong, and stonde unteid in lusty lese,
Withouten jalousye or swich debat.
Shall non housbande say to me "check mat!"
For either they ben full of jalousye,
Or maisterful, or loven novelrye.

'What shall I don? to what fin live I thus?
Shall I nat love, in cas if that me leste?
What, pardieux, I am nat religious!
And though that I myn herte sette at reste
Upon this knight, that is the worthieste,
And kepe alway myn honour and my name,
By alle right it may do me no shame.'

But right as whan the sunne shineth brighte,
In March that chaungeth ofte time his face,
And that a cloude is put with wind to flighte
Which oversprat the sunne as for a space,
A cloudy thought gan thurgh hir soule pace
That overspradde hir brighte thoughtes alle,
So that for fere almost she gan to falle.

That thought was this: 'Allas, sith I am free,
Sholde I now love and putte in jupartye

751 after] of *J*. **estat** station in life.
752 unteid in lusty lese untethered in rich pasture.
753 debat strife.
756 maisterful domineering. **novelrye** change.
757 fin end.
758 if] be *J*. **me leste** it please me.
759 religious A 'religious' is one bound by monastic vows; here, a nun.
760–3 Cf. *Filostrato* 2.69: 'If perhaps honour forbids me this, I will be prudent and keep my desire so hidden that it will not be known that I have ever had love in my heart.' Boccaccio's Criseida is generally franker and less romantic than Chaucer's.
761 Unrevised version in *J* etc: 'Unwist of him that is the worthyeste.'
763 By alle right by rights.
765 Cf. No. 23 line 62 and *n*.
766 put with wind to flighte driven along (*not* away) by a wind.
767 oversprat overspreads.
768 pace move.
772 jupartye jeopardy.

My sikernesse, and thrallen liberté?
Allas, how durste I thinke that folye?
May I nat well by other folk espye
Her dredful joye, her constrainte and her paine?
There loveth non that she nath why to plaine.

'For love is yit the moste stormy lif
Right of himself that ever was begunne;
For ever som mistrust or nice strif
There is in love: som cloude is over that sunne.
Therto we wrecched women no thing cunne,
Whan us is wo, but wepe and sitte and thinke;
Oure wreche is this, oure owne wo to drinke.

'Also thise wicked tonges ben so prest
To speke us harm. Eke men ben so untrewe
That right anon as cessed is her lest
So cesseth love, and forth to love a newe.
But harm ydon is don, whoso it rewe;
For though thise men for love hem first torende,
Full sharp beginninge breketh ofte at ende.

'How ofte time hath it yknowen be,
The tresoun that to women hath be do!

773 sikernesse security. **thrallen** enslave.

776 dredful joye The same oxymoron ('joy full of fear') is applied to love in *Parlement of Foules* 3. **constrainte** affliction.

777 'There is no woman in love who has not some reason to complain.' *why* is apparently used as a noun, but only 2 MSS. have this reading; 3 others rewrite, and the rest (including *J*) have *wey* ('way'? 'woe'??).

780 nice strif foolish conflict.

782 cunne can do.

784 wreche punishment. **drinke** The verb has the same unusual meaning ('to take suffering without bothering others') in *House of Fame* 1879–80: 'For what I drye or what I thinke, | I will myselven all hit drinke.'

785 wicked tonges gossips. 'Wicked-Tonge' in the English *Romaunt* 3027 etc. translates 'Male Bouche', the name of one of the Lover's chief adversaries in *R. de la Rose*. **prest** quick.

787 lest desire.

789 Proverbial: Whiting H134. **rewe** regret.

790 torende tear to pieces.

791 Proverbial: Whiting B201. **sharp** eager, enthusiastic.

792 Unrevised version, in *J* and 7 MSS: 'How ofte tyme may men rede and sen', revised to avoid identical rhyme: see 516 *n.*

To what fin is swich love I can nat see,
Or where becomth it whan it is ago.
There is no wight that wot, I trowe so,
Where it becomth. Lo, no wight on it sporneth.
That erst was no thing, into nought it torneth.

'How bisy, if I love, eke moste I be
To plesen hem that jangle of love and dremen,
And coye hem that they sain no harm of me.
For though there be no cause, yit hem semen
All be for harm that folk her frendes quemen.
And who may stoppen every wicked tonge,
Or soun of belles whil that they be ronge?'

And after that hir thought began to clere,
And saide, 'He which that no thing undertaketh
No thing acheveth, be him loth or dere.'
And with another thought hir herte quaketh:
Then slepeth hope, and after drede awaketh;
Now hot, now cold; but thus betwixen twaye
She rist hir up and went hir forto playe.

794–8 Gordon *Double Sorrow* 30 comments on 'the irony that gives this proof of the falsity of worldly happiness to the one who was to be the instrument of the proof in action.'

795 where becomth it where does it go to.

797 on it sporneth trips over it.

798 erst at first.

800 jangle gossip maliciously. **dremen** imagine things. 6 MSS. read *demen*: see 802–3 *n.*

801 coye hem keep them quiet.

802–3 yit . . . quemen 'Yet all things that people do to please their friends seem to these persons harmful' (Root). A crux. It is not easy to see the subject of plural verb *semen* in *all* ('all things' Root). *J* reads *they semen*, *Gg hem semeth*, neither convincingly. One would expect *they demen*. Perhaps Chaucer revised *demen* to *dremen* at 800 (see *n.*) to release the former for use here? But there is no sign of *demen* in MS. tradition here.

804–5 The sense 'clapper of a bell', recorded for *tongue* from C16, probably lies behind the comparison here.

806 clere clear up – resuming the meteorological metaphor of 764–9.

807–8 Proverbial: Whiting N146.

808 be him loth or dere whether he likes it or not.

810–11 Criseide's indecision sounds very like love, conventionally accompanied by rapid alternations between hope and fear, heat and cold, etc: cf. *C.T.* I 1528–39 and *Troilus* 5.1102: 'But often was his herte hoot and cold.'

812 rist rises. **went hir** goes (pres. tense). **hir]** *J* omits (corrector adds).

Adown the staire anon right tho she wente
Into the gardin with hir neces three,
And up and down they maden many a wente,
Flexippe and she, Tarbe and Antigoné,
To playen that it joye was to see;
And other of hir women a gret route
Hir folwed in the gardin all aboute.

This yerd was large, and railed all th'aleyes,
And shadwed well with blosmy bowes grene,
And benched newe and sonded all the weyes,
In which she walketh arm in arm betwene,
Till at the laste Antigoné the shene
Gan on a Troyan song to singen clere
That it a hevene was hir vois to here.

She saide: 'O Love, to whom I have and shall
Ben humble, subgit, trewe in myn entente,
As I best can, to you, lorde, yive I all

813 Adown] And doun *J.*
814 the] hir *J.*
815 wente turn.
816 They walk arm in arm (823) in pairs (but some MSS. omit the first *and*). The nieces are Chaucer's invention. The name *Antigone* is borrowed, as Prof. Fowler points out, from *Met.* 6.93–7, where Ovid tells the story of Antigone, Priam's sister, who was turned into a stork for contending with Juno. The sources of the other two names are unknown.
818 route company.
820 yerd garden. **railed all th'aleyes** all the paths railed off.
822 And benched] I benched *J.* The reference is to benches of earth, with plank or brick sides, topped with turf which would be renewed each spring: cf. *Floure and the Leafe* 50–1 and *n.* in D. A. Pearsall's edn (1962). **sonded** sanded.
824 shene bright.
825 song] lay *J.*
827–75 In 3.1737–71 Troilus, in a garden, sings a song in praise of love. The source of that episode, *Filostrato* 3.73–89, perhaps suggested the introduction of a corresponding woman's song here. The song itself is based on Guillaume de Machaut's *Paradis d'amour: Poésies lyriques* ed. V. Chichmaref (Paris 1909) 2.345–51. For the parallels (not very close) see Meech 439–40. Much of Antigone's song (esp. 862–75) harks back to, and answers, Criseide's doubts and fears (esp. 780–91): see Borthwick *MLQ* 22 (1961) 232–4. Gordon *Double Sorrow* 98–102 finds 'oblique allusions' to Boethian philosophy in the song.
828 subgit obedient.
829 you] whom *J.*

For ever mo myn hertes lust to rente;
For never yit thy grace no wight sente
So blissful cause as me my lif to lede
In alle joye and seurté, out of drede.

'Ye, blissful god, han me so well beset
In love, ywis, that all that bereth lif
Imaginen ne coude how to be bet;
For, lorde, withouten jalousye or strif
I love oon which that is most ententif
To serven well, unwery or unfeined,
That ever was, and leest with harm desteined,

'As he that is the welle of worthinesse,
Of trouthe ground, mirour of goodlihede,
Of wit Appollo, ston of sikernesse,
Of vertu roote, of lust finder and hede,
Thurgh which is alle sorwe fro me dede.
Ywis, I love him best, so doth he me;
Now good thrift have he, wherso that he be.

'Whom sholde I thonken but you, god of love,
Of all this blisse in which to bathe I ginne?
And thonked be thou, lorde, for that I love.
This is the righte lif that I am inne,
To flemen alle manere vice and sinne.
This doth me so to vertue for t'entende
That day by day I in my will amende.

'And whoso saith that forto love is vice
Or thraldom, though he feele in it destresse,

830 lust desire. **to rente** as payment due.
833 seurté security.
834 Ye] The *J*. **beset** placed.
837 or] and *J*.
838 that] *J* omits. **ententif** diligent.
839 unfeined without deceit (or 'without shirking'?).
840 desteined stained.
842 mirour ideal.
843 Appollo God of intelligence. **sikernesse** trustworthiness. *J* and other MSS. read *secre(t)nesse*.
844 hede head, originator.
847 thrift success.
852 flemen put to flight.
853 'This causes me so much to seek after virtue.'
856 The bearing of the concessive clause is quite unclear. In view of what follows, Antigone can hardly mean that the defamer of love nevertheless feels something of its pains. A hidden corruption in the text may be suspected.

He outher is envious or right nice,
Or is unmighty for his shrewednesse
To love; for swich manere folk, I gesse,
Defamen Love as no thing of him knowe.
They speken, but they benten never his bowe.

'What is the sunne wors of kinde right
Though that a man for feblesse of his eyen
May nat endure on it to see for bright?
Or love the wors though wrecches on it cryen?
No wele is worth, that may no sorwe dryen.
And forthy, who that hath a hed of verre,
Fro cast of stones war him in the werre.

'But I with all myn herte and all my might,
As I have said, woll love unto my laste
My deere herte and all myn owne knight,
In which myn herte growen is so faste,
And his in me, that it shall ever laste.
All dredde I first to love him to beginne,
Now wot I wele there is no peril inne.'

And of hir song right with that word she stente,
And therwithal, 'Now, nece,' quod Criseide,
'Who made this song now with so good entente?'
Antigoné answerde anon and saide:
'Madame, ywis, the goodlieste maide

857 outher either. **nice** silly.
858 unmighty incapable. **shrewednesse** wickedness.
859 for swich] lo wech *J*.
861 Cf. Whiting R156: 'Many men speak of Robin Hood that never bent his bow.' The witty application to Cupid the archer of the proverb about Robin was recognized by the scribe of MS. *Ph*, who notes 'of robyn hode'.
862 of kinde right in its proper nature.
864 it] him *J*. **for bright** because of its brightness: see 656 *n*.
866 'Who cannot endure sorrow deserves no joy' (Skeat). Proverbial: Whiting W143 (and W137).
867–8 'And so, if a man has a head of glass, let him beware of stones cast in battle', i.e. if a man wants to avoid the inevitable sorrows of love, let him stay away from it altogether. The reference is to stone balls thrown, especially at sieges, by engines of war. Proverbial: see Robinson's *n.* to *C.T.* VII 2372.
868 Fro] For *J*. **war]** wer *J*.
874 All dredde I although I was afraid.
876 stente ceased.
879 answerde anon] anon answerde *J*.

Of gret estat in all the town of Troye,
And let hir lif in most honour and joye.'

'Forsothe, so it semeth by hir song,'
Quod tho Criseide, and gan therwith to sike,
And saide, 'Lorde, is there swich blisse among
Thise loveres as they conne faire endite?'
'Yea, wis,' quod freshe Antigoné the white,
'For all the folk that han or ben on live
Ne conne well the blisse of love discrive.

'But wene ye that every wrecche wot
The parfit blisse of love? Why, nay, ywis!
They wenen all be love yif oon be hot.
Do way, do way, they wot no thing of this!
Men mosten axe at saintes yif it is
Aught fair in hevene – why? for they can telle –
And axen fendes is it foul in helle.'

Criseide unto that purpos naught answerde,
But saide, 'Ywis, it woll be night as faste.'
But every word which that she of hir herde
She gan to prenten in hir herte faste,
And ay gan love hir lasse for t'agaste
Than it dide erst, and sinken in hir herte,
That she wax somwhat able to converte.

882 let (one who) leads.

884 sike sigh. The assonantal rhyme with *endite* is remarkable. Skeat suggested a conjectural emendation to *site* 'grieve'; but this seems to be a non-London word.

886 endite describe.

887 Yea] Yis *J*. **wis** indeed. **white** fair. A poetic epithet for ladies; cf. 'White' in *Book of Duchess*. Imagery of light and dark is frequent in this book of *Troilus*. For whiteness, cf. 55, 908, 926.

889 discrive describe.

894 mosten axe must ask.

895 Aught at all.

897 unto that purpos naught] no thing ther to hir *J*.

898 as faste immediately. The coming of evening has already been suggested at 681: see *n*.

900 prenten imprint.

901 agaste frighten.

903 converte be converted. Again, the Religion of Love.

The dayes honour and the hevenes ye,
The nightes fo – all this clepe I the sunne –
Gan westren faste and downward forto wrye,
As he that hadde his dayes cours yrunne,
And white thinges wexen dimme and dunne
For lack of light, and sterres for t'apere,
That she and all hir folk in wente yfere.

So when it liked hir to gon to reste,
And voided weren tho that voiden oughte,
She saide that to slepen well hir leste.
Hir women sone unto hir bed hir broughte.
Whan all was hust, tho lay she stille and thoughte
Of all this thing the manere and the wise.
Reherse it nedeth naught, for ye ben wise.

A nightingale up on a cedre grene
Under the chaumber wall theras she lay
Full loude song ayain the moone shene
Paraunter in his briddes wise a lay
Of love, that made hir herte fresh and gay.
That herkened she so longe in good entente
Till at the laste the dede slepe hir hente;

904–9 Such periphrastic indications of time belong to the Latin rhetorical tradition: see Curtius 275–6. The humorous turn of the explanation in 905 is like *C.T.* V 1017–8. Curtius traces the tradition of joking about such periphrases back to Seneca, *Ep.* 122.11–13.
906 wrye turn.
908 dunne dun. The unrevised version gets less in: 'And white thinges gan to waxen donne' (*J* etc).
910 yfere together.
912 'And those had left the chamber who ought to have left.'
915 hust hushed.
917 Reherse repeat.
918–22 The nightingale singing to Criseide in her joy recalls and contrasts with the swallow singing to Pandarus at the beginning of the day. Recollections of the fate of Philomela, evoked at 69, perhaps shadow the idyll here: see Owen *Med. Stud.* 22 (1960) 366–70.
918 cedre The lofty and exotic cedar is the queen of trees, as the eagle (926) is the king of birds: see Trevisa in *OED* s.v. *Cedar*. Cedars (with laurels) were regarded as trees appropriate to high-style narratives concerned with kings and princes: see 'Virgil's wheel' in Faral 87.
920 ayain against, in the face of. **shene** bright.
922 Nightingales are universally associated with love in medieval poetry. The unrevised version (*J* and 4 MSS.) reads, 'Of love weche that made his herte gay'. But in the revision Criseide is referred to.
923 That] Hym *J*. **in good entente** attentively.
924 hente seized.

And as she slep, anonright tho hir mette
How that an egle, fethered white as bon,
Under hir brest his longe clawes sette
And out hir herte rente, and that anon,
And dide his herte in to hir brest to gon,
Of which she naught agros ne no thing smerte;
And forth he fleigh, with herte left for herte.

925–31 Criseide's dream of the eagle balances Troilus's nightmare of the boar (5.1234–41), from whose Italian original (*Filostrato* 7.23–4) Chaucer takes the idea of the painless tearing-out of a heart. See Meech 43–4 and Spearing *Criticism* 139–47.
925 anonright straight away. **tho**] ther *J.* **hir mette** she dreamed (impersonal verb).
926 The eagle, king of birds, represents the royal lover Troilus: cf. *Parlement of Foules*, where eagles represent aristocratic, or royal, lovers. **white as bon** white as a bone. A traditional simile, here powerfully used to suggest splendour, fleshless purity, and death.
929 dide caused.
930 'At which she felt no fear or pain at all.' Spearing *Criticism* 145 cites Freud: 'In a dream I may be in a horrible, dangerous and disgusting situation without feeling any fear or repulsion.'
931 fleigh flew. 'The garden, the song, the nightingale, and the dream, are all conventional medieval properties of love allegory, but Chaucer mingles them without effort in an atmosphere that seems as we read it as naturalistic as Chekhov's', J. O. Bayley *Characters of Love* (Constable 1960) 97.

13 To Rosemounde

The form is that of the ballade, as practised by Machaut and especially Deschamps in C14 France: French examples and discussion in Wilkins. Nos. 14 and 17 below are other Chaucerian ballades (No. 16 may be considered a double ballade). Cf. also two ballades by Charles d'Orléans (Nos. 24.1, 24.4). The form requires three stanzas (followed in Nos. 17 and 24 by an envoy) linked by refrain and normally by common rhymes also. See Friedman, *Med. Aev.* 27 (1958) 95–110. Chaucer, apparently the first to write ballades in English, favours either the eight-line '*Monk's Tale* stanza' (cf. No. 24.4) as here, rhyming *ababbcbc*, or the seven-line rhyme royal (Nos. 14 and 17), rhyming *ababbcc* – both used in ballades by Machaut and Deschamps. The need for twelve different *b*-rhymes on *-ounde* here leads to some unusual diction (*mapamounde* 2, *jocounde* 5, *affounde* 21). Each stanza divides sharply into two quatrains, linked by the *b*-rhyme. Like many French ballades, *Rosemounde* is a love poem; but the conventional courtly sentiments (simply to see the lady is an 'ointment' to love's wound, for example) are touched with humour, especially in the images at the beginning of the second and third stanzas.

Geoffrey Chaucer [13]

Text *Rosemounde* is attributed to Chaucer in the sole MS., Bodleian Rawlinson Poet. 163, where it follows *Troilus*. On text etc. see Kökeritz *MLN* 63 (1948) 310–18.

Ma dame, ye ben of all beauté shrine
As fer as cercled is the mapamounde,
For as the crystal glorious ye shine
And like ruby ben your chekes rounde.
Therwith ye ben so mery and so jocounde
That at a revel whan that I see you daunce
It is an oinement unto my wounde,
Though ye to me ne do no daliaunce.

For though I wepe of teres full a tine,
Yet may that wo myn herte nat confounde.
Your semy vois, that ye so small out-twine,
Maketh my thoght in joy and bliss habounde.
So curtaisly I go with love bounde
That to myself I say in my penaunce,
'Suffiseth me to love you, Rosemounde,
Though ye to me ne do no daliaunce.'

Nas never pik walwed in galauntine
As I in love am walwed and ywounde;
For which full ofte I of myself devine

1–2 All beauty is contained in Rosemounde like a saint in a reliquary (*shrine*), and all the world honours her.
1 Ma dame form of address to a mistress.
2 mapamounde *mappa mundi*. Medieval maps represent the earth (i.e. N. hemisphere) as a circle.
3–4 Reliquaries were often made of crystal, to display the relic, and adorned with precious stones (*L.G.W.* 672–4). Hence the conventional images of 'crystal' eyes and 'ruby' cheeks carry on the conceit of line 1.
7 See No. 15.1 lines 1–3 *n*.
8 do no daliaunce show no favour.
9 tine tub, vat. The hyperbole carries the tone into comedy.
11 semy thin i.e. low. **small** softly (fynall MS.). **out-twine** spin out, utter (suggesting threadlike delicacy).
13 curtaisly without churlish resentment, joyously.
15 Rosemounde No convincing identification has been proposed. The name suggests beauty and splendour by its associations (Fair Rosamond, mistress of Henry II) and supposed etymology (*rosa mundi* 'rose of the world', or *rosa munda* 'pure rose').
17 pik walwed in galauntine pike immersed (rolled) in galantine sauce. A medieval recipe (quoted by Skeat) directs that the thick sauce should be applied to both sides of the fish, 'that he be all yhid'.
19 devine believe *or* declare.

That I am trewe Tristam the secounde.
My love may not refreide nor affounde;
I brenne ay in an amorous plesaunce.
Do what you list, I will your thrall be founde,
Though ye to me ne do no daliaunce.

20 Tristam a type of devotion and fidelity in his love for Iseult.
21 refreide cool off (*be* inserted in MS. above line before *refreide*). **affounde** become exhausted.
22 brenne burn.

14 'Hide, Absolon, thy gilte tresses clere'

This ballade (see headnote to No. 13) is inset in the Prologue to Chaucer's *Legend of Good Women* (F version 249–69, G version 203–23). In F version the narrator sings it in praise of 'his lady', the queen Alceste, whom he sees in his dream in company with Cupid. In the (probably revised) version G, the song is sung like a carole by ladies dancing round the daisy, again in praise of the daisy-queen Alceste. The present text is based on Bodleian MS. Fairfax 16, one of seven MSS. attesting the F version. The G version is preserved only in Cambridge Univ. Libr. MS. Gg. 4. 27, from which main variants are recorded here. The F version probably dates from the mid 1380s.

Earlier French ballades of courtly devotion resemble this poem in using the eulogistic device of comparison with 'exemplary figures' (Curtius 59 ff., 362 ff.) from classical and biblical antiquity: e.g. the ballades by Machaut and Froissart, Nos 17 and 36 in Wilkins. But Chaucer's list of classical examples of fidelity and suffering in love (beginning with Lucretia, line 9) serves also to introduce heroines of the Legends which follow – 'good women' who, like Alceste herself, were ready to die for love. Prof. Fowler points out to me that the whole set of exemplary figures, together with Alceste, totals 21, which is also the number of lines of the poem, and that 21 is the number representing human perfection: Bungus *Numerorum mysteria* (Paris 1617) 434.

Hide, Absolon, thy gilte tresses clere;
Ester, lay thou thy mekenesse all adown;
Hide, Jonathas, all thy frendly manere;

1 Absolon 'But in all Israel there was not a man so comely, and so exceedingly beautiful as Absalom', 2 *Sam.* 14.25. Because of his long (traditionally golden) hair, Absalom became a type of female as well as male beauty: see Beichner *Med. Stud.* 12 (1950) 222–33, referring to the effeminate Absolon of *Miller's T.* (*C.T.* I 3312 f.).
2 Ester Esther, type of meekness also e.g. in *Merchant's T.* (*C.T.* IV 1744–5) as well as in ballades of Deschamps, because of the humility which found favour with K. Ahasuerus (*Esther*, *passim*).
3 Jonathas Jonathan, as type of friendship (1 *Sam.* 19), was coupled with Absalom, as type of beauty, in medieval moral verse, e.g. by Lydgate in No. 23 below, lines 69–71. Hence his rather surprising appearance here: see Beichner 228–9.

Penalopé and Marcia Catoun,
Make of your wifhod no comparisoun;
Hide ye your beautés, Ysoude and Eleyne:
My lady cometh that all this may disteine.

Thy faire body, lat it nat appere,
Lavyne; and thou Lucresse of Rome town
And Polixene, that boughten love so dere,
And Cleopatre with all thy passioun,
Hide ye your trouthe of love and your renown;
And thou Tisbé, that hast for love swich peine:
My lady cometh that all this may disteine.

Herro, Dido, Laudomia alle yfere,
And Phillis hanging for thy Demophoun,
And Canacé espied by thy chere,
Ysiphile betrayed with Jasoun,

4 Penalopé Penelope, faithful wife of Ulysses. **Marcia Catoun** 'Marcia Catonis', 'Cato's Marcia'. On Marcia, faithful wife of Cato of Utica, cf. Lucan *Pharsalia* 2.326 f. and Dante *Purg*. 1.78–87. See R. P. Hamilton *MP* 30 (1933) 361–4, with refs to earlier discussions.

6 Ysoude and Eleyne Iseult and Helen of Troy.

7 disteine make dim, outshine. Cf. lines following the ballade in F Prol. 274–5: 'For as the sunne wole the fir disteine, | So passeth all my lady sovereine.' The refrain is altered in *G*: 'Alceste is here that all that may desteine.'

9 Lavyne Lavinia, wife of Aeneas and heroine of the latter part of Virgil's *Aeneid*. **Lucresse** Lucretia, wife of Tarquinius Collatinus, committed suicide after being raped by Sextus Tarquinius: see her story in *L.G.W.* 1680–1885.

10 Polixene Polyxena, Priam's daughter, killed because of the love between her and Achilles. **boughten** plural verb: both Lucretia and Polyxena paid for their fidelity (*trouthe* 12) with their lives.

11 passioun martyrdom. The 'legend' of Cleopatra, Love's 'martyr', is in *L.G.W.* 580–705.

13 Tisbé Thisbe, who killed herself for love of Pyramus: *L.G.W.* 706–923.

15 All three heroines killed themselves for love: Hero for Leander, Dido for Aeneas, Laodamia for Protesilaus. Dido's story is in *L.G.W.* 924–1367. **yfere** together.

16 The story of the suicide of Phyllis after being deserted by Demophon is in *L.G.W.* 2394–561.

17 Canace's tragic love for her brother was first discovered, according to Ovid *Heroides* 11.25 f, by an old nurse who observed her pallor and thinness: so, 'Canace, detected by your appearance'.

18 The story of Hypsipyle, who died for love of Jason, occurs in *L.G.W.* 1396–1579.

Make of your trouthe neither boost ne soun,
Nor Ypermystre or Adriane, ye tweine:
My lady cometh that all this may disteine.

19 neither boost] in love no bost *G*.
20 Ypermystre Hypermnestra, punished for refusing to kill her husband, is the subject of the last, unfinished legend, *L.G.W.* 2562–723. **Adriane** Ariadne, abandoned on Naxos by Theseus: *L.G.W.* 1886–2227. **ye tweine**] ne pleyne *G*.

15 Two Roundels

Chaucer was apparently the first English poet to write roundels, in imitation of Fr. rondeaux. The rondeau was developed as a *forme fixe* (often set to music) by such C14 poets as Machaut and Froissart, and became especially popular in C15 France: see examples from Charles d'Orléans, Nos 24.2 and 24.3 below. The form (best discussed and illustrated by Wilkins) traditionally comprised four sections: refrain; new text + first part of refrain; new text; refrain. In Chaucer's *Parlement of Foules* 680–92 the birds sing a roundel to a tune 'made in France'. In *L.G.W.* F Prol. 422–3 Alceste says that Geoffrey has written many 'hymns' for Love's holidays, 'balades, roundels, virelayes'. Some are no doubt lost.

Three roundels (the second omitted here) appear only in Magdalene Coll. Cambridge MS. Pepys 2006, following a series of short Chaucer items (*Scogan*, *Balade de Bone Conseyl* etc.). Though not ascribed to Chaucer in the MS., they are almost certainly his. Who else could have written them? The three poems are treated as one in the Pepys MS. Index (where they are entitled *Merciles Beauté*) and modern editions; but they are formally unconnected. For comparison with Deschamps see J. L. Lowes *MLR* 5 (1910) 33–9. The second roundel (which must be later than 1389: see *n.* to line 1) exhibits a theme not uncommon in courtly verse: rebellion against Love.

15.1 'Your eyen two . . .'

Your eyen two woll slee me sodenly,
I may the beauté of hem not sustene,
So woundeth hit thurghout my herte kene.

1–3 The conceit of the 'wound' of love inflicted by the lady's eyes on the lover's heart had a basis in medieval physiology. Love was caused by an 'influence' emanating from the eyes and travelling to the heart: cf. *Knight's Tale*, *C.T.* I 1096–7.

1 eyen two] two yen MS. (but cf. 6, 10).

3 kene keenly.

And but your word woll helen hastily
My hertes wounde while that hit is grene,
Your eyen two woll slee me sodenly.

Upon my trouthe, I say you faithfully
That ye ben of my lif and deth the quene,
For with my deth the trouthe shall be sene.

Your eyen two woll slee me sodenly,
I may the beauté of hem not sustene,
So woundeth hit thurghout my herte kene.

4 but unless.
5 grene fresh (unmortified and therefore still curable).
6 Here and at line 10 the scribe (following common practice: Wilkins 136) abbreviates the refrain to 'Your yen etc'. Normal C14 usage requires the whole refrain at the end and the first part of the refrain here in the second section. Skeat and Robinson repeat lines 1 and 2 here; but a single-line refrain at this point makes the syntax more lively, esp. in No. 15.2.
9 trouthe truth of my condition (and 'my fidelity'? cf. 7).

15.2 'Syn I fro Love . . .'

Syn I fro Love escaped am so fat,
I never thenk to ben in his prison lene;
Syn I am free, I counte him not a bene.

He may answere and saye this and that;
I do no fors, I speke right as I mene,
Syn I fro Love escaped am so fat.

Love hath my name ystrike out of his sclat,
And he is strike out of my bokes clene
For evermo, there is non other mene.

1 A cynical ballade written in 1389 by the middle-aged Duc de Berry (Wilkins No. 45) provided Chaucer with this spirited opening: 'Puiz qu'à Amours suis si gras eschappé.' Chaucer (approaching 50, even if the Fr. ballade reached him at once) enjoyed alluding to his own stoutness: cf. No. 16 below, lines 27, 31. Lovers were supposed to become lean: 'Who loveth trewe hath no fatnesse' (*Romaunt of the Rose* 2686). **Syn** since.
2 thenk intend. **in his prison** Skeat smoothes the metre by omitting MS. *in*, supposing that a scribe failed to recognize ME *prison* 'prisoner'.
5 I do no fors I do not care at all.
6 Here and at line 10 the scribe abbreviates the refrain to 'Syn I fro love etc'. See *n.* to line 6 in No. 15.1.
7 sclat slate. Slates were much used for temporary records of all kinds. Did gaolers use them to list prisoners in their charge?
9 there] this MS. **mene** course of action.

Syn I fro Love escaped am so fat,
I never thenk to ben in his prison lene;
Syn I am free, I counte him not a bene.

16 Envoy to Scogan

'Envoy' here means 'missive', 'letter' (see title in MS. *Gg* below). The poem is a verse epistle in seven stanzas (perhaps significantly: see 3) of ordinary rhyme royal. 'The command of urbane conversational syntax and style, of sly and playful use of mythology, of structural indirection, together with the Horatian borrowing [see *n.* to 39], marks Chaucer out as the first English poet to master the essentials of the Augustan verse epistle' (Norton-Smith *Chaucer* 220). Chaucer approaches the last, 'begging', stanza obliquely, with abrupt, humorous changes of style (Kean 1.33–5). A. David *Ch. R.* 3 (1969) 265–74, stresses the moral strain in the poem, regarding it as a humorous variant of moral ballades such as No. 17; but *Scogan* is only loosely a (double) ballade. Its date is about 1393 (see *n.* to 14).

Text and attribution The poem is attributed to Chaucer in all three MSS: Bodleian MS. Fairfax 16 (= *F*), where it is headed 'Lenvoy de Chaucer a Scogan'; Magdalene Coll. Cambridge MS. Pepys 2006 (= *P*), with same heading; Cambridge Univ. Libr. MS. Gg. 4. 27 (= *Gg*), headed 'Litera directa de Scogon per G.C.' The present text is based on *F*.

Tobroken ben the statuts hye in hevene
That creat were eternally to dure,
Syn that I see the brighte goddes sevene
Mowe wepe and waile and passion endure
As may in erthe a mortal creature.
Allas, fro whennes may this thing procede,
Of which errour I deie almost for drede?

By word eterne whilom was yshape
That fro the fifte cercle in no manere
Ne mighte a drope of teres down escape;

1 Tobroken shattered (*to-* is intensive). Inversion of subject and verb contributes to the mock heroic style of the opening, as does the order adj–noun–adj in 3.
3 Syn that since. **goddes** the seven planetary deities.
4 Mowe may. **passion endure** suffer emotion; also perhaps 'suffer themselves to be acted upon' (*passion* = passivity)? Divine *statut* decrees that everything beyond the moon's sphere should be impassible and unchanging, unlike sublunary, *mortal* creatures (5).
7 errour aberration. **deie** die.
8 yshape decreed (it shape *Gg P*).
9 fifte cercle sphere of Venus (fifth of the seven planetary spheres in the Ptolemaic system, counting inwards).

But now so wepeth Venus in hir spere
That with hir teres she woll drenche us here.
Allas, Scogan, this is for thyn offence,
Thou causest this diluge of pestilence.

Hastow not said in blaspheme of the goddis,
Thurgh pride or thurgh thy grete rakelnesse,
Swich thing as in the lawe of love forbode is –
That for thy lady saw not thy distresse,
Therfore thou yave hir up at Michelmesse?
Allas, Scogan, of olde folk ne yonge
Was never erst Scogan blamed for his tonge.

Thou drowe in scorn Cupide eke to record
Of thilke rebel word that thou hast spoken,
For which he woll no lenger be thy lord;
And, Scogan, though his bowe be not broken,
He woll nat with his arwes ben ywroken
On thee, ne me, ne non of oure figure;
We shull of hem have neither hurt ne cure.

11 Rain-storms were commonly ascribed to planetary influence; but the identification of rain with Venus' tears (cf. *Knight's Tale C.T.* I 2666) seems more like a courtly fancy. **spere** sphere.
12 drenche drown.
13 Scogan Henry Scogan (1361 ?–1407) was himself a poet. As tutor to Henry IV's sons, he addressed to them a poem in which he speaks of Chaucer as his master and quotes his *Gentilesse*. **thyn** The singular pronoun (as against more formal *you*) reinforces the intimate tone throughout.
14 diluge of pestilence pestilential deluge: perhaps alluding to the great storms and pestilences of 1393.
15 the goddis] *Gg P*; this goddis *F* (i.e. Venus).
16 rakelnesse rashness.
17 forbode forbidden.
18–19 The *lawe of love* demanded eternal constancy, however pitiless the mistress.
19 Michelmesse Michaelmas, a quarterday, at which property might be given up.
21 erst previously.
22 'You also contemptuously called on Cupid as your witness.' **drowe** drew.
23 thilke that same.
25 his] *Gg P*; thy *F*.
26 ywroken revenged.
27 oure] *Gg P*; youre *F*. **figure** shape, appearance: compare 31 and No. 15.2 line 1 and *n*.
28 hem] *P*; him *F Gg*. But it is Cupid's arrows that can cure as well as hurt: English *Romaunt* 1885–1926.

Now certes, frend, I drede of thyn unhap,
Lest for thy gilt the wreche of Love procede
On alle hem that ben hore and rounde of shap,
That ben so likly folk in love to spede;
Then shall we for oure labour han no mede.
But well I wot thou wolt answere and saye,
'Lo, olde Grisel list to ryme and playe!'

Nay, Scogan, say not so, for I m'excuse:
God helpe me so, in no ryme doutelees
Ne thinke I never of slep to wake my muse,
That rusteth in my shethe stille in pees.
While I was yong, I put it forth in prees;
But all shall passe that men prose or ryme;
Take every man his turn, as for his time.

Scogan, that knelest at the stremes hed
Of grace, of all honour and worthinesse,

29 unhap misfortune.

30 wreche vengeance. Cupid will not use his arrows (26). Perhaps he may ensure that Scogan and other middle-aged poets (like Chaucer) will fail when they try to help others to success in love by their compositions. The poets will then get no rewards.

31 hore grey.

32 Probably: 'Who are so well qualified to help lovers to success.' Otherwise: 'Who are people so well qualified to succeed in love.' But the irony of the latter seems rather pointless here.

33 mede reward. See 30 *n*.

35 olde] *Gg P*; tholde *F*. 'You see, old Greyhair likes writing verse and amusing himself' – Scogan's imagined way of dismissing the previous stanzas. Grisel was a horse-name: cf. *Confessio* 8.2407.

36 m'excuse declare myself innocent.

38 of from. **muse** The word is first recorded in English in Chaucer; cf. *Troilus* 2.9. Gower also speaks of '*my* muse', as here: *Confessio* 8.3140.

39 The image of the pen as a weapon laid aside and rusting seems to come from Horace *Sat*. 2.1.39–44: see Norton-Smith *Chaucer* 216–18.

40 it] *F Gg*; her *P*. **in prees** in the crowd, i.e. in open competition.

43 stremes hed] *F P*; wellis hed *Gg*. The MSS. write 'Wyndesore' against this line and 'Grenewich' against 45. Chaucer, who was living at Greenwich at the time of composition, sent his letter to Scogan, who was with the court at Windsor, upstream from Greenwich. The *streme* is both literal and metaphorical.

In th'end of which strem I am dull as ded,
Forgete in solitarye wildernesse,
Yet, Scogan, thenke on Tullius kindnesse:
Minne thy frend there it may fructifye.
Farewell, and loke thou never eft Love defye.

45 ded death. An unusual form in Chaucer, perhaps used for rhyme. Or did he write *dull as led* (Whiting L121)?
46 Forgete forgotten.
47 Tullius Cicero's. Referring to the well-known treatise on true friendship, *De amicitia*.
48 'Take thought of (*Minne*) your friend, in a place where it [the thought] can bear fruit.' Chaucer asks Scogan to put in a good word for him where it will count. Scogan was a member of Richard II's household.
49 eft again.

17 Balade de Bone Conseyl

This poem (otherwise known as *Truth*) is a ballade (see headnote to No. 13) in rhyme royal. The fourth stanza corresponds to the envoy introduced into the French ballade at the time of Deschamps, whose moral ballades were Chaucer's chief model; but Chaucer was the first to use the same stanza form for envoy as for the rest. In the first three stanzas, abrupt, paratactic syntax (contrasting with the smooth periodic syntax of the envoy) and elliptical expression combine to produce a grave, proverbial effect. The pseudo-proverbs appealed to later poets: cf. Lydgate's imitations (Whiting C553, P369, P377). Chaucer's main sources were the Bible, Boethius (see B. L. Jefferson *Chaucer and the Consolation of Philosophy* (Princeton U.P. 1917) 104–19) and Seneca. Kean 1.38–42 shows that the combination of pithy style and stoic sentiment points specially to the *Moral Essays* of Seneca. Du Boulay, in Brewer *Geoffrey Chaucer* 46–7, identifies the religious feeling as 'orthodox evangelical', the kind of feeling which, in several of Chaucer's associates, shaded off into Lollardry: see *n.* to 22. The tradition that Chaucer composed the poem on his deathbed goes back to C15, but is suspect. A more likely date is the late 1380s: see *n.* to 22.

Text and attribution This was the most popular of Chaucer's shorter poems, on MS. evidence: 22 survive (2 with two copies each; so 24 MS. copies). Considerable variations appear in the text, some apparently going back to Chaucer's revisions (e.g. 2, 6, 7). The present text is based (with correction of non-Chaucerian forms) on Cambridge Univ. Libr. MS. Gg. 4. 27 (= *Gg*), except for the last stanza, which is found only in B.L. MS. Additional 10340. The poem is attributed to Chaucer in 10 MSS. Its common title, *Truth*, is C19. I have preferred that of *Gg*, which finds support in 10 MSS. and defines the poem exactly: as a ballade of good counsel.

[17] Geoffrey Chaucer

Flee from the press and dwelle with sothfastnesse.
Suffise unto thy thing though it be small,
For hord hath hate, and climbing tikelnesse,
Press hath envye, and wele blent overall.
Savour no more than thee behove shall.
Werke well thyself, that other folk canst rede,
And trouthe shall delivere, it is no drede.

Tempest thee nought all croked to redresse
In trust of hir that turneth as a ball,
Gret reste stant in littel bisinesse.
And eke be war to sporne agains an all,
Strive not as doth the crocke with the wall.
Daunte thyself, that dauntest otheres dede,
And trouthe shall delivere, it is no drede.

1 press throng (at court?). **sothfastnesse** half-personified, like its synonym *trouthe* in the refrain.
2 Source and explanation for this line lie in a pseudo-Senecan saying quoted by Gower in a marginal note to *Confessio* 5.7735–9 (see Macaulay's note there for its source): 'Si res tuae tibi non sufficiant, fac ut rebus tuis sufficias', 'If your things do not suffice you, see to it that you suffice your things'. 17 MS. copies have *good* 'possessions' for the laconic *thing*, possibly representing Chaucer's own second thought. 3 MSS., boggling at the odd use of *suffise*, read 'suffise thee thy good' etc. See No. 19 below, lines 1128–9 and *n*.
3 hord hath hate Cf. Chaucer's *Boece* Bk 2 prose 5 lines 15–6: 'For avarice maketh alway mokereres [hoarders] to ben hated.' **tikelnesse** unsteadiness.
4 wele blent overall prosperity everywhere makes men blind.
5 'Have an appetite for no more than is your due.'
6 Werke] *Gg*+4 MSS.; do 10 MSS.; reule 7 MSS.; rede 2 MSS. *reule* may be Chaucerian – perhaps a revision? – but it duplicates *daunte* 13. **rede** counsel, give advice to.
7 Cf. *John* 8.32 'veritas liberabit vos' ('the truth shall make you free'). Apart from *Gg*+3 MSS., all other copies show a pronoun in the refrain: 'thee shall deliver', or 'shall thee deliver'. This is metrically superfluous (*trouthe* has 2 syllables) but may be a Chaucerian variant.
8 Tempest thee nought do not work yourself up. Sixteen copies have *peyne* for the unusual *tempest*.
9 Fortune is commonly associated with a turning sphere.
10 stant stands, resides.
11 sporne kick. **all** awl (piercing tool used by shoemakers etc). The phrase is a variant, for rhyme, of biblical and proverbial 'kick against the pricks' (*Acts* 9.5).
12 crocke pot. A fable about an earthenware pot rashly assaulting a wall seems to be implied by this line; but it is not in Aesop. Cf. *Ecclesiasticus* 13.3.
13 Daunte subdue, control.

That thee is sent, receive in buxomnesse,
The wrastling for this world axeth a fall.
Here nis non home, here nis but wildernesse.
Forth, pilgrim, forth! forth, beste, out of thy stall!
Knowe thy contré, loke up, thank God of all,
Hold the hye way and lat thy gost thee lede,
And trouthe shall delivere, it is no drede.

Therefore, thou Vache, leve thyn old wrecchednesse,
Unto the world leve now to be thrall;
Crye him mercy that of his hye goodnesse
Made thee of nought, and in especial
Drawe unto him and pray in general
For thee and eke for other hevenlich mede,
And trouthe shall delivere, it is no drede.

15 That what. **in buxomnesse** submissively.

16 for] *Gg*+3 MSS.; of 16 MSS.; with 4 MSS. **axeth** asks for.

17–20 Commonplace ideas. Man in the world is an exile from heaven, his true home (*Boece* Bk 1 prose 5). Like the people of Israel, he is a wanderer in the wilderness. His life should be a pilgrimage to God (*Heb.* 11.13).

18 beste beast. See 22 *n.*

19 Knowe thy contré loke up] *Gg*+6 MSS.; Loke up on hye and 15 MSS. **loke up** Only man, according to Boethius (Bk 5 metre 5), naturally carries his head erect. Beasts (cf. 18) hang their heads and gaze at the ground. Cf. Ovid *Met.* 1.84–6.

20 Hold the hye way] *Gg*+6 MSS.; Weyve thy lust 13 MSS. (*weyve* 'set aside'). **gost** spirit.

22 thou Vache Sir Philip de la Vache, a near-contemporary (1346–1408) of Chaucer and son-in-law of Chaucer's friend Clifford, was a country gentleman who suffered eclipse at court during the same period (1386–89) as Chaucer, and perhaps for the same reason (the disfavour of Gloucester). This poem may date from that period: E. Rickert *MP* 11 (1913–14) 209–25. The form of address, with pronoun, suggests word play on Fr. *vache* 'cow', which would link up with the *beste* of 18. K. B. McFarlane shows that de la Vache was associated with the 'Lollard Knights': *Lancastrian Kings and Lollard Knights* (Oxford U.P. 1972) 161, 185. This association throws light on the tone of sincere and deliberately simple piety which marks Chaucer's poem.

23 leve cease.

27 mede reward. Word play on *mede* 'meadow', continuing the word play of 22 and 18, has been plausibly suggested.

18 The Canterbury Tales: extract

The plan of *The Canterbury Tales*, as projected in the Host's speech in *General Prologue* I 790–5, required the 29 pilgrims assembled at the Tabard Inn to tell two stories each on the way to Canterbury and two more on the way back. This implies a total of 120 tales (allowing 4 for the Canon's Yeoman, who joins the pilgrims on the road). Of these, Chaucer completed only 22, leaving 2 unfinished (*Cook's T.*, *Squire's T.*). The fragmentary condition of *C.T.*, and the unfinished condition of some of the fragments, appear clearly in the MSS., studied by J. M. Manly and E. Rickert *Text of the Canterbury Tales* 8 vols. (Univ. of Chicago P. 1940). The 55 more or less complete MSS. (there are also 8 imperfect MSS. and 19 containing selections) represent a number of attempts by friends or early editors to put in order a work which Chaucer evidently left in a mess. The extant tales fall into 'Fragments' (otherwise called 'Groups'), i.e. tales or strings of tales not linked to others by authentic Prologues or Epilogues. The two most elaborately worked Fragments are I (where *Gen. Prol.* is followed by the tales of Knight, Miller, Reeve and Cook) and VII. The two tales here edited occur at the beginning of Fragment VII, which continues with Chaucer's own tales of *Thopas* and *Melibee*, *Monk's T.* and *Nun's Priest's T.* They illustrate the principle of extreme contrast between neighbouring tales: cf. tales of Knight and Miller (too long to include here) in Fragment I. The order of tales within Fragments is, by definition, established with authentic Chaucerian 'links' (e.g. 435–52 here); but the order of the Fragments themselves in MSS. is the work of scribes and early 'editors'. The order represented by the numbering with roman numerals used here is that of Ellesmere and other MSS. The recovery of Chaucer's intentions in this matter (so far as he had formed them) is difficult: see, beside Manly and Rickert 2.475–94, W. W. Lawrence *Chaucer and the C.T.* (Columbia U.P. 1950) Ch. 4 and R. A. Pratt *PMLA* 66 (1951) 1141–67.

Early enthusiasm for *C.T.* is evidenced by the large number of MSS. and by apocryphal tales composed in C15 (e.g. *Tale of Beryn*). Caxton printed *C.T.* twice (*c.* 1478 and *c.* 1484); but *Troilus* was more highly praised in Renaissance times. Dryden modernized three tales in *Fables* (1700). His *Preface* is, with Blake's *Descriptive Catalogue* (1809), still valuable. Modern criticism begins with G. L. Kittredge *Chaucer and His Poetry* (Harvard U.P. 1915). Kittredge emphasizes the 'dramatic' character of *C.T.*, and sees the tales as reflecting pilgrims' antipathies (see *n.* to 643) and opinions (especially in the 'Marriage Group', Fragments III–V, where Kittredge first saw a consecutive discussion of marital relations). A similar approach is in R. M. Lumiansky *Of Sondry Folk* (Univ. of Texas P. 1955). R. Baldwin *Unity of the C.T.* (Copenhagen, Rosenkilde and Bagger 1955) attempts to show that the work as it stands has unity, based on the theme of pilgrimage raised to a higher power (Canterbury = Heavenly Jerusalem, cf. X 48–51). See also P. Ruggiers, *The Art of the C.T.* (Univ. of Wisconsin P. 1965). What would these critics have made of the return journey to Southwark, if Chaucer had lived to describe it? Muscatine Ch. 6 sees the juxtaposition of conventional and naturalistic elements in *C.T.* as an example of 'Gothic form'.

Sources The 22 completed tales already represent an omnium gatherum of different literary types: romance, Breton lay, saint's life, miracle of the Virgin, penitential treatise, tragedy, exemplum, beast fable, fabliau. Sources of individual tales are therefore extremely various. The standard work is W. F. Bryan and G. Dempster, eds. *Sources and Analogues of Chaucer's C.T.* (Univ. of Chicago P. 1941). Ch. 1 discusses Chaucer's precedents for 'framing' stories in a narrative setting. The closest analogues come from C14 Italy: Boccaccio's *Decameron*, which probably never came Chaucer's way, and the *Novelle* of Giovanni Sercambi (1347–1424), which he possibly knew. Sercambi represents himself as telling stories to a group of travellers banded together to escape the plague.

Date Chaucer probably conceived *C.T.* not long after completing *Troilus* (1386?). He apparently abandoned his other story collection, *Legend of Good Women*, in its favour about 1387. At least two tales were already in existence as separate pieces: *Knight's T.* and *Second Nun's T.*, both referred to in Prologue to *L.G.W.* (F 420, 426). Other tales which may antedate 1387 are those of the Monk, Man of Law, Physician and Manciple. But most were written for the Canterbury collection between *c.* 1387 and Chaucer's death in 1400.

Editions Besides edns of the complete works by Skeat and Robinson, see J. M. Manly's *C.T.* (N.Y., Holt 1928; London, Harrap 1928), E. T. Donaldson's *Chaucer's Poetry*: *an anthology for the modern reader* (N.Y., Ronald 1958), and R. A. Pratt's *Tales of Canterbury* (Boston, Houghton Mifflin 1974). Donaldson and Pratt present the best texts. A convenient glossed edn is A. C. Cawley's in the Everyman Libr. (1958). A selection of articles on *C.T.* is given in Schoeck and Taylor (see Chaucer headnote) vol. 1.

Fragment VII, lines 1-690

The Shipman's Tale

Shipman's Tale belongs to a clearly defined literary type: the short, comic verse tale, developed in C12 France and known as 'fabliau'. The standard study is P. Nykrog *Les Fabliaux* (Copenhagen, Munksgaard 1957), which questions the older description of fabliau as a 'genre bourgeois' (adopted e.g. by Muscatine), and represents it rather as a species of burlesque poetry often intended for courtly audiences. Most French fabliaux belong to C13. The genre was dead in France by Chaucer's time. Four other Canterbury Tales belong to the same type: *Miller's T.*, *Reeve's T.*, *Summoner's T.*, *Merchant's T.* See discussion of Chaucer's fabliaux, with bibl., by D. S. Brewer in B. Rowland, ed. *Companion to Chaucer Studies* (Oxford U.P. 1968) Ch. 14. *Shipman's T.* resembles the French type especially closely, having much dialogue, little set description, and no learned digression: see W. W. Lawrence *Spec.* 33 (1958) 56–68.

Chaucer's exact source for his beautifully machined plot is not known. The story belongs to a folk-tale type 'The Lover's Gift Regained', which appears frequently in medieval and Renaissance comic writing. For analogues, see J. W. Spargo in Bryan and Dempster Ch. 18; texts with translations in L. D. Benson and T. M. Andersson, eds. *The Literary Context of Chaucer's Fabliaux* (Bobbs–Merrill, Indianapolis 1971). The nearest analogues are two Italian *novelle*: Boccaccio *Decameron* 8.1, and its derivative Sercambi *Novelle* 19.

Chaucer may have known either or both of these (though his knowledge of *Decameron* is unproved): R. Guerin *ES* 52 (1971) 412–19. Or he may have taken the story from oral tradition, or have followed a lost French fabliau (so Spargo). The nearest (not very close) surviving fabliau is *Le Bouchier d'Abevile* (trans. in Benson and Andersson). In any case, Chaucer clearly recognized the story as fabliau material, and treated it accordingly.

Till recently interpretation has been dominated by controversy about the original teller of the tale, started by the C18 editor Tyrwhitt. He detected a female speaker (it could only be the Wife of Bath) in line 12 (see *n.*). So Kittredge 170 read the poem according to his conception of the Wife: it is 'frankly sensual – unmoral, if you like, – but too hearty and too profoundly normal to be unwholesome.' Similarly W. W. Lawrence *art. cit.* contrasts the *novelle*, where the wives are subject to moral criticism (and have to pay back the money), with a pro-feminine *Shipman's T.* F. Tupper, by contrast, interprets the pronouns of 12–19 as 'clever mimicry', believes the tale to have been written for the Shipman, and reads it as antifeminist in tendency: *JEGP* 33 (1934) 352–72. Other critics see the tale as more impartially 'cruel', 'cynical', 'sordid': e.g. G. Dempster *Dramatic Irony in Chaucer* (Stanford U.P. 1932) 39–42; A. H. Silverman 'Sex and money in Ch's *Sh. T.*' *PQ* 32 (1953) 329–36; Donaldson *Chaucer's Poetry* 930–2. The best balanced view of this enigmatic poem is that of M. Copland, *Med. Aev.* 35 (1966) 11–28.

Date Generally assigned to the *C.T.* period, *c.* 1387–1400. If originally meant for Wife of Bath, it may antedate her Prologue, which itself cannot be later than 1396: see R. A. Pratt 'The development of the W. of B.' in MacE. Leach, ed. *Studies in Medieval Literature in Honor of A. C. Baugh* (Univ. of Pennsylvania P. 1961) 45–79.

Manuscripts The tale is in 55 MSS., representing 8 separate lines of descent, according to Manly and Rickert 2.341–50. 'The large number of copies derived independently, mainly, no doubt, through lost intermediaries, from the original MS. would indicate immediate popularity of the tale' (2.350). The present text is based on the 'Hengwrt MS.', Nat. Libr. of Wales MS. Peniarth 392 D (= *Hg*). *El* = Ellesmere MS.

Here beginneth the Shipmannes Tale.

A marchant whilom dwelled at Saint Denis
That riche was, for which men helde him wis.
A wif he hadde of excellent beauté,
And compaignable and revelous was she,
Which is a thing that causeth more dispence

1 Saint Denis Saint-Denis, about 6 km. north of Paris, famous for its abbey and fair. The cloth trade was carried on there in C14.

4 revelous fun-loving. A rare word, first recorded here by *OED*. 27 MSS. read *reverent*!

5–19 The Wife of Bath quotes her old husband's opinions on gay clothing and gadding about (*C.T.* III 337–56). The parallel has been used as evidence that Chaucer originally intended this tale for the Wife; but the latter does not mention cost, the chief point of this passage.

5 dispence expense.

Than worth is all the cheere and reverence
That men hem don at festes and at daunces.
Swich salutacions and contenaunces
Passen as doth a shadwe upon the wall.
But wo is him that payen mot for all!
'The sely housbonde algate he mot paye,
He mot us clothe and he mot us arraye,
All for his owene worship richely,
In which array we dauncen jolily;
And if that he noght may, paraventure,
Or elles list no swich dispence endure,
But thinketh it is wasted and ylost,
Thenne mot another payen for oure cost,
Or lene us gold, and that is perilous.'
This noble marchant heeld a worthy hous,
For which he hadde alday so gret repair
For his largesse, and for his wif was fair,
That wonder is; but herkneth to my tale.
Amonges alle his gestes grete and smale
There was a monk, a fair man and a bold,
I trowe a thritty winter he was old,
That ever in oon was drawing to that place.

6 cheere friendly treatment.
8 contenaunces civilities.
9 Chaucer uses the same simile elsewhere, of the gifts of Fortune (*C.T.* IV 1315) and the riches of the world (*C.T.* X 1068). The latter's source refers to *Job* 14.1–2, 'Man . . . fleeth as a shadow'; but the wall is not biblical.
11 sely poor. **algate** in any case.
12 us First-person pronouns here and at 14, 18, 19, suggest a female speaker. Either Chaucer failed to revise a tale intended originally for the Wife of Bath (so Kittredge, Robinson, etc.), or the Shipman is mimicking a female speaker. The latter opinion is convincingly supported by M. Copland *Med. Aev.* 35 (1966) 25–6, comparing lines 68–9 below (and see 312) and Skelton's *Magnificence* 461. Cf. also *Troilus* 3.531.
13 worship reputation.
16 no] nat 27 MSS., giving tighter syntax for 15–16: 'if he cannot, or else will not, suffer such expense.'
19 lene lend.
20 heeld a worthy hous maintained his household generously.
21 alday continually. **so gret repair** so many visitors.
22 largesse generosity. A noble quality, hence uncharacteristic of merchants in medieval literature. On this merchant's generosity (cf. 282 f.), see Copland 17–23.
26 a thritty winter about thirty years. See Mustanoja 1.265 on indefinite article with 'implication of an approximate estimation'.
27 'Who was always visiting that house.'

This yonge monk that was so fair of face
Aquainted was so with the goode man
Sith that her firste knowliche began,
That in his hous as famulier was he
As it is possible any freend to be.
And for as muchel as this goode man
And eek this monk of which that I began
Were bothe two yborn in oo village,
The monk him claimeth as for cosinage,
And he again he saith nat ones nay,
But was as glad therof as fowel of day;
For to his herte it was a gret plesance.
Thus ben they knit with eterne alliance,
And ech of hem gan other for t'assure
Of bretherhede whil that her lif may dure.
  Free was daun John and manly of dispence,
As in that hous, and full of diligence
To don plesance and also gret costage.
He nat forgat to yeve the leeste page
In all that hous, but after her degré
He yaf the lord and sith all his meiné,
Whan that he cam, som manere honeste thing;

29 goode man master of the house: see *MED* s.v. *God man* phr. and n. 2(a). Cf. 33, 107 and 92.
30 Sith that ever since. **knowliche** acquaintance.
31 famulier 'like one of the family'. A loan word often used by Chaucer in sinister contexts: cf. *C.T.* IV 1784 'famulier foo' (from *familiaris inimicus* in Boethius).
34 of which that I began of whom I began to speak.
35 oo a single, the same. *village* suggests humble origins for both monk and merchant: cf. *C.T.* IV 483.
36 'The monk claims him as a blood relation.' Fisher *N & Q* 12 (1965) 168–70 proposes a pun on *cozen* 'cheat'; but the word is not recorded so early.
37 again in return.
38 A popular simile: cf. 51, *C.T.* I 2437 etc.
42 *bretherhede* suggests that the *alliance*, or bond of friendship, approaches that of sworn brothers. In *Knight's T.* Palamon and Arcite are both cousins by birth (cf. 36 here) and sworn brothers.
43 daun a title for monks (cf. Modern 'Dom'). **manly]** *Hg*+13 MSS.; namely *El*+36 MSS. The latter reading gives good Chaucerian English (*namely* meaning 'particularly') but weak sense, since *free* does not here stand to be particularized by mention of *dispence*. *manly* has a rare sense 'generous': cf. *Piers* B 5.260, 10.87, Hoccleve *Regement of Princes* 720. See Donaldson in Brewer *Geoffrey Chaucer* 106–7.
45 'To give pleasure and incur expense.'
48 sith afterwards. **meiné** household.
49 honeste suitable.

For which they were as glad of his coming
As fowl is fain whan that the sonne up riseth.
Namore of this as now, for it suffiseth.
But so befell this marchant on a day
Shoop him to make redy his array
Toward the town of Brugges forto fare,
To byen there a porcion of ware;
For which he hath to Paris sent anon
A messager, and prayed hath daun John
That he sholde come to Saint Denis and pleye
With him and with his wif a day or tweye,
Ere he to Brugges wente, in alle wise.
This noble monk of which I you devise
Hath of his abbot as him list licence,
By cause he was a man of heigh prudence
And eek an officer, out forto ride
To seen her granges and her bernes wide,
And unto Saint Denis he comth anon.
Who was so welcome as my lord daun John,
Oure deere cosin, full of curteisye?
With him broghte he a jubbe of malvesye
And eek another full of fin vernage
And volatil, as ay was his usage.
And thus I lete hem ete and drinke and pleye,
This marchant and this monk, a day or tweye.

54 'Got ready to make his preparations.'
55 Brugges Bruges, great mercantile centre in Flanders, where many foreign merchants had dealings. See J. A. Van Houtte 'The rise and decline of the market of Bruges' *Economic History Review* 19 (1966) 29–47.
56 ware The commodity is not specified, but may be thought of as cloth: *OED* s.v. *Ware* sb.[3] 3b and Van Houtte 37–8.
59 pleye relax. But the next line suggests a sexual pun: cf. 117, 422.
62–5 The monk holds some office (perhaps that of cellarer) in his monastery which requires him to do business with the outside world. Hence, like the Monk on the pilgrimage, he is an *outridere* (I 166). Such monks were held in suspicion by moralists.
66 granges outlying farms. **bernes** barns.
68 my See 12 *n*.
69 Oure the 'domestic *our*': see Mustanoja 1.159. The expression is unusually frequent in this Tale: cf. 107, 356, 363.
70 jubbe a vessel capable of holding (*Miller's T.* I 3628) a day's supply of ale for three. **malvesye** malmsey (15 MSS. have forms with *-m-*), a sweet wine, originally from Greece.
71 vernage the most costly of the sweet wines imported from the Mediterranean (mod. Ital. *vernaccia*).
72 volatil wild fowl, game. **usage** custom.

The thridde day this marchant up ariseth
And on his nedes sadly him aviseth,
And up in to his countour-hous goth he
To rekene with himselven, well may be,
Of thilke yere how that it with him stood,
And how that he despended hadde his good,
And if that he encressed were or noon.
His bokes and his bagges many oon
He layth beforn him on his counting-bord.
Full riche was his tresor and his hord,
For which full faste his countour-dore he shette;
And eek he nolde that no man sholde him lette
Of his acountes for the mene time.
And thus he sit till it was passed prime.
Daun John was risen in the morwe also
And in the gardin walketh to and fro,
And hath his thinges said full curteisly.
This goode wif cam walking privély
In to the gardin there he walketh softe,
And him salueth as she hath don ofte.
A maide child cam in hir compaignye,
Which as hir list she may governe and gye,

76 sadly seriously. **him aviseth** deliberates.
77 countour-hous counting-house. Chaucer perhaps had in mind the 'hall-house' type of town house favoured by English merchants: a central hall with a two-storey block at each end. The counting-house might then be above (cf. 156, 250) buttery and pantry in the 'service' block.
78 himselven] 9 MSS.; hymself *Hg* etc. The missing syllable is restored in 27 MSS. reading 'as well may be'.
79 thilke that same.
81 encressed increased in wealth.
86 nolde did not wish. **lette** disturb.
87 for the mene time for the time being.
88 prime 9 a.m. The wife is later said to leave the monk at prime (206); but her visit to the kitchens means that it is 'passed prime' before she disturbs her husband.
90 gardin] gardyns *Hg*.
91 thinges devotions. **curteisly** Variants ('coriously', 'devoutely', holily') suggest that scribes disapproved of the worldly epithet ('more appropriate to the smoothness of the lady's man than to the holy matter in hand', Copland 13).
92 goode wif See 29 *n*.
95–7 The little girl plays no further part in the story. Wives of wealthy merchants, like other gentlewomen, usually took a girl to wait upon them when they went out.
96 gye guide.

For yet under the yerde was the maide.
'O deere cosin myn, daun John,' she saide,
'What aileth you so rathe forto rise?'
'Nece,' quod he, 'it oghte ynow suffise
Five houres forto slepe upon a night,
But it were for an old apalled wight,
As ben thise wedded men that lie and dare,
As in a forme sit a wery hare
Were all forstraught with houndes grete and smale.
But deere nece, why be ye so pale?
I trowe certes that oure goode man
Hath you laboured sith the night began,
That you were nede to resten hastily.'
And with that word he lough full mirily,
And of his owene thoght he wex all reed.
This faire wif gan forto shake hir heed
And saide thus, 'Yea, God wot all,' quod she,
'Nay, cosin myn, it stant nat so with me;
For by that God that yaf me soule and lif,
In all the reaume of France is there no wif
That lasse lust hath to that sory pley;
For I may singe allas and weilawey
That I was born; but to no wight,' quod she,

97 yet under the yerde still subject to the discipline of the rod.
99 rathe early.
100–5 The monk boasts about his toughness. The amount of sleep needed by a person was held to vary according to age, 'complexion', diet, etc.; but even those with 'warm complexion' and good digestion were said to need 6 or 8 hours: Arnold of Villanova *De regimine sanitatis* Pt 2 Ch. 8, in *Opera omnia* (Basle 1585) cols. 699–701. So the monk's five hours represents an extravagant claim for the warmth of his complexion.
102 apalled pale and languid: cf. *C.T.* V 365 and IX 55 (both in connection with lack of sleep).
103 dare cower.
104 'As a weary hare sits in a lair.' The Monk on the pilgrimage is fond of hare-hunting: I 191.
105 forstraught driven to its wits' end (recorded only here in *MED*).
108 laboured put to work: used with a sexual sense in *Merchant's T.*, 'Thus laboureth he till that the day gan dawe' (*C.T.* IV 1842). Cf. *R. de la Rose* 19523.
110 lough laughed.
111 wex grew. Cf. No. 12 above, line 652.
113 wot knows. Proverbial: Whiting G245.
114 stant stands.
117 'Who takes less pleasure in . . .' **pley** See 59 *n.*
118 weilaway woe, alack.

'Dar I nat telle how it stant with me.
Wherfore I thinke out of this land to wende,
Or elles of myself to make an ende,
So full am I of drede and eek of care.'
This monk began upon this wif to stare
And saide, 'Allas, my nece, God forbede
That ye for any sorwe or any drede
Fordo yourself; but telleth me your grief.
Paraventure I may in your meschief
Conseille or helpe, and therfore telleth me
All your anoy, for it shall ben secré.
For on my portehors I make an oth
That never in my lif, for lief ne loth,
Ne shall I of no conseil you bewreye.'
'The same again to you,' quod she, 'I seye.
By God and by this portehors I swere,
Thogh men me wolde all into peces tere,
Ne shall I never, for to gon to helle,
Bewreye a word of thing that ye me telle –
Nat for no cosinage ne alliance,
But verraily for love and affiance.'
Thus ben they sworn, and hereupon they kiste,
And ech of hem tolde other what hem liste.
'Cosin,' quod she, 'if that I hadde a space,

120 how] how that *Hg* + 8 MSS. But final *-e* does not necessarily elide before *how*.
127 Fordo destroy.
130 anoy trouble.
131 portehors breviary (cf. 91). The trisyllabic Fr. form, though found in none of the MSS. (which spell variously, *porthors* in *Hg*, most often *portos*), appears to be what Chaucer wrote here and at 135, perhaps as a touch of local colour (cf. 214). By substituting disyllabic Eng. forms, scribes created metrical difficulties, solved e.g. by adding *here* after *portos* in 131 (9 MSS.) or *you* before *swere* in 135 (8 MSS.).
132 for lief ne loth for friend or foe, i.e. in any circumstances. **ne]** or *Hg*.
133 conseil secret. **bewreye** betray.
135 portehors See 131 *n*.
136 At 193–4 the wife refers to the traitor Ganelon, who was torn to pieces by warhorses.
137 for to gon to helle even though I have to go to hell for it.
140–1 Their new relationship of intimacy and mutual trust (*affiance*) makes their dubious 'cousinhood' irrelevant (cf. 36, 149).
141 The kiss seals the bargain.
143 The wife addresses John as *cousin*, despite 139; but the term is not used again between them after 149–50, whereas the monk uses it four times to the merchant in 257–80. **space** time.

As I have non, and namely in this place,
Thenne wolde I telle a legende of my lif,
What I have suffred sith I was a wif
With myn housbonde, all be he your cosin.'
'Nay,' quod this monk, 'by God and saint Martin,
He is namore cosin unto me
Than is this leef that hangeth on the tree!
I clepe him so, by saint Denis of France,
To han the more cause of aquaintance
Of you, which I have loved specially
Aboven alle wommen sikerly.
This swere I you on my professioun.
Telleth your grief, lest that he come adown,
And hasteth you, and goth away anon.'
'My deere love,' quod she, 'O my daun John,
Full lief were me this conseil forto hide,
But out it mot, I may namore abide.
Myn housbonde is to me the worste man
That ever was sith that the world began.
But sith I am a wif, it sit nat me
To tellen no wight of oure priveté,
Neither abedde ne in non other place.
God shilde I sholde it tellen, for his grace!
A wif ne shall nat sayn of hir housbonde
But all honour, as I can understonde –
Save unto you thus muche I tellen shall:
As help me God, he is noght worth at all

144 namely especially.
145 legende properly the story of the life and sufferings (cp. 146) of a saint. The wife dramatizes her situation: see A. B. Thro *Ch. R.* 5 (1970) 106–8.
147 all be he although he is.
148 Martin Bp of Tours, a famous saint of France—a common oath, especially in rhyme, in Eng. romances and Fr. fabliaux.
151 clepe call. **Denis** Bp of Paris, patron saint of France—a common oath, but especially apt here, since his remains were preserved in the Benedictine Abbey of Saint-Denis.
154 sikerly certainly.
155 professioun monastic vow (a solemn form of oath).
159 Full lief were me I should be very glad.
160 But out it mot but it must come out. I] *Hg* + 15 MSS.; it 36 MSS.
163 it sit nat me it is not fitting for me.
164 privetė private doings.
166 shilde forbid.
167–8 'A wife must not report anything about her husband except what is entirely to his credit . . .'

In no degree the value of a flye.
But yet me greveth most his nigardye.
And well ye wot that wommen naturelly
Desiren thinges sixe, as well as I:
They wolde that her housbondes sholde be
Hardy and wise and riche and therto free
And buxom unto his wif and fresh abedde.
But by that ilke lord that for us bledde,
For his honour myself forto arraye
A Sonday next I moste nedes paye
An hundred frankes, or elles am I lorn.
Yet were me levere that I were unborn
Than me were don a sclaundre or vileinye;
And if myn housbonde eek mighte it espye
I nere but lost; and therfore I you preye,
Lene me this somme or elles mot I deye.
Daun John, I saye, lene me thise hundred frankes.
Pardee, I woll noght faile you, my thankes,
If that you list to don that I you praye,
For at a certain day I woll you paye,
And don to you what plesance and servise
That I may don, right as you list devise.

171 The theme of male sexual inadequacy is found in French fabliaux: Nykrog 189.
173–7 Similar statements of what women desire in their husbands occur in *C.T.* VII 2912–7 (2914 resembles 176 here), and III 1258–64 (1259 resembles 177 here); and cf. III 925 ff. But these passages do not number the desirable qualities. The hexadic form may derive from Irish lists of 'the six excellences': see Smith, *Journal of Celtic Studies* 1 (1949–50) 98–104, and generally Curtius, Excursus 16 on 'Numerical apothegms'.
176 Hardy bold. **free** generous. The four qualities form two pairs: boldness and wisdom represent a rare but desirable combination, as do wealth and generosity. The same may be said of the two qualities in 177, to judge by the history of the Wife of Bath's marriages.
177 buxom obedient, submissive.
180 'On Sunday next . . .' Cf. 307.
181 frankes. Like the shield (331 *n.*), the franc provides local colour (it is not found elsewhere in Chaucer). The 'franc à cheval' was first issued in 1360, and established itself as an important French gold coin, equivalent in Chaucer's day to 3s4d sterling. Thus the wife owed something over £15 for her *array* – a very considerable sum. **lorn** lost.
183 sclaundre slander. **vileinye** discourtesy.
185 'I would be simply lost . . .'
186 somme sum (first here in *OED*).
188 my thankes willingly, i.e. if I can help it.
190 certain day fixed date.
192 devise specify.

And but I do, God take on me vengeance
As foul as ever hadde Genelon of France.'
This gentil monk answerde in this manere:
'Now trewely, myn owene lady deere,
I have,' quod he, 'on you so gret a routhe
That I you swere and plighte you my trouthe
That whan your housbonde is to Flandres fare
I woll delivere you out of this care,
For I woll bringe you an hundred frankes.'
And with that word he caughte hir by the flankes
And hir embraceth harde and kiste hir ofte.
'Goth now your way,' quod he, 'all stille and softe,
And lat us dine as soone as that ye may,
For by my chilindre it is prime of day.
Goth now and beth as trewe as I shall be.'
'Now elles God forbede, sire,' quod she,
And forth she goth as jolif as a pye
And bad the cookes that they sholde hem hye
So that men mighte dine, and that anon.
Up to hir housbonde is this wif ygon
And knocketh at his countour boldely.
'Qui la?' quod he; 'Peter, it am I!'
Quod she. 'What, sire, how longe woll ye faste?
How longe time woll ye rekene and caste

194 Ganelon was the traitor who caused Roland's death at Roncesvalles. He was torn to pieces by four warhorses, according to *Chanson de Roland* 3964 f.
197 routhe pity.
199 is . . . fare has gone.
205–6 Dinner, the first big meal of the day, was usually taken some time between *prime* (9 a.m.) and noon.
206 chilindre 'a portable sun dial in the shape of an upright cylinder' (*MED* s.v.): 'a new and fashionable gadget', Bennett *Chaucer* 72.
208 'Now God forbid that it should be otherwise . . .'
209 jolif as a pye merry as a magpie. The Wife of Bath uses the same simile of her younger self: *C.T.* III 456.
210 hem hye hurry up.
212 Up See 77 *n*. **this**] his *Hg*.
214 Qui la] who ther *Hg*+4 MSS. *Hg* corrects to *who is ther* (the reading of 12 MSS.) and adds *qi la* as a marginal gloss. The same gloss is found in 3 other MSS.; but the majority of MSS. have *qui la* in the text, no doubt rightly. Presumably *who* (*is*) *there* was originally itself a marginal gloss. This is the only place in Chaucer's works where a fragment of foreign speech is used as local colour, as if to recall that the characters would in fact have been speaking French. Contrast e.g. the Fr. phrases in *Summoner's T.*, *C.T.* III 1832, 1838. **Peter** an oath by the porter of heaven (not the merchant's name). The wife speaks with unnatural vehemence.
216 caste calculate. The merchant is drawing up annual accounts: cf. 78–87.

Your sommes and your bokes and your thinges?
The devel have part on all swich rekeninges!
Ye have ynogh, pardee, of Goddes sonde.
Com down today, and lat your bagges stonde.
Ne be ye nat ashamed that daun John
Shall fasting all this day elenge gon?
What, lat us here a masse and go we dine.'
 'Wif, 'quod this man, 'littel canstow devine
The curious bisynesse that we have;
For of us chapmen, also God me save,
And by that lord that cleped is saint Ive,
Scarsly amonges twelve ten shull thrive
Continuelly, lasting unto oure age.
We may well make cheere and good visage
And drive forth the world as it may be
And kepen oure estat in priveté,
Till we be dede, or elles that we playe
A pilgrimage, or gon out of the waye.

217 thinges Cf. 91: both men have their business to attend to.
218 'The Devil take . . .' A phrase imitated from Fr. 'que le diable ait part en', whence the peculiar use of *on* (some scribes substitute *of*, others *in*).
219 sonde gift, 'sending'. The wife's reproach recalls Christian themes: cf. the old widow in *Nun's Priest's T.*, who lives 'by housbondrye of swich as God hir sente' (*C.T.* VII 2828).
222 elenge miserable.
224–48 Merchants were notorious for their worrying: cf. the character of Winner in No. 7 above, and see Stillwell in *RES* 20 (1944) 1–18.
224 devine guess.
225 'The painstaking activity which is our lot.'
226 chapmen merchants. **also** as.
227 The line is identical with *C.T.* III 1943, where *Ive* again rhymes with *thrive*. Of several candidates, St Ivo of Chartres is to be preferred to St Yves of Brittany or St Ives of Huntingdonshire, on grounds of apt nationality (cf. 148, 151): see Cline *MLN* 60 (1945) 482.
228 The numbers vary in the MSS: 'The confused mass of readings here seems to have originated in efforts by the scribes to adjust the proportion of thrivers to their ideas of the facts', Manly and Rickert 4.497. The choice lies between ten-out-of-twelve (*Hg* + 14 MSS.) and two-out-of-twelve (20 MSS.). I prefer the former for its unobtrusive humour: the anxious merchant cannot bring himself even to contemplate more than two failures in twelve.
230–4 Difficult. 'We have every reason to put on a good appearance, make the best we can of things, and look after our affairs quietly, until the time comes for us to die, or else take time off on a pilgrimage, or else keep out of sight.' *playe a pilgrimage* presents problems. *playe*, if transitive, must mean something like 'make pretence of' (to escape creditors?); but in the ME phrase *goon a pilgrimage*, *a* represents the preposition *on* in reduced stress, and 6 MSS. in fact read *on* here. Hence my translation. *gon out of the waye* may imply absconding, or else being 'unavailable for comment'.

And therfore have I gret necessité
Upon this queinte world t'avise me,
For evermo we mote stonde in drede
Of hap and fortune in oure chapmanhede.
To Flandres woll I go tomorwe at day
And come again as soone as ever I may.
For which, my deere wif, I thee beseke
As be to every wight buxom and meke,
And forto kepe oure good be curious,
And honestly governe well oure hous.
Thou hast ynow in every manere wise
That to a thrifty houshold may suffise.
Thee lacketh non array ne no vitaille;
Of silver in thy purs shaltow nat faille.'
And with that word his countour-dore he shette,
And down he goth, no lenger wolde he lette,
But hastily a masse was there said,
And spedily the tables were ylaid,
And to the diner faste they hem spedde,
And richely this monk the chapman fedde.
   At after-diner daun John sobrely
This chapman took apart and privély
He saide him thus: 'Cosin, it standeth so
That well I see to Brugges woll ye go.
God and saint Austin spede you and gide!
I pray you, cosin, wisly that ye ride.
Governeth you also of your diete

236 'To take thought about this strange world.'
238 hap chance.
241 beseke beseech.
242 buxom gracious, ready to help.
243 curious careful.
244 honestly honourably, in a creditable way.
246 thrifty prosperous (modern sense not before C16).
247 vitaille food.
250 lette delay.
252 ylaid Referring to the setting up of the customary trestle tables (*MED* s.v. *Leien* v.(1) 4(c)).
255 At] *Hg* + 5 MSS.; And 46 MSS. The rarer phrase in *Hg* etc. is certainly right (cf. *C.T.* V 918, 1219); but it is uncertain whether *after* is part of a compound preposition *at-after* (see *OED* s.v. *After* adv. and prep. D1, and *At* prep. 40) or of a compound noun or phrase *after*(-)*dinner*. See Mustanoja 1.366–7.
259 Austin Augustine.

Atemprely, and namely in this hete.
Betwix us two nedeth no strange fare;
Farewell, cosin, God shilde you fro care.
And if that any thing by day or night,
If it lie in my power and my might,
That ye me woll comande in any wise,
It shall be don right as ye woll devise.
Oo thing ere that ye gon, if it may be,
I wolde praye you: forto lene me
An hundred frankes for a wike or tweye,
For certain bestes that I moste beye
To store with a place that is oures.
God help me so, I wolde it were youres!
I shall nat faille surely of my day,
Nat for a thousand frankes, a mile way.
But lat this thing be secré, I you preye,
For yet tonight thise bestes mot I beye.
And fare now well, myn owene cosin deere;
Grant mercy of your cost and of your cheere.'
This noble marchant gentilly anon
Answerde and saide, 'O cosin myn, daun John,
Now sikerly this is a small requeste.
My gold is youres whan that it you leste,
And nat only my gold, but my chaffare.
Tak what you list, God shilde that ye spare.
But oo thing is, ye knowe it well ynow,
Of chapmen that her moneye is her plow.

262 Atemprely in moderation. Medical authorities such as Galen recommend moderation in eating especially in hot weather. Cf. No. 11.1 above, lines 259–75.
263 strange fare formal behaviour, as of one stranger to another.
265 by day or night The conventional expression acquires extra point here.
267 That marks the resumption of the conditional clause after a parenthesis.
273 'With which to stock one of our places', i.e. one of the farms with which the 'outriding' monk was concerned.
276 a mile way i.e. by as much time as it takes to walk a mile (20 mins. according to Chaucer's *Astrolabe* 1.16: '3 mile-way maken an houre').
277–8 The monk, afraid that the wife might hear of the loan and discover the trick, suggests that his deal might be prejudiced (by an increase in the asking-price?) if the loan became public knowledge: cf. *privély* 256, 294. No parallel in Boccaccio or Sercambi.
278 yet tonight this very evening.
280 Grant mercy many thanks. **cheere** hospitality.
285 chaffare merchandise.
286 shilde forbid.
288 Proverbial? See *OED* s.v. *Plough* sb.[1] 1c.

We may creance whil we han a name,
But goldlees forto ben, it is no game.
Pay it again whan it lith in your ese;
After my might full fain woll I you plese.'
Thise hundred frankes he fette forth anon,
And privély he took hem to daun John.
No wight in all this world wiste of this lone
Saving this marchant and daun John allone.
They drinke and speke and rome a while and pleye,
Till that daun John rideth to his abbeye.
  The morwe cam, and forth this marchant rideth
To Flandres-ward; his prentis well him gideth,
Till he cam in to Brugges murily.
Now goth this marchant faste and bisily
Aboute his nede, and byeth and creanceth.
He neither playeth at the dees ne daunceth,
But as a marchant, shortly forto telle,
He let his lif, and there I lete him dwelle.
  The Sonday next the marchant was agon,
To Saint Denis ycomen is daun John,
With crowne and berd all fresshe and newe shave.
In all the hous there nas so littel a knave,
Ne no wight elles, that he nas full fain
That my lord daun John was come again.
And shortly to the point right forto gon,

289–90 'We can raise money on credit for as long as our credit lasts; but it is no joke to be without ready money.' **creance** raise money on credit. See 328–34 *n*.

291 The request for prompt repayment has been noted as one of the points which Chaucer's tale shares with Sercambi's against Boccaccio's: Pratt *MLN* 55 (1940) 142–5. **it lith in your ese** it is convenient.

293 fette fetched.

294 took handed.

297 rome stroll.

300 prentis apprentice. One of his jobs was evidently to act as courier.

304 Dice and dancing figure among the activities of the feckless apprentice in *Cook's T., C.T.* I 4370, 4384.

306 let leads. A contracted form (OE *lætt*) obsolescent in Chaucer's day. *Hg* has *t* over erasure, and other MSS. read *ledith*, *lad* etc.

307 'The Sunday immediately after the merchant had gone.'

309 crowne tonsure.

310 knave houseboy.

311 that he nas who was not.

312 That The MSS. divide almost evenly between *That* and *For that*; but Manly and Rickert regard the latter as a scribal correction of a nine-syllable line.

This faire wif acorded with daun John
That for thise hundred frankes he sholde all night
Have hir in his armes bolt upright.
And this acord parfourned was in dede;
In mirthe all night a bisy lif they lede
Till it was day, that daun John wente his way
And bad the meiné 'farewell, have good day.'
For non of hem, ne no wight in the town,
Hath of daun John right no suspecioun,
And forth he rideth hom till his abbeye,
Or where him list; namore of him I seye.
This marchant, whan that ended was the faire,
To Saint Denis he gan forto repaire,
And with his wif he maketh feste and cheere
And telleth hir that chaffare is so deere
That nedes moste he make a chevissance,
For he was bounden in a reconissance
To paye twenty thousand sheelde anon.
For which this marchant is to Paris gon
To borwe of certaine freendes that he hadde
A certain frankes, and some with him he ladde.
And whan that he was come in to the town,
For greet chierté and greet affeccioun

316 bolt upright stretched out supine as straight as an arrow (*bolt*).
325 The merchant comes home when the *faire*, i.e. the particular gathering of buyers and sellers which concerned him, was over.
328–34 In Bruges the merchant had to raise a short-term loan of 20,000 *écus* in order to buy up merchandise selling at unexpectedly high prices there. He now has to go to Paris to raise another loan from his associates in order to repay the debt incurred in Bruges.
329 make a chevissance raise a loan.
330 reconissance the same as the *bond* of 368. For the financial background, see R. de Roover *Money, Banking and Credit in Medieval Bruges* (Cambridge, Mass., Mediaeval Academy of America 1948).
331 sheelde Like the franc (181 *n.*), the shield (Fr. *écu*) was a French gold coin. It was used as a unit of account in Bruges trade (de Roover 59). At the end of C14 the London–Bruges exchange rate was 25 old pence sterling to the écu (de Roover 78, cf. *Gen. Prol.* I 278). At that rate 20,000 shield = over £2000, which would make the merchant a very big operator. But 20,000 is a conventional large number in Chaucer, e.g. *C.T.* III 1143.
334 'A certain number of francs, and some he took with him.' The merchant, having called in at home to pick up his ready money, took this on to Paris, where he supplemented it with a second loan in order to repay the first. The point for the story is that he should have occasion to see his wife before he sees the monk.
336 chierté fondness.

Unto daun John he first goth him to pleye;
Nat forto axe or borwe of him moneye,
But forto wite and seen of his welfare
And forto tellen him of his chaffare,
As freendes don whan they ben met yfeere.
Daun John him maketh feste and murye cheere,
And he him tolde again full specially
How he hadde well yboght and graciously,
Thanked be God, all hool his marchandise;
Save that he moste, in alle maner wise,
Maken a chevissance as for his beste,
And thenne he sholde ben in joye and reste.
Daun John answerde, 'Certes, I am fain
That ye in heele are comen hom again.
And if that I were riche, as have I blisse,
Of twenty thousand sheeld sholde ye nat misse,
For ye so kindely this other day
Lente me gold, and as I can and may
I thanke you, by God and by saint Jame.
But nathelees, I took unto oure dame,
Your wif at hom, the same gold again
Upon your bench; she wot it well, certain,
By certain tokenes that I can you telle.
Now, by your leve, I may no lenger dwelle.
Oure abbot woll out of this town anon,

338 axe ask.
339 wite know.
341 yfeere together.
343 again in return. **full specially** in great detail.
345 all hool his marchandise all the merchandise he was intending to buy.
347 'Raise a loan so as to serve his interests best.'
350 heele health (cf. 260–2).
355 Jame St James of Compostella.
356 took gave.
357 the same gold In Sercambi (Bryan and Dempster 446) the lover tells the husband that he returned the borrowed florins to the wife 'not being able to spend them'. So perhaps here: not merely 'the same amount in gold', but 'the identical gold pieces'.
358 bench 'the table or desk of a merchant, a counting table', *MED* s.v. *Bench(e* 3(a), giving only this example. The sense is borrowed from cognate Italian *banca*/*banco*.
359 tokenes circumstantial details given as evidence for some statement or claim (cf. *C.T.* IX 258). The monk is enjoying a private joke: 'She will be forced to admit it by certain details which I am able to mention to you.' See 390, 403. In Skelton's *Tunning of Elinour Rumming* 497 *token* means 'female pudendum', a sense which may be involved here. **you]** hir 32 MSS.

And in his compaignye mot I gon.
Greet well oure dame, myn owene nece swete,
And fare well, deere cosin, till we mete.'
  This marchant, which that was full war and wis,
Creanced hath and payed eek in Paris
To certain Lombardes redy in her hond
The somme of gold, and gat of hem his bond;
And hom he gooth murye as a papinjay,
For well he knew he stood in swich array
That nedes moste he winne in that viage
A thousand frankes aboven all his costage.
His wif full redy mette him at the gate,
As she was wont of old usage algate;
And all that night in mirthe they besette,
For he was riche and cleerly out of dette.
  Whan it was day, this marchant gan embrace
His wif all newe, and kiste hir on hir face,
And up he goth and maketh it full tough.
'Namore,' quod she, 'by God, ye have ynough!'
And wantounly again with him she plaide,
Till at the laste this marchant saide:
'By God,' quod he, 'I am a littel wroth
With you, my wif, although it be me loth,
And wot ye why? By God, as that I gesse,
That ye han made a manere strangenesse
Betwixen me and my cosin daun John.

365 war prudent.
366 Creanced raised a loan (from the 'friends' of 333).
367 The merchant redeems his bond from the Paris branch of the Italian bank which had lent him 20,000 shields in Bruges. 'The great Italian banking houses were the principal lenders and practically dominated the money market', de Roover 55. **redy in her hond** promptly and in cash (*OED* s.v. *Ready* a., adv. and sb. 12).
369 papinjay parrot.
370 array state.
371 viage journey.
372 costage expenses.
374 usage custom. **algate** always.
375 besette employed.
379 maketh it full tough is very (sexually) demanding.
382 Scribes attempted to smooth this line: e.g. 10 MSS. read 'Til at the laste that this . . .' But Chaucer may have intended a slight pause after *laste*.
384 you The merchant addresses his wife with the reproachfully formal plural pronoun here and in 385, 386, 388, 389. Previously he has always used *thou*, to which he returns in 395. **loth** disagreeable.
386 a manere strangenesse a sort of estrangement.

Ye sholde han warned me ere I had gon
That he you hadde a hundred frankes payed
By redy tokne; and heeld him ivele apayed
For that I to him spak of chevissance;
Me semed so, as by his contenance.
But nathelees, by God oure hevene king,
I thoghte nat to axe of him no thing.
I pray thee, wif, ne do namore so;
Tell me alway, ere that I fro thee go,
If any dettour hath in myn absence
Ypayed thee, lest thurgh thy necligence
I mighte him axe a thing that he hath payed.'
This wif was nat afered ne afrayed,
But boldely she saide, and that anon,
'Marie, I defye the false monk daun John!
I kepe nat of his toknes never a deel;
He took me certain gold, this wot I weel.
What, ivel theedom on his monkes snoute!
For God it wot, I wende withouten doute
That he hadde yeve it me by cause of you,
To don therwith myn honour and my prow,
For cosinage, and eek for bele cheere
That he hath had full ofte times heere.
But sith I see I stande in this disjoint,
I woll answere you shortly to the point.
Ye han mo slacker dettours than am I;
For I woll paye you well and redily
Fro day to day; and if so be I faile,
I am your wif, score it up on my taile,

388 ere I had gon i.e. before I left for Paris.
390 By redy tokne 'by clear evidence' (Baugh), i.e. he has paid you and is ready to prove it (referring to 359, and cf. 403).
394 'I had no intention of asking him for anything.'
403–4 'He does not need to produce his evidence; I am quite ready to confess that he did give me a certain amount of gold.'
405 ivel theedom bad luck.
406 wende supposed.
408 prow advantage.
409 bele cheere good cheer, hospitality.
411 I stande] it stant *Hg* + 12 MSS. **disjoint** predicament.
416 score it up on my taile mark it up on my tally, charge it to my account. A tally was a stick on which debts were recorded by notches (cf. *C.T.* I 570). A pun is intended on *tail* 'sexual member' (*OED* s.v. *Tail* sb.[1] 5c), as in *Wife of Bath's T.*, *C.T.* III 466. See C. Jones *MLN* 52 (1937) 570; R. A. Caldwell *MLN* 55 (1940) 262–5; A. H. Silverman *PQ* 32 (1953) 329–36. Cf. 434 below. The interchangeability of sex and money in the Tale is summed up in the pun.

And I shall paye as sone as ever I may;
For by my trouthe I have on myn array,
And nat in wast, bestowed every deel.
And for I have bestowed it so weel
For your honour, for Goddes sake, I saye,
As be nat wroth, but lat us laughe and playe.
Ye shall my joly body han to wedde;
By God, I woll noght paye you but abedde.
Forgive it me, myn owene spouse deere.
Turn hiderward, and maketh bettre cheere.'
  This marchant saugh there was no remedye,
And forto chide it nere but folye,
Syn that the thing may nat amended be.
'Now, wif,' he saide, 'and I foryeve it thee;
But by thy lif, ne be namore so large.
Keep bet thy good, this yeve I thee in charge.'
Thus endeth my tale, and God us sende
Tailling ynough unto oure lives ende.

Here endeth the Shipmannes Tale.

Herke the mirye wordes of the worthy Hoost.

'Well said, by corpus dominus,' quod oure Hoost,
'Now longe mot thou saille by the coost,
Sire gentil maister, gentil mariner.
God yeve the monk a thousand last quade yere!
A ha, felawes, beth war of swich a jape!

423 my joly body In *C.T.* II 1185 this phrase is used without physical suggestion, as its French source 'mon cors' may mean just 'myself'; cf. Mustanoja 1.148–9. But here, as in *Gawain* 1237, the sexual potential of the phrase is released. **to wedde** as security for the debt.
428 it nere but folye it would be merely foolish.
431 large generous.
432 thy] *Hg*+19 MSS.; oure *El*; my 30 MSS. Ellesmere is recalling 243. The majority reading arose from failure to catch a nuance. The merchant, who sees no point in getting angry, accepts the wife's claim that she thought the money was given to her personally (406–7), and simply suggests that she should perhaps not spend so much of her own money on dress (418–19).
433–4 Here, as in *Wife of Bath's T.*, the prayer on behalf of the company (a common kind of ending in *C.T.*) is adapted to the context.
434 Tailling dealing by tally, on credit, with pun on *tail* as above, 416 ***n.***
435 corpus dominus the body of the Lord. *dominus* for *domini* reflects the Host's lack of schooling. Swearing by the body of Christ was especially deplored by moralists: Elliott 270–3.
437 Sire] Thow *Hg* etc.
438 a thousand last quade yeer a thousand cartloads of bad years.

The monk putte in the mannes hood an ape,
And in his wives eke, by saint Austin.
Draweth no monkes more into your inn.
  But now passe over, and lat us seke aboute:
Who shall now telle first of all this route
Another tale?' And with that word he saide,
As curteisly as it had ben a maide:
'My lady Prioresse, by your leve,
So that I wiste I sholde you nat greve,
I wolde demen that ye telle sholde
A tale next, if so were that ye wolde.
Now woll ye vouche sauf, my lady deere?'
'Gladly,' quod she, and saide as ye shall heere.

440 'The monk duped the man'. The phrase is an elaborated version (recorded only here) of the idiom 'make an ape of': cf. *C.T.* I 3389.

441 Austin Augustine (echoing 259?)

442 The drawing of 'morals' like this is characteristic of Fr. fabliaux: Nykrog 100–3, 248–52. There is a close parallel at the end of *Gombert*: 'This tale shows us by its example that a man who has a pretty wife should never allow, despite his prayers, a clerk to sleep in his house' (184–7, trans. Benson and Andersson 99). Cf. the Cook's reaction to the *Reeve's T.*, *C.T.* I 4330–4. **inn** house.

444 route company.

447 your polite plural (contrast *thou* 436).

448 So that provided only that.

451 vouche] vouche it *Hg* etc.

The Prioress's Tale

Prioress's Tale is a miracle of the Virgin. Stories of miracles performed by Mary on behalf of her devotees were collected together in England in earlier C12 (see R. W. Southern *Medieval and Renaissance Studies* 4 (1958) 176–216) and became popular from C12 to C15. Vernacular English examples are edited by B. Boyd *The ME Miracles of the Virgin* (San Marino, Calif., Huntington Library 1964).

The miracle of the boy who sings in praise of Mary even after he has been killed by the Jews was popular in various forms. Carleton Brown's standard study, in Bryan and Dempster Ch. 19, lists 33 versions, divided into three main groups. See also M. H. Statler *PMLA* 65 (1950) 896–910. The story had assumed very much the form Chaucer knew by about 1215 (the date of Carleton Brown's version C1); but his exact source is untraced. He evidently followed it closely, since many of his details are matched in the analogues.

The chief critical problem is to define the nature and extent of Chaucer's irony (if any). Those who see Chaucer as hostile to the Prioress stress the sentimental sweetness of her religious feeling (comparing the 'littel clergeon' with the 'smale houndes' of her portrait, *Gen. Prol.* I 146–50) and also what

Wordsworth (who modernized the tale) called the 'fierce bigotry' of her treatment of the Jews. So e.g. I. Robinson *Chaucer and the English Tradition* (Cambridge U.P. 1972) 147–53. R. J. Schoeck, in Schoeck and Taylor (see Chaucer headnote) vol. 1, 245–58, calls the tale 'cruelly anti-Semitic' and credits Chaucer with more humane feelings. However, the tale is remote, as its 'Asian' setting suggests, from English social and political realities. Since Edward I banished them in 1290 there were no Jews in England: C. Roth *History of the Jews in England* (Oxford U.P. 1941). In the poem Jews play an ancillary role as followers of Satan and adversaries of Christ: see *n.* to 558–64. The conflict is conceived in orthodox theological terms: see S. Hawkins *JEGP* 63 (1964) 599–624 and A. B. Friedman *Ch. R.* 9 (1974) 118–29. The expressions of religious feeling (especially towards Mary) draw on the Bible, the liturgy (see *nn.* to 453–87, 580–5), and Dante (*n.* to 474–80). The strength of this poetry is best brought out by Kean, Vol. 2 Ch. 5, who also recognizes its limitations: 'the tale is fitted to the teller through a certain contrived simplicity and deliberate restriction of scope (in which it is in contrast to the *Second Nun's T.*)'. A similarly balanced view is presented by F. H. Ridley *The Prioress and the Critics* (Berkeley, Univ. of California 1965).

Date Unlike its companion piece, *Second Nun's T.*, which was composed before *C.T.* period, *Prioress's T.* was evidently written specifically for the Prioress: witness 'quod she' at 454 and 581. It therefore belongs to the *C.T.* period, after about 1387.

Manuscripts The tale is in 62 MSS., representing 10 separate lines of descent, according to Manly and Rickert 2.351–60. Like some other Canterbury Tales (e.g. *Melibee*), *Prioress's T.* circulated as a separate item. It occurs, for example, in the C15 collection of religious writings MS. Harley 1704. The present text is based on the 'Hengwrt MS.', Nat. Libr. of Wales MS. Peniarth 392 D (= *Hg*). *El* = Ellesmere MS.

The Proheme of the Prioresse Tale.

Domine dominus noster

O lord, oure lord, thy name how merveilous
Is in this large world ysprad – quod she –
For nat only thy laude precious
Parfourned is by men of dignité,
But by the mouth of children thy bounté
Parfourned is, for on the brest soukinge
Somtime shewen they thyn heryinge.

453–87 The Prioress's *Proheme* or prologue draws heavily on the Bible and liturgy, as well as on Dante. See discussion in Kean 2.188 f. The chief source is the Little Office of Our Lady, the abbreviated form in which the Divine Office was best known to laymen such as Chaucer: see Sister Madaleva *Chaucer's Nuns* (New York, Appleton 1925) 29–33. The Invocation to Mary (467–87) formed a conventional opening to a miracle story or saint's legend. Cf. the 'Invocatio ad Mariam' at the beginning of Chaucer's earlier work, the Second Nun's tale of St Cecilia (*C.T.* VIII 29–77), upon which part of the present invocation is based. [*See further notes on facing page*]

Wherfore in laude, as I best can or may,
Of thee and of the white lilye flour
Which that thee bar and is a maide alway,
To telle a storye I woll do my labour;
Nat that I may encressen hir honour,
For she hirself is honour and the rote
Of bounté, next hir sone, and soules bote.

O moder maide, O maide moder free!
O bush unbrent, brenning in Moises sighte,
That ravishedest down fro the deité,
Thurgh thyn humblesse, the gost that in th'alighte,
Of whos vertu, whan he thyn herte lighte,
Conceived was the fadres sapience,
Help me to telle it in thy reverence!

453–9 Closely modelled on *Ps*. 8.2–3 (A.V. 1–2): 'O Lord our Lord: how admirable is thy name in the whole earth! For thy magnificence is elevated above the heavens. Out of the mouth of infants and of sucklings thou hast perfected praise.' This was the opening Psalm at Matins in the Little Office and was also used on Holy Innocents' Day: see 580–5 *n*.

454 ysprad spread.

455 laude praise (Vulgate 'laudem').

456 Parfourned made perfect (Vulgate 'perfecisti').

457 bounté goodness.

459 heryinge praise. An example (mentioned at 514) is the infant St Nicholas, who was said to have sucked only once on Wednesdays and Fridays.

461 lilye an image of the Virgin, deriving from *Song of Sol*. 2.2: 'As the lily among thorns, so is my love among the daughters.'

462 bar bore.

466 bote remedy.

468 unbrent unburnt. The burning bush on Sinai (*Exod*. 3.2) was an acknowledged O.T. type of the Virgin, alluded to in an antiphon in the Little Office: 'In the bush which Moses saw burning without being consumed, we acknowledge the preservation of thy admirable virginity.' See also Chaucer's *ABC of Virgin* 89–96, compared by Kean 2.194–6.

469 ravishedest The word implies the force exerted by Mary's humility on God. **deité** a rare and stylistically elevated word in Chaucer.

470 the gost that in th'alighte the Holy Spirit that alighted in thee.

471 vertu power. **lighte** illuminated.

472 sapience Cf. Dante *Inf*. 3.5–6, where the three persons of the Trinity are identified as divine Power (the Father), supreme Wisdom (*Sapienza*, the Son) and primal Love (the Holy Spirit). All three are involved in the Dantesque intricacies of the Prioress's allusion to the Incarnation. Cf. also *Piers* B 16.36–7. The tradition goes back to *1 Cor*. 1.24.

Lady, thy bounté, thy magnificence,
Thy vertu and thy grete humilité,
There may no tonge expresse in no science;
For somtime, lady, ere men praye to thee,
Thou goost beforn of thy benignité
And getest us the light of thy prayere
To giden us unto thy sone so dere.

My conning is so waik, O blisful quene,
Forto declare thy grete worthinesse,
That I ne may the weighte nat sustene;
But as a child of twelf month old or lesse
That can unethe any word expresse
Right so fare I; and therfore I you praye,
Gideth my song that I shall of you saye.

Here beginneth the Prioresse Tale of Alma Redemptoris Mater.

There was in Asie in a gret cité
Amonges Cristen folk a Jewerye,

474–80 Based on Dante *Par*. 33.16–21. Chaucer recalled his earlier, closer, rendering of Dante in *Second Nun's T., C.T.* VIII 50–6: see Pratt *MLQ* 7 (1946) 259–61.

476 in no science using the language of any branch of human learning (?). *science* is stressed on the second syllable.

477–80 Close to Dante *Par*. 33.16–18: 'Thy kindness (*benignità*) not only succours whoever asks, but often freely foreruns (*precorre*) asking.' The idea (which seems to have no special application to the Prioress's story) goes back to *Wisdom of Sol*. 6.14: 'She [Wisdom] preventeth [i.e. anticipates] them that covet her, so that she first sheweth herself unto them.'

478 goost beforn go on in front, anticipate.

479–80 'And procure for us, by your prayer, the light (of the Holy Ghost? cf. 471) to help us on our way to your beloved Son.' The ambiguity of 479 is resolved in some MSS., which read *thurgh* for *of*.

481 conning ability.

484–6 The whole stanza follows rhetoricians' recommendations for writers to express incapacity at the beginning of works (Curtius 83–5); but these lines link the Prioress's 'laud' of the Virgin with that of the infants of 457 and the innocent of the Tale.

485 unethe hardly.

487 Gideth guide (imperative).

488 Asie probably Asia Minor.

489 Jewerye Jewish quarter. 493 shows that it was simply a street occupied by Jews (the usual meaning of the word in England; cf. 'Jewry' as a street name). 'This was not a Ghetto in the technical sense, nor were the Jews confined to it by law', Roth *History of the Jews in England* 123.

Sustened by a lord of that contré
For foul usure and lucre of vileinye,
Hateful to Crist and to his compaignye;
And thurgh this strete men mighte ride and wende,
For it was free and open at either ende.

A littel scole of Cristen folk there stood
Down at the ferther ende, in which there were
Children an heep, ycomen of Cristen blood,
That lerned in that scole yeer by yere
Swich manere doctrine as men used there,
This is to sayn, to singen and to rede,
As smale children don in hir childhede.

Among thise children was a widwes sone,
A littel clergeon seven yeer of age,
That day by day to scole was his wone,
And eke also, where as he say th'image
Of Cristes moder, hadde he in usage,
As him was taught, to knele adown and saye
His Ave Marie as he goth by the waye.

Thus hath this widwe hir littel sone ytaught
Oure blisful lady, Cristes moder dere,
To worshipe ay, and he forgat it naught,

490–1 Jewish communities in medieval Europe were often 'sustained' by the King for financial reasons, against considerable popular hostility. See Roth (above) for English examples.
491 usure usury. Christians were not allowed to lend money at interest. **lucre of vileinye** glossed in *Hg* etc. *turpe lucrum*, i.e. 'filthy lucre', from *1 Tim.* 3.8. The phrase became technical in canon law, denoting inordinate profit from sales. It is therefore distinct from, and complementary to, *usure*. See Yunck *N & Q* 7 (1960) 165–7.
495 The school is an ordinary primary school, not a choir school: see Carleton Brown *MP* 3 (1905–6) 467–91.
497 heep large number.
499 doctrine teaching, i.e. school subjects.
500 rede i.e. read Latin. Cf. No. 36 below, line 29.
503 clergeon schoolboy, young scholar (diminutive of 'clerk'). **seven yeer** In the analogues, the boy is older: 10 or more. The 'innocent' age of infancy ended at 7, according to medieval reckoning (cf. 538, 566, 635). 7 was also the customary age at which children began school. The boy is in his first term: see 540 *n*.
504 'Whose custom was to go to school every day.'
505 say saw. **image** The reference is to images of Mary in niches etc. on the street.
511 worshipe honour.

For sely child woll alway soone lere.
But ay whan I remembre on this matere,
Saint Nicholas stant evere in my presence,
For he so yong to Crist dide reverence.

This littel child his littel book lerninge,
As he sat in the scole at his primer,
He *Alma redemptoris* herde singe,
As children lerned her antiphoner;
And as he dorste, he drow him ner and ner
And herkned ay the wordes and the note,
Till he the firste vers coude all by rote.

Nat wiste he what this Latin was to saye,
For he so yong and tendre was of age;
But on a day his felawe gan he praye
T'expounden him this song in his langage
Or telle him why this song was in usage:
Thus prayde he him to construe and declare
Full ofte time upon his knowes bare.

His felawe, which that elder was than he,
Answerde him thus: 'This song, I have herd saye,
Was maked of oure blisful lady free,

512 'For a good child will always be quick to learn.' Proverbial: Whiting C219.
514–15 St Nicholas, patron of children, fasted even in his infancy: 459 *n.* He also learned more quickly than any other child: *Southern English Legendary* ed. Horstmann EETS o.s. 87 (1887) p. 240.
514 stant stands.
516 littel . . . littel The most striking repetition of an epithet very characteristic of both tale and teller: cf. 495, 503, 509 etc.
517 primer a Latin book of devotions (including the Little Office), here used as a reader: see Brown (*cit* 495 *n.*).
518 ***Alma redemptoris*** 'Gracious [mother] of the Redeemer', a popular anthem in praise of Mary as Virgin Mother and help of sinners, sung at Lauds, Vespers and Compline.
519 antiphoner anthem book. In another part of the schoolroom, older children (530) are learning to 'sing' (500), i.e. liturgical singing. Chanting Marian anthems was a school exercise.
520 'And, as much as he dared, he drew nearer and nearer.'
521 note tune.
522 vers line. **coude** knew.
523 'He did not know what this Latin meant.'
525 felawe companiōn.
528 construe Regularly stressed on first syllable in early use.
529 knowes knees.
532 free noble.

Hir to salue, and eke hir forto praye
To ben oure help and socour whan we deye.
I can namore expounde in this matere;
I lerne song, I can but small gramere.'

'And is this song maked in reverence
Of Cristes moder?' saide this innocent.
'Now certes I woll do my diligence
To conne it all ere Cristemasse is went.
Thogh that I for my primer shall be shent,
And shall be beten thries in an houre,
I woll it conne oure lady forto honoure.'

His felawe taughte him homward privély,
Fro day to day, till he coude it by rote;
And thenne he song it well and boldely,
Fro word to word, acording with the note.
Twies a day it passed thurgh his throte,
To scoleward and homward whan he wente.
On Cristes moder set was his entente.

As I have said, thurghout the Jewerye
This littel child, as he cam to and fro,
Full murily wolde he singe and crye
O alma redemptoris ever mo.
The swetnesse his herte perced so
Of Cristes moder, that to hir to praye
He can nat stinte of singing by the waye.

533–4 Salutation and prayer are precisely the two purposes of the anthem; but it does not call for Mary's help at the time of death.

536 'I am learning singing; I know only a little Latin (*gramere*).'

538 innocent cf. 503 *n*. The term associates the boy with the Holy Innocents massacred by Herod: see 574, 580–5, 627 *n*.

540 'To learn it all before the Christmas feast is ended', i.e. before the beginning of next term. The boy is in the first (Michaelmas) term of his first year.

541 'Even though I am punished for neglecting my primer.'

544 homward on the way home.

547 i.e. with every word rightly matched with the music.

550 entente intent, heart.

553 wolde] than wolde 22 MSS. (repairing halting metre).

555 his] hath his 24 MSS. (again for metrical reasons; but the characteristic word *swetnessė* is to be dwelt on).

557 stinte of cease from.

Oure firste foo, the serpent Sathanas,
That hath in Jewes herte his waspes nest,
Up swal and saide, 'O Hebraic peple, alas,
Is this to you a thing that is honest,
That swich a boy shall walken as him lest,
In your despit, and singe of swich sentence
Which is agains oure lawes reverence?'

Fro thennes forth the Jewes han conspired
This innocent out of this world to chace.
An homicide therto han they hired,
That in an aleye hadde a privé place;
And as the child gan forby forto pace,
This cursed Jew him hente and heeld him faste
And cutte his throte and in a pit him caste.

I saye that in a wardrobe they him threwe,
Wheras thise Jewes purgen her entraille.
O cursed folk of Herodes all newe,
What may your ivel entente you availle?
Morder woll out, certain it woll nat faille,
And namely theras th'honour of God shall sprede;
The blood out crieth on your cursed dede.

558–64 The intimate relation between the Jews and Satan in medieval thought is discussed by J. Trachtenberg *The Devil and the Jews* (Yale U.P. 1943).

560 Up swal swelled up (with indignation).

561 honest honourable.

562 boy a rare, colloquial word, usually contemptuous as here. Elsewhere the boy is called *child*, *innocent*, etc. **him lest** it pleases him.

563 In your despit in defiance of you. **swich sentence** such matters.

564 oure Satan and the Jews share one law, as God and Christians share another. See 558–64 *n*. 34 MSS. read *youre*.

568 hadde] at *Hg* etc.

569 'And as the child was going past.'

570 hente seized.

572 wardrobe Because the same room was often used as clothes room and latrine, the word originally designating the former came to be applied euphemistically to the latter. The Merchant (*C.T.* IV 1954) more robustly says 'privy'

574 The reference to *Herodes* (Chaucer regularly uses the Vulgate form) recalls the Massacre of the Innocents: see 580–5 *n*. The Jews who kill the boy re-enact (*all newe*) what 'Herod's folk' did.

576 The proverb 'Murder will out' (Whiting M806) is later echoed by the Prioress's priest: *C.T.* VII 3052, 3057.

577 namely especially.

O martyr souded to virginité,
Now maystow singen, folwing ever in oon
The white lamb celestial – quod she –
Of which the grete evangelist saint John
In Pathmos wroot, which saith that they that gon
Beforn this lamb and singe a song all newe,
That never fleshly womman they ne knewe.

This poure widwe awaiteth all that night
After hir littel child, but he cam noght;
For which, as soone as it was dayes light,
With face pale of drede and bisy thoght
She hath at scole and elleswhere him soght,
Till finally she gan so fer espye
That he last seen was in the Jewerye.

With modres pité in hir brest enclosed,
She goth as she were half out of hir minde
To every place where she hath supposed
By liklihede hir littel child to finde,
And ever on Cristes moder meke and kinde

579 souded puzzled the scribes (who have *sounded*, *sounyng*, *ostendid* etc.) understandably enough. The choice lies between *OED Sold* v.[1] 'to enlist or retain for service' and *OED Sold* v.[2] 'to solder . . . to unite firmly or closely'. *OED* places this use under v.[1] ('enlisted in the service of virginity'); but v.[2] is equally possible ('inseparable from virginity'). Matthew Arnold misquoted to illustrate the special charm of Chaucer: 'O martyr, souded in virginitee' ('The study of poetry' *Essays in Criticism*: *Second Series*).

580–5 The virgin martyr has now joined the company of 144,000 virgin followers of the Lamb, described by St John in *Rev*. 14.1–5. (The little girl in *Pearl* joins the same company.) These were specially associated with the Holy Innocents massacred by Herod, and the passage from *Revelation* was read at Mass on Holy Innocents' Day, 28 Dec. M. P. Hamilton *MLR* 34 (1939) 1–8 (reptd in Wagenknecht) notes other echoes from this Mass: *Ps*. 8 (see 453–9 *n*.) provided the Introit; and the story of Herod was read, ending with the quotation from *Jeremiah* about Rachel (below 627). However, the passage from *Rev*. is cited in a Latin gloss opposite these lines (in *Hg*+4 MSS.) in a form which suggests that Chaucer was recalling Jerome *Adversus Iovinianum*: see Brennan *SP* 70 (1973) 243–51.

580 ever in oon constantly.

583 Pathmos Patmos, where John wrote his Revelation.

585 fleshly adverbial, glossed *carnaliter* in *Hg*.

589 bisy anxious.

591 gan so fer espye got so far as to discover.

595 where] wher as *Hg*+13 MSS.

She cride, and at the laste thus she wroghte:
Among the cursed Jewes she him soghte.

She fraineth and she prayeth pitously
To every Jew that dwelte in thilke place
To telle hir if hir child wente oght forby.
They saide nay; but Jesu of his grace
Yaf in hir thought inwith a littel space
That in that place after hir sone she cride
Where he was casten in a pit beside.

O grete God, that parfournest thy laude
By mouth of innocents, lo here thy might!
This gemme of chastité, this emeraude,
And eke of martirdom the ruby bright,
There he with throte ycorven lay upright,
He *Alma redemptoris* gan to singe
So loude that all the place gan to ringe.

The Cristen folk that thurgh the strete wente
In comen forto wondre upon this thing,
And hastily they for the provost sente.
He cam anon withouten tarying,
And herieth Crist that is of hevene king,
And eke his moder, honour of mankinde;
And after that the Jewes leet he binde.

This child with pitous lamentacioun
Up taken was, singing his song alway;
And with honour of gret processioun

600 fraineth asks.
601 thilke that same.
602 wente oght forby had by any chance been past.
604 'Within a short time put it into her mind.'
607–8 See *nn.* to 453–9 and 580–5. Jesus quoted the same verse after throwing out the money-changers (*Matt.* 21.16).
607 parfournest See 456 *n.*
608 lo here behold.
609 According to the lapidaries, the emerald is a 'clean' stone which 'voideth lechery': *English Mediaeval Lapidaries* ed. J. Evans and M. S. Serjeantson EETS o.s. 190 (1933) 20–1, 40, 121.
610 Red is the colour of martyrdom. See No. 23 below, line 110.
611 ycorven cut. **upright** flat on his back.
616 provost chief magistrate (a term used in referring only to foreign towns).
618 herieth praises (poetic and somewhat archaic in C14).
620 leet he binde he caused to be bound.
623 The solemn procession is appropriate to translation of a saint's remains.

They carien him unto the nexte abbay.
His moder swouning by his beere lay.
Unethe mighte the peple that was there
This newe Rachel bringen fro his beere.

With torment and with shameful deth echon
The provost doth thise Jewes forto sterve
That of this mordre wiste, and that anon.
He nolde no swich cursednesse observe.
Ivel shall have that ivel woll deserve.
Therfore with wilde hors he dide hem drawe,
And after that he heng hem by the lawe.

Upon his beere ay lith this innocent
Beforn the chief auter whil the masse laste;
And after that, the abbot with his covent
Han sped hem forto buryen him full faste;
And whan they holy water on him caste,
Yet spak this child whan spreind was holy water
And song *O alma redemptoris mater*.

This abbot, which that was an holy man
As monkes ben, or elles oghten be,
This yonge child to conjure he began,

624 nexte nearest.
625 beere bier.
627 Rachel *Matthew* (2.18) represents the Massacre as a fulfilment of Jeremiah's prophecy (*Jer*. 31.15): 'A voice in Rama was heard, lamentation and great mourning; Rachel bewailing her children and would not be comforted, because they are not'. See 580–5 *n*. **newe** Here as at 574, implies the typological idea that modern people and events are foreshadowed in the Bible.
629 doth causes. **sterve** die.
630 wiste had knowledge.
631 'He had no wish to countenance such wickedness.'
632 Apparently proverbial: Whiting E178.
633 he dide hem drawe he had them drawn. Traitors were dragged through the streets to the place of hanging.
634 heng hanged.
636 auter altar. Corpses of laymen were ordinarily set down in the nave. **masse** Requiem Mass.
637 covent convent, company of monks.
639 Sprinkling the corpse with holy water forms part of the burial ritual following the Requiem Mass.
640 spreind sprinkled.
643 A reproachful allusion to the Shipman's disrespectful portrait of a monk?
644 conjure appeal to.

And saide, 'O dere child, I halsen thee
In vertu of the holy Trinité,
Tell me what is thy cause forto singe,
Sith that thy throte is cut, to my seminge?'

'My throte is cut unto my necke boon,'
Saide this child, 'and as by way of kinde
I sholde have died, yea, longe time agoon;
But Jesus Crist, as ye in bokes finde,
Woll that his glorye laste and be in minde;
And for the worship of his moder dere
Yet may I singe *O alma* loude and clere.

'This welle of mercy, Cristes moder swete,
I loved alway as after my conninge;
And whan that I my lif sholde forlete,
To me she cam, and bad me forto singe
This antheme verraily in my deyinge
As ye han herd; and whan that I had songe,
Me thoughte she laide a grain upon my tonge.

'Wherfore I singe, and singe mot, certain,
In honour of that blisful maiden free,
Till fro my tonge off taken is the grain;
And after that, thus saide she to me:
"My littel child, now woll I fecche thee
Whan that the grain is fro thy tonge ytake.
Be nat agast, I woll thee nat forsake".'

645 halsen implore (*MED* s.v. *Halsnen* v.).
648 to my seminge as it seems to me. Idiomatic: *OED* s.v. *Seeming* vbl sb. 1c.
650 as by way of kinde in the way of nature.
653 Woll wills.
654 worship honour.
657 loved praised (OE *lofian*, distinct from OE *lufian*, Modern *love*). **after** according to.
658 sholde forlete was to lose.
662 grain In one analogue a lily is found in the boy's throat; in two others a jewel and pebble are found in place of the cut-out tongue (see Bryan and Dempster). Robinson thinks *grain* means 'little pearl' here; but *MED* s.v. *Grain* 3 hardly supports this. Beichner *Spec.* 36 (1961) 302–7 more plausibly suggests 'grain of Paradise', a granular spice (cardamom) chewed to sweeten the breath (cf. *C.T.* I 3690, where Absolon uses it) and to soothe the throat: 'The image therefore is that of a loving mother who uses medicine to relieve the pain and distress of the injured throat of her child.' See also *Spec.* 40 (1965) 63–73, for a bizarre anatomical possibility.

This holy monk, this abbot, him mene I,
His tonge out caughte and took away the grain,
And he yaf up the gost full softely.
And whan this abbot hadde this wonder sein,
His salte teres trickled down as rain,
And gruf he fil all plat upon the grounde,
And stille he lay as he hadde lain ybounde.

The covent ek lay on the pavement
Wepinge, and herien Cristes moder dere;
And after that they rise and forth ben went
And toke away this martir from his beere,
And in a tombe of marbelstones clere
Enclosen they this littel body swete.
There he is now, God leve us forto mete!

O yonge Hugh of Lincoln, slain also
With cursed Jewes, as it is notable,
For it is but a littel while ygo,
Praye ek for us, we sinful folk unstable,
That of his mercy God so merciable
On us his grete mercy multiplye,
For reverence of his moder Marie. Amen.

Here endeth the Prioresse Tale.

671 caughte pulled.

672 yaf gave.

673 sein seen.

675 gruf prostrate. **plat** flat (*Hg*+4 MSS. read *flat*).

676 lain] *Hg*+12 MSS.; been 42 MSS. The high authority of some of the 13 MSS. reading *lein/lain*, set against the awkward verbal repetition involved, leaves the original in doubt.

678 herien praise. Most MSS. have *herying*; but how could *herien* have arisen as an error in *Hg*, *El* and 5 other MSS?

679 rise rose.

681 clere bright.

682 this] *Hg*+33 MSS.; his *El*+20 MSS.

683 'Where he is now (i.e. in Paradise) may God grant us to meet.'

684–90 The anonymous boy martyr cannot be invoked by name; so the Prioress instead invokes the prayers of St Hugh of Lincoln, an English boy thought to have suffered the same fate. Nine-year-old 'little St Hugh' was found dead in Lincoln in 1255, supposedly martyred by Jews. His relics were venerated at Lincoln Cathedral. See G. Langmuir *Spec.* 47 (1972) 459–82.

John Gower

Life Born 1330, according to tradition. His family were of the gentry, owning land especially in Yorkshire and Kent. His title 'esquire of Kent' (in a document of 1382) is borne out by Kentish features in his dialect and by records of land purchases in Kent. He perhaps practised law; but 'from about 1377 until his death in 1408, [he] lived a semiretired life in St Mary's Priory [Southwark], devoting his time mainly to his books and his friends': so J. H. Fisher *John Gower: moral philosopher and friend of Chaucer* (New York U.P. 1964; London, Methuen 1965), the most complete biographical study (p. 60). He remained a layman, residing at the Priory as a pious sympathizer and (perhaps) benefactor. His London friends included Chaucer. In 1378 Chaucer appointed Gower one of his legal representatives during his absence in Italy. In the mid 1380s Chaucer 'directed' *Troilus* (5.1856–7) to 'moral Gower' and 'philosophical Strode' (the latter an Oxford logician and London lawyer). About 1390 Gower in the first version of *Confessio Amantis* (VIII 2941*–57*, not in revised versions) makes Venus speak of Chaucer as her 'disciple' and 'poet'. Venus asks Gower to tell Chaucer 'upon his latere age' to 'sette an ende of alle his werk' and make his 'testament of love'. A similar humorous tone marks what appears to be Chaucer's allusion to *Confessio Amantis* in *Canterbury Tales* II 77–89. Gower died in 1408.

Works and editions Gower confesses to *fols ditz d'amours* ('foolish amorous ditties') in youth, some of which may survive in the sequence of his French *Cinkante balades*. His first major work was also in French: *Mirour de l'omme*, a long didactic poem on virtues and vices (late 1370s). This was followed by the Latin *Vox clamantis*, lamenting the evils of society in the age of Richard II and referring to the Peasants' Revolt (1381): trans. E. W. Stockton *The Major Latin Works of John Gower* (Univ. of Washington P. 1962). His last major work was the English *Confessio Amantis*, on which see below. The standard edn of Gower's works (French, Latin, and English) is by G. C. Macaulay, 4 vols (Oxford U.P. 1899–1902). See also J. A. W. Bennett, ed. *Selections from John Gower* (Oxford U.P. 1968).

Reputation C15 and C16 references regularly couple Gower with Chaucer (and Lydgate) as a member of the first and greatest generation of English 'makers': so Dunbar in C15 (No. 33 lines 49–51) and Puttenham in C16 (*cit.* Introd. xvi). *Confessio Amantis* was printed by Caxton (1483) and Berthelette (1532, 1554). Shakespeare draws on *Confessio Amantis* in *Pericles*, where the Prologue imitates Gower's octosyllabic couplets: 'To sing a song that old was sung, | From ashes ancient Gower is come, | Assuming man's infirmities | To glad your ear and please your eyes'. Ben Jonson, in his English Grammar, cites more examples from Gower than from any other author. The C18 literary historian Thomas Warton praised him for extensive reading and 'knowledge of life'. But Coleridge called him 'almost worthless', and he has not appealed to Romantic tastes. The two classic modern studies are W. P. Ker *Essays on Medieval Literature* (1905) Ch. 5 and C. S. Lewis *Allegory of Love* Ch. 5. J. H. Fisher's book (above) traces Gower's critical reputation (Ch. 1), and considers him chiefly as moral commentator on contemporary society. See also A. B. Ferguson *The Articulate Citizen and the English Renaissance* (Duke U.P. 1965) Ch. 2.

19 Confessio Amantis: extract

Confessio Amantis proposes (Prol. 17–19) to steer a 'middle way' between entertainment (*lust*) and teaching (*lore*). The entertainment derives chiefly from the courtly conceit of the Religion of Love: see Lewis *Allegory of Love* Ch. 1. John Gower, represented as an unhappy lover (Amans), sees Cupid and Venus in a vision. He is commanded to confess his sins to the priest of Venus, Genius (Nature's priest in *R. de la Rose* and in Alanus *De planctu Naturae*: see Lewis App. 1). His confession is organized round the scheme of the Seven Deadly Sins, as confessions commonly were: see M. W. Bloomfield *The Seven Deadly Sins* (Michigan State U.P. 1952). Each sin occupies a book. Genius illustrates different species of sin with stories, and questions Amans about his conduct. The present extract comes from the Book of Sloth. The serious moral teaching (*lore*) in the *Confessio* is represented especially in the Prologue (on discords in contemporary society), in Bk 7 (devoted to a survey of 'philosophy'), and above all in the beautiful closing scenes (8.2029–end), where Amans is brought by Venus and Genius to recognize that he is too old for love, and receives a string of black beads 'por reposer' as a sign of his newly achieved philosophic calm. See, besides Lewis and Fisher, J. A. W. Bennett in J. Lawlor, ed. *Patterns of Love and Courtesy* (E. Arnold 1966) 107–21.

Gower is the greatest ME master of the octosyllabic couplet (cf. No. 2), a form developed in C12 France as a medium of narrative and employed by Gower much in the French way; his 'plain style' (Lewis) is equally well suited for narrative. See D. Pearsall 'Gower's narrative art' *PMLA* 81 (1966) 475–84. Stylistically, Gower is the most correct and polished of ME poets. Thomas Warton, in C18, observed his 'critical cultivation of his native language'.

Manuscripts and versions The 49 MSS. exhibit *Confessio Amantis* in several states. After first finishing the poem, Gower subjected his master copy to a complex process of revision over several years. Copies (as in the case of *Troilus*) were taken for 'publication' at various stages. The first version, completed about 1390, contains praises of Richard II and an allusion to Chaucer. Within the next year or two, the passage about Richard was excised. The third version (1393) is dedicated to the future Henry IV. See Macaulay's edn (preceding headnote) for details. The present text is based, like Macaulay's, on Bodleian MS. Fairfax 3, a copy of the third version made in the last decade of C14, perhaps at the scriptorium of St Mary's, Southwark, under the poet's supervision. It is exceptionally careful, preserving the delicate verbal and metrical art of the poem almost flawlessly, and may be regarded as a monument to Gower's passion for 'correctness'.

[19] John Gower

Book IV 1083–1462

CONFESSOR:

'Among these othre of Slouthes kinde,
Which alle labour set behinde
And hateth alle besinesse,
There is yit oon, which Idelnesse
Is cleped, and is the norrice
In mannes kinde of every vice,
Which secheth eases manifold.
In winter doth he noght for cold,
In somer may he noght for hete;
So whether that he frese or swete,
Or he be inne or he be oute,
He woll ben idel all aboute,
Bot if he playe oght atte dees.
For who as ever take fees
And thenkth worshipe to deserve,
There is no lord whom he woll serve,
As forto dwelle in his servise,
Bot if it were in such a wise
Of that he seeth per aventure
That by lordshipe and coverture
He may the more stonde stille
And use his idelnesse at wille.
For he ne woll no travail take
To ride for his lady sake,
Bot liveth all upon his wishes;

1083 Slouthes kinde the family of Sloth. In this Fourth Book, the Confessor expounds the various types of sloth: forgetfulness, negligence, etc. See S. Wenzel *The Sin of Sloth* (N. Carolina U.P. 1967).

1084 set behinde puts aside (*set* = *setteth*).

1085 besinesse strenuous activity. 'Business' is the conventional ME opposite of sloth (e.g. *Castle of Perseverance* 1641–53): cf. 1119, 1151, 1155 etc. The form with *e* in first syllable is Kentish, reflecting Gower's origins.

1087 norrice nurse. Cf. 'The ministre and the norice unto vices, | Which that men clepe in English idelnesse', *C.T.* VIII 1–2. See Wenzel 103.

1093 'Indoors or out.'

1095 'Unless he plays a bit of dice'; *atte* is disyllabic ('at the').

1096–1103 'For whoever else may receive rewards and set out to win a reputation, *he* [Sloth] will not serve any lord – not so as to stay any length of time in his service – unless it so happens, maybe, that he sees he can do less work under the cover of his lord's protection.'

1105 ff. The Confessor turns to idleness in love.

And as a cat wolde ete fishes
Withoute weting of his cles,
So wolde he do, bot natheles
He faileth ofte of that he wolde.
My sone, if thou of such a molde
Art made, now tell me plain thy shrifte.'

AMANS:

'Nay, fader, God I yive a yifte,
That toward love, as by my wit,
All idel was I never yit,
Ne never shall, whil I may go.'

CONFESSOR:

'Now, sone, tell me thenne so,
What hast thou don of besishipe
To love and to the ladiship
Of hire which thy lady is?'

CONFESSIO AMANTIS

'My fader, ever yit ere this
In every place, in every stede,
What so my lady hath me bede,
With all myn herte obedient
I have therto be diligent;
And if so is she bidde noght,
What thing that thenne into my thoght
Comth ferst, of that I may suffise.
I bowe and profre my servise,
Somtime in chambre, somtime in halle,

1108–9 A medieval Lat. proverb, Englished in C14: Whiting C93. Cf. *House of Fame* 1783–5, Shakespeare *Mac.* 1.7.44–5. See Wenzel 105.
1109 cles claws.
1113 plain fully, completely. Confession (*shrift*) had to be full.
1114 'No, father, I pledge my word to God.' Idiomatic: see *OED* s.v. *Give* v. 8.
1117 go walk.
1120 to the ladiship to the honour as a lady.
1122–1223 'The Lover appears even more servile and plaintive – one is tempted to use the word degraded – than is usually the case in courtly literature', D. Schueler *Med. Aev.* 36 (1967) 158, who attributes this to Amans's advanced age (cf. Thomas Mann's *Death in Venice*).
1123 stede place.
1124 bede commanded.
1127 if so is if it happens that.
1128–9 'Then I can be satisfied with whatever (service) comes first into my mind.' This unusual use of *suffice* occurs also in No. 17 above, line 2: see *n.*

Right as I see the times falle;
And whan she goth to hiere masse,
That time shall noght overpasse
That I n'aproche hir ladihede
In aunter if I may hir lede
Unto the chapel and ayain.
Then is noght all my waye in vain:
Somdel I may the bettre fare,
Whan I, that may noght fele hir bare,
May lede hir clothed in myn arm.
Bot afterward it doth me harm
Of pure imaginacioun;
For thenne this collacioun
I make unto myselven ofte
And saye, "Ha, lord, how she is softe,
How she is round, how she is small!
Now wolde God I hadde hir all
Withoute danger at my wille!"
And thenne I sike and sitte stille,
Of that I see my besy thoght
Is torned idel into noght.
Bot for all that lete I ne may,
Whan I see time another day,
That I ne do my besinesse
Unto my lady worthinesse.
For I therto my wit afaite
To see the times and awaite

1132 times falle occasions arise. Not being 'idle', Amans does not waste 'times' or opportunities: cf. 1134, 1154, 1158, 1160.
1133 hiere hear.
1135 That I n'aproche without my approaching.
1136 In aunter if on the chance that.
1137 ayain back again.
1139 Somdel somewhat.
1144 collacioun reflection.
1147 small slender.
1149 Withoute danger without any standoffishness on her part. The personification Danger in *R. de la Rose* is one of the Lover's enemies (English *Romaunt* 3018). Cf. No. 12 above, line 384 and *n.*
1150 sike sigh.
1151 Of that because.
1152 idel uselessly. Word play on *idel* and *besy*: see *n.* to 1085.
1153 lete refrain.
1156 lady lady's (regular possessive form).
1157 my wit afaite direct my mind.

What is to done and what to leve;
And so, whan time is, by hir leve,
What thing she bit me don, I do,
And where she bit me gon, I go,
And whan hir list to clepe, I come.
Thus hath she fulliche overcome
Myn idelnesse till I sterve,
So that I mot hir nedes serve,
For as men sain, nede hath no lawe.
Thus mot I nedly to hir drawe;
I serve, I bowe, I loke, I loute,
Myn yë folweth hir aboute;
What so she wole, so woll I,
Whan she woll sitte, I knele by,
And whan she stant, then woll I stonde.
Bot whan she takth hir werk on honde
Of weving or enbrouderye,
Then can I noght bot muse and prye
Upon hir fingres longe and smale;
And now I thenke, and now I tale,
And now I singe, and now I sike,
And thus my contenaunce I pike.
And if it falle as for a time
Hir liketh noght abide bime,
Bot besien hir on othre thinges,
Then make I othre taryinges

1159 done do (inflected infinitive).
1161 bit bids (= *biddeth*).
1163 hir list to clepe it pleases her to call.
1165 sterve die.
1166 mot must.
1167 A legal maxim ('Necessitas non habet legem') which became proverbial: Whiting N51.
1168 nedly of necessity. The word play on derivatives from the same root (*nedes*, *nede*, *nedly*) is a rhetorical artifice (*annominatio*).
1169 loute make obeisance.
1176 muse and prye gaze and peer (*prye* does not imply improper curiosity).
1177 Long slender (*smale*) fingers characterize aristocratic ladies: cf. No. 11.1 above, lines 10–12.
1178 tale converse.
1180 Difficult. *pike* perhaps means 'select carefully' (*OED* s.v. *Pick* v.[1] 7, citing *Confessio* 3.500): 'And thus I choose exactly how I will behave' (i.e. to create the best impression)? Macaulay, comparing 1.698, suggests: 'thus I keep up a pretence (for staying)'.
1182 bime 'by me', in my company.

To drecche forth the longe day,
For me is loth departe away.
And then I am so simple of port
That forto feigne som desport
I playe with hir littel hound
Now on the bed, now on the ground,
Now with hir briddes in the cage;
For there is non so littel page,
Ne yit so simple a chamberere,
That I ne make hem alle chere,
All for they sholde speke wel.
Thus mow ye seen my besy whel
That goth noght ideliche aboute.
And if hir list to riden oute
On pelrinage or other stede,
I come, though I be noght bede,
And take hir in myn arm alofte
And sette hir in hir sadel softe,
And so forth lede hir by the bridel,
For that I wolde noght ben idel.
And if hir list to ride in char,
And then I may therof be war,
Anon I shape me to ride
Right evene by the chares side;
And as I may, I speke among,
And otherwhile I singe a song
Which Ovide in his bokes made

1185 drecche forth while away.
1187 port bearing, behaviour.
1193 chamberere chambermaid.
1194–5 'That I do not treat them in the most friendly way, and all in order that they may speak well of me.' The monk employs a similar technique in Chaucer's *Shipman's T.*, No. 18 above, lines 43–9.
1196 mow may. **whel** mill-wheel.
1199 pelrinage pilgrimage.
1200 bede invited.
1202 softe gently.
1205 char carriage.
1207 shape me prepare.
1209 among from time to time.
1211 Ovide The paradoxical character and irresistible power of love were ancient themes. Gower's references to his authorities are not always reliable; but cf. oxymorons such as Ovid's *Amores* 2.9.26: 'dulce puella malum est' ('a woman is a sweet evil'). Chaucer describes love in similar oxymorons: *Troilus* 1.411; *Parlement of Foules* 3. Cf. No. 12 above, line 776.

And saide, "O whiche sorwes glade,
O which wofull prosperité
Belongeth to the propreté
Of Love, who so woll him serve!
And yit therfro may no man swerve,
That he ne mot his lawe obeye."
And thus I ride forth my weye,
And am right besy overall
With herte and with my body all,
As I have said you hertofore.
My goode fader, tell therfore
Of idelnesse if I have gilt.'

CONFESSOR:

'My sone, bot thou telle wilt
Oght elles than I may now here,
Thou shalt have no penance here.
And natheless a man may see
How nowadayes that there be
Full many of suche hertes slowe,
That woll noght besien hem to knowe
What thing love is, till atte laste
That he with strengthe hem overcaste,
That malgré hem they mote obeye
And don all idelshipe aweye,
To serve well and besiliche.
Bot, sone, thou art non of swiche,
For love shall thee well excuse;
Bot otherwise, if thou refuse
To love, thou might so per cas
Ben idel, as somtime was
A kinges doughter unavised,
Till that Cupide hir hath chastised.

1214 propreté nature.
1216 swerve turn aside.
1224 bot unless.
1226 here i.e. in this matter of idleness.
1229 slowe slothful.
1232 overcaste throws down. Love's revenge on those who refuse to serve him is illustrated in *Troilus* Bk 1. See also No. 16 above, lines 29–33.
1233 malgré hem despite themselves.
1236 swiche such.
1239 per cas perhaps.
1241 unavised thoughtless.

Wherof thou shalt a tale here
Acordant unto this matere.
  Of Armenye, I rede thus,
There was a king which Herupus
Was hote, and he a lusty maide
To doughter hadde, and as men saide
Hir name was Rosiphelee,
Which tho was of gret renomee
For she was bothe wis and fair,
And sholde ben hir fader heir.
Bot she hadde o defalte of slouthe
Towardes love, and that was routhe;
For so well coude no man saye
Which mighte sette hir in the waye
Of loves occupacion
Thurgh non imaginacion –
That scole wolde she noght knowe.
And thus she was oon of the slowe
As of such hertes besinesse,
Till whanne Venus the goddesse,
Which loves court hath forto reule,
Hath broght hir into betre reule,
Forth-with Cupide and with his might.
For they merveille how such a wight,
Which tho was in hir lusty age,
Desireth nother mariage

1244 'Appropriate to this subject.'
1245–1462 Closest analogues to the story of Rosiphelee are in the Breton lay (see headnote to No. 2) *Lai du Trot* and Andreas Capellanus *De amore* (trans. J. J. Parry as *The Art of Courtly Love* (Columbia U.P. 1941), 74–8). Andreas has three companies (faithful mistresses, promiscuous women, scorners of love), whereas the scornful lady in G. is a solitary outcast. For other analogues, see W. A. Neilson *Romania* 29 (1900) 85–93.
1245 Armenye Armenia.
1247 hote called. **lusty** in the full vigour of youth (cf. 1267, 1271).
1250 renomee fame.
1252 'And was to be her father's heir.'
1253 o defalte one fault.
1259 scole discipline.
1261 See *n.* to 1085.
1263–4 Rhyme of noun with formally identical verb conforms to rules of 'rime equivoque' (punning rhyme) as recommended by late-medieval French treatises on poetry: E. Langlois, ed. *Recueil d'arts de seconde rhétorique* (Paris 1902) Index s.v. *Equivocques*. Cf. here 1159–60, 1365–6 etc.
1265 Forth-with together with.

Ne yit the love of paramours,
Which ever hath be the comun cours
Amonges hem that lusty were.
So was it shewed after there;
For he that hihe hertes loweth
With firy dartes which he throweth,
Cupide, which of love is god,
In chastising hath made a rod
To drive away hir wantounesse,
So that withinne a while, I gesse,
She hadde on such a chance sporned
That all hir mood was overtorned
Which ferst she hadde of slow manere.
For thus it fell, as thou shalt here.
  Whan come was the monthe of May,
She wolde walke upon a day,
And that was ere the sunne ariste,
Of wommen bot a fewe itwiste;
And forth she wente privély
Unto the park was faste by,
All softe walkende on the grass,
Till she cam there the launde was,
Thurgh which there ran a gret rivere.
It thoghte hir fair, and saide, "Here
I woll abide under the shawe",
And bad hir wommen to withdrawe,
And there she stood all one stille
To thenke what was in hir wille.
She sih the swote floures springe,
She herde glade foules singe,

1269 love of paramours passionate love. The Confessor here speaks as priest of Venus.
1273 So Cupid humbles the pride of Troilus: *Troilus* 1.211 ff.
1277 wantounesse naughtiness. The image is of a parent 'chastising' a child.
1279 sporned tripped.
1280 mood disposition.
1281 of slow manere of a slothful kind.
1285 the sunne ariste the rising of the sun.
1286 'Together with only a few women': See *MED* s.v. *Itwix*.
1288 park specifically, an enclosed area in which beasts of chase are kept: cf. 1300.
1290 launde glade.
1292 thoghte seemed.
1293 shawe wood.
1295 one alone.

She sih the bestes in her kinde,
The buck, the do, the hert, the hinde,
The madle go with the femele;
And so began there a querele
Betwen love and hir owne herte,
Fro which she couthe noght asterte.
And as she caste hir ye aboute
She sih clad in o suite a route
Of ladis where they comen ride
Along under the wodes side.
On faire amblende hors they sete
That were all white, fatte and grete,
And everichon they ride on side.
The sadles were of such a pride,
With perle and gold so well begon,
So riche sih she never non.
In kertles and in copes riche
They weren clothed alle liche,
Departed even of whit and blew.
With alle lustes that she knew
They were enbrouded overall.

1299–1301 The deer go together according to species (*kinde*): fallow deer (*buck*, male; *do*, female) and red deer (*hert*, male; *hinde*, female).
1301 madle male. This line echoes *R. de la Rose* 18975, where Nature is complaining that animals obey her law of the reproduction of the species, but men do not. The whole passage is relevant to Rosiphelee.
1302 querele state of hostility.
1304 asterte escape.
1305 ff. Bennett compares this visionary company of ladies with that seen by Sir Orfeo (No. 2 above, lines 303 f.), and with the company of fairy knights and ladies on white steeds in that poem (143 f.). G. gives more descriptive detail, without dispelling the sense of mystery.
1306 in o suite in matching attire: cf. 1316–17. Matching fabrics figure commonly in medieval accounts of courtly and fairy luxury: *Gawain* 180, 191, 859; *Orfeo*, No. 2 above, 145–6. **route** company.
1309 amblende hors horses walking gently.
1310–14 See Wimberly 186–9 on the Fairy Steed, which is usually white and richly accoutred.
1311 on side side-saddle: 'like Chaucer's elegant Prioress in the Ellesmere drawings – not like the Wife of Bath' (Bennett *Gower*).
1313 begon adorned.
1315 kertles gowns. **copes** cloaks.
1316 liche alike.
1317 Departed even equally divided. White symbolizes purity, blue fidelity – colours appropriate for the 'livery' of true servants of Love.
1318 lustes pleasant things.

Her bodies weren long and small;
The beauté faye upon her face
Non erthly thing it may desface.
Corones on her hed they bere
As ech of hem a queene were,
That all the gold of Cresus halle
The leste coronal of alle
Ne mighte have boght after the worth.
Thus come they ridende forth.
  The kinges doughter which this sih
For pure abaisht drough hir adrih,
And held hir clos under the bough
And let hem passen stille inough;
For as hir thoghte in hir avis,
To hem that were of such a pris
She was noght worthy axen there
Fro when they come or what they were.
Bot lever than this worldes good
She wolde have wist how that it stood,
And putte hir hed a littel oute;
And as she lokede hir aboute
She sih comende under the linde
A womman up an hors behinde.
The hors on which she rod was black,
All lene and galled on the back,

1321–2 G. apparently revised this couplet twice. First version: 'The beauté of hir face shon | Well brighter than the crystal stone' (cf. No. 13 above line 3). Second version: 'The beauté of hir faire face | There may non erthly thing deface' (*faye* for *faire* in one MS.). See Lewis *Allegory* 204.
1321 faye otherworldly.
1322 desface disfigure (i.e. outshine?).
1327 after the worth at its true value.
1330 'Drew back out of sheer astonishment.' On the construction, see *n.* to No. 12 above, line 656.
1331 clos hidden.
1333 hir thoghte it seemed to her. **avis** opinion.
1334 pris excellence.
1336 when whence.
1337 lever rather.
1341 linde trees.
1342 womman First identified as a 'woman', servant, rather than 'lady'; but her beauty, the horse's star and the rich bridle create a puzzling impression, reflected in Rosiphelee's guarded manner of addressing her as 'sister' (1369, 1383). **up** upon.
1344 galled having sores.

And haltede as he were encluyed,
Wherof the womman was annuyed.
Thus was the hors in sory plit,
Bot for all that a sterre whit
Amiddes in the front he hadde.
Hir sadel eke was wonder badde
In which the wofull womman sat,
And natheless there was with that
A riche bridel for the nones
Of gold and preciouse stones.
Hir cote was somdel totore.
Aboute hir middel twenty score
Of horse haltres and well mo
There hingen atte time tho.
Thus whan she cam the lady nih,
Then took she betre hede and sih
This womman fair was of visage,
Fresh, lusty, yong and of tendre age;
And so this lady, there she stood,
Bethoghte hir well and understood
That this which com ridende tho
Tidinges couthe telle of tho
Which as she sih tofore ride,
And putte hir forth and prayde abide
And saide, "Ha, suster, let me here,
What ben they that now riden here
And ben so richeliche arrayed?"
This womman, which com so esmayed,
Answerde with full softe speche
And saith, "Ma dame, I shall you teche.
These are of tho that whilom were

1345 'And limped as if he was crippled by a nail in the hoof.'
1347 **plit** condition.
1348 The white star, a good point in itself, links the thin black horse with the fat white ones.
1349 **front** brow.
1353 **for the nones** a tag for rhyme; roughly 'for the time being'.
1355 **somdel totore** somewhat tattered.
1357 The halters are to be used for tethering the horses at a stopping-place. **mo** more.
1363 **there** where.
1368 **putte hir forth** stepped out.
1369 **suster** See *n.* to 1342.
1372 **esmayed** downcast.
1375 **of tho** some of those.

Servants to Love, and trouthe bere
There as they hadde her herte set.
Fare well, for I may noght be let.
Ma dame, I go to my servise,
So moste I haste in alle wise.
Forthy, ma dame, yif me leve,
I may noght longe with you leve."
"Ha, goode suster, yit I praye,
Tell me why ye ben so beseye
And with these haltres thus begon."
"Ma dame, whilom I was oon
That to my fader hadde a king;
Bot I was slow, and for no thing
Me liste noght to Love obeye,
And that I now full sore abeye.
For I whilom no love hadde,
Myn hors is now so feble and badde,
And all totore is myn aray;
And every yeer this freshe May
These lusty ladis ride aboute,
And I mot nedes suie her route
In this manere as ye now see,
And trusse her haltres forth with me,
And am bot as her horse knave.
Non other office I ne have,
Hem thenkth I am worthy no more,
For I was slow in loves lore
Whan I was able forto lere,

1376 trouthe bere kept faith. Cf. the company of faithful ladies following Cupid in Chaucer's *L.G.W.* F Prol. 282 f.
1378 let interrupted.
1379 The woman's service to the servants of love recalls the humble title adopted by Popes, 'servus servorum Dei', and adapted by Chaucer: 'For I, that God of Loves servantz serve', *Troilus* 1.15.
1382 leve remain.
1384 beseye dressed, equipped.
1385 begon bedecked.
1390 abeye pay for.
1391 For because.
1396 suie her route follow their company.
1398 trusse carry.
1399 'And am nothing but their groom, as it were.'
1401 Hem thenkth it seems to them.
1402 loves lore learning about love.
1403 lere learn.

And wolde noght the tales here
Of hem that couthen love teche."
"Now telle me thenne, I you beseche,
Wherof that riche bridel serveth."
With that hir chere away she swerveth
And gan to wepe, and thus she tolde:
"This bridel which ye now beholde
So riche upon myn horse hed –
Ma dame, afore, ere I was ded,
Whan I was in my lusty lif,
There fell into myn herte a strif
Of love, which me overcom,
So that therafter hede I nom
And thoghte I wolde love a knight.
That laste well a fourtenight,
For it no lenger mighte laste,
So nigh my lif was atte laste.
Bot, now, allas, to late war!
That I ne hadde him loved ar!
For deth cam so in haste bime,
Ere I therto hadde eny time,
That it ne mighte ben achieved.
Bot for all that I am relieved
Of that my will was good therto,
That Love soffreth it be so
That I shall swich a bridel were.
Now have ye herd all myn answere.
To God, ma dame, I you betake,
And warneth alle for my sake,
Of love that they ben noght idel,
And bid hem thenke upon my bridel."

1404 tales speeches, instructions.
1408 'With that she turns her face aside.'
1414 strif contest.
1416 hede I nom I took heed.
1418 laste lasted.
1420 atte laste to its end.
1421 'Too late aware!', a proverbial expression of regret: see *n.* to No 12 above, 398.
1422 'If only I had loved him sooner.'
1423 bime 'by me', to me.
1427 Of that because.
1429 were have the use of.
1431 betake commit.
1433–4 The rhyme clinches the connection between story and theme.

And with that word all sodeinly
She passeth, as it were a sky,
All clene out of this lady sighte.
And tho for fere hir herte afflighte,
And saide to hirself, "Helas!
I am right in the same cas.
Bot if I live after this day,
I shall amende it, if I may."
And thus homward this lady wente,
And changede all hir ferste entente
Within hir herte and gan to swere
That she none haltres wolde bere.

Lo, sone, here might thou taken hede
How idelnesse is forto drede,
Nameliche of love, as I have write.
For thou might understonde and wite
Among the gentil nacion
Love is an occupacion
Which forto kepe his lustes save
Sholde every gentil herte have.
For as the lady was chastised,
Right so the knight may ben avised
Which idel is and woll noght serve
To Love, he may per cas deserve
A gretter paine than she hadde
Whan she aboute with hir ladde
The horse haltres; and forthy
Good is to be well war therby.'

1436 sky cloud.
1438 afflighte became distressed.
1444 entente intent, purpose.
1449 Nameliche particularly.
1451 the gentil nacion those who are noble: *OED* s.v. *Nation* sb.[1] 6, 'A particular class, kind, or race of persons.'
1453 forto kepe his lustes save 'to keep its desires on the true path' (Bennett *Gower*). Opposite this passage the MS. has a marginal note: 'Non quia sic se habet veritas, sed opinio Amantum' ('Not that this is the truth, but it is the opinion of lovers'). This note, probably authorial, baldly states what the poem itself implies: that there is a 'veritas' beyond the 'opiniones' of Amans and his Confessor.
1456 the knight i.e. any knight who is slothful in love's service. **ben avised** take thought.
1458 per cas by chance.
1461 forthy for that reason.
1462 war warned.

20 This World Fares as a Fantasy

This is a religious meditation on the mutability and uncertainty of life, based largely on *Ecclesiastes*: see G. Sitwell, *Dominican Studies* 3 (1950) 284–90. It draws also on other 'vanity' passages in the Bible (*nn.* to lines 4, 42, 69–71), as well as on scientific (Aristotelian) teaching about generation and corruption in nature (*nn.* to 16, 39, 53–6). The meditation has three phases: sts 1–6, mutability in man and nature; sts 7–9, the vanity of controversial theology; sts 10–11, moral conclusion. Discussion in Gray 212–16 and A. B. Cottle *The Triumph of English* (Blandford Press 1969) 188–93. My st. 5 appears in both MSS. at the end of the poem, causing an abrupt reversion to an earlier phase in the argument. I assume that a scribe missed it out as a result of eyeskip (specially likely in a refrain poem) and added it at the end. In its present position (lines 49–60) it fits neatly. The exemplum of the tree complements those of gnat and moth in the previous stanza (cf. 58 with 38 and 44); and mention of 'hors and hounde' links with the following stanza. The new last stanza begins with a unique opening repetition of the refrain words (121) and ends with the appropriate exhortation to prayer.

Metrical form The stanza form is as in *Pearl*, No. 9 above: *ababababbcbc* with refrain. The line also resembles that of *Pearl*: short, four-stressed, with considerable variation of syllable count. Alliteration, though not as frequent as in *Pearl*, is marked: most often 2 alliterating sounds, sometimes 3 or 4, but sometimes none (e.g. 29).

Manuscripts Two closely allied MSS., the 'Vernon MS.', Bodleian MS. Eng. Poet. a 1 (on which this text is based) and 'Simeon MS.', B.L. MS. Additional 22283, both made 1380–1400, contain a set of moralizing refrain poems known as the 'Vernon lyrics': ed. F. J. Furnivall in EETS o.s. 117 (1901) 658–746. For discussion of MSS., see A. I. Doyle *Robbins Studies* 328–41, who says the refrain poems 'would fit best into the mouth of a friar or of a secular priest' (335). See also Woolf *Lyric* 111–2. The poem is No. 106 in Brown *XIVth-Century Religious Lyrics* and No. 83 in Gray *Selection.*

I wolde witen of som wis wight
Witterly what this world were.
It fareth as a fowles flight,
Now is hit henne, now is hit here.
Ne be we never so muche of might,
Now be we on benche, now be we on bere;
And be we never so war and wight,

1 witen know.

2 Witterly for sure.

4 henne far away. The traditional comparison between man's life and a bird (e.g. *Wisdom of Sol.* 5.11) here refers to birds like swallows which dart to and fro. This introduces the sudden changes of 5 ff.

6 bere bier.

7 war and wight vigilant and active.

Now be we seke, now be we fere.
Now is oon proud withouten pere,
Now is the selve yset not by;
And whoso woll alle thing hertly here,
This world fareth as a fantasy.

The sunnes cours, we may well kenne,
Ariseth est and goth down west;
The rivers into the see they renne
And it is never the more almest;
Windes rosheth here and henne;
In snow and rain is non arest.
Whon this woll stunte who wot, or whenne,
But only God on grounde grest?
The erthe in oon is ever prest,
Now bedropped, now all drye;
But uche gome glit forth as a gest:
This world fareth as a fantasye.

Kunredes come and kunredes gon
As joineth generacions;

8 seke sick. **fere** healthy.
10 'Now the same person is thought nothing of.'
11 hertly seriously.
12 fantasy illusion. The form of this keyword appears to vary according to whether its rhyme companion has final *-e* (*drye* 22) or not (*by* 10). Forms without *-e* were increasingly current in less formal C14 speech.
13–28 Cf. *Eccles*. 1.4–7: '4 One generation passeth away, and another generation cometh [25–8 here]: but the earth standeth for ever [21]. 5 The sun riseth, and goeth down, and returneth to his place: and there rising again, 6 Maketh his round by the south, and turneth again to the north [13–4]: the spirit (A.V. wind) goeth forward, surveying all places round about, and returneth to his circuits [17]. 7 All the rivers run into the sea, yet the sea doth not overflow [15–6].'
16 Here *Eccles*. 1.7 coincides with Aristotle *Meteorologica* 2.2. **almest** hardly.
17 here and henne hither and thither.
18 arest cessation.
19 'Who knows when this will stop, or from what cause' (*whenne* 'whence'). Nature is 'eterne in mutabilitie', Spenser *Faerie Queen* 3.6.47.
20 on grounde grest the greatest of all.
21 'The earth is always in the same condition of readiness.' Cf. *Eccles*. 1.4, cited above.
23 'But every man glides away (departs) like a visitor', i.e. no one stays on earth as if he really belonged there.
25 Kunredes generations: *MED* s.v. *Kinrede* n. 5.
26 joineth follow each other.

But alle heo passeth everichon
For all her preparacions;
Som are foryete clene as bon
Among alle maner nacions.
So shull men thenken us nothing on
That now han the occupacions,
And alle these disputacions
Ideliche all us occupye;
For Crist maketh the creacions,
And this world fareth as a fantasye.

Whuch is mon who wot, and what,
Whether that he be ought or nought?
Of erthe and air groweth up a gnat,
And so doth mon, whon all is sought;
Thaugh mon be waxen gret and fat
Mon melteth away so deth a mought.
Monnes might nis worth a mat,
But nyeth himself and turneth to nought.
Who wot, save he that all hath wrought,
Where mon becometh whon he shall die?
Who knoweth by dede ought, bote by thought?
For this world fareth as a fantasye.

27 heo they.

29 foryete forgotten. Cf. *Eccles.* 1.11, 2.16, 9.5–6. 'Clean as bone' is more than merely proverbial (Whiting B442) in this context.

31 thenken us nothing on take no thought of us.

32 occupacions positions of power.

33–4 Cf. *Eccles.* 6.11: 'There are many words that have much vanity in disputing.'

34 Ideliche in vain, uselessly.

35 maketh the creacions makes created things (or 'performs the acts of creation'?).

37 'Who knows the nature of man, and what he is?'

39 Gnats were held to originate by spontaneous generation in slimy places: Aristotle *Historia animalium* 5.19, followed by medieval encyclopaedists.

42 so deth a mought as a moth does. Cf. *Ps.* 39.11 (A.V.): 'thou makest his beauty to consume away like a moth: surely every man is vanity.'

43 mat an unusual type of worthlessness. 'Probably the humble (and sometimes verminous) woven straw sleeping-mat' (Cottle 189).

44 nyeth vexes.

46 becometh goes to. Similar agnosticism in *Eccles.* 3.21, 9.5.

47 'Who knows anything (about life after death) by experience, or in any way save by speculation?' Cf. Chaucer's *L.G.W.* F Prol. 1–9.

By ensaumple men may see,
A gret tree groweth out of the grounde;
Nothing abated the erthe woll be
Thaugh hit be huge, gret and rounde.
Right there woll roten the selve tree
Whon elde hath made his kinde aswounde;
Thaugh there were rote suche three
The erthe woll not encrece a pounde.
Thus waxeth and wanieth mon, hors and hounde,
From nought to nought thus henne we hie;
And here we stunteth but a stounde,
For this world is but fantasye.

Dieth mon and beestes die
And all is oon ocasion,
And alle o deth bos bothe drie
And han oon incarnacion:
Save that men beth more slye
All is o comparison.
Who wot yif monnes soule stie
And beestes soules sinketh down?

49 ensaumple an exemplum, in the manner of contemporary sermons: an item of natural history applied allegorically to man's life. On the position of this stanza, see headnote.

53–6 'That same tree will rot in the same spot, when old age has enfeebled its natural powers; but even though three such trees were to rot there, the soil will not be a pound heavier.' The notion that soil neither loses weight from plants' growth nor gains it from their decomposition must come from a scientific source. I cannot find it in Aristotle. Prof. Fowler refers me to Spenser *Faerie Queen* 5.2.39–40.

57 wanieth wanes (wanteth MSS.).

58 hie journey.

59 stunteth stop. **stounde** time.

61–6 Cf. *Eccles*. 3.19: 'Therefore the death of man and of beasts is one: and the condition of them both is equal. As man dieth, so they also die.'

62 ocasion occurrence.

63 'And both have to suffer the same death' (*bos* 'behoves': *hos* MS.).

64 incarnacion conception.

65 slye intelligent.

67–8 'Who knoweth if the spirit of the children of Adam ascend upward, and if the spirit of the beasts descend downward?', *Eccles*. 3.21.

67 stie ascend.

[20]

Who knoweth beestes entencioun,
On her creatour how they crye,
Save only God, that knoweth her soun?
For this world fareth as a fantasye.

Uche secte hopeth to be save
Baldely by her beleve,
And uchon upon God heo crave.
Why sholde God with hem him greve?
Uchon troweth that other rave;
But alle heo choseth God for cheve,
And hope in God uchon they have,
And by her wit her worching preve.
Thus mony maters men don meve,
Sechen her wittes how and why;
But Goddes mercy is alle biheve,
For this world fareth as a fantasy.

For thus men stumble and sere her wit
And meveth maters mony and fele;
Som leveth on him, som leveth on hit,
As children lerneth forto spele.
But non seeth non that abit
Whon stilly deth woll on him stele.
For he that hext in hevene sit

69–71 Cf. *Rom.* 8.18–22, esp. 20 'For the creature was made subject to vanity' and 22 'For we know that every creature groaneth and travaileth in pain, even till now'; cf. also *Joel* 1.20.
69 entencioun meaning i.e. what animals have in mind. Only God understands their language. Perhaps he does not consign them to oblivion, as it seems to us.
71 her soun their utterances.
73 secte sect or religion. **save** safe, saved.
74 Baldely confidently.
75 crave call in supplication.
76 him greve bother himself.
78 cheve chief, lord.
80 'And by their reasoning justify their practices.'
81 meve move, raise for discussion.
82 Sechen explore.
83 is] us MSS. **biheve** necessary.
85 sere wither, blight.
86 fele numerous.
87 Som leveth one believes. **hit** it.
89 'But no one sees anyone who will stand his ground.'
90 stilly silently (or adj?).
91 hext highest.

He is the help and hope of hele;
For wo is ende of worldes wele –
Uch lif loke wher that I lie –
This world is fals, fickel and frele,
And fareth but as a fantasye.

Wharto wilne we forto knowe
The pointes of Goddes privetė?
More than him lust us forto showe
We sholde not knowe in no degré;
An idel bost is forto blowe,
A maister of divinité.
Thenk we live in erthe here lowe
And God an hye in mageste.
Of material mortualité
Medle we, and of no more maistrye:
The more we trace the trinité
The more we falle in fantasye.

But leve we ure disputisoun
And leve on him that all hath wrought:
We mowe not preve by no resoun
How he was born that all us bought.
But hool in oure entencioun
Worshipe we him in herte and thought,

92 hele salvation.

94 'Let every person judge whether I am lying.'

97 Wharto to what end. **wilne** wish.

98 privetė secret purposes. Sitwell (see headnote) suggests that this refers to C14 disputes about providence and freewill.

99 him lust it pleases him. **lust us]** *Simeon*; lustnes *Vernon*.

101–2 'It is a worthless boast to utter, that one is a Master of Divinity.'

104 an hye on high.

105 'Of material and mortal matters.' *mortual* (see *OED* s.v.) is a ME form of *mortal*.

106 Medle we let us concern ourselves. **maistrye** knowledge which constitutes a Master (cf. 102), science.

110 leve believe (*leve* 109 = leave).

111 mowe can.

112 Referring to philosophical speculations about the 'double nature', divine and human, of Christ.

113 'But single-mindedly.'

[20]

For he may turne kindes upsedown,
That alle kindes made of nought.
Whon all oure bokes ben forth brought,
And all oure craft of clergye,
And all oure wittes ben thorwout sought,
Yit we fareth as a fantasye.

Of fantasye is all oure fare,
Olde and yonge and alle yfere;
But make we murye and slee care,
And worshipe we God whil we ben here,
Spende oure good and littel spare,
And uch mon cherise otheres chere.
Thenk how we, comen hider all bare,
Oure way-wending is in a were.
Pray we the prince that hath no pere
Take us hool to his mercy
And kepe oure concience clere,
For this world is but fantasy.

115–16 'For he who made all species from nothing is able to turn species upside down.' Emphasis on the absolute power of God (he could make lions timid, black white) is characteristic of C14 thought, often leading to the same fideistic conclusion as here: God cannot be known, he can only be trusted and worshipped.

118 'And all our skill in learning.'

119 thorwout sought searched through, ransacked.

121 The repetition of refrain words uniquely at the beginning of this stanza confirms that it *is* the last. See headnote.

122 yfere together.

123–6 Cf. *Eccles*. 3.12–3: 'And I have known that there was no better thing than to rejoice and to do well in this life. For every man that eateth and drinketh, and seeth good of his labour, this is the gift of God.'

125 *Spende* and *spare* (save) are traditionally opposed: cf. No. 6 above, lines 1–2.

126 cherise otheres chere gladden others' hearts.

127 Punctuation after *we* in Vernon MS. suggests that it is not subject of *comen* (to be taken as past participle), but introduces colloquially *Oure* 128. **bare** See *Eccles*. 5.14: 'As he came forth naked from his mother's womb, so shall he return.'

128 'Our departure (the time of our death) is uncertain.' **were** state of uncertainty: *OED* s.v. *Were* sb.[3] 6.

21 Mum and the Sothsegger: extract

The extract forms part of a fragment of 1751 lines of alliterative verse, B.L. MS. Additional 41666, which came to light in 1928. The fragment deals with the government of the kingdom under Henry IV, and refers to an event in 1402. The first part treats Henry's household, emphasizing the need for the King to be told the truth. There follows a 'disputation' between the narrator and Mum, who represents the principle of keeping your mouth shut. The narrator then examines the 'matter of Mum' in society (see *n.* to 842), with such depressing results that he grows faint and dreams of a wise old gardener (954 ff. here) who condemns Mum and praises the rival principle of the truth-teller (*sothsegger* 'sooth-sayer'). The narrator wakes and, encouraged by his dream, opens a 'bag' of writings which will tell Henry the truth about his subjects. Here the fragment breaks off. For discussion, see V. J. Scattergood *Politics and Poetry in the C15* (Blandford Press 1971) and A. B. Ferguson *The Articulate Citizen and the English Renaissance* (Duke U.P. 1965) Ch. 3. Scattergood 124 compares the contrast between Mum and the truthteller with that between Placebo and Justinus in Chaucer's *Merchant's T.* The ideal of 'truth', embodied in the old gardener and the narrator, owes much to Langland, as does the style and manner generally. The fragment is uneven and apparently rather rambling; but it is the best of the C15 pieces descending from *Piers Plowman.* Its high point is the Vision of England (876–951), a passage which may remind a modern reader of Samuel Palmer.

The B.L. fragment was first edited by M. Day and R. Steele, EETS 199 (1936), and identified by them as a later part of a poem (entitled by them *Mum and the Sothsegger*) previously known only in another fragment of 857 lines of alliterative verse in Cambridge Univ. Lib. The Cambridge fragment had been edited by W. W. Skeat as *Richard the Redeless* and assigned by him to Langland. But a poem beginning exactly like the Cambridge fragment was known to John Bale in C16 as 'Mum, Soth Segger'; and the part played by Mum and the 'sothsegger' in the B.L. fragment make likely some association with the Cambridge fragment (in which neither appears). However, it is by no means certain that the two fragments belong to the same poem, as Day and Steele thought. The Cambridge fragment appears to have been composed in the last year of Richard II (d. 1400). It refers specifically and exclusively to Richard's misrule (the bad influence of royal favourites etc.). It is possible, but not easy, to imagine how this would be connected with the B.L. fragment's discussion of Henry. For arguments against linking the two fragments, see D. Embree *N & Q* 22 (1975) 4–12.

Lines 841–991

Thenne wax I wounder wroth, as I well might,
And drow me to the dorward and dwelled no lenger,

842 'And made my way towards the door . . .' The poet has visited academics, clergy, courtiers and citizens, ending up here at a mayor's banquet. He finds that all serve Mum – the principle of keeping your mouth shut.

[21]

But romed forth reedless, remembring ofte
That Mum was such a maister among men of good.
And as I loked the logges along by the streetes,
I saw a sothsegger, in sothe as me thought,
Sitte in a shop and salven his woundes.
Thenne was I full-come, and knew well the sothe
That Mum upon molde mirrier life had
Than the sothsegger, asay whoso woll;
But the better barn to abide stille
And to live with a lord to his lifes ende
Is the sothsegger, asay whoso woll.
Yit was I not the wiser for way that I wente;
This made me all mad, as I moste nede,
And well fleuble and faint, and fell to the grounde,
And lay down on a linche to lithe my bones,
Rolling in remembrance my renning aboute
And alle the perillous pathes that I passed had,
As priories and personages and pluralités,
Abbayes of Augustin and other holy places,
To knightes courtes and crafty men many,
To mayers and maisters, men of high wittes,
And to the felle freres, alle the foure ordres,

843 reedless in bewilderment.
844 good substance.
845 loked the logges looked at the houses.
846 sothsegger truthteller. Unlike its opposite, the principle of speaking out the truth is represented, not by a personification, but by individuals such as this one and the poet himself.
847 A Lat. sidenote cites *Matt*. 5.10: 'Blessed are they that suffer persecution for justice' sake.' **salven** anoint.
848 full-come 'perfected (in knowledge)' (Day and Steele).
849 Mum was present at the mayor's banquet. **molde** earth.
850 asay whoso woll test it if you like.
851 barn man.
853 The echo of 850 clinches the antithetical statement.
854–70 The lead-in to the following dream imitates Langland's *Piers*, where intellectual dissatisfaction leads to madness (B 15.1 f.) or faintness (B 5.1 f.), followed by sleep.
854 for way that I wente for all my travels.
855 as I moste nede as I could not fail to be.
856 fleuble feeble.
857 linche strip of unploughed land between fields. **lithe** relieve, rest.
858 renning running.
860 personages parsonages. **pluralités** benefices held in plurality.
861 Augustin i.e. Augustinian canons.
862 courtes households. **crafty men** skilled workmen.
863 maisters scholars.
864 felle wicked. **ordres** Dominican, Franciscan, Augustinian, Carmelite.

And other hobbes a heep, as ye herd have,
And nought the neer by a note! This noyed me ofte,
That thurgh construing of clerkes that knewe alle bokes
That Mum sholde be maister most upon erthe.
And ere I were ware, a wink me assailled,
That I slepte sadly seven houres large.

Thenne mette I of mervailles mo than me luste
To telle or to talke of till I see time;
But som of the sildcouthes I woll shewe here-after,
For dreme is no dwele, by Danieles wordes,
Though Caton of the contrarye carpe in his bokes.
Me thought I was in wildernesse walking all oon,
There bestes were and briddes and no barn elles,
In a cumbe cressing on a creste wise,
All grass grene that gladed my herte,
By a cliff un-yknowe, of Cristes owen making.

865 'And a crowd of other fellows.' *hobbe*, familiar for 'Robert', is colloquial and contemptuous.
866 neer nearer (to the truth). **note** nut.
867 thurgh construing of clerkes in the judgment of learned men (?).
869 wink sleep.
870 sadly soundly. **large** full.
871 mette dreamed. **mo than me luste** more than I would want.
873 sildcouthes marvels.
874–5 Again recalling Langland, who also contrasts the opinions of 'Cato' and Daniel on dreams: *Piers* B 7.149–58.
874 Daniel's interpretation of Nebuchadnezzar's dream: *Dan.* 2.27 f. **dwele** illusion.
875 The 'Distichs of Cato' was a common elementary Latin schooltext. See Boas II 31: 'somnia ne cures' ('take no notice of dreams'). The gloss to this distich cites Daniel (Boas 142), which perhaps accounts for Langland's coupling. **carpe** speaks.
876–951 Such rich and detailed descriptions of countryside are uncommon in ME poetry. Particularly unusual is the presence of a moving observer, first climbing the hill (881–4), then enjoying the view from the top (885–931), descending into the vale (932–43) and approaching the franklin's house (944–51). The handling of point of view recalls the *Gawain*-poet: e.g. Gawain's view of the Green Chapel in No. 10 above. The panorama here is much fuller than that in *Piers* B 11.315 f., but the intention is similar: to invoke a vision of the bountiful order of nature (including a garden 948 f. and a hive 982 ff.) and so expose the pettiness of human perversity.
876 wildernesse uncultivated land. **all oon** alone.
878 'In a valley widening out in the manner of a crest.' Referring perhaps to bird's crests, or to crests on helmets. Day and Steele suggest 'tail of a comet'; but this use of *crest* is rare.
880 un-yknowe unfamiliar.

[21]

I lepte forth lightly along by the hegges
And moved forth mirrily to maistrie the hilles;
For till I came to the coppe couthe I not stinte
Of the highest hill by half of alle other.
I tourned me twies and toted aboute,
Beholding hegges and holtes so grene,
The mansions and medwes mowen all newe,
For such was the saison of the same yere.
I lifte up my eye-ledes and loked ferther
And saw many swete sightes, so me God helpe:
The wodes and the waters and the welle-springes
And trees ytrailed fro toppe to th'erthe,
Coriously ycovred with curtel of grene,
The flours on feeldes flavring swete,
The corn on the croftes ycropped full faire,
The renning riviere rushing faste,
Full of fish and of frye of felefold kind,
The breres with their beries bent over the wayes,
Als honysoucles honging upon eche half;
Chesteines and chiries that children desiren
Were logged under leves, full lusty to seen.
The hawthorne so holsom I beheld eke,
And how the benes blowed and the brome-floures.
Peres and plummes and pesecoddes grene,
That ladies lusty loken muche after,

882 maistrie master, surmount.
883 coppe top. **stinte** stop.
884 'Of the hill, which was higher than all the others by half as much again.' MS. omits second *of*.
885 toted peered.
886 holtes woods.
887 mansions homesteads (not so grand as in later use). Once out of the uncultivated mountain valley, the poet sees a landscape on which farmers, hunters and gardeners have imposed order.
892 ytrailed adorned with trailing greenery.
893 Coriously exquisitely. **curtel** tunic.
894 flavring smelling.
895 croftes enclosed fields. **ycropped** harvested.
897 frye young fish. **felefold** manifold.
898 breres briars.
899 Als also (as MS.). **eche half** every side.
900 Chesteines chestnuts.
901 logged lodged, sheltered.
903 blowed blossomed.
904–5 Here, as in Touchstone's speech in Shakespeare *A.Y.L.I.* 2.4.43–52, there lurks an improper pun on 'peasecods' (*cod* also means 'scrotum').

Were gadred for gomes ere they gunne ripe.
The grapes growed agrete in gardins aboute,
And other fruites felefold in feldes and closes –
To nempne alle the names hit nedeth not here.
The coninges fro covert covred the bankes
And raughte out a raundon and retourned againes,
Played forth on the plain and to the pit after,
But any hound hente thaim, or the hay-nettes.
The hare hied him faste and the houndes after,
For kissing of his croupe acauntwise he wente;
For nad he tourned twies, his tail had be licked,
So ernestly Ector icched him after.
The shepe fro the sunne shadwed thaimself,
While the lambes laiked along by the hegges,
The cow with hir calf, and coltes full faire;
And high hors in haras hurteled togeder
And praised the pasture that primesaute thaim made.
The dere on the dale drowe to their dennes,
Ferked forth to the ferne and felle down amiddes;
Hertes and hindes a hundred togeder
With reindeer and roobuck runne to the wodes,
For the kenettes on the cleere were un-ycoupled;
And buckes full burnished that baren good grece,
Four hundred on a herde yheeded full faire,

906 gomes men. **gunne** began to.
907 agrete in profusion.
908 closes enclosures.
909 nempne name.
910 'The rabbits, coming out from shelter, ranged over the slopes.'
911 raughte out a raundon came out in a rush.
912 pit burrow.
913 But unless. **hente** captured. **hay-nettes** nets to catch rabbits, stretched in front of their holes: *OED* s.v. *Hay* sb.[3].
915 'He turned in zig-zag fashion for fear of having his hindquarters kissed.'
916 nad had he not.
917 Ector Hector (hound name). **icched** ran.
919 laiked sported.
921 haras 'an enclosure or establishment in which horses and mares are kept for breeding' *OED* s.v. *Haras*.
922 primesaute 'vigorous, spirited' (Day and Steele).
923 drowe drew.
924 'Hurried out into the ferns and settled down among them.'
927 'For the hunting-dogs were unleashed in a clearing.'
928 burnished having polished the velvet off their antlers. **baren good grece** had a good depth of fat.
929 yheeded headed, antlered.

[21]

Layen lowe in a launde along by the pale,
A swete sight for sovereins, so me God helpe.
   I moved down fro the mote to the midwardes
And so adown to the dale, dwelled I no longer.
But such a noise of nestlinges ne so swete notes
I herde not this halfe yere, ne so hevenly sounes,
As I dide on that dale adown among the hegges,
For in every bush was a brid that in his beste wise
Babled with his bille, that blisse was to here.
So cleerly they chirmed and chaunged their notes
That what for flavour of the fruit and of the somer floures
The smelling smote as spices, me thought,
That of my travail trewly took I no kepe,
For all was vaneshed me fro thurgh the freshe sightes.
   Thenne lepte I forth lightly and loked aboute,
And I behelde a faire hous with halles and chambres,
A frankeleines freeholde all freshe newe.
I bente me aboute and bode atte dore
Of the gladdest gardin that gome ever had.
I have no time trewly to telle alle the names
Of impes and herbes and other feele thinges
That growed on that gardin, the ground was so noble.
I passed inne privély and pulled of the fruites
And romed th'aleys round all aboute;

930 launde clearing. **pale** palisade surrounding a game preserve.
931 sovereins lords.
932 mote hill. **midwardes** i.e. middle slopes.
935 sounes sounds. MS. omits; but metre requires some word here. Day and Steele supply.
939 cleerly loudly. **chirmed** sang. **chaunged** varied.
940 flavour scent.
941 smote was penetrating.
942 travail laborious journey. **kepe** notice.
944 'Then I ran quickly forward . . .'
945 halles and chambres public and private rooms.
946 A franklin was a gentleman landowner, comparable to the local squire of Fielding's times: cf. Chaucer's portrait, *C.T.* I 331–60, where the riches of the Franklin's estate are emphasized, as here.
947 bente me aboute turned aside. **bode** stopped.
950 impes trees. **herbes** plants. **feele** many.
951 ground soil.
953 th'aleys the alleys: cf. description of the railed 'alleys' in Criseide's garden, No. 12 above, 820 ff.

[21]

But so semely a sage as I saw there
I saw not sothly sith I was bore:
An old auncien man of a hundred winter,
Yweded in white cloth and wisely ymade,
With hore heres on his heed more than half white,
A fair visage and a vresh and vertuous to sene.
His eyen were all ernest, egged to non ille,
With a brood besmed berd, balled a lite,
As comely a creature as ever kinde wroughte.
He was sad of his semblant, soft of his speche,
Proporcioned at alle pointes and pithy in his time,
And by his stature right strong and stalworth on his dayes.
He hoved over a hive the hony forto kepe
Fro dranes that destrued hit and dide not elles;
He thraste thaim with his thumbe as thicke as they come,
He lafte non alive for their lither tacches.
I wondred on his workes, as I well might,
And ever I neyed him nere, as ney as me oughte,
And halsed him as hendily as I had lerned;
And he me grette again right in a good wise,
And asked what I wolde, and anon I tolde

954 ff. The wise old gardener is a descendant of Piers Plowman (who also has a garden, B 16.13 ff.) and ancestor of the Gardener in Shakespeare *R.2* 3.4. Here as in Shakespeare, the well-ordered garden contrasts with a disordered kingdom.
954 sage A gloss in MS. interprets this as *segge* 'man', probably wrongly.
955 sith since.
957 Yweded attired. The gardener's white dress seems an unrealistic touch, perhaps recalling the white robes of the Elders of the Apocalypse (*Rev.* 4.4). Or cf. *Dan.* 7.9.
958 hore grey.
959 vresh fresh, hale. **sene** look at (seme MS.).
960 ernest grave. **egged** aroused.
961 besmed shaped like a besom or broom (unique use). **balled** bald.
962 kinde Nature.
963 sad of his semblant grave in appearance.
964 pithy in his time vigorous for his age.
966 hoved stood.
967 dranes drones.
968 thraste crushed.
969 lither tacches evil ways.
971 'And I edged nearer to him all the time, as near as was fitting.'
972 halsed greeted. **hendily** politely.

[21]

My will was to wite what man he were.
'I am gardiner of this garth,' quoth he, 'the ground is myn owen
Forto digge and to delve and to do such deedes
As longeth to this leightone; the law woll I do,
And wrote up the wedes that wirwen my plantes;
And wormes that worchen not but wasten my herbes,
I dashe thaim to deeth and delve out their dennes.
But the dranes don worst, deie mote they alle:
They haunten the hive for hony that is inne,
And lurken and licken the liquor that is swete,
And travelen no twinte, but taken of the beste
Of that the bees bringen fro blossomes and floures.
For of all the bestes that breden upon erthe,
For qualité ne quantité, no question, I trowe,
The bee in his bisiness best is allowed,
And proved in his proprieté passing alle other,
And pretiest in his wirching to profit of the peuple.'

975 wite know.
976 garth garden (gate MS.).
978 'As pertain to this garden (*leightone*); I want to do what is right.' *longeth* may be a corruption of *longing* 'belonging': '[such deeds] as, pertaining to this garden, the law wills me to do.'
979 wrote dig. **wirwen** destroy.
980 wormes 'any animal that creeps or crawls' (*OED* s.v. *Worm* 2), e.g. slugs.
982 ff. Exposition of the habits of bees, as a model for human society, continues up to line 1086. Cf. Shakespeare *H.5* 1.2.187 ff: 'so work the honey bees, | Creatures that by a rule in nature teach | The act of order to a peopled kingdom'. The source is Bartholomeus Anglicus *De proprietatibus rerum* (quoted by Day and Steele 79–81); but the literary tradition goes back to Virgil *Georg*. 4.
982 mote must.
984 lurken skulk about.
985 travelen no twinte do no work at all (*twinte* 'jot').
986 A side-note here has 'Qui non laborat non manducet' ('He who does not work, let him not eat'), a version of *2 Thess.* 3.10 also found in a gloss to *Piers* B Prol. 39.
989 allowed esteemed.
990 proved approved of. **proprieté** natural disposition: cf. title of encyclopaedia cited in *n.* to 982 ff. above.
991 pretiest most skilful.

Thomas Hoccleve

Life Born 1368 or 1369, perhaps of a Bedfordshire family. He entered the Privy Seal Office *c.* 1387, as one of the clerks who were chiefs (under the Keeper) of the secretariat: see T. F. Tout 'Literature and learning in the English civil service in the C14' *Spec.* 4 (1929) 365–89. He continued living in London and working in the Privy Seal Office in Westminster until 1423. In 1399 he received a £10 annuity from Henry IV (a regular way of rewarding civil servants), and in 1409 an annuity of £13 6s 8d, which continued to be paid until his death in 1426. On the date of his death, see *RES* n.s. 8 (1957) 218. Hoccleve claims to have lived a gay London life in his youth. He was acquainted with Chaucer, who talked with him about poetry: 'fader Chaucer fain wold han me taght, | But I was dull and lerned lite or naght' (*Regement of Princes* 2078–9). He praises Chaucer in three passages of the *Regement* (1958–74, 2077–2107, 4978–98), and caused a famous portrait of Chaucer to be introduced into *Regement* MSS. His marriage barred him from ecclesiastical preferment. He suffered a mental breakdown in 1416.
Works and editions Hoccleve's best-known work was *Regement of Princes*, a treatise on the right conduct of a prince, addressed to the future Henry V in 1412, and prefaced by a lengthy autobiographical prologue: ed. F. J. Furnivall EETS e.s. 72 (1897). Other works are available in *Minor Poems* ed. F. J. Furnivall and I. Gollancz, rev. J. Mitchell and A. I. Doyle EETS e.s. 61 and 73 in one vol. (1970), with biographical materials. The two most remarkable are *La Male Regle de T. Hoccleve* (1406), an autobiographical piece lamenting his bad habits, bad health and irregular income, and the 'Series', on which see below.
Studies Biographical account in H. S. Bennett *Six Medieval Men and Women* (Cambridge U.P. 1955) Ch. 3. The study by J. Mitchell, *Thomas Hoccleve: a study in early C15 English poetic* (Univ. of Illinois P. 1968), is chiefly valuable for its annotated bibliography. The best short critical discussions are: W. J. Courthope *History of English Poetry* (1895) 1.333–40; Mathew 55–8; and I. Robinson *Chaucer's Prosody* (Cambridge U.P. 1971) 190–9, demonstrating H's powers as a metrist.

22 Hoccleve's Complaint: extract

In 1421–2 Hoccleve produced a group of pieces addressed to Humphrey Duke of Gloucester. Hammond 69 called this the 'Series', describing it as a 'partially-linked set of poems and prose moralizations'. *Hoccleve's Complaint*, the first part of which is edited here, is followed by *Dialogue with a Friend*, which introduces a story from *Gesta Romanorum*, Jereslaus' Wife. There follows (without link) a moral piece *Learn to Die*, which is linked by further dialogue with the same friend to a second *Gesta* story, Jonathas and Fellicula. The Series represents an attempt to organize narrative and didactic material into a single 'book', within an autobiographical rather than narrative framework. The Chaucerian precedent is *Legend of Good Women* rather than *Canterbury Tales*; but Hoccleve is much more directly autobiographical. He describes the circumstances and anxieties attending the compilation of the book that he is to present to his patrons. Courthope compares Pope's *Epistle to Arbuthnot*.

Complaint The Complaint or *Planctus* was a common medieval genre: see Cresseid's Complaint in Henryson's *Testament of Cresseid*, No. 30 below, lines 407–69 and *n.* A. G. Rigg *Spec.* 45 (1970) 564–74 identifies the book consulted by H. in the later part of the *Complaint* as the *Synonyma* of Isidore of Seville, suggesting that 'this book may have helped to shape the organization of his *Complaint*, which may accordingly be viewed as belonging to the genre of *Consolatio*', that is, as a consolation for sorrow and a justification of God's ways. Doob Ch. 5, studying 'conventions of madness in ME literature', emphasizes conventional elements in H's account of his breakdown, which she suggests may never have really occurred. But H's other 'self-revelations' turn out true, when they can be checked (e.g. he did work in the Privy Seal, line 296); nor would he have described a real breakdown in other than conventional terms. It may be argued, too, that the obsessively repetitive style of the *Complaint* is symptomatic of H's illness: it is, at least, a highly appropriate style. The documents do in fact suggest that H. was ill in 1416: *RES* n.s. 20 (1967) 482.

Metre and style The stanza is rhyme royal. H's style is plainer than Chaucer's. He renders conversation with almost mannered naturalness (especially in the Dialogues). He tends to be rambling and repetitive; but his syntax (unlike Lydgate's) is energetic and controlled.

Manuscripts The Series survives, wholly or in part, in 8 MSS. The present text is based on Durham Univ. Lib. MS. Cosin V. iii. 9. This MS. (= *D*) is one of four surviving autograph Hoccleve MSS: H. C. Schulz 'Thomas Hoccleve, Scribe' *Spec.* 12 (1937) 71–81. But the first part (including *Complaint*) was lost and is supplied in the hand of John Stowe, the C16 chronicler. Four other MSS. have been consulted: Coventry City Record Office MS. Accession 325/1 (= *C*), and Bodleian MSS. Bodley 221 (= *B*), Laud Misc. 735 (= *L*) and Selden Sup. 53 (= *S*).

Lines 1–308

After that hervest inned had his sheves,
And that the brown sesoun of Mihelmesse
Was come, and gan the trees robbe of her leves
That grene had ben and in lusty freshnesse,
And hem into colour of yelownesse
Had dyed and down throwen under fote,
That chaunge sank into myn herte rote;

1–9 The syntax recalls the opening of *Canterbury Tales*. For metrical analysis, see I. Robinson *Chaucer's Prosody* 190–1. Autumn is the appropriate season for thoughts of transience. Being the season in which the melancholy humour increases in strength, it disposes man to melancholy madness: Doob 20, 220. Cf. the decorum of the winter setting in No. 34 below (see *n.* to line 6 there) and Henryson's *Testament of Cresseid*. [*See further notes on facing page*]

For freshly broughte it to my remembraunce
That stablenesse in this world is there non.
There is no thing but chaunge and variaunce.
How welthy a man be or well begon,
Endure it shall not, he shall it forgon.
Deth under fote shall him thrist adown:
That is every wightes conclusioun,

Which for to waive is in no mannes might,
How riche he be, strong, lusty, fresh and gay.
And in the ende of November, upon a night,
Sighing sore as I in my bedde lay,
For this and other thoughts which many a day
Before I took, sleep cam non in myn ye,
So vexed me the thoughtful maladye.

I sy well, sithen I with sicknesse last
Was scourged, cloudy hath ben the favour
That shon on me full bright in times past.
The sunne abated and the derke shour
Hilded down right on me and in langour
Me made swimme, so that my spirite
To live no lust had, ne delite.

1 hervest the usual word for autumn in ME. **inned** got in.
2 brown] brome *D C*. The reading *brown* in *S B L* is convincing; but agreement of *D* and *C* is remarkable, perhaps representing some derivative of Lat. *bruma* 'winter' or Fr. *brume* 'mist' (cf. *OED* s.v. *Brumal*, *Brume*). *S* also could be read not *broun* but *bromi* (*bromy*); but no such word for 'misty' is recorded in dictionaries, still less an adj. *brome*. So the more difficult reading seems, at present, too difficult. **Mihelmesse** Michaelmas, 29 Sept.
8 it] *D* omits.
10 but without.
11 well begon well provided.
12 forgon give up.
13 thrist thrust (cf. 6).
15 waive avoid.
16 How however. **lusty** vigorous.
22 sy saw: the regular past form here (*D* reads *see*). **sithen** since.
23 favour Referring implicitly to the 'favour of Fortune' (e.g. Chaucer *C.T.* I 2682). H. recalls Chaucer's image of Fortune covering her bright face with a cloud: *C.T.* VII 2766.
24 on] *D* omits.
26 Hilded poured. **langour** misery.
27 Me] He *D*. **spirite]** wite *D*.
28 lust motive.

The greef about my herte so swal
And bolned ever too and too so sore,
That nedes out I moste therewithal.
I thought I nolde it kepe clos no more,
Ne lette it in me forto elde and hore;
And forto preve I cam of a woman,
I braste out on the morwe and thus began.

Here endeth my Prologe and foloweth my Complaint.

Almighty God, as liketh his goodnesse,
Visiteth folk alday, as men may see,
With loss of good and bodily sicknesse,
And among other he foryat not me –
Witnesse upon the wilde infirmité
Which that I hadde, as many a man well knew,
And which me out of my self caste and threw.

It was so knowen to the peple and couth
That counseil was it non, ne non be mighte;
How it with me stood was in every mannes mouth,
And that full sore my frendes affrighte:
They for myn helthe pilgrimages highte,

29 so] *D B C*; ran so *L* (with *ran* expuncted); so sore *S* (*sore* inserted above line). The *S* correction might be adopted on metrical grounds. **swal** swelled.
30 bolned swelled. **too and too** intolerably much: cf. *OED* s.v. *Too* adv. 4.
31 'So that I had of necessity to give expression to it.'
32 nolde would not.
33 lette it in me dam it up inside myself. **elde and hore** grow old and grey.
34 i.e. to show that I was flesh and blood. The question of whether H. should give expression to his state of mind, and if so how, runs right through the Series.
35 braste burst. **morwe** next day.
36–8 On the idea of disease and madness as visitations of God, see Doob *passim*. Rigg *Spec.* 45 (1970) 571 compares Isidore *Synonyma*.
37 folk] folks *D*.
39 foryat forgot.
40 Witnesse upon witness: regular ME idiom (*OED* s.v. *Witness* sb. 7b). **infirmité** H. nowhere specifies the nature of the illness which had made him mad five years earlier.
42 caste and threw Such word pairs are characteristic of H's style: cf. *knowen . . . and couth* 43. See Mitchell 66–70.
44 counseil a secret.
46 affrighte alarmed.
47 highte vowed. When Charles VI of France went mad, his Queen made pilgrimages on his behalf: Doob 221.

And soughte hem, som on hors and som on fote –
God yelde it hem – to gette me my bote.

But although the substaunce of my memorye
Wente to playe, as for a certain space,
Yit the lord of vertue, the king of glorye,
Of his hye might and beninge grace,
Made it to retourne into the place
Whennes it cam, which was at All-halwe-messe,
Was five yeer, neither more ne lesse.

And ever sithen, thanked be God oure lord
Of his good reconsiliacioun,
My wit and I have ben of such accord
As we were or the alteracioun
Of it was; but by my savacioun,
That time have I be sore set on fire
And lived in grete tourment and martire;

For though that my wit were hoom come again,
Men wolde it not so understond or take;
With me to dele hadden they disdain.
A riotous person I was, and forsake;
Myn olde frendship was all overshake;
No wight with me list make daliaunce;
The world me made a straunge countenaunce,

48 soughte hem went on them.

49 'May God reward them for it . . .' **my]** *D* omits. **bote** recovery.

51 'Went off to amuse itself elsewhere for a short time.'

55 Whennes whence. **was]** *S* omits. **All-halwe-messe** the feast of All Saints, 1 Nov. Writing at the end of November (line 17), H. looks back to the fifth anniversary of his recovery, at the beginning of the same month. For evidence of H's illness in the summer of 1416, five years before composition of the poem, see *RES* n.s. 20 (1967) 482.

56 Was five yeer five years ago.

58 good] good and gracious *S B L C.*

60 or before.

62 That time during that period (*S* has *Sith that time* over erasure).

63 martire suffering.

64 ff. H. traces his present melancholy to his friends' and acquaintances' refusal to believe that he is really recovered from madness. Doob cites the old saying 'once mad, always half-mad' (48, cf. 221–2).

67 riotous dissolute. **forsake** deserted.

68 overshake shaken off.

69–70 'No one chose to have any friendly conversation with me; everyone treated me like a stranger.'

Which that myn herte sore gan to tourmente;
For ofte whan I in Westminster Halle
And eke in London among the prees wente,
I sy the chere abaten and apalle
Of hem that weren wont me forto calle
To companye: her hede they caste awry
When I hem mette, as they not me sy.

As said is in the Sauter, might I say:
They that me sy fledden away from me;
Foryeten I was, all out of mind away,
As he that dede was from hertes cherté.
To a lost vessel likened might I be,
For many a wight aboute me dwelling
Herde I me blame and putte in dispraising.

Thus spake many oon and saide by me:
'Although from him his sicknesse savage
Withdrawen and passed as for a time be,
Resort it woll, namely in such age
As he is of.' And thenne my visage
Began to glowe for the wo and fere:
The wordes, hem unwar, cam to myn ere.

71 Which] with *S B L C*. But H. likes beginning stanzas with relatives (cf. 15), and no intransitive use of *torment* is recorded.
72 H's office, the Privy Seal, was in Westminster, where the Hall was a great place of resort and business.
73 London and Westminster were separated by a green belt in C15. **prees** crowd.
74–146 *L* omits by loss of leaf.
74 'I saw the countenance fall and grow indifferent.'
76 caste awry turned away.
77 as as if.
78–84 Three of the five MSS. consulted (*L* has missing leaf; *D* lacks glosses throughout) cite as a gloss *Ps.* 30 (A.V. 31) 12–4: 'They that saw me without fled from me. I am forgotten as one dead from the heart. I am become as a vessel that is destroyed. For I have heard the blame of many that dwell round about.' Rigg 571 cites a passage from Isidore; but the present passage is very close to the Psalm.
81 from hertes cherté out of the heart's affection: Vulgate 'mortuus a corde' ('dead from the heart').
85 by concerning.
88 Resort return. **namely** particularly. **age** In the following *Dialogue* H. says he is 53 years old (246). Middle age was the melancholic stage of life when madness was likely to occur: Doob 221.
91 hem unwar without their knowing (absolute construction).

'Whan passing hete is,' quod they, 'trusteth this,
Assaile woll him again that maladye.'
And yit, pardé, they token hem amiss;
Non effect at all took her prophecye.
Many someres ben past sithen remedye
Of that God of his grace me purvayde;
Thanked be God, it shoop nought as they saide.

What falle shall, what men so deme or gesse,
To him that wot every mannes secré
Reserved is. It is a lewednesse
Men wiser hem pretende than they be.
And no wight knoweth, be it he or she,
Whom, how, ne whan, God woll him visite:
It happeth ofte whan men wene it lite.

Som time I wende as lite as any man
Forto have falle into that wildenesse;
But God, whan him list, may, woll and can
Helthe withdrawe and sende a wight sicknesse.
Though man be well this day, no sickernesse
To him behight is that it shall endure.
God hurte now can, and now hele and cure.

He suffreth longe, but at the last he smit,
Whan that a man is in prosperité.
To drede a fall coming it is a wit.
Whoso that taketh hede ofte may see

92 passing hete great heat. 'Summer was considered the most dangerous time for madmen of all kinds' Doob 221.
94 'And yet, by God, they were mistaken.'
97–8 Lines transposed in *D*.
97 purvayde provided.
98 shoop turned out.
99–101 'Whatever men judge or guess, knowledge of what will come to pass is reserved for him who knows every man's secrets . . .'
100 mannes] hertis *S C*. **secré**] secrete *B*: perhaps correct, representing trisyllabic *secreté*, a form of *secrecy* (see *OED* s.v. *Secrecy* sb. 3 'a secret').
101 lewednesse form of ignorance.
104 Syntax would be improved by emending *Whom* to *Where* (Kern).
105 wene it lite little expect it.
110 sickernesse certainty.
111 behight promised.
113 Proverbial: Whiting G264. **but**] *D* omits. **smit** smites.
115 a wit an act of wisdom.

This worldes chaunge and mutabilité
In sondry wise – how, nedeth not expresse;
To my matere streght woll I me dresse.

Men saide I loked as a wilde steer,
And so my look aboute I gan to throwe;
Myn hede too hye another saide I beer,
'Full buckish is his brain, well may I trowe';
And saide the thirde, 'and apt is in the rowe
To sitte of hem that a resounless rede
Can geve – no sadnesse is in his hede.'

Chaunged had I my pas, som saiden eke,
For here and there forth stirte I as a ro,
Non abode, non arrest, but all brain-seke.
Another spake, and of me saide also,
My feet weren ay waving to and fro
Whan that I stonde sholde and with men talk,
And that myn eyen soughten every halk.

I laide an ere ay to as I by wente
And herde all, and thus in myn herte I caste:
'Of long abiding here I may repente.
Lest of hastinesse I at the laste

119 'I will address myself directly to my subject.' *matter* is a favourite word of Chaucer's in such contexts: e.g. *Troilus* 1.53, 'For now will I gon streght to my matere.'
120–33 Doob 221 cites Bartholomeus Anglicus *De proprietatibus rerum* trans. Trevisa Bk 7 Ch. 5 on symptoms of madness: 'woodness and continual wakinge, mevinge and castinge aboute the eyen, raginge, stretchinge and castinge of hondes, mevinge and wagginge of heed.'
120 steer young ox. Cf. Whiting B593: 'As wood (mad) as a wild bullock.'
122 beer carried.
123 buckish 'haughty, overbearing' (*MED*). The second speaker compares H's carriage of his head to a male deer with its proud head of antlers.
124 And Kern would omit this, but it can stand. The third speaker adds that H. is not to be looked to for advice. **rowe** company (*OED Row* sb.[1] 2).
125 resounless rede unreasonable piece of advice.
126 sadnesse gravity.
127 pas way of walking.
128 stirte jumped. **ro** roe deer, proverbially swift-footed. The three successive animal comparisons (ox, buck, deer) suggest H's degradation (like Nebuchadnezzar) to a bestial state.
129 'No staying anywhere, no stopping, but entirely brain-sick.' A fine example of H's metrical boldness.
133 halk corner of a room. H. is thought not to look straight at people.
135 caste considered.

Answere amiss, best is hens hie faste;
For if I in this prees amiss me gye,
To harm woll it me turne and to folye.'

And this I demed well and knew well eke:
Whatsoever I sholde answer and say,
They wolden not han holde it worth a leke.
Forwhy, as I had lost my tonges key,
Kepte I me cloos, and trussed me my way
Drouping and hevy and all wo-bestad.
Small cause had I, me thoughte, to be glad.

My spirites laboureden bisily
To painte countenaunce, chere and look,
For that men spake of me so wonderingly;
And for the verray shame and fere I quook.
Though myn herte had be dipped in the brook,
It wete and moist ynow was of my swot,
Which was now frosty cold, now firy hot.

And in my chaumbre at home when I was,
Myself alone, I in this wise wroughte:
I streite unto my mirrour and my glass
To loke how that me of my chere thoughte,
If any other were it than it oughte;

138 hens hie to go hence.

139 amiss me gye behave badly.

143 leke leek, proverbial type of worthlessness: Whiting L185.

144–5 'For which reason I kept myself to myself as if I had lost the key to my tongue, and took myself off.'

146 wo-bestad woebegone.

148 laboureden] laboryd *D C*; labouriden ever ful *S* (over erasure); hem labured then full *B L*.

149 painte simulate. On his way home, H. tries to make his appearance (*countenaunce*), expression (*chere*) and looks seem normal.

150 For that because.

151 quook trembled.

153 i.e. 'It would not have been any wetter than it already was with my sweat.' **ynow** enough.

157 streite stretched. *OED* s.v. *Stretch* v. 9: 'To make one's way (rapidly or with effort).' *B* and *L* read *sterte*.

158 'To see how my expression looked to me.'

159 other] *D* omits.

For fain wolde I, if it had not be right,
Amended it to my cunning and might.

Many a saut made I to this mirrour,
Thinking, 'If that I loke in this manere
Amonge folk as I now do, non errour
Of suspect look may in my face appere.
This countenaunce, I am sure, and this chere
If I forth use, is no thing reprevable
To hem that han conseites resonable.'

And therwithall I thoughte thus anon:
'Men in her owne case ben blind alday,
As I have herd say many a day agon,
And in that same plite I stonde may.
How shall I do, which is the beste way
My troubled spirit forto bringe at rest?
If I wist how, fain wolde I do the best.'

Sithen I recovered was have I full ofte
Cause had of anger and impacience,
Where I borne have it esely and softe,
Suffering wrong be don to me, and offence,
And nought answered again, but kept silence,
Lest that men of me deme wolde and sain,
'See how this man is fallen in again.'

As that I ones fro Westminster cam,
Vexed full grevously with thoughtful hete,

161 'Have improved it so far as I knew how or was able.'
162 saut leap.
167 'If I go on using, there is nothing to object to.'
168 conseites ideas.
169–75 This soliloquy puts the other side of the case stated in 163–8. Another pair of opposed soliloquies follows: 185–9 and 191–3. Cf. also 275–80. The device may derive from Chaucer's presentation of Criseide's uncertain reaction to Troilus' suit: No. 12 above, lines 703–63 and 771–805.
170 alday always.
172 same] *D* omits. **plite** condition.
175 wist knew.
178 esely mildly.
180 again back. **silence** Rigg 572 compares the grieving man in Isidore *Synonyma* (Migne *P.L.* 83.831), who also complains of enforced silence.
181 deme judge.
183 Westminster See *n.* to 72. H. seemingly refers to some occasion (distinct from that in 145 f.) when he was walking home after a day at the office.
184 hete heat. Painful thoughts are often represented as 'hot' in ME.

Thus thoughte I, 'A grete fole I am
This paviment adayes thus to bete,
And in and out laboure faste and swete
Wondring and hevinesse to purchace,
Sithen I stonde out of all favour and grace.'

And then thoughte I on that other side:
'If that I not be seen amonge the prees,
Men deme woll that I myn hede hide
And am worse than I am, it is no lees.'
O lord, so my spirit was restelees;
I soughte reste and I not it fond,
But ay was trouble redy at myn hond.

I may not lette a man to imagine
Fer above the mone, if that him list;
Thereby the sothe he may not determine;
But by the prefe ben things knowen and wist.
Many a doom is wrapped in the mist.
Man by his dedes, and not by his lokes,
Shall knowen be, as it is written in bokes.

By taste of fruit men may well wite and knowe
What that it is – other prefe is there non;
Every man wot well that, as that I trowe.
Right so they that demen my wit is gon
(As yit this day there demeth many a oon

186 adayes every day.
187 swete sweat.
188 Wondring anxiety. Cf. *wondering* (or *wandering*) coupled with *woe* in *Death and Life* 250 etc. and *Parliament of the Three Ages* 257. See Offord's note on latter line (EETS 246 (1959) 51–2), comparing earlier *wandreth and wo*, where *wandreth* is an Old Norse loan meaning 'distress'. **purchace** obtain.
193 lees lie.
194–5 An echo of *Matt*. 12.43, applied to the poet after his recovery: 'And when an unclean spirit is gone out of a man, he walketh through dry places seeking rest and findeth none.' The whole *Complaint* depicts such a 'dry place'.
197 ff. Rigg 572 cites Isidore *Synonyma* (Migne *P.L.* 83.830), where the grieving man complains that no one bothers to investigate the truth of false reports current about him.
197 lette prevent.
198 mone moon. Proverbial: Whiting M657.
200 prefe putting to the test.
201 doom judgment, estimate.
202–3 Three MSS., *S B L*, cite in the margin *Matt*. 7.16: 'By their fruits you shall know them.' Cf. 204–5.

I am not well) may, as I by hem go,
Taste and assay if it be so or no.

Upon a look is hard men hem to grounde
What a man is – thereby the sothe is hid.
Whether his wittes seke ben or sounde
By countenaunce it is not wist nor kid.
Though a man harde have ones ben betid,
God shilde it sholde on him continue alway.
By communing is the best assay.

I mene, to commune of thinges mene,
For I am but right lewed, douteless,
And ignoraunt, my cunning is full lene;
Yet homly resoun know I nevertheless.
Not hope I founden be so resounless
As men demen – Marie, Crist forbede!
I can no more; preve may the dede.

If a man ones fall in dronkenesse,
Shall he continue therin ever mo?
Nay, though a man do in drinking excesse
So ferforth that not speke he ne can ne go,
And his wittes welny ben reft him fro
And buried in the cuppe, he afterward
Cometh to himself again, elles were it hard.

210 Taste put to the proof (*OED* s.v. *Taste* v. 2). This sentence illustrates H's control of verse syntax.
211–12 'It is unfair for men to base their opinion of what a person is like upon a glance . . .'
214 'It is not known or manifested in his appearance.'
215 'Though a man has once had a hard time.'
216 shilde forbid.
217 'Holding a conversation is the best kind of test.'
218 commune talk. **mene** ordinary.
219 lewed uneducated.
220 cunning intelligence. **lene** lean, limited.
221 homly everyday.
224 'I cannot say more than that; actions can show the truth.'
225–31 Doob 22 cites Chaucer's Pardoner (*C.T.* VI 492–7) on the kinship between drunkenness and madness. Cf. Whiting M60: 'A drunken man is likened to a wood (mad) man.'
228 So ferforth to such an extent. **go** walk.
229 reft taken.
231 elles were it hard it would be dreadful if it were not so.

Right so, though that my wit were a pilgrime
And wente fer fro hoom, he cam again.
God me voided of this grevous venime
That had enfected and wilded my brain.
See how the curteis leche most soverein
Unto the sicke yeveth medicine
In nede, and him releveth of his pine.

Now lat this passe. God wot, many a man
Semeth full wise by countenaunce and chere,
Which, and he tasted were what he can,
Men mighten liken him to a foles pere;
And som man loketh in foltish manere
As to the outward doom and jugement,
That at the prefe discreet is and prudent.

But algates, how so be my countenaunce,
Debate is now non betwix me and my wit,
Although there were a disseveraunce,
As for a time, betwixe me and it.
The gretter harm is myn, that never yit
Was I well lettred, prudent and discreet;
There never stood yit wise man on my feet.

The sothe is this: such conceit as I had
And understonding, all were it but small,

232 that] *D* omits.
234 voided emptied. **venime** 'either a direct consequence of his profligate living – overeating and drinking produces "fumosity" which causes frenzy – or the "venyme" of melancholy and thought, which the Beggar in the *Regement* [*Regement of Prices* 271] warns against', Doob 222.
235 wilded An unusual expression, which puzzled some scribes (wilkyd *B*; weldid *L*).
236–8 H's preoccupation with God as 'leech' or healer is discussed by Doob 211.
238 pine] *C*; peyne *D*; grevous pine *S* (over erasure) *B L*.
241 'Who, if he were tested to see what he was capable of.'
242 foles pere fool's peer, i.e. no better than a fool. H. puns on *peer/pear*, like Langland *Piers* B 16.71 ('angeles peres'). The pun matches previous word play on *taste* (204, 210). Pears were proverbial types of worthlessness: Whiting P78–85. They often seem good when they are rotten.
243 foltish stupid.
245 discreet rational.
246 algates at any rate.
247 Debate dispute.
251 lettred educated.
253 conceit power of mind.
254 all although.

Before that my wittes weren unsad –
Thanked be oure lord Jesu Crist of all –
Such have I now; but blowe is ny overall
The reverse, wherethurgh is the morning
Which causeth me thus sigh in complaining.

Sithen my good fortune hath chaunged his chere,
Hye time is me to crepe into my grave.
To live joyeless, what do I here?
I in myn herte can no gladnesse have;
I may but small say but if men deme I rave.
Sithen other thing than wo may I non gripe,
Unto my sepulture am I now ripe.

My wele, adieu! Farewell, my good fortune!
Out of your tables me planed have ye.
Sithen well ny any wight forto commune
With me loth is, farewell, prosperité!
I am no lenger of your liveré,
Ye have me put out of your retenaunce.
Adieu, my good aventure and good chaunce!

And as swithe after, thus bethoughte I me:
'If that I in this wise me despaire,
It is purchase of more adversité.
What nedeth it my feble wit appaire?
Sith God hath made myn helthe home repaire,

255 unsad unsettled.
257–8 '. . . but the opposite (report) has spread almost everywhere, from which derives the sorrow.'
260 his] hir *S B L C*. Fortune was commonly feminine.
264 'I can say very little without men thinking that I am raving.'
265 gripe grasp, get.
267 wele prosperity.
268 Writing was removed from wax tablets by smoothing ('planing') the surface. Cf. metaphor in No. 15.2 above, lines 7–8.
271 liveré 'A suit of clothes, formerly sometimes a badge or cognizance . . . bestowed by a person upon his retainers or servants' (*OED* s.v. *Livery* 2): hence 'following, faction' (*OED* 3b).
272 retenaunce] remembraunce *D*. The reading of *S B L C* continues the metaphor of 271: H. no longer belongs to Prosperity's retinue.
273 aventure fortune.
274 as swithe immediately.
276 'It is simply a way of bringing more adversity down upon myself.'
277 'What need is there to weaken my already feeble mind?'
278 repaire return. Cf. 233.

Blessed be he; and what men deme or speke,
Suffre it thenke I, and me not on me wreke.'

But somdel had I rejoising amonge
And gladnesse also in my spirit
That, though the peple toke hem mis and wronge,
Me deming of my sicknesse not quit,
Yit for they complained the hevy plit
That they had seen me in with tendrenesse
Of hertes cherté, my greef was the lesse.

In hem putte I no default but oon:
That I was hool they not ne deme coude.
And day by day they sy me by hem gon
In hete and cold, and neither still nor loude
Knew they me do suspectly – a derke cloude
Her sight obscured within and withoute –
And for all that were they in such a doute.

Axed han they full ofte sith and freined
Of my felawes of the Privy Seel
And prayed hem to telle hem with hert unfeined
How it stood with me, whether ill or well;
And they the sothe told hem every dell.
But they helden her wordes not but lees;
They mighten as well have holden her pees.

This troubly lif hath all too longe endured;
Not have I wist how in my skin to tourne;
But now my self to my self have ensured

280 'I intend to endure it, and not take vengeance on myself.'
281 somdel somewhat. **amonge** between whiles.
283 toke hem See 94 and *n*.
287 hertes cherté See 81 and *n*.
289 hool whole, recovered.
294 for all that notwithstanding all this (i.e. the evidence referred to in 290–2)? **they**] *D C*; ay *S B L*.
295 sith since. **freined** inquired.
296 See *n*. to 72, and headnote.
297 with hert unfeined honestly.
299 dell part, bit.
300 not but lees nothing but a lie.
303 This vivid expression is not recorded elsewhere.
304 ensured guaranteed.

For no such wondring after this to mourne.
As long as my lif shall in me sojourne
Of such imagining I not ne recche.
Lat hem deme as hem list, and speke and drecche.

305 wondring See 188 and *n*.
307 I not ne recche I shall take no notice at all (emphatic double negative).
308 deme] drem *D*. Since key words are commonly repeated in this poem, the use of *deme* to denote other people's inferences and guesses at 99, 181, 192, 208, 223, 264 etc supports the reading of *S B L C*. But *dreme* can mean 'speculate' in ME: *MED* s.v. *Dremen* v.(2) 2(b). Cf. textual problem in No. 12 above, line 800 and *n*. **drecche** speculate? *MED* s.v. *Drecchen* v. 1(e).

John Lydgate

Life Born *c.*1370 in Suffolk, and recruited as a boy to the neighbouring abbey of St Edmund at Bury, a prosperous and influential Benedictine house with a famous library. He spent his life as a monk (Dunbar calls him 'the Monk of Bery', No. 33 line 51), but much of it outside the cloister: he studied at the Benedictine college at Oxford; may have met Chaucer, whose works he admired and imitated; travelled widely (e.g. he was in Paris in the late 1420s). He enjoyed the patronage of royalty and nobility: Henry V and his brother Humphrey, Duke of Gloucester, Henry VI, the Earl of Salisbury, the Countess of Suffolk, etc. During the 1420s and early 1430s, he achieved almost laureate status, receiving many commissions for municipal, court and national occasions. About 1434 he returned permanently to Bury, where he lived a more retired life until his death in 1449 or 1450.
Reputation C15 writers commonly couple Lydgate with Chaucer and Gower as the first masters of English verse: so Dunbar, No. 33 lines 49–51. His works were frequently copied, and exerted great influence on both content and style (his example encouraged the development of 'aureate' or Latinate diction) of C15 poetry in England and Scotland. He was early printed (e.g. *Temple of Glass*, Caxton 1477) and continued to be read in C16: for example *Mirror for Magistrates* is a continuation of his *Fall of Princes*. Puttenham (1589) called him 'one that wrate in good verse' (see also Introd. xvi). Some antiquarian-minded readers still liked him in C18, notably Thomas Warton and Thomas Gray: for the latter's essay, see *Works* ed. E. Gosse 1 (1884) 387–409. But in 1802 Joseph Ritson called him 'this voluminous, prosaick and driveling monk' – an opinion with which many modern readers continue to concur, despite recent attempts at rehabilitation.
Works and editions There is no collected edition of L.'s 145,000 lines of verse. Well-annotated selections in Hammond 77–187 and J. Norton-Smith, ed. *Poems* (Oxford U.P. 1966). His two biggest poems are *Troy Book* ed. H.

Bergen EETS e.s. 97, 103, 106, 126 (1906–35), intended as a standard English treatment of the siege of Troy, undertaken for the future Henry V in 1412, completed 1420; and *Fall of Princes* ed. Bergen EETS e.s. 121–4 (1924–27), a version of Boccaccio's collection of 'tragedies' (cf. Chaucer's *Monk's T.*) made for Humphrey of Gloucester between 1431 and 1438/9. Courtly works in Chaucer's manner (mostly before *c.* 1420?) include *Complaint of the Black Knight* (imitating *Book of the Duchess*), *Temple of Glass* (imitating *House of Fame*) and *Flower of Courtesy*. *Siege of Thebes* ed. A. Erdmann and E. Ekwall EETS e.s. 108, 125 (1911, 1920) is a readable appendage to *Troy Book*, composed 1420–22 and presented as a new Canterbury Tale. Minor poems are ed. H. N. MacCracken EETS e.s. 107, o.s. 192 (1910, 1934). A version of *Secreta Secretorum* was left unfinished at L.'s death.

Studies Two modern studies see in L. a movement towards the humanism and political consciousness of the Renaissance: W. F. Schirmer *John Lydgate: a study in the culture of the C15* (Tübingen 1952; trans. Keep, Methuen 1961), and A. Renoir *The Poetry of John Lydgate* (Routledge 1967). Schirmer's book is useful on biography, canon etc.; but the account of L. as a 'transitional' poet has been convincingly demolished by D. Pearsall *John Lydgate* (Routledge 1970), who gives an admirable account of L. as a paradigmatic specimen of medieval poetic methods: 'In him we can see, at great length, and in slow motion, the medieval mind at its characteristic work.' This was more or less what Joseph Ritson saw; but Pearsall is more interested. See also Norton-Smith's volume of selections.

23 As a Midsummer Rose

The poem belongs to a group of 20 Lydgate poems described by MacCracken as 'little homilies with proverbial refrains': see Pearsall 204–16. Chaucer's moral ballades (e.g. No. 17 above) provided precedent, as did anonymous moral poems such as No. 20. The 8-line '*Monk's Tale* stanza' (*ababbcbc*) is similarly used by Henryson, with refrain, in the *Moralitas* to No. 31.2 below. L.'s manner here is characteristic of such 'little homilies': end-stopped lines, much proverbial matter, examples piled up to 'prove' the theme. The first section, lines 1–64, offers examples of contrast and change in Nature. Lines 65–96 add examples from human history. Lines 97–120 describe how change may be transcended through martyrdom or meditation on Christ's Passion.

Text 7 MSS. The present text is based on B.L. MS. Harley 2255 (= *H*), a copy perhaps written under L.'s direction at Bury. Bodleian MS. Ashmole 59 (= *A*) represents a variant (earlier?) version, from which some readings are recorded here. They give glimpses of L.'s methods of working. For fuller variants, see MacCracken *Minor Poems* 2.780–5, and Norton-Smith 136–42 (whose sigils I use).

Lat no man boste of conning nor vertu,
Of tresour, richesse nor of sapience,
Of worldly support, for all cometh of Jesu,

1 conning knowledge.
3 support backing (witte *A*).

[23] John Lydgate

Counseil, confort, discrecioun and prudence,
Provisioun, forsight and providence,
Like as the lord of grace list dispose:
Som man hath wisdom, som man hath eloquence;
All stant on chaunge like a midsomer rose.

Holsom in smelling be the sote floures,
Full delitable outward to the sight;
The thorn is sharp, cured with fresh coloures;
All is nat gold that outward sheweth bright;
A stockfish bon in dirknesse yeveth a light:
Twen fair and foul, as God list dispose
A difference atwix day and night,
All stant on chaunge like a midsomer rose.

Floures open up on every grene
Whan the larke, messager of day,
Salueth the uprist of the sunne shene
Most amerously in April and in May;
And Aurora, again the morwe gray,

5 All three words mean 'foresight' (*OED* s.v. *Provision* sb. 1, *Providence* sb. 2). *Providentia* in this sense was an aspect of prudence (line 4): see No. 31.1 below, line 137 and *n. A* reads *promocioun* for *provisioun*, reducing the tautology.
6 list pleases to.
7 *A*: 'As summe man hath ful directe elloquence.'
8 In *H* etc. the refrain is unvaried, except for 32, until the last three stanzas. *A* varies it more: see *nn.* to 24, 48, 52–6, 69–72. **stant on** stands on. See *OED* s.v. *Stand* v. 74c: 'To be grounded or based on. Also, to be contingent on; to consist in.' The combination of an abstract sense with the physical notion of standing on slippery ground (or Fortune's turning wheel) makes *stant on* preferable to *stant in* (in *A* etc).
9 Holsom pleasant. **sote** sweet.
11 cured covered. **coloures** i.e. petals.
12 Proverbial: Whiting G282.
13 stockfish codfish etc 'cured by splitting open and drying hard in the air without salt' (*OED* s.v.). The luminosity of an old fishbone is another example of 'fair' appearances masking 'foulness'.
14–16 Punctuation and sense uncertain. Perhaps: 'Everything varies between beauty and ugliness, just as God has chosen to establish a variation between day and night' (cf. next st.).
18 Chaucerian echo: 'The bisy larke, messager of day', *Knight's T.*, *C.T.* I 1491.
19 uprist uprising. **shene** bright.
21 again to welcome (*OED* s.v. *Again* prep. 3b). **morwe gray** cf. again *Knight's T. C.T.* I 1492.

Causeth the dayeseye hir crown to unclose:
Worldly gladnesse is medled with affray;
All stant on chaunge like a midsomer rose.

Atwen the cuckow and the nightingale
There is a maner straunge difference;
On fresh braunches singeth the wodewale;
Jayes in music have small experience;
Chatering pyes, whan they come in presence,
Most malapert their verdit to purpose:
All thing hath favour, brefly in sentence,
Of soft or sharp, like a midsomer rose.

The royal lioun lete calle a parlement,
All bestes aboute him environ.
The wolf of malis, being there present,
Upon the lamb complained, again resoun,
Said he made his water unholsom,
His tender stomak to hinder and undispose:

22 In *Legend of Good Women*, Chaucer goes out in May to see the daisy 'agen the sunne sprede, | Whan it up riseth by the morwe shene' (G. Prol. 48–9). *crown* also recalls *L.G.W.*, where Alceste's crown corresponds to the petals of the daisy which she represents.
23 medled mingled. **affray** fear.
24 All] And *A*.
25–6 Cuckoo and nightingale oppose each other e.g. in J. Clanvowe's *Boke of Cupide* (*Works* ed. Scattergood). L. alludes to the difference between the cuckoo's 'foule voise' (*Boke* 94) and the nightingale's song.
26 maner kind of.
27 wodewale a bird (Golden Oriole?) noted for the beauty of its song.
29 Magpies conventionally *chatter*: Whiting P179.
30 'To propose their judgment very presumptuously': recalling Chaucer's *Parlement*, where various orders of bird give their *verdit* (503) on a disputed case in the *presence* (307) of Nature.
31 favour ? disposition, leaning, one way or other. But L. may have written *savour*. **in sentence** in substance. Lydgatean tag: see *OED* s.v. *Sentence* sb. 7b.
33–9 The Aesopian fable of the Wolf who devoured the Lamb for muddying his drinking-water is narrated in Lydgate's *Isopes Fabules* ed. MacCracken *Minor Poems* Pt 2 EETS o.s. 192 (1934) 574–8 and in Henryson's *Fables*. L. evidently associated the fable with others in which a case is brought before the Lion in council, e.g. Henryson's *Trial of the Fox*.
33 lete calle caused to be summoned.
34 environ in a circle.
36 again against. The Wolf's complaint is unreasonable because the Lamb drank from the stream at a point below where he was drinking.

Raveinours reign, the innocent is bore down;
All stant on chaunge like a midsomer rose.

All worldly thing braideth upon time:
The sunne chaungeth, so doth the pale mone,
The aureat noumbre in kalenderes set for prime.
Fortune is double, doth favour for no bone,
And who that hath with that queen to done
Contrariously she will his chaunce dispose:
Who sitteth highest, most like to falle sone;
All stant on chaunge like a midsomer rose.

The golden chaar of Phebus in the air
Chaseth mistes blake that they dar nat appere,
At whos uprist mountains be made so fair
As they were newly gilt with his bemes clere;
The night doth folwe, appalleth all his chere,
Whan western wawes his stremes overclose.
Reckne all beauté, all freshnesse that is here:
All stant on chaunge like a midsomer rose.

Constraint of cold maketh floures dare
With winter frostes, that they dar nat appere;
All clad in russet, the soil of grene is bare;

39 *A*: 'By ravynours a reame is offt undone.' **Raveinours** plunderers. In L.'s *Fabules* the story is told 'ayenst ravein and tiranny'.
41 braideth upon time changes in course of time.
43 The Golden Number (Med. Lat. *aureus numerus*), otherwise called the Prime, is the 'number of any year in the Metonic lunar cycle of nineteen years', included in ecclesiastical calendars to help in computation of movable feasts: *OED* s.v. *Golden* a. 6 and *Prime* sb.[1] 4.
44 bone request, prayer.
47 Proverbial in Lydgate: Whiting S357.
48 *A*: 'For al in chaunge stont lyche a midsomer roose.'
49 chaar chariot.
50 they] *A* etc; day *H* etc.
52–6 *A* has a different (and inferior: see *n.* in Norton-Smith) version: 'Soone affter that the clowdes assemble in feere | And night folowethe, it is wele seene to here; | It chaungethe offt what thing that man purpose, | Leve this soothe, beo it far or neere, | The worlde chaungethe as a midsomer roos.'
53–4 'The night follows and dims all his (the sun's) countenance, when western waves close over his rays.' See *OED* s.v. *Stream* sb. 7.
57–64 *A* omits this stanza.
57 dare shrink.
58 Cf. 50.

Tellus and Jove be dulled of their chere
By revolucioun and turning of the yere.
As gery March his stoundes doth disclose,
Now rain, now storm, now Phebus bright and clere,
All stant on chaunge like a midsomer rose.

Where is now David, the most worthy king
Of Juda and Israel, most famous and notable?
And where is Salomon, most soverein of conning,
Richest of bilding, of tresour incomparable?
Face of Absolon, most fair, most amiable?
Reckne up echon, of trouthe make no glose,
Reckne up Jonathas, of frenship immutable:
All stant on chaunge like a midsomer rose.

Where is Julius, proudest in his empire,
With his triumphes most imperial?
Where is Porrus, that was lord and sire
Of all Ind in his estat royal?
And where is Alisaundir that conquered all?

60 Tellus Earth. **Jove**] Imo *H*; Ymo *J T*; Iuno *h*; Yone *P*. Norton-Smith 137 shows that *Imo* does not exist: the readings of *h* and *P* point to a conjectural original *Jove* ('Ioue'). 'Jove was a common designation for the heavens in classical and medieval Latin verse.'

62 'As changeable March manifests its phases.' The changeableness of March is a L. commonplace (Whiting M373); and cf. No. 12 above, line 765.

65-96 L.'s catalogue of great men now dead takes the form of a series of questions, 'Where is . . . ?' This formula originated in Latin homiletic writings (*Ubi sunt . . .* ?); whence it became common in the vernacular, e.g. Brown *XIIIth-Century Lyrics* 85–7 and Henryson, No. 30 below, lines 416 ff. See further Gray 183–90.

66 *A*: 'Of al Iuda the prince mooste notable.'

68 bilding referring to the building of the Temple.

69–72 Cf. Chaucer's ballade, No. 14 above, lines 1 and 3, where Absalom and Jonathan appear together. *A* reads: 'Fayre Absolon of face mooste amyable, | Rekken hem alle by trouthe and make no gloose, | Of Ionathas, and make ful mutable, | Al is in chaunge lyche a midsomer roos.'

70 'Count them all, without disguising the truth.'

73 Julius Julius Caesar.

75 Porrus Porus, King of India and one of the chief adversaries conquered by Alexander. The ref. to India and the proximity of Alexander establish *A*'s reading *Porrus* against *H*'s *Pirrus*.

76 all] *A*; *H* etc. omit.

77 Alisaundir Alexander, who figures in other *ubi sunt* catalogues: Cary 310.

Failed leiser his testament to dispose.
Nabugodonosor or Sardonapal?
All stant on chaunge like a midsomer rose.

Where is Tullius with his sugred tonge?
Or Crisistomus with his golden mouth?
The aureat ditės that be red and songe
Of Omerus in Grece both north and south?
The tragedyes divers and uncouth
Of moral Senek, the mysteryes to unclose?
By many example this matere is full couth:
All stant on chaunge like a midsomer rose.

Where ben of Fraunce all the dozeperes,
Which that in Gaule had the governaunce?
Vowes of the Pecock, with all their proude cheres?
The worthy nine with all their high bobbaunce?

78 'There was no time to arrange his will.' Alexander died suddenly and prematurely (by poison), but not intestate. For a Testament of Alexander see Cary 312–13.
79 Nabugodonosor the usual medieval form of Nebuchadnezzar. **Sardonapal** Sardanapalus, King of Assyria, who burned himself to death.
81 Tullius Marcus Tullius Cicero, a chief authority on rhetoric in medieval curricula. This stanza is devoted to those who owe their fame to verbal, rather than martial, arts (two Latin and two Greek).
82 Crisistomus St John Chrysostom (a nickname meaning 'golden-mouthed'), a C4 Church Father.
83 aureat golden, eloquent. A literary term apparently coined by Lydgate: see Norton-Smith 192–5. **ditės** compositions.
85 uncouth strange.
86 Senek Seneca the Younger, dramatist and philosopher. **mysteryes** 'i.e. "riddles or enigmas connected with divine authority": the oracle and plague in *Oedipus*, the ghost of Tantalus in *Thyestes*, etc.', Norton-Smith 141.
87–8 *A*: 'Bynsaumple of theos thinges here nowthe | They beon far chaunged as a somer roos.'
87 couth well-known.
89 dozeperes the 'twelve peers', the lords closest to Charlemagne (including Roland).
91 Vowes of the Pecock An early-14C Alexander romance, *Les Voeux du paon* by Jacques de Longuyon, describes how Porus (see 75) and others made vows to a roast peacock before a battle.
92 The Nine Worthies (four already alluded to by L.) first appear as a set in Longuyon's poem (see *n.* to 91): Alexander, Hector and Julius Caesar; Joshua, David and Judas Maccabeus; Arthur, Charlemagne and Godfrey of Bouillon. The motif is closely linked to the *ubi sunt* tradition, as in the ME *Parliament of the Three Ages* 297–583: ed. Offord EETS 246 (1959). See Offord's Introd. p. xl. **bobbaunce** pride.

Trojan knightes, grettest of alliaunce?
The flees of gold, conquered in Colchos?
Rome and Cartage, most soverein of puissance?
All stant on chaunge like a midsomer rose.

Put in a sum all marcial policye,
Compleet in Affrick and boundes of Cartage;
The Theban legioun, example of chevalrye,
At Rodanus river was expert their corage:
Ten thousand knightes born of high parage,
Their martirdom rad in metre and prose,
Their golden crownes made in the hevenly stage,
Fresher than lilies or ony somer rose.

The remembraunce of every famous knight,
Ground considered, is bilt on rightwisnesse.
Race out ech quarel that is not bilt of right;
Withoute trouthe, what vaileth high noblesse?
Laurer of martirs, founded on holynesse!

93 grettest of alliaunce most highly connected.

95 puissance power.

96 *A*: 'Thus alle beo chaunged as the somers roos.'

97 Put in a sum equivalent to the 'reckon up' of 55, 70, 71.

99–101 A legion of Christian soldiers from Egyptian Thebes was massacred by the Emperor Maximian for refusing to sacrifice to idols. The massacre occurred beside the R. Rhone (*Rodanus*). Cf. Aelfric *Lives of the Saints* (No. 28) and *Golden Legend*.

100 expert clearly demonstrated: *MED* s.v. *Expert* ppl. 3(b).

101 parage lineage.

103 The image is of martyrs sitting crowned in their heavenly thrones. See *OED* s.v. *Stage* sb. 2 'Station, position, seat', citing *Kingis Quair* 549–50: 'martris and confessouris, | Ech in his stage.'

104 The imagery of lilies and roses, white and red, here and in 110–12, may be compared with the rose and lily crowns given to the chaste martyrs in Chaucer's *Second Nun's T.*, *C.T.* VIII 220 f. Both poets recall associations between roses and martyr's blood, lilies and chastity: see Robinson's note.

106 Ground considered if one considers what it is based upon. The latinate absolute construction contributes to the higher style of these last stanzas.

107–8 'Eliminate from consideration every enterprise which is not built upon justice – for what use is great nobility without truth?'

109 The contrast between Christian chivalry 'founded on holiness' and secular chivalry, which at best is 'built upon justice', was implicit in the previous st. **Laurer** laurel, i.e. the laurel of martyrdom.

Whit was made red their triumphes to disclose,
The white lilye was their chast clennesse,
Their bloody suffraunce was no somer rose.

It was the rose of the bloody feeld,
Rose of Jericho, that grew in Beedlem,
The five roses portrayed in the sheeld,
Splayed in the baner at Jerusalem.
The sunne was clips, and dirk in every rem,
Whan Crist Jesus five welles list unclose
Toward Paradis, called the rede strem,
Of whos five woundes prent in your hert a rose.

110–12 See *n.* to 104 above.

112 *A*: 'Theire martirdome was lyke the rede roose.' *H* reverts to an idea implied in 104: the roses of martyrdom and lilies of chastity transcend the natural flowers.

113–20 The martyrdom of the Theban Legion is identified with Christ's Passion.

113 feeld Golgotha; but also the heraldic 'field' upon which are displayed the roses which form the arms of Christ the Knight.

114 Rose of Jericho L. alludes to what was considered a prophecy of Christ, *Ecclesiasticus* 24.18: 'I was exalted like a palm tree in Cades, and as a rose plant in Jericho.'

115 The ref. here and in 118 is to the five wounds of Christ, on which see D. Gray *N & Q* 10 (1963) 50–1, 82–9, 127–34, 163–8. The idea of a Christ–Knight bearing a blazon of the Five Wounds on his shield was traditional (Gray 88), as was the image of wounds as roses (Woolf *Lyric* 233, Gray 85). The two ideas were combined before L. in a C14 poem (found in Vernon MS.), where Christ's coat-armour bears, on a red field (cf. L.'s line 113), five red roses representing the wounds: *Christ's Testament* ed. Furnivall EETS o.s. 117 (1901) lines 215–24.

116 Splayed] *A* etc. ('displayed'); splayned *H*.

117–20 *A*: 'The sunne was derke almoste with bright beeme | Whane Ihesu Crist fyve wellis list unclose, | Called the ryver with the red streme: | To Paradyse-wardes unto Ihesu oure roos.'

117 clips eclipsed. **rem** realm: 'There was darkness over the whole earth' *Matt*. 27.45.

118 The Wounds are frequently called 'wells' in devotional poetry: Gray *N & Q* 10 (1963) 50–1, 129–34, 163–7.

119 Gray *art. cit.* 132–3 notes cases where the blood from the Wounds was identified with the four rivers of Paradise flowing from the Fountain of Life.

120 The imprint of a five-petalled rose on the heart is an image of meditation upon the Wounds: cf. the five-petalled roses in the Buxheim altarpiece (*c.* 1500): Schiller 2. 195 and Pl. 668.

Charles d'Orléans

Life Born 1394, son of Louis d'Orléans and nephew of King Charles VI of France. In 1406 married Isabella, child-widow of King Richard II. After being captured at Agincourt (1415), Charles was held prisoner in England for 25 years, in the charge of various English knights and lords. The Earl of Suffolk, husband of Chaucer's granddaughter and himself a poet, was his custodian from 1432 to 1436. In 1440 he was released, married for a third time (his second wife, Bonne, having died while he was in captivity), and spent much of the rest of his life at Blois, dying in 1465. Biographical studies: P. Champion *Vie de Charles d'Orléans* (Paris 1911); E. McLeod *Charles of Orleans: prince and poet* (Chatto 1969).

French poems Charles was one of the masters of the late-medieval high courtly French lyric, on which see D. Poirion *Le Poète et le prince* (Paris 1965). His ballades, complaints, rondeaux and chansons survive in many MSS., of which the most important is Charles's own personal copy in Bibliothèque Nationale (MS. fr. 25458), which also contains some English poems (printed by Hammond 221–3). This MS., prepared after Charles's return to France, orders his French lyrics into a sequence representing, in highly conventionalized form, the 'history' of the lover-prisoner. This is the 'Livre de prison'. The French poems are edited by P. Champion, 2 vols. (Paris 1923–7), studied by J. Fox *The Lyric Poetry of Charles d'Orléans* (Oxford U.P. 1969).

English poems B.L. MS. Harley 682 contains a collection of more than 200 English poems, corresponding in many ways to the French sequence: ed. R. Steele and M. Day *The English Poems of Charles of Orleans* EETS 215, 220 (1941, 1946), reprinted with new bibliography 1970. About two-thirds of the English poems have French equivalents; and the order and shape of the collection resembles that of Charles's personal copy. The question of the authorship of the Harley poems has been much debated, and is still unresolved. The English poems generally derive from the French, but they are not literal translations. They are more varied in mood and style than the French. Echoes of Chaucer (No. 24.4 lines 25–7) and of Lydgate and Gower (No. 24.3 line 4), alternate with slangy expressions (No. 24.1 lines 5, 22) and violent outbursts (No. 24.2 lines 11–12). For an analysis of Charles's 'abstract style', see P. Gradon *Form and Style in Early English Literature* (Methuen 1971) 336–47. R. Steele, in Introd. to his edn of the English poems, argues strongly for Charles's authorship, as does J. Fox *Romania* 86 (1965) 433–62. For the opposite opinion see Hammond 214–15. Excellent critical suggestions in Stevens *Music and Poetry* Chs. 9 and 10. Survey of more recent work by C. Clark *Med. Aev.* 40 (1971) 254–61.

24 Four Lyrics from the 'Livre de prison'

These come from the sole MS., B.L. Harley 682 (see above).

No. 24.1 belongs to the first section of the book, which describes a love affair between Charles and an unnamed 'Lady Beauty'. It is a ballade (Ballade 6 in Steele's edn) with common rhymes and envoy: see headnote to No. 13. The corresponding French poem is Ballade 6 in Champion's edn.

No. 24.2 belongs to the second, central section, where Charles entertains other lovers to a 'banquet' of love songs. It is a roundel (Roundel 48 in Steele): see headnote to No. 15. The corresponding French poem is Chanson 48 in Champion: 'Vostre bouche dit: Baisiez moy, | Se m'est avis quant la regarde; | Mais Dangier de trop prés la garde, | Dont mainte doleur je reçoy. || Laissiez m'avoir, par vostre foy, | Un doulx baisier, sans que plus tarde. | Vostre . . . | Se m'est . . . || Dangier me heit, ne sçay pourquoy, | Et tousjours Destourbier me darde [Hindrance throws darts at me]; | Je prie a Dieu que mal feu l'arde! | Il fust temps qu'il se tenist coy [kept quiet]. | Vostre bouche . . .'

No. 24.3 is another roundel (57 in Steele) from the same section. No French equivalent is known. The poem 'charmingly catches the spirit of Gower's penitential dialogue' in *Confessio Amantis* (Bennett).

No. 24.4 belongs to the third and last section of the 'Livre', which describes a second love-affair. It is another ballade (Ballade 97 in Steele), employing the '*Monk's Tale* stanza' used by Chaucer in No. 13 above and also by French balladiers. No French equivalent is known.

Date If the English version of the 'Livre de prison' is by Charles himself, it was presumably made before his departure to France in 1440.

24.1 'Not long ago . . .'

Not long ago I hied me apace
In secret wise myn hert forto counsail
Himsilf forto withdraw, as for a space,
Out of loves painful thought and travail;
To which he said me, 'Nay, set there a nail,
Speke me no more therof, I hertly pray,
For, God wot, to love I shall me pain,
For I have chose the fairist that be may,
As me reported hath myn eyen twain.'

'Now pardon me,' I said, 'as in this case,
Forwhy I say hit for oure both avail

5 set there a nail go no further, make a stop there (?). Obscure, unparalleled in the French, or elsewhere in ME.

7 me pain take pains.

11 Forwhy because. **oure both avail** the benefit of us both.

With all the power that good will in me has,
That in good trouthe thou dost me to mervail.
Seest thou not well that fortune doth us fail?
Hast thou good lust to live in sorow?' 'Nay,
Ywis,' he said, 'I trust more to attain.
I had a praty look yit yestirday,
As me reported hath myn eyen twain.'

'Allas,' said I, 'thou fonnest, as have I grace,
That for oon look thy lif lust to bewail.
For countenaunce or lokes of hir face
Knowest thou hir thought?' 'Yea, cast me lo a kail!
O pese,' quod he, 'now, good, I list not rail
Nor I beleve no word thou dost me say;
For trewly serve I shall, and never fain,
Of good which is the best – leve this aray –
As me reported hath myn eyen twain.'

O ywis, madame, in this maner aray
Myn hert and I thus have ye brost atwain;
But what, swete hert, as gide us such a way
As me reported hath myn eyen twain.

13 dost cause.

15 lust desire.

16 Ywis indeed.

17 praty nice. **yit yestirday** only yesterday.

19 thou fonnest you are going mad.

20 lust are willing.

21 countenaunce favourable manner: 'un doulx acointement' in the Fr.

22 Yea cast me lo a kail that's right, abuse me! MS. *ye* is *yea* not *ye*: the poet and his heart address each other with the familiar sing. *thou*. The odd placing of *lo* is characteristic of these poems. *kail* means 'ninepin', and *cast me a kail* was apparently slang: 'knock down one of my skittles', i.e. 'abuse me'. See *MED* s.v. *Keile* n., first quotation. Perhaps the French prince did not realize just how slangy some of his English was: cf. 5. The Fr. here has simply 'Taisiez vous'.

23 good my dear fellow.

25 fain spare, hold back.

26 leve this aray let this matter drop.

28–31 The Fr. original of this ballade has no envoy. The address to the mistress is a characteristic topic of envoys.

29 brost atwain burst apart.

[24] Charles d'Orléans

24.2 'Your mouth hit saith . . .'

Your mouth hit saith me 'Bas me, bas me, sweet'
When that I you behold, this semeth me.
But Daunger stant so nigh hit may not be,
Which doth me sorow gret, I you beheet.

But by your trouthe, gef me hit now we meet,
A privé sweet sweet cosse, two or three.
Your mouth hit saith me 'Bas me, bas me, sweet'
When that I you behold, this semeth me.

Daunger me hateth – why, I can not weet –
And laboureth ay my gret adversité.
God graunt me ones forbrent I may him see,
That I might stamp his ashes with my feet.

Your mouth hit saith me 'Bas me, bas me, sweet'
When that I you behold, this semeth me.
But Daunger stant so nigh hit may not be,
Which doth me sorow gret, I you beheet.

1 Bas me kiss me. MS. omits second *me*, probably by error. Cf. Skelton's *Speke, Parott* 104: 'Bas me, swete Parrot, bas me, swete swete'; and Chaucer *C.T.* I 3709. The allusion is evidently to a popular song. The Fr. version simply has 'Baisiez moy'.

3 Daunger a hostile personification, deriving from *R. de la Rose*, and representing either the Lady's own standoffishness, or some suspicious or jealous third party, or indeed 'any factor that comes between the poet and his desires' (Fox). **stant** stands.

4 beheet promise.

5 gef give.

6 cosse kiss.

7–8 The scribe writes only the first words of the refrain lines.

9 weet discover.

10 laboureth labours to bring about.

11 forbrent burnt right up (*for-* is an intensive prefix).

12 This violent, memorable line has no equivalent in the Fr., which says merely 'It is time that he kept quiet'.

13–16 The scribe indicates only two refrain lines, as at 7–8; but I assume that Charles intended a regular 16-line roundel, like Wilkins No. 94.

24.3 'My gostly fader . . .'

My gostly fader, I me confess
First to God and then to you
That at a window, wot ye how,
I stale a cosse of gret swetnesse,

Which don was out avisiness;
But hit is don, not undon, now.
My gostly fader, I me confess
First to God and then to you.

But I restore it shall doutless
Again, if so be that I mow,
And that God I make a vow,
And elles I axe foryefness.

My gostly fader, I me confess
First to God and then to you
That at a window, wot ye how,
I stale a cosse of gret swetnesse.

1 gostly fader spiritual father, father confessor. The poet speaks as if in the confessional. The conception is the same as Gower's: a Lover's Confession.

3 wot ye how you know how.

4 stale a cosse stole a kiss: a phrase first recorded in a similar context in Gower's *Confessio Amantis*, where the Confessor asks Amans whether he has ever 'stolen kisses' (5.6543 f.).

5 out avisiness without premeditation. Absence of premeditation reduces the gravity of a fault, as manuals of confession point out.

7–8 The scribe writes only the first words of the refrain lines.

9 restore A penitent cannot be absolved unless he 'restores' (cf. No. 10 above, line 2354) wrongfully acquired goods, or at least, as here, expresses a firm intention of making such restitution. Charles here plays upon one of the cardinal points of confessional theory.

10 mow may.

11 Perhaps *to* is lost before *God* (Steele).

12 'And for the rest, I ask pardon.'

13–16 The scribe indicates only two refrain lines, as at 7–8; but I assume that Charles intended a regular 16-line roundel, like Wilkins No. 94.

24.4 'O sely anker . . .'

O sely anker, that in thy cell
Yclosed art with stoon and gost not out,
Thou maist ben gladder so forto dwell
Than I with wanton wandring thus about,
That have me piked amonges the rout
An endless wo withouten recomfort,
That of my poore lif I stond in dout.
Go, dull complaint, my lady this report.

The anker hath no more him forto greve
Than sool alone upon the walles stare;
But welaway, I stond in more mischeve,
For he hath helth and I of helth am bare.
And more and more, when I come where there are
Of faire folkes to see a goodly sort,
A thousand-fold that doth encrese my care.
Go, dull complaint, my lady this report.

It doth me think, 'Yonder is fair of face,
But what, more fair yet is my lady dere.
Yond oon is small, and yond streight sides has,
Hir foot is lite, and she hath eyen clere.
But all there stained my lady, were she here.'
Thus think I, lo, which doth me discomfort.
Not for the sight, but for I nare hir nere.
Go, dull complaint, my lady this report.

1 sely anker fortunate anchorite.
4 wanton uncontrolled.
5 me piked picked out for myself. **rout** crowd.
6 recomfort consolation.
7 dout fear.
8 dull sad.
10 sool solitary. Charles's sketch of an anchorite's life, ostensibly to be preferred to his own, shows a pleasing touch of court arrogance.
11 welaway alas. **mischeve** distress.
14 'A goodly company of fine folk to be seen.'
17 doth makes.
19 small slender.
20 lite small.
21 'But my lady would put everyone there into the shade, if she were here.' Cf. Chaucer's use of *disteine*, No. 14 above, line 7.
23 'Not because of what I see, but because I may not be near her.'

Wo worth them which that raft me hir presence,
Wo worth the time to I to hir resort,
Wo worthis me to be thus in absence!
Go, dull complaint, my lady this report.

25–7 The anaphora (same word beginning several lines) in this envoy is imitated from Chaucer's *Troilus*, No. 12 above, lines 344–5.
25 Wo worth woe betide. **raft** deprived . . . of.
26 to I to hir resort until I come to her.
27 Wo worthis me wretched am I. The verb shifts here from optative to indicative.

25 Five Sloane Lyrics

Manuscript B.L. MS. Sloane 2593, dated first half of C15: descriptions in Greene *Carols* 330 and *Selection* 173–4 ('from Bury St Edmunds, almost certainly from the great Benedictine monastery there'). The majority of the contents are in 'carol' form (see below), and are printed by Greene. The complete contents (74 items, preponderantly religious) were ed. T. Wright *Songs and Carols from a MS. in the British Museum* (1856). Wright's ascription of the MS. to a professional minstrel (followed by Robbins *Secular Lyrics* pp. xxvi–xxvii) was just a guess; but the MS. is clearly a song-book of some sort, despite absence of music. Fowler 33–42 considers it 'an important early folksong collection'.
Metre Sloane MS. (the sole authority) sets out all five poems as printed here, i.e. in long rhyming couplets (with burden in No. 25.1). Editors sometimes print the couplets as quatrains, normally rhyming *abcb*, very occasionally *abab* (e.g. 25.3 lines 23–4). The caesura is certainly very strong; and in Nos. 25.4 and 25.5 the scribe marks it with a point (here an extra space). The first half-line, most often of 6, 7 or 8 syllables, is generally longer than the second, whose main range lies between 5 and 7 syllables. The line is at its longest and loosest in 25.3, at its shortest and tightest in 25.5.
No. 25.1 A 'carol' (No. 457 in Greene *Carols*). Up to C16, 'carol' is a purely formal term, denoting 'a song on any subject, composed of uniform stanzas and provided with a burden' (Greene *Carols* p. xxiii). The burden was performed at the beginning and then after each stanza, where in this poem it is introduced by the refrain 'Kyrieleison': 'One of the burden-lines will often be found as the last line of a stanza, as a refrain' (Greene *Carols* pp. xlix–l). Cf. No. 1.2 above. On the carol generally see Greene's Introductions to *Carols* and *Selection*.
No. 25.2 A riddle-song. On early riddle-songs see Fowler 21–9. A nursery rhyme recorded in 1838 resembles this song closely in structure and content: 'I have four sisters who sent me four presents . . . a chicken without a bone, a cherry without a stone, a book no man could read, a blanket without a thread . . . How can there be a chicken . . . etc.? When the chicken is in the shell, the cherry in bud, the book in the press, the blanket in the fleece': I. and P. Opie *Oxford Dictionary of Nursery Rhymes* (Oxford U.P. 1951) No. 478. The substitution of book and blanket for the briar and love of Sloane turns

the poem from a love-song into a children's riddle. A similar set of three riddles forms part of the resistance offered by the laird of Bristol's daughter to Captain Wedderburn in the ballad *Captain Wedderburn's Courtship* (Child No. 46): 'You must get me a cherry without a stone, a chicken without a bone, and a bird without a gall.' The answer to the last is dove: cf. line 4 here. The nursery-rhyme and ballad analogues, as well as the repetitive style, suggest close connections with folksong.

No. 25.3 Child's inclusion of this poem as a ballad (his No. 22) is disputed by Fowler 41, who considers it, however, 'representative of that body of folksong which was of such great importance in the shaping of the ballad tradition'. It is accepted as a ballad by M. J. C. Hodgart *The Ballads* (Hutchinson 1950) 71 and G. H. Gerould *The Ballad of Tradition* (Oxford U.P. 1932) 37. The style of narrative, with incremental repetition and abrupt dialogue, is much like that of later ballads. On analogues to the story, see Child 1.233–41, 505–6. The apocryphal miracle of the cock is associated with Stephen the first martyr in Scandinavian tradition. Elsewhere it is associated with the Magi (Child No. 55), St James and (earliest of all) Judas.

No. 25.4 A song centring on the paradox of the Fortunate Fall, a paradox formulated in the *Exultet* of Easter Eve: 'O happy fault, O necessary sin of Adam'. Woolf *Lyric* 290–1 and Davies 21–3 observe how the poet expresses this learned idea in a popular, 'ballad-like' style.

No. 25.5 A song of the virgin birth, partly based (first and last couplets: see notes) on a C13 Virgin lyric, Brown *XIIIth-Century Lyrics* No. 31: see *MP* 7 (1909–10) 165–8 and *N & Q* 9 (1962) 134–7. In the middle 3 couplets, the imagery of dew, grass, flower and spray is based on O.T. texts associated with the Virgin esp. in antiphons for Advent and Christmas: B. Raw *MLR* 55 (1960) 411–14. See also Woolf *Lyric* 287, Davies 14–19, Gray 101–6. S. Manning *Wisdom and Number* (Univ. of Nebraska P. 1962) 158–67 suggests that the 5 couplets may allude to the 5 joys of Maria and the 5 letters of her name. They 'contain' the 3 couplets describing the incarnation, which in turn may allude to the Trinity.

25.1 'Kyrie, so kyrie'

Kyrie, so kyrie,
Jankin singeth mirie,
With aleison.

1–3 The 'burden' of the carol. *Kyrie eleison* (Gk 'Lord, have mercy') appears again in customary run-together form as a refrain (6, 12 etc.). It occurs early in the Mass. Introducing new words between the words of the liturgy was customary. Greene *Selection* 259 quotes one such 'trope' of the *Kyrie:* '*Kyrie* – Rex pie – Da nobis hodie – Veniae – Munus et gratiae – *Eleison.*' The poem, recalling a Christmas Mass, follows the order of service from Introit and *Kyrie*, through Epistle, *Sanctus* and *Agnus Dei*, to the closing *Benedicamus Domino* and *Deo Gratias*.

2 Jankin a conventional name: cf. Wife of Bath's 'joly clerk, Jankin', Chaucer *C.T.* III 628. In both cases Jankin is a parish clerk. Among his duties were to sing the *Kyrie*, read the Epistle (16), sing the *Sanctus* (22), and carry the 'pax brede' (34). **mirie** sweetly. [*See further note on facing page.*]

As I went on Yol day in our procession
Knew I joly Jankin by his merry ton:
Kyrieleison.
Kyrie, so kyrie,
Jankin singeth mirie,
With aleison.

Jankin began the offis on the Yol day
And yit me thinketh it dos me good, so merry gan he say
Kyrieleison.
Kyrie, so kyrie,
Jankin singeth mirie,
With aleison.

Jankin red the pistil full fair and full well
And yit me thinketh it dos me good, as ever have I sel,
Kyrieleison.
Kyrie, so kyrie,
Jankin singeth mirie,
With aleison.

Jankin at the Sanctus cracketh a merry note
And yit me thinketh it dos me good, I payed for his cote,
Kyrieleison.
Kyrie, so kyrie,
Jankin singeth mirie,
With aleison.

Jankin cracketh notes an hundred on a knot
And yit he hacketh hem smaller than wortes to the pot,
Kyrieleison.
Kyrie, so kyrie,

3 aleison The form with *a-* instead of *e-*, unparalleled in ME, points to a pun on 'Alisoun' (appropriately the name of the Miller's heroine in *C.T.*). The meaning of the Greek, 'have mercy', is also ambiguous, being the conventional plea of lovers.
5 ton tone i.e. in the processional singing.
10 offis the Introit sung at the beginning of Mass: see *OED* s.v. *Office* sb. 6b.
11 'And it seems to do me good still, so sweetly did he say.'
16 pistil Epistle.
17 sel happiness.
22 cracketh sings with quick short notes: cf. 28–9. Bennett *Chaucer* 44 compares the singing of another parish clerk, Absolon in *Miller's T.*, *C.T.* I 3377.
28 on a knot in a cluster.
29 hacketh applied to quick singing also in *Towneley Plays*: see *MED* s.v. *Hakken* v. 3(a). **wortes** vegetables.

Jankin singeth mirie,
With aleison.

Jankin at the Angnus bereth the pax brede,
He twinkeled but said nowt and on myn foot he trede,
Kyrieleison.
Kyrie, so kyrie,
Jankin singeth mirie,
With aleison.

Benedicamus Domino, Crist fro shame me shilde,
Deo gratias therto, alas, I go with childe!
Kyrieleison.
Kyrie, so kyrie,
Jankin singeth mirie,
With aleison.

34 pax brede 'the disk of silver or gilt with a handle and a sacred symbol used in giving the "kiss of peace" to the congregation', Greene.
35 twinkeled winked. Absolon takes similar advantage of his duties: Chaucer *C.T.* I 3340–3. **trede** trod (possibly with sexual innuendo: *tread* can mean 'copulate', *OED* s.v. 8).
40 'Let us bless the Lord, Christ shield me from shame.'
41 Deo gratias therto Thanks be to God, in addition.

25.2 'I have a yong suster...'

I have a yong suster fer beyonden the sea;
Many be the drowryes that she sente me.

She sente me the cherry withouten ony ston,
And so she did the douve withouten ony bon.

She sente me the brer withouten ony rind,
She bad me love my lemman withoute longing.

How shuld ony cherry be withoute ston?
And how shuld ony douve ben withoute bon?

How shuld ony brer ben withoute rind?
How shuld I love myn lemman withoute longing?

2 drowryes keepsakes.
4 the douve the dove (MS. omits *the*). Nursery-rhyme and ballad versions have 'chicken' here; but the ballad has 'dove' as answer to another riddle ('a bird without a gall'). See headnote.
5 brer briar. **rind** bark.
6 lemman sweetheart.
10 I] MS. omits.

Whan the cherry was a flour, then hadde it non ston.
Whan the douve was an ey, then hadde it non bon.

Whan the brer was on brerd, then hadde it non rind.
Whan the maidin hath that she loveth, she is withoute longing.

12 ey egg.
13 on brerd] onbred MS. MS. reading is accepted by editors as 'unbred', i.e. in the seed; but *bred* probably represents *OED Braird* sb. 'the first shoots of grass, corn or other crops' – a northern word, found in Henryson: cf. No. 31.1 below, line 175 and *n*. So: 'When the briar was first shooting.'

25.3 'Saint Steven was a clerk . . .'

Saint Steven was a clerk in King Heroudes halle
And served him of bred and cloth as every king befalle.

Steven out of kechoun cam with bores hed on honde,
He saw a storre was fair and bright over Bedlem stonde.

He kist adown the bores hed and went into the halle:
'I forsake thee, King Heroudes, and thy werkes alle,

'I forsake thee, King Heroudes, and thy werkes alle,
There is a child in Bedlem born is better than we alle.'

'What aileth thee, Steven, what is thee befalle?
Lacketh thee either mete or drink in King Heroudes halle?'

'Lacketh me neither mete ne drink in King Heroudes halle,
There is a child in Bedlem born is better than we alle.'

'What aileth thee, Steven, art thou wood or thou ginnest to
brede?
Lacketh thee either gold or fee or ony riche wede?'

1 Heroudes The nominative is also *Heroudes* (6 etc.), from the Vulgate form *Herodes*: cf. No. 18 above, line 574.
2 of bred and cloth at table (laying out tablecloth and bread). **befalle** would befit.
3 bores hed The traditional Christmas delicacy is here being served on the very day of Christ's birth. E. K. Chambers thinks the poem a Christmas piece: *English Literature at the close of the Middle Ages* (Oxford U.P. 1945) 153.
4 storre star. **was** which was. **Bedlem** Bethlehem.
5 kist cast, threw.
6 forsake repudiate.
13 'Are you mad, or are you beginning to be a grumbler?': see *MED* s.v. *Breiden* v.(2) 'find fault'.
14 fee goods. **wede** clothing.

'Lacketh me neither gold ne fee ne non riche wede,
There is a child in Bedlem born shall helpen us at our nede.'

'That is all so soth, Steven, all so soth ywis
As this capoun crowe shall that lith here in my dish.'

That word was not so sone said, that word in that halle,
The capoun crew 'Christus natus est' among tho lordes alle.

'Riseth up, myn turmentoures, by two and all by one,
And ledeth Steven out of this town and stoneth him with stone.'

Token he Steven and stoned him in the way,
And therfore is his even on Cristes owen day.

17 all so just as. **ywis** indeed.

18 capoun capon (castrated cock).

19 not so sone no sooner.

20 Christus natus est 'Christ is born', from the invitatory at the beginning of Christmas Matins.

23 he they. **way** road.

24 even eve. St Stephen's Day is 26 Dec.

25.4 'Adam lay ybounden . . .'

Adam lay ybounden   bounden in a bond,
Four thousand winter   thought he not too long,

And all was for an appil   an appil that he took,
As clerkes finden writen   in her book.

Ne hadde the appil take ben   the appil taken ben,
Ne hadde never our lady   a ben hevene quen.

Blissed be the time   that appil take was,
Therfore we moun singen   Deo gratias.

2 Adam was harrowed out of Hell by Christ between Good Friday and Easter. Many different calculations of the age of the world at the time of Christ were current in the C15, several of them approximating to 4,000 years (e.g. 3,971 in Peter Comestor).

4 her their. The division of this line follows the MS. pointing. Editors sometimes put *writen* in the second half.

5 Ne hadde had not.

6 'Our Lady would never have (*a* = have) been Queen of Heaven.'

8 moun may. **Deo gratias** Thanks be to God.

25.5 'I singe of a maiden . . .'

I singe of a maiden that is makeless,
King of alle kinges to hir sone she ches.

He cam also stille there his moder was
As dew in April that falleth on the grass.

He cam also stille to his moderes bour
As dew in April that falleth on the flour.

He cam also stille there his moder lay
As dew in April that falleth on the spray.

Moder and maiden was never non but she;
Well may swich a lady Goddes moder be.

1–2 Cf. the related C13 Virgin lyric (see headnote) 3–4: 'Of on ic wille singen that is makeless, | The king of alle kinges to moder he hire ches.'
1 singe] syng a MS. **makeless** matchless *and* mateless.
2 ches chose: 'aptly describes her voluntary decision at the Annunciation' Gray 102. The C13 poem has the more obvious 'to moder he hire ches'.
3 also stille as silently. **there** where.
4 Several O.T. passages involving fall of dew or rain were interpreted (and used in the liturgy) as prophecies of Christ's coming: *Judg.* 6.36–40 (Gideon's fleece) taken with *Ps.* 71 (A.V. 72) 6 ('He shall come down like rain upon the fleece: and as showers falling gently upon the earth'), *Deut.* 32.2 and *Isa.* 45.8: 'Drop down dew, ye heavens, from above . . . Let the earth be opened and bud forth a saviour.' See Raw (headnote) and cf. No. 36 below, line 1.
6 flour Mary was identified with the 'flower of the field' of *Song of Sol.* 2.1. See also next *n.*
8 spray Mary was the *virga* or rod coming out of the root of Jesse: 'and a flower shall rise up out of his root', *Isa.* 11.1.
9–10 Cf. the related C13 Virgin lyric 19–20: 'Maiden and moder nas never non wimon boten he [she]: | Well mitte he berigge [bearer] of Godes sune be.'

26 God Speed the Plough

This poem was apparently composed as five 6-line stanzas (*aabaab*) and is so printed here. However, the sole MS., Bodleian Arch. Seld. B.26, a mid-C15 collection of English and Latin songs with musical settings, sets it out as a carol (see headnote to No. 25.1 above), with lines 1–3 acting as the burden, to be repeated every three lines (i.e. after 6, 9, 12 etc.): see J. Stevens, ed. *Medieval Carols* (2nd edn, Stainer and Bell 1958) 112–3 and 124, followed by Greene *Selection* No. 85. But the carol arrangement is poetically weak. The splitting of each stanza into two disrupts the sense (9–10, 27–8) and makes the *b*-rhymes pointless. It also defuses rhetorical effects such as the parallelisms within St. 3 (lines 15 and 18), and between Sts. 2 and 4 (lines 12 and 24), or 4 and 5 (lines 19 and 21, 25 and 27).

Occasion Stevens 124 suggests that the poem 'belongs to the Christmas season and is, in fact, a carol for Plough Monday', i.e. the first Monday after Epiphany. 'Plough Monday celebrations and feasts are recorded into modern times from many parts of England, frequent features being the drawing through the village streets of a decorated plough. . . . This carol, of course, is intended for more sophisticated performance, probably by choir-boys' (Greene *Selection* 244).

The merthe of all this londe
Maketh the gode husbonde
With ering of his plow;
Yblessed be Cristes sonde
That hath us sent in honde
Merthe and joy ynow.

The plow goth mony a gate
Both erly and eke late
In winter in the clay
About barly and whete,
That maketh men to swete.
God spede the plow all day!

Brown, Morel and Gore
Drawen the plow full sore
All in the morwening;

2 husbonde husbandman, farmer (subject of *maketh*). In the sung version final *-e* is syllabic in all *a*-rhymes.
3 ering ploughing.
4 sonde 'sending', gift.
6 ynow enough, in abundance.
7 gate way.
10 About busy with: *MED* s.v. *Aboute*(*n*. prep. 7(a).
11 swete sweat.
12 A proverbial expression (Whiting G239) occurring e.g. in the Paston Letters. Another ME poem (*Index* 363) has the refrain 'I praye to God, spede wele the plough.' **spede** prosper.
13–15 A medieval plough team consisted of 4, or even 8, oxen or horses (Homans 45–6). Line 13 presumably contains three common ploughmen's horse (or ox) names. *Morel* (*OED* s.v. *Morel* a. and sb.[4]) meaning 'dark-coloured' is recorded as a horse name; but *Gore* is unparalleled. Stevens guesses 'dark-coloured', Robbins 'gray'; but Greene cites modern dialect *gore* 'goad' (see *EDD* s.v. *Gore* sb.[3]) – referring either to a sluggish beast, or to one commonly yoked on the left side where the driver walked with his goad.
14 full sore with great difficulty.

Rewarde hem therfore
With a shefe or more
All in the evening.

Whan men begin to sowe
Full well her corn they knowe
In the month of May.
How ever Janiver blowe,
Whether hye or lowe,
God spede the plow all way!

Whan men beginneth to wede
The thistle fro the sede,
In somer whan they may,
God let hem well to spede;
And long good life to lede,
All that for plowmen pray.

17 'The injunction to reward the oxen with sheaves is figurative and apparently equivalent to saying, "Treat them like the human labourers", the men's bonus at harvest-time being reckoned in sheaves', Greene *Selection* 245. Or are *sheaves* simply bundles of hay and straw?
20 knowe judge.
22 Janiver January (Old French *Jenever*). The reference to January has special point if (as Greene suggests, see headnote) the poem is a 'carol for Plough Monday', celebrated on the first Monday after Epiphany (6 Jan.).
28 let grant.
29–30 'And (God grant that) all who pray for ploughmen may have a long and happy life.'

27 Corpus Christi Carol

Versions The version printed here is found only in Balliol Coll. Oxford MS. 354, a commonplace book of Richard Hill, grocer of London, compiled 1503–36 (cf. No. 28 below). In form it is a 'carol' (see No. 25.1 above), with burden and an unusual carol stanza of two short 4-accent lines: Greene *Carols* pp. liv–lvi. Some editors (Fowler 12) take the burden as an 'internal refrain' alternating with the stanza lines, as in the Staffs. version below. Four other versions have been recorded from oral tradition, three printed by Greene (*Carols* No. 322, *Selection* 67). The earliest was recorded by James Hogg, the Ettrick Shepherd, first in 1807, later in the following form in *The Bridal of Polmood* (*Winter Evening Tales*, Edinburgh 1820):

The Herone flewe eist, the Herone flewe weste,
The Herone flewe to the fayir foryste!
And ther scho sawe ane gudelye bouir,
Was all kledde ouir with the lille flouir:

And in that bouir ther was ane bedde,
With silkine scheitis, and weile dune spredde;
And in thilke bed ther laye any knichte,
Hos oundis [whose wounds] did bleide beth day and nicghte:
And by the bedde-syde ther stude ane stene,
And thereon sate ane leil maydene,
Withe silvere nedil, and silkene threde,
Stemmynge the oundis quhan they did blede.

See E. C. Batho *The Ettrick Shepherd* (Cambridge U.P. 1927); comparison with Hill version in *EC* 5 (1955) 299–314. The second version, recorded in Staffs., was printed in 1862 in *N & Q* (lines 2 and 4 to be repeated in each stanza):

1
Over yonder's a park, which is newly begun,
  All bells in Paradise I heard them a-ring;
Which is silver on the outside, and gold within,
  And I love sweet Jesus above all things.

2
And in that park there stands a hall,
Which is covered all over with purple and pall.

3
And in that hall there stands a bed,
Which is hung all round with silk curtains so red.

4
And in that bed there lies a knight,
Whose wounds they do bleed by day and by night.

5
At that bed side there lies a stone,
Which is our blessed Virgin Mary then kneeling on.

6
At that bed's foot there lies a hound,
Which is licking the blood as it daily runs down.

7
At that bed's head there grows a thorn,
Which was never so blossomed since Christ was born.

The third version, recorded in Derbyshire in 1908, is similar to Staffs., but lacks sts. 1, 4 and 6, and includes two other stanzas, one of which adapts the poem for Christmas: first printed, with tune, *Journal of Folk-Song Society* 4 (1910–13) 63. A fourth version is reported from N. Carolina in *Journal of the English Folk Dance and Song Society* 4 (1942) 122–3. This has a unique Christmas refrain; but otherwise it resembles the Derbyshire version, except in having one extra stanza and not omitting the wounded 'lord'. Like No. 25.2 above, this poem evidently came down in folk tradition (Hill's version was not printed until 1895).

Interpretation A. G. Gilchrist, when first printing the Derbyshire version, interpreted the poem as a version of the Grail. The orchard is Avalon, 'isle of apples' (cf. refs. to Glastonbury thorn in folk versions), the hall is the Castle of the Grail, the bleeding knight is Amfortas (wounded Keeper of the Grail), the weeping maiden is the Grail Damsel. Gray 164–7 connects the stone of line 23 with the tradition that the Grail was a stone, as in Wolfram's *Parzival*: see A. D. Horgan *Med. Stud.* 36 (1974) 354–81. E. C. Batho *E & S* 9 (1924) 93–5 interprets the poem as 'a meditation on the Eternal Sacrifice', with Christ as the wounded knight and Mary as the weeping maiden. The central tableau is then a kind of *pietà*. Eucharistic symbolism may also be present: see Gray, and Davies 364. R. L. Greene suggests that the Hill poem represents an original adapted by addition of burden to refer to the displacement of Catherine of Aragon from Henry VIII's affections by Anne Boleyn, whose heraldic badge was a white falcon: *Med. Aev.* 29 (1960) 10–21, 33 (1964) 53–60. The central tableau accordingly would represent the deserted Catherine at her devotions – a weak reading. But Greene's interpretation is strong on the burden, where Grail, Passion and Eucharist interpretations are weak (identifying the falcon with Joseph of Arimathea, or Death). The relationship between burden and tableau, unconvincingly rationalized in Hogg's version, is the unsolved crux of the poem.

Lully, lulley, lully, lulley,
The faucon hath born my mak away.

He bare him up, he bare him down,
He bare him into an orchard brown.
Lully, lulley, lully, lulley,
The faucon hath born my mak away.

1 A common refrain (cf. Greene *Carols* pp. cxlii–cxliii on lullay burdens), usually addressed by mother to child, as in No. 4 above. Fowler 58–64 proposes that the whole poem is basically a lullaby carol, in which the Virgin Mary, rocking Christ, prophetically describes his death and her own sorrow. But Greene *Med. Aev.* 33 (1964) 54–5 cites instances of *lullay* as 'colloquial expression connected with misfortune in love': cf. *OED* s.v. *Lullaby* int. and sb. 1b, 'Used for "farewell", "good-night"'. The whole burden was possibly taken from an older folk-song.

2 mak mate.

3–4 Greene observes that this stanza 'has the air of having been composed to link the burden and the second stanza.' It has no equivalent in the later versions.

4 brown dark, shady. A well-established use: see *OED* s.v. *Brown* adj. 1, and cf. Milton *Par. Lost* 4.246. The thick 'brown' shade of the orchard would harmonize with the luxurious hall and bed. Otherwise, if *brown* is taken as 'ungreen', i.e. withered, autumnal, the orchard may recall the barren Waste Land of the Grail legend.

In that orchard there was an hall,
That was hanged with purpil and pall.
   Lully, lulley, lully, lulley,
   The faucon hath born my mak away.

And in that hall there was a bed,
Hit was hanged with gold so red.
   Lully, lulley, lully, lulley,
   The faucon hath born my mak away.

And in that bed there lith a knight,
His woundes bleding day and night.
   Lully, lulley, lully, lulley,
   The faucon hath born my mak away.

By that beddes side there kneleth a may,
And she wepeth both night and day.
   Lully, lulley, lully, lulley,
   The faucon hath born my mak away.

And by that beddes side there stondeth a ston,
'Corpus Christi' writen theron.
   Lully, lulley, lully, lulley,
   The faucon hath born my mak away.

8 purpil and pall purple cloth and costly fabric. A customary collocation (*OED* s.v. *Purpur* sb. 1), associated with great nobility and luxury. *Pall* also meant 'altar-cloth' and 'cloth spread over a coffin' in C15 (*OED* s.v. *Pall* sb.[1] 3 and 4); but collocation with *purple* would largely neutralize such suggestions. The primary reference here is certainly to wall-hangings.

12 The four-poster bed has hangings of gold cloth.

19 may maiden.

23 The mysterious stone has been inconclusively identified with the paten covering the chalice at Mass, with the stone covering Christ's sepulchre, with an altar-stone (Gray) and with the Grail (Horgan). In other versions, the maiden sits (Hogg) or kneels (Staffs. and Derbys.) on the stone, or 'atones' on it (Carolina).

24 The inscription presumably refers to the bleeding knight, identified as the Body of Christ.

28 'Farewell, this world . . .'

The farewell of a dead (14) or dying (30) man to the world and his friends. He is apparently a king (10 and *n.*); but kingship here simply represents 'pride of life'. The poem is a Dead Man's Lament, to be considered alongside other late-medieval lyrics concerned with death: see Gray 205–6, Woolf *Lyric* 323–4. It draws on Lydgate's *Dance of Death* (*nn.* to 2, 7, 12), and shares motifs with the play of *Everyman*. On late-medieval preoccupations with death, see J. Huizinga *The Waning of the Middle Ages* trans. F. Hopman (E. Arnold 1924).

Metrical form Five stanzas of rhyme royal.

Text and date The present text, like No. 27 above, is from Balliol Coll. Oxford MS. 354, a commonplace book of Richard Hill, grocer of London, compiled 1503–36. An incomplete text, breaking off at 25, is in Trinity Coll. Cambridge MS. 1157 (=*T*), printed as No. 149 in Brown *XVth-Century Religious Lyrics*, and as No. 89 in Gray *Selection*. The last stanza appears separately as 'Epitaphium' in B.L. MS. Lansdowne 762, and appears as an actual epitaph in seven C15 examples, all printed by D. Gray *N & Q* 8 (1961) 132–5. The Maldon epitaph (No. VII in Gray) includes also a version of St. 1, suggesting that the epitaphs derived from the poem rather than vice versa. If so, the date of the earliest datable epitaph, 1487, provides a latest date for the poem, which is doubtless mid-C15.

Farewell, this world! I take my leve for ever;
I am arrested to appere afore Goddes face.
O merciful God, thou knowest that I had lever
Than all this worldes good, to have an owr space
Forto make asseth for my gret trespace;
My hert, alas, is broken for that sorow.
Som be this day that shall not be tomorow.

This world, I see, is but a cherry fair;
All thinges passeth, and so moste I algate.
This day I sat full royally in a chair

2 The image of Death as 'fell sergeant', or officer of God's court, who 'arrests' man (closely akin to the image of Death as summoner) developed in later C14: Woolf *Lyric* 323. It became popular: e.g. Lydgate *Dance of Death* 137, *Troy Book* 5.2935.

3 merciful] myghtyfull *T*. **lever** rather.

4 worldes good] world *T* (metrically preferable). **owr space** space of an hour. Davies 348 cites the widely read C12 *Meditationes* of William of Tournai (Woolf *Lyric* 76), where a summoned soul pleads: 'Give me the space of just one hour (*unius horae spatium*)' (Migne *P.L.* 184.488).

5 make asseth make amends. From Fr. 'assez feire': see *MED* s.v. *Asseth* n.

7 Proverbial: Whiting T351. Cf. Lydgate *Dance of Death* 360: 'Some bene today that shulle not be tomorwe.'

8 world] lyfe *T*. **cherry fair** 'a fair held in cherry-orchards for the sale of the fruit' (*OED* s.v.): a common image of transience in C14 and C15 verse (Whiting W662).

9 algate i.e. whatever I do.

10 chair throne: *MED* s.v. *Chaier(e* 2(a). The speaker is imagined as a king, as in much *memento mori* literature.

[28]

Till sotil deth knocked at my gate,
And unavised he said to me 'checkmate'.
Lo how sodeinly he maketh a devorce!
And, wormes to fede, here he hath laid my corse.

Speke soft, ye folkes, for I am laid aslepe,
I have my dreme, in trust is mich treason.
From dethes hold fain wold I make a lepe,
But my wisdom is turned into feble reason.
I see this worldes joy lasteth but a season.
Wold God I had remembred this beforne!
I say no more, but be ware of an horne.

This feckil world so false and so unstable
Promoteth his lovers but for a littel while;
But at last he giveth them a bable
Whan his painted trouth is torned into gile.
Experience causeth me the trouth to compile,
Thinking this – to late, alas, that I began!
For foly and hope disseiveth many a man.

11 sotil insidious, subtle. The image of the knock continues that of Death the sergeant: see *n.* to 2, and Woolf *Lyric* 323, who also refers to Horace *Carm.* 1.4, 'Pale death with equal force knocks on the hovels of the poor and the halls of kings.'

12 unavised without warning. **checkmate** Another conventional image (Whiting C169): e.g. Lydgate *Dance of Death* 459.

13 devorce i.e. between soul and body.

14 corse corpse.

15–21 'The middle stanza is . . . strikingly unlike typical medieval style, for it gains its effect, not by startling lucidity, but by the romantically half-concealed', Woolf *Lyric* 324.

16 The relation between the two parts of the line is enigmatic. Perhaps the true 'dream' which the sleep of death brings is contrasted with the illusory dreams of life. The dead man now realizes that faith in mundane things is always betrayed. The second half-line is proverbial: Whiting T492.

17 hold stronghold. The prime image is one of escaping from a castle or prison.

21 Death summons man by a trumpet-blast in *Everyman* 843 (Woolf *Lyric* 354).

22 feckil] febyll *T*.

24 bable bauble, trifle.

25 The *T* text ends with this line at the bottom of a page.

26 compile formulate.

27 Syntax aud punctuation uncertain. Perhaps: 'Reflecting on the fact that I began (to realize the truth) too late, alas!'

Farewell, my frendes! the tide abide h no man;
I moste departe hens, and so shall ye.
But in this passage the best song that I can
Is *Requiem eternam*: I pray God grant it me.
Whan I have ended all myn adversité,
Graunte me in paradise to have a mancion
That shed his blood for my redempcion.

29 the tide time. Proverbial: Whiting T318.

30 I moste departe] I am departed *Epitaphs*. See headnote.

31 passage journey. **can** know.

32 ***Requiem eternam*** 'Eternal rest (grant them, O Lord)': opening of the Introit in the Mass for the Dead. **I pray God**] now Jesu *Epitaphs*.

35 That he who. **his**] thy *Epitaphs*. Balliol MS. adds 'Beati mortui qui in Domino moriuntur. Humiliatus sum vermis' ('Blessed are the dead who die in the Lord. I am brought low as a worm').

29 Christ Triumphant

Three short but weighty couplets, spoken by the dead Christ. 'The figure of the triumphant Christ who has conquered sin and death is not so favoured by the devotional poets as that of the suffering Lord, but the poems which use it often show a remarkable power', Gray *Selection* 120. Cf. No. 37 below. The touch of menace in the last couplet prompts comparison with the Old English *beot* or battle-vaunt (Gray 147). The poem survives in one copy, N.L.S. MS. Advocates' 19.1.11, on an end leaf after Hoccleve's *De Regimine Principum*.

I have labored sore and suffered deth,
And now I rest and draw my breth;
But I shall come and call right sone
Heven and erth and hell to dome;
And then shall know both devil and man
What I was and what I am.

2 Christ's death is rest after labour also in OE *Dream of the Rood* 64–5: 'He rested himself there for a time, weary after the great struggle.' Both poems stress Christ's triumph through the Passion; but the mundane suggestion that Christ has to get his breath back (see *MED* s.v. *Drauen* 1c) is characteristic of ME as against OE poetry.

4 dome the Last Judgement.

Robert Henryson

Life On the title page of two early surviving printed editions of his *Fables* (1570) and *Testament of Cresseid* (1593), Robert Henryson is styled 'Schoolmaster of Dunfermline'. Dunfermline was an important town in C15 Scotland, with a grammar school controlled by the Benedictine Abbey. In his *Lament* (No. 33 below, line 82), Dunbar refers to 'Maister Robert Henrisoun', a title which suggests that Henryson was an M.A.; but of what university is not known. He may have spent some time in Italy: see R. D. S. Jack *Italian Influence on Scottish Literature* (Edinburgh U.P. 1972) 7–14. He may also have been a notary public. He was certainly dead before *c.*1508, when Dunbar's *Lament* was printed; and probably before 1505, when Stobo died (cf. *Lament* 86): 1500 seems a likely rough date. The date of his birth is unknown. Sir Francis Kynaston, in 1639, reported that he was 'very old' when he died: see the anecdote printed in Harvey Wood's edn, pp. xii–xiii.
Works and editions Henryson's two main works, *The Testament of Cresseid* and *Moral Fables*, are both represented here. Other works include a version of the Orpheus and Eurydice story, a short pastoral poem (*Robene and Makyne*) and a short allegorical romance of the Redemption (*The Bludy Serk*). The standard large edn is by G. Gregory Smith (STS 3 vols. Edinburgh 1906–14). Complete poems ed. in one vol. by H. Harvey Wood (2nd edn, Edinburgh, Oliver and Boyd 1958). Selections ed. C. Elliott (2nd edn, Oxford U.P. 1974).
Studies Like Dunbar, Henryson belongs to the 'Scottish Chaucerians', on whom see D. Fox in D. S. Brewer, ed. *Chaucer and Chaucerians* (Nelson 1966) 164–200. The influence of Chaucer is strong. Thus *Testament of Cresseid* is attached to Chaucer's *Troilus*, and the Fable of the Cock and the Fox reworks the *Nun's Priest's T.* But the main recent study J. MacQueen, *Robert Henryson: a study of the major narrative poems* (Oxford U.P. 1967), rightly stresses H.'s place in the general late-medieval learned tradition, representing him as 'in some sense a humanist' and 'the first of the University Wits'. Despite a tendency to over-allegorize, MacQueen's study is much superior to M. W. Stearns *Robert Henryson* (Columbia U.P. 1949). The best short account, apart from Fox (above), is Edwin Muir *Essays on Literature and Society* (2nd edn, Hogarth Press 1965) 10–21. See also H. J. C. Grierson, 'Robert Henryson' in *Essays and Addresses* (Chatto 1940).

30 The Testament of Cresseid: extract

The *Testament* begins with the narrator, an old man on a cold spring night, sitting by the fire and taking up first Chaucer's *Troilus*, then 'ane uther quair [book]'. In this 'uther quair' (which has never been identified, and is presumably an invention) he finds the story of how Cresseid, after betraying Troilus and losing Diomeid, becomes promiscuous, suffers leprosy and dies. Henryson's poem depends heavily on Chaucer's *Troilus*, to which it provides a kind of supplement by giving a description of the end of Cresseid (last seen in Chaucer 'loving' Diomede, 5.1746) to set beside Chaucer's account of Troilus's end. It also draws on Chaucer's own pendant to *Troilus*, *Legend of Good Women*, for the idea of a 'blasphemy' against Cupid (the poet's in Chaucer, Cresseid's in Henryson) punished by the angry god.

The conception of the *Testament* owes much to the conventions of courtly love narrative, as represented in Chaucer and Gower. Thus the narrator serves Venus (22–6) and reads the great 'poet of Venus' Chaucer. His story concerns a daughter of a priest of Venus (Calchas, who in Chaucer serves Apollo), who sins against Venus and Cupid by her infidelity and promiscuousness, blasphemes against them (126–40), suffers punishment, and dies repenting both' sin' and 'blasphemy'. See D. L. Noll *SSL* 9 (1971) 16–25. As in much courtly love writing, 'worship of Venus' coexists here with a robust clerkly antifeminism (notably in the unflattering description of Venus herself, 218–38); but it is not clear whether this points to a consistent deeper Christian significance. E. M. W. Tillyard *Poetry and Its Background* (Chatto 1955) 5–29 saw in the poem 'a second plot, that of Cresseid's inward purification', her 'salvation according to the Christian scheme'; and Fox also sees Cresseid as 'redeemed' and stresses the Christian 'condemnation of earthly love' implicit in the end of the *Testament* (Introd. to his edn, *cit.* below). In Ch. 3 of his general study (above), MacQueen proposes an allegorical interpretation, with Troilus representing the 'habit of moral virtue' and Cresseid the 'appetitive power of the soul'. But Spearing points out some difficulties in extreme Christian readings, *Criticism* Ch. 7 (which also contains a good account of Henryson's 'concise' style). Here, as in Gower's *Confessio Amantis*, the relationship of courtly foreground to Christian background is difficult to bring into focus. Some faults and inconsistencies are pointed out in J. A. W. Bennett 'Henryson's *Testament*: a flawed masterpiece' *Scottish Literary Journal* 1 (1974) 5–16.

Text and edition The separate edn by D. Fox (Nelson 1968) discusses fully the sources of the text, distinguishing five texts with authority: the Charteris print of 1593 (= *C*), upon the only surviving copy of which (in B.L.) the present text is founded; the 1532 printed edn of Chaucer by Thynne (= *T*); the Anderson printed edn of 1663 (= *A*); the *Book of the Dean of Lismore* of 1512–29 (= *L*), containing only lines 561–7; and one other MS. fragment. Introd. and notes in Fox are of fundamental importance.

Date *Testament* was probably in circulation by 1492, since *Spektakle of Luf*, completed in that year, refers to Cresseid who 'went common amang the Grekis', probably echoing *Testament* 76–7 and 82: B. J. Whiting *MLR* 40 (1945) 46–7.

Authorship The attribution of *Testament* to Henryson in *C* is not to be questioned. However, Thynne's inclusion of the poem in his 1532 *Works of Geoffrey Chaucer* immediately after *Troilus* ('Thus endeth the fifth and last book of Troilus: and here followeth the pitiful and dolorous testament of fair Creseyde') led C16 readers to regard it as Chaucer's. It played an important part in the development of the Troilus story up to Shakespeare: H. E. Rollins *PMLA* 32 (1917) 383–429. Francis Kynaston translated the poem into Latin in 1639, together with *Troilus*, and provided interesting annotations (see Henryson *Works* ed. G. Smith vol. 1 pp. xcvii–clxii). Kynaston ascribed the poem to H.; but 'it was not until the C19 . . . that the poem was universally recognized as Henryson's, not Chaucer's' (Fox 19).

[30] Robert Henryson

Lines 400–616

The day passit and Phebus went to rest,
The cloudis black overheled all the sky.
God wait gif Cresseid was ane sorrowfull gest,
Seeing that uncouth fair and harbery.
But meit or drink sho dressit hir to ly
In ane dark corner of the hous allone,
And on this wise, weiping, sho maid hir mone.

The Complaint of Cresseid

'O sop of sorrow, sonkin into cair,
O cative Cresseid! for now and ever mair
Gane is thy joy and all thy mirth in eird;
Of all blitheness now art thou blaiknit bair;
Thair is na salve may saif thee of thy sair.
Fell is thy fortoun, wickit is thy weird,
Thy bliss is baneist, and thy baill on breird.
Under the eirth God gif I gravin wer
Whair nane of Grece nor yit of Troy micht heir'd.

401 overheled covered over. *C A* read 'ouirquhelmit'.
402 God wait gif God knows that.
403 uncouth fair unfamiliar fare. The contrast between the leper-house food and what Cresseid is used to is pointed in 440–1. **harbery** lodging-place.
404 But without. **dressit hir** prepared herself.
407–69 The Complaint or *Planctus* is frequent in medieval poetry: cf. No. 22 above, *Hoccleve's Complaint*. The 9-line stanza, rhyming *aabaabbab*, which distinguishes Cresseid's Complaint from the rest of the *Testament*, derives from the Complaint of Anelida in Chaucer's *Anelida and Arcite* 211–55, 272–316, 333–50 (though H. adds much alliteration). Chaucer's love complaints (on which see Norton-Smith *Chaucer* Ch. 2) were no doubt H.'s chief model.
407 sop piece of bread soaked usually in wine. Cresseid is soaked and immersed (*sonkin*) in sorrow.
408 cative wretched.
409 Gane gone. **eird** earth.
410 blaiknit bair made pale and bare. *T* has 'blake and bair'. Fox compares Chaucer *Anelida* 213: 'Myn herte, bare of bliss and black of hewe'.
411 salve remedy. **saif** probably a form of *salve* 'heal' (*OED* v.[1] 2). **sair** sickness.
412 Fell cruel. **weird** fate (OE *wyrd* 'fate').
413 baneist banished. **thy baill on breird** your sorrow is sprouting (*DOST* s.v. *Abreird* adv.).
414 gif grant. **gravin** buried.
415 heir'd hear it. *It* is sometimes reduced to *'d* in Middle Scots (*DOST* s.v. *'d*).

'Whair is thy chaumer wantounly besene,
With burely bed and bankours browderit bene;
Spicis and wine to thy collatioun,
The coupis all of gold and silver shene;
The sweit meitis, servit in plaittis clene,
With saipheron saus of ane gud sessoun;
Thy gay garments with mony gudely goun,
Thy plesand lawn pinnit with goldin prene?
All is areir, thy greit royall renoun.

'Whair is thy gardin with thir gressis gay
And freshe flouris, whilk the quene Floray
Had paintit plesandly in every pane,
Whair thou was wont full merrily in May
To walk and tak the dew by it was day,
And heir the merle and mavis mony ane,
With ladyis fair in carrolling to gane,
And see the royal rinks in their array,
In garments gay garnishit on every grane?

416 The *whair is* formula used here and at 425 recalls the *ubi sunt* formula frequent in Lat. meditations on transitoriness: see No. 23 above, lines 65–96 and *n.* Cresseid later (452 ff.) represents herself to other ladies as a 'model or type of the mortal creature subjected to Fortune's whims': E. D. Aswell 'The role of Fortune in the *Testament*' *PQ* 46 (1967) 471–87, emphasizing the theme of mutability throughout the poem. **chaumer** chamber. **wantounly besene** luxuriously furnished.
417 'With handsome bed and furniture covered with fine embroidery.' *Bankours* were covers for benches and chairs.
418 Spicy delicacies (e.g. ginger) were eaten with wine as a snack or *collatioun* late at night: cf. No. 31.2 below, line 45.
419 **coupis** goblets. **shene** bright.
420 **sweit meitis** dainty foods.
421 'With saffron sauce of a good flavour.' **sessoun**] facioun *T* (but *sessoun* 'seasoning' is preferable).
423 **lawn** fine linen. **prene** pin, brooch.
424 **areir** behind i.e. past.
425 **thir** these. **gressis** plants.
426 **Floray** Flora, goddess of flowering plants. Cf. No. 31.1 below, line 59.
427 **pane** part.
429 Dew was thought to wash the complexion clear. **by** as soon as.
430 **merle and mavis** blackbird and songthrush.
431 A 'carol' was a ring-dance (much favoured by courtly ladies) in which the dancers sang: cf. 443. **gane** go.
432 **rinks** men: a poetic word, belonging to the ancient diction of alliterative verse (OE *rinc*).
433 **garnishit on every grane** ornamented in every smallest part. *Grane* is obscure: perhaps 'grain'.

'Thy greit triumphand fame and hie honour,
Whair thou was callit of eirdly wichtis flour,
All is decayit, thy weird is welterit so;
Thy hie estait is turnit in darkness dour.
This lipper ludge tak for thy burely bour,
And for thy bed tak now ane bunch of stro;
For waillit wine and meitis thou had tho
Tak mowlit breid, peirrie and ceder sour.
Bot cop and clapper, now is all ago.

'My cleir voice and courtly carrolling,
Whair I was wont with ladyis forto sing,
Is rawk as ruik, full hiddeous, hoir and hace;
My plesand port, all uthers precelling,
Of lustiness I was hald maist conding –
Now is deformit the figour of my face;
To luik on it na leid now liking has.
Sowpit in site, I say with sair siching,
Ludgit amang the lipper leid, "allace!"

'O ladyis fair of Troy and Grece attend
My miserie, whilk nane may comprehend,
My frivol fortoun, my infelicitie,
My greit mischief whilk na man can amend.
Be war in time, approchis neir the end,

435 eirdly wichtis earthly creatures.
436 welterit overturned.
438 lipper ludge leper house. **burely bour** fine chamber.
439 stro straw (implicitly contrasted with the feather beds of the wealthy).
440 waillit choice.
441 mowlit mouldy. **peirrie** perry, cider made from pears.
442 Bot except for. The leper's 'cup' (bowl) was for alms; his 'clapper' (rattle) was to give warning of his approach.
445 rawk raucous (*T A* read 'rank'). **ruik** rook. **hoir and hace** harsh and hoarse.
446 port bearing. **precelling** surpassing: a typical late medieval literary Latinism ('aureate term').
447 lustiness delightfulness. **hald** held. **conding** worthy.
448 figour form, outline.
449 leid person. **liking** pleasure.
450–1 'Worn out with grief and lodged among the leper folk, I say with bitter sighing "allas!"' **Sowpit** worn out (*OED* s.v. *Sowp* v.[1])? But see also *OED Sowp* v.[2] 'to soak or saturate', and cf. 407 above.
454 frivol fickle (pronounced as monosyllable).
456–60 Cresseid addresses the ladies much as the dead address the living in medieval *memento mori* writings: 'Such as I am, so shall you be.' See Fox 44–6; and cf. No. 28 above.

And in your mind ane mirrour mak of me:
As I am now, peradventure that ye
For all your micht may come to that same end,
Or ellis war, gif ony war may be.

'Nocht is your fairness bot ane faiding flour,
Nocht is your famous laud and hie honour
Bot wind inflat in uther mennis eirs;
Your roising reid to rotting sall retour.
Exempil mak of me in your memour,
Whilk of sic thingis wofull witness beirs:
All welth in eird away as wind it weirs:
Be war thairfoir, approchis neir the hour.
Fortune is fickil when sho begins and steirs.'

Thus chidand with hir drery desteny
Weiping sho woik the nicht fra end to end;
Bot all in vane – hir dule, hir cairfull cry,
Micht not remeid, nor yit hir murning mend.
Ane lipper lady rais and till hir wend

457 mirrour A common figure for a warning example held up for others' instruction: cf. *Mirror for Magistrates*: Fox 46.

459 micht might, power.

460 war worse. **gif** if.

462 laud praise.

463 inflat puffed: recalling Boethius *De consolatione* 3 prose 6, where some MSS. translate incorrectly a passage quoted by Boethius in the original Greek from Euripides: 'O gloria, gloria, in milibus hominum nihil aliud facta nisi auribus inflatio magna' ('O fame, fame, amounting to nothing more in many cases than a great blowing in the ears').

464 roising reid rosy redness, i.e. pink complexion. Fox conjectures an original *rude* or *ruid*, 'complexion'. **retour** return.

467 welth well-being. **weirs** passes away.

468 Cf. 456.

469 steirs may represent either *steer* 'govern' or *stir* 'bestir oneself' (*OED Stir* v. 14b). The latter suits the context better, since Fortune is always in control, but only intermittently acts to throw men down. So: 'Fortune is fickle once she begins to bestir herself.' See article cited in *n.* to 416 above.

471 woik lay awake through.

472 dule sorrow.

473 remeid bring relief. **mend** remedy.

474 rais got up. **wend** went.

And said, 'Why spurnis thou aganes the wall,
To sla thyself and mend nathing at all?

'Sen thy weiping doubils bot thy wo,
I counsal thee mak vertew of ane neid:
Go leir to clap thy clapper to and fro,
And leif efter the law of lipper leid.'
Thair was na buit, bot furth with thame sho yeid
Fra place to place, whill cauld and hounger sair
Compellit hir to be ane rank beggair.

That samin time, of Troy the garnisoun,
Whilk had to chiftane worthy Troilus,
Throw jeopardie of weir had stricken doun
Knichtis of Grece in number marvellous.
With greit triumph and laud victorious
Agane to Troy richt royally they raid
The way whair Cresseid with the lipper baid.

475–80 The old leper woman's words unexpectedly expose a vanity in Cresseid's previous moralizing reflections on Vanity.

475 Kicking against a wall was a proverbial image of useless rebellion: Whiting W20. Cf. No. 17 above, lines 11–12.

476 sla kill.

477 'Since your weeping only doubles your sorrow.' The placing of *bot* ('but') after the word it governs is unusual, but not impossible. *T* reads 'thy wepyng but doubleth'.

478 The proverbial 'make virtue of necessity' (Whiting V43) appears in Chaucer *Troilus* 4.1586 and *Knight's T., C.T.* I 3042.

479 Go] *T A*; To *C* (perhaps rightly). **leir** learn.

480 leif live. A conjectural emendation: *C A* read 'leir' (from 479); *T* reads 'lerne'. **leid** people.

481 buit remedy ('there was nothing for it . . .'). **yeid** went.

482 whill until.

483 rank absolute, downright. Lepers were customarily beggars; but Cresseid is now 'not strong enough to go from place to place, but must sit at one spot': Bennett, *art. cit.* (headnote) 13.

484 ff. This scene ironically recalls the scene in *Troilus* where Criseide sees Troilus riding back from a victorious skirmish: No. 12 above, lines 610–86. See Moran *N & Q* 10 (1963) 11–12.

484 garnisoun garrison.

486 jeopardie of weir (good) fortune in war.

489 raid rode.

490 'Along the road where Cresseid waited with the lepers.'

Seeing that company come, all with ane stevin
They gaif ane cry, and shuik coppis gude speid;
Said, 'Worthy lordes, for Goddis lufe of hevin,
To us lipper part of your almous deid!'
Than to their cry nobil Troilus tuik heid;
Having pietie neir by the place can pass
Whair Cresseid sat, not witting what sho was.

Than upon him sho kest up baith hir ene,
And with ane blenk it com into his thocht
That he somtime hir face befoir had sene;
Bot sho was in sic plye he knew hir nocht;
Yit than hir luik into his mind it brocht
The sweit visage and amorous blenking
Of fair Cresseid, somtime his awin darling.

Na wonder was, suppois in mind that he
Tuik hir figure sa sone, and lo now why:

491 that company come] *T*; that companie thai come *C*; the troup they came *A*. Fox conjectures that *come* arose by dittography from *company*, and reads 'Seing that companie, all with ane steuin'. **ane stevin** one voice.
492 The cry of lepers contrasts with the excited cries of the people in *Troilus*: cf. No. 12, lines 611 f., 646. **gude speid** vigorously.
494 'Give a share of your alms to us lepers.'
496 pietie pity (the same word, historically). **can pass** passed.
497 witting knowing.
498 The reference to '*both* her eyes', conventional in verse, acquires extra implications here: Cresseid shifts and focuses her bloodshot eyes (cf. Cynthia's threat: 'Thy cristal ene mingit with blude I mak' 337) with difficulty. See MacQueen 91.
499–501 Bennett *art. cit.* (headnote) 13–14 compares the scene in Malory 501 where Isode encounters Tristram in his madness, thinks she has seen him before, but does not recognize him.
499 blenk glance. Troilus glances quickly at her.
501 plye condition.
503 blenking glances.
505–11 It is part of the scene's horror and pathos that a learned explanation is required for the fact that Troilus recognizes Cresseid at all, and that his recognition can only be explained as a form of delusion. Stearns *Robert Henryson* 98–105 cites Aristotle *De somniis* 460b: 'We are easily deceived respecting the operations of sense-perception when we are excited by emotions, and different persons according to their different emotions; for example, the coward when excited by fear, the amorous person by amorous desire; so that, with but little resemblance to go upon, the former thinks he sees his foes approaching, the latter, that he sees the object of his desire.' So Chaucer's Troilus mistakes the 'fare cart' for the returning Criseide in *Troilus* 5.1158–62
505–6 'It was no wonder that he conceived her image so quickly in his mind, and see now why.' **suppois** if.

The idol of ane thing in cace may be
Sa deip imprentit in the fantasy
That it deludes the wittis outwardly
And sa appeirs in form and like estait
Within the mind as it was figurait.

Ane spark of lufe than till his hart culd spring
And kendlit all his body in ane fire.
With hait fevir, ane sweit and trimbling
Him tuik, whill he was reddy to expire;
To beir his sheild his breist began to tire;
Within ane while he changit mony hew;
And nevertheless not ane ane uther knew.

For knichtly pietie and memorial
Of fair Cresseid, ane girdil can he tak,
Ane purs of gold and mony gay jowal,
And in the skirt of Cresseid doun can swak,
Than raid away, and not ane word he spak,

507–8 The 'fantasy', or *vis imaginativa*, records and stores sense impressions: Stearns 100. *Idol* corresponds to *idolum*, the scholastic term for an impression or image stored by the *vis imaginativa*: e.g. St Thomas Aquinas *Summa theologica* I 85.2 *ad.* 3: 'Vis imaginativa format sibi aliquod idolum rei absentis' ('The imaginative power forms for itself a certain image of the absent thing'). Jean de Meun couples *ydoles* with *fantasie* in the same technical sense: *R. de la Rose* 18229–37.
507 in cace may be may chance to be.
509 wittis senses. **outwardly** externally, i.e. the image takes the delusive appearance of an external object.
510 estait condition.
511 figurait formed.
512 culd spring sprang.
514 hait hot. **sweit** sweat.
515 whill until.
517 Rapid changes of colour, like hot flushes, trembling and weakness, were recognized symptoms of love. Fox compares *Troilus* 1.441: 'sexty time a day he loste his hewe'.
518 Cresseid's failure to recognize Troilus has been variously explained. Fox 47 says that Cresseid never really knew Troilus for what he was; but this hardly accounts for the physical fact. I prefer MacQueen's explanation, that Cresseid is 'half-blind' with leprosy (see *n.* to 498), but not his allegorical interpretation ('appetite, deformed by sin, cannot recognize Virtue', 91). In any case, Cresseid must be too absorbed in her own miserable situation, and too ashamed of it, to pay much attention to her benefactors.
520–1 Fox: 'Probably a purse hanging from a jewelled girdle'.
522 swak fling.
523 he] *C* omits.

Pensive in hart, whill he com to the toun,
And for greit cair oft syis almaist fell doun.

The lipper folk to Cresseid than can draw
To see the equal distributioun
Of the almous; bot when the gold they saw,
Ilk ane to uther prevély can roun,
And said, 'Yon lord hes mair affectioun,
How ever it be, unto yon lazarous
Than to us all; we knaw by his almous.'

'What lord is yon,' quod sho, 'have ye na feill,
Hes done to us so greit humanitie?'
'Yis,' quod a lipper man, 'I knaw him weill;
Shir Troilus it is, gentil and free.'
When Cresseid understude that it was he,
Stiffer than steil thair stert ane bitter stound
Throwout hir hart, and fell doun to the ground.

When sho owircom, with siching sair and sad,
With mony cairfull cry and cald ochane:
'Now is my breist with stormy stoundis stad,
Wrappit in wo, ane wretch full will of wane!'
Than fell in swoun full oft ere she wolde fane,
And ever in hir swouning cryit sho thus:
'O fals Cresseid and trew knicht Troilus!

'Thy lufe, thy lawtie and thy gentilness
I countit small in my prosperitie,

525 oft syis often.
529 'Every one began to murmur quietly to the other.'
531 How ever it be for whatever reason. The implication is cruel.
533 feill idea.
536 Shir Sir. **gentil and free** noble and generous.
538–9 The *stound*, or pang, is imagined as a steel blade piercing Cresseid's heart – and, in effect, killing her.
540 owircom revived. **siching** sighing.
541 cald cold. The epithet is associated with care (rather than fear) in older English. **ochane** Gaelic *ochòin*, a cry of sorrow: *OED* s.v. *Ohone*. Henryson, like the other Lowland poets, uses very few Gaelic words.
542 stoundis sorrows. **stad** beset.
543 will of wane bewildered, hopeless (an established alliterative phrase).
544 full oft ere she wolde fane] *A* and (with *fone* for *fane*) *T*. *C* reads 'oft or scho culd refrane'; but this most likely arose from not understanding *fane*, a form perhaps related to *fine* 'stop'. Fox observes that *fane* ought to be the past tense of this verb (*DOST Fine* v.[1]). He emends: 'full oft or euer scho fane.'
547 lawtie fidelity.

Sa elevait I was in wantoness,
And clam upon the fickil wheill sa hie.
All faith and lufe I promissit to thee
Was in the self fickil and frivolous.
O fals Cresseid and trew knicht Troilus!

'For lufe of me thou keipit continence,
Honest and chaist in conversatioun;
Of all wemen protectour and defence
Thou was, and helpit thair opinioun.
My mind in fleshly foul affectioun
Was inclinit to lustis lecherous.
Fy, fals Cresseid; O trew knicht Troilus!

'Lovers be war and tak gude heid about
Whom that ye lufe, for whom ye suffer pain.
I lat you wit, thair is richt few thairout
Whom ye may traist to have trew lufe agane;
Preif when ye will, your labour is in vain.
Thairfoir I reid ye tak thame as ye find,
For they are sad as widdercock in wind.

549 elevait] efflated *A*; effated *T*. Fox adopts *A*'s *efflated* ('puffed out'); but *efflate* is not recorded before 1634 in *OED*, and *C*'s *elevait* is metrically better.

550 clam climbed. A common image: men clambering to get to the top of Fortune's wheel. See *n.* to 416 above.

552 the self itself.

554 continence self-restraint ('gude continence' *C*).

555 conversatioun dealings with others.

557 opinioun reputation.

558 affectioun desire.

561–74 'Her advice to (male) lovers is not that they reject all earthly love but rather that they be wary of fickle women', Noll *SSL* 9 (1971) 23.

561–7 This stanza appears as a separate item in the *Book of the Dean of Lismore* (N.L.S. Gaelic MS. XXXVII): printed by Fox 132. Fox suggests that the compilers of *L* included the stanza because of their 'taste for anti-feminist verse'. The *Testament* as a whole has a marked anti-feminist streak.

562 for whom] *C A*; for whan *T*; quhairfor *L*.

563 I lat you wit I give you to know. **thairout** about.

564 agane back from.

565 Preif try.

566 reid advise.

567 sad steadfast, constant. The comparison with a weathercock was proverbial: Whiting W157–60. Cf. Chaucer's *Against Women Unconstant* 12–13.

'Becaus I knaw the greit unstabilness,
Bruckil as glass, into my self I say,
Traisting in uther als greit unfaithfulness,
Als unconstant and als untrew of fay,
Thocht som be trew, I wait richt few are they;
Wha findis treuth, lat him his lady ruse.
Nane but myself as now I will accuse.'

When this was said, with paper sho sat doun
And on this maneir maid hir testament:
'Heir I beteiche my corps and carioun
With wormis and with taidis to be rent;
My cop and clapper, and mine ornament,
And all my gold, the lipper folk sall have,
When I am deid, to bury me in grave.

'This royal ring, set with this ruby reid,
Whilk Troilus in drowry to me send,
To him agane I leif it when I am deid,
To mak my cairfull deid unto him kend.

569 Bruckil brittle. **into my self I say** (which) I find by experience in myself. *say* is probably *OED Say* v.^{2}, an aphetic form of *assay*. Cresseid has learned her own 'unstableness' and concludes that, if other women are as bad (570–1), there can be very few faithful mistresses (572).
570 Traisting assuming. **unfaithfulness**] *C A*; brutelnesse *T*.
571 fay faith.
572 Thocht though. **wait** know.
573 ruse praise: *OED Roose* v.
574 Earlier Cresseid blamed Cupid and Venus for her plight: 124–40.
575–91 'Testaments' are quite common in medieval literature: Fox 48. Cf. Piers's 'bequest' in *Piers Plowman*, No. 11.1 above, lines 86–105: esp. *Testament* 577–8 with *Piers* 92, and *Testament* 587–8 with *Piers* 88. Langland's pious, moralized testament contrasts with Henryson's secular, neoclassical version, from which all explicit Christian suggestions have been expunged.
577 beteiche commit (bequeth *T A*). **carioun** dead body.
578 taidis toads.
579 ornament What adornments are intended? Presumably the *gold* of 580 is that just given by Troilus; so *mine ornament* may be the jewelled purse (520–1 and *n.*). Or are the lepers to reclaim burial expenses from jewelry of Cresseid's still kept by her father?
582–3 Apparently a confused allusion to *Troilus* 3.1366–72, where Troilus and Criseide exchange rings, and Criseide gives Troilus a gold brooch set with a ruby. But Troilus does possess a ruby ring (2.1087); and the image of ruby in ring is used by Pandarus to express the lovers' union: see No. 12 above, line 585 (and cf. *Troilus* 5.549). The ring here symbolizes Troilus's fidelity.
583 in drowry as a love token.
585 kend known.

Thus I conclude shortly and mak ane end:
My spreit I leif to Diane, whair sho dwells,
To walk with hir in waist woddis and wells.

'O Diomeid, thou hes baith broche and belt
Whilk Troilus gave me in takening
Of his trew lufe,' and with that word sho swelt.
And sone ane lipper man tuik off the ring,
Syne buryit hir withouttin tarying.
To Troilus furthwith the ring he bair,
And of Cresseid the deith he can declair.

When he had hard hir greit infirmitie,
Hir legacie and lamentatioun,
And how sho endit in sic povertie,
He swelt for wo and fell doun in ane swoun,
For greit sorrow his hart to brist was boun;
Siching full sadly, said, 'I can no moir.
Sho was untrew, and wo is me thairfoir.'

Som said he maid ane tomb of merbel gray,
And wrait hir name and superscriptioun,
And laid it on hir grave whair that sho lay,
In goldin letters, conteining this ressoun:
'Lo, fair ladyis, Cresseid of Troyis town,
Somtime countit the flour of womanheid,
Under this stane, lait lipper, lyis deid.'

587–8 By bequeathing her soul to Diana, goddess of chastity and traditional rival of Venus (see e.g. Chaucer *Parlement of Foules* 281 f.), Cresseid relinquishes at last her service of the latter. Fox 57 says 'Diana is a fairly obvious surrogate for God'. Why?
588 The huntress Diana spends her time in uninhabited (*waist*) woodlands. **wells** springs.
589–91 Troilus gave Criseide a brooch on her departure from Troy 'in remembraunce of him and of his sorwe' (5.1663); but she gave it to Diomede (5.1040–1). Chaucer mentions no belt; but belts are common love tokens in romances. In *Gawain* the Lady offers Gawain two 'druries', a ring with a precious stone and a 'love-lace' or belt.
590 in takening as a token.
591 swelt lost consciousness (death here, a swoon at 599).
600 to brist was boun was ready to burst.
601 I can no moir there is no more I can do.
603 tomb tombstone.
604 superscriptioun inscription.
606 ressoun statement.
607 Troyis] Troy the *T A*. Both readings reflect the difficulty of finding a metrical equivalent to Chaucer's 'Troyė town'.
609 lait formerly.

Now, worthy wemen, in this ballet short,
Maid for your worship and instructioun,
Of cheritie, I monish and exhort,
Ming not your lufe with fals deceptioun.
Beir in your mind this short conclusioun
Of fair Cresseid, as I have said befoir.
Sen sho is deid, I speik of hir no moir.

610–15 The address to worthy women recalls Chaucer's address to ladies in *Troilus* 5.1772–85. Although 613 resembles Chaucer's later condemnation of earthly love (e.g. 5.1835–48), Henryson makes no serious reference to the love of Christ. Indeed, he may even be held to say no more than that women should be faithful to their lovers.
610 ballet poem. The word implies shortness: 'In this context it is a deprecatory term' (Fox).
611 for your worship in honour of you. Cf. Chaucer's protestation (*Troilus* 5.1772–85) that his account of Criseide's infidelity is not meant to reflect discredit on women.
612 Of cheritie for the love of God. **monish** admonish.
613 Ming mingle.
614 short] *C A*; sore *T*.
616 The poem ends here, with deliberate abruptness.

31 Moral Fables

'The Morall Fabillis of Esope the Phrygian' (so entitled in the Bassandyne print) is a collection of 13 Aesopic animal fables, probably left unfinished by Henryson, with the order of fables unfixed. The Latin Aesop was a standard 'curriculum author' (Curtius 48–54) used for elementary instruction in medieval schools, and therefore particularly familiar to the Schoolmaster of Dunfermline. Of the 13 fables, 7 (including both the present examples) are based on a C12 Latin verse *Aesop* by Gualterus Anglicus, with additional material from the French versions (the *Isopets*); the other 6 mostly derive from the beast-epic tradition associated with the name of Reynard the Fox. Henryson generally fills out his traditional stories with narrative detail, much of it realistic and humorous in character: see brief but excellent discussion by G. Tillotson *Essays in Criticism and Research* (Cambridge U.P. 1942) 1–4. He also adds an allegorizing and/or moralizing *Moralitas* (e.g. here No. 31.2 lines 204–35), the importance of which is stressed by MacQueen *Robert Henryson* Ch. 4 and by D. Fox *ELH* 29 (1962) 337–56. See also H. E. Toliver *ES* 46 (1965) 300–9.
Date MacQueen *Robert Henryson* App. 1 and D. K. Crowne *JEGP* 61 (1962) 583–90 attempt to date *Fables* by the presence or absence of echoes from Caxton's *Reynard* (1481) and *Aesop* (1484), concluding that some fables were written before, and some after, these dates. But D. Fox *JEGP* 67 (1968) 586–93 shows that there is no evidence of H.'s using *Reynard* and little of his knowing *Aesop*. The date of *Fables* therefore remains uncertain.

[31] Robert Henryson

Text Five authorities: N.L.S. MS. Asloan (= *A*), dated *c*.1515, mutilated, contains only 'The Tale of the Uplandis Mous and the Borowstown Mous', upon which copy the present text of this Fable is based; Bannatyne MS., N.L.S. MS. Advocates' 1.1.6 (= *Ban*), dated 1566–8, base-text for 'The Preiching of the Swallow' here; B.L. MS. Harley 3865 (= *H*), dated 1571 over an erasure on titlepage; print by Charteris (= *C*), 1569 or 1570; print by Bassandyne (= *Bas*), 1571. *H*, *C* and *Bas* all derive from an ancestor with Protestant emendations: D. Fox *N & Q* 14 (1967) 348–9. There is much textual variation. G. G. Smith in his STS edn prints all authorities separately, except *Bas* (the base-text of Wood and Elliott).
No. 31.1 'The Preiching of the Swallow' is much expanded from Gualterus Anglicus's Fable 25: ed. J. Bastin *Recueil général des Isopets* SATF 2 vols. (Paris 1929–30) 2.26. Henryson also used the French version in *Isopet I* (Bastin 2.242–4). D. Fox *ELH* 29 (1962) 337–56, in an excellent discussion, stresses the importance of the *Moralitas*, omitted here (summarized in *n.* to 266). The Fable itself is governed by the moral theme of prudence, already present in Gualterus: see *nn.* to 1, 5–7, 137, 263; and Burrow *EC* 25 (1975) 25–37. The prudent man, by recalling the past and observing the present, anticipates the future. Thus the theme of prudence involves the theme of time, represented by the four seasons (54–91; and see *n.* to 204–10).
No. 31.2 'The Tale of the Uplandis Mous and the Borowstown Mous' is based on Gualterus Anglicus's Fable 12 (Bastin 2.15–16), with use of the French version in *Isopet de Lyon* (Bastin 2.105–7) and other sources (*nn.* to 164–91 and 211). The old fable of the Town and Country Mice (narrated by Horace *Sat*. 2.6.79–117) is given, in the *Moralitas*, its natural twist towards praise of the contented simple life. Cf. the version by Sir Thomas Wyatt (*Collected Poems* ed. Muir and Thomson, 91–5), deriving from a sung version perhaps also known to Henryson: D. Fox *N & Q* 18 (1971) 203–7.

31.1 The Preiching of the Swallow

The hie prudence and wirking mervellous,
The profound wit of God omnipotent,
Is so perfite and so ingenious,
Excelland fer all mannis argument,
Forwhy till him all thing is ay present

1 prudence Prudence is the main moral topic of the Fable, here as in Gualterus Anglicus (cf. Bastin 2.26, lines 15–7): see Burrow *art. cit.* (headnote). It signifies the capacity to see future and past, as well as present: cf. E. Panofsky 'Titian's *Allegory of Prudence*' in *Meaning in the Visual Arts* (Penguin 1970) 184–6.
2 wit intellect.
3 ingenious discerning (ingeing *Ban*).
4 argument reasoning (jugement *Bas C H*).
5–7 The supreme 'prudence' of God consists in having past, present and future eternally present in his sight. A classic statement of the presentness of all time to God was Boethius *De consolatione* 5 prose 6.
5 Forwhy because. **ay]** *Ban* omits.

Richt as it is or ony time sall be,
Befoir the sicht of his devinité.

Thairfore oure saul with sensualitie
So fettrid is in presoun corporal,
We may nocht cleirly undirstand nor see
God as he is, a thing celestial:
Oure mirk and deidly cors material
Blindis the spiritual operatioun,
Like as man war bundin in presoun.

In Metaphisik Aristotle sayis
That mannis saul is like ane bakkis ee,
Whilk lurkis still as lang as licht of day is
And in the gloming comis furth to flee:
Hir eine are waik, the sun sho may nocht see.
So is oure saul with phantesy opprest
To knaw the things in nature manifest.

For God is in his power infinite,
And mannis saul is febil and owir small,
Of undirstanding waik and unperfite,
To comprehend him that contenis all.
Non suld presume, by reasoun natural,
To serche the secrets of the Trinitie,
Bot trow fermly and lat dirk resouns be.

8–14 The soul is imprisoned in the body (a traditional image) and can only see God so far as the limits of man's sensual nature permit, just as a prisoner can see little in a dark cell.
11 a thing] nor thingis *Bas C H* (to avoid calling God a 'thing'?)
12 'Our dark and mortal physical body.' **material]** naturall *Bas C H*.
14 bundin confined.
15–18 Cf. Aristotle *Metaphysics* 993b: 'For as the eyes of bats are to the blaze of day, so is the reason in our soul to the things which are by nature most evident of all.'
16 bakkis bat's.
17 'Which (i.e. the bat) lies low . . .'
18 gloming twilight.
19 'Her eyes are weak . . .'
20–1 'In the same way our soul is prevented by illusion from knowing those things which are manifest in nature.' Cf. *n.* to 15–18 above. The illusory 'reality' of the natural world prevents our seeing the true realities of God manifest in it (cf. 29–49 below).
23 owir 'over', too (monosyllabic).
24 waik weak.
26–8 Cf. No. 20 above, esp. lines 107–8.
28 trow believe. **dirk resouns** obscure arguments.

Yit nevertheless we may have knawleging
Of God almichty by his creatours,
That he is guid, fair, wis and bening.
Exemple takis by thir joly flours,
Richt sweit of smell and plesand of colours,
Som grene, som blew, som purpur, white and reid,
Thus distribute by gift of his godheid.

The firmament paintit with starris cleir
Fra eist to west rolland in circil round,
And every planet in his propir sphere
In moving makand armony and sound,
The fire, the air, the watter and the ground –
Till understand it is eneuch, ywis,
That God in all his warkis witty is.

Luik we the fish that sowmis in the sea;
Luik we in erd all kind of bestiall;
The foulis fair, so forcély they flee,
Sheddand the air with pennis grit and small;
Syne luik to man, whilk God maid last of all,

29 knawleging knowledge.
31 bening benevolent.
32 'Learn a lesson from these beautiful flowers.'
35 distribute distributed.
36–9 The *firmament*, or sphere of the fixed stars, represents the furthest limits of human perception. Within it are the seven planetary spheres. All eight spheres are carried each day through one complete revolution from E. to W. by the *Primum mobile*, which contains them all, although their own proper motions are from W. to E.
38 propir own particular.
39 According to ancient belief, the planets' motion produced musical sounds inaudible to human ears because of the 'mirk and deidly cors material'. Cf. Chaucer *Parlement of Foules* 60–4 and *Troilus* 5.1812–13.
40 The world below the lowest of the spheres (the moon's) was composed of four elements, here cited in descending order, *ground* (earth) being lowest of all.
41–2 'This is enough, certainly, to enable us to understand that God is wise in all his works.'
43 Luik we let us consider (Luke weill *Bas C H*, here and at 44). **sowmis** swim.
44 'Let us consider all species of animals on the earth.'
45 forcély vigorously.
46 Sheddand cutting. **pennis** feathers.
47 Syne then.

Like till his image and his similitude:
By thir we knaw that God is fair and guid.

All creatours he maid for the behuif
Of man and till his supportatioun,
In to this erd, baith under and abuif,
In number, wecht and dew proportioun,
The differens of time and ilk seasoun
Concordand to oure oportunitie,
As daily by experiens we may see:

The Somer with his joly mantil grene,
With flouris fair furrit on every fent,
Whilk Flora goddess, of the flouris quene,
Hes to that lord as for his seasoun lent,
And Phebus with his gowdin beamis gent

48 Like till like unto. **image** See *Gen*. 1.27.

49 thir these (things).

50 behuif benefit.

51 till his supportatioun for his preservation.

52 In to this erd in this earth.

53 Cf. 'Thou hast ordered all things in measure, and number, and weight', *Wisdom of Sol*. 11.21. This was a key text in medieval cosmology: Curtius 504.

54–91 The variety of the seasons (*differentia temporum*) is introduced as a further example of the ordered variety of Nature. MacQueen 160 compares Boethius *De consolatione* 1 metre 5. See also Fox *ELH* 29 (1962) 349–50 (good on the Prologue generally). The theme is developed according to the rhetoricians' precepts for *descriptio temporum*. It begins with summer and ends with spring, so that the description of the latter can serve as traditional spring opening for the following narrative. On the seasons, see N. E. Enkvist *The Seasons of the Year* (Helsingfors 1957) and R. Tuve *Seasons and Months* (reissued Cambridge, Brewer 1974).

54–5 'The varieties of time and season agreeing with our need': *OED* s.v. *Opportunity* 5.

56 may] do *Ban*.

57 The seasons were commonly personified. Henryson clearly personifies Summer and Spring; but in the descriptions of autumn and winter the main personification is replaced by associated figures (Ceres, Bacchus, Copia, Eolus). **joly** fine.

58 furrit on every fent trimmed (literally 'furred') at every opening. Summer has every slit (at neck, sleeve, side, etc.) decorated, where fur trimmings would normally be, with Flora's flowers.

59 the] everye *Ban*.

61 his] *Ban* omits. **gowdin beamis gent** gracious golden beams.

Hes purfillit and paintit plesandly
With heat and mosture stilland fra the sky.

Syne hervest hait, when Ceres that goddess
Hir barnis benit hes with abundance,
And Bacchus, god of wine, renewit hes
The tume pipis in Italy and France
With winis wicht and liccour of pleasance,
And *Copia temporis* to fill hir horn
That nevir wes full of wheit nor uthir corn.

Syne winter wan, when austern Eolus,
God of the wind, with blastis borial,
The grene garment of somer glorious
Hes all to-rent and revin in peicis small;
Than flouris fair faidit with frost most fall,
And birdis blithe changis thair notis sweit
In still murning, neir slane with snaw and sleit.

Thir dailis deip with dubbis drownit is,
Baith hill and holt heilit with frostis hair,

62 purfillit bordered, edged.
63 stilland falling as a distillation.
64 hervest hait hot autumn ('autumn' is a loan-word not much used in ME). **Ceres** the corn-goddess, commonly coupled with Bacchus.
65 'Has filled her barns full with abundance'. *abundance* is stressed on first and third syllables.
66 Bacchus god of autumn, as well as wine.
67 The tume pipis the empty casks (*Ban* has *Hir* for *The*).
68 wicht strong.
69 ***Copia temporis*** the richness of the season. Copia is goddess of abundance in classical literature. Her attribute is the horn of plenty, or 'cornucopia' (see *OED* s.v.). Cf. Ovid *Met*. 9.85–92. MacQueen 162 notes the Renaissance character of this stanza. Cf. John Ford *The Sun's Darling* 4.1 (of autumn): 'In the year's revolution | There cannot be a season more delicious, | When Plenty, Summer's daughter, empties daily | Her cornucopia fill'd with choicest viands.'
71 wan pale. **austern** severe.
72 borial northern.
74 to-rent ripped up. **revin** torn.
75 most must.
77 'Into quiet lamentation, nearly killed by snow and sleet.' Cf. *Gawain* 729, 'Ner slain with the slete', and 746–7. **In still**] Intill *Ban*.
78 'These deep dales are drowned in puddles.'
79 holt wood. **heilit** covered. **hair** hoar, white.

And bewis bene are bethit bair of bliss.
By wickit windis of the winter wair,
All wild beistis than fra the bentis bair
Drawis for dreid unto thair dennis deip
Couchand for cauld in covis thame to keip.

Syne comis Ver, when winter is away,
The secretar of Somer with his seill,
When columbie up keikis throw the clay
Whilk fleit was before with frostis feill.
The mavis and the merle begins to meill;
The lark on loft, with uthir birdis smale,
Than drawis furth fra derne, on doun and dale.

That samin seasoun, into a soft morning,
Richt blith tha bitter blastis were ago,
Unto the wod, to see the flouris spring
And heir the mavis sing and birdis mo,
I passit furth, syne luikit to and fro,
To see the suil that was richt seasonable,
Sappy, and to resave all seidis hable.

Movand thusgait, grit mirth I tuik in mind
Of lauborers to see the besiness,

80 bewis bene goodly boughs. **bethit** dried up, withered: *DOST* s.v. *Bethit*. A rare word. *Bas H* read *laifit*, *C* has *baissit*.
81 'Warned (*wair*) by the wicked winter winds.' See *MED* s.v. *Iwar* adj. 2(c).
82 bentis open ground.
84 'Lying down in caves to avoid the cold.'
85 Ver Spring (the common term in late ME, from Lat.).
86 The 'secretary', or officer who conducted a lord's correspondence, would have use of his seal.
87 columbie columbine. **up keikis** peeps up.
88 'Which had previously been frightened by severe frosts.' The columbine has been afraid (*DOST* s.v. *Fle* v.[3]) to appear earlier. For *feill* ('fell, severe') see *DOST* s.v. *Fell* a. 4.
89 'The thrush and the blackbird begin to sing.' See *DOST* s.v. *Mele* v. and *Mell* v.[2]: the collocation with *mavis* and *merle* is quite common.
91 derne hiding.
92 ff. Going out on a spring morning, often to the woods, is a common narrative opening in *chansons d'aventure* and other kinds of medieval poem (e.g. Gower *Confessio* 1.98 f.). See *n.* to 153–4 below, and headnote to No. 38.
92 samin same.
93 tha those. **ago** gone.
97 suil soil.
98 'Moist and capable of receiving any kind of seed.'
99 thusgait in this way.

Som makand dike, and som the pleuch can wind,
Som sawand sedis fast fra place to place,
The harrows hoppand in the sawers trace.
It was grit joy to him that lufit corn
To see thame labour sa at evin and morn.

And as I baid under a bank full bene,
In hert gritly rejosit of that sicht,
Unto a hege, under a hawthorn grene,
Of small birdis thair com a ferly flicht
And doun belive can on the levis licht
On every side about me whair I stude,
Richt mervelous, a mekle multitude.

Amang the whilk a swallow loud coud cry,
On that hawthorn heich in the crop sittand:
'O ye birdis on bewis here me by
Ye sall weill knaw and wisly undirstand,
Whair danger is and perrell appeirand,
It is grit wisdom to provide before
It to devoid, for drede it hurt you more.'

'Shir swallow,' quod the lark agane, and leuch,
'What have ye sene that causis you to drede?'

101 dike a ditch. **the pleuch can wind** guided the plough.
103 sawers trace tracks of the sower.
105 sa so.
106 baid lingered. **bene** pleasant.
108 Unto beside. **hawthorn** The element *haw* means 'hedge'.
109 ferly flicht marvellous flock.
110 belive straightaway. **licht** settle.
112 mekle great.
113 The swallow's role as spokesman of prudence, here and in Gualterus, probably derives from the C12 Bestiary, which praises the swallow for its wisdom and second sight in nest-building, and also for its *prudens intellectus* in curing its children's eye-trouble: trans. T. H. White as *The Book of Beasts* (Cape 1954) 147–8; deriving from Isidore *Etym.* 12.7.70 and St Ambrose *Hexaemeron* 5.17 (Migne *P.L.* 14.244). **coud** did.
114 heich in the crop high in the top.
117 appeirand 'evident; likely (to be or befall) to all appearance' *DOST* s.v. *Apperand* 2.
119 'To avert it, for fear it does you more damage.' **for]** or *Ban.*
120 Shir Sir. **agane** in reply. **leuch** laughed. The lark plays a similar part in *Isopet I* (Bastin 2.243, line 19), a French version of Gualterus Anglicus; it does not appear in the Lat. original. On H's use of the *Isopet*, see MacQueen App. 2.

'See ye yon churl,' quod sho, 'beyond yon pleuch,
Fast sawand hemp, lo, see! and linget sede?
Yon lint will grow in litil time of dede,
And thairof will yon churl his nettis mak,
Under the whilk he thinkis us to tak.

'Thairfore, I rede, pass we when he is gone,
At evin, and with oure nailis sharp and small
Out of the erd scraip we yon sede anon
And ete it up; for gif it grows, we sall
Have caus to weip hereftir ane and all.
See we remede thairfore furthwith instante,
Nam levius laedit quicquid providimus ante.

'For clerkis says it is nocht sufficient
To consider that is befoir thine ee;
Bot prudence is ane inward argument
That gars a man provide befoir and see

123 lo see and] *Ban C*; and gude *Bas H*. **linget** 'lint', i.e. flax.
124 of dede indeed (*DOST* s.v. *Dede* n.[1]). *Bas C H* have *in deid*.
125 The *churl* is a bird-catcher, or fowler.
126 'Under which he intends to catch us.'
127 rede advise.
128 small narrow.
130 gif if.
131 ane one.
132 'Let us prepare a remedy for it immediately and at once.' **instante** 'apparently Lat. *instante*, abl. of *instans*, used instead of *instanter*' (*DOST*). A legalism?
133 This Latin maxim, occurring at the numerological centre of the fable (266 lines without *Moralitas*), is the second line of one of the 'Distichs of Cato', a reading text much used in schools and therefore familiar to the schoolmaster poet: 'Prospice qui veniant casus: hoc esse ferendos; | Nam levius laedit quidquid praevidimus ante' ('Anticipate events that are to come, and consider that they will have to be borne; for whatever we see in advance does us less harm'), Boas II 24. The distich was imitated by Gualterus (Bastin 2.26, line 10), and H. no doubt pointed out the imitation to his pupils. **providimus]** *Ban*; praevidimus *Bas C H*: see *n*. to 137 below.
134 nocht] *Ban* omits.
135 consider probably stressed on first syllable. **that** that which.
136–7 'But prudence is an interior process of reasoning (?) which makes a man foresee in advance and observe.' See *n*. to line 1.
137 provide cf. 118. *Providentia* is one of the three parts of prudence in Cicero's analysis, *De inventione* 2.160: *memoria* for things past, *intellegentia* for things present, *providentia* for things future. Cf. No. 23 above, line 5. *Ban* reads *providimus* at 133 (following some MSS. of 'Cato': Boas 131), where the other MSS. have the more usual reading *praevidimus*.

What guid, what evil is likly forto be
Of every thingis at the final end,
And so fro perrell ether him defend.'

The lark lauchand the swallow thus coud scorn,
And said sho fishit lang befoir the net:
'This barn is eith to busk that is unborn;
All growis nocht that in the ground is set;
The neck to stoup when it the strake sall get
Is sone eneuch; dede on the feyest fall.'
Thus scornit they the swallow ane and all.

Despising thus hir hailsom document,
The fowlis fersly tuke their flicht anon;
Som with a bir they braidit owr the bent,
And som agane are to the grenewod gone.
Upon the land, whair I wes left allone,
I tuke my club and hamewart coud I cary,
So ferliand as I had sene a fary.

We furth passit whill June, that joly tide,
And sedis that war sawin of beforn

139 every thingis The unusual use of *every* ('all severally', *OED* s.v. *Every* a. 2) puzzled scribes. Hence: Off everilk thing behald the fynall end *Bas H*.
140 ether more easily (*DOST Eith* adv.). *Bas C H* read *the better*, an obvious gloss.
142–6 The lark's comic misapplication of proverbs may be compared with that of Chaucerian characters such as the Carpenter in *Miller's T.*: D. MacDonald *Med. Aev.* 39 (1970) 21–7.
142 Proverbial: Whiting N91. Especially apt here where another kind of net is in question.
143 'The child who is not yet born is easy to dress.' Proverbial: Whiting B12.
144 Evidently proverbial, though not in Whiting.
145–6 'It is soon enough to bend the neck when it is about to receive the stroke; let death fall on those most ready for it.' Both proverbial: Whiting M157, D90.
148 hailsom document salutary teaching (the usual meaning of *document* in ME).
149 fersly furiously.
150 'Some with a rush darted off over the field.'
153–4 'I took up my staff and made my way home, as much amazed as if I had seen magic.' Cf. *Piers* Prol. 6: 'Me befell a ferly, of fairy me thoughte.' Evidently Langland's dream prologue was in H's mind: 92 above recalls Prol. 1.
155 'The time passed for us until June, that happy time.' Text in doubt here. *Bas C H* read 'Thus passit furth quhill June . . .'
156 sawin of sown. *of* is apparently redundant.

War growin heich, that haris micht thame hide
And als the quailye crakand in the corn.
I movit furth, betwene midday and morn,
Unto the hege under the hawthorn grene
Whair I befoir the said birdis had sene.

And as I stude, by aventure and cais,
The samin birds as I haif said you air –
I hope becaus it was their hanting place,
Mair of succour or yit mair solitare –
They lichtit doun; and when they lichtit ware,
The swallow swithe put forth a piteous pime,
Said, 'Wo is him can nocht be war in time.

'O blind birdis, and full of negligence,
Unmindfull of your awin prosperitie,
Cast up your sicht and tak guid advertence;
Luik to the lint that growis on yon lee,
Yon is the thing I bad furthwith that we,
Whill it was seid, had tane it out of the eird;
Now is it lint, now is it heich on breird.

'Go yit, whill it is tendir, young and small,
And pull it up, let it no moir increis.
My flesh growis, my body quakis all;
Thinkand on it I may nocht sleip in peis.'
They cryit all and baid the swallow ceis
And said, 'Yon lint heireftir will do guid,
For linget is to litil birdis fuid.

157 heich high. **haris** hares.
158 quailye 'quail' (? corncrake).
159 The later hour of day (cf. 92) matches the later season.
162 by aventure and cais 'by fortune and chance', i.e. it so happened.
163 air previously.
164–5 'I think because it was their customary place of resort, being safer or else more solitary.'
167 swithe immediately (swift *Ban*). **pime** ? cry (pryme *Ban*).
170 awin own (*Ban* omits).
171 advertence notice.
173 bad commanded.
174 had tane it out of the eird should have taken it out of the earth. Text doubtful. *Bas C H* read 'suld rute furth off the eird', which is smoother and more forceful, but doubtfully appropriate to newly sown seeds.
175 heich on breird high and sprouting (see *DOST* s.v. *Abreird* adv.).
178 growis shudders.
182 to] a *Ban*.

'We think, when that yon lint bowis are ripe,
To mak us feist and fill us of the seid,
Mawgré yon churl, and on it sing and pipe.'
'Weill,' quod the swallow, 'freindis, hardly bei'd,
Do as ye will; bot certane, sair I dreid
Heirefter ye sall find als sour as sweit,
When ye are speldit on yon cairlis speit.

'The awner of yon lint ane fowler is,
Richt cautelous and full of subtletie.
His prey full seindil timis will he miss,
Bot gif we birdis all the warrer be;
For mony of our kin he hes gart dee,
And thocht it bot ane sport till spill their blude.
God keip me fra him, and the halye rude.'

Thir small birdis haifand bot litil thocht
Of perrell that micht fall by aventure,
The counsal of the swallow set at nocht,
Bot tuik their flicht and on togidder fure,
Som to the wod, som markit to the mure.
I tuke my staff, when this was said and done,
And walkit hame, whill it drew neirhand none.

183 bowis seed-pods.
185 Mawgré yon churl in defiance of that churl. The tradition of birds defying the fowler is reflected in *L.G.W.* F Prol. 130–9, where birds sing about 'the foule cherl': 'The foweler we deffye, | And all his craft.'
186 hardly bei'd 'by all means let it be so' (G. Smith). *bei'd* is a regular Scots form of 'be it': see *DOST* s.v. *Beid*. *Ban* has *beit*, which spoils the rhyme.
187 sair sorely.
188 'You will find it hereafter as sour as it is sweet.'
189 speldit skewered. Small birds were trapped for food, especially in winter (cf. *L.G.W.* Prol. 133). The swallow anticipates roasting. **cairlis speit** fellow's spit.
190 awner owner.
191 cautelous cunning.
192 seindil timis seldom.
193 'Unless all we birds are more careful.'
194 hes] *Ban* omits. **gart dee** caused to die.
196 'God and the Holy Rood preserve me from him.'
198 by aventure by chance, in the course of things.
200 on togidder fure went away together.
201 markit went. **mure** moor.
202 staff the 'club' or walking-stick of 153.
203 neirhand none nearly noon: cf. 159.

This lint ripit, the carl pullit the line,
Ripplit the bowis and in beitis set,
It steipit in the burn and dryit syne,
And with a bitill knockit it and bet,
Syne scutchit it weill and heclit it in the flet.
His wife it span and twane it into threid,
Of whilk the fouler nets war maid indeid.

The winter cam, the wickit wind can blaw,
The woddis grene war wallowit with the weit,
Baith firth and fell with frostis war maid faw,
Slonkis and slack maid sliddery with the sleit.
The foulis fair for falt they fell of feit;
On bewis bair it was na bute to bide,
Bot hyit on in housis thame to hide.

Som in the bern, som in the stack of corn
Their ludging tuke and maid their residence.
The fouler saw and grit aiths hes he sworn
They suld be tane trewly for their expence.
His nettis he hes set with diligence,

204–10 This description of how thread was manufactured from flax (in autumn – all four seasons are represented in the story) is technically precise. The fowler uproots the ripe flax plants (*line*), removes the seeds from the pods (*ripplit the bowis*) for sowing next year, ties the stalks in bundles (*beitis*), soaks them in a stream to loosen the fibres, and dries them. He then beats them with a mallet (*bitill*), separates the fibres from the woody substance (*scutchit*) and combs them out (*heclit*). His wife spins them and twists them into thread.

208 scutchit] swingillit *Bas C H* (a synonymous technical term). **in the flet** indoors.

210 war maid] *Bas C H* omit *war*, perhaps rightly (with *fouler* as subject). In *Ban*, *fouler* is used attributively: *DOST* s.v. *Foular* n. b.

212 wallowit swamped (*OED Wallow* v.[1]). **weit** wet.

213 firth wood (poetic word). **faw** glittering.

214 'Hollows and dells made slippery with the sleet.'

215 'For lack of food (*falt*) the beautiful birds could not keep their footing.' G. Smith glosses *of feit* 'in fact'; but the phrase is not in *DOST*.

216 On] Quhen *Ban* (but an intrans. verb *bare* is unparalleled). **na bute** no use.

217 hyit on they hurried on.

219 Their] The *Ban*.

220 aiths oaths.

221 tane taken, caught. **for their expence** 'for their pains' (*DOST*). Or 'because of the losses they caused (by eating grain)'?

And in the snaw he shulit hes a plane
And healit it attowr with caff agane.

Thir small birdis seeand the caff was glad;
Trowand it had bene corn, they lichtit doun;
Bot of the nettis na presume they had,
Nor of the foulers fals intentioun;
To scraip and seik their meit they maid thame boun.
The swallow on a litil branch neir by,
Dredand for gile, thus loud on thame coud cry:

'Into this caff scraip whill your nailis bleid,
Thair is na corn, ye laubour all in vain.
Trow ye yon churl for pietie will you feid?
Na, na, he hes it layit heir for a train.
Remove, I reid, or ellis ye will be slain.
His nettis he hes set full privély
Reddy to draw; in time be war for thy.

'Grit fule is he that puttis in dangeir
His life, his honour, for a thing of nocht.
Grit fule is he that will nocht glaidly heir
Counsal in time, whill it avail him mocht.
Grit fule is he that na thing hes in thocht

223 shulit hes a plane has shovelled a clear space.
224 'And covered it all over again with chaff.' **attowr**] all ouer *Bas C H*; but see *DOST* s.v. *Atour* prep. and adv.
226 Trowand thinking.
227 presume inkling.
229 maid thame boun prepared themselves.
230 on a litil branch neir by] into a branche litill by *Ban*. *litill by* may represent a rare expression meaning 'not too close', otherwise unrecorded. *branch* here means 'seedling tree' (see *MED* s.v. *Braunch* 4(c)): cf. 251, when the swallow takes refuge 'up in a tree'.
231 coud did.
232 'Scrape in this chaff until your nails bleed.' 'The poem produces a strong feeling of approaching danger and of a blindness that no warning can pierce. It is filled with pity and a sort of second-sight which makes one think of Cassandra', Muir *Essays on Literature* 16–7.
234 pietie pity (both words derive from Lat. *pietas*).
235 layit laid. **train** snare.
236 reid] ride yow *Ban*.
238 be war for thy be warned of that.
239–45 Editors have taken this stanza as authorial moralizing; but it is probably part of the swallow's speech.
240 nocht no worth.
242 mocht The reading *nocht* in *Bas H* makes sense ('until it cannot serve him') but a bad identical rhyme.

Bot thing present, and eftir what may fall
Nor of the end hes na memorial.'

Thir small birdis, for hunger famist neir,
Full bisy scraipand forto seik their fude,
The counsal of the swallow wald nocht heir,
Suppois their laubour did thame litil guid.
When sho their fulish hertis understude
So indurate, up in a tree sho flew.
With that the churl owir thame his nettis drew.

Alace, it was richt grit herts sair to see
That bludy boucher beit tha birdis doun,
And forto heir, when they wist weill to dee,
Their cairful sang and lamentatioun.
Som with ane staff he straik to erd in swoun,
Som off the heid, of som he brak the craig,
Som half on live he stappit in his bag.

And when the swallow saw that they war deid,
'Lo!' quod sho, 'thus it happins oftin syis
Of thame that will nocht tak counsal nor reid
Of prudent men or clerkis that are wis.
This grit perrell I tauld thame mair than thryis;
Now are they deid, and wo is me thairfore!'
Sho tuik hir flicht, bot hir I saw no moir.

244–5 '. . and takes no thought of what may occur afterwards, nor of the end.'
246 famist neir nearly starved.
249 Suppois although.
251 indurate hardened, obstinate.
252 owir over (monosyllabic).
253 sair pain.
254 'That bloody butcher strike those birds down.'
255 wist weill to dee knew well they were to die.
256 cairful sorrowful.
257 straik to erd in swoun struck unconscious to the earth.
258 'He struck the head off some, and broke the neck (*craig*) of others.' *Bas C H* read 'Off sum the heid he straik, off sum he brak the crag'. This makes the first phrase less abruptly forceful, and produces a six-foot line.
259 on live alive. **stappit** stuffed.
261 syis times.
262 reid advice.
263 The topic of prudence is stated for the last time.
266 One might have expected the narrator to return home a wiser man; but H. liked abrupt endings: cf. *Testament*, No. 30 above, line 616. In the *Moralitas* which follows here, the fable is interpreted in a spiritual sense. The fowler is the Devil; the seed is wicked thoughts growing into sinful acts; the chaff is the vain pleasure of earth; the birds are worldly wretches; the swallow is the 'holy preacher'. Cf. Fox *ELH* 29 (1962) 353–4.

[31] Robert Henryson

31.2 The Tale of the Uplandis Mous and the Borowstown Mous

Heir beginnes the Tale of the Uplandis Mous and the Borowstown Mous.

Isope myn auctor makis mencioun
Of twa mise, and they war sisters deir,
Of whom the elder in a borowstown,
The younger wonnit upon land wele neir,
Richt solitar, while under busk and breir,
While in the corn in uther mennis scaith,
As outlaws dois, and levit on hir waith.

This rural mous in to the winter tide
Had hunger cauld, and tholit gret distress.
The tother mous, that in the burgh couth bide,
Gild brother was and maid ane free burgess,
Toll-free also, but custom mare or less,
And licence had to gang wharever sho list
Amang the cheis and meil in ark and kist.

A time when sho was full and unfutsair
Sho tuke in mind hir sister upon land,
And langit sar to heir of hir welfair,

Title: Uplandis country. **Borowstown** town possessing borough rights. Here 'urban'.
1 Isope On Henryson's 'Aesopic' sources, see headnote.
3 The verb is to be understood from 4. *Ban Bas C H* add *dwelt* before *in.*
4 wonnit lived. **upon land** in the country. **wele neir** very thriftily (*OED Near* adv.[2] 10). Or 'quite near'?
5–6 'Quite alone, sometimes under bush and briar, sometimes in the corn to the detriment of other men.' **corn in]** corn and *Bas C H.*
7 levit on hir waith lived on her spoils ('levis on thair waith', *Ban Bas C H*, referring to the outlaws).
9 tholit suffered.
10 that in] in to *A.* **couth bide** remained.
11 The town mouse is a freeman and member of one of the powerful merchant guilds which controlled C15 Scots burghs: see W. C. Dickinson *Scotland from the Earliest Times to 1603* (Nelson 1961) Ch. 24.
12 but without. The great ('mare') custom was levied on export of wools and hides (*magna custuma*), the petty on market goods (*parva custuma*). Such exemptions were unusual, to say the least.
13 licence] fredome *Ban Bas C H.* The burgess was 'free in his person and could come and go as he wished' (Dickinson 115).
14 meil meal. **ark** bin. **kist** chest.
15 unfutsair not footsore.
17 sar sorely.

To see what life sho led under the wand.
Bairfute, alone, with pikestaff in hir hand
As pure pilgrim sho passit out of toun
To seik hir sister baith owr dail and doun.

Throw mony wilsome wayis couth sho walk,
Throw mure and moss, throw bank, busk and brere,
Fra fur to fur, cryand fra balk to balk:
'Come furth to me, my awn swet sister deir,
Cry "pepe" anis!' With that the mous couth heir,
And knew hir voce, as kinnismen will do,
By verray kind, and furth sho com hir to.

The hartly cheir, lord God!, gif ye had sene,
Was kithit when thir sisters twa war met!
The welcoming was shawin thame betwene!
For whiles they leuch and whiles for joy they gret,
Whiles kissit sweit and whiles in armis plet;
And thus they fure whill soberit was their mude,
Syne fute for fute unto their chaumer yude.

18 under the wand in the greenwood: *OED* s.v. *Wand* sb.^{2}.

19–20 The pikestaff was a spiked stick specially associated with pilgrims. It is not clear why the prosperous town mouse assumes this poor and penitential guise, unless to avoid being robbed.

21 owr over.

22 wilsome bewildering.

23 mure moor. *A* omits the first *and*, possibly intending *mure* for 'moory': *DOST* s.v. *Mury*. **moss** bog. **busk** bush.

24 'From furrow to furrow, calling out at each ridge.' So *Ban*. The sudden switch to the Lilliputian world of the mouse, labouring up and down the ridge and furrow of a ploughed field, puzzled scribes: Cryand on hir fra balk to balk *A* (unmetrical); Scho ran cryand quhill scho come to a balk *Bas H*.

26 anis just once. **couth heir** heard. *Ban* has 'quod', in which case *heir* is 'here!'

28 By verray kind by simple nature, i.e. by natural affinity.

29–30 'Would to God you had seen the heartfelt joy which was shown when these two sisters had met!'

31 The welcoming] Quhilk that oft syis *Ban*; And grit kyndnes *Bas C H*.

32 leuch laughed. **gret** wept.

33 plet embraced.

34 fure went on. **whill** until. **mude** mood.

35 'Then, keeping pace together, they went to their chamber.'

As I hard say, it was a semple wane,
Of fog and farn full misterlik war maid,
Ane sely sheld under ane erdfast stane,
Of whilk the entré was nocht hie nor braid.
In they went samin, but more abaid,
Withoutin fire or candil birnand bricht –
For commonly sik pickers lufs no licht.

When they war lugit thus, the sely mise,
The youngest sister unto the buttry hyid,
Brocht furth nuttis and peis insteid of spyis:
If thar was weilfar, I do'd on thame beside.
This burgess mous prompit furth in pride
And said, 'Sister, is this your daly fude?'
'Why nocht?' quod she, 'think ye this meit nocht gude?'

'Nay, by my saul, I think it bot a scorn.'
'Madame,' quod she, 'ye be the more to blame.
My moder said, efter that we war born,
That ye and I lay baith in till ane wame.
I kepe the rite and custom of my dame
And of my sire, liffand in poverté,
For landis haf we nane in properté.'

36 semple wane simple dwelling.
37 'Such as might be made in a very impoverished fashion from moss and fern.' *misterlik* is probably from *mister* 'need' (*DOST* s.v. *Misterlyk* adv.): *maisterlig* (*Ban*) is a misreading, *febilie* (*Bas C H*) a gloss.
38 sely sheld poor hovel. **erdfast** fixed in the earth.
39 braid broad.
40 samin together. *Ban Bas C H* read: 'And in the samin [the same] thay went . . .' **but more abaid** without more delay.
42 sik pickers such pilferers. Proverbial: Whiting E184.
43 lugit lodged. **sely** simple.
44 hyid hurried.
45 peis peas. The reading of *Bas C H*, 'candill', has apparently strayed in from the feast in the town house (125–6), where it is appropriate. Cf. 41, 61. **spyis** delicacies such as ginger and licorice, normally eaten after a meal: cf. 126 below, No. 30 line 418, and *Gawain* 979.
46 'I leave it for them to decide whether there was good food there' (*do'd* = 'do it').
47 prompit furth ? burst out.
50 scorn insult.
53 in till ane wame within a single womb (i.e. as part of the same litter). MacQueen 122 sees a human application: poor and rich are alike descended from Adam.
54 rite usage ('rate' in *Bas C H*, with same sense). **dame** mother.
55 sire father.
56 in properté of our own.

'My fair sister,' quod sho, 'hald me excusit,
This rude diet and I can nocht accord.
Till tender meit my stomok ay is usit,
Forwhy I fare als wele as ony lord.
Thir widderit peis and nuts, or they be bord,
Will brek my teith and mak my wame full sklender,
Whilk usit is befor with metis tender.'

'Weil, weil, sister,' quod the rural mous,
'Gif it you pleis, sic thing as ye see heir,
Baith meit and drink, herbery and hous,
Sall be your awn, will ye remane all yeir.
Ye sall it have with blithe and hartly chere,
And that suld mak the messis that are rude,
Amang frendis, baith tender, sweit and gud.

'What plesans is in festis delicate
The whilk are gevin with a gloumand brow?
A gentil hart is better recreate
With blithe visage than set till him a cow.
A modicum is fer mair till allow,
Sa at gud will be carvour at the deis,
Than thrawin vult with mony spicit meis.'

57 ff. 'The town mouse has to speak out – one can see her contracting her offended body within her dress, rising in considered rejection', Tillotson (see headnote) 2. Henryson's are very much *female* mice (Horace's are male).
59 'My stomach has always been accustomed to delicate food.'
60 Forwhy for.
61 widderit shrivelled, i.e. dried. *A* reads: 'Thir rude nuittis and pess'. **or they be bord** before they are broken open.
62 wame belly.
63 usit . . . with accustomed to (*OED* s.v. *Use* v. 18).
66 herbery lodging.
67 Sall be your awn] Ye sall it haue *A* (from 68). **will ye** even if you wish to.
68 Ye sall it have with] With richt gud will baith *A*.
69 messis dishes.
70 frendis relatives.
71–7 Elliott compares *Prov.* 15.17: 'It is better to be invited to herbs with love, than to a fatted calf with hatred.'
72 gloumand scowling.
73 recreate refreshed.
74 visage stressed on second syll. **than set till him a cow** than if you set before him a whole cow: referring to the 'fatted calf' of *Prov.* **set**] seith ('boil') *Ban Bas H*.
75–6 'A small amount is much more to be praised, provided that Good Will is in attendance to carve at the high table.'
77 thrawin vult bad-tempered face. **meis** dish.

For all this mery exhortacioun
The burgess mous had litil will to sing;
Bot hevély sho kest hir browis doun,
For all the dantes that sho couth till hir bring.
Yit at the last sho said, half in hething:
'Sister, this vittal and your ryall feist
May weil suffyis for sic a rural beist.

'Lat be this hole, and come unto my place.
I shall you shaw by trew experiens
My Gudfriday is better na your Pace.
My dish-lickings is worth your hale expens.
Housis ynewe I have o gret defence;
Of cat na trap na fall I haf na dreid.'
'I grant,' quod sho, and on togidder yeid.

In skugry ay, throw rankest gers and corn,
Under covert full prevély couth they crepe.
The eldest mous was gide and yeid beforn,
The younger till hir wayis tuk gud kepe.
On nicht they ran, and on the day they slepe,
Till in a morning, or the laverok sang,
They fand the town, and in gladly can gang.

81 dantes dainties. *Ban* omits 'that'; *Bas C H* omit 'till'. But *dantes* in *A* may be an early example of the monosyllabic form of 'dainty' (see *OED* s.v. *Daint* a. and sb.), in which case the metre is correct.
82 hething scorn.
83 your] this *A*. **ryall** royal.
87 'My Good Friday (a fast) is better than your Easter (a feast).'
88 your hale expens everything you spend.
89 ynewe enough. **o gret defence** very secure.
90 fall a kind of mousetrap, perhaps differing from *trap* in involving a trap-door.
91 yeid they went.
92 In skugry ay] *Ban*; In stowthry ay *A*; In stubbill array *Bas C H* (omitting *rankest*). H. probably used the colloquial phrase in *Ban*, meaning 'in secrecy': see *OED* s.v. *Scuggery*. *stowthry* ('stealing, stolen goods') seems an intelligent scribal guess. *In stubbill array* could mean 'in awkward fashion' (Elliott), but is also probably scribal. **gers** grass.
93 Under covert full] And wondir sly full *Ban*; And under buskis *Bas C H*. I cannot account for these variants. **they]** *A* omits (perhaps rightly).
95 tuk gud kepe paid careful attention (cautiously making sure she knew the way back).
97 a] *Ban*; the *A Bas C H*. But several days are suggested by 96. Again, scribes fail to gauge the scale: cf. *n*. to 24 above. **or** before. **laverok** lark.
98 can gang went.

Nocht fer fra thine, unto a worthy wane
The burgess brocht thame syne whar they suld be.
Without God speid their herbery was tane
In till a spence with vittal gret plenté,
Baith cheis and butter upon skelfis hie,
Flesh and fish yneuch, baith fresh and salt,
And seckis full of grotis, meil and malt.

Eftir, when they disposit war to dine,
Withoutin grace they wosh and went to meit –
All kind of coursis that cukes couth devine,
Mutoun and beif strikin in talyeis grete.
A lordis fair thus can they counterfeit,
Except a thing, they drank the watter cleir
Insteid of wine, bot yit they maid gud chere.

With blith upcast and merry countenance
The eldest sister sperit at hir gest
Gif that sho thocht by resoun difference
Betwix that chalmer and hir sary nest.
'Ye, dame,' quod she, 'how lang now will this lest?'
'Evirmore, I wait, and lenger too.'
'Gif it sa be, ye are at eis,' quod sho.

99 thine thence (this *A*). **wane** dwelling.

100 syne afterwards (sone *Ban Bas C H*).

101 Without God speid without receiving any greeting (from the human master of the house, i.e. without his knowledge). Cf. 107. *A* reads: 'In till ane innes' ('in a place of lodging').

102 spence pantry.

103 Baith] *A* omits. **skelfis** shelves.

105 seckis sacks. **grotis** groats.

108 devine devise.

109 strikin in talyeis grete cut in big slices.

110 'Thus they imitated a lord's fare.'

111–12 Wine would not be kept in the pantry.

111 a one.

113 upcast ? banter (*OED* s.v. *Upcast* sb. 2). Or 'lifted' (of the face)?

114 sperit asked.

116 that] hir *A*.

117 lest last.

118 Evirmore] For evermair *Ban Bas C H*. But the headless line may be original, reflecting the town mouse's emphasis. **wait** know.

119 'If it is so, you are well off . . .'

Till eik the cheir the surcharge furth sho brocht,
A plait of grotis and a dish of meill;
Thref caikis, as I trow, sho sparit nocht
Haboundantly about hir forto deill;
Furmage full fine sho brocht insteid of geill;
A white candill out of a coffer stall
Insteid of spice to creish their teiths withall.

Thus maid they merry whill they micht na mair
And 'Hail, Yule, hail!' they cryit upon hie.
Eftir joy ofttimis comis care,
And truble eftir gret prosperitie.
Thus as they sat in all their jolisé,
So com the spenser with keyis in till hand,
Opinit the dure and thame at diner fand.

They taryit nocht to wesh, as I suppose,
Bot on to go wha that micht formast win.
The burgess had a hole, and in sho gois;
Hir sister had no hole to hide her in.
To see this sely mous it was gret sin
So desolate and will of a gud reid:
For verray dreid sho fell in swoun nere deid.

120–6 *A* omits; supplied from *Ban*.
120 'To add to the entertainment, she brought out an extra course.'
122 Thref caikis oat-cakes. **as]** *Ban* omits.
123 deill distribute.
124 Furmage full fine excellent cheese. So *Ban*. The common ancestor of *Bas C H* apparently read: 'And mane full fyne' ('and excellent white bread'). It would seem natural for the mice to eat cheese (103). **geill** jelly.
125 stall stole. But this may be the noun *stall*, going with *coffer* to mean 'a stand of boxes'.
126 spice See *n*. to 45. **creish their teiths** grease their teeth (with the candle tallow): *DOST* s.v. *Cresch(e* v. *Bas C H* read 'gust thair mouth', where *gust* means 'please with a relish' (*DOST*).
128 upon hie loudly.
129–30 These mock-heroic reflections on mutability recall Chaucer's *Nun's Priest's T.*, esp. VII 3205–6: 'For evere the latter ende of joye is wo. | God woot that worldly joye is soone ago.'
131 jolisé jollity: *DOST Jolisie* n.
132 spenser steward, who would hold the keys of the locked pantry.
135 'But whoever could get in front, made off.' **on to]** unto *A*. **that]** *A Ban* omit.
139 will of a gud reid having no idea what to do. **a]** all *Ban*; ane *Bas C H*. The *a* of *A* may represent *all* (*a'*).

Bot as God wald, it fell a happy case:
The spenser had na lasere forto bide,
To sers, to seik, to char nor yit to chase,
Bot on he went and left the dure up wide.
This bald burgess his passage wele has spyid;
Out of hir hole sho com and cryit on hie:
'How, fair sister? Cry "pepe" wharever ye be.'

This rural mous lay flatlings on the ground
And for the deid full sore sho was dredand,
For till hir hart straik mony wilsome stound;
As in a fever trimblit fute and hand.
When she hir sister in to sic plite fand,
For verray peté sho began to grete,
Syne comfort hir with wordis hony swete.

'Why ly ye sa? Rise up, my sister deir,
Come to your meit, this perrell is owr-past.'
The tother answerd with a hevy cheir:
'I may nocht eit, I am so sair agast.
I had lever thir fourty days haf fast
With watter-caill, and gnawe benis and peis,
Than all your fest in this dreid and diseis.'

With fair trety yit sho gart hir rise,
And unto burd togiddir baith they sat.

142 lasere leisure.

143 sers search. **char** drive.

144 up open.

145 passage departure.

148 flatlings flat.

149 deid death.

150 'For many bewildering pangs struck at her heart.' Cf. No. 30, lines 538–9. **wilsome]** wofull *Ban Bas C H*.

151 The feverish trembling is a detail from the version by Gualterus: 'Ille tamen febrit, teste timore tremit' ('But he is in a fever, and trembles in the head with fear').

152 in to sic plite in such a state.

154 comfort comforted.

156 owr-past passed over.

159 Referring to the forty days of fasting at Lent.

160 watter-caill vegetable soup (*caill* 'kale') without meat or fat.

161 your] this *A*. **diseis** uneasiness.

162 trety entreaty.

Scantly had they drunkin anes or twyis
When in com Gib Hunter, our joly cat,
And bad God speid. The burgess up with that,
In at hir hole sho fled as fire of flint.
Bauderonis the tother by the back has hint.

Fra fute to fute sho kest hir to and fra,
While up, while down, als tait as ony kid;
Whiles wald sho lat hir rin under the stra,
Whiles wald sho wink and play with hir buckheid.
Thus to the sely mous gret pain sho did,
Till at the last, throw fair fortune and hap,
Betwene the dosore and the wall sho crap.

Syne up in haist behind the parrelling
So hie sho clame that Gilbert micht nocht get hir,
And by the clukes richt craftély can hing
Till he was gone – hir cher was all the better –
Syne down sho lap when thair was nane to let hir.
Upon the burgess mous loud couth sho cry:
'Fair wele, sister, thy feist heir I defy!

164–91 In Gualterus and his French derivatives, the country mouse has a single encounter, with the steward, before deciding to leave. Jamieson *N & Q* 14 (1967) 403–5 suggests that the second encounter, with the cat, derives from a version of the story in Odo of Cheriton's *Fabulae* (*c.* 1320). H. appears to have combined the cat version with the steward version to strengthen the climax.

164 Scantly scarcely.

165 Gib a form of 'Gilbert', a popular cat-name: see *MED* s.v. *Gib(be*. **our** the 'domestic *our*': see No. 18 above, line 69 and *n*.

166 God speid the greeting which the mice previously lacked: 101.

167 as fire of flint a proverbial type of swiftness: Whiting F190.

168 Bauderonis another familiar cat-name, of obscure origin. **hint** caught.

169 sho *Bas C H* have *he* for the cat throughout this stanza; *A Ban* have *sho*, changing to *he* at 179.

170 MacQueen 127 observes that this passage 'combines realistic observation with verbal reminiscences of stock descriptions of Fortune and her wheel'. **While** now. **tait** playful (*Bas C H* read *cant* 'frisky').

171 stra straw (used as floor-covering).

172 wink shut her eyes. **buckheid** blindman's buff.

175 dosore wall-hanging (cf. *courtin* 187). *dressour* in *Ban* is a homoeograph; *burde* in *Bas C H* was apparently carried back from 176. **crap** crept.

176 parrelling ? wainscot (*OED* s.v. *Parelling* vbl. sb.).

177 clame climbed.

178 clukes claws.

180 lap leapt (come *A*). **let** stop.

182 defy renounce.

'Thy mangerie is mengit all with cair,
Thy guse is gud, thy ganesall sour as gall,
The surcharge of thy service is bot sair;
Sa sall thou find hereftirwart, may fall.
I thank yon courtin and yon parpell wall
Of my defence now fra yon cruel beist.
Almichty God kepe me fra sic ane feist.

'War I anes in the kith that I come fra,
For weil nor wo I suld never come agane.'
With that sho tuke hir leif and furth can ga,
Whiles throw the corn and whilis throw the plane.
When sho was furth and free, sho was full fane,
And merrily sho markit unto the mure.
I can nocht tell how eftirwart sho fure.

Bot I herd say sho passit till hir den,
Als warm as woll, suppos it was nocht grete,
Full benely stuffit baith but and ben
Of nuttis, pes, benis, ry and wheit.
Whenevir sho list sho had yneuch till eit,
In quiet and eis, withoutin ony dreid;
Bot till hir sisters fest no mor sho yeid.

183 mangerie feast. **mengit** mingled.
184 guse goose. **ganesall** garlic sauce: Whiting G378.
185 surcharge] suchardis *A*; ?sachngis *Ban*; subcharge *Bas C H*. Cf. 120, where *Bas C H* again have *subcharge* for *surcharge* 'extra course'. **service** meal.
186 may fall it may happen. *Bas C H* read *na fall* 'without fail'.
187 courtin curtain (the wall-hanging of 175). **parpell wall** partition wall.
190 'If I were once back in the land I come from.'
191 nor] and *A*.
193 plane open ground.
194 furth away.
195 markit went.
196 fure fared.
198 as] in *A*. **suppos** even though.
199 'Very well supplied, both in outer and inner rooms.' In Scottish cottages, the room entered from the external door was 'but', the next one being 'ben' (OE *butan* 'outside' and *binnan* 'inside'). **Full]** Alss *A*.
202 ony] *A Ban* omit.

Moralitas

Frendis, heir may ye find, will ye tak heid,
In this fabil ane gud moralité.
As fitchis mengit are with noble seid,
Sa intermellit is adversité
With erdly joys, so that no stat is free
Without truble or som vexacioun,
And namly they whilk climmis up most hie
And nocht content of small possessioun.

Blissit be simpil lif withoutin dreid,
Blissit be sobir feist in quieté;
Who has yneuch, of no mor has he neid,
Thocht it be litil in to quantité.
Gret haboundans and blind prosperité
Oft timis makes ane evil conclusioun.
The swetest lif, thairfoir, in this cuntré
Is sekerness with small possessioun.

O wantoun man, whilk usis forto feid
Thy wame, and makis it a god to be,
Luke to thyself; I warn thee weil on deid,
The cat comis and to the mous has ee.

Moralitas For his moral conclusion, H. departs from the 7-line rhyme-royal stanza and adopts the 8-line stanza (rhyming *ababbcbc*) used by Chaucer in the *Monk's T.* and in some ballades (e.g. No. 13 above, and *The Former Age*). The use of refrain and of repeated rhymes also suggests imitation of Chaucer's ballades. *Balade de Bone Conseyl* (No. 17 above) is evidently in his mind throughout. Lydgate also wrote moral poems in the '*Monk's Tale* stanza' with refrain: see No. 23 above. Cf. also Dunbar's *Resurrection*, No. 37 below, and headnote. See Introd. xviii–xix.
204 will] quhill ('while') *A*.
206 fitchis vetches. **mengit** Cf. 183.
207 intermellit intermingled.
210 namly particularly.
211 Cf. No. 17 above, line 2. G. Smith compares Lydgate *Isopes Fabules* 427: 'Than glad povert with small possession'.
213 in] and *A*.
216 haboundans abundance.
218 Supplied from *Ban. A* repeats 226 here.
219 *A* exchanges this line with 227. **sekerness** security.
220 usis are accustomed.
221 Cf. *Phil.* 3.19: 'Whose end is destruction: whose God is their belly.'
222 on deid indeed.
223 and to] unto A.

What is avale thy feist and ryalté
With dreidful hart and tribulacioun?
Tharfor best thing in erd, I say for me,
Is merry hart with small possessioun.

Thy awn fire, frend, thocht it be bot a gleid,
It warmis weil and is worth gold to thee.
As Salamon sayis, and thou will it reid,
'Under the hevin I can nocht better see
Than ay be blithe and live in honesté.'
Whairfoir I may conclud by this resoun:
Of erdly joy it beris mast degré,
Blitheness in hert with small possessioun.

224 What is avale of what use is: *avale* probably represents 'of vail' (*OED Vail* sb.[1] 2). *Ban* reads 'dois awaill'; *Bas H* read 'vaillis than'; *C* lacks whole stanza. **and]** in *A*.

227 *A* exchanges this line with 219. *Bas H* read 'Is blyithnes in hart with small possessioun'; but the resemblance to 235 is suspicious, since Henryson appears to be varying his refrain at each occurrence.

228 thocht though (*sa* 'provided that' *Bas C H*). **gleid** ember.

230 and if.

231–2 Alluding to *Eccles*. 3.22: 'And I [the Preacher, identified as Solomon] have found that nothing is better than for a man to rejoice in his work: and that this is his portion.'

231 I can nocht better see] thair can not better be *Bas C H*.

232 honesté] quiete *A*. But *quieté* would be a unique exception (cf. 213) to the rule that rhyme-words are not repeated in this ballade.

233 resoun proposition.

234 beris mast degré holds highest place.

32 The Hunting of the Cheviot

Border warfare between Harry Percy or 'Hotspur' (1364–1403), son of the E. of Northumberland, and James, second E. of Douglas (1358?–88), was a favourite subject of popular song: 'Certainly, I must confess my own barbarousness, I never heard the old song of Percy and Douglas that I found not my heart moved more than with a trumpet; and yet is it sung but by some blind crowder [fiddler], with no rougher voice than rude style' (Philip Sidney *Apology for Poetry* ed. Shepherd 118). Texts of three such songs survive in C16 and C17 copies: *The Hunting of the Cheviot*, here edited (Child No. 162, MS. mid-C16, title from lines 107 and 291); *The Battle of Otterburn* (Child No. 161, MS. C16 early or mid); and *Chevy Chase* (Child No. 162B, Percy

Folio MS., mid-C17). The fullest study is by O. Arngart *Two English Border Ballads* (Lund 1973), who dates *Otterburn* in second or third quarter of C15 and *Cheviot* towards end of C15. *Otterburn* is generally considered the older (though see Fowler 108–14). Its account of the battle of Otterburn (1388), which *Cheviot* also claims to describe (280–1), is much closer to contemporary reports. According to Froissart and other chroniclers, the battle arose from a raid by the Scots under Douglas (as in *Otterburn*), not a hunting expedition by the English under Percy (as in *Cheviot*). *Chevy Chase* is an early C17 street ballad version of *Cheviot*. It provided the subject of two notable essays (Nos. 70 and 74) in the 1711 *Spectator*, where Joseph Addison considers it, quite properly, as a heroic poem, and praises its naturalness and nobility.

Metre and style The MS. presents *Cheviot* in long rhyming couplets, here arranged as 4-line 'ballad stanzas' rhyming *abcb* or *abab*. In 5 cases, the MS. long lines rhyme in triplets, expanded by Child into 6-line stanzas. Experimentally here these are expanded into two 4-line stanzas, with repetition of the MS. second line (5–6, 69–70, 101–2, 161–2, 265–6). Arngart and D. Hamer *RES* n.s. 20 (1969) 1–21 suggest that *Cheviot* was originally composed in 8-line stanzas rhyming *abababab* (or variants), preserved e.g. in lines 117–32. Hamer also prints a text heavily corrected to yield more regular alternation of four- and three-stress lines; but it is hard to distinguish textual corruptions from genuine minstrel licences. Like many genuinely early ballads, *Cheviot* shares some stylistic features with medieval minstrel romances: e.g. use of tags such as *verament* (39), asseverations (50), addresses to the audience (107–8). See Fowler Ch. 4 and E. K. Wells *The Ballad Tree* (New York, Ronald 1950) 209–10. Alliteration is common, especially in description of hunting and battle. The dialect was originally northern (Yorkshire?). For general discussions of ballad, see G. H. Gerould *The Ballad of Tradition* (Oxford U.P. 1932) and M. J. C. Hodgart *The Ballads* (Hutchinson 1950).

Manuscript and editions One MS: Bodleian Library MS. Ashmole 48, a miscellany copied by various hands, mainly 1557–65. The text of *Cheviot* ends with an attribution to 'Rychard Sheale', a contemporary northern minstrel who composed some other poems in the MS. No doubt *Cheviot* formed part of his repertoire. Fowler 95–108 discusses the MS. as a specimen of the 'new minstrelsy' of C15 and C16. *Cheviot* was first printed in 1719, and was the first item in Bp Percy's *Reliques of Ancient English Poetry* (1765). Modern edns by W. W. Skeat in *Specimens of English Literature* (2nd edn, Oxford U.P. 1879), Child (No. 162) and Arngart.

First Fit

The Persé out of Northomberlond
An avow to God made he
That he wold hunte in the mountains
Of Cheviat within days three,

2 An avow] and a vowe MS. Redundant *and* is common in ballad style; but this example, attached to the first verb of the ballad, is suspect.
4 Cheviat The Cheviot hills lie across the Border from Northumberland.

That he wold hunte in the mountains
Of Cheviat within days three
In the magger of doughty Doglas
And all that ever with him be.

The fattest hartes in all Cheviat, he said,
He wold kill and cary them away.
'By my faith,' said the doughty Doglas again,
'I will let that hunting if that I may.'

Then the Persé out of Banborow cam,
With him a mighty meany,
With fifteen hondrith archeres bold of blood and bone,
They were chosen out of shires three.

This began on a Monenday at morn,
In Cheviat the hillis so hye;
The child may rue that is unborn,
It was the more pité.

The drivers thorow the woodes went
Forto raise the deer;
Bowmen bickered upon the bent
With their broad arrows clear.

5–6 Lines not repeated in MS. See headnote.

7 In the magger of in spite of (cf. 64, 72). *magger* is a form of *maugré* 'ill will, spite'.

9 he said Taken by Child at the beginning of the next line. The metre would run better, here as at 67, 95, 255, 263, without the phrase: cf. *Chevy Chase* st. 4, 'The cheefest harts in Chevy Chase | To kill and beare away.'

11 again in reply.

12 let hinder, prevent.

13 Banborow Bamburgh, a stronghold on the Northumb. coast.

14 meany company.

15 of blood and bone Derives from a traditional phrase reinforcing a superlative (cf. No. 2 above, line 54): equivalent to 'the boldest alive'.

16 shires three three districts in Northumberland, known as 'shires': Bamburghshire (cf. *Otterburn* stanza 6), Islandshire, Norhamshire.

17 Monenday] Monday MS. Form adopted from 30 for metrical reasons.

21 drivers men who drove deer into clearings for the archers to shoot: cf. *Gawain* 1150 f.

23 bickered let fly. **bent** field. Alliteration is strong in this hunt passage.

24 clear bright (i.e. the heads).

[32]

Then the wild thorow the woodes went
On every side sere;
Grehondes thorow the grevis glent
Forto kill their deer.

This began in Cheviat the hills abone
Yerly on a Monenday;
By that it drew to the ower of none
A hondrith fat hartes ded there lay.

They blew a mot upon the bent,
They sembled on sidis sere;
To the quirry then the Persé went
To see the britling of the deer.

He said, 'It was the Doglas promis
This day to meet me here;
But I wiste he wold faille, verament.'
A great oth the Persé swear.

At the last a squier of Northomberlond
Lokid at his hand full ny;
He was war o the doughty Doglas commande,
With him a mighty meany,

Both with spear, briny and brand,
It was a mighty sight to see;
Hardier men both of hert nar hand
Were not in Cristianté.

25 wild wild animals: cf. *Gawain* 1150.
26 every side sere every single side.
27 'Greyhounds slipped through the thickets.'
29 the hills abone up in the hills.
30 Yerly early.
31 'By the time that it was approaching noon.' Cf. 206.
33 mot a note on a hunting horn, here used to summon the scattered hunting party for the 'brittling'.
34 'They assembled from various directions.'
35 quirry collection of killed deer.
36 britling the breaking-up of the carcases: an occasion of importance and ceremony: cf. *Gawain* 1327 ff.
39 wiste knew. **verament** truly (a favourite minstrel word).
42 at his hand on his side (?'shading his eyes with his hand', Child).
43 o the] ath the MS. **commande]** commynge MS. The northern pres. partic. form restores an *abab* stanza (Hamer).
45 briny corslet. Skeat and Child emend MS. *brylly* to *bylle* ('bill'); but *bryny* is nearer the MS. form. **brand** sword.
47 Hardier more courageous. **nar** nor.

They were twenty hondrith spearmen good
Withouten any fale;
They were born along by the watter o Twide
I' the boundes of Tividale.

'Leave off the britling of the deer,' he said,
'And to your bows look ye taik good hede;
For never sith ye were o your mothers born
Had ye never so mickle nede.'

The doughty Doglas on a stede
He rode all his men beforn;
His armor glitterid as did a glede,
A bolder barn was never born.

'Tell me whos men ye are,' he says,
'Or whos men that ye be.
Who gave you leave to hunte in this Cheviat chais
In the spit of myn and of me?'

The first man that ever him an answer made
It was the good lord Persé:
'We will not tell thee whos men we are,' he says,
'Nor whos men that we be,

'We will not tell thee whos men we are,
Nor whos men that we be;
But we will hunte here in this chais
In the spit of thyn and of thee.

49 The contrast between the Scots with their spears and the English with their bows is present throughout.
50 Withouten] Withoute MS. The asseveration is typical of the alternating 'weak lines' in minstrel balladry.
51–2 The R. Tweed and Teviotdale lie on the Scotch side of the Cheviots. 'The country of the Scotch warriors, described in these two last verses [*Chevy Chase*: All men of pleasant Tivydale | Fast by the river Tweede'], has a fine romantic situation, and affords a couple of smooth words for verse' (Addison).
55 sith since. **o**] on MS.
59 glede hot coal.
60 barn warrior.
61 whos Hamer would emend to *what*, here and at 69; but double insistence on the intruder's allegiance is appropriate in feudal times.
63 chais hunting-ground. Hunting rights were jealously guarded; and tracts of unfenced land, or *chases*, were reserved.
69–70 Lines not repeated in MS. See headnote.

'The fattest hartes in all Cheviat we have killed,
And cast to carry them away.'
'By my troth,' said the doughty Doglas again,
'Therfor the ton of us shall de this day.'

Then said the doughty Doglas
Unto the lord Persé:
'To kill all these giltless men, alas,
It were great pité.

'But, Persé, thou art a lord of land,
I am a yerl callid within my contré;
Let all our men upon a party stand,
And do the battel of thee and of me.'

'Now Cristes cors on his crown,' said the lord Persé,
'Whosoever therto says nay!
By my troth, doughty Doglas,' he says,
'Thou shalt never see that day,

'Neither in Inglond, Scotlond nar France,
Nor for no man of a woman born,
But, and fortune be my chance,
I dar meet him oon man for oon.'

Then bespake a squier of Northomberlond,
Richard Witherington was his name:
'It shall never be told in Sothe Inglond,' he says,
'To King Henry the Fourth for shame.

74 cast intend.
76 ton one.
82 yerl earl.
83 upon a party stand stand aside.
84 'And let you and me fight the battle.'
85 'Now may Christ's curse fall on his head . . .'
87–92 Hamer takes this as Douglas's answer; but in *Chevy Chase* the corresponding lines belong to Percy, though at an earlier stage of the encounter (sts 15–16). There seems no reason why the chivalrous Percy should not address his adversary as *doughty*.
90 Cf. 152. In *Otterburn* (Herd's version, sts 10–12) Percy is commanded by Montgomery to yield to 'yon braken-bush' where Douglas is to be buried. Bland *N & Q* o.s. 194 (1949) 335–6 finds in both passages traces of the sort of 'riddling trick' played by the Witches on Macbeth.
91 'But, if good fortune come to me.'
92 oon man for oon man for man, in single combat.
95 Sothe south.
96 Henry IV reigned 1399–1413. He was not king at the time of the Battle of Otterburn (1388).

'I wat you ben great lordes twa,
I am a poor squier of land;
I will never see my captain fight on a felde
And stand my self lookande,

'I will never see my captain fight on a felde
And stand my self lookande;
But while I may my wepon welde
I will not fail both hert and hand.'

That day, that day, that dredful day!
The first fit here I finde.
And you will here any more o the hunting o the Cheviat
Yet is there more behinde.

Second Fit

The Inglish men had their bows ybent,
Their hertes were good ynough.
The first of arrows that they shot off
Seven score spearmen they slough.

Yet bidis the yerl Doglas upon the bent,
A captain good ynough,
And that was sene verament,
For he wrought hom both woo and wough.

The Doglas partid his ost in three
Lyk a chefe cheften of pride;
With suer spears of mighty tree
They come in on every side;

97 wat know.
100 lookande] and loocke on MS. Hamer's emendation restores the rhyme. The northern pres. partic. ended in *-ande*: cf. 43.
101–2 Lines not repeated in MS. See headnote.
103 A heroic formula, found in OE poetry: 'Tha hwile the hi waepna wealdan moston' ('For such time as they could wield their weapons'), *Maldon* 83.
104 fail] MS. omits.
106 fit a favourite minstrel's term for a section of verse story. **finde** Skeat suggested a corruption of *fine* 'I finish'; but the line was probably intended for the reciter: 'At this point I find the first fit completed.' Compare, with this and the following lines, Chaucer's ending of a 'fit' in his parody of minstrel romance, *Thopas*: 'Lo, lordes mine, heere is a fit! | If ye woll any moore of it, | To telle it woll I fonde', *C.T.* VII 2078–80.
107 And if.
108 behinde i.e. to come.
113 bidis remains.
116 wough injury.
118 chefe outstanding.
119 'With trusty spears of strong wood'. **suer** 'sure'.

[32]

Thorow our Inglish archery
Gave many a wound full wide;
Many a doughty they garde to dy,
Which ganid them no pride.

The Inglish men let their bowes be
And pulde out brandes that were bright;
It was a hevy sight to see
Bright swordes on basnetes light.

Thorow rich male and miniplé
Many sterne they strok down streght;
Many a freke that was full free
There under foot did light.

At last the Doglas and the Persé met
Lyk to captains of might and of main;
They swapte together till they both swat
With swordes that wer of fyn millain.

These worthé frekes forto fight
Therto they were full fain,
Till the blood out of their basnetes sprent
As ever did hail or rain.

'Yelde thee, Persé,' said the Doglas,
'And i' faith I shall thee bringe
Where thou shalt have a yerls wagis
Of Jamy our Scottish kinge.

121 Thorow through.
123 garde caused.
124 Obscure and perhaps corrupt. 'Their pride availed them not' (Skeat)? The modern verb *gain* (OED *Gain* v.[2]) is not recorded until C16. ME *gain* (*OED* v.[1]) means 'avail, serve'.
128 basnetes helmets. **light** descend.
129 male chainmail. **miniplé**] myne ye ple MS. Perhaps a corruption of Fr. *manople* 'armoured gauntlet' (Skeat).
130 sterne i.e. stern warriors.
131 freke warrior (poetic word already in OE).
132 light alight, fall.
133–41 Closely corresponding to *Otterburn* sts 50–1.
135 swapte together exchanged blows. **swat** sweated.
136 millain steel used by Milanese armourers.
139 sprent spurted.
143 yerls earl's.
144 Jamy The first James to be K. of Scotland came to the throne in 1406.

'Thou shalt have thy ransom free,
I hight thee here this thing,
For the manfullest man yet art thou
That ever I conquerid in filde fighting.'

'Nay,' said the lord Persé,
'I told it thee beforn,
That I wold never yeldid be
To no man of a woman born.'

With that there cam an arrow hastély
Forth of a mighty wane,
Hit hath streken the yerl Doglas
In at the brest-bane.

Thorow liver and longes bathe
The sharp arrow is gane,
That never after in all his lif-days
He spake mo wordes but ane,

That never after in all his lif-days
He spake mo wordes but ane,
That was, 'Fight ye, my mirry men, whilis ye may,
For my lif-days ben gane.'

The Persé leanid on his brand
And saw the Doglas de;
He took the dede man by the hand
And said, 'Wo is me for thee.

'To have savid thy lif I wold have partid with
My landes for yeares three,
For a better man of hert nar of hand
Was nat in all the north contré.'

145 Percy will be released without ransom if he surrenders, and accepts 'wages' to fight for James.

146 hight promise.

152 See *n.* to 90.

154 wane obscure. Skeat takes as the Northern form of *OED Wone* sb.[3], 'a multitude'; the arrow which kills Douglas comes from a huge flight of arrows (despite 125) shot by the English. Hamer 20 attempts emendation.

156 bane bone.

157 longes lungs.

161–2 Lines not repeated in MS. See headnote.

165 ff. 'Earl Percy's lamentation over his enemy is generous, beautiful, and passionate' (Addison).

169 partid with i.e. 'surrendered all the profits of' (Hamer).

[32]

Of all that see a Scottish knight,
Was callid Sir Hewe the Mongombirry,
He saw the Doglas to the deth was dight,
He spendid a spear o trusty tree.

He rode upon a corsiere
Through a hondrith archery,
He never stintid nar never blane
Till he cam to the good lord Persé.

He set upon the lord Persé
A dint that was full sare;
With a suer spear of a mighty tree
Clean thorow the body he the Persé bare,

O the tother side that a man might see
A large cloth-yard and mare.
Two better captains were nat in Cristianté
Than that day slain were there.

An archer of Northomberlond
Say slain was the lord Persé.
He bar a bend bow in his hond
Was made of trusty tree.

An arrow that a cloth-yard was lang
To the hard stele haled he,
A dint that was both sad and sare
He set on Sir Hewe the Mongombirry.

173 'A Scottish knight saw all that.'
174 In *Otterburn*, Sir Hugh Montgomery is exchanged for Percy in an exchange of prisoners after the battle (st. 69).
175 dight put.
176 spendid grasped. o] a MS. (cf. 192). **tree** wood.
177 corsiere courser, charger.
179 'He never drew up or stopped.'
182 dint blow. **sare**] soare MS. Hamer's emendations here and at 184 (bare] ber) restore the original rhyming northern forms: cf. 197, 199.
186 The yard by which cloth was measured (36 inches) was the length of a long-bow arrow: cf. 193.
190 Say saw.
191 bend bent i.e. strung.
193 See 186 and *n.*
194 haled drew back.
196 set] sat MS.

The dint it was both sad and sare
That he on Mongombirry set;
The swan fethers that his arrow bare
With his hert-blood they were wet.

There was never a freke one foot wold flee,
But still in stour did stand,
Hewing on iche other while they might dree
With many a balful brand.

This battel began in Cheviat
An ower befor the none,
And when even-song bell was rang
The battel was nat half done.

They toke strokes on ether hand
By the light of the mone;
Many had no strength forto stand
In Cheviat the hillis abone.

Of fifteen hondrith archers of Inglond
Went away but seventy and three;
Of twenty hondrith spearmen of Scotlond
But even five and fifty.

But all were slain Cheviat within,
They had no strenge to stand on hye;
The child may rue that is unborn,
It was the more pité.

There was slain with the lord Persé
Sir Johan of Agerstone,
Sir Roger the hinde Hartly,
Sir William the bold Hearone.

198 on] of MS.
199 The arrow, which was drawn up to its steel head, sinks in up to its feathers. The Northumb. archer is another heroic figure.
202 stour combat. This stanza is like *Otterburn* st. 58.
203 dree endure.
204 balful destructive.
209 strokes] MS. omits. Skeat supplied *the fight* and *Oxford Book of Ballads* supplies *a stand*. 'Took strokes' means 'struck blows': see *OED* s.v. *Take* v. 5.
213–6 Cf. *Otterburn* sts 62 and 65.
218 strenge strength: an authentic form (*OED* s.v. *Strengh* sb.). **on hye** upright.
219–20 Repeated from 19–20.
222 Sir John of Agerstone is named among the dead Scots in *Otterburn* st. 60.
223 hinde gracious (ME *hende*).
224 'The bold Sir William Heron.'

[32]

Sir Jorg the worthy Loumlé,
A knight of great renown,
Sir Raff the riche Rugbé,
With dintes were beaten down.

For Witherington my hert was wo
That ever he slain shold be;
For when both his leggis were hewen in two
Yet he kniled and fought on his knee.

There was slain with the doughty Doglas
Sir Hewe the Mongombirry,
Sir Davy Lwdale, that worthy was,
His sisters son was he,

Sir Charls o Murré in that place,
That never a foot wold flee;
Sir Hewe Maxwell, a lord he was,
With the Doglas did he de.

So on the morrow they made them biers
Of birch and hasel so gray;
Many wedows, with weping tears,
Cam to feche their makes away.

Tividale may carpe of care,
Northomberlond may make great mone,
For two such captains as slain were there
On the March party shall never be none.

Word is comen to Edenburrow,
To Jamy the Scottish king,
That doughty Doglas, lifftenant of the Marches,
He lay slain Cheviat within.

225 Loumlé Lumley.
227 'The wealthy Sir Ralph Rugby.'
229 Witherington See 94 above.
231–2 A heroic motif, documented in Child's note, III 306.
235 Lwdale This obscure name seems to correspond to the 'Lambwell' of *Chevy Chase* st. 52.
236 The relationship of sister's son, linking Sir David with Montgomery (or Douglas?), was held to be especially close in heroic tradition.
242 gray] gay MS. Cf. the corresponding stanza in *Otterburn* (st. 67): 'Of byrch and haysell graye.'
244 makes mates.
245 carpe speak.
248 On the March party in the region of the Marches, i.e. the Borderland.
251 lifftenant lieutenant, King's representative: an official position in the Marches of Wales and Scotland.

His handes did he weal and wring,
He said, 'Alas and woe is me!
Such another captain Scotland within,' he said,
'I' faith shold never be.'

Word is comen to lovly London,
Till the fourth Harry our king,
That lord Persé, chefe tenant of the Marches,
He lay slain Cheviat within.

'God have mercy on his soule,' said King Harry,
'Good lord, if thy will it be!
I have a hondrith captains in Inglond,' he said,
'As good as ever was he,

'I have a hondrith captains in Inglond
As good as ever was he;
But, Persé, and I brook my lif,
Thy deth well quit shall be.'

As our noble king made his avow,
Like a noble prince of renown,
For the deth of the lord Persé he did
The battel of Hombildown,

Where six and thritty Scottish knights
On a day were beaten down;
Glendale glittered o their armor bright
Over castel, tower and town.

253 weal ? 'clench so as to leave marks' (Child: cf. *OED* s.v. *Wale* v.[2]). Skeat suggested that the familiar 'wring and wail' (e.g. Chaucer *C.T.* IV 1212) got reversed in transmission.
257 'Lovely London', or 'leve London', was a ballad formula.
258 See *n.* to 96.
259 The parallel with 251 suggests emendation; but Percy would be the King's tenant-in-chief in the Marches.
263–4 The pointed contrast with 255–6 establishes beyond doubt the English origins of the ballad (though Fowler 114 regards lines 249 to the end as a late interpolation in a basically Scottish ballad).
265–6 Lines not repeated in MS. See headnote.
267 and I brook my lif if I enjoy my life; if I live.
268 quit avenged.
272 Hombildown The Battle of Homildon did take place in the reign of Henry IV, in 1402; but it had nothing to do with the death of Percy, who survived Otterburn, led the English forces (with his father, the E. of Northumberland) and defeated the Scots at Homildon.
275 Glendale The district of Northumb. to which Homildon Hill belongs. **o]** on MS.

This was the hunting of the Cheviat;
That ear began this spurn!
Old men that know the ground well ynough
Call it the battel of Otterburn.

At Otterburn began this spurn
Upon a Monenday;
There was the doughty Doglas slain,
The Persé never went away.

There was never a time on the March partés
Syn the Doglas and the Persé met,
But it is mervel and the red blud ronne not
As the rean does in the stret.

Jesu Crist our balis bete
And to the bliss us bringe.
Thus was the hunting of the Cheviat.
God send us all good ending.

278 'Alas, that ever this fray began!' The MS. reading 'That tear begane this . . .' is obscure. I take *that* to introduce an exclamation of grief (*OED That* conj. 1e) and *tear* to represent '(tha)t e'er': cf. *ton* for 'one' at 76. **spurn** ? fray.
280 The old men should have known that Otterburn is in Percy's own Northumb., not in Cheviot. The battle of Otterburn (1388) in fact took place as the result of an incursion by Douglas. See headnote.
285 See 248 and *n*.
287 'When it was other than a matter of wonder if the red blood did not flow.'
288 rean Skeat takes this as 'rain', which is possible in Sheale's spelling; but it is more probably *OED Rean* 'gutter'. Cf. *Siege of Jerusalem* 12 'Till he all on rede blode ran, as rain in the strete'. In *Siege* 560 streams of blood run 'as goteres'.
289 our balis bete put an end to our troubles. A traditional phrase.

William Dunbar

Life Born in Lothian, Scotland, in later 1450s (?1456), into some branch of the Earls of Dunbar and March. 'William Dunbar' received B.A. at St Andrews University in 1477 (M.A. 1479). There is no evidence for the period 1479–1500: Dunbar says he wore 'Friar's weed' (*How Dumbar wes Desyrd to be Ane Freir* 36), but see A. G. Rigg *RES* n.s. 14 (1963) 269–73. He moved in court circles, and probably travelled abroad. In 1500 he received a 'pension' from King James IV of Scotland, which was paid out until the Battle of Flodden (1513). Unlike e.g. Hoccleve, D. based his claim to money from the

King partly on his services as poet or 'maker' (*Remonstrance to the King* 25–34); but he was also a priest and chaplain (first mass 1503), and a royal secretary who joined in embassies. He was in London in 1501 in connection with James's marriage to Margaret, a marriage celebrated in the laureate poem *The Thrissil and the Rois*, which illustrates D.'s courtly allegorical style. There is no record of D. after Flodden: he may have died then, or soon after. He was probably long dead by 1530, when Sir David Lindsay lamented 'Dunbar, whilk language had at large'. The standard biographical study (not very critical) is J. W. Baxter *William Dunbar* (Edinburgh, Oliver and Boyd 1952). See also D. Fox 'The chronology of D.' *PQ* 39 (1960) 413–25.

Works and editions D.'s poems (mostly short) exhibit a wide range of subjects and styles, all skilfully and vigorously handled. The main types are: public court poems (*Thrissil and Rois*, *Goldyn Targe*); private and petitionary poems referring to his own circumstances, often moralizing (Nos. 33 and 34 here); poems of moral reflection (No. 35); religious poems (Nos. 36 and 37); and comic poems (No. 38). The standard large edn is by J. Small (STS 3 vols. Edinburgh 1884–93). Complete poems ed. in one vol. by W. M. Mackenzie (2nd edn, Faber 1960). Selections ed. J. Kinsley (Oxford U.P. 1958).

Studies Like Henryson, Dunbar is commonly classed among the 'Scottish Chaucerians', on whom see D. Fox in D. S. Brewer, ed. *Chaucer and Chaucerians* (Nelson 1966) 164–200; but specific Chaucerian influence appears only sporadically (e.g. in No. 38). The best short account of his work is by C. S. Lewis, *English Literature in the C16* (Oxford U.P. 1954) 90–8, comparing him with Horace and Dryden (all 'men of strongly masculine genius, professional to the point of virtuosity, and much in love with the languages they write'). J. Leyerle distinguishes 'two voices' in D., the formal poetic voice and the comic 'eldritch' voice: *UTQ* 31 (1962) 316–38. See also E. Morgan *EC* 2 (1952) 138–58. The book-length study by T. Scott, *Dunbar: a critical exposition of the poems* (Edinburgh, Oliver and Boyd 1966) is valuable chiefly for annotated bibliography.

33 Lament: When He Wes Sek

The basic idea of this poem, that Death takes men from all 'estates' (17), connects it with the Dance of Death, on which see J. M. Clark *The Dance of Death* (Glasgow, Jackson 1950). Lydgate's *Dance of Death* was a famous literary expression of the theme, probably known to Dunbar (*n.* to 39). The catalogue of members of the 'faculty' of poetry in the latter part of the poem (49–92) also recalls the *ubi sunt* tradition (see No. 23 above, lines 65–96 and *n.*), where individual dead are listed. The absence here of any consoling reference to poets' immortality through their verse marks D.'s treatment as essentially medieval, and remote from the ideas of classical humanism. On ME death-literature generally, see Woolf *Lyric* Ch. 3 and Gray Ch. 10. Parallels with Villon simply illustrate the international currency of death themes: see J. M. Smith *The French Background of Middle Scots Literature* (Edinburgh, Oliver and Boyd 1934) 69–74.

Metre Stanzas of four four-foot lines rhyming *aabb*, with refrain – a form used several times by D., e.g. in No. 35 below. The use of a familiar liturgical text as refrain is common in ME religious lyric (cf. Nos. 36 and 37). There are several other poems, including one by Lydgate, in which the present refrain occurs: see *n.* to 4.

Text The earliest authority is a print (also containing No. 38) of unknown date and provenance, but probably Scottish, *c.*1508: facsimile and discussion in W. Beattie, ed. *The Chepman and Myllar Prints*, Edinburgh Bibliog. Soc. (1950). The present text is based on this print (=*P*), with variants from the two much later MSS: Bannatyne MS., N.L.S. MS. Advocates' 1.1.6 (=*B*), and Maitland MS., Magdalene Coll. Cambridge MS. Pepys 2553 (=*M*).

Title All three authorities ascribe the poem to D., the print as follows: 'quod Dunbar when he wes sek etc.' The title 'Lament for the Deth of the Makaris', devised by Lord Hailes in 1770, somewhat misrepresents the poem, which laments the death of everyone.

Date Between the death of 'Stobo' in 1505 (line 86) and the print of *c.*1508: a period when sickness was rife in Edinburgh. Dunbar lived for at least another five years, however.

The Catalogue of Poets (49–92) D. begins with Chaucer, Lydgate ('Monk of Bury') and Gower, generally regarded as the great originators by C15 and C16 poets. He then turns to 'this country' (55) and lists 21 Scottish poets. Five of these remain mere names: 'Heryot' (54), 'James Afflek' (58), 'Clerk of Tranent' (65), 'Sandy Traill' (69), and 'Roull of Aberdene' (77). The rest, in D.'s order (not consistently chronological), are as follows: Sir Hugh of Eglinton (d. 1377), not known as a poet (53); Andrew of Wyntoun, Prior of Lochleven until 1422, author of *Oryginale Chronykil of Scotland* (54); John Clerk, possible author of several poems ascribed in *B* to 'Clerk' (58); Sir Richard Holland (*c.*1420–*c.*1490), author of *Buke of the Howlat* (61); John Barbour, Archdeacon of Aberdeen (d. 1395), author of *The Bruce* (61); Sir Mungo Lockhart of the Lee (d. 1489 ?), a Lanarkshire knight not known for poetry (63); Sir Gilbert Hay, C15 translator of an Alexander romance (67); Blind Harry (*c.*1440–*c.*1492), author of *The Wallace* (69); Patrick Johnston (d. 1494/5), playwright (71); Mersar, whose name appears under three poems in *B* (73); Roull of Corstorphin, possible author of 'The Cursing of Sir John Rowlis upon the Steilaris of his Fowlis' in *M* and *B* (78); Robert Henryson, see above Nos. 30, 31 (82); Sir John the Ross of Montgreenan (d. 1493/4: see M. P. McDiarmid, *SHR* 33 (1954) 50, 88), not known for poetry, but named by D. as his second in his *Flyting* with Kennedy (83); John Reid, alias 'Stobo' (d. 1505), royal secretary, colleague and friend of D., poems unidentified (86); Quintin Shaw, author of a poem in *M*, still alive in 1504 (86); Walter Kennedy (*c.*1460–*c.*1508), D.'s adversary in the *Flyting*, author of several poems in *M* and *B* (89). For further biographical details, see Baxter *William Dunbar* App. 5.

I that in heill wes and glaidness
Am trublit now with gret seikness
And feblit with infermité;
Timor mortis conturbat me.

1 heill health.

3–13 Cf. Lydgate *Testament* 197–208 (*Minor Poems* ed. MacCracken EETS e.s. 107 p. 336), a passage which combines references to the poet's 'infirmity', the frailty of the flesh (cf. 7), the cunning malice of the Devil (7) and the mutability of things (9–11). [*See further note on facing page*]

Our plesance heir is all vane glory,
This fals warld is bot transitory,
The flesh is bruckle, the fend is slee;
Timor mortis conturbat me.

The stait of man dois change and vary,
Now sound, now seik, now blith, now sary,
Now dansand mirry, now like to dee;
Timor mortis conturbat me.

No stait in erd heir standis sickir;
As with the wind wavis the wickir,
Wavis this warldis vanité;
Timor mortis conturbat me.

On to the deid gois all estates,
Princis, prelotes and potestates,
Baith riche and pure of all degré;
Timor mortis conturbat me.

He takes the knichtis in to feild,
Anarmit under helm and sheild;
Victour he is at all mellé;
Timor mortis conturbat me.

4 The refrain, like those of Nos. 36 and 37, comes from the Liturgy – here, the Office of the Dead: 'Fear of death troubles me.' The phrase occurs commonly in death-literature and epitaphs. Lydgate used it as refrain for a lyric (*Minor Poems* ed. MacCracken EETS o.s. 192 pp. 828–32), as did other poets: Woolf *Lyric* 333–6.

7 bruckle brittle, frail. **slee** sly.

10 sary sad.

11 like to dee on the point of death.

13 erd earth. **sickir** sure.

14 wickir branch of willow. Imitated by Burns, *Poem on Life* 15–7: 'flickering, feeble, and unsicker . . . Ay wavering like the willow wicker.'

15 Wavis] So wannis *B*; Swa waveris *M*. But the reversed foot (/ x) gives a stronger opening.

17 deid death. **estates** The emphasis in 17–47 on all 'estates' (orders) of society suffering death connects this part of the poem with the Dance of Death. See headnote.

18 potestates lords.

21 in to in (the).

22 Anarmit armed.

23 at all mellé in every fight.

That strang unmerciful tirand
Takes on the moders breist sowkand
The bab full of benignité;
Timor mortis conturbat me.

He takes the campioun in the stour,
The capitane closit in the tour,
The lady in bour full of bewté;
Timor mortis conturbat me.

He spares no lord for his piscence
Na clerk for his intelligence;
His awful strak may no man flee;
Timor mortis conturbat me.

Art-magicians and astrologs,
Rhetors, logicians and theologs,
Thame helpis no conclusions slee;
Timor mortis conturbat me.

In medecine the most practicians,
Lechis, surrigians and phisicians,
Thame self fra deid may not supplé;
Timor mortis conturbat me.

26 Takes] Tak *P.* **sowkand** sucking.

27 benignité graciousness, meekness.

29–31 Fox *Chaucer and Chaucerians* 185 notes the 'logical progression' of this stanza, from the danger of the battlefield, to the warlike security of the castle, to the peacetime security of the lady's bower.

29 campion champion. **stour** battle.

33 piscence puissance, power.

34 clerk The term included all educated men capable of practising learned arts such as those specified in the next stanza.

35 strak stroke.

37 Art-magicians men skilled in the arts of magic. **astrologs** astrologers.

38 Rhetoric and logic formed, with grammar, the trivium on which medieval schooling was based.

39 'No subtle reasonings will help them.' Nichols compares Lydgate's *Dance of Death*, where Death says to the Tregetour (Illusionist): 'Nought may availe all thy conclusions' (ed. Hammond, line 518).

41 most greatest (or ironical: 'majority of'?).

42 Lechis physicians. **surrigians** surgeons. The power of Death even over physicians is noted in *R. de la Rose* 15927–34.

43 'Cannot deliver themselves from Death.'

I see that makers amang the laif
Plays heir their pageant, syne gois to graif;
Sparit is nocht their faculté;
Timor mortis conturbat me.

He has done petuously devour
The noble Chaucer, of makers flour,
The Monk of Bery and Gower, all three;
Timor mortis conturbat me.

The gude Sir Hew of Eglintoun,
And eik Heryot, and Wyntoun,
He hes tane out of this cuntré;
Timor mortis conturbat me.

That scorpioun fell hes done infek
Maister John Clerk and James Afflek
Fra ballat making and trigidé;
Timor mortis conturbat me.

Holland and Barbour he hes berevit;
Allace, that he nocht with us levit
Sir Mungo Lokert of the Lee;
Timor mortis conturbat me.

45 makers poets. **laif** rest.
46 'Act their piece here, then go to the grave.' Alluding to dramatic productions (miracle plays, civic shows to welcome royal visitors, etc.) in which 'pageants' were separately undertaken by various crafts.
47 faculté profession, occupation.
49–92 On the poets mentioned here, see headnote 'The Catalogue of Poets'.
49 'He has devoured in pitiable fashion.'
50 The pageant of dead poets begins precisely half way through the 100-line poem. On the use of mathematical centres in Renaissance poems, see A. D. S. Fowler *Triumphal Forms* (Cambridge U.P. 1970).
54 And eik *P* reads 'Et eik', *et* being used for *and* in *P* generally, presumably as a result of foreign printers expanding *&*. The readings 'Ettrik' (*B*) and 'Etrik' (*M*) apparently arose from misunderstanding the early print, though Ettrick (the place in Selkirk) provides a possible epithet. Nothing is known of 'Heryot'.
55 'This country' marks the transition from England to Scotland.
57 'That cruel scorpion has poisoned.' Death has a 'sting': *1 Cor.* 15.55.
58 Affleck phonetic spelling of the name customarily spelled 'Auchinleck'. *M* reads 'auchinlek'.
59 ballat song. **trigidé** Chaucer calls *Troilus* a 'tragedy' because it ends unhappily. The term does not necessarily imply dramatic form; but cf. No. 34 line 5.
61 berevit taken away by force.

Clerk of Tranent eik he hes tane,
That maid the Anteris of Gawane;
Sir Gilbert Hay endit hes he;
Timor mortis conturbat me.

He hes Blind Hary and Sandy Traill
Slain with his shour of mortal haill,
Whilk Patrick Johnestoun might nocht flee;
Timor mortis conturbat me.

He hes reft Merseir his endite
That did in luf so lifly write,
So short, so quick, of sentence hie;
Timor mortis conturbat me.

He hes tane Roull of Aberdene
And gentil Roull of Corstorphin;
Two bettir fallows did no man see;
Timor mortis conturbat me.

In Dumfermelyne he hes done roun
With Maister Robert Henrisoun;
Sir John the Ros enbrast hes he;
Timor mortis conturbat me.

He hes now tane last of aw
Gud gentil Stobo and Quintyne Shaw,
Of wham all wichtis hes peté;
Timor mortis conturbat me.

65 Clerk] The clerk *M*.
66 Anteris Adventures. Referring to an unidentified Gawain romance.
67 Hay] gray *B*.
70 his shour] his schot *B*; the schour *M*. God uses hail to kill people in the O.T.: *Exod.* 9.25, *Josh.* 10.11.
73 'He has deprived Merseir of his powers of composition.'
74 lifly vividly.
75 In praising the conciseness, energy and nobility of Merseir's love poetry, Dunbar recalls Chaucer's description of the Clerk of Oxford's speech: 'short and quick and full of hy sentence' (*C.T.* I 306). **quick** vigorous, lively.
79 fallows fellows, companions.
81 done roun had a whispered conversation. *Roune* is a verb (cf. 49, 57), corresponding to *round* 'whisper' in Elizabethan English. *B* reads 'tane broun' (a poet called Brown?).
83 enbrast embraced. The gentle approaches of Death in this stanza resemble No. 34, lines 31–5.
85 aw all.
87 'Whom everyone is sorry to lose.'

Gud Maister Walter Kennedy
In point of deid lyis veraly;
Gret reuth it wer that so suld be;
Timor mortis conturbat me.

Sen he hes all my brether tane,
He will nocht lat me lif alane;
On forse I man his next pray be;
Timor mortis conturbat me.

Sen for the deid remeid is none,
Best is that we for deid dispone,
Eftir our deid that lif may we;
Timor mortis conturbat me.

91 so suld be it should be so (*M* reads 'he suld de').
93 brether brethren.
95 'Of necessity I must be his next victim.'
97 remeid remedy.
98 dispone make our dispositions.

34 Meditatioun in Wyntir

Editors classify the *Meditatioun* under 'Personal' rather than 'Moralizings', and rightly. The personifications who 'assay' the poet suggest a morality play; but Patience and Prudence, who might have provided a moral conclusion, take their place in the middle of the poem among other causes of depression; and the poem ends only with the hope of Spring. See the masterly analysis in *TLS* (1958) 208.
Metre Stanzas of five 4-foot lines, rhyming *aabba*, used elsewhere by D., e.g. *On his Heid-Ake*, deriving from the 'cinquain' of Fr. poets.
Text The only two copies are in the Maitland MS., Magdalene Coll. Cambridge MS. Pepys 2553 (copied 1570–85). The first copy (= *M1*) occurs on p. 3 of an earlier MS. fragment now part of the Maitland MS., and lacks lines 1–22 by loss of leaf. The second copy (= *M2*), on pp. 318–19 of Maitland, provides the present text. The MS. ascribes the poem to D., but gives no title. The title is C18.

In to thir dirk and drubly days
Whone sabil all the hevin arrays

1–10 There is a similar matching of season and poetic mood at the opening of Henryson's *Testament*, where the 'dooly season' of winter corresponds to the tragic tale of Cresseid (lines 1–2). Hoccleve claims to have composed his *Complaint* in late November: No. 22 above, lines 1–35.
1 'In these dark and cloudy days.'
2 Whone when. **sabil** sable, black (a favourite poetic epithet in Dunbar).

With misty vapours, cluds and skys,
Nature all curage me denys
Of sangis, ballats and of plays.

Whone that the nicht dois lenthin hours
With wind, with hail and havy shours,
My duly spreit dois lurk for shoir;
My hairt for languor dois forloir
For laik of simmer with his flours.

I wake, I turn, sleip may I nocht,
I vexit am with havy thocht;
This warld all owir I cast about,
And ay the mair I am in dout
The mair that I remeid have socht.

I am assayit on every side:
Despair says ay, 'In time provide,
And get som thing whairon to leif,
Or with grit trouble and mischeif
Thou sall in to this court abide.'

Than Patience says, 'Be not agast;
Hald hoip and treuth within thee fast,

3 skys clouds.
4–5 curage . . . Of heart for.
5 ballats songs. **plays** There was much theatrical entertainment at the Scottish court (pageants, 'mummings', etc.). D. is not necessarily referring to his own compositions, but to the indoor amusements of winter.
6 Autumn, when nights grow longer, was the season when the humour melancholy gathered strength in the body, according to medical authorities: Klibansky Ch. 1, and No. 22 above, *n.* to lines 1–9.
8 'My dismal spirit cowers under the threat.' **duly** (dule MS.) represents *DOST Doly* adj. **shoir** is *OED Shore* sb.^{2}.
9 languor misery. **dois forloir** is lost (*DOST Forlore* v.).
10 simmer summer.
13 owir over (monosyllabic). **cast about** consider.
14 mair more. **dout** anxiety.
15 remeid a remedy.
16–40 The conception of the poet assailed on every side by allegorical figures suggests the morality plays. Dunbar has his own private 'play' inside his head.
16 assayit put to the test, assailed (*DOST Assay* v. 1 and 3).
18 leif live.
19 mischeif hardship.
20 in to in. **court** i.e. the royal court of James IV of Scotland.
22 hoip hope.

And lat Fortoun wirk furth hir rage;
Whone that no rasoun may assuage,
Whill that hir glass be run and past.'

And Prudence in my eir says ay:
'Why wald thou hald that will away,
Or craif that thou may have no space,
Thou tending to ane uther place,
A journay going every day?'

And than says Age, 'My freind, com neir
And be not strange, I thee requeir;
Com, brodir, by the hand me tak;
Remember thou hes compt to mak
Of all thy time thou spendit heir.'

Syne Deid casts up his yettis wide,
Saying, 'Thir oppin sall thee abide;
Albeid that thou were never sa stout,
Undir this lintal sall thou lout:
Thair is nane uther way beside.'

For feir of this all day I droup;
No gold in kist, nor wine in coup,

23–5 'And let Fortune work off her violence, when there is no reasonable way of mitigating it, until . . .' Mackenzie emends *M2 Quhone* (*M1 quhen*, Craigie) to *Quhome*; but 'when' makes as good sense as 'whom'.
25 glass hourglass, an attribute of Time, not Fortune. The idea is that Fortune's time eventually runs out.
27 Proverbial: Whiting H413, citing *Troilus* 4.1628: 'For who may holde a thing that woll away?'
28 'Or crave that which thou canst not keep for any length of time' (Kinsley).
30 journay Specifically, a day's journey (Fr. *jour*-).
31–5 Age (rather than Death) here evokes memories of the Dance of Death. 'No one knows better than Dunbar how to touch a personification into life' (C. S. Lewis).
32 'And do not act like a stranger, I beg you.'
34 compt an account (*M1 ane compt*). The rendering of accounts (*Rom.* 14.12) is a key image in the death-play *Everyman*.
36 'Then Death throws his gates wide open.' Cf. No. 12, line 615 and *n*.
37 'Saying "These will remain open for you".'
38 Albeid although. **stout** strong.
39 lintal lintel. **lout** stoop. The idea of the grave as a low house, with the roof pressing down on a man's nose etc., is common in lyrics on death: Woolf *Lyric* 84.
41 droup am dejected.
42 kist treasure-chest. **coup** goblet.

No ladeis bewty, nor luiffis bliss,
May lat me to remember this,
How glaid that ever I dine or soup.

Yit whone the nicht begins to short
It dois my spreit som part confort,
Of thocht oppressit with the shours.
Com, lusty simmer, with thy flours,
That I may leif in som disport.

44 lat prevent.
45 soup sup.
46 Cf. 6. According to medical authorities, 'autumn-engendered pains would be relieved by spring'. Spring, being 'warm and moist', reduced the strength of the 'cold and dry' humour melancholy: Klibansky 9.
50 disport pleasure.

35 All Erdly Joy Returns in Pane

This poem is a stripped-down version of a favourite type of moral poem, opening like a *chanson d'aventure* (see headnote to No. 38 below) with the poet coming upon a moralizing speaker in a wood or other country setting. The moralist is a bird in several other ME lyrics: Brown *XIVth-Century Religious Lyrics* Nos. 117 and 121, and Greene *Carols* Nos. 370, 378, 389. Bird-narrators also occur in continental *chansons d'aventure*.
Metre Same as in No. 33 above.
Text Two MSS: Bannatyne MS., N.L.S. MS. Advocates' 1.1.6 (= *B*), where the poem occurs, with ascription to D., in the section of the MS. devoted to 'verry singular ballatis full of wisdome and moralitie'; and Maitland MS., Magdalene Coll. Cambridge MS. Pepys 2553 (= *M*). The present text is based on *B*.

Of Lentren in the first morning,
Airly as did the day up spring,
Thus sang ane bird with voce upplane:
'All erdly joy returns in pane.

1 Lentren Lent, season of penance and birdsong.
3 upplane] out plane *M*. *B*'s reading has been taken as a form of *upland* 'rustic, unpolished'; but *DOST* will take *up-* as reinforcing *plane*: 'very loudly, very clearly'.
4 erdly earthly. **returns in** changes into (*OED* s.v. *Return* v. 4d).

'O man, haif mind that thou mon pas,
Remembir that thou art bot as
And sall in as revert agane:
All erdly joy returns in pane.

'Haif mind that eild follows youth,
Deth follows life with gaipand mouth
Devoring fruct and flouring grane:
All erdly joy returns in pane.

'Welth, wardly gloir and rich array
Are all bot thorns laid in thy way
Owrcoverd with flours laid in ane trane:
All erdly joy returns in pane.

'Com nevir yit May so fresh and grene,
Bot Januar com als wood and kene;
Wes nevir sic drouth bot anis com rane:
All erdly joy returns in pane.

'Evirmair unto this warldis joy
As nerrest heir succeidis noy;
Thairfoir, when joy ma nocht remane,
His verry heir succeidis pane.

'Heir helth returnis in seikness,
And mirth returns in haviness,
Toun in desert, forest in plane:
All erdly joy returns in pane.

5 mon must.
6 as ashes.
7 revert] *M*; return *B*. *B* anticipates 8. Dunbar is recalling *Gen.* 3.19: 'Quia pulvis es, et in pulverem *reverteris*' ('For dust thou art, and into dust thou shalt return'). Cf. poem No. 74 in Mackenzie's edition.
8 erdly Here and at 12, 16, 20, 28, 32, and 40, *M* reads *warldlie*.
9 eild Age.
11 grane grain, seed.
13 gloir glory.
14 laid] *M* omits.
15 Owrcoverd covered over. **in ane trane** as a snare. Cf. the imagery in Henryson, No. 31.1, line 235.
18 als wood as furious.
19 'There was never such a drought but that rain came at some time.'
22 'Trouble succeeds as the nearest heir.'
23 ma may.
24 verry true.
26 haviness dreariness.
27 plane open country.

'Fredom returns in wrechitness,
And treuth returns in doubilness
With fenyeit words to mak men fane:
All erdly joy returns in pane.

'Vertew returnis in to vice,
And honour in to avarice;
With cuvatice is consciens slane:
All erdly joy returns in pane.

'Sen erdly joy abidis nevir,
Wirk for the joy that lestis evir,
For uder joy is all bot vane:
All erdly joy returns in pane.'

31 fenyeit feigned. **fane** happy.
35 cuvatice covetousness.
37 Sen since. The turn of this stanza resembles that of the last stanza in No. 33.

36 Of the Nativitie of Christ

This exultant hymn of joy at the Nativity draws chiefly on liturgical sources: see *nn.* to 1, 8, 9–10, 10, 12, 25 f., 33 f., 53. The anonymous critic in *TLS* (1958) 208, in the best discussion of the poem, calls it 'a poetic expansion of the triumphant words from *Psalm* 95, spoken at the Offertory of the first Mass on Christmas Day: "Laetentur coeli, et exultet terra ante faciem domini: quoniam venit" ["Let the heavens rejoice, and let the earth be glad before the face of the Lord, because he cometh"]'. Woolf *Lyric* 306–7 stresses the influence of the *Te Deum* (comparing carols where *Te Deum* is used to celebrate the Nativity). The poem belongs to a common type of ME religious lyric that uses a familiar liturgical text as refrain: cf. Nos. 33 and 37.
Metre The rhyme scheme is that of the '*Monk's Tale* stanza' (*ababbcbc*); but the use of a 4-foot line, instead of the more usual 5-foot line (as in No. 37), helps to make the poem less weighty and more rapid.
Text One MS. only: Bannatyne MS., N.L.S. MS. Advocates' 1.1.6, with ascription to Dunbar. The title is C18.

Rorate coeli desuper,
Hevins distill your balmy shours,

1 'Drop down dew, ye heavens, from above: [and let the clouds rain the just. Let the earth be opened and bud forth a saviour]', *Isa.* 45.8, words repeated at Vespers throughout Advent as a prophecy of Christ's birth: cf. No. 25.5 above. 'Unlike the personal Nativity poems of Donne and Crashaw, Dunbar's is a public act of worship, and it is fitting that it should open with words which everyone in his audience would recognize', *TLS* (1958) 208.

For now is risin the bricht day ster
Fro the rose Mary, flour of flours;
The cleir sone whom no clud devours,
Surmunting Phebus in the est,
Is comin of his hevinly tours,
Et nobis Puer natus est.

Archangels, angels and dompnations,
Trones, potestates and marteirs seir,
And all ye hevinly operations,
Ster, planeit, firmament and speir,
Fire, erd, air and watter cleir,
To him gife loving most and lest,
That com in to so meik maneir,
Et nobis Puer natus est.

3–4 The connection between dew and daybreak perhaps prompted the image of Christ as day-star: 'I am the root and stock of David, the bright and morning star', *Rev.* 22.16. This passage in turn may have suggested D.'s bold combination of star and plant imagery.
4 rose a traditional epithet for Mary, deriving from *Ecclesiasticus* 24.18: 'I was exalted . . . as a rose plant in Jericho.' See Woolf *Lyric* 287–9. **flour of flours** Cf. Chaucer *ABC of Virgin* 4: 'Glorious virgine, of alle floures flour.'
5–7 The ancient image of Christ as rising sun ('Oriens ex alto' *Luke* 1.78) occurs in the Sarum Breviary immediately after *Rorate coeli*, in an antiphon for Vespers on the Second Sunday of Advent: 'Orietur sicut sol Salvator mundi' ('The saviour of the world will arise like the sun').
5 clud cloud.
7 Is comin has come. **tours** towers.
8 'Puer natus est nobis' ('Unto us a Son is born', cf. *Isa.* 9.6) was part of the Introit of the Great Mass on Christmas Day.
9–10 Archangels, angels, dominations, thrones and powers were 5 of the 9 orders of heavenly beings. *TLS* (1958) 208 cites the Preface to the Mass used from Nativity to Epiphany: 'Et ideo cum Angelis et Archangelis, cum thronis et dominationibus, cumque omni militia caelestis exercitus, hymnum gloriae tuae canimus' ('And so with angels and archangels, with thrones and dominations, and with all the army of the heavenly host, we sing a hymn of thy glory'). There is a similar passage in the *Te Deum.*
10 marteirs seir various martyrs. Cf. *Te Deum*: 'The noble army of Martyrs praise thee.'
11 operations agencies.
12 In the outer 'firmament' are the fixed 'stars'; in each of the seven 'spheres', a 'planet'. Cf. the *Benedicite*: 'O ye Sun and Moon . . . O ye Stars of Heaven, bless ye the Lord.'
13 The four elements (*erd* earth).
14 gife loving give praise: *MED Loven* v.(2), distinct from modern *love*.
15 com in to came in.

[36] William Dunbar

Sinners be glaid and penance do
And thank your maker hairtfully,
For he that ye micht nocht come to
To you is comin full humly,
Your saulis with his blude to by
And lows you of the feinds arrest,
And only of his awin mercy
Pro nobis Puer natus est.

All clergy do to him incline
And bow unto that bairn bening,
And do your observance devine
To him that is of kingis king;
Ensence his altar, reid and sing
In haly kirk, with mind degest,
Him honouring attowr all thing
Qui nobis Puer natus est.

Celestial foulis in the air
Sing with your nottis upoun hicht,
In firthis and in forrests fair
Be mirthful now, at all your micht;
For passit is your dully nicht,
Aurora hes the cluddis perst,
The son is risin with glaidsom licht,
Et nobis Puer natus est.

18 hairtfully from your hearts.

22 lows release. **arrest** detention.

25 f. Cf. *Te Deum*: 'The holy Church throughout all the world doth acknowledge thee.'

26 bairn child. **bening** gracious (a regular ME form).

29 Ensence burn incense before.

30 degest grave, settled (literally 'digested').

31 attowr above.

33 f. Cf. *Benedicite*: 'O all ye Fowls of the Air, bless ye the Lord.'

34 nottis notes. **upoun hicht** on high, loudly.

35 firthis woods (poetic).

36 at all your micht as much as you can.

37–9 The association between birdsong and dawn brings back the imagery of the first stanza.

37 dully dismal.

38 Aurora Dawn. **perst** broken through ('pierced').

Now spring up, flouris, fra the rute,
Revert you upwart naturaly,
In honour of the blissit frute
That rais up fro the rose Mary;
Lay out your levis lustily,
Fro deid tak life now at the lest
In wirship of that prince wirthy
Qui nobis Puer natus est.

Sing, hevin imperial most of hicht,
Regions of air mak armony;
All fish in flude and foul of flicht
Be mirthful and mak melody;
And *Gloria in excelsis* cry,
Hevin, erd, see, man, bird and best:
He that is crounit abone the sky
Pro nobis Puer natus est.

42 Revert you reflexive: 'Of plants etc: To spring up afresh', *OED* s.v. *Revert* v. 1c. **naturaly** The natural movement upwards of plants (as against the more common downward direction of natural movement – e.g. falling stones) is here given a spiritual value.
43 blissit frute 'Blessed is the fruit of thy womb', *Luke* 1.42.
46 deid death. **at the lest** at last.
49 The highest heaven, where God dwells, is the 'empyreal' heaven, or heaven of fire: see *OED* s.v. *Empyreal* a. (citing forms spelled 'imperial', as here).
50 The 'regions of air' are below the moon, whose sphere is nearest the earth. D. recapitulates the theme of the four elements here.
53 ***Gloria in excelsis*** the angels' song at the Nativity ('Glory to God in the highest'), as used in the Missal.
55 abone above.

37 Of the Resurrection of Christ

A poem celebrating the triumph of Christ: cf. No. 29 above, and No. 39 in Gray *Selection*. Its 'exultant energy' (C. S. Lewis) derives from a rich variety of traditional images contained in a strictly patterned syntax (see *nn.* to 17–9 and 33–8). The refrain is a familiar liturgical text, as in Nos. 33 and 36.
Metre '*Monk's Tale* stanza' (eight 5-foot lines rhyming *ababbcbc*): 'Dunbar's most favoured form for short pieces of a heroic or festal character' (STS edn). Cf. here Nos 13, 23, 24.4 and 31.2 (*Moralitas*). K. James VI calls this 'Ballat Royal', judging it suitable for 'any heich and grave subjectis, specially drawin out of learnit authouris': *Treatise* (1584), ed. G. G. Smith *Elizabethan Critical Essays* (Oxford U.P. 1904) 1.222.
Text Like No. 36, one MS. only: Bannatyne MS., N.L.S. MS. Advocates' 1.1.6, with ascription to Dunbar. The title is C18.

[37] William Dunbar

Done is a battel on the dragon black,
Our campioun Christ confoundit hes his force;
The yets of hell are brokin with a crack,
The sign triumphal rasit is of the croce,
The divils trimmillis with hiddous voce,
The sauls are borrowit and to the bliss can go,
Christ with his blude our ransons dois indoce:
Surrexit Dominus de sepulchro.

Dungin is the deidly dragon Lucifer,
The crewel serpent with the mortal stang,
The auld kene tegir with his teith on char,
Whilk in a wait hes lyne for us so lang,
Thinking to grip us in his clowis strang;
The merciful lord wald nocht that it wer so,
He maid him forto failye of that fang:
Surrexit Dominus de sepulchro.

1 Cf. *Rev.* 20.2: 'And he laid hold on the dragon, the old serpent, which is the devil and Satan, and bound him for a thousand years.' The passage was understood to refer to the Harrowing of Hell by Christ, between Crucifixion and Resurrection, narrated in the apocryphal *Gospel of Nicodemus*. Cf. No. 11.2 above, where Langland describes Christ's battle with Satan. On the biblical and patristic idea of Christ the Conqueror (preserved in the Easter liturgy), see G. Aulén *Christus Victor* (London, S.P.C.K. 1931).
2 campioun champion.
3 yets gates. Cf. Langland, No. 11.2 above, line 260 and *n.* The present passage may also recall *Isa.* 45.2, 'I will break in pieces the gates of brass.'
4 croce cross: perhaps suggesting a banner raised on the battlements of a captured stronghold.
5 trimmillis tremble.
6 borrowit ransomed.
7 dois indoce endorses (*OED Endoss*). The image of a legal document or charter is often used in connection with the redemption: Woolf *Lyric* 210–14.
8 'The Lord has risen from the tomb': a phrase from the Easter liturgy, used also as first line of another Resurrection poem ascribed to Dunbar (STS edn No. 37).
9 Dungin knocked down.
10 stang sting: referring to the wound inflicted by the old serpent on mankind in Eden. Cf. *1 Cor.* 15.55–6.
11 'The fierce old tiger with his teeth ajar.' Biblical tigers (e.g. *Job* 4.11) are identified with the Devil in patristic sources cited by Hyde, *MLR* 51 (1956) 489.
12 'Which has lain in wait so long for us.'
15 'He caused him to fail in that capture.' **fang** 'taking'.

He for our saik that sufferit to be slane
And like a lamb in sacrifice wes dicht,
Is like a lion risin up agane
And as gyane raxit him on hicht;
Sprungin is Aurora radius and bricht,
On loft is gone the glorious Apollo,
The blisful day depairtit fro the nicht:
Surrexit Dominus de sepulchro.

The grit victour agane is risin on hicht
That for our querrel to the deth wes woundit;
The sone that wox all pail now shinis bricht,
And, dirkness clerit, our faith is now refoundit;
The knell of mercy fra the hevin is soundit,
The Cristin are deliverit of their wo,
The Jowis and their errour are confoundit:
Surrexit Dominus de sepulchro.

The fo is chasit, the battel is done ceis,
The preson brokin, the jevellours fleit and flemit;

17–9 The two relative clauses, postponing the main verb to line 19, create a special effect of sustained power in a poem where at the end of all other lines the sense is complete.
18 dicht prepared.
19 'When a lioness gives birth to her cubs, she brings them forth dead and lays them up lifeless for three days – until their father, coming on the third day, breathes in their faces and makes them alive. Just so did the Father Omnipotent raise Our Lord Jesus Christ from the dead on the third day. Quoth Jacob: "He shall sleep like a lion, and the lion's whelp shall be raised"': a C12 Bestiary trans. T. H. White as *The Book of Beasts* (Cape 1954) 8–9, citing *Gen.* 49.9.
20 'And has stretched himself on high like a giant.' Christ at the Harrowing is called a giant by Langland: No. 11.2 above, line 251 and *n*. The allusion is to Vulg. *Ps.* 18.6.
21–3 Cf. No. 36, lines 37–9.
21 radius radiant: an aureate term, first recorded here by *OED*.
22 On loft aloft.
23 depairted (is) separated.
26 querrel cause.
27 wox grew: alluding to the darkness at noon during the Crucifixion.
28 refoundit re-established.
29 'An allusion to the ringing of bells on Easter Sunday' (Kinsley). Cf. Langland, No. 11.2 above, line 424. *Knell* does not necessarily have funereal associations in early use.
33–8 The syntax shifts from a regular one subject per line to a regular two.
33 done ceis brought to an end.
34 jevellours gaolers. **fleit and flemit** scared away.

The weir is gon, confermit is the peis,
The fetters lowsit and the dungeoun temit,
The ransoun maid, the presoners redemit;
The feild is win, owrcomin is the fo,
Dispulit of the tresur that he yemit:
Surrexit Dominus de sepulchro.

35 weir war.
36 lowsit loosed. **temit** emptied.
38 owrcomin overcome.
39 Dispulit dispoiled. **yemit** guarded. Dragons guard treasure.

38 The Tretis of the Twa Mariit Wemen and the Wedo: extract

Structurally this poem follows the conventions of the French lyric type known as *chanson d'aventure*, in which a narrator sets out and encounters in some lonely place (near a wood, often) some person or persons whose speech he reports. See the fundamental study by H. E. Sandison, *The 'Chanson d'Aventure' in ME* (Bryn Mawr, Penn. 1913), with discussion of this poem (53–6). A relevant kind of *chanson d'aventure* is the *chanson de mal mariée*, where wives are overheard complaining about their husbands, as here. Sandison 13–14 cites one short French example quite close to D. It describes three wives, in a meadow, garlanded, one dressed in green for summer; the youngest still likes her husband, and gets scolded by the other two, who do not. Sandison 50–3 also refers to three other late medieval Scots examples, none very like D. The type is amplified by D. to 530 lines, in the manner of alliterative narrative verse, and enriched with anti-matrimonial material, much of it from Chaucer (especially *Wife of Bath's Prol.*, see *n.* to 50–145). The speeches of the three women display varieties of wife less clearly than varieties of husband (two old, one young, one middle-aged); but the poem ends with a conventional *question d'amour* addressed to male members of the audience: If you had to marry one of these three women, which would you choose?

The poem, with its explosively unstable mixture of outdoor romance and domestic reality, has been variously understood. J. Speirs *Scrutiny* 7 (1938) 56–68 sees it as a prime expression of D.'s exuberant delight in 'nature and instinct'; and A. D. Hope *A Midsummer Eve's Dream* (Edinburgh, Oliver and Boyd 1970) suggests relationships with the sexual mores and fairy beliefs of old Scotland. J. Leyerle *UTQ* 31 (1962) 316–38 and P. Bawcutt *Robbins Studies* 196–9 see in the poem a 'scarification of women' and an exposé of an 'unnatural perverted state of affairs'. So also J. Kinsley *Med. Aev.* 23 (1954) 31–5: Dunbar 'draws a satirical contrast between [the women's] superficial beauty and delicacy, and their essential coarseness and corruption'. But C. S. Lewis stresses the 'sheer preposterousness' of the poem: 'it is no nearer to real "satire on women" than the impossibly red nose of an old-fashioned comedian is to real satire on drunkenness' (*English Literature in C16*, 94). The introduc-

tion of the women's coarseness within the delicately courtly setting seems to subvert neither courtliness nor women. The effect is one of burlesque gaiety and carnival, rather than one of satire. This is often the case with medieval 'parody': see P. Zumthor *Essai de poétique médiévale* (Paris 1972) 104–5.
Metre and style D. employs unrhymed alliterative lines (a rarity in Scotland, whose poets preferred alliterative verse rhymed in stanzas), correctly alliterated (70 per cent alliterate *aaax*), with many lines linked by common alliteration (1–2, 5–6, 7–8, 9–10, 11–14 etc.). See Introd. p. xxii. Scottish poets tended to use alliterative verse for burlesque or low purposes: James VI calls it 'Tumbling verse for flyting' (i.e. invective) in his *Treatise* (1584), ed. G. G. Smith *Elizabethan Critical Essays* (Oxford U.P. 1904) 1.218. See W. Craigie 'The Scottish alliterative poems' *PBA* 28 (1942) 217–36. But the form was also associated traditionally with romance and lavish descriptions. D. exploits both potentialities: compare e.g. the high style of 17 ff. with the low 'flyting' style of 89 ff. See Leyerle's article (above). Bawcutt (above) points out that the low style is marked here by pervasive animal imagery.
Text The earliest authority is a print (also containing No. 33, see headnote there) of unknown date and provenance, but probably Scottish, *c.*1508. The poem also appears in the Maitland MS., Magdalene Coll. Cambridge MS. Pepys 2553. The present text is based on Maitland (= *M*) for lines 1–103, which are lacking in the print by loss of two leaves, and thereafter on the print (= *P*). The title is as in *M*. Both authorities ascribe the poem to Dunbar, whose longest surviving work it is.

Lines 1–149

Apon the midsummer evin, mirriest of nichtis,
I muvit furth till ane meid, as midnicht wes past,
Beside ane gudly grene garth full of gay flouris,
Hegit of ane huge hicht with hawthorn treis,
Whairon ane bird on ane branch so birst out hir notis
That never ane blithfuller bird was on the beuch hard.
What throw the sugarat sound of hir sang glaid

1–40 On the *chanson d'aventure* opening, see headnote.
1 midsummer evin the night of 23–24 June, a time of revelry and licence: see A. K. Moore *ES* 32 (1951) 56–62 and Hope 15–16. The prescribed revelries came to a head at midnight, which is past when the poem opens (2). The narrator and the women are presumably relaxing afterwards.
2 till ane meid] allane meid MS. (reinked). Editors have emended MS. *meid* 'meadow' to *neir* 'near', giving weak sense and a light first half-line. *meid* alliterates, and line 514 refers to 'the meid'.
3 garth garden.
4 'Hedged to a great height . . .' The narrator in Henryson's *Preiching* (No. 31.1 above) also lurks under a hawthorn hedge: see 108 there (and *n.*).
6 beuch bough. **hard** heard.
7 What throw what with. **sugarat** a Latinized form (Med. Lat. *sugaratus*) of *sugared*, a term used by Lydgate in the sense 'mellifluous': see *OED* s.v. *Sugared* 2c.

And throw the savour sanative of the sweit flouris,
I drew in dern to the dyk to dirkin eftir mirthis.
The dew donkit the dail, and dinnit the foulis.
I hard under ane holin hevinly grene hewit
Ane hie speich at my hand with hautand wordis.
With that in haist to the hege so hard I inthrang
That I was heildit with hawthorn and with heind levis.
Throw pikis of the plet thorn I presandly luikit,
Gif ony persoun wald approche within that plesand gardin.
I saw three gay ladeis sit in ane grene arbeir,
All grathit in to garlandis of fresh gudly flouris:
So glitterit as the gold wer their glorious gilt tressis,
Whill all the gressis did gleme of the glaid hewis;
Kemmit was their cleir hair and curiously shed,
Attowr their shulderis doun shire shining full bricht,
With curches cassin there abone of kirsp cleir and thin.

8 sanative healing. The old belief in the healing power of scented flowers is still to be observed in hospitals.
9 'I made my way in secret to the wall to get entertainment without being seen.' **dirkin** lie hidden: see *DOST* s.v.
10 'The dew made the dale damp, and the birds clamoured.' Awkwardly introduced here. The references to dew and mass birdsong (as against the single nightbird of 5) would fit better in the dawn scene at the end of the poem (512–22). The line may have been misplaced.
11 holin holly tree: presumably referring to the 'green arbour' (17) under which the ladies sit. **hewit** hued.
12 hautand haughty.
13 inthrang pressed in.
14 heildit concealed. **heind** pleasant.
15 pikis prickles. **plet** plaited, intertwined. **presandly** at once.
17–29 The description of the ladies, with yellow hair in garlands, green mantles, and pink and white complexions, is a conventional courtly portrayal of damsels *en fête* (cf. e.g. Dunbar's *Goldyn Targe* 58–63). Its conventionality prepares for the burlesque joke of their incongruous frankness.
17 arbeir arbour.
18 grathit in to arrayed in.
19 wer wire. A favourite Lydgate simile, found also in Henryson (*Testament* 177).
20 Whill until, so that. **gressis** grass.
21 Kemmit combed. **curiously shed** carefully parted.
22 Hope 10–12, observing that married women and widows did not normally wear their hair down, concludes that these are fairies, or women pretending to be fairies. But the hair style matches the style of conversation: in both the women emancipate themselves from their everyday roles. **Attowr** over. **shire** bright.
23 'With kerchiefs thrown over (i.e. over their hair) of transparent and delicate fabric (*kirsp*).' Cf. 138 below.

Their mantillis grene war as the gress that grew in May sesoun,
Fetrit with their white fingeris about their fair sidis.
Of ferliful fine favour war their faces meik
All full of flurist fairheid as flouris in June,
White, seimly and soft, as the sweit lillies
New upspred upon spray, as new spinist rose;
Arrayit ryally about with mony rich vardour,
That nature full nobilly annamalit with flouris
Of alkin hewis under hevin that ony heind knew,
Fragrant, all full of fresh odour finest of smell.
Ane cumly tabil coverit wes befoir tha cleir ladeis,
With ryal coupis apon rawis full of rich winis.
And of thir wlonkes whit, twa weddit war with lordis,
Ane was ane wedow, ywis, wantoun of laitis.
And as they talk at the tabil of mony tail sindry,
They wauchtit at the wicht wine and waris out wordis,

25 Fetrit fastened.

26 ferliful wonderfully. **favour** appearance.

27 flurist blossoming.

28-38 From here to the bottom of the leaf in *M*, staining and fading spreads increasingly from the left margin, especially after line 34.

29 spray stalk. **spinist** opened out, blown (*OED* s.v. *Spanish* v.[1]). The second simile is introduced abruptly; but the blending of white and red, lily and rose, in a beautiful face was familiar.

30–3 The ladies are surrounded by the June flowers which they resemble.

30 vardour verdure.

31 annamalit enamelled, inlaid, adorned. An early example of a poeticism common in early modern poetry: see *OED* s.v. *Enamel* sb. 4, v. 1c.

32 alkin all kinds of. **heind** gentle, or courteous, person.

34 coverit wes was laid with a cloth. **tha** those. **cleir** fair.

35 coupis goblets. **apon rawis** in rows.

36 thir these. **wlonkes** noble creatures. Craigie reports 'fair wlonkes' as the reading of *M*; but there is no room for *fair*. *thir* is apparently followed by a deletion. **whit** white (cf. 28). *M* reads *with*, understood by editors as a preposition, and generally omitted. But forms like *whith* and *wytht* are recorded for 'white' by *OED* in this period.

37 ywis certainly. **wantoun of laitis** wanton in her behaviour. The ambiguity of *wanton* ('sportive' or 'lewd') is deliberate.

38 tail topic of conversation. **sindry** sundry (MS. reading uncertain).

39 'They knocked back the strong wine, and speak freely'. *waucht* (*OED* s.v. *Waught*) implies large draughts. *waris out* means literally 'spend freely', implying thoughtless chatter, in contrast to the more serious discussion introduced in the next line.

And syne they spak more spedely and sparit no materis.
 'Bewry,' said the wedow, 'ye woddit wemen ying,
What mirth ye fand in mariage sen ye war mennis wifis:
Reveil gif ye rewit that rackless conditioun,
Or gif that ever ye lufit leid upon life mair
Nor thame that ye your faith hes festinit for ever,
Or gif ye think, had ye chois, that ye wald cheis better?
Think ye it nocht ane blist band that bindis so fast
That none undo it a deil may bot the deith ane?'
 Than spak ane lusty belife with lusty effeiris:
'It that ye call the blist band that bindis so fast
Is bair of bliss and bailful and greit barrat wirkis.
Ye speir, had I free chois, gif I wald cheis better.
Chenyeis ay are to eschew, and changeis are sweit:
Sic cursit chance till eschew had I my chois anis,
Out of the chenyeis of ane churl I chaip suld for ever.
God gif matrimony wer made to mell for ane yeir!
It war bot merrens to be mair, bot gif our mindis pleisit.

40 syne afterwards. **spedely** to the purpose. After this line, *M* has a heading: 'Aude viduam iam cum interrogatione sua' ('Hear now the widow and her question').
41 Bewry make known. **woddit** wedded.
42 sen since.
43 rewit rued, regretted. **rackless** 'reckless', ill-advised.
44 leid upon life living man.
45 Nor than. **that** i.e. to whom.
46 cheis choose.
47 blist blessed.
48 'That nothing can unfasten it even a little, except only death.' After this line, *M* has a heading: 'Responsio primae uxoris ad viduam' ('The reply of the first wife to the widow').
49 ane lusty one merry (woman). A proposed emendation to *lufly* here avoids the repetition. **belife** at once. **effeiris** bearing.
50–145 The first wife's account of her life with her old husband owes much to Chaucer, esp. *Wife of Bath's Prol.* and *Merchant's T*: see *nn.* to 53, 70–5, 81–8, 89–145, 94–5, 131–44.
51 'Is completely lacking in joy, and quite miserable, and causes great distress.'
52 speir ask.
53 Chenyeis chains. The image of the chains of marriage is Chaucerian (*Envoy to Bukton* 9), but not the jingle with 'changes' **to eschew** to be escaped from.
54 'If I was once free to escape from such an accursed fate.'
55 chaip escape.
56 God gif God grant. **mell** have sexual intercourse.
57 'It would be just a nuisance for it to last longer, unless we felt like it.' See *DOST* s.v. *Merrans* n.

It is agane the law of lufe, of kind and of nature,
Togidder hartis to strene that strivis with uther.
Birdis hes ane better law na bernis, by meikil,
That ilk yeir with new joy joyis ane maik,
And fangis thame ane fresh feir, unfulyit and constant,
And lattis their fulyit feiris flie whair they pleis.
Crist gif sic ane consuetude war in this kith haldin!
Than weill war us wemen that ever we war born!
We suld have feiris as fresh to fang when us likit,
And gif all larberis their levis when they lack curage.
My self suld be full seimly in silkis arrayit,
Gimp, joly and gent, richt joyous and gentil.
I suld at fairis be found, new facis to see,
At playis and at preichingis and pilgrimages greit,

58 kind synonymous with *nature*. Cf. No. 8 above, line 259. Men living under the Law of Nature, before the Old Law was revealed to Moses, were allowed more than one wife (e.g. Jacob); but this is no precedent for men living under the New Law of Christ. Even birds (60), according to Langland *Piers* B 11 326 ff., are governed by reason and moderation in their sex life. The wife here expounds a heretical theory of 'natural' free love similar to that put forward by la Vieille in *R. de la Rose* 13845–14130. See J. A. W. Bennett *The Parlement of Foules: an interpretation* (Oxford U.P. 1957) Appendix, on Nature and Kind.
59 'To fasten tightly together hearts which are at strife with each other.'
60–3 The idea that birds choose new mates each year on St Valentine's Day appears first in C14 courtly writings, e.g. the *Parlement of Foules* – in which, however, Chaucer does not stress the uncourtly fact that the birds' choice is for one year only.
60 'Birds have a better law than men, by a long way.'
61 ilk each. **joyis** enjoys. **maik** mate.
62–71 The readings of *M* are often hard to decipher (even under ultraviolet light) from here to the bottom of the leaf.
62 fangis takes. **feir** mate. **unfulyit** unspoiled, fresh. **constant** MS. so read by Craigie, but now indecipherable. It seems uncharacteristic of the wife to be concerned about constancy.
64–5 'Christ grant that such a custom might be observed in this country! Then we women would be glad to be alive!' Only an initial *b* of the last word is visible. ME idiom would lead one to expect *born*: cf. No. 9 above, line 239.
66 feiris] freiris *M* (protestantizing?). **fang** take.
67 larberis impotent men. **curage** spirit, sexual vigour.
69 'Dainty, pretty and elegant . . .' **gentil**] gent *M*. The repetition is very suspect.
70–5 The Wife of Bath dresses up and goes to similar gatherings in the absence of her fourth husband: *Wife of Bath's Prol. C.T.* III 555–9.
71 playis The Wife of Bath visits 'playes of miracles', III 558. *Cf. R. de la Rose* 13492–5.

To shaw my renoun royaly whair press was of folk,
To manifest my makdom to multitude of pepil,
And blaw my bewty on breid whair bernis war mony,
That I micht cheis and be chosin, and change when me likit.
Than suld I waill ane full weil, owr all the wide realm,
That suld my womanheid weild the lang winter nicht;
And, when I gottin had ane grome ganest of uther,
Yaip and ying in the yoke ane yeir forto draw,
Fra I had previt his pith the first plesand moneth,
Than suld I cast me to keik in kirk and in markat
And all the cuntré about, kingis court and uther,
Whair I ane galland micht get aganis the nixt yeir,
Forto perfurneis furth the werk when failyit the tother,
A forky fure, ay furthwart and forsy in draucht,
Nother febil nor fant nor fulyit in labour,
Bot als fresh of his form as flouris in May –
For all the fruit suld I fang, thocht he the flour burgeoun.

72 royaly MS. so read by Craigie, now indecipherable. **press** crowd.

73 makdom beauty.

74 on breid abroad. **bernis** men. Lines 72–4 illustrate the stylistic trick in alliterative verse of saying the same thing several times with a different alliterating letter, like playing the same tune in a different key.

76 waill choose. **owr** over.

77 weild possess.

78 grome man. **ganest** most suitable.

79 Yaip keen. **yoke** The conventional image of marital union (cf. Chaucer *C.T.* IV 1285, 1837) is here converted into an image of farm-horse labour.

80 Fra once. **previt his pith** tested his vigour.

81–8 The Wife of Bath, on the death of her fourth husband, is already provided with another (*C.T.* III 591). D.'s wife outdoes her (as elsewhere) by making provision after only one month of marriage.

81 cast me to keik set out to look.

83 aganis 'against', in preparation for.

84 perfurneis carry out.

85 'A lusty fellow, always full of promise, and a strong puller.' *draucht* recalls the farm-horse image of 79.

86 fant faint, weak. **fulyit** worn out.

88 'For I would take all the fruit, even though he caused the flower to bud', i.e. I will get all the pleasure, but he will do all the work (with phallic suggestion in *burgeoun*?). After this line, *M* has a heading: 'Aude ut dicet de viro suo' ('Hear what she says about her husband').

I have ane wallidrag, ane worm, ane auld wobat carl,
A waistit wolroun na worth bot wordis to clatter,
Ane bumbart, ane dronbee, ane bag full of flewm,
Ane scabbit skarth, ane scorpioun, ane scutard behind.
To see him scart his awin skin, grit scunner I think;
When kissis me that caribald, than kindilis all my sorow:
As birs of ane brim bair his berd is als stiff,
Bot soft and soupil as the silk is his sary lume –
He may weill to the sin assent, bot sackless is his deidis.
With goris his twa grim ene are gladderit all about
And gorgit like twa gutteris that war with glar stoppit.
Bot when that glowrand gaist grippis me about
Than think I hiddowus Mahoun hes me in armes.
Thair may na saning me save fra that auld Sathan,
For thocht I croce me all clein fra the croun doun,
He will my corse all beclip and clap to his breist.

89–145 The type of the old lover (*senex amans*) was well established in medieval literature as an object of disgust or ridicule. D. recalls, among others, the three old husbands of the Wife of Bath and old January in *Merchant's T*.

89–92 'I have a weakling, a worm, an old caterpillar man, a worn-out boar, good for nothing but chatter, a lazy fellow, a drone bee, a bag full of phlegm, a scabby monster, a scorpion, a shit-breech.' The ancient idea of the poet as master of abuse survived with special vigour in Scotland: cf. 'flytings' (slanging-matches) such as D.'s *Flyting of Dunbar and Kennedie*, where similar sequences of inventive (and often obscure) insult occur.

91 flewm The four bodily humours supposedly prevailed in the Four Ages of Man, as follows: blood in childhood, red choler in adolescence, melancholy in maturity, phlegm in old age. Phlegm was cold and not conducive to sexual power.

93 scart scratch. **scunner** cause of disgust.

94–5 This, like 105–10, recalls the bristly old husband January in *Merchant's T., C.T.* IV 1823–7. See Bawcutt in *Robbins Studies* 192–3.

94 caribald 'an abusive term of doubtful origin and meaning' (*DOST* s.v.).

95 birs bristles. **brim bair** fierce boar.

96 sary 'sorry', wretched. **lume** sexual member, 'tool'.

97 sackless innocent.

98–108 MS. damaged.

98 goris slimes (*M* 'gor is'). **ene** eyes. **gladderit** besmeared.

99 gorgit clogged up. **glar** slime.

100 glowrand staring.

101 Mahoun Mahomet, used as name of the devil: cf. 102, 112.

102 saning crossing myself.

103 'For though I cross myself all over, from the top of my head down.'

104 The first surviving leaf of the print of ?1508 begins with this line. My text is hereafter based on this print (*P*), with variants from *M*. **beclip** embrace. **clap]** clap me *M*.

When shaven is that ald shaik with a sharp rasour
He shovis on me his shevil mouth and sheddis my lippis,
And with his hard hurchon skin sa hecklis he my chekis
That as a glemand gleid glowis my chaftis:
I shrenk for the sharp stound, bot shout dar I nocht
For shore of that auld shrew – shame him betide!
The lufe-blenkis of that bogil, fra his blerit ene,
As Belzebub had on me blent abasit my spreit;
And when the smy on me smirkis with his smake smolet
He fepillis like a farcy aver that flirit on a gillot.
When that the sound of his saw sinkis in my eris
Than ay renewis my noy, or he be neir cumand.
When I heir nemit his name than mak I nine crocis
To keip me fra the cummerans of that carl mangit,
That full of eldning is and anger and all evil thewis.
I dar nocht luke to my luf for that lene gib,

105–10 See *n.* to 94–5.
105 shaik (schak *M*) probably a slang word meaning 'tramp' or 'wreck'. Editors substitute the poetic word 'shalk'; but see *OED* s.v. *Shake* sb.[2] and *Shack* sb.[2]
106 on] *M* omits. **shevil** twisted. **sheddis** parts.
107 hurchon hedgehog. **hecklis** scratches. The 'heckle' was an instrument for combing flax: cf. Henryson's description, No. 31.1 above, lines 204–10.
108 gleid live coal. **chaftis** jaws.
109 stound assault.
110 shore threat, fear.
111 lufe-blenkis love-glances. **bogil** goblin.
112 'Cast down my spirits, as if Beelzebub had given me a look.'
113 smy wretch. **smake smolet** miserable little penis (?). The editor of *DOST* suggests to me that *smolet* is a corruption of *smolt*, mod. Scots dialect *smowt* 'little fellow', here used colloquially of the penis. P. T. Ingham and E. J. Dobson *Med. Aev.* 36 (1967) 38–9 emend to *smakes mollet* 'little rogue's mouth', taking *mollet* as derived from *mull* 'lip'.
114 'He dribbles (?) like a diseased horse (*aver*) leering at a mare.' *farcy* is a disease of horses, causing swelling and discharge.
115 saw speech. The rest of the line illustrates a collocation established in alliterative usage: 'The grete soun of Sodamas sinkes in myn eres' (*Cleanness* 689).
116 'Then I always feel miserable again, before he comes anywhere near me.'
117 crocis crosses: cf. 102–3.
118 cummerans annoyance. **carl mangit** imbecile old man.
119 eldning jealousy. The morbid jealousy of old husbands was a commonplace: cf. January in *Merchant's T.*, or the Carpenter in *Miller's T.* **thewis** qualities.
120 'I dare not so much as glance at my beloved for fear of that skinny tomcat.' For *gib*, cf. No. 31.2 above, line 165 and *n.*

He is sa full of jelusy and engine fals,
Ever imagining in mind materis of evil,
Compassand and castand cacis a thousand
How he sall tak me, with a train, at trist of ane other.
I dar nocht keik to the knaip that the cop fillis
For eldning of that ald shrew that ever on evil thinkis;
For he is waistit and worn fra Venus werkis
And may nocht beit worth a bene in bed of my misters.
He trowis that young folk I yerne, yeild for he gane is,
Bot I may yuke all this yeir or his yerd help.
Ay when that caribald carl wald clim on my wamb
Than am I dangerous and daine and dour of my will.
Yit leit I never that larber my leggis ga betwene
To file my flesh na fummil me without a fee gret;
And thocht his pene purly me payis in bed,
His purse pays richly in recompense efter:
For, or he clim on my corse, that caribald forlane,

121 engine ingenuity.
123–4 'Devising and working out a thousand ways by which he can catch me, by a trick, at an assignation with another man.' The emendation of *P*'s *trawe* (*trew* in *M*) to *train* 'trick' is due to C. Singh *N & Q* 21 (1974) 163. Both authorities give *at trist* as one word. If *atrist* were past participle of an unrecorded verb, it would explain the *of*: 'being dated by another man'.
125 keik to peep at. **knaip** lad. **cop** cup.
128 'And what he does to relieve my needs (*misters*) in bed is not worth a bean.' Cf. *Shipman's T.*, No. 18.1 above, lines 170–1.
129 'He thinks that I long for young people because he has gone sterile.' *yeild* appears to represent *OED Yeld* a. ('barren, dry, sterile'), though word order is awkward. For the sense of *gane* 'become', see *DOST* s.v. *Ga* v. 5c. Cf. *Twa Mariit Wemen* 293: 'the churl wes gane chaist or the child wes gottin' ('the wretch had "gone chaste" – i.e. become impotent – before the child was begotten'). **I yerne yeild for**] *P*; I warne yeild quhair (?) *M*.
130 yuke itch. **or** before. **yerd** sexual member.
131–44 The Wife of Bath laid down similar conditions to her old husbands: *C.T.* III 409–16.
131 clim climb.
132 dangerous standoffish. **daine** haughty (dane *M*, dame *P*), coupled with *dangerous* in *C.T.* I 517: 'Ne of his speche daungerous ne digne'. **dour** obstinate.
133 larber impotent man.
134 file defile. **fummil** See *OED* s.v. *Fumble* v. 4 for associations with sexual impotence.
135 pene sexual member. Probably a form of *pen*, used colloquially in this sense: Partridge s.v. But the unusual spelling in *P* ('pen' in *M*) perhaps recalls Latin *penis*. **purly** poorly. **payis** can mean 'satisfies' as well as 'pays' (see 136) in ME.
137 corse body. **forlane** worthless.

I have conditioun of a curche of kersp allther finest,
A goun of engranit claith richt gaily furrit,
A ring with a ryal stane or other rich jowel –
Or rest of his rousty raid, thocht he were red wood.
For all the buddis of John Blunt, when he abone climis,
Me think the baid deir aboucht, sa bawch are his werkis.
And thus I sell him solace, thocht I it sour think.
Fra sic a sire God you saif, my sweit sisteris deir.'
    When that the semely had said hir sentence to end,
Than all they leuch apon loft with laitis full mery
And raucht the cop round about full of rich winis
And ralyit lang, or they wald rest, with riatous speche.

138 'I make it a condition that I receive a kerchief of the very finest fabric.'
139 engranit dyed in grain.
141 'Otherwise he must desist from his unpractised onslaught, even though he is stark mad for it.' *rousty* is apparently 'rusty' in *OED* sense 5. **wood**] wod *M*; wmyod *P*. See *OED* s.v. *Red-wood* a. *P* apparently incorporates a *my* misplaced in printing.
142 buddis bribes. **John Blunt** a proverbial name, with abusive connotations. **abone** above.
143 'It seems to me I pay a high price for the delay, so feeble (*bawch*) are his doings.' Obscure. If *baid* means 'delay' (so *DOST*), the wife may be suggesting (ironically?) that if she had yielded at once she might have got more satisfaction, or else that (in spite of the money) it was not worth breaking off from whatever else she was doing.
146 sentence opinion.
147 leuch apon loft laughed loudly. **laitis** words.
148 raucht passed.
149 ralyit joked. After this line, *M* has a heading (not in *P*): 'Hic bibent et inde vidua interrogat alteram mulierem et illa respondet ut sequitur' ('Here they drink, and then the widow asks the other woman, and she replies as follows').

Select Bibliography

[*ALMA*] LOOMIS, R. S., ed. *Arthurian Literature in the Middle Ages*, Oxford U.P. 1959.

BASTIN, J., ed. *Recueil général des Isopets*, 2 vols, Paris, Société des Anciens Textes Français, 1929–30.

[Bennett] BENNETT, J. A. W., ed. *'Piers Plowman': The Prologue and Passus I–VII*, Oxford U.P. 1972.

[Bennett *Chaucer*] BENNETT, J. A. W. *Chaucer at Oxford and at Cambridge*, Univ. of Toronto P., Oxford U.P. 1974.

[Bennett *Gower*] BENNETT, J. A. W., ed. *Selections from John Gower*, Oxford U.P. 1968.

BENSON, L. D. *Art and Tradition in 'Sir Gawain and the Green Knight'*, Rutgers U.P. 1965.

BISHOP, I. B. *'Pearl' in its Setting*, Oxford, Blackwell 1968.

[Blanch] BLANCH, R. J., ed. *'Sir Gawain' and 'Pearl': critical essays*, Indiana U.P. 1966.

[Blanch *Style*] BLANCH, R. J., ed. *Style and Symbolism in 'Piers Plowman': a modern critical anthology*, Univ. of Tennessee P. 1969.

BLOOMFIELD, M. W. *'Piers Plowman' as a Fourteenth-Century Apocalypse*, Rutgers U.P. 1961.

BOAS, M., ed. *Disticha Catonis*, Amsterdam, 1952.

BORROFF, M. *'Sir Gawain and the Green Knight': a stylistic and metrical study*, Yale U.P. 1962; repr. N.Y., Shoe String Press 1967.

BREWER, D. S., ed. *Geoffrey Chaucer* (Writers and Their Background), G. Bell 1974.

[Brown *XIIIth-Century Lyrics*] BROWN, CARLETON, ed. *English Lyrics of the XIIIth Century*, Oxford U.P. 1932.

[Brown *XIVth-Century Religious Lyrics*] BROWN, CARLETON, ed. *Religious Lyrics of the XIVth Century*, 2nd edn rev. G. V. Smithers, Oxford U.P. 1952.

[Brown *XVth-Century Religious Lyrics*] BROWN, CARLETON, ed. *Religious Lyrics of the XVth Century*, Oxford U.P. 1939.

BROWN, CARLETON, and ROBBINS, R. H., eds. *The Index of Middle English Verse*, New York, Index Soc. 1943; *Supplement*, ed. R. H. Robbins and J. L. Cutler, Univ. of Kentucky P. 1965.

BRYAN, W. F., and DEMPSTER, G., eds. *Sources and Analogues of Chaucer's 'Canterbury Tales'*, Chicago U.P. 1941; Atlantic Highlands N.J., Humanities Press 1958.

[Burrow *Reading*] BURROW, J. A. *A Reading of 'Sir Gawain and the Green Knight'*, Routledge 1965.

[Burrow *Ricardian Poetry*] BURROW, J. A. *Ricardian Poetry: Chaucer, Gower, Langland and the 'Gawain' Poet*, Routledge 1971.

CARY, G. *The Medieval Alexander*, Cambridge U.P. 1956.

[*Castle of Perseverance*] ECCLES, M., ed. *The Macro Plays*, EETS, o.s. 262, London, 1969.

[*Chester Cycle*] LUMIANSKY, R. M., and MILLS, D., eds. *The Chester Mystery Cycle*, EETS, suppl. ser. 3, London, 1974.

CHILD, F. J., ed. *The English and Scottish Popular Ballads*, 5 vols, Boston and New York, 1882–98.

Select Bibliography

[Clanvowe] *The Works of Sir John Clanvowe*, ed. V. J. Scattergood, Cambridge, D. S. Brewer 1975.

CURRY, W. C. *Chaucer and the Mediaeval Sciences*, 2nd edn, New York, Barnes & Noble 1960.

CURTIUS, E. R. *European Literature and the Latin Middle Ages*, trans. W. R. Trask, Routledge 1953.

DAVIES, R. T., ed. *Medieval English Lyrics: a critical anthology*, Faber 1963.

[Donaldson *Chaucer's Poetry*] DONALDSON, E. T., ed. *Chaucer's Poetry: an anthology for the modern reader*, New York, Ronald 1958.

[Donaldson *Piers*] DONALDSON, E. T. *Piers Plowman: the C-Text and its poet*, 2nd edn, London, Cass 1966.

DOOB, P. B. R. *Nebuchadnezzar's Children: Conventions of Madness in Middle English literature*, Yale U.P. 1974.

[*DOST*] *A Dictionary of the Older Scottish Tongue from the Twelfth Century to the End of the Seventeenth*, ed. W. A. Craigie and A. J. Aitken, Oxford U.P. and Chicago U.P. 1931–69; Chicago U.P. 1970–

DRONKE, P. *The Medieval Lyric*, Hutchinson 1968.

[*EDD*] *The English Dialect Dictionary*, ed. J. Wright, London, 1896–1905.

ELLIOTT, R. W. V. *Chaucer's English*, Deutsch 1974.

EMPSON, W. *Seven Types of Ambiguity*, 2nd edn, Chatto 1947.

EVERETT, D. *Essays on Middle English Literature*, ed. P. M. Kean, Oxford U.P. 1955.

FARAL, E., ed. *Les Arts Poétiques du XIIe et du XIIIe Siècle*, Paris, Champion 1924.

FOWLER, D. C. *A Literary History of the Popular Ballad*, Duke University Press 1968.

FOX, D., ed. *Robert Henryson: Testament of Cresseid*, Nelson 1968.

GORDON, I. L. *The Double Sorrow of Troilus*, Oxford U.P. 1970.

GRAY, D. *Themes and Images in the Medieval English Religious Lyric*, Routledge 1972.

[Gray *Selection*] GRAY, D., ed. *A Selection of Religious Lyrics*, Oxford U.P. 1975.

[Greene *Carols*] GREENE, R. L., ed. *The Early English Carols*, Oxford U.P. 1935.

[Greene *Selection*] GREENE, R. L., ed. *A Selection of English Carols*, Oxford U.P. 1962.

HAMMOND, E. P., ed. *English Verse between Chaucer and Surrey*, Duke University Press 1927; repr. N.Y., Octagon 1965.

HOCCLEVE, T. *The Regement of Princes*, ed. F. J. Furnivall, EETS, e.s. 72, London, 1897.

HOMANS, G. C. *English Villagers of the Thirteenth Century*, Harvard U.P. 1941.

[*Index*] *The Index of Middle English Verse*, see BROWN, CARLETON and ROBBINS, R. H.

JAMES, M. R., trans. *The Apocryphal New Testament*, Oxford U.P. 1924.

KANE, G., and DONALDSON, E. T., eds. *Piers Plowman: the B version*, Athlone Press 1975.

KEAN, P. M. *Chaucer and the Making of English Poetry*, 2 vols, Routledge 1972.

KITTREDGE, G. L. *Chaucer and his Poetry*, Harvard U.P. 1915.

[Klibansky] KLIBANSKY, R., PANOFSKY, E., and SAXL, F. *Saturn and Melancholy*, Nelson 1964.

LEWIS, C. S. *The Allegory of Love*, Oxford U.P. 1936.

LOOMIS, R. S., ed. *Arthurian Literature in the Middle Ages*, Oxford U.P. 1959.

[*Ludus Coventriae*] BLOCK, K. S., ed. *Ludus Coventriae*, EETS, e.s. 120, London, 1922.

MACQUEEN, J. *Robert Henryson: a study of the major narrative poems*, Oxford U.P. 1967.

MALORY, SIR THOMAS *Works*, ed. E. Vinaver, 3 vols, Oxford U.P. 1947.

MANLY, J. M., and RICKERT, E. *The Text of 'The Canterbury Tales'*, 8 vols, Univ. of Chicago P. 1940.

MATHEW, G. *The Court of Richard II*, John Murray 1968.

[*MED*] *Middle English Dictionary*, ed. H. Kurath, S. M. Kuhn and J. Reidy, Univ. of Michigan P. 1954–

MEECH, S. B. *Design in Chaucer's 'Troilus'*, Syracuse U.P. 1959.

[Migne *P.L.*] MIGNE, J.-P., ed. *Patrologia Latina*, 221 vols, Paris, 1844–90.

MITCHELL, J. *Thomas Hoccleve: a study in early fifteenth-century English poetic*, Univ. of Illinois P. 1968.

MUSCATINE, C. *Chaucer and the French Tradition*, Univ. of California P. 1957.

MUSTANOJA, T. F. *A Middle English Syntax, Part I: Parts of Speech*, Helsinki, 1960.

[Norton-Smith] NORTON-SMITH, J., ed. *John Lydgate: poems*, Oxford U.P. 1966.

[Norton-Smith *Chaucer*] NORTON-SMITH, J. *Geoffrey Chaucer*, Routledge 1974.

NYKROG, P. *Les Fabliaux*, Copenhagen, Munksgaard 1957.

[*OED*] *Oxford English Dictionary*.

OWST, G. R. *Literature and Pulpit in Medieval England*, 2nd edn, Oxford, Blackwell 1961.

PARTRIDGE, E., ed. *A Dictionary of Slang and Unconventional English*, 2 vols, 7th edn, Routledge 1970.

PATCH, H. R. *The Other World According to Descriptions in Medieval Literature*, Harvard U.P. 1950; repr. N.Y., Octagon 1970.

PEARSALL, D. *John Lydgate*, Routledge 1970.

[*R. de la Rose*] *Le Roman de la Rose*, ed. F. Lecoy, 3 vols, Paris, Champion 1965–70.

RÉAU, L. *Iconographie de l'art chrétien*, 4 vols, Paris, Presses Universitaires de France 1955–59.

[Robbins *Secular Lyrics*] ROBBINS, R. H., ed. *Secular Lyrics of the XIVth and XVth Centuries*, Oxford U.P. 1952.

[*Robbins Studies*] ROWLAND, B., ed. *Chaucer and Middle English Studies in Honour of R. H. Robbins*, Allen & Unwin 1974.

ROBERTSON, D. W. *A Preface to Chaucer*, Princeton U.P. 1963.

ROBINSON, F. N., ed. *The Works of Geoffrey Chaucer*, 2nd edn, Boston, Mass., Houghton Mifflin; Oxford U.P. 1957.

SCHILLER, G. *Iconography of Christian Art*, trans. J. Seligman, Lund Humphries, Vol. 1, 1971; Vol. 2, 1972.

[*Schlauch Studies*] BRAHMER, M., and others, eds. *Studies in Language and Literature in Honour of Margaret Schlauch*, Warsaw, 1966.

[Sisam] SISAM, K., ed. *Fourteenth Century Verse and Prose*, Oxford U.P. 1921.

[Sisam *Med. Eng. Verse*] SISAM, K., and SISAM, C., eds. *The Oxford Book of Medieval English Verse*, Oxford U.P. 1970.

[*Sources and Analogues*] see BRYAN, W. F., and DEMPSTER, G.

Select Bibliography

[Spearing] SPEARING, A. C. *The 'Gawain'-Poet: a critical study*, Cambridge U.P. 1970.

[Spearing *Criticism*] SPEARING, A. C. *Criticism and Medieval Poetry*, 2nd edn, E. Arnold 1972.

SPEIRS, J. *Medieval English Poetry: the non-Chaucerian tradition*, Faber 1957.

STEVENS, J. E. *Music and Poetry in the Early Tudor Court*, Methuen 1961.

TILLEY, M. P., ed. *A Dictionary of the Proverbs in England in the Sixteenth and Seventeenth Centuries*, Univ. of Michigan P. 1950.

[*Towneley Plays*] ENGLAND, G., and POLLARD, A. W., eds. *The Towneley Plays*, EETS, e.s. 71, London, 1897.

[*Utley Studies*] MANDEL, J., and ROSENBERG, B. A., eds. *Medieval Literature and Folklore Studies in Honor of F. L. Utley*, New Brunswick, N.J., 1970.

WHITING, B. J., ed. *Proverbs, Sentences, and Proverbial Phrases From English Writings Mainly before 1500*, Harvard U.P., Oxford U.P. 1968.

WICKHAM, G. *Early English Stages*, Vol. I: 1300 to 1576, Routledge 1959.

WILKINS, N., ed. *One Hundred Ballades, Rondeaux and Virelais from the Late Middle Ages*, Cambridge U.P. 1969.

WILSON, R. M. *The Lost Literature of Medieval England*, 2nd edn, Methuen 1970.

WIMBERLY, L. C. *Folklore in the English and Scottish Ballads*, Univ. of Chicago P. 1928; repr. N.Y., Dover 1965.

[Woolf *Lyric*] WOOLF, R. *The English Religious Lyric in the Middle Ages*, Oxford U.P. 1968.

[Woolf *Mystery Plays*] WOOLF, R. *The English Mystery Plays*, Routledge 1972.

[*York Plays*] SMITH, L. T., ed. *York Plays*, Oxford U.P. 1885.

Index of Titles and First Lines

Adam lay ybounden bounden in a bond 300
After that hervest inned had his sheves 266
All Erdly Joy Returns in Pane 372
Alnight by the rose, rose 3
A marchant whilom dwelled at Saint Denis 202
Among these othre of Slouthes kinde 236
Apon the midsummer evin, mirriest of nichtis 381
As a Midsummer Rose (Lydgate) 281

Balade de Bone Conseyl (Chaucer) 197
Bot then kerpede the king, said, 'Kithe what ye hatten 33

Canterbury Tales, The (Chaucer) 200
The Shipman's Tale 201
The Prioress's Tale 221
Christ Triumphant 309
Confessio Amantis (Gower) 235
Corpus Christi Carol 303

Done is a battel on the dragon black 378

Envoy to Scogan (Chaucer) 194

Farewell, this world! I take my leve for ever 306
Flee from the press and dwelle with sothfastnesse 198

God Speed the Plough 301
Gold and all this werdis win 31

Hide, Absolon, thy gilte tresses clere 190
Hit betidde somtime in the termes of Judé 48
Hoccleve's Complaint (Hoccleve) 265
Hunting of the Cheviot, The 349

Ich am of Irlaunde 2
I have a yong suster fer beyonden the sea 298
I have labored sore and suffered deth 309
In May, that moder is of monthes glade 150
In to thir dirk and drubly days 369
I singe of a maiden that is makeless 301

Index of Titles and First Lines

Isope myn auctor makis mencioun 338
I that in heill wes and glaidness 364
I wolde witen of som wis wight 250
I would be Clad in Christ's Skin 31

Kyrie, so kyrie 296

Lament: When He Wes Sek (Dunbar) 363
Lat no man boste of conning nor vertu 281
Livre de prison (Charles d'Orléans) 290
Lollay, lollay, littel child, why wepestow so sore 29
Loverd, thou clepedest me 28
Lully, lulley, lully, lulley 305

Ma dame, ye ben of all beauté shrine 189
Maiden in the mor lay 2
Meditatioun in Wyntir (Dunbar) 369
Moral Fables (Henryson) 323
Mum and the Sothsegger 257
My gostly fader, I me confess 293

Not long ago I hied me apace 290
Now neghes the New Yere and the night passes 78

Of everykune tree 2
Of Lentren in the first morning 372
Of the Nativitie of Christ (Dunbar) 374
Of the Resurrection of Christ (Dunbar) 377
O lord, oure lord, thy name how merveilous 222
O sely anker, that in thy cell 294

Patience 47
Pearl 61
Penny 31
Piers Plowman (Langland) 105
Prioress's Tale, The (Chaucer) 221

Rawlinson Lyrics 1
Rorate coeli desuper 374
Roundels (Chaucer) 192

Saint Steven was a clerk in King Heroudes halle 299
Shipman's Tale, The (Chaucer) 201
Sir Gawain and the Green Knight 76
Sir Orfeo 4

Index of Titles and First Lines

Sloane Lyrics 295
Spende, and God shall sende 31
Syn I fro Love escaped am so fat 193

Testament of Cresseid, The (Henryson) 310
The day passit and Phebus went to rest 312
The dubbement dere of down and dales 63
The hie prudence and wirking mervellous 324
The merthe of all this londe 302
Thenne wax I wounder wroth, as I well might 257
The Persé out of Northomberlond 350
This were a wicked way, but whoso hadde a gide 107
This World Fares as a Fantasy 250
Thole a Little 28
Tobroken ben the statuts hye in hevene 194
To Rosemounde (Chaucer) 188
Tretis of the Twa Mariit Wemen and the Wedo, The (Dunbar) 380
Troilus (Chaucer) 147

We reden ofte and finde ywrite 5
Winner and Waster 32
Wolleward and wete-shoed went I forth after 123

Your eyen two woll slee me sodenly 192
Your mouth hit saith me 'Bas me, bas me, sweet' 292